Ranma 1/2

Ranma 1/2
2-in-1 Edition
Vol. 3

STORY AND ART BY
RUMIKO TAKAHASHI

RANMA 1/2 Vol. 5, 6
by Rumiko TAKAHASHI
© 1988 Rumiko TAKAHASHI
All rights reserved.
Original Japanese edition published by SHOGAKUKAN Inc.
English translation rights in the United States of America,
Canada, United Kingdom, Ireland, Australia and New Zealand
arranged with SHOGAKUKAN.

English Adaptation/Gerard Jones, Matt Thorn, Toshifumi Yoshida
Touch-up Art & Lettering/Deron Bennett
Design/Yukiko Whitley
Editors/(First Edition) Satoru Fujii, Trish Ledoux; (Second Edition)
Julie Davis; (2-in-1 Edition) Hope Donovan

The stories, characters and incidents mentioned in
this publication are entirely fictional.

Printed in the U.S.A.

Published by VIZ Media, LLC
P.O. Box 77010
San Francisco, CA 94107

10 9 8 7 6 5 4 3 2 1
First printing, July 2014

www.viz.com   WWW.SHONENSUNDAY.COM

Ranma ½

5·6

CAST OF CHARACTERS

THE SAOTOMES

Ranma Saotome
Martial artist with an ego that won't let him quit. Changes into a girl when splashed with cold water.

Genma Saotome
Ranma's irresponsible father, recently returned from training his son in China. Changes into a panda.

STORY SO FAR

The Tendos are an average, run-of-the-mill Japanese family—at least on the surface. Soun Tendo is the owner and proprietor of the Tendo Dojo, where "Anything-Goes Martial Arts" is practiced. Like the name says, anything goes and usually does.

When Soun's old friend Genma Saotome comes to visit, Soun's three lovely young daughters—Akane, Nabiki and Kasumi—are told that it's time for one of them to become the fiancée of Genma's teenage son, as per an agreement made between the two fathers years ago. Youngest daughter Akane—who says she hates boys—is quickly nominated for bridal duty by her sisters.

Unfortunately, Ranma and his father have suffered a strange accident. While training in China, both plunged into one of many cursed springs at the legendary martial arts training ground of Jusenkyo. These springs transform the unlucky dunkee into whoever—or whatever—drowned there hundreds of years ago.

From then on, a splash of cold water turns Ranma's father into a giant panda, and Ranma becomes a beautiful, busty young woman. Hot water reverses the effect…but only until next time.

Although their parents are still determined to see Ranma and Akane marry and carry on the dojo, both seem to have a talent for accumulating suitors. Will the two ever work out their differences and get rid of all these extra people, or will they just call the whole thing off? And will Ranma ever get rid of his curse?

THE TENDOS

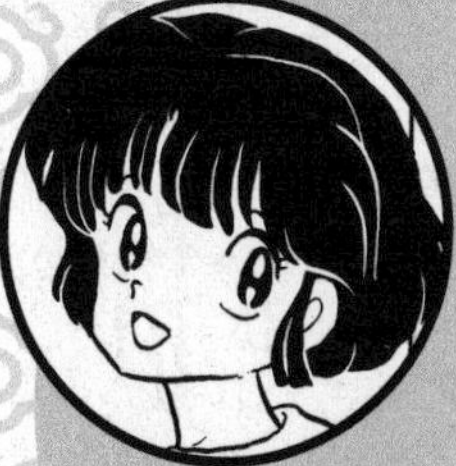

Akane Tendo
A martial artist, tomboy and Ranma's reluctant fiancée. Has no clue who "P-chan" really is.

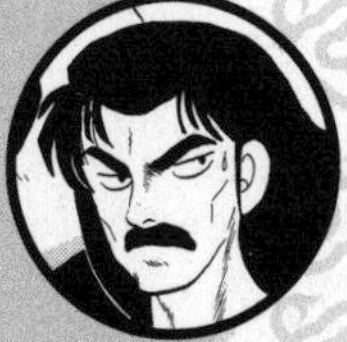

Soun Tendo
Head of the Tendo household and owner of the Tendo Dojo.

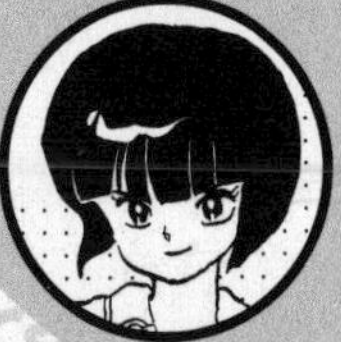

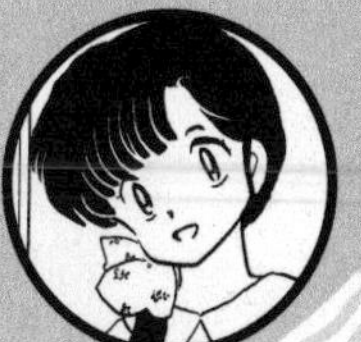

Kasumi Tendo
Sweet-natured eldest daughter and substitute mother figure for the Tendo family.

Nabiki Tendo
Always ready to make a buck off others' suffering, coldhearted capitalist Nabiki is the middle Tendo daughter.

THE SUITORS

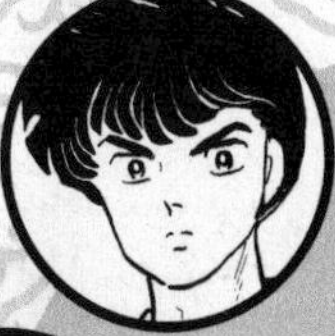

Tatewaki Kuno
Blustering upperclassman who is the kendo team captain. In love with both Akane and girl Ranma.

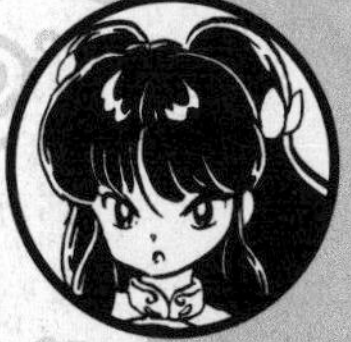

Shampoo
Chinese Amazon warrior who wants to kill girl Ranma and marry boy Ranma.

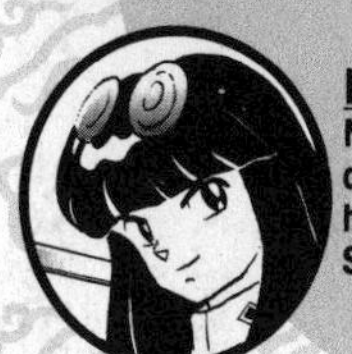

Mousse
Nearsighted martial arts master of hidden weapons. Shampoo's suitor.

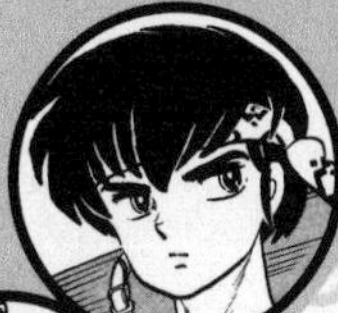

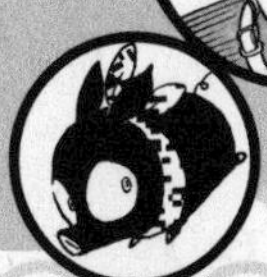

Ryoga Hibiki
A martial artist with a grudge against Ranma, a crush on Akane and no sense of direction. Changes into a piglet Akane calls "P-chan."

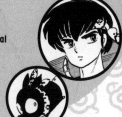

AND IN THIS CORNER...

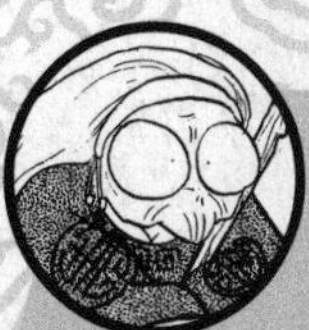

Cologne
Shampoo's great-grandmother, a martial artist and devious matchmaker.

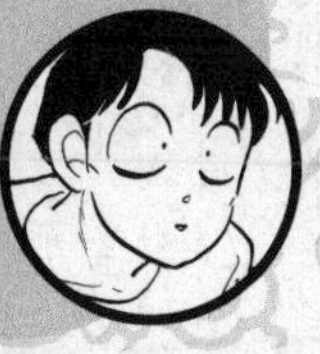

Gosunkugi
Creepy guy with a crush on Akane.

Contents

PART 1
LOOKING FOR A WEAK SPOT

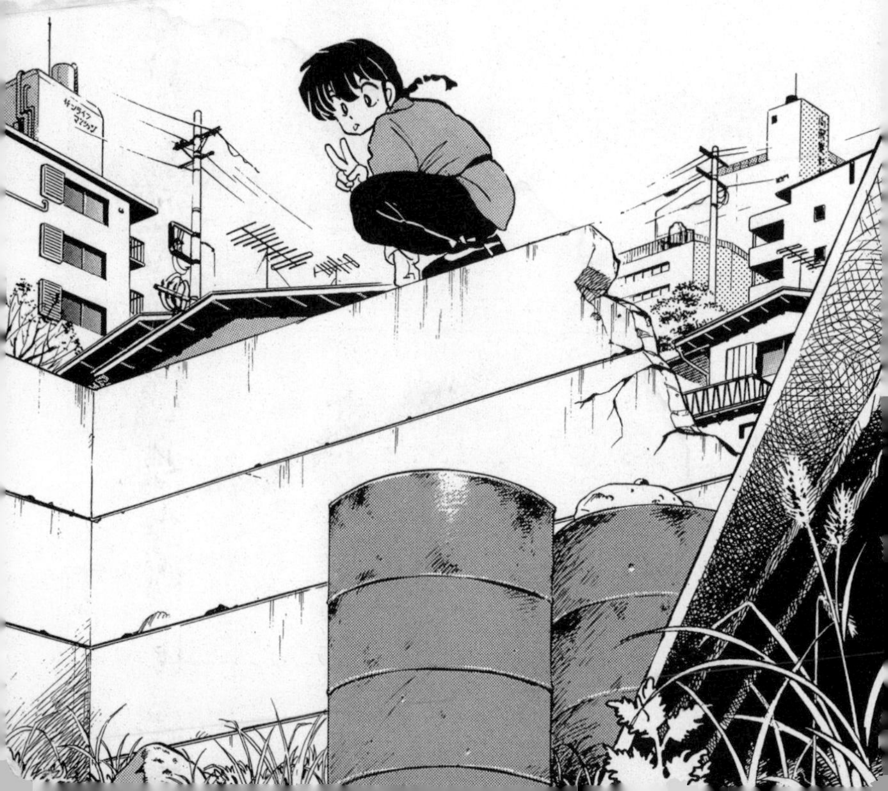

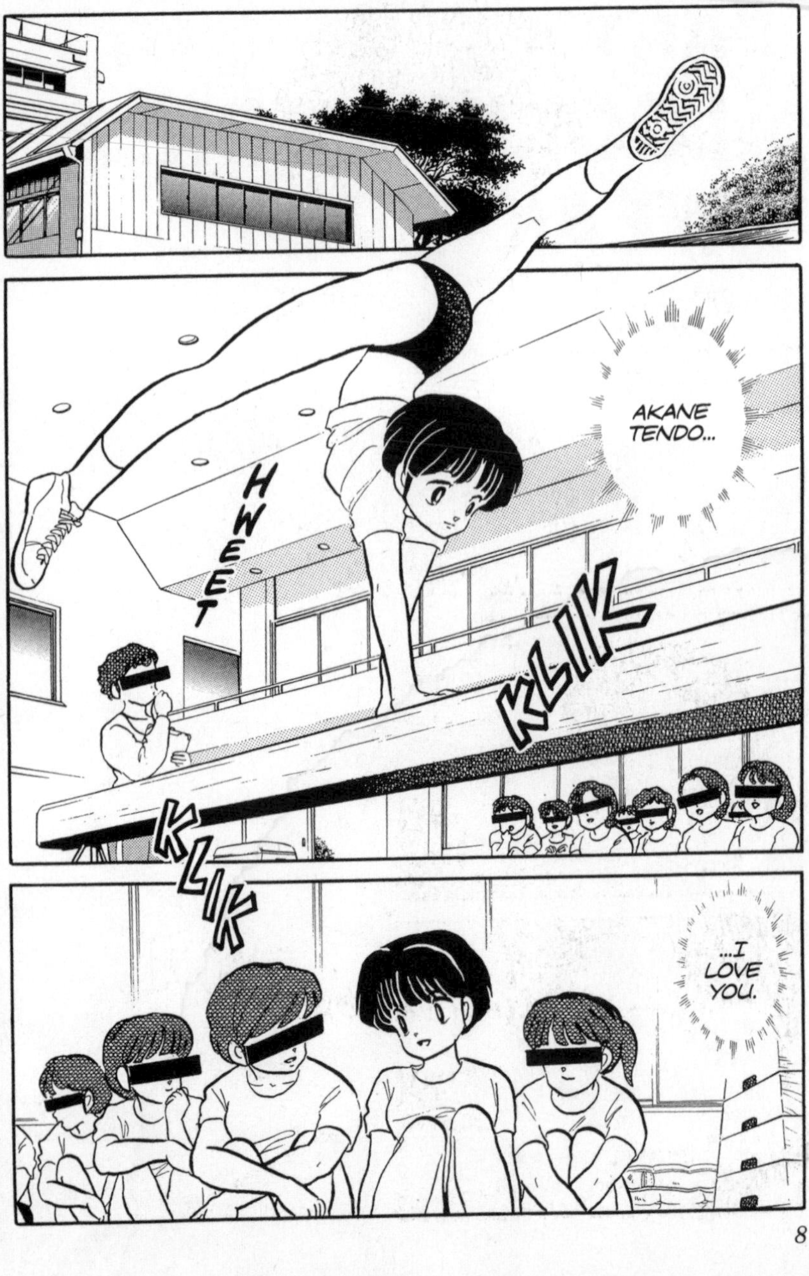
AKANE TENDO...
HWEET
KLIK
KLIK
...I LOVE YOU.

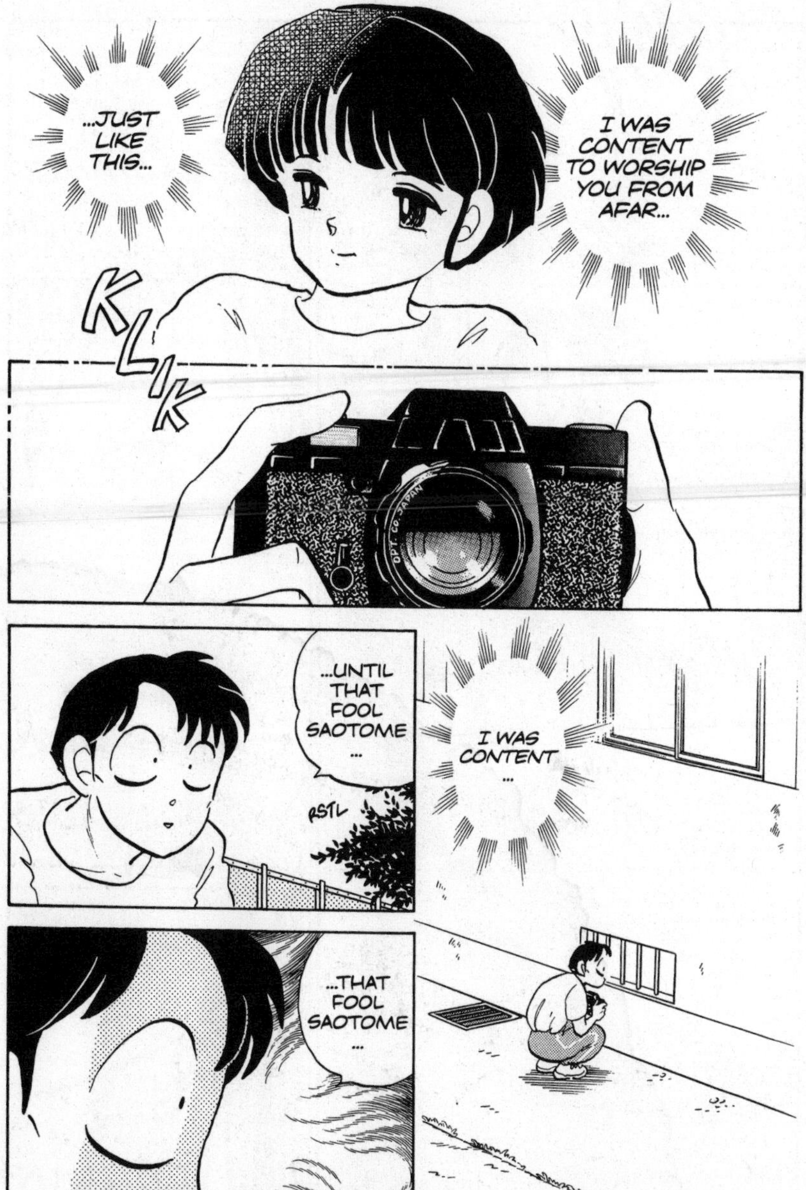
I WAS CONTENT TO WORSHIP YOU FROM AFAR...
...JUST LIKE THIS...
KLIK
I WAS CONTENT ...
...UNTIL THAT FOOL SAOTOME ...
RSTL
...THAT FOOL SAOTOME ...

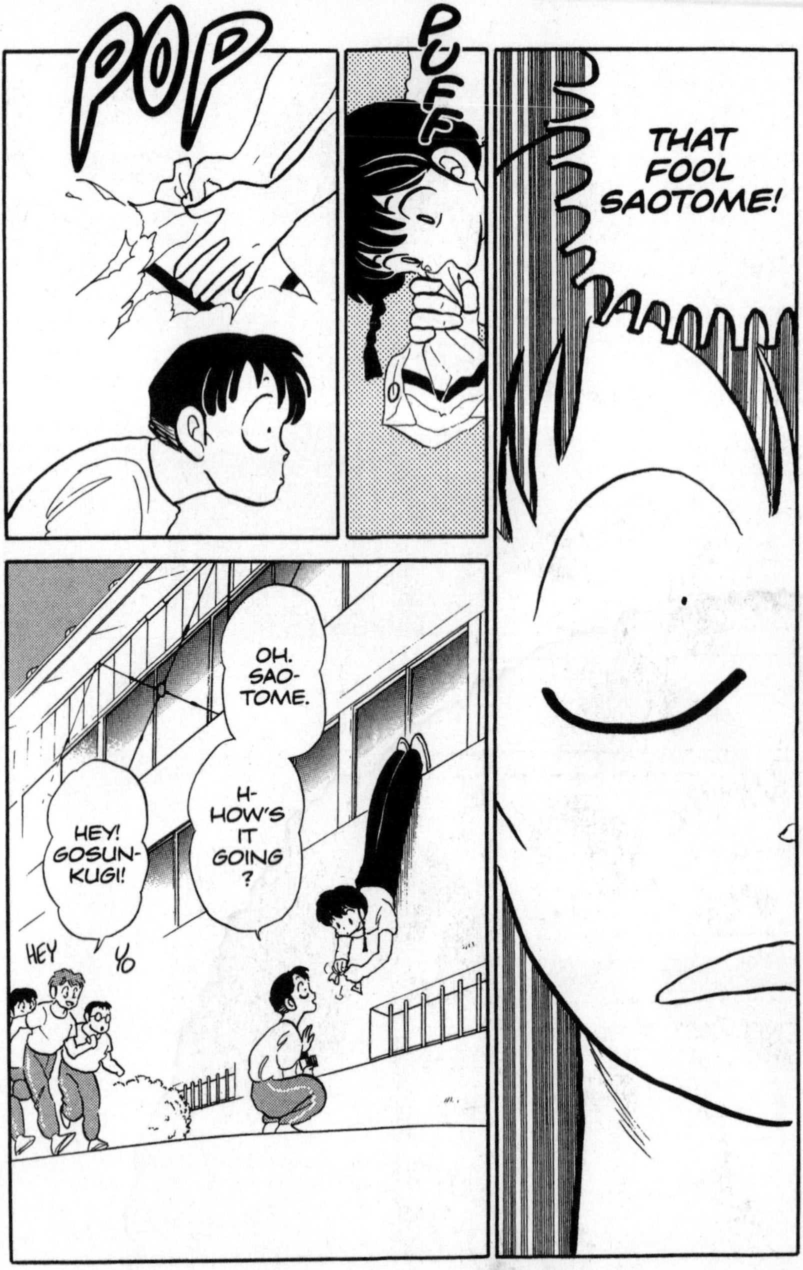
THAT FOOL SAOTOME!
AAAAAA
PUFF
POP
OH. SAO-TOME.
H-HOW'S IT GOING?
HEY! GOSUN-KUGI!
YO
HEY

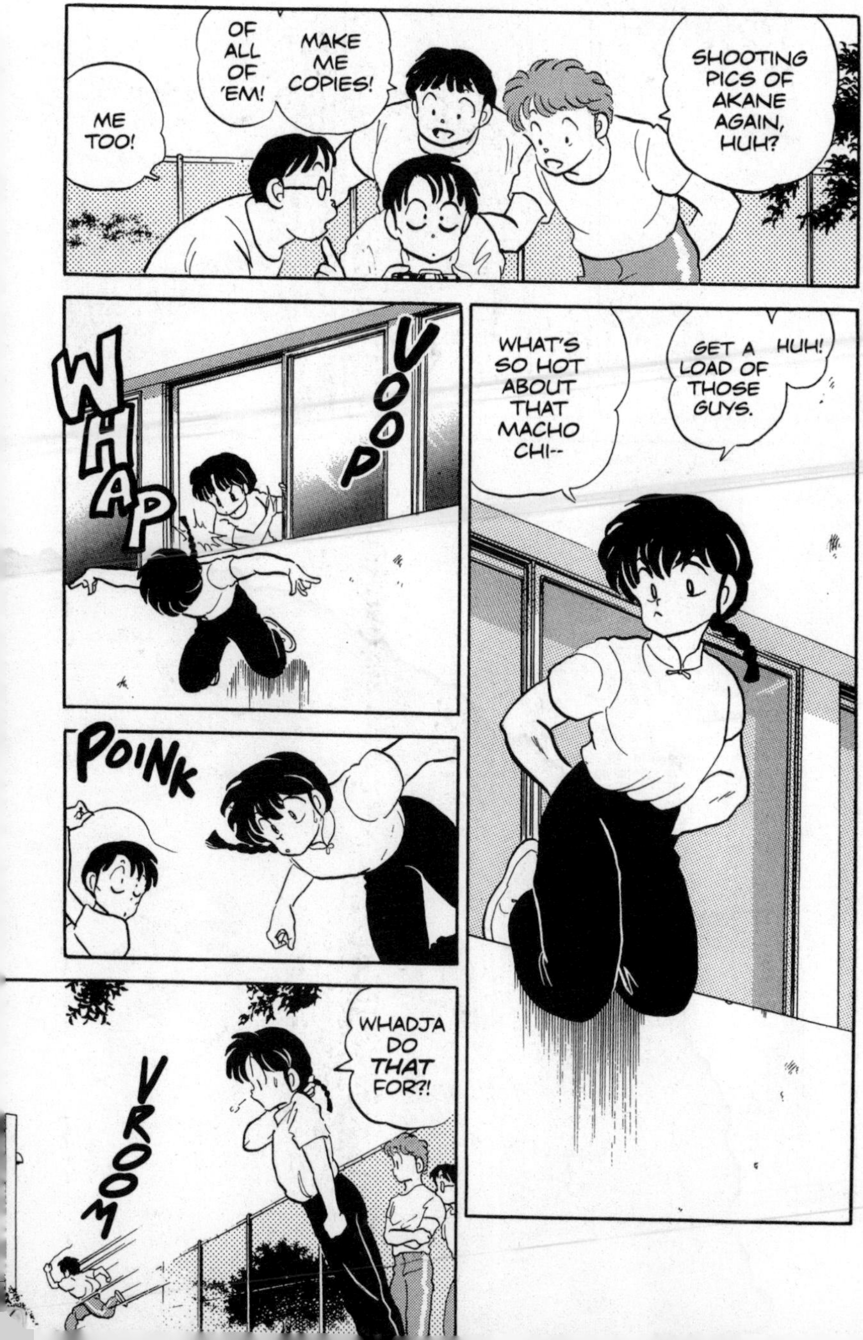
SHOOTING PICS OF AKANE AGAIN, HUH?
MAKE ME COPIES!
OF ALL OF 'EM!
ME TOO!
HUH!
GET A LOAD OF THOSE GUYS.
WHAT'S SO HOT ABOUT THAT MACHO CHI--
VOOP
WHAP
POINK
WHADJA DO THAT FOR?!
VROOM

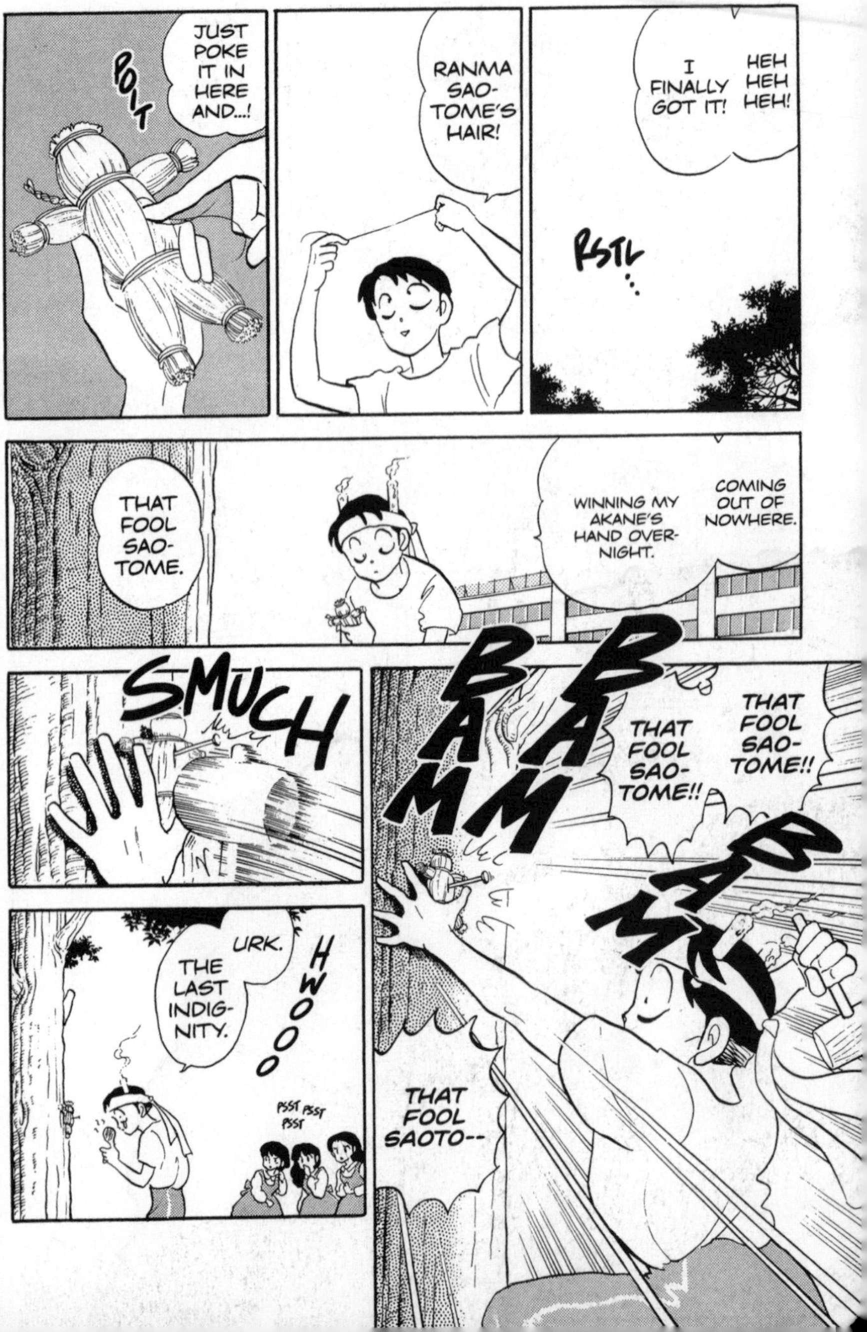
HEH HEH HEH!
I FINALLY GOT IT!
RSTL...
RANMA SAOTOME'S HAIR!
JUST POKE IT IN HERE AND...!
POIT
COMING OUT OF NOWHERE.
WINNING MY AKANE'S HAND OVERNIGHT.
THAT FOOL SAOTOME.
BAMM
BAMM
THAT FOOL SAOTOME!!
THAT FOOL SAOTOME!!
BAM
THAT FOOL SAOTO--
SMUCH
URK.
THE LAST INDIGNITY.
HWOOOO
PSST PSST PSST

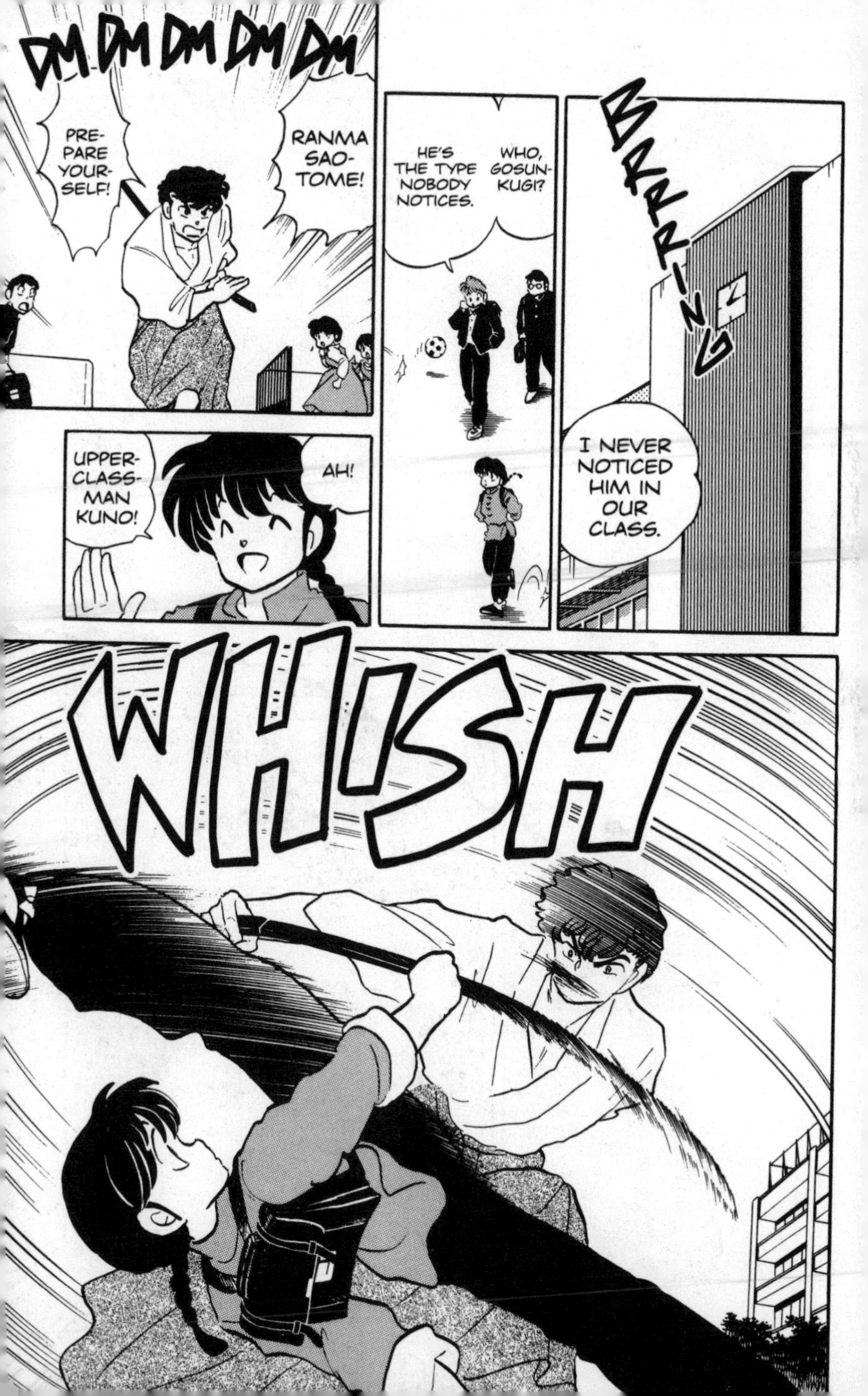
BRRRING
I NEVER NOTICED HIM IN OUR CLASS.
WHO, GOSUNKUGI?
HE'S THE TYPE NOBODY NOTICES.
DM DM DM DM DM
RANMA SAOTOME!
PRE-PARE YOUR-SELF!
AH!
UPPER-CLASS-MAN KUNO!
WHISH

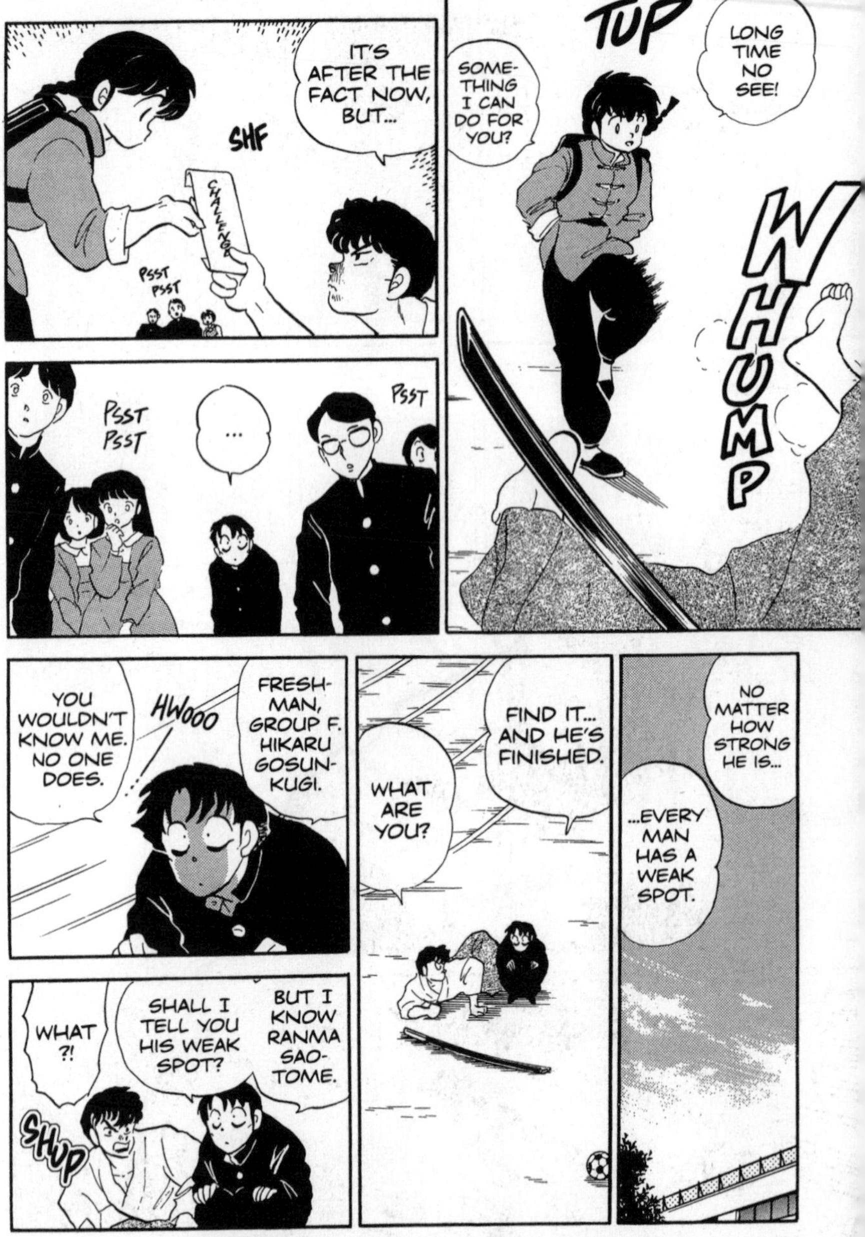
TUP
LONG TIME NO SEE!
SOME-THING I CAN DO FOR YOU?
WHUMP
IT'S AFTER THE FACT NOW, BUT...
SHF
CHALLENGE
PSST PSST
PSST
...
PSST PSST
NO MATTER HOW STRONG HE IS...
...EVERY MAN HAS A WEAK SPOT.
FIND IT... AND HE'S FINISHED.
WHAT ARE YOU?
FRESH-MAN, GROUP F. HIKARU GOSUN-KUGI.
HWOOO
YOU WOULDN'T KNOW ME. NO ONE DOES.
BUT I KNOW RANMA SAO-TOME.
SHALL I TELL YOU HIS WEAK SPOT?
WHAT?!
SHUP

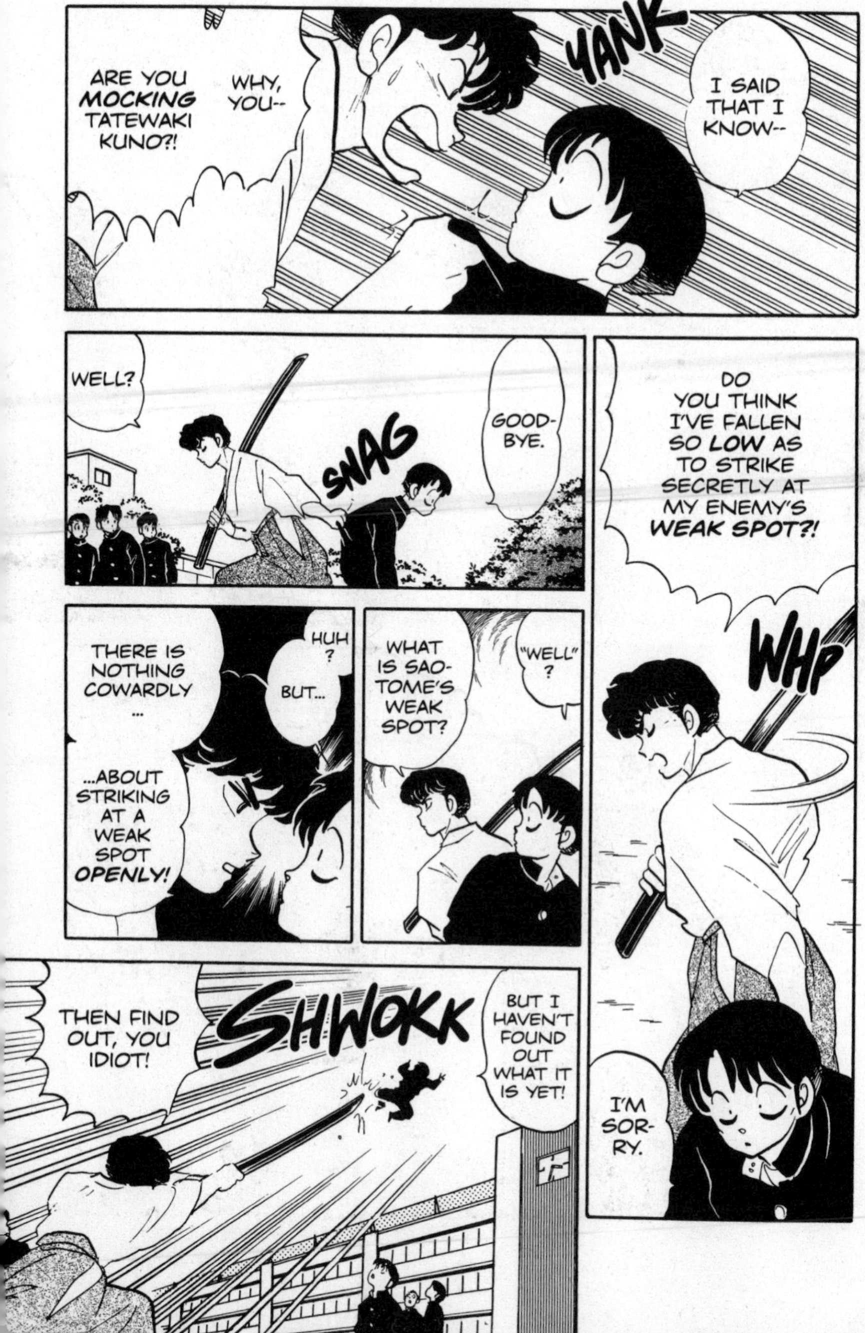
YANK
I SAID THAT I KNOW--
WHY, YOU--
ARE YOU MOCKING TATEWAKI KUNO?!
DO YOU THINK I'VE FALLEN SO LOW AS TO STRIKE SECRETLY AT MY ENEMY'S WEAK SPOT?!
WHP
I'M SORRY.
GOOD-BYE.
SNAG
WELL?
"WELL"?
WHAT IS SAOTOME'S WEAK SPOT?
HUH? BUT...
THERE IS NOTHING COWARDLY ...
...ABOUT STRIKING AT A WEAK SPOT OPENLY!
BUT I HAVEN'T FOUND OUT WHAT IT IS YET!
SHWOKK
THEN FIND OUT, YOU IDIOT!

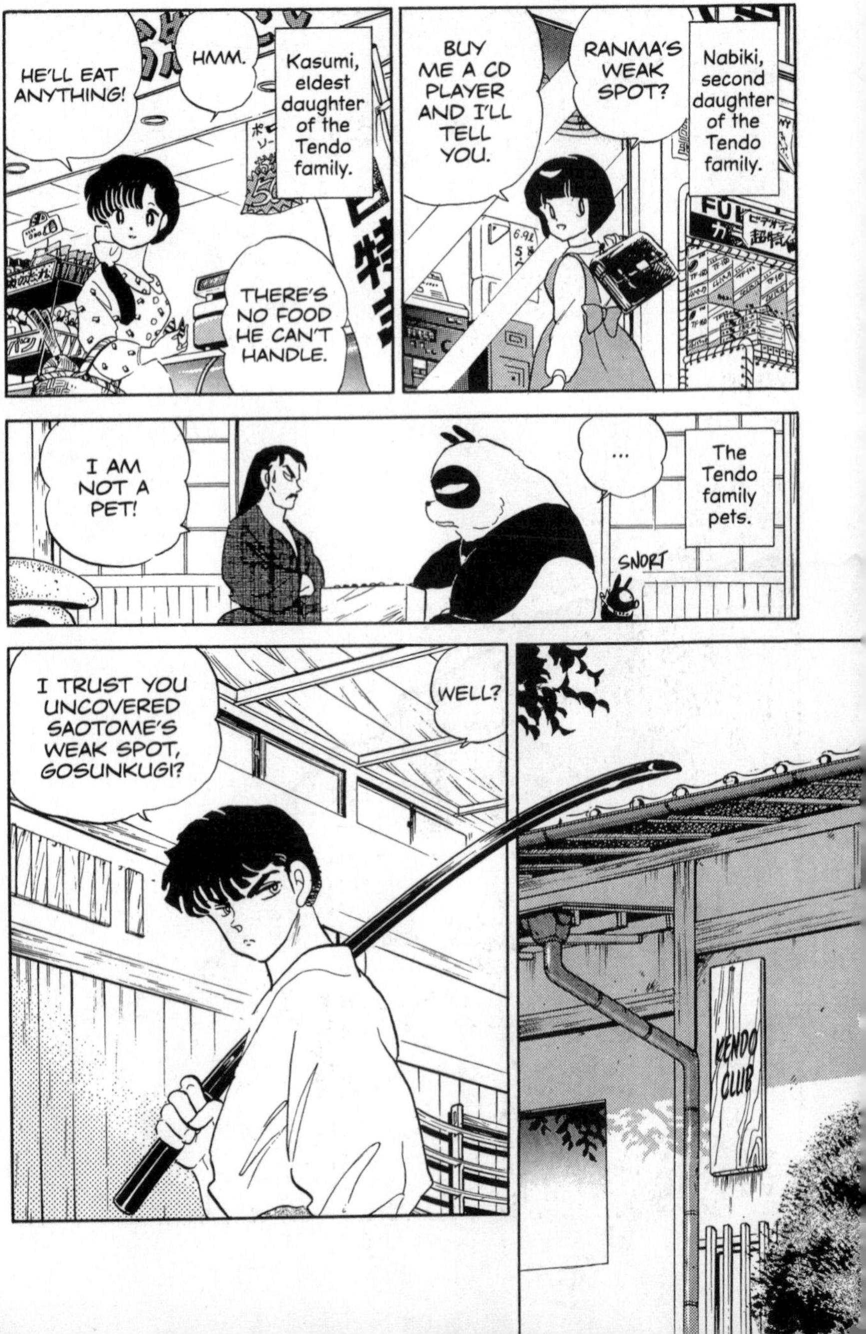
Nabiki, second daughter of the Tendo family.
RANMA'S WEAK SPOT?
BUY ME A CD PLAYER AND I'LL TELL YOU.
Kasumi, eldest daughter of the Tendo family.
HMM.
HE'LL EAT ANYTHING!
THERE'S NO FOOD HE CAN'T HANDLE.
The Tendo family pets.
...
SNORT
I AM NOT A PET!
KENDO CLUB
WELL?
I TRUST YOU UNCOVERED SAOTOME'S WEAK SPOT, GOSUNKUGI?

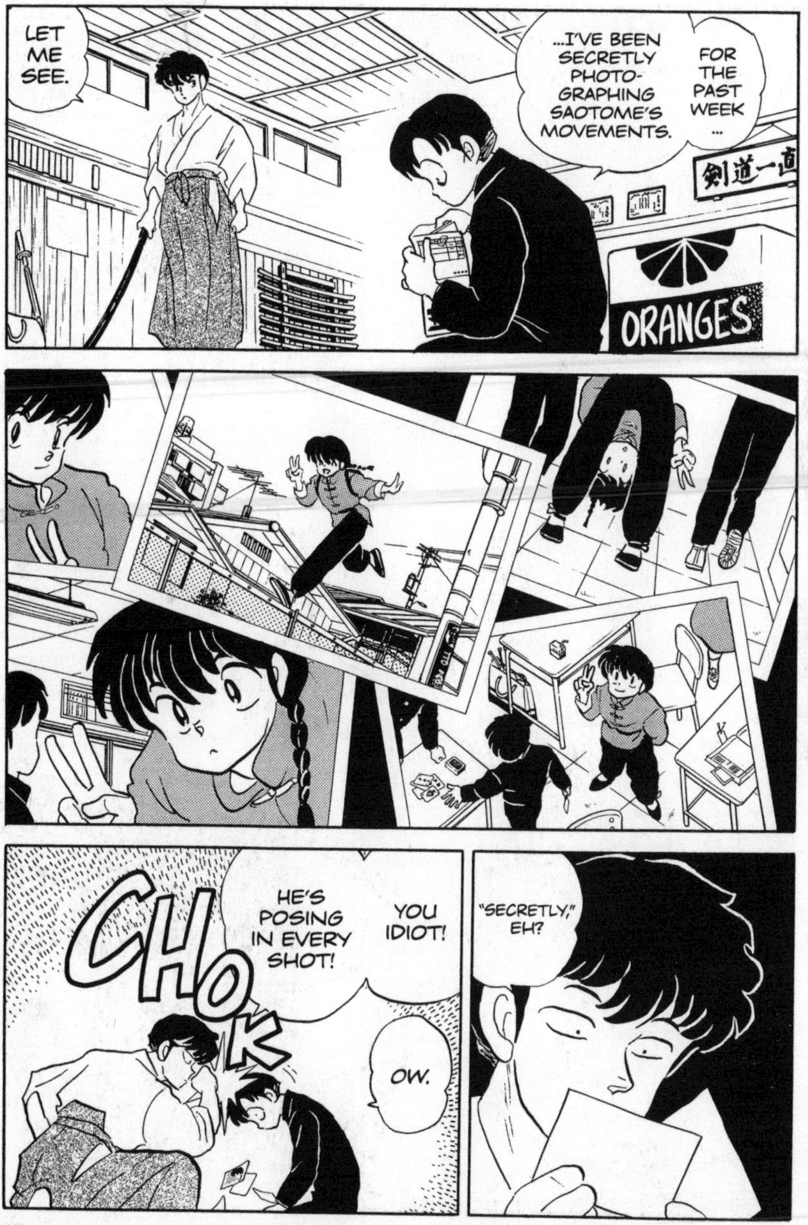

FOR THE PAST WEEK ...
...I'VE BEEN SECRETLY PHOTOGRAPHING SAOTOME'S MOVEMENTS.
剣道一直
ORANGES
LET ME SEE.
"SECRETLY," EH?
YOU IDIOT!
HE'S POSING IN EVERY SHOT!
CHOK
OW.

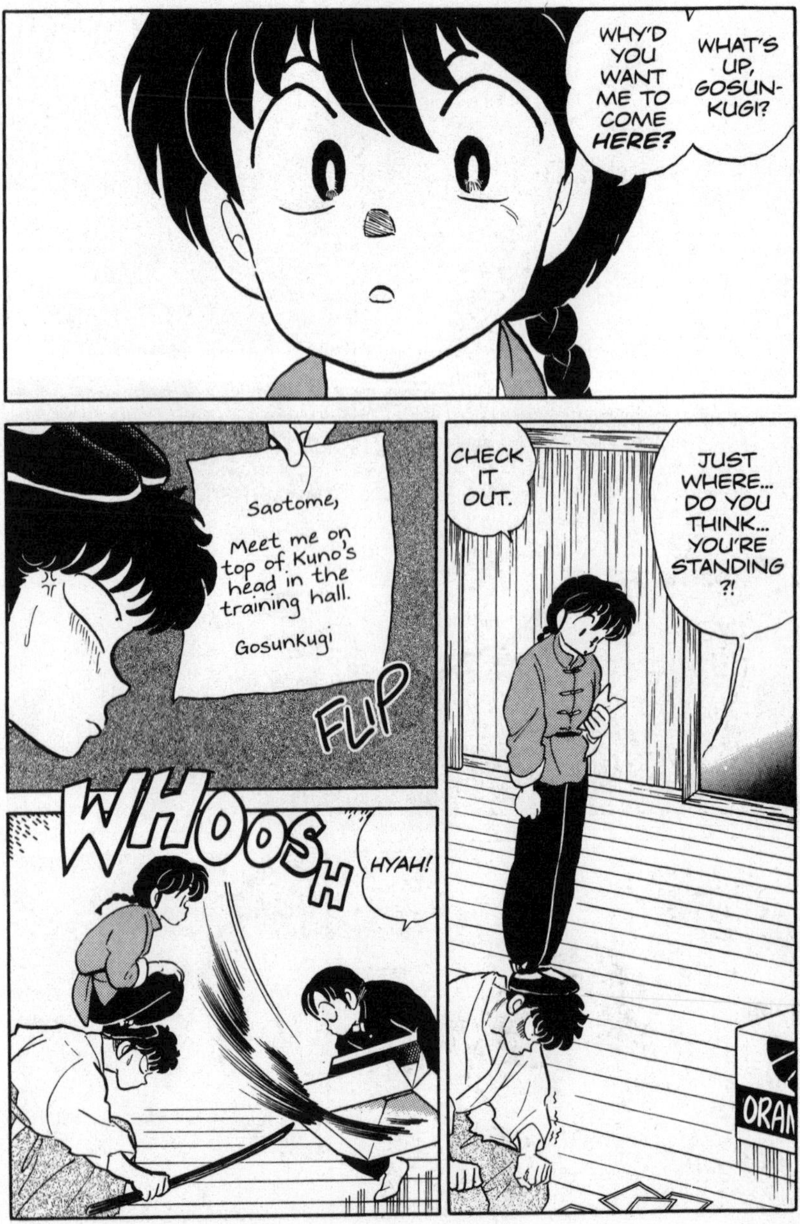
WHAT'S UP, GOSUNKUGI?
WHY'D YOU WANT ME TO COME HERE?
JUST WHERE... DO YOU THINK... YOU'RE STANDING?!
CHECK IT OUT.
ORAN
Saotome,
Meet me on top of Kuno's head in the training hall.
Gosunkugi
FLIP
WHOOSH
HYAH!

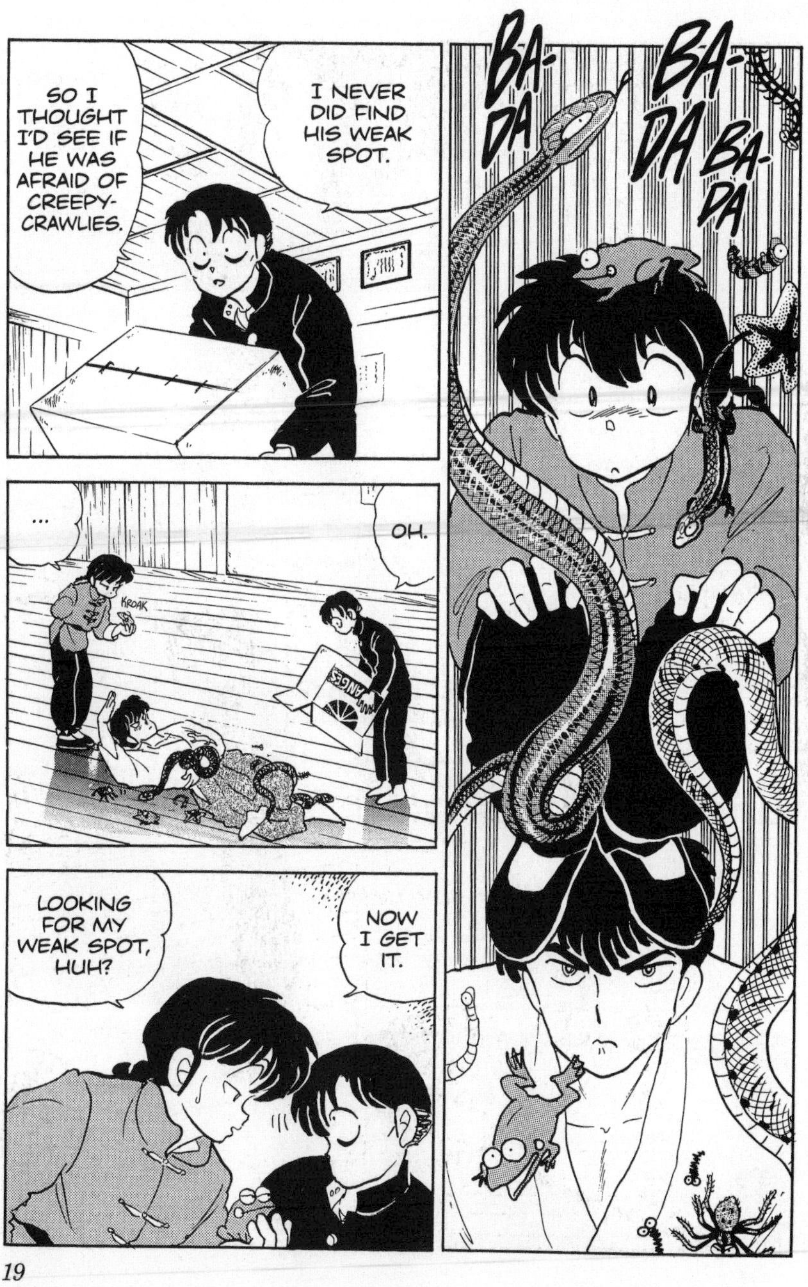
BA-DA
BA-DA
BA-DA
I NEVER DID FIND HIS WEAK SPOT.
SO I THOUGHT I'D SEE IF HE WAS AFRAID OF CREEPY-CRAWLIES.
OH.
...
KROAK
NOW I GET IT.
LOOKING FOR MY WEAK SPOT, HUH?

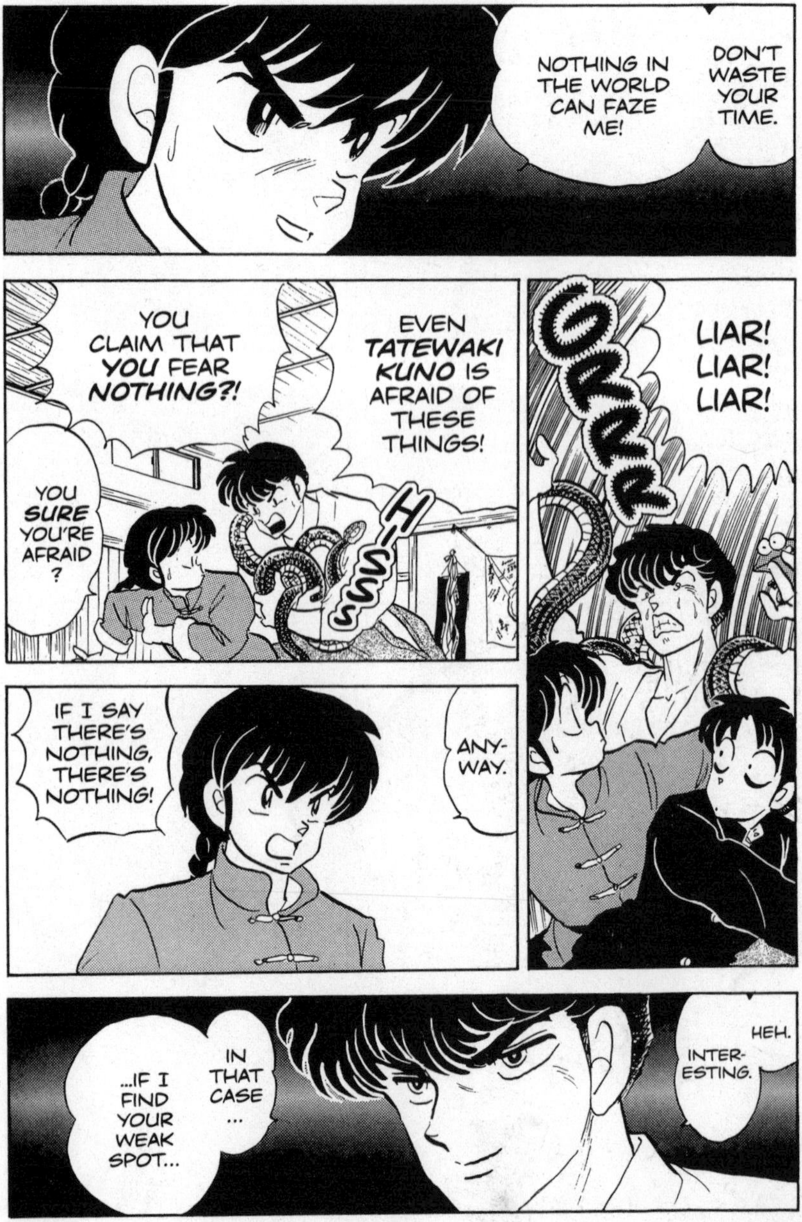
DON'T WASTE YOUR TIME.
NOTHING IN THE WORLD CAN FAZE ME!
LIAR! LIAR! LIAR!
GRRR
EVEN TATEWAKI KUNO IS AFRAID OF THESE THINGS!
YOU CLAIM THAT YOU FEAR NOTHING?!
H-SSSS
YOU SURE YOU'RE AFRAID?
ANY-WAY.
IF I SAY THERE'S NOTHING, THERE'S NOTHING!
HEH.
INTER-ESTING.
IN THAT CASE...
...IF I FIND YOUR WEAK SPOT...

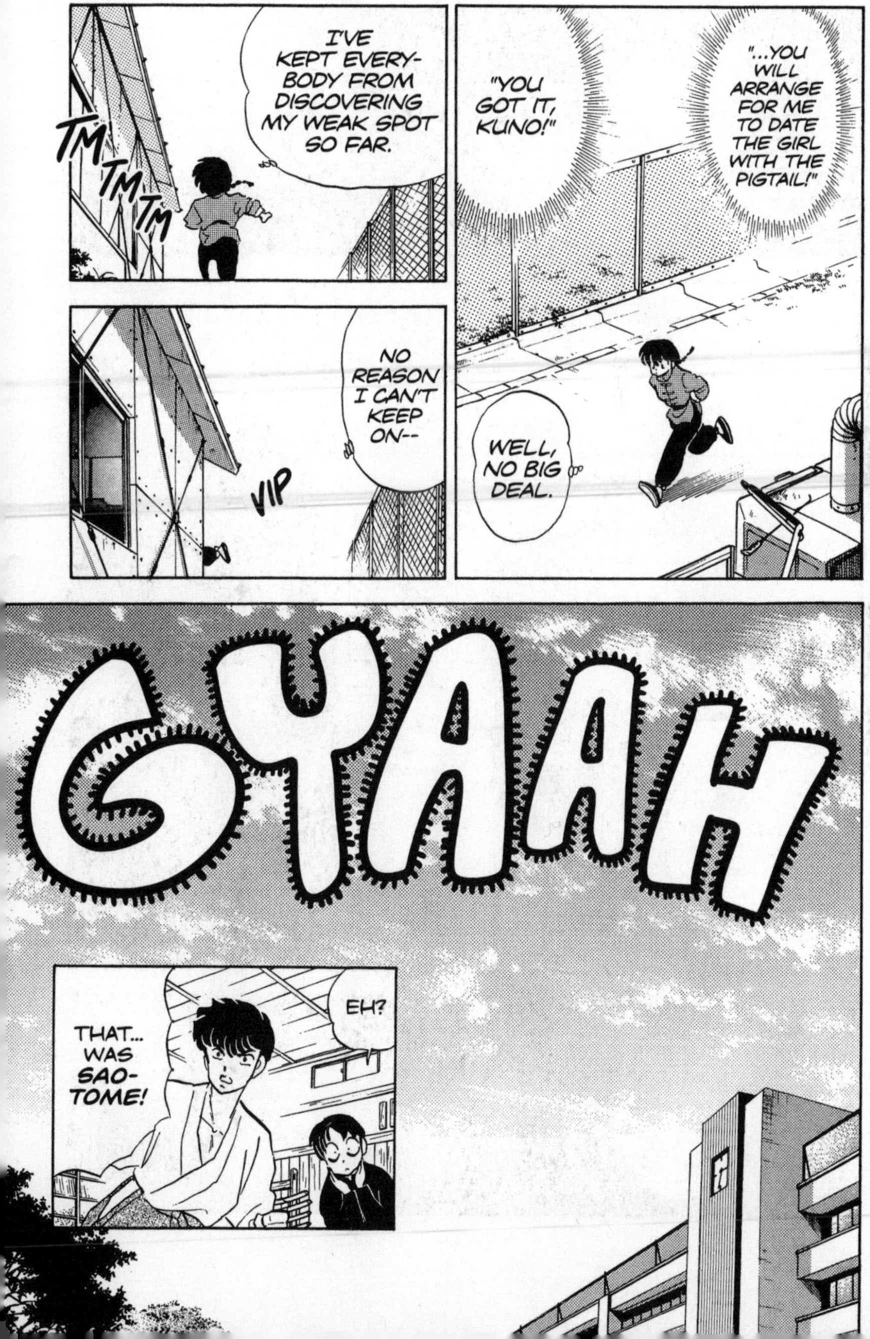
"...YOU WILL ARRANGE FOR ME TO DATE THE GIRL WITH THE PIGTAIL!"
"YOU GOT IT, KUNO!"
WELL, NO BIG DEAL.
I'VE KEPT EVERY-BODY FROM DISCOVERING MY WEAK SPOT SO FAR.
TM TM TM
NO REASON I CAN'T KEEP ON--
VIP
GYAAH
EH?
THAT... WAS SAO-TOME!

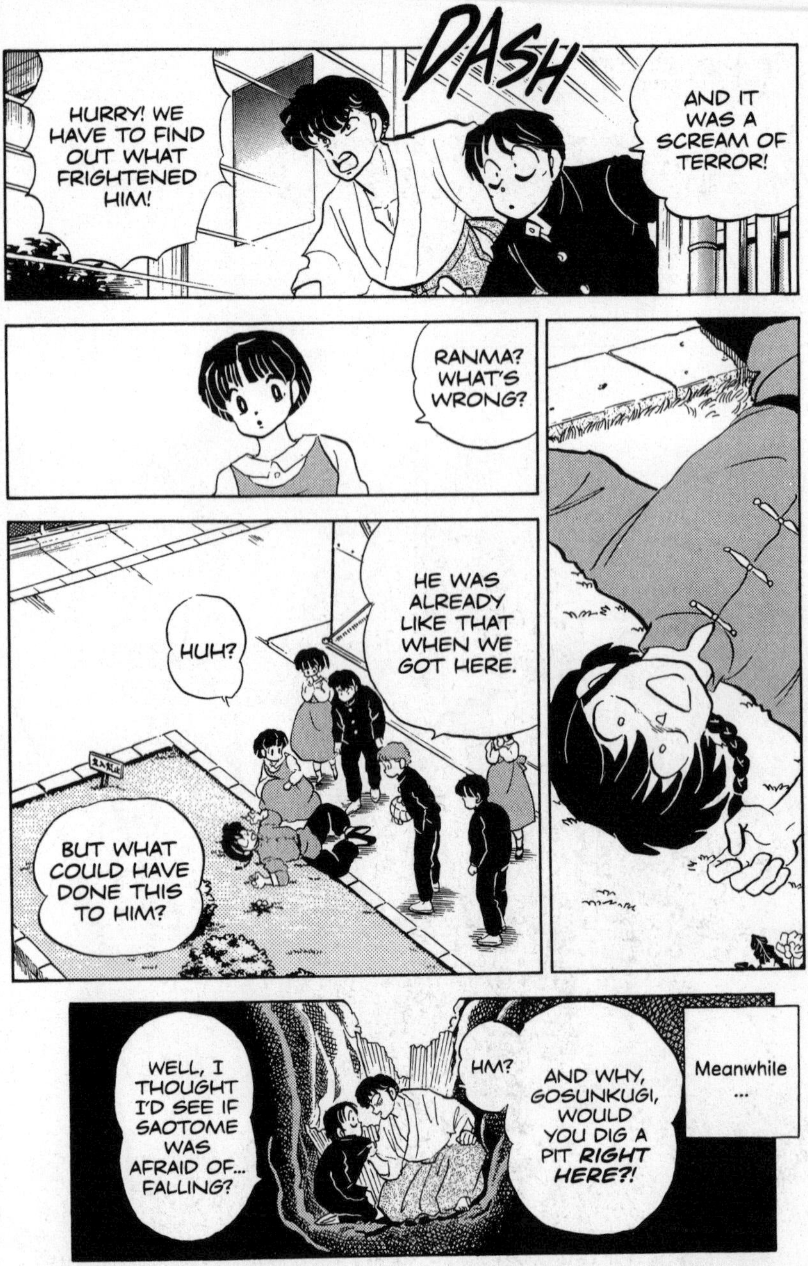
DASH
AND IT WAS A SCREAM OF TERROR!
HURRY! WE HAVE TO FIND OUT WHAT FRIGHTENED HIM!
RANMA? WHAT'S WRONG?
HE WAS ALREADY LIKE THAT WHEN WE GOT HERE.
HUH?
BUT WHAT COULD HAVE DONE THIS TO HIM?
Meanwhile ...
AND WHY, GOSUNKUGI, WOULD YOU DIG A PIT RIGHT HERE?!
HM?
WELL, I THOUGHT I'D SEE IF SAOTOME WAS AFRAID OF... FALLING?

PART 2
WEAK SPOT—FOUND!

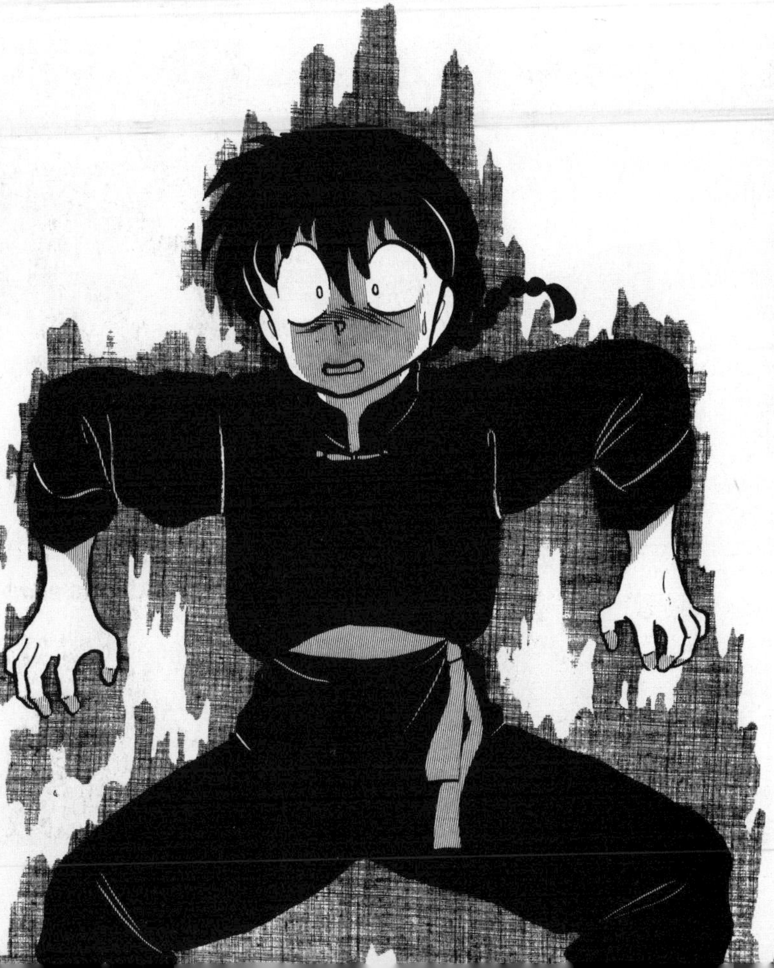

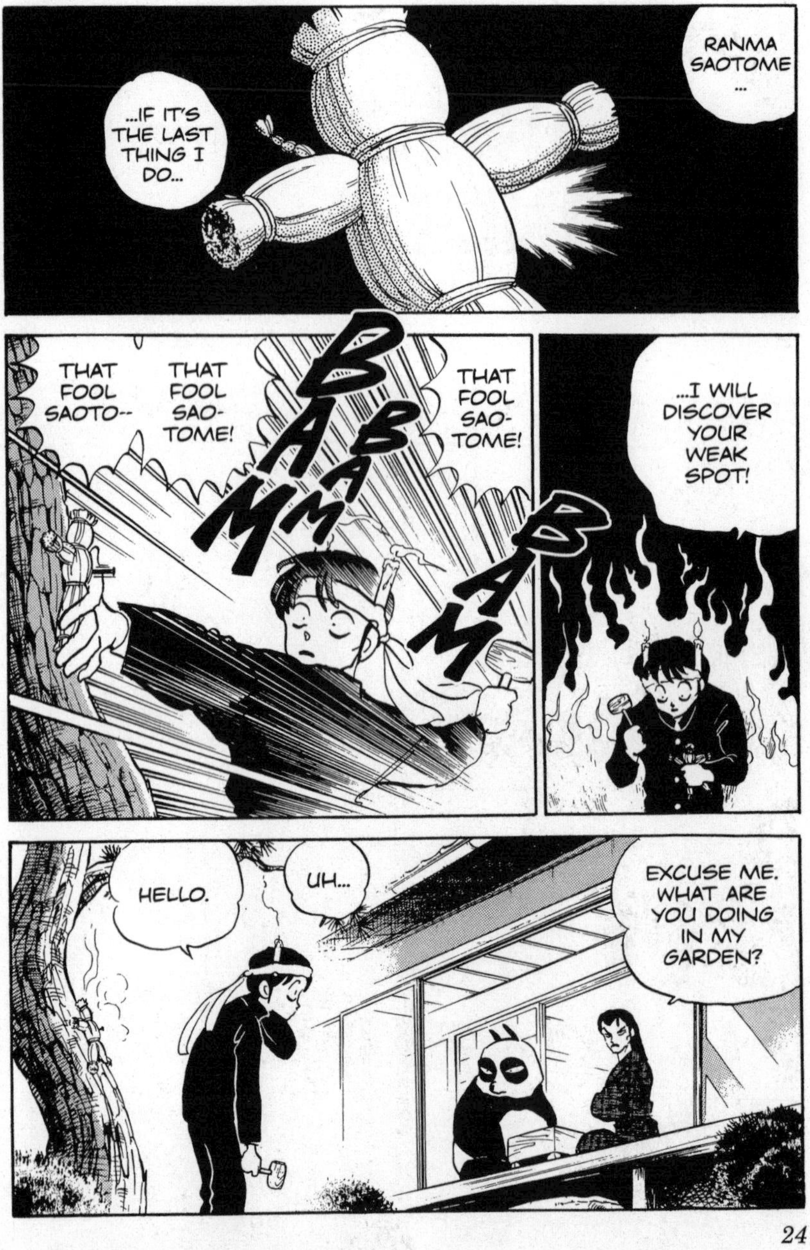
RANMA SAOTOME ...
...IF IT'S THE LAST THING I DO...
...I WILL DISCOVER YOUR WEAK SPOT!
BAM
THAT FOOL SAO-TOME!
BABAMM
THAT FOOL SAO-TOME!
THAT FOOL SAOTO--
EXCUSE ME. WHAT ARE YOU DOING IN MY GARDEN?
UH...
HELLO.

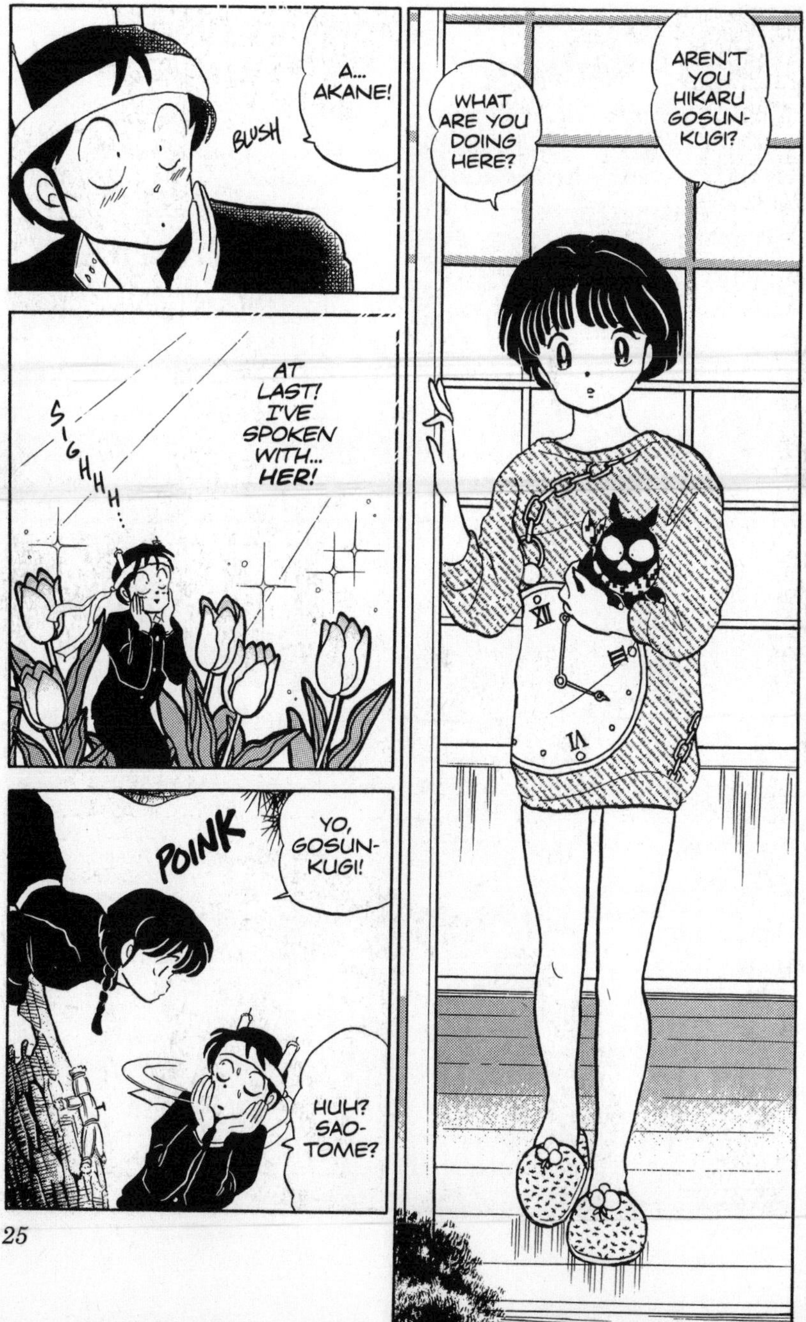
AREN'T YOU HIKARU GOSUN-KUGI?
WHAT ARE YOU DOING HERE?
A... AKANE!
BLUSH
AT LAST! I'VE SPOKEN WITH... HER!
SIGHHH...
YO, GOSUN-KUGI!
POINK
HUH? SAO-TOME?

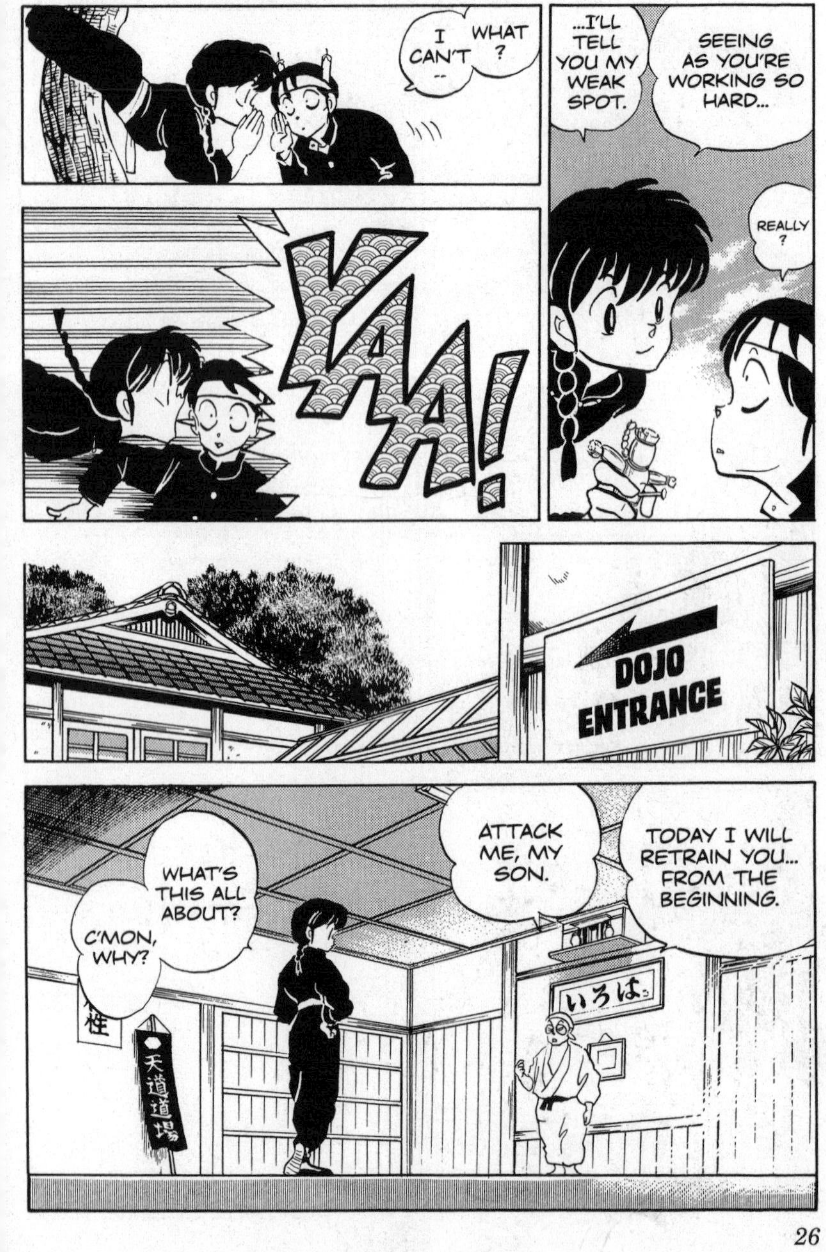
SEEING AS YOU'RE WORKING SO HARD...
...I'LL TELL YOU MY WEAK SPOT.
WHAT?
I CAN'T --
REALLY?
YAA!
DOJO ENTRANCE
TODAY I WILL RETRAIN YOU... FROM THE BEGINNING.
ATTACK ME, MY SON.
いろは
WHAT'S THIS ALL ABOUT?
C'MON, WHY?
天道道場

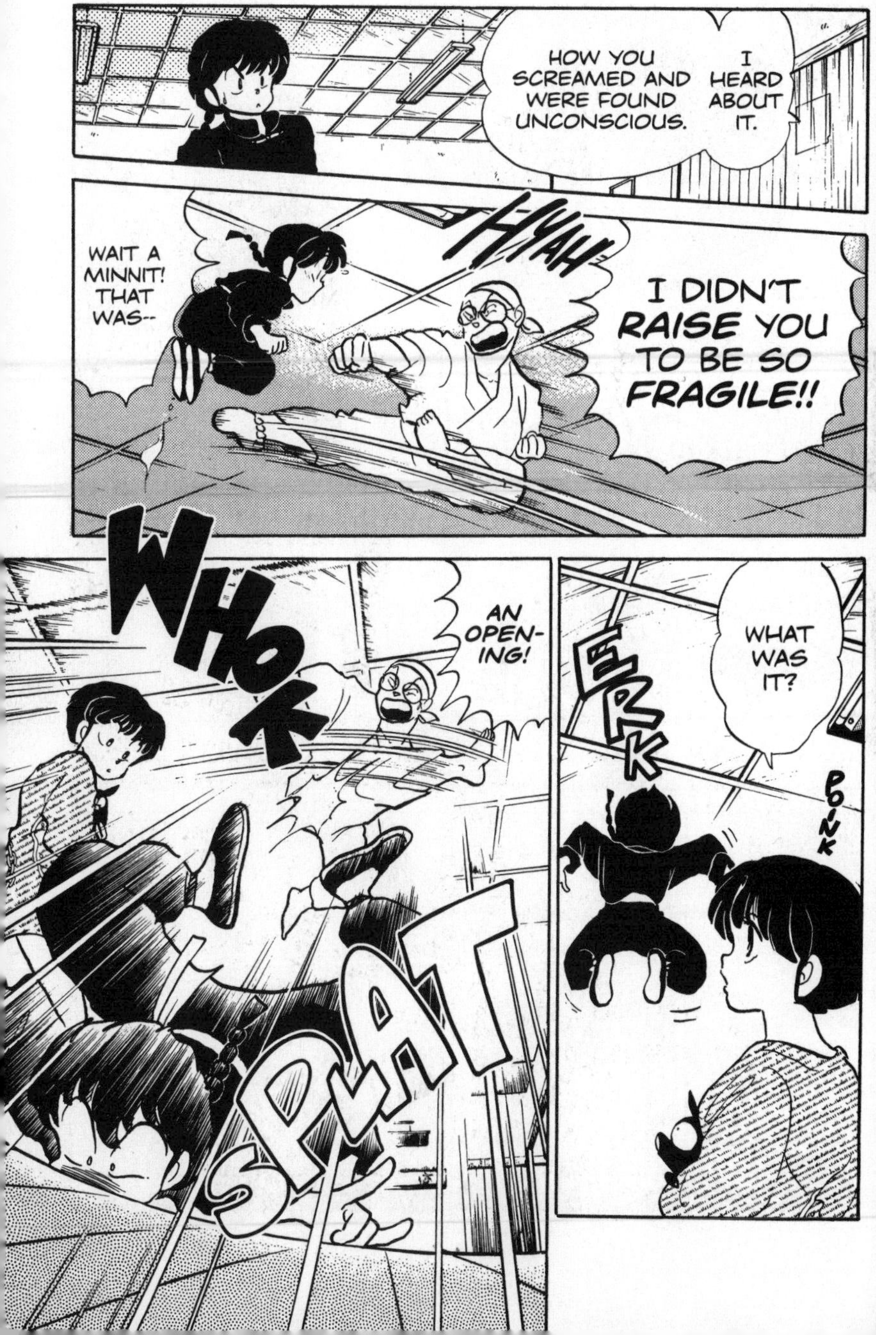
I HEARD ABOUT IT.
HOW YOU SCREAMED AND WERE FOUND UNCONSCIOUS.
HIYAH
I DIDN'T RAISE YOU TO BE SO FRAGILE!!
WAIT A MINNIT! THAT WAS--
WHAT WAS IT?
ERK
POINK
AN OPEN-ING!
WHOK
SPAT

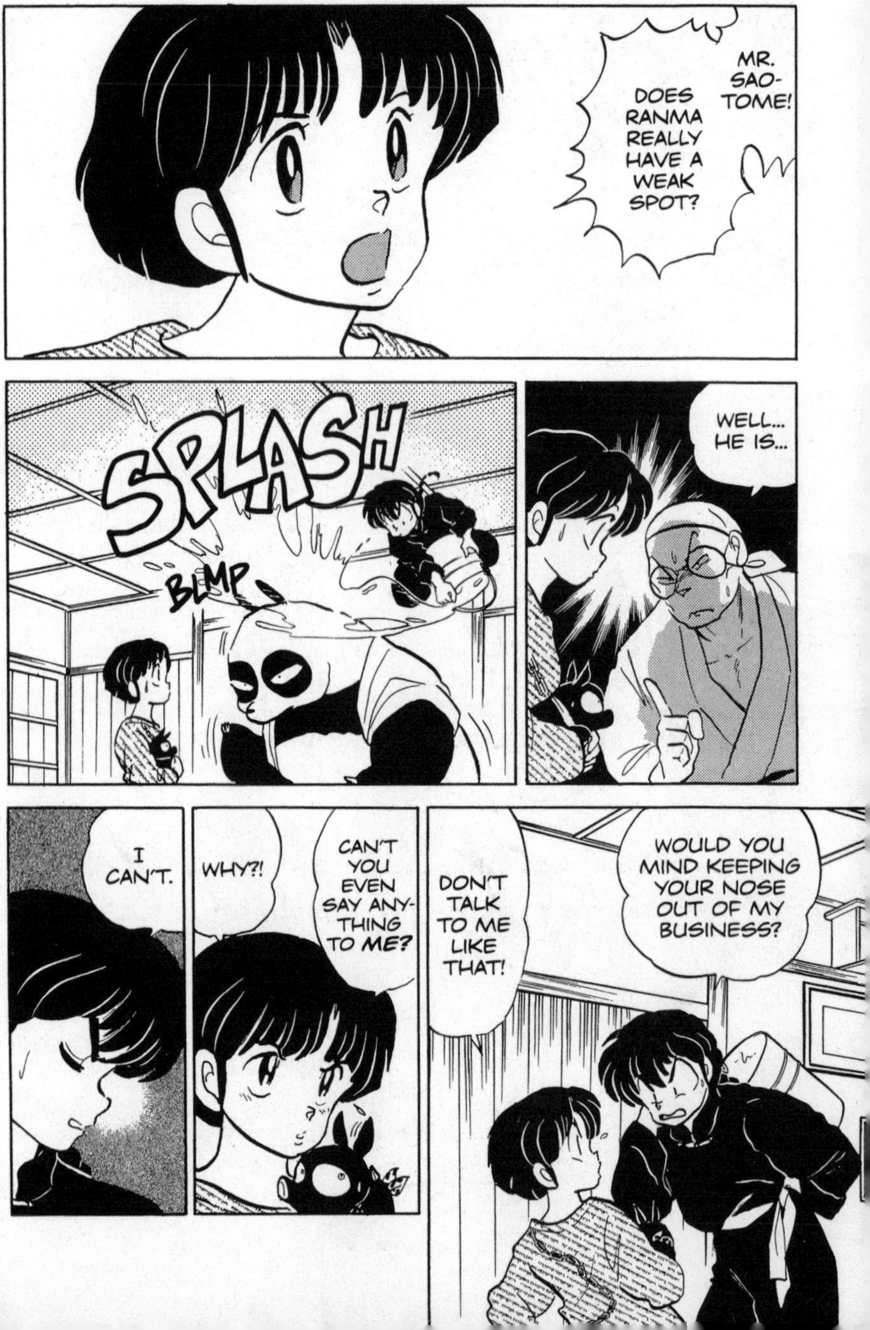
MR. SAOTOME!
DOES RANMA REALLY HAVE A WEAK SPOT?
WELL... HE IS...
SPLASH
BLMP
WOULD YOU MIND KEEPING YOUR NOSE OUT OF MY BUSINESS?
DON'T TALK TO ME LIKE THAT!
CAN'T YOU EVEN SAY ANYTHING TO *ME*?
WHY?!
I CAN'T.

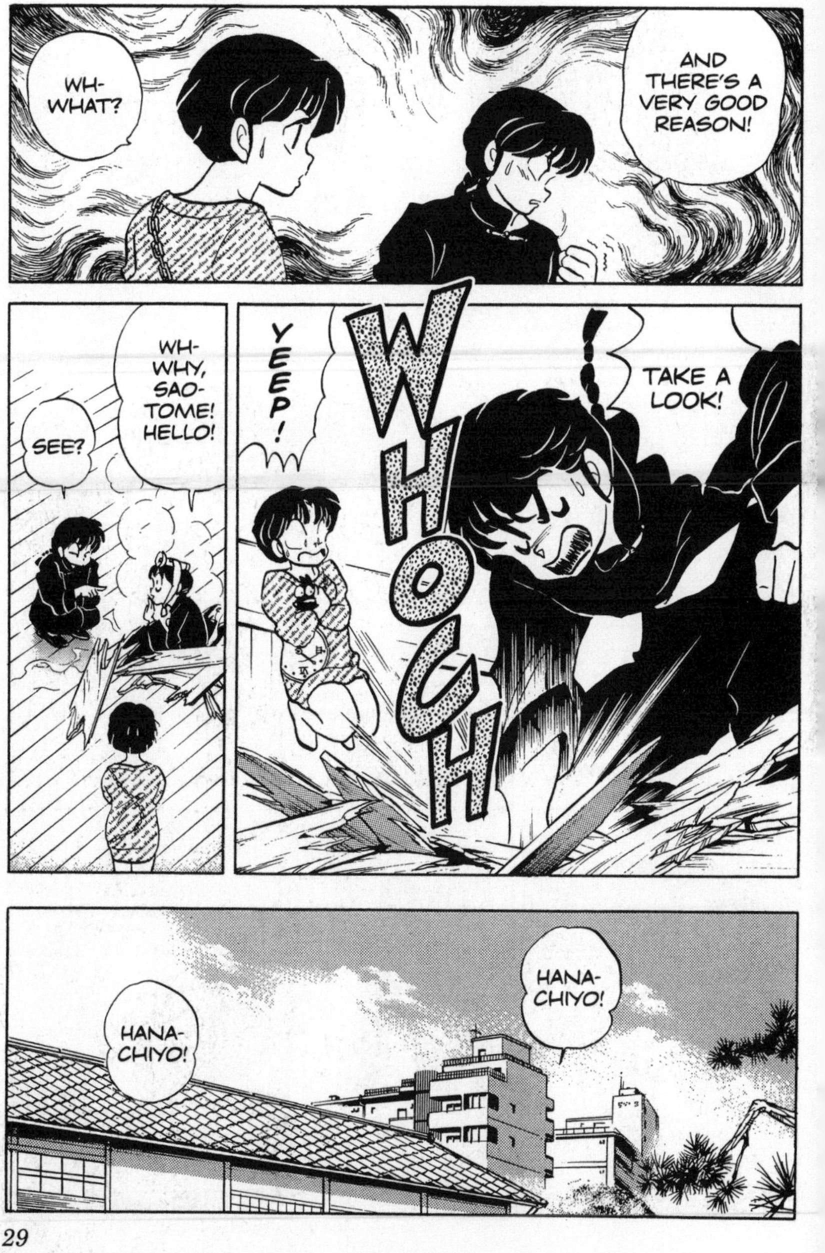
AND THERE'S A VERY GOOD REASON!
WH- WHAT?
TAKE A LOOK!
WHOUCH
YEEP!
WH- WHY, SAO- TOME! HELLO!
SEE?
HANA- CHIYO!
HANA- CHIYO!

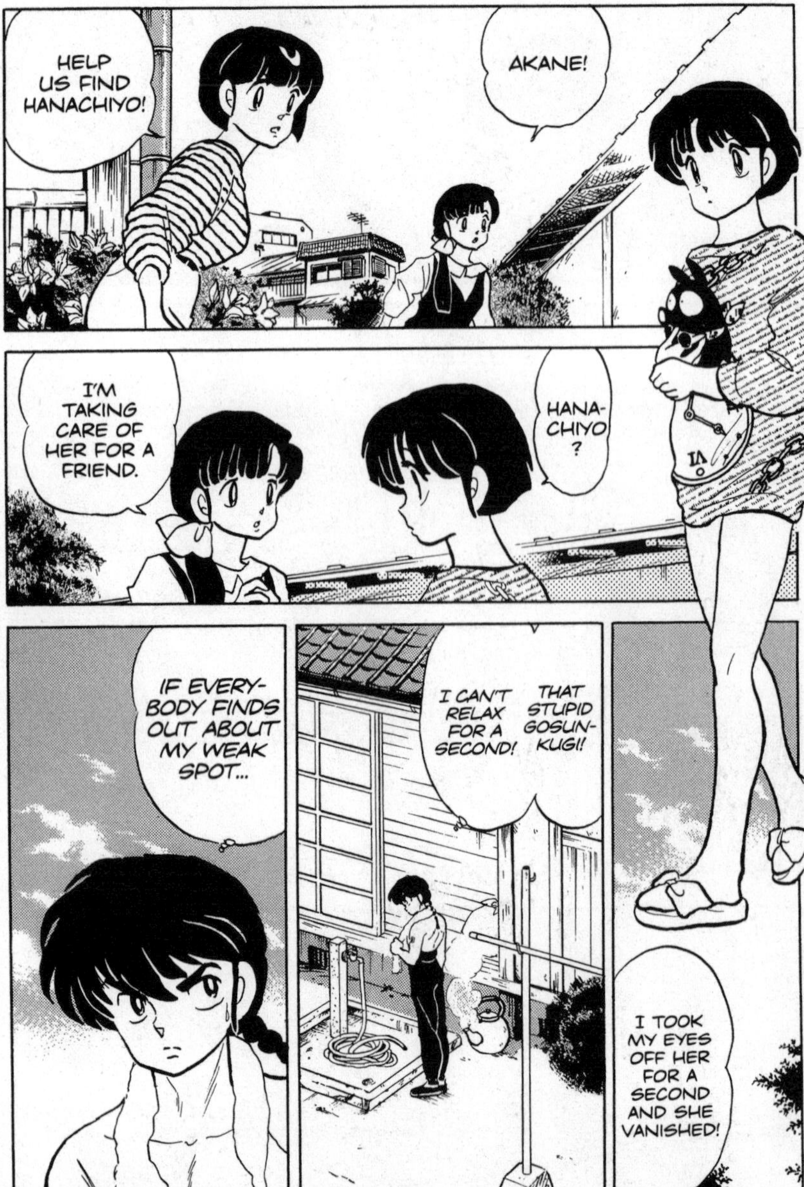
AKANE!
HELP US FIND HANACHIYO!
HANA-CHIYO?
I'M TAKING CARE OF HER FOR A FRIEND.
I TOOK MY EYES OFF HER FOR A SECOND AND SHE VANISHED!
I CAN'T RELAX FOR A SECOND! THAT STUPID GOSUNKUGI!
IF EVERY-BODY FINDS OUT ABOUT MY WEAK SPOT...

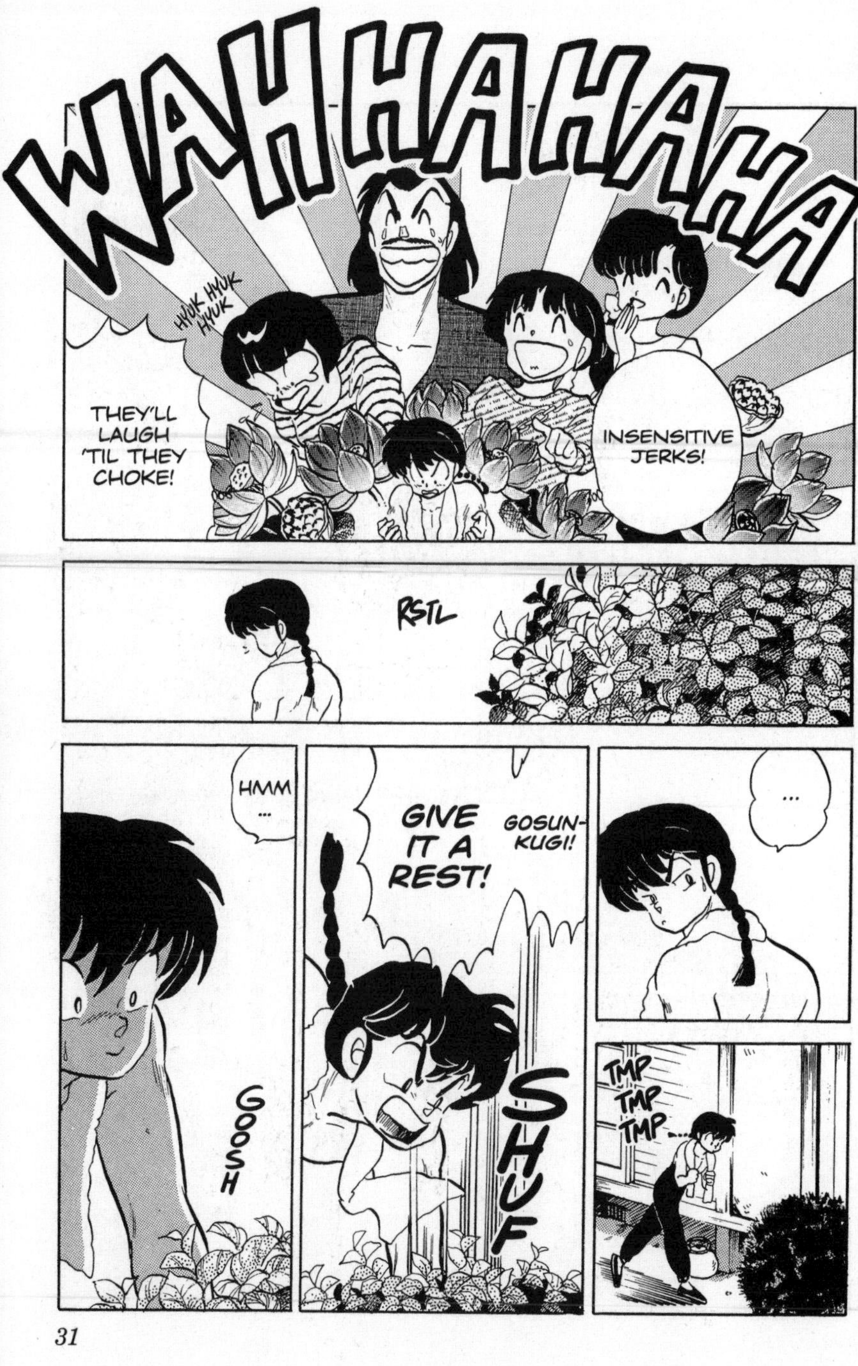
WAHHAHAHAHA
INSENSITIVE JERKS!
HYUK HYUK HYUK
THEY'LL LAUGH 'TIL THEY CHOKE!
RSTL
...
TMP TMP TMP
GOSUN-KUGI!
GIVE IT A REST!
SHUF
HMM ...
GOOSH

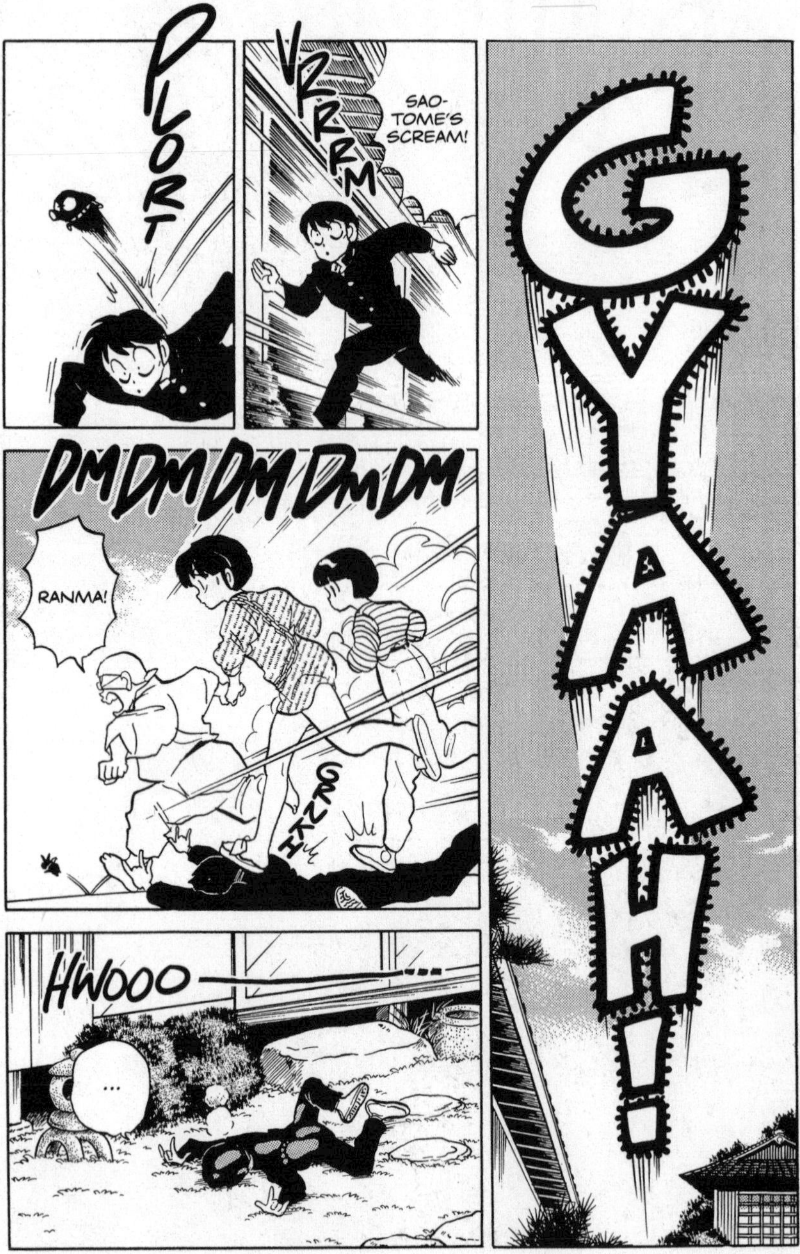
GYAAAH!
VRRRM
SAO-TOME'S SCREAM!
PLORT
DM DM DM DM DM
RANMA!
GRNKH
HWOOO
...

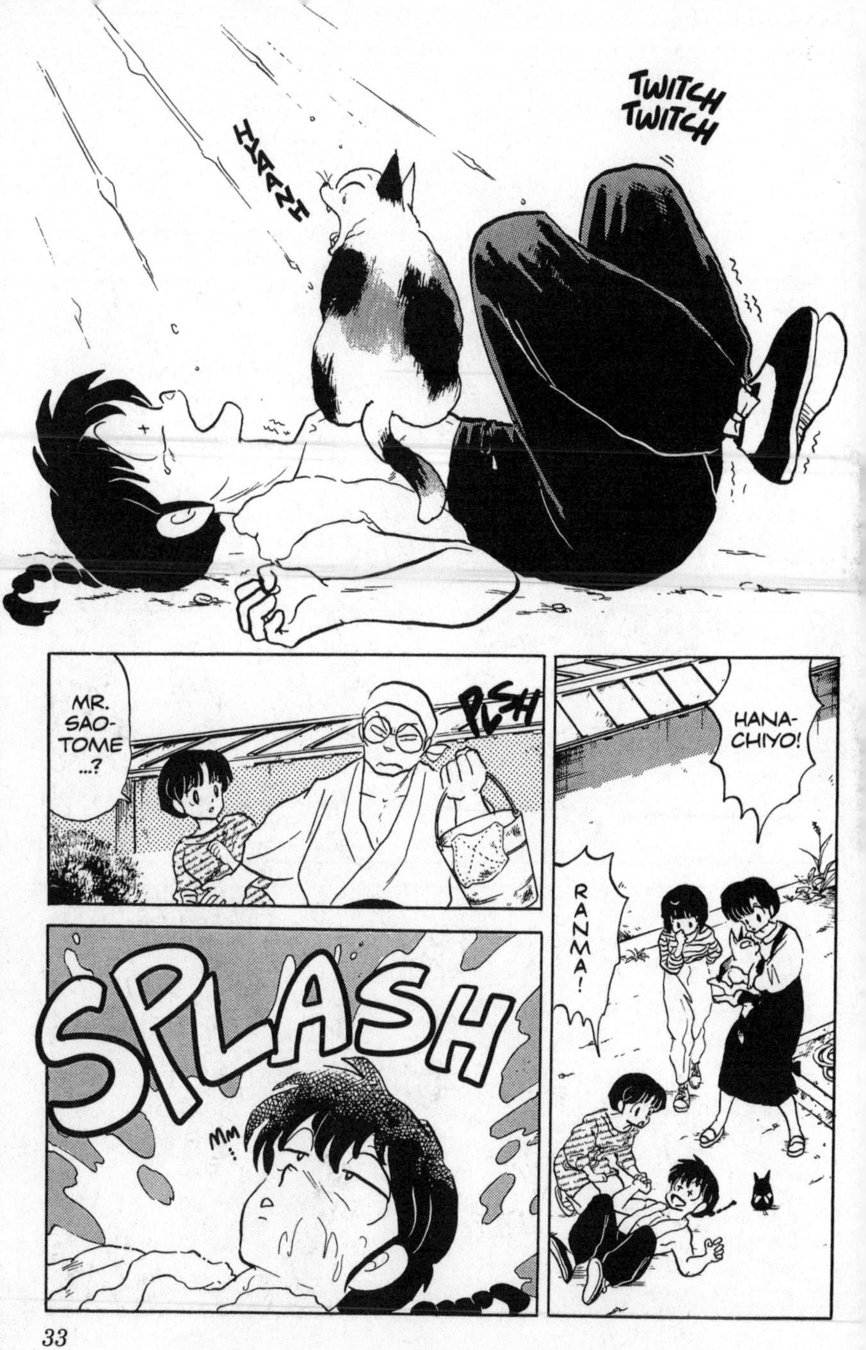
TWITCH TWITCH
HYAAAH!
HANA-CHIYO!
MR. SAO-TOME ...?
PLSH
RANMA!
SPLASH
MM...

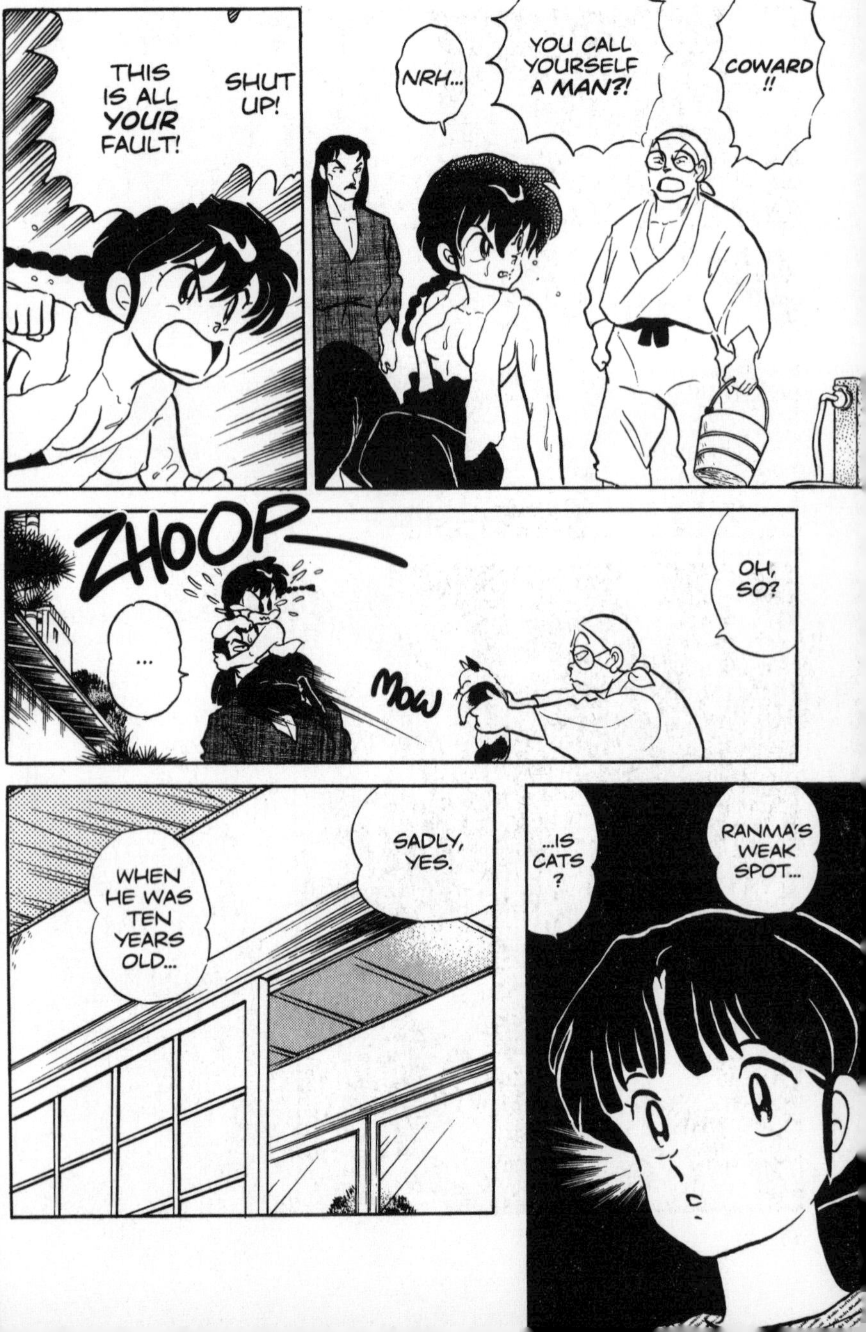
COWARD !!
YOU CALL YOURSELF A MAN?!
NRH...
SHUT UP!
THIS IS ALL YOUR FAULT!
OH, SO?
MOW
ZHOOP
...
RANMA'S WEAK SPOT...
...IS CATS ?
SADLY, YES.
WHEN HE WAS TEN YEARS OLD...

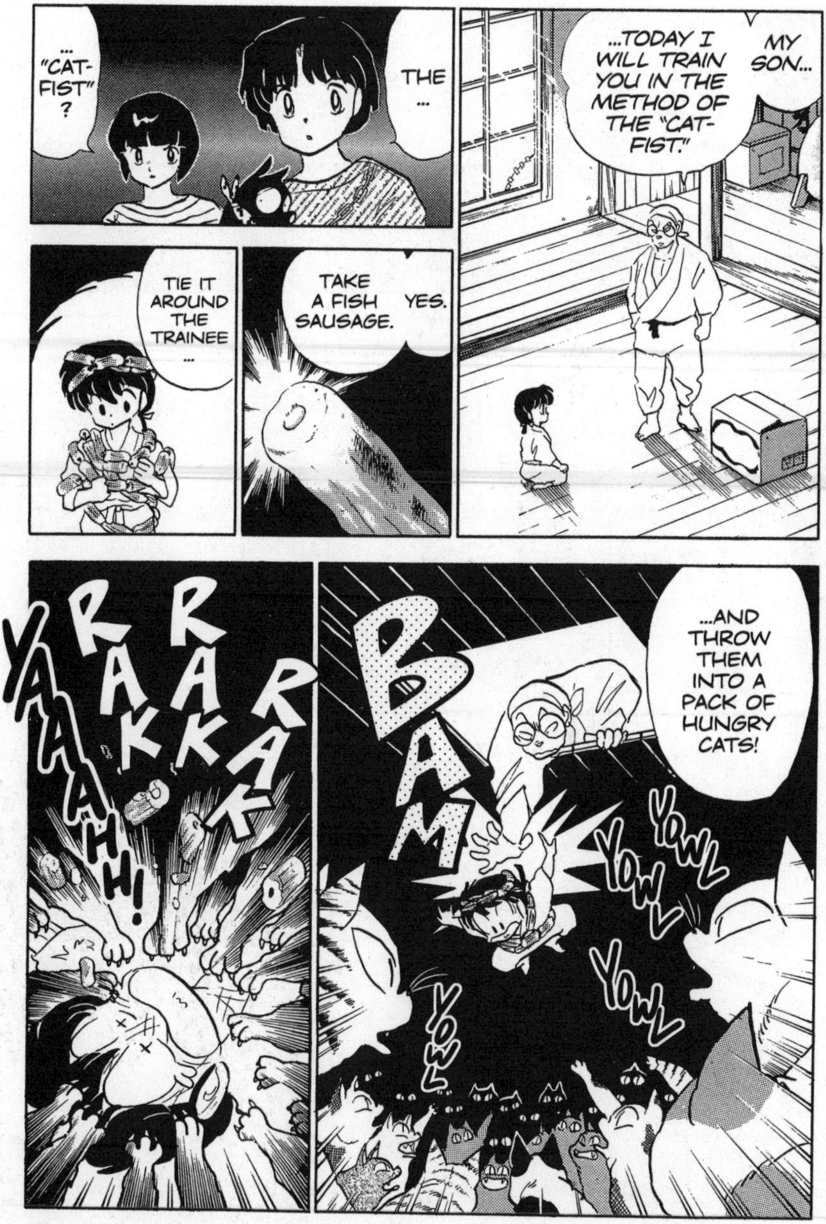
MY SON...
...TODAY I WILL TRAIN YOU IN THE METHOD OF THE "CAT-FIST."
THE ...
... "CAT-FIST"?
YES.
TAKE A FISH SAUSAGE.
TIE IT AROUND THE TRAINEE ...
...AND THROW THEM INTO A PACK OF HUNGRY CATS!
BAM
YOWL
YOWL
YOWL
YOWL
YAAAAHH!
RRAAKKRAK

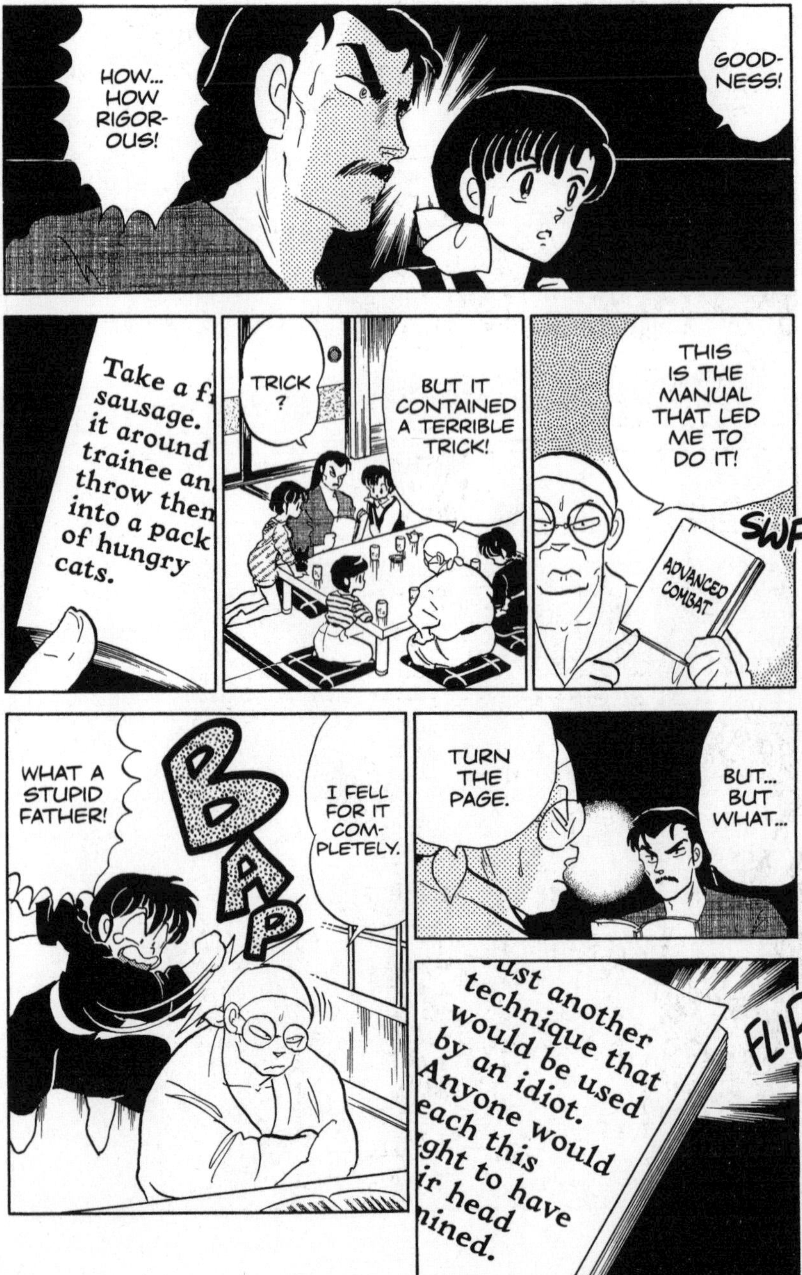
GOOD-NESS!
HOW... HOW RIGOR-OUS!
THIS IS THE MANUAL THAT LED ME TO DO IT!
SWF
ADVANCED COMBAT
BUT IT CONTAINED A TERRIBLE TRICK!
TRICK ?
Take a f sausage. it around trainee an throw then into a pack of hungry cats.
BUT... BUT WHAT...
TURN THE PAGE.
FLIP
ust another technique that would be used by an idiot. Anyone would each this ght to have ir head nined.
I FELL FOR IT COM-PLETELY.
BAP
WHAT A STUPID FATHER!

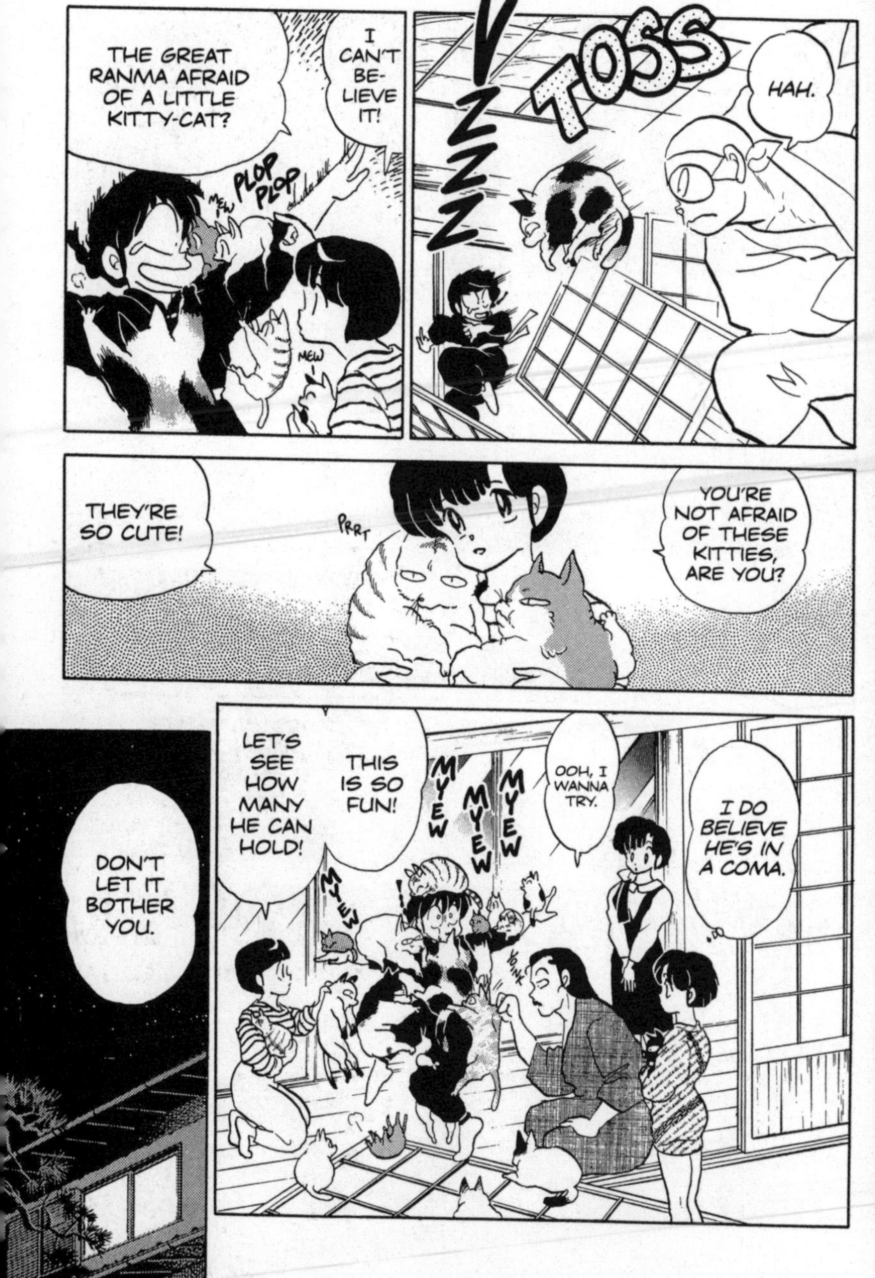
TOSS
HAH.
I CAN'T BE-LIEVE IT!
THE GREAT RANMA AFRAID OF A LITTLE KITTY-CAT?
PLOP PLOP
MEW
MEW
YOU'RE NOT AFRAID OF THESE KITTIES, ARE YOU?
PRRT
THEY'RE SO CUTE!
I DO BELIEVE HE'S IN A COMA.
OOH, I WANNA TRY.
MYEW
MYEW
MYEW
THIS IS SO FUN!
LET'S SEE HOW MANY HE CAN HOLD!
MYEW
YOINK
DON'T LET IT BOTHER YOU.

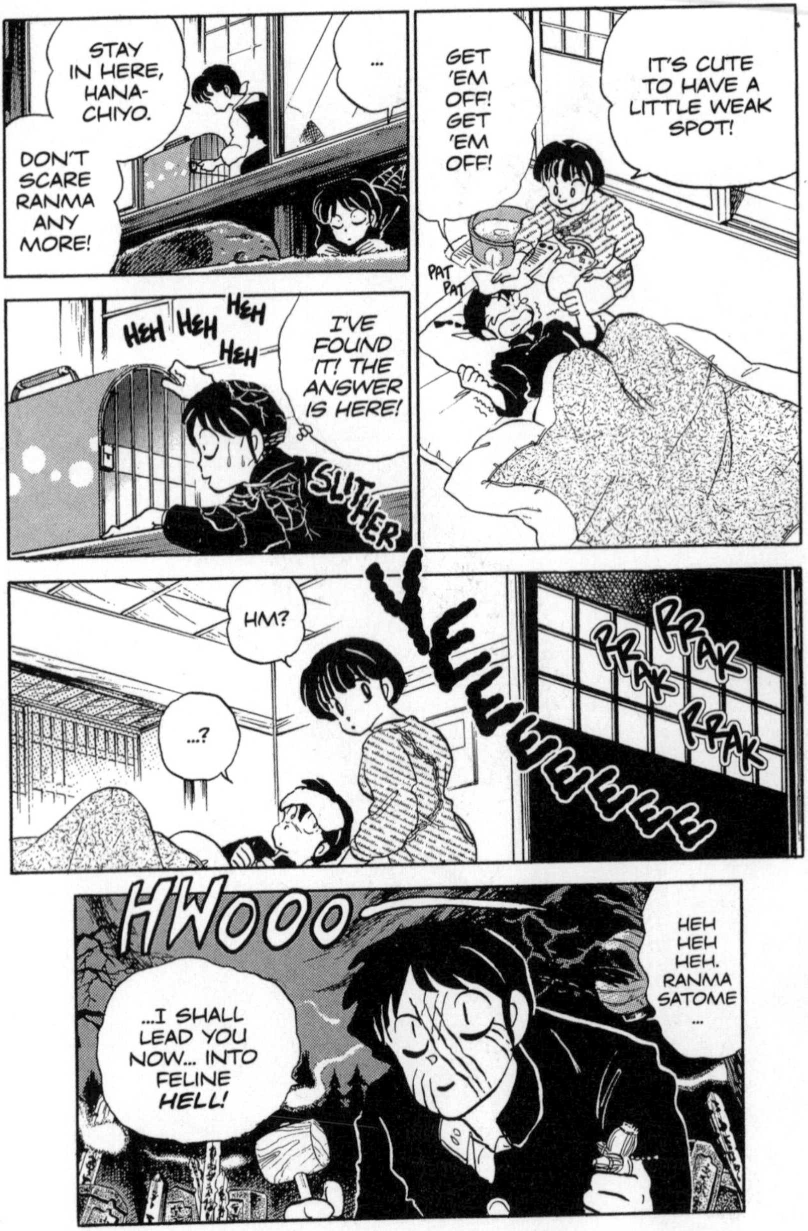
IT'S CUTE TO HAVE A LITTLE WEAK SPOT!
GET 'EM OFF! GET 'EM OFF!
PAT PAT
...
STAY IN HERE, HANA-CHIYO.
DON'T SCARE RANMA ANY MORE!
I'VE FOUND IT! THE ANSWER IS HERE!
HEH HEH HEH HEH
SLITHER
RRAK RRAK RRAK RRAK
YEEEEEEEEE
HM?
...?
HWOOO
HEH HEH HEH. RANMA SATOME ...
...I SHALL LEAD YOU NOW... INTO FELINE HELL!

PART 3
CAT HELL

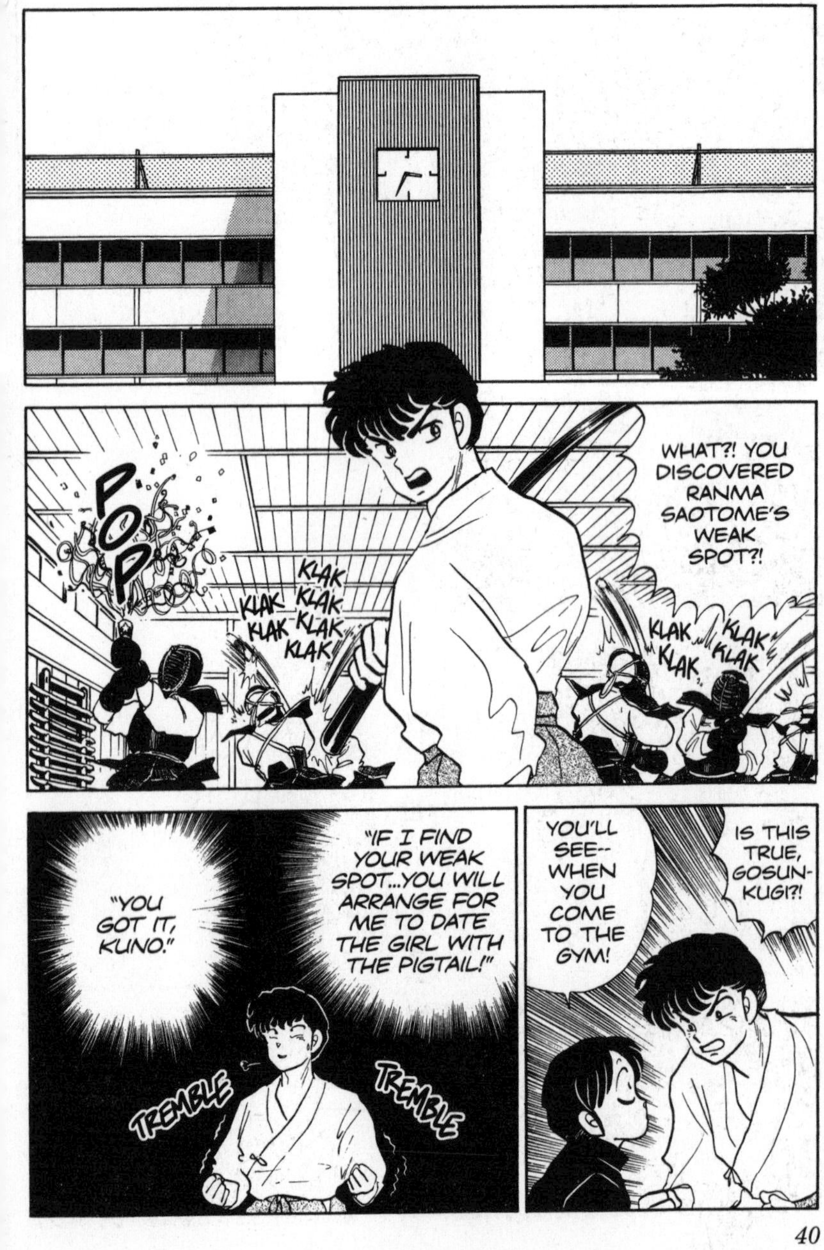
WHAT?! YOU DISCOVERED RANMA SAOTOME'S WEAK SPOT?!
KLAK KLAK KLAK KLAK
POP
KLAK KLAK KLAK KLAK KLAK KLAK
IS THIS TRUE, GOSUN-KUGI?!
YOU'LL SEE-- WHEN YOU COME TO THE GYM!
"IF I FIND YOUR WEAK SPOT...YOU WILL ARRANGE FOR ME TO DATE THE GIRL WITH THE PIGTAIL!"
"YOU GOT IT, KUNO."
TREMBLE
TREMBLE

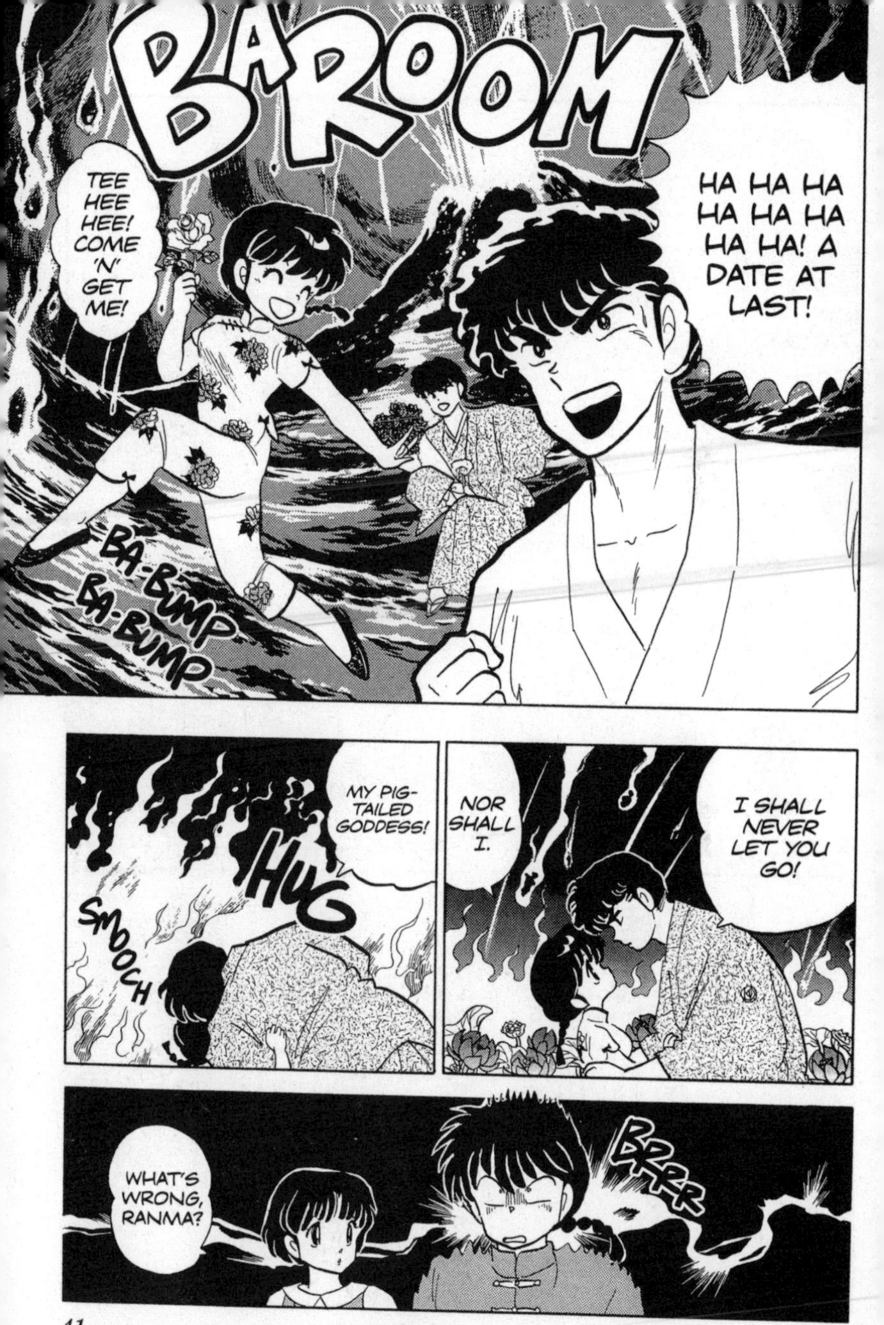
BAROOM
HA HA HA HA HA HA HA HA! A DATE AT LAST!
TEE HEE HEE! COME 'N' GET ME!
BA-BUMP BA-BUMP
I SHALL NEVER LET YOU GO!
NOR SHALL I.
MY PIG-TAILED GODDESS!
HUG
SMOOCH
BRRR
WHAT'S WRONG, RANMA?

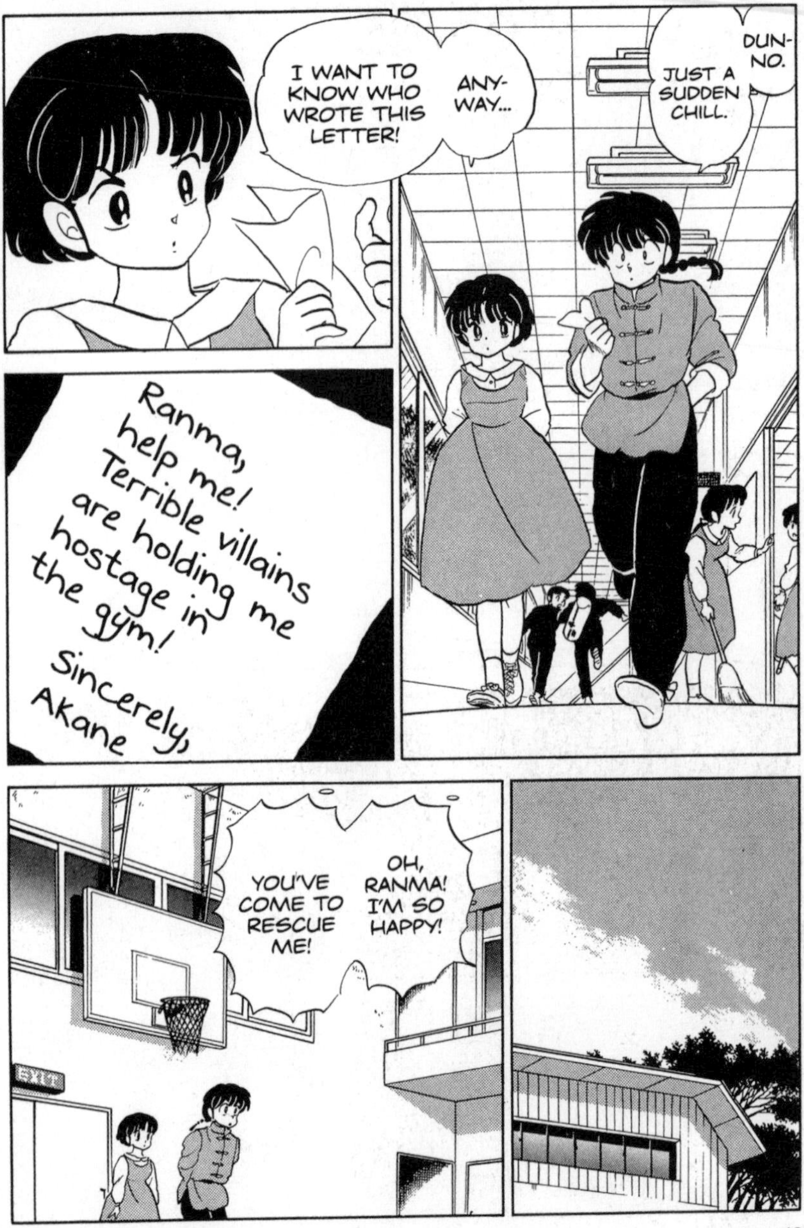
DUN-NO.
JUST A SUDDEN CHILL.
ANYWAY...
I WANT TO KNOW WHO WROTE THIS LETTER!
Ranma, help me! Terrible villains are holding me hostage in the gym! Sincerely, Akane
OH, RANMA! I'M SO HAPPY!
YOU'VE COME TO RESCUE ME!
EXIT

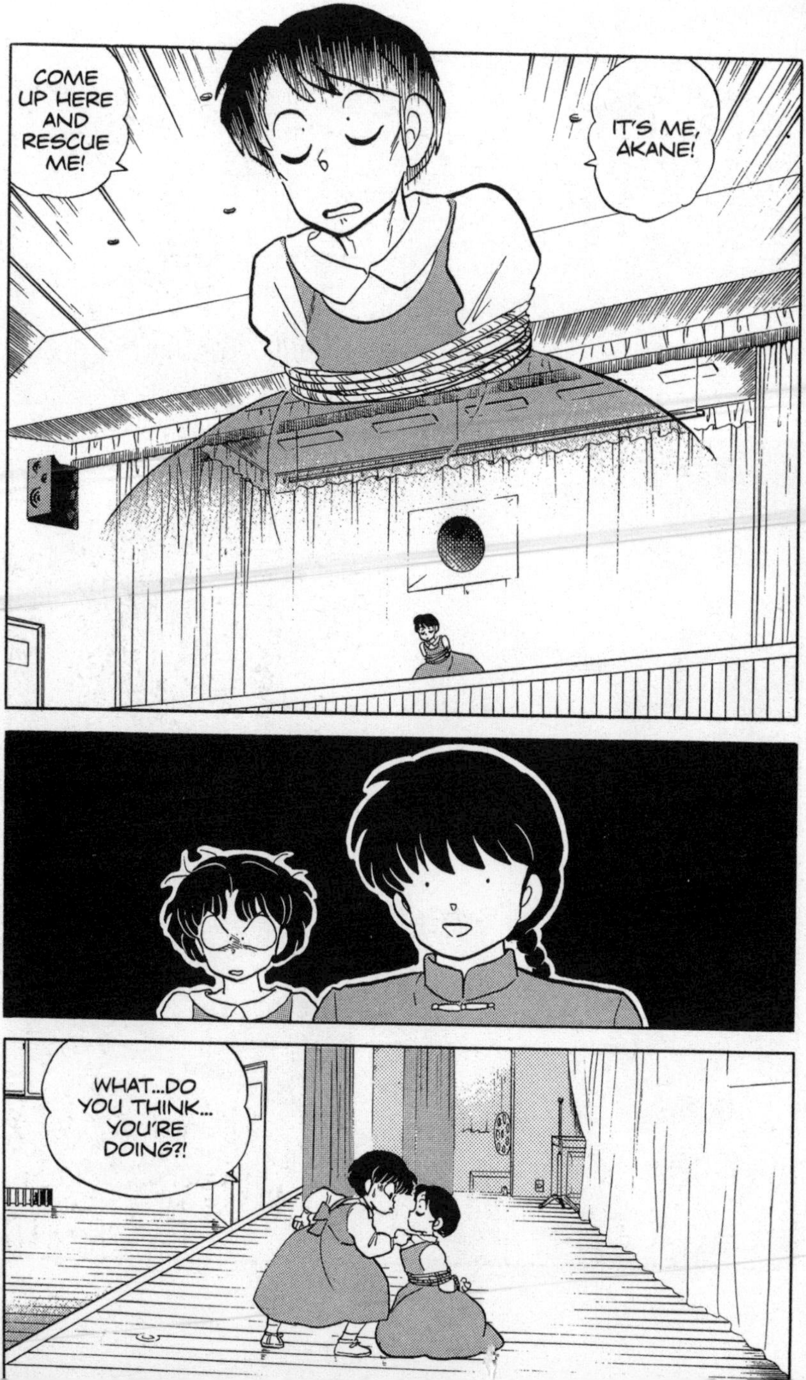
IT'S ME, AKANE!
COME UP HERE AND RESCUE ME!
WHAT...DO YOU THINK... YOU'RE DOING?!

AKANE! SHE SPOKE TO ME AGAIN!
S~GH
WAH HA HA! YOU'VE FALLEN INTO MY TRAP, SAOTOME!
LISTEN ...
SLIP
YOINK
VOOOP
UH... OH...
WHAT IS THIS ?!
AND JUST WHO WAS IT YOU WANTED TO DROP?

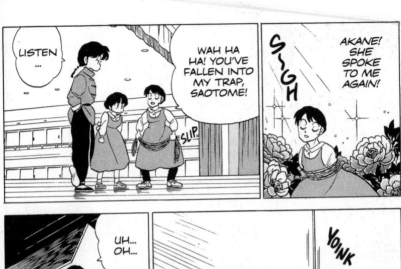

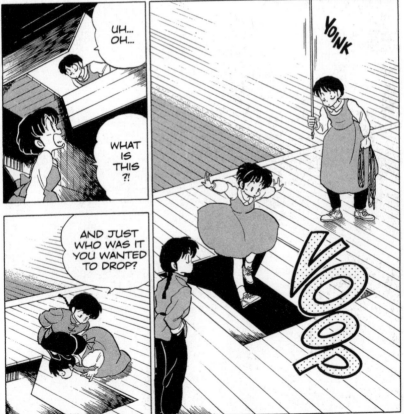

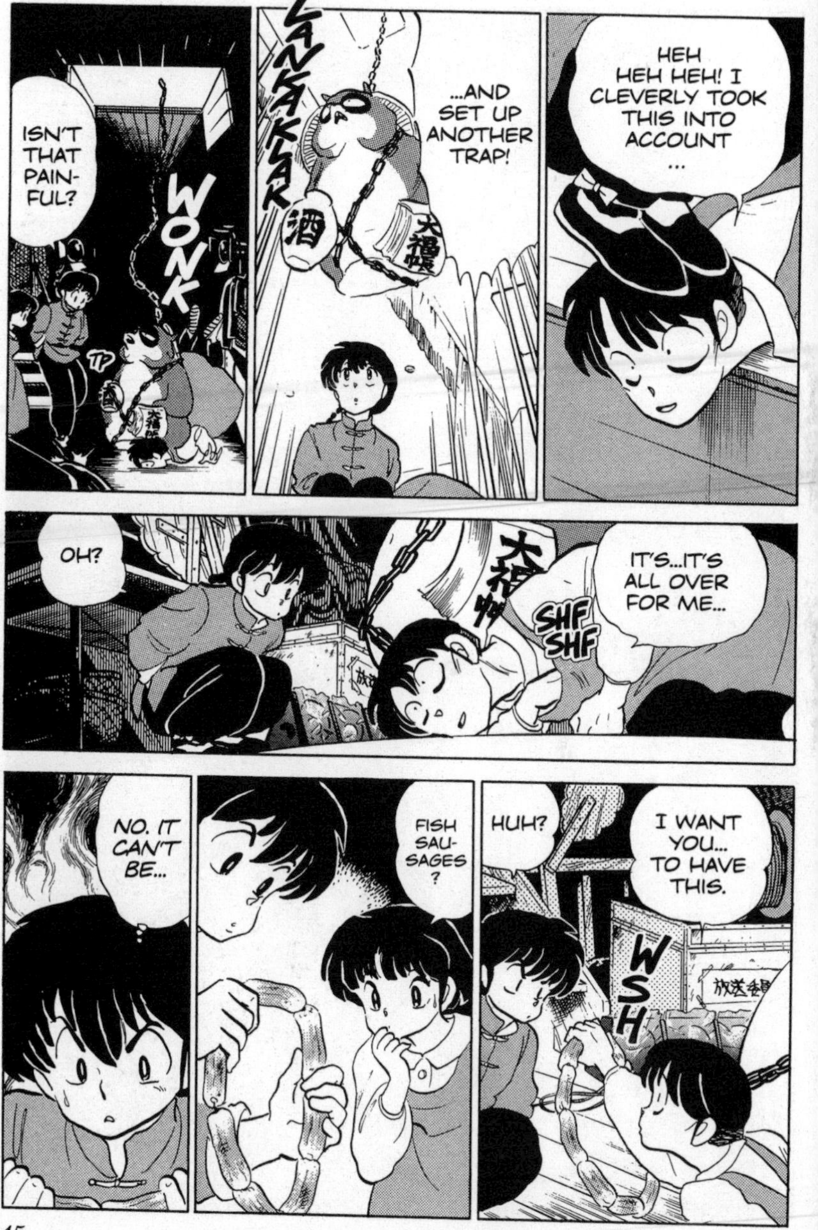
HEH HEH HEH! I CLEVERLY TOOK THIS INTO ACCOUNT ...
CLANKAKLAK
...AND SET UP ANOTHER TRAP!
酒
大福帳
ISN'T THAT PAIN-FUL?
WONK
TP
IT'S...IT'S ALL OVER FOR ME...
SHF SHF
OH?
I WANT YOU... TO HAVE THIS.
WSH
HUH?
FISH SAU-SAGES?
NO. IT CAN'T BE...

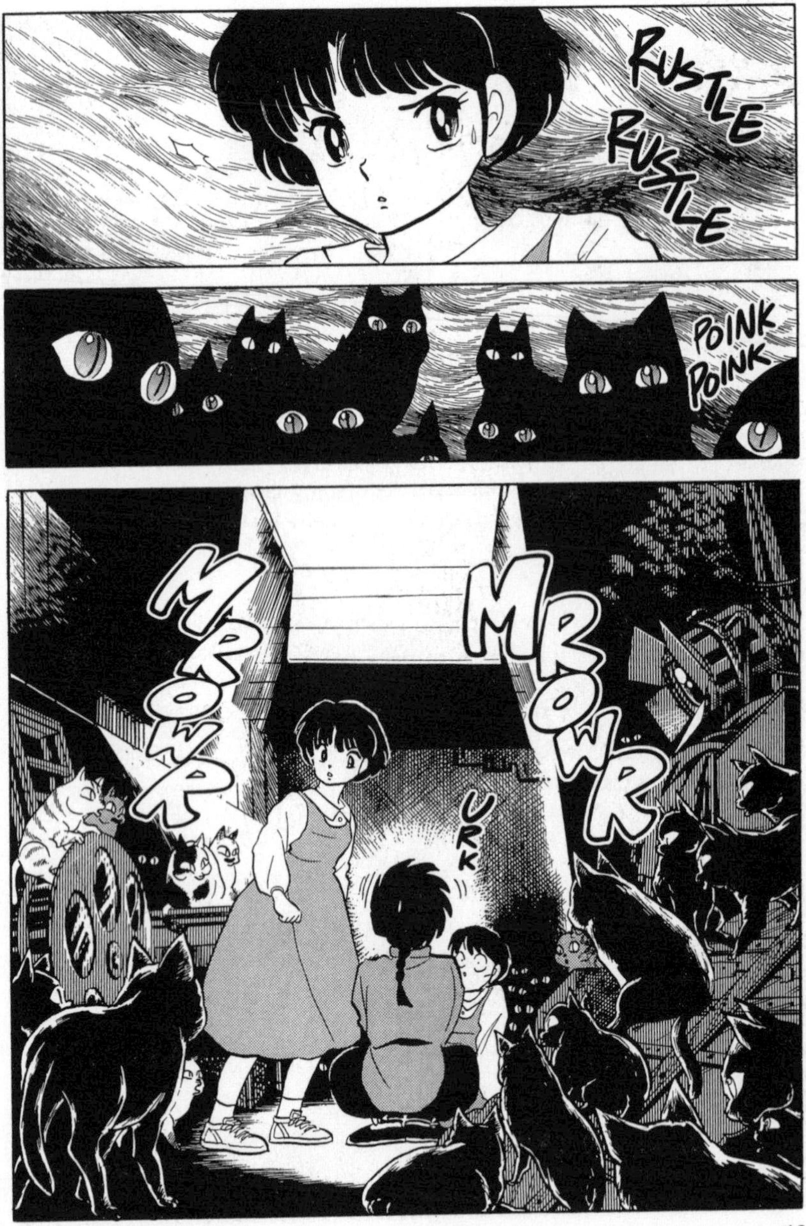
RUSTLE
RUSTLE
POINK
POINK
MROWR
URK
MROWR

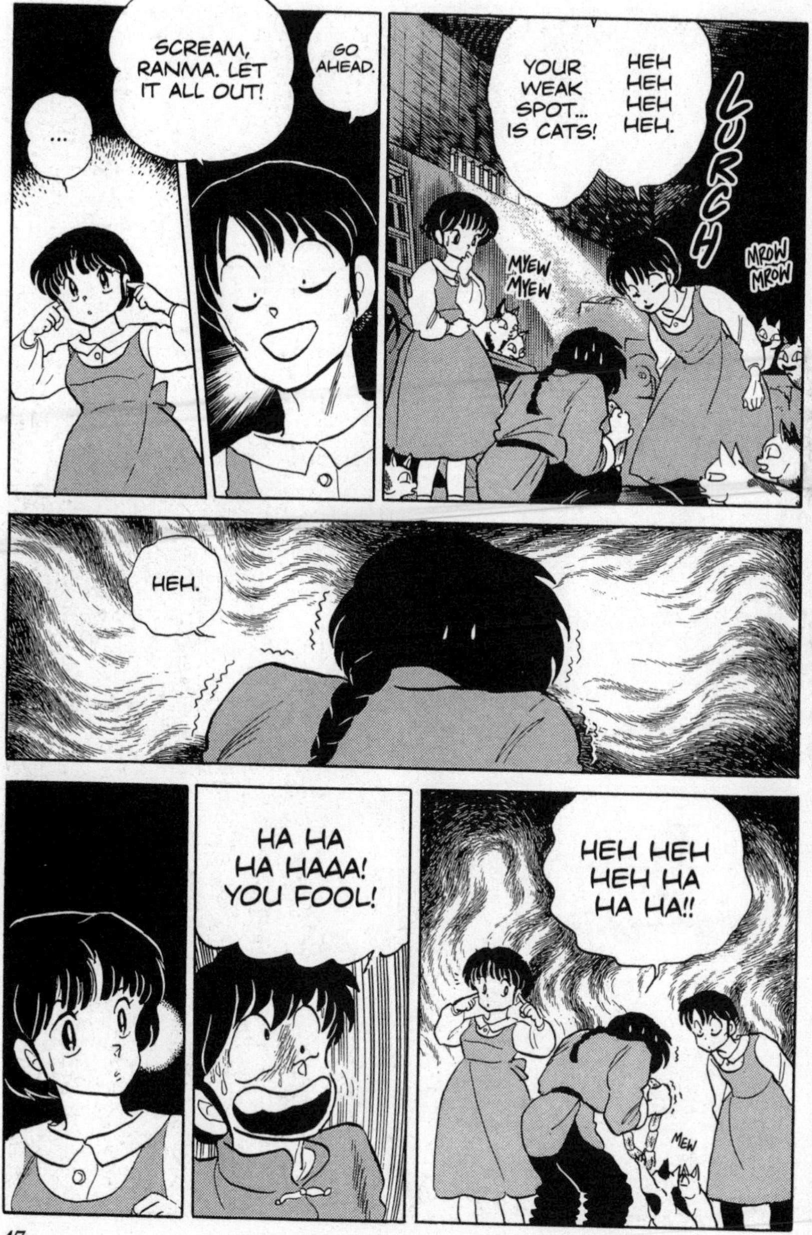
HEH HEH HEH HEH.
YOUR WEAK SPOT... IS CATS!
LURCH
MROW MROW
MYEW MYEW
GO AHEAD.
SCREAM, RANMA. LET IT ALL OUT!
...
HEH.
HEH HEH HEH HA HA HA!!
MEW
HA HA HA HAAA! YOU FOOL!

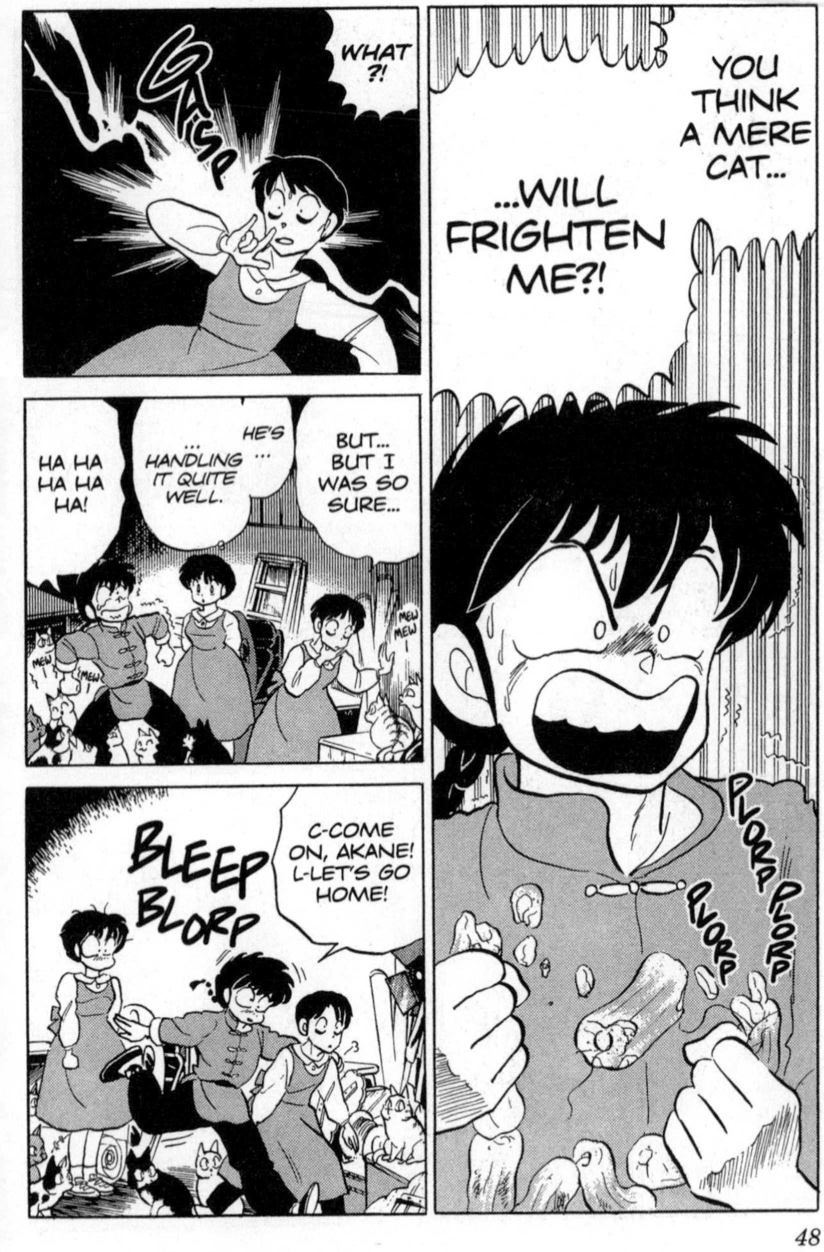
YOU THINK A MERE CAT...
...WILL FRIGHTEN ME?!
PLORP PLORP
PLORP
WHAT ?!
GASP
BUT... BUT I WAS SO SURE...
HE'S ...
... HANDLING IT QUITE WELL.
HA HA HA HA HA!
MEW MEW
MEW
MEW
C-COME ON, AKANE! L-LET'S GO HOME!
BLEEP BLORP

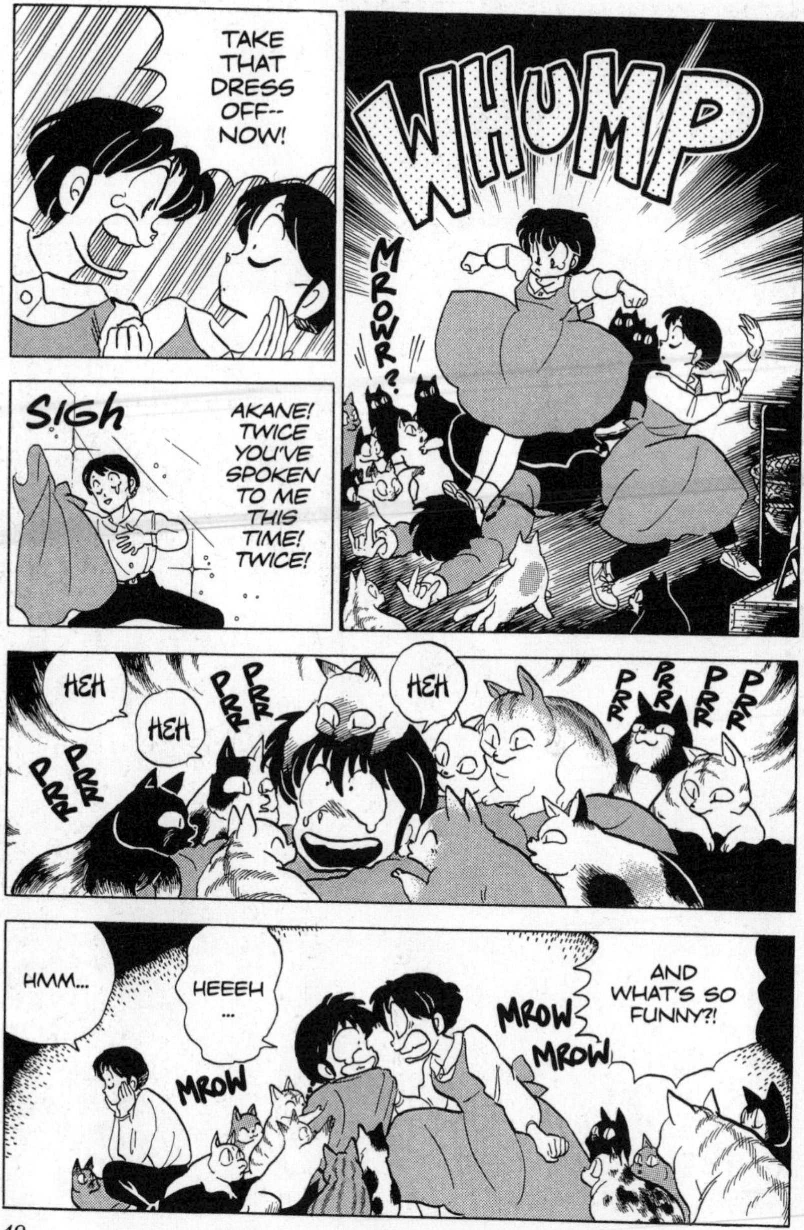
WHUMP
MROWR?
TAKE THAT DRESS OFF-- NOW!
SIGH
AKANE! TWICE YOU'VE SPOKEN TO ME THIS TIME! TWICE!
PRR PRR
PRR
PRR
PRR
HEH
PRR PRR
HEH
HEH
PRR PRR
AND WHAT'S SO FUNNY?!
MROW
MROW
MROW
HEEEH ...
HMM...

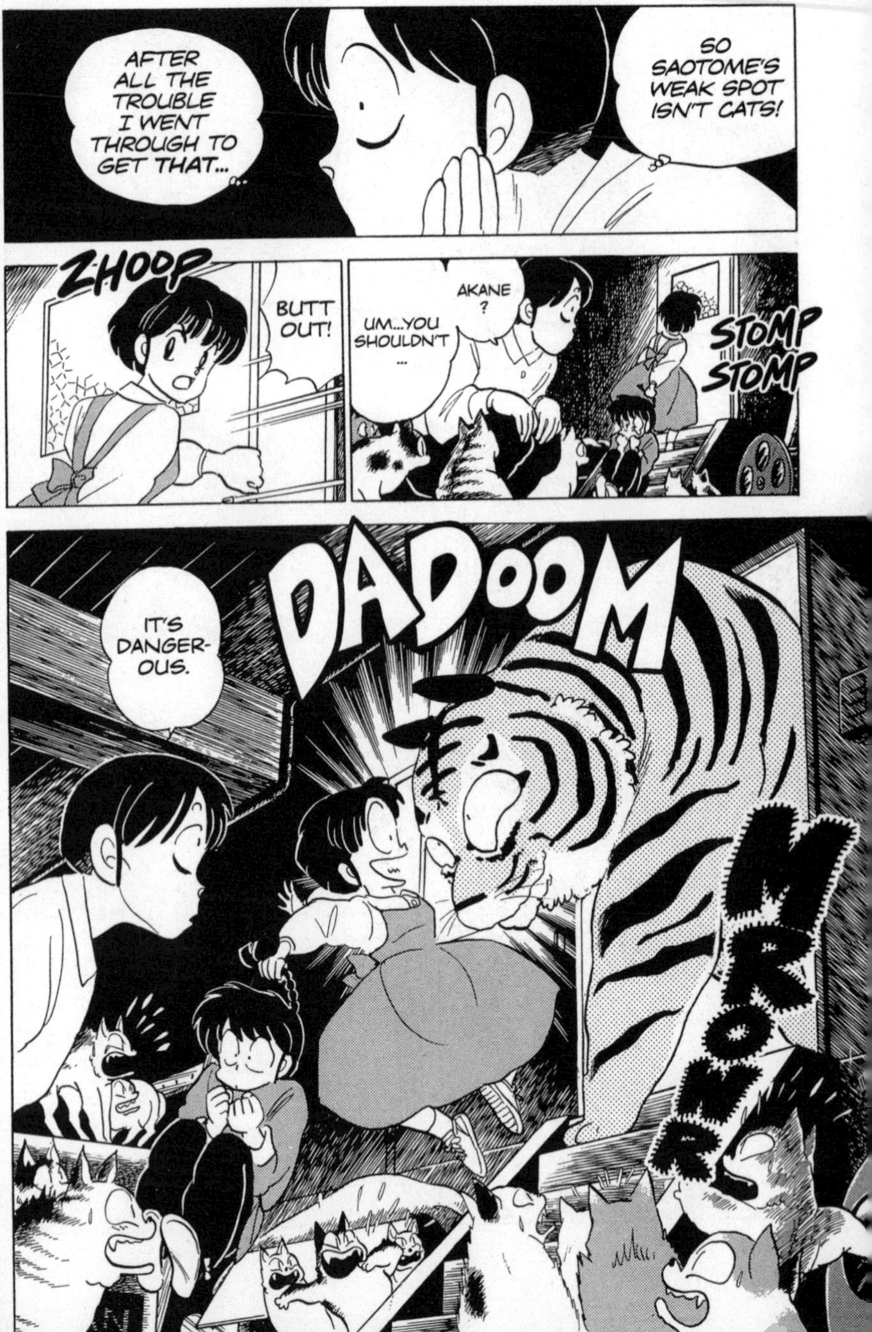
SO SAOTOME'S WEAK SPOT ISN'T CATS!
AFTER ALL THE TROUBLE I WENT THROUGH TO GET THAT...
STOMP STOMP
AKANE ?
UM...YOU SHOULDN'T ...
Z-HOOP
BUTT OUT!
DADOOM
IT'S DANGER-OUS.

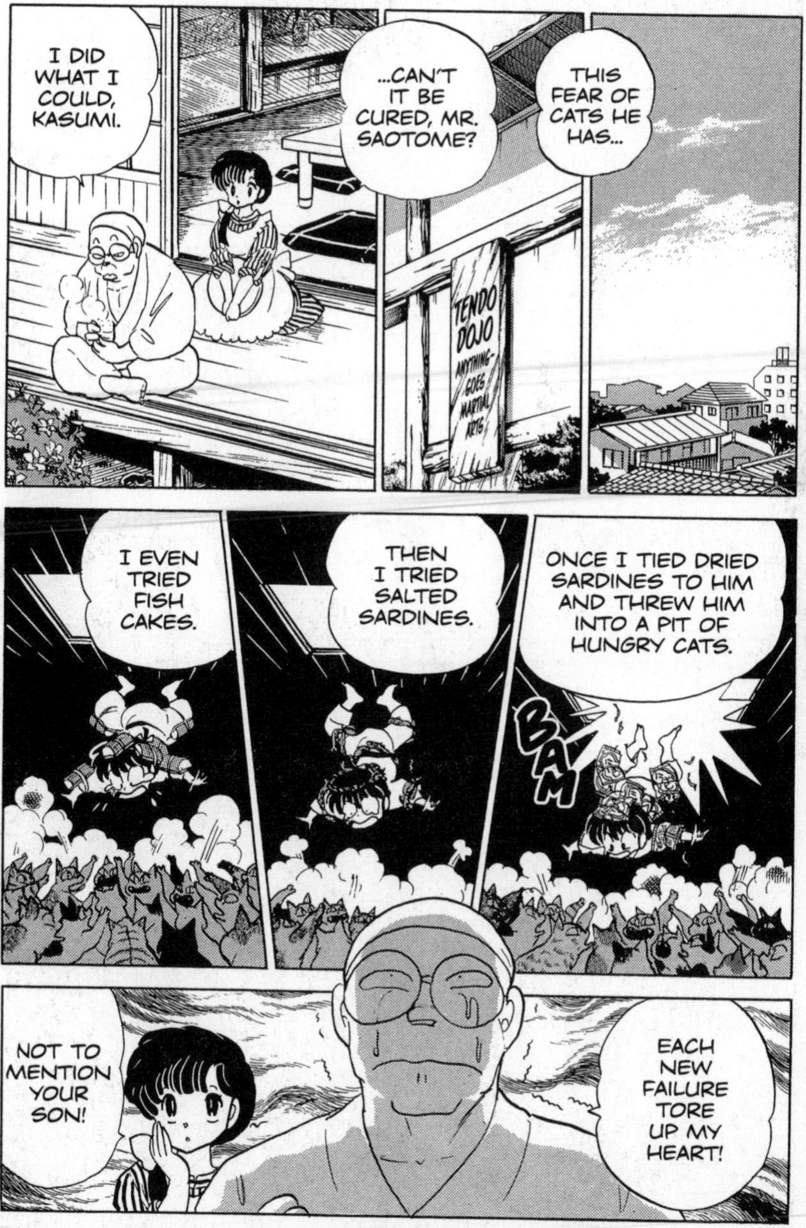
THIS FEAR OF CATS HE HAS...
...CAN'T IT BE CURED, MR. SAOTOME?
TENDO DOJO ANYTHING-GOES MARTIAL ARTS
I DID WHAT I COULD, KASUMI.
ONCE I TIED DRIED SARDINES TO HIM AND THREW HIM INTO A PIT OF HUNGRY CATS.
BAM
THEN I TRIED SALTED SARDINES.
I EVEN TRIED FISH CAKES.
EACH NEW FAILURE TORE UP MY HEART!
NOT TO MENTION YOUR SON!

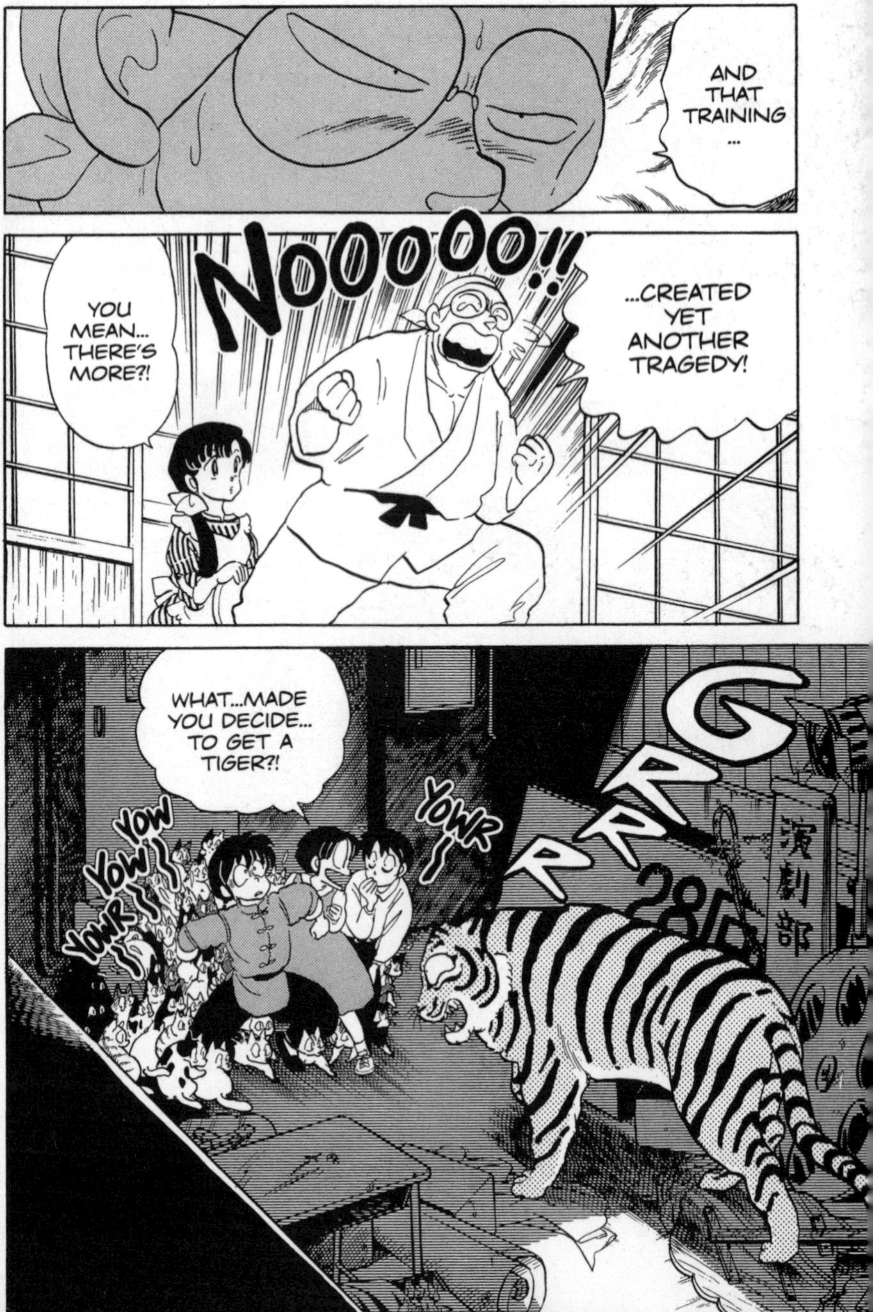
AND THAT TRAINING ...
...CREATED YET ANOTHER TRAGEDY!
NOOOOO!!
YOU MEAN... THERE'S MORE?!
GRRR
演劇部
YOWR
WHAT...MADE YOU DECIDE... TO GET A TIGER?!
YOW
YOW
YOWR

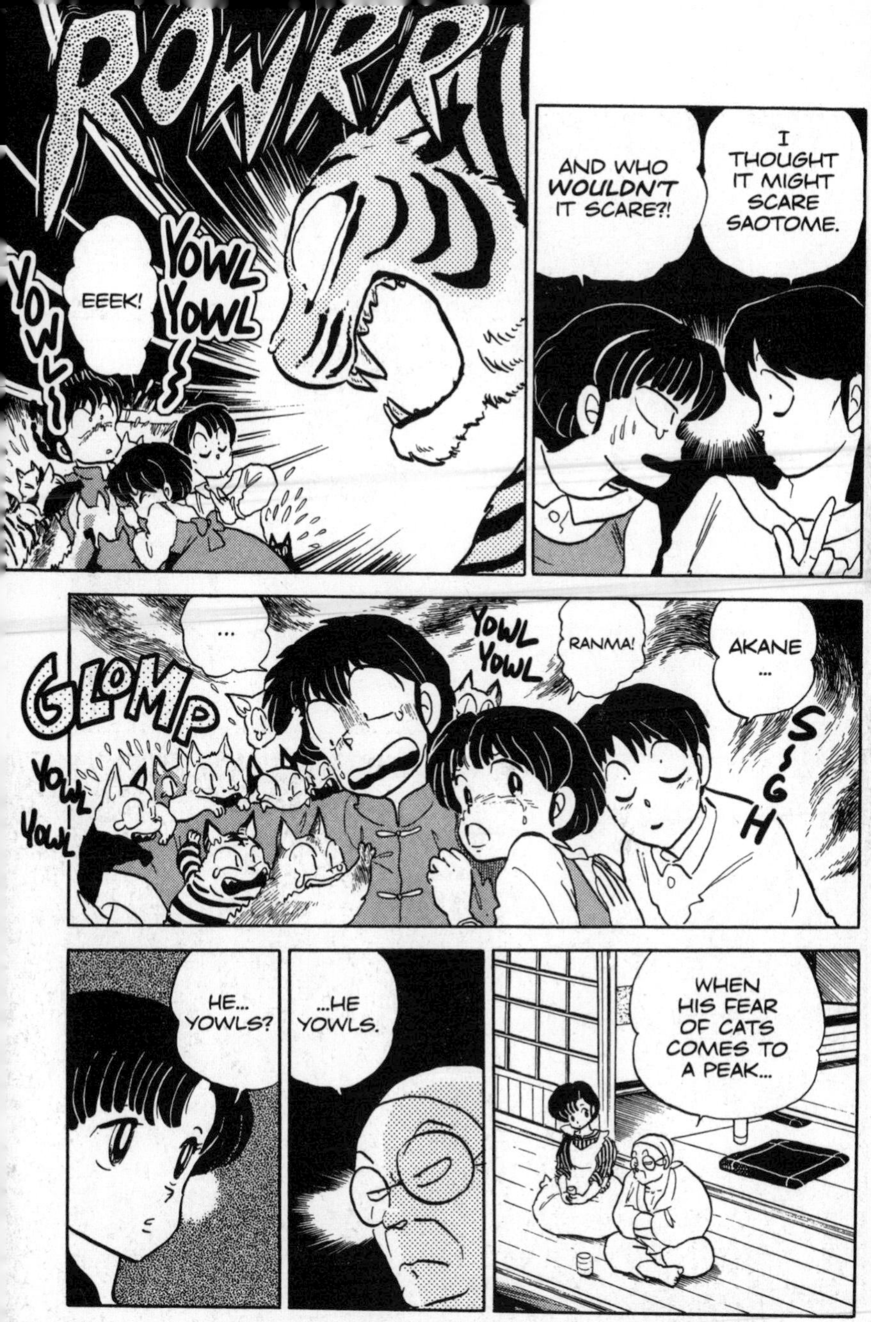
I THOUGHT IT MIGHT SCARE SAOTOME.
AND WHO WOULDN'T IT SCARE?!
ROWRR!
YOWL YOWL
EEEK!
YOWL
AKANE ...
SIGH
RANMA!
YOWL YOWL
...
GLOMP
YOWL YOWL
WHEN HIS FEAR OF CATS COMES TO A PEAK...
...HE YOWLS.
HE... YOWLS?

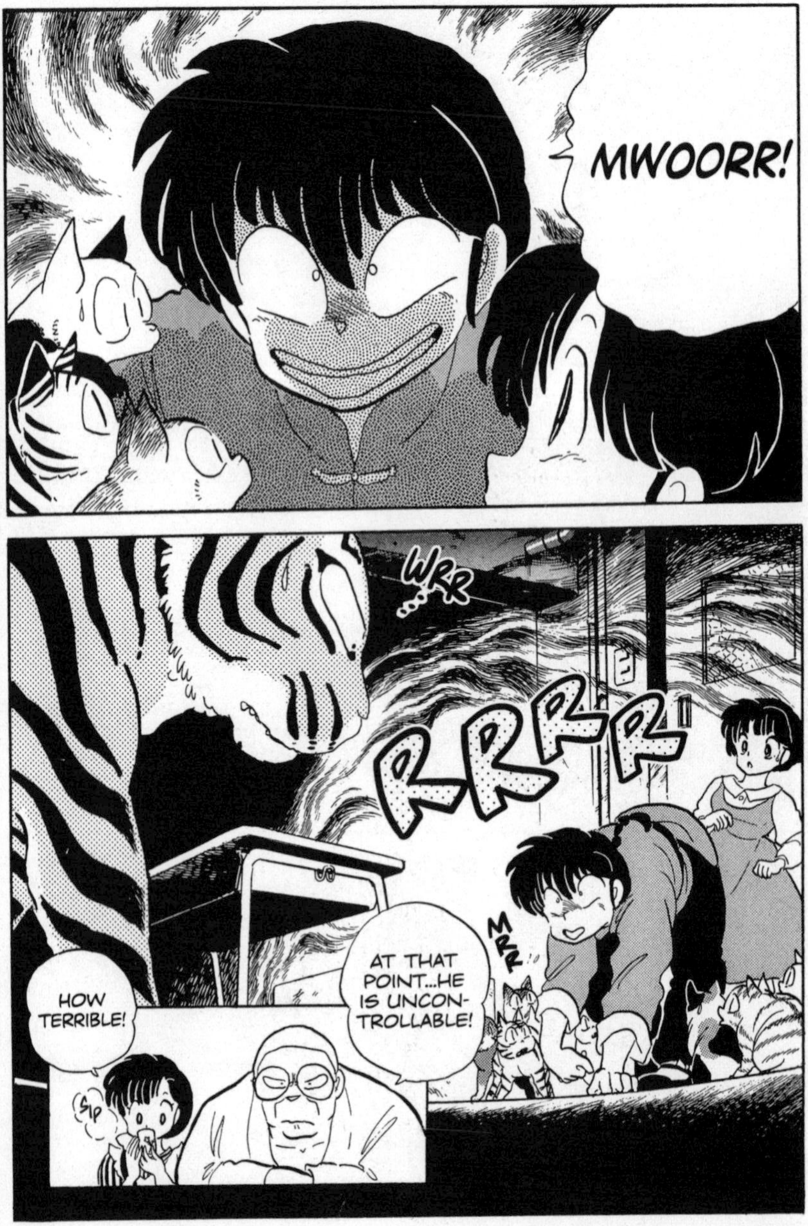
MWOORR!
...WRR
RRRR
MRR
AT THAT POINT...HE IS UNCONTROLLABLE!
HOW TERRIBLE!
SIP

PART 4
CAT-FU

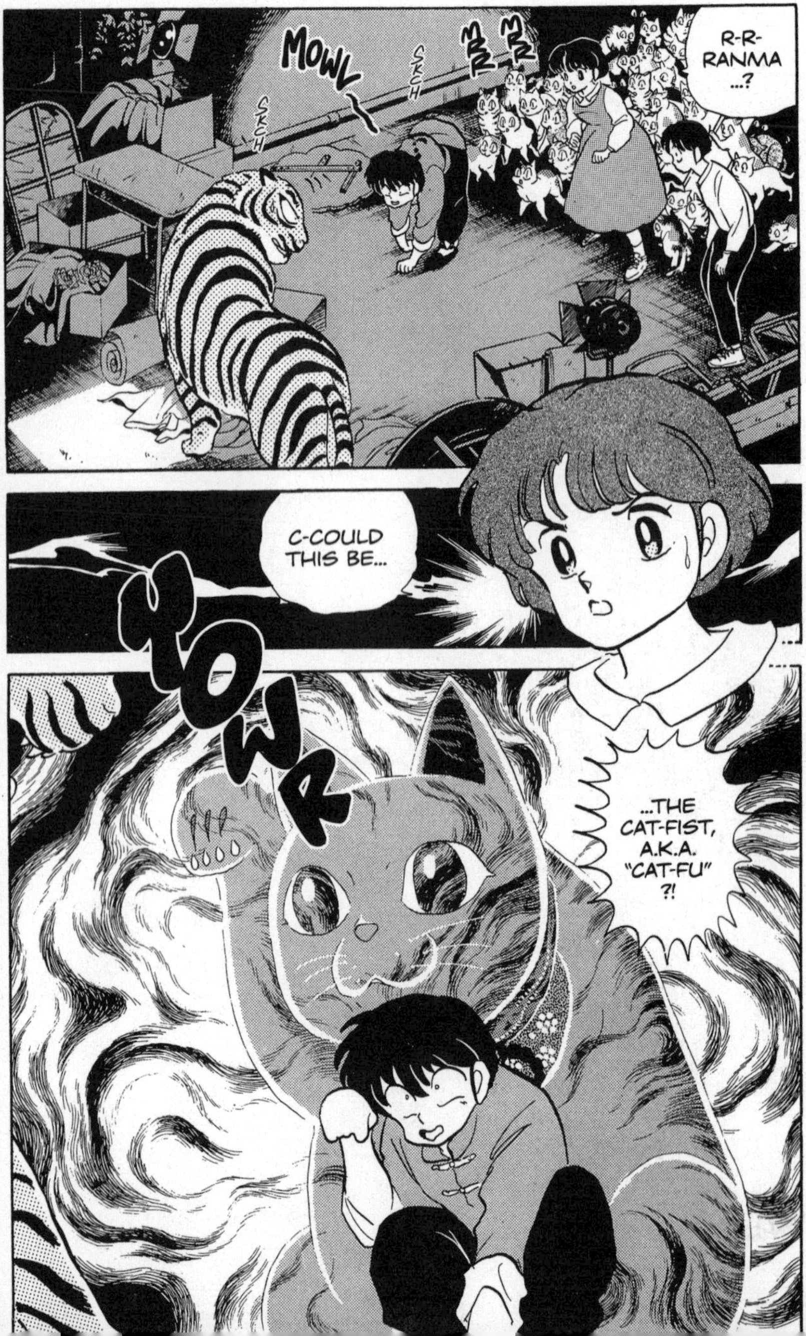
R-R-RANMA ...?
MRR
MRR
SKCH
MOWL~
SKCH
C-COULD THIS BE...
YOWR
...THE CAT-FIST, A.K.A. "CAT-FU" ?!

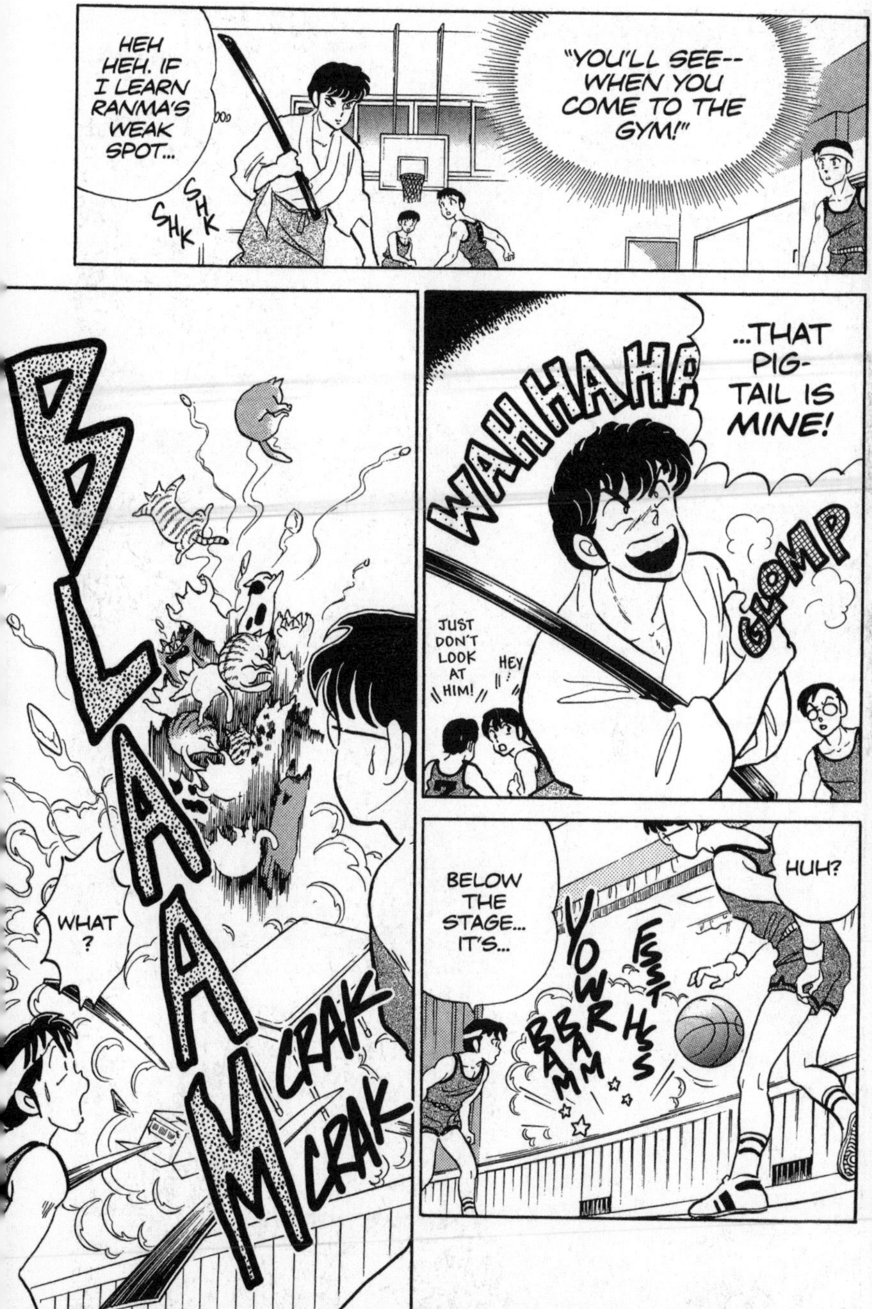
"YOU'LL SEE-- WHEN YOU COME TO THE GYM!"
HEH HEH. IF I LEARN RANMA'S WEAK SPOT...
SHK SHK
WAHHAHA
...THAT PIG-TAIL IS MINE!
GLOMP
HEY
JUST DON'T LOOK AT HIM!
HUH?
BELOW THE STAGE... IT'S...
FSSST HSSS
YOWR
BRAAMM
BLAAAM
WHAT?
CRAK CRAK

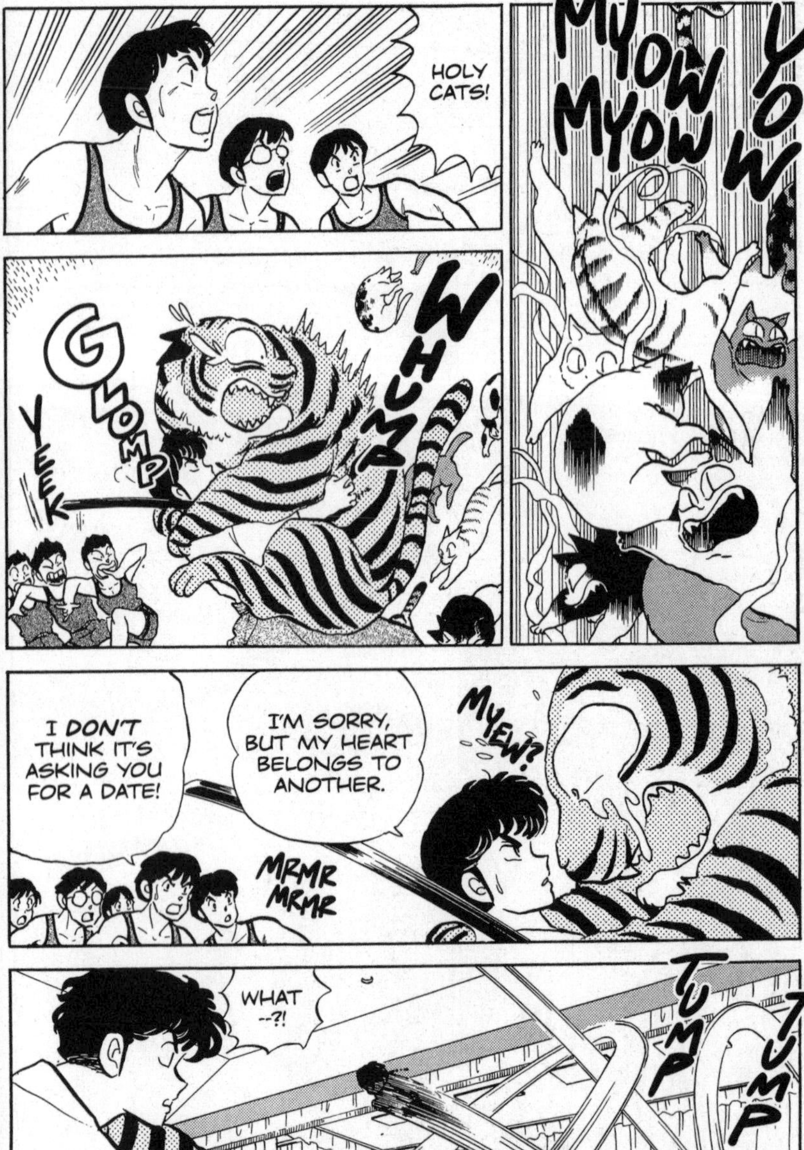
MYOW MYOW
YOW YOW
HOLY CATS!
WHUMP
GLOMP
YEEEK
MYEW?
I'M SORRY, BUT MY HEART BELONGS TO ANOTHER.
I *DON'T* THINK IT'S ASKING YOU FOR A DATE!
MRMR MRMR
TUMP TUMP
WHAT --?!

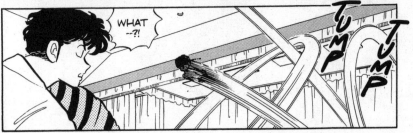

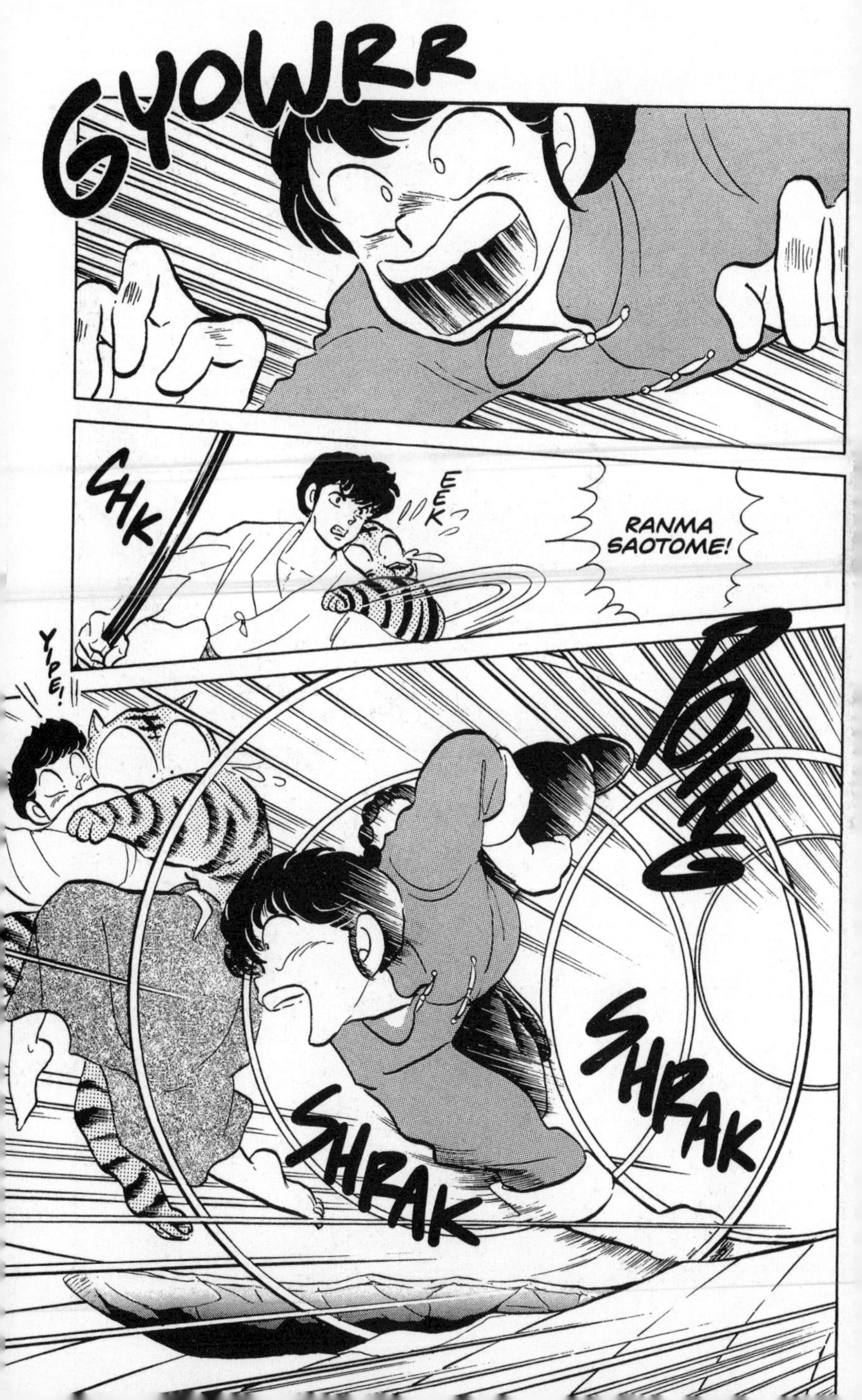
GYOWRR
RANMA SAOTOME!
EEK
CHK
BOWNG
SHRAK
SHRAK
YIPE!

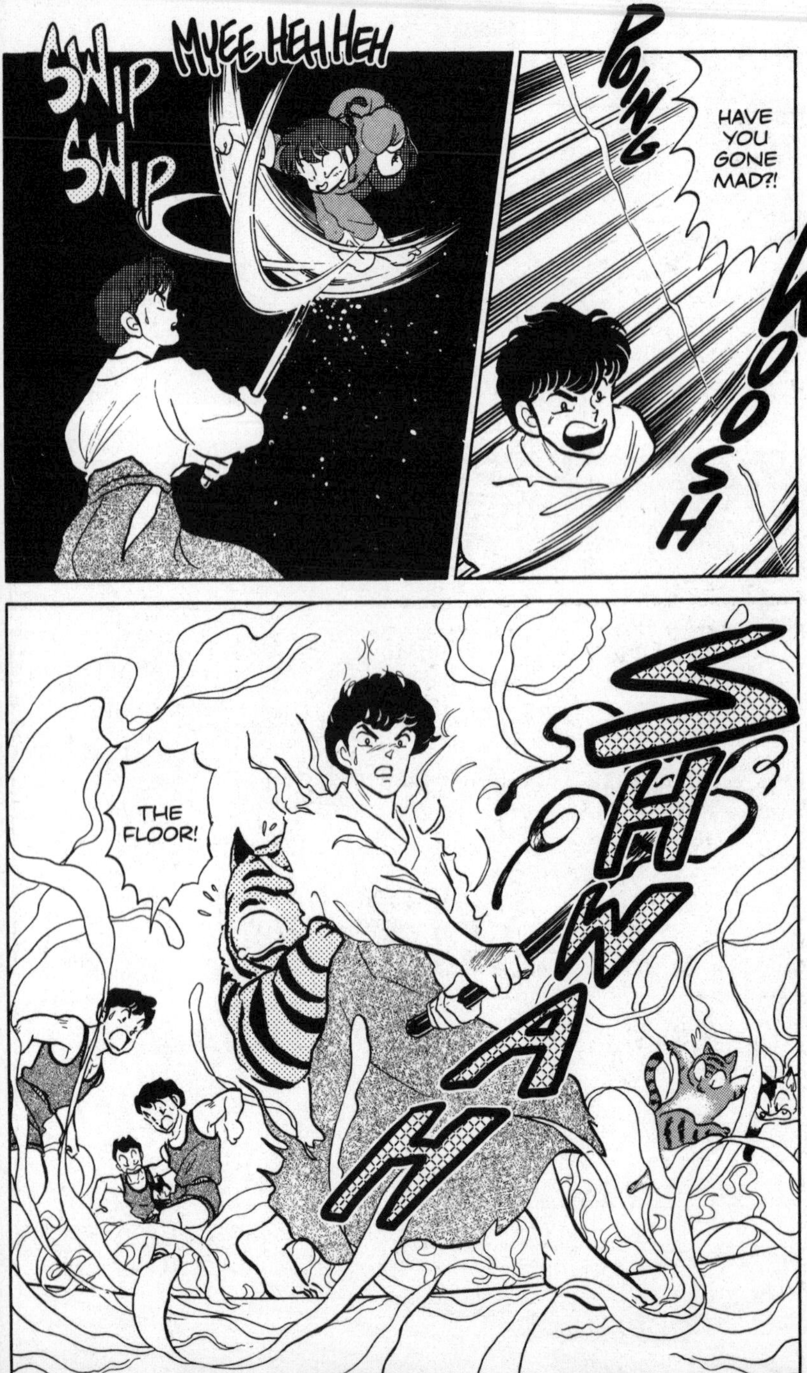
POING
HAVE YOU GONE MAD?!
WOOOSH
MYEE HEH HEH
SWIP SWIP
SHWAAH
THE FLOOR!

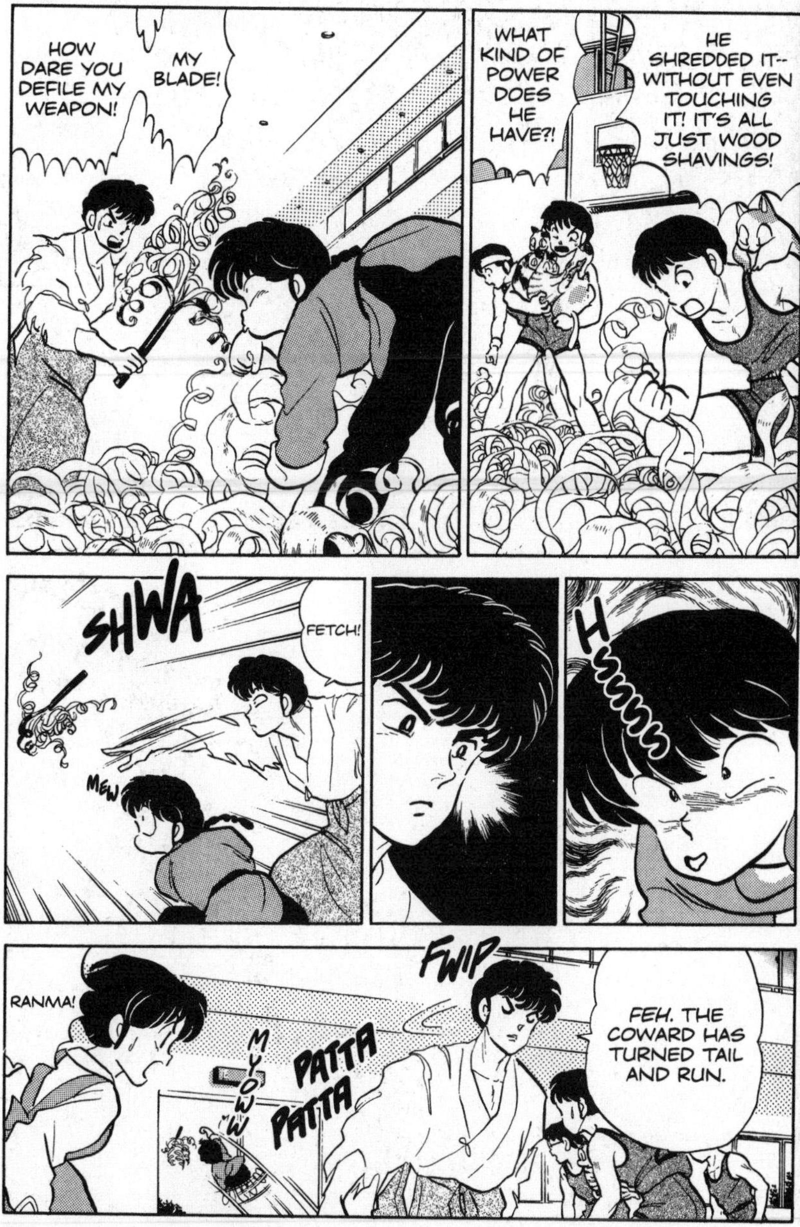
HE SHREDDED IT-- WITHOUT EVEN TOUCHING IT! IT'S ALL JUST WOOD SHAVINGS!
WHAT KIND OF POWER DOES HE HAVE?!
MY BLADE!
HOW DARE YOU DEFILE MY WEAPON!
HSSSSS
FETCH!
SHWA
MEW
FEH. THE COWARD HAS TURNED TAIL AND RUN.
FWIP
PATTA PATTA
MYOWWW
RANMA!

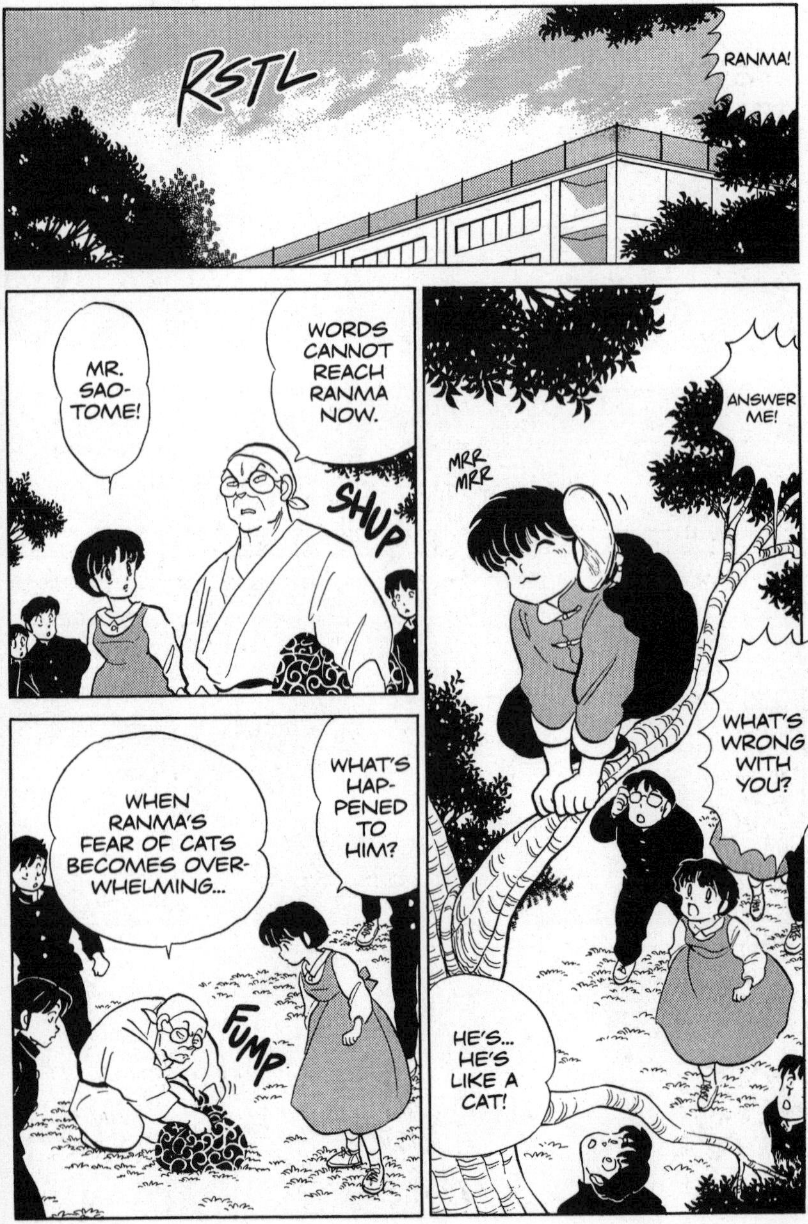
RANMA!
RSTL
ANSWER ME!
MRR MRR
WHAT'S WRONG WITH YOU?
HE'S... HE'S LIKE A CAT!
WORDS CANNOT REACH RANMA NOW.
MR. SAO-TOME!
SHUP
WHAT'S HAP-PENED TO HIM?
WHEN RANMA'S FEAR OF CATS BECOMES OVER-WHELMING...
FUMP

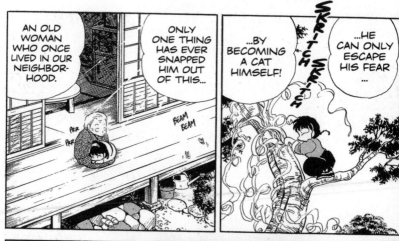

...HE CAN ONLY ESCAPE HIS FEAR ...
SKRITCH SKRITCH
...BY BECOMING A CAT HIMSELF!
ONLY ONE THING HAS EVER SNAPPED HIM OUT OF THIS...
AN OLD WOMAN WHO ONCE LIVED IN OUR NEIGHBOR-HOOD.
BEAM BEAM
PRR PRR
THEN WE HAVE TO GO FIND THAT WOMAN!
NO. *I'LL* HAVE TO DO.
WEEYAAA

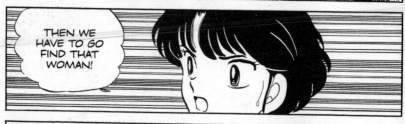

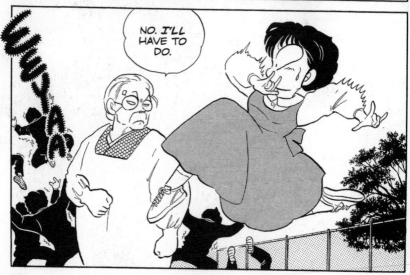

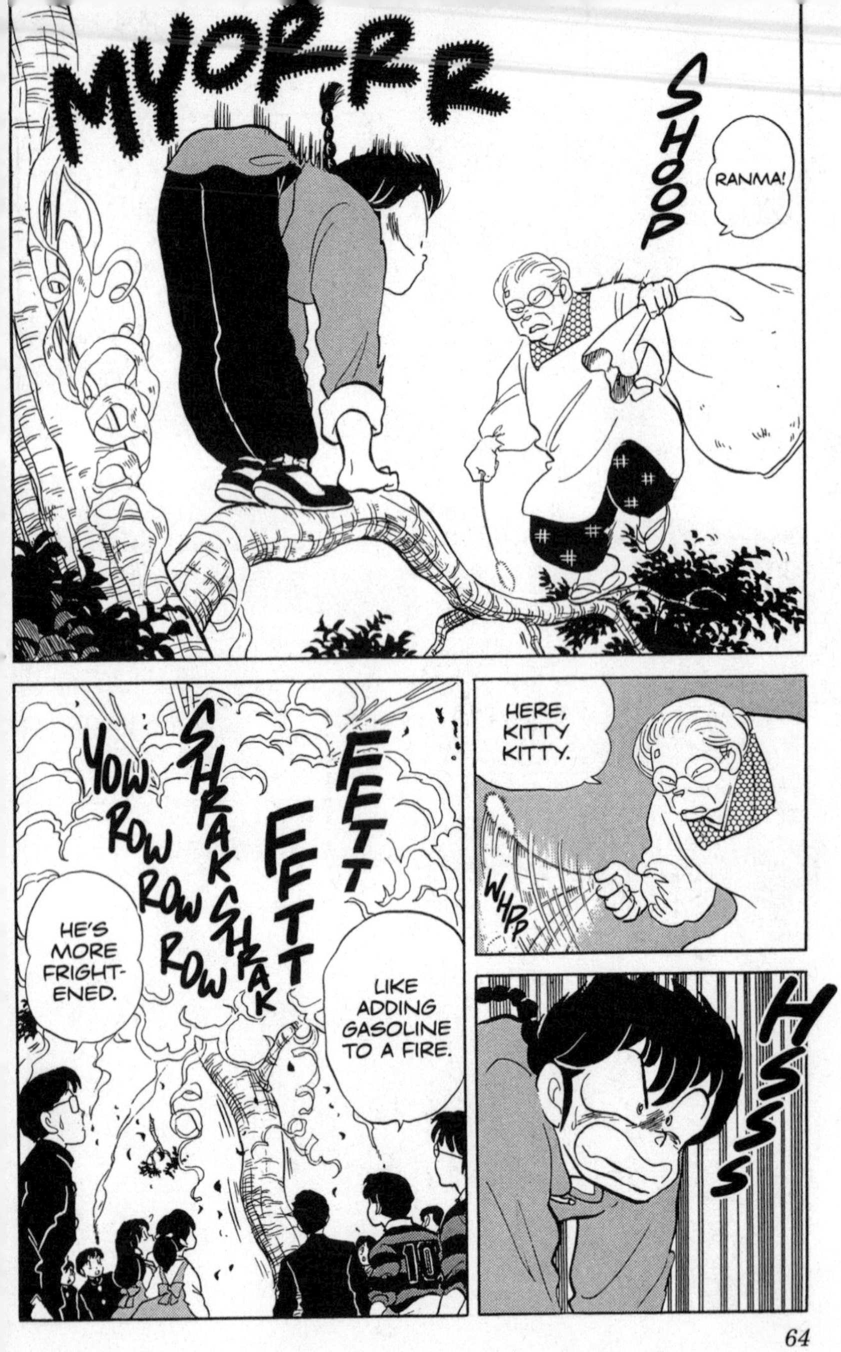
MYOPRR
SHOOP
RANMA!
HERE, KITTY KITTY.
WHPP
HSSSS
FFTT
FFTTT
SHRAK SHRAK
YOW ROW ROW ROW
LIKE ADDING GASOLINE TO A FIRE.
HE'S MORE FRIGHT-ENED.

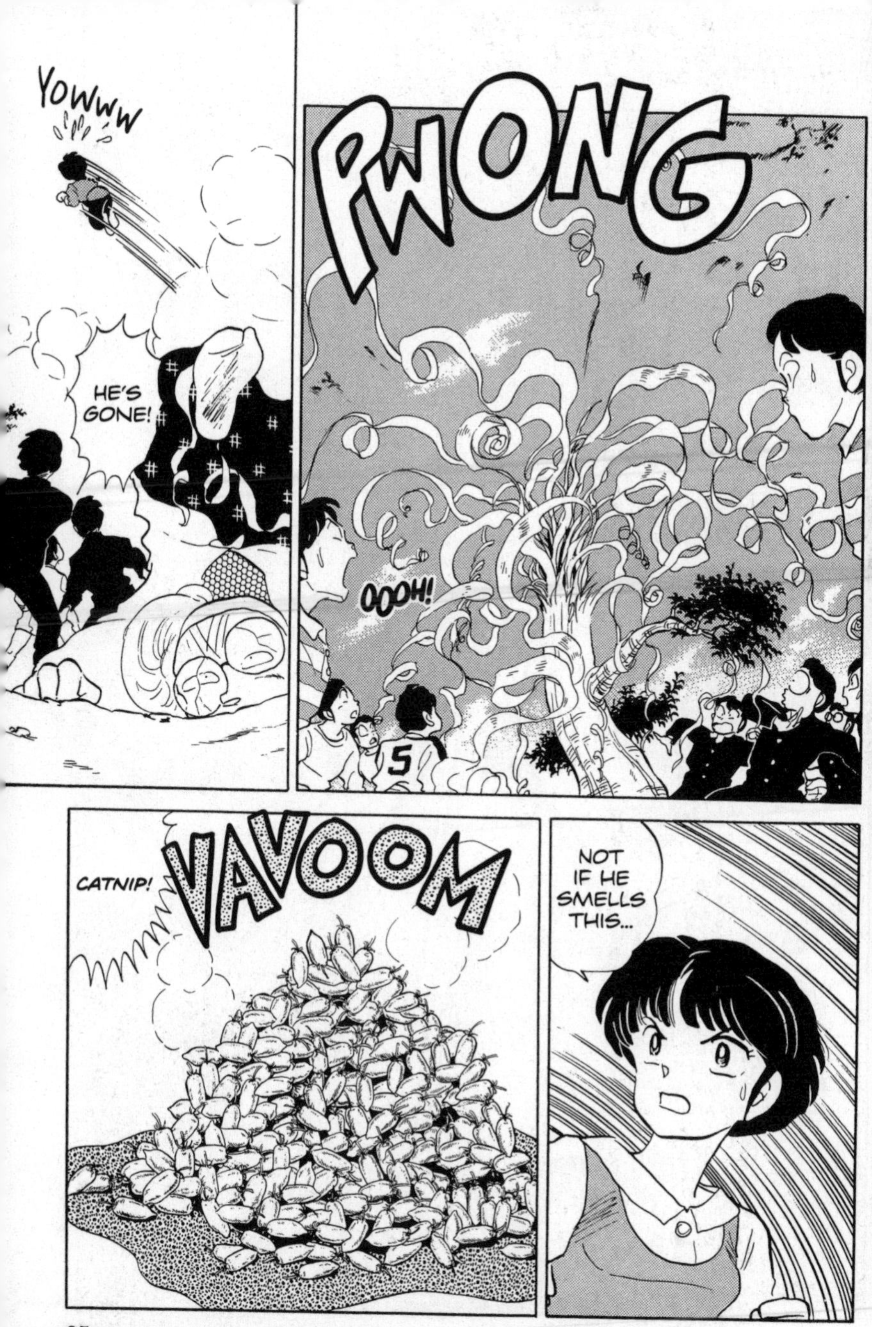
PWONG
OOOH!
YOWWWW
HE'S GONE!
NOT IF HE SMELLS THIS...
VAVOOM
CATNIP!

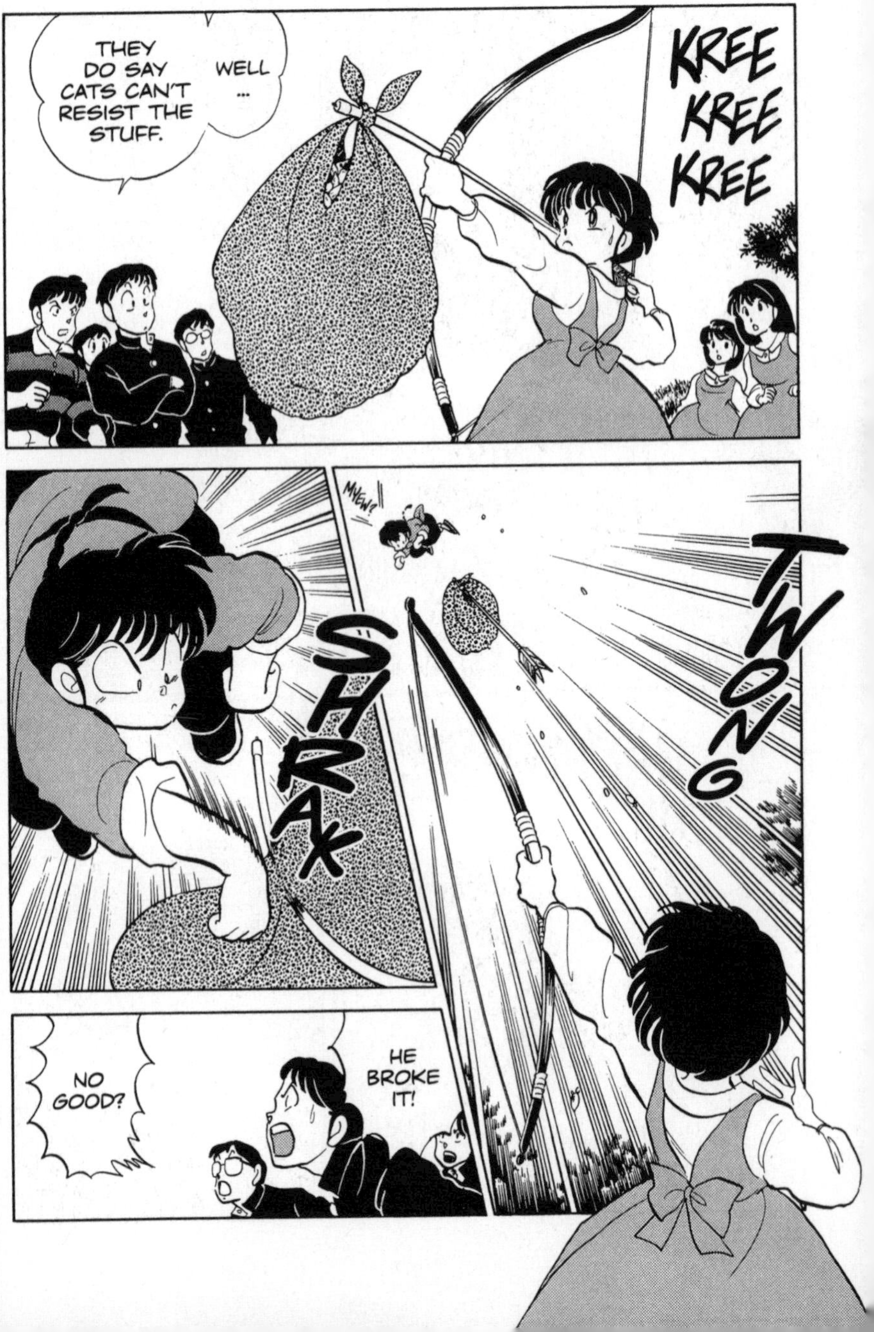
KREE KREE KREE
WELL ...
THEY DO SAY CATS CAN'T RESIST THE STUFF.
TWONG
MYEW?
SHRAK
HE BROKE IT!
NO GOOD?

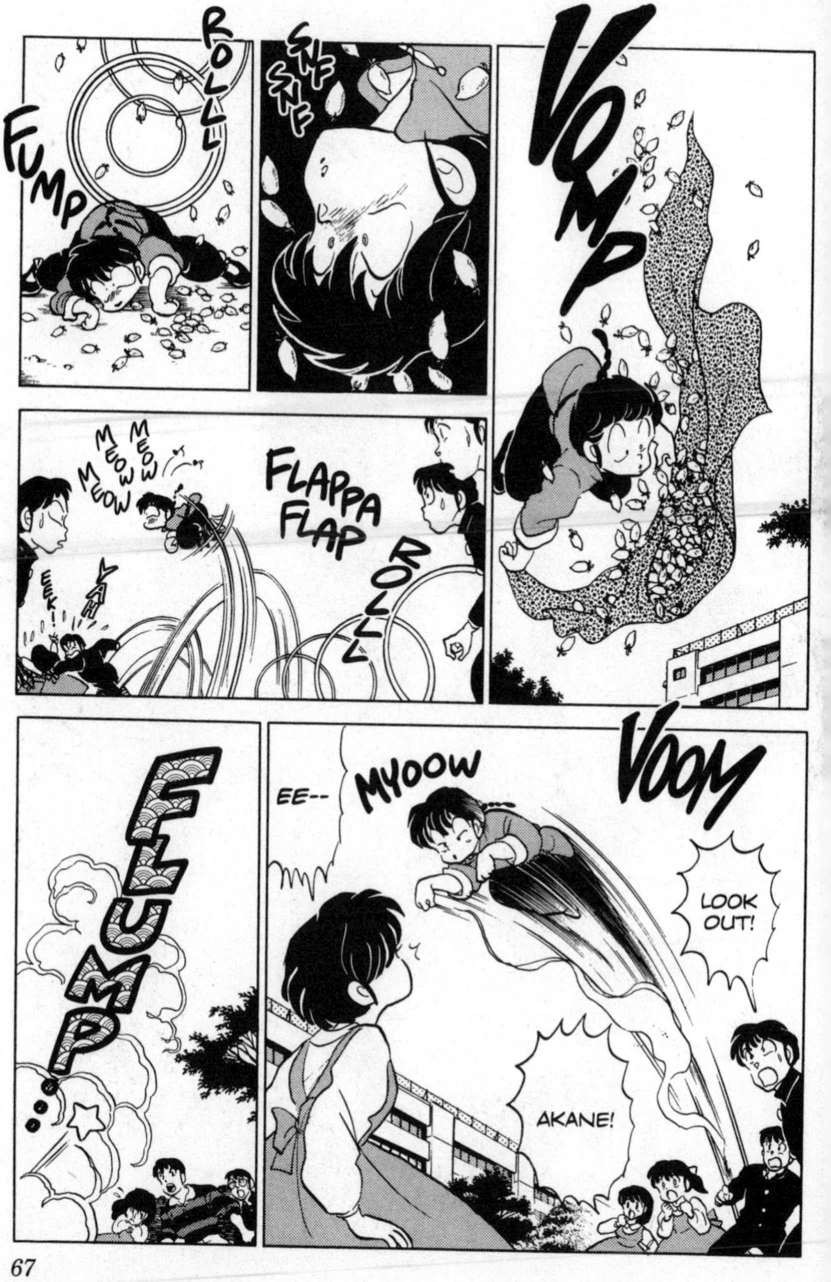
VOMP
SNIF SNIF
ROLLL
FUMP
FLAPPA FLAP
ROLLL
MEOW MEOW MEOW
YAH
EEK!
VOOM
LOOK OUT!
MYOOW
EE--
AKANE!
FLUMP...

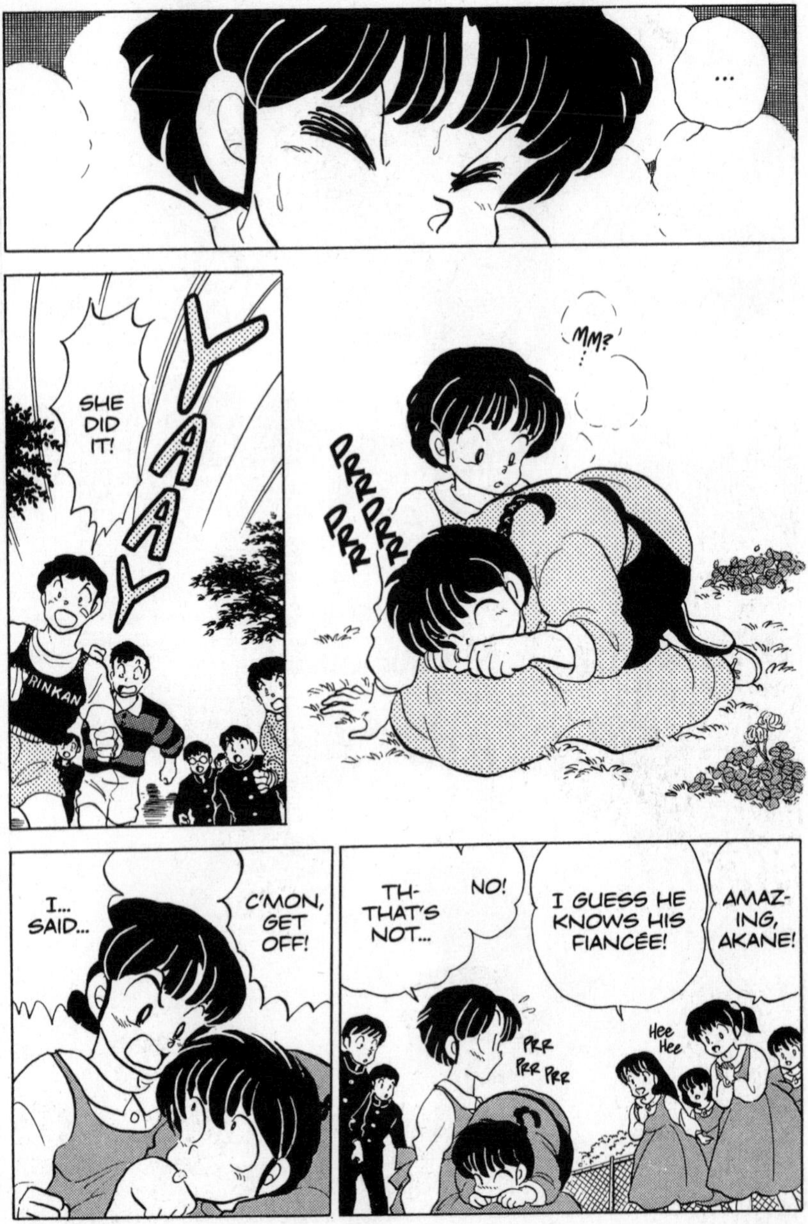
...
MM?
PRRR PRRR PRR
YAAAAY
SHE DID IT!
AMAZ-ING, AKANE!
I GUESS HE KNOWS HIS FIANCÉE!
NO!
TH- THAT'S NOT...
Hee Hee
PRR PRR PRR
C'MON, GET OFF!
I... SAID...

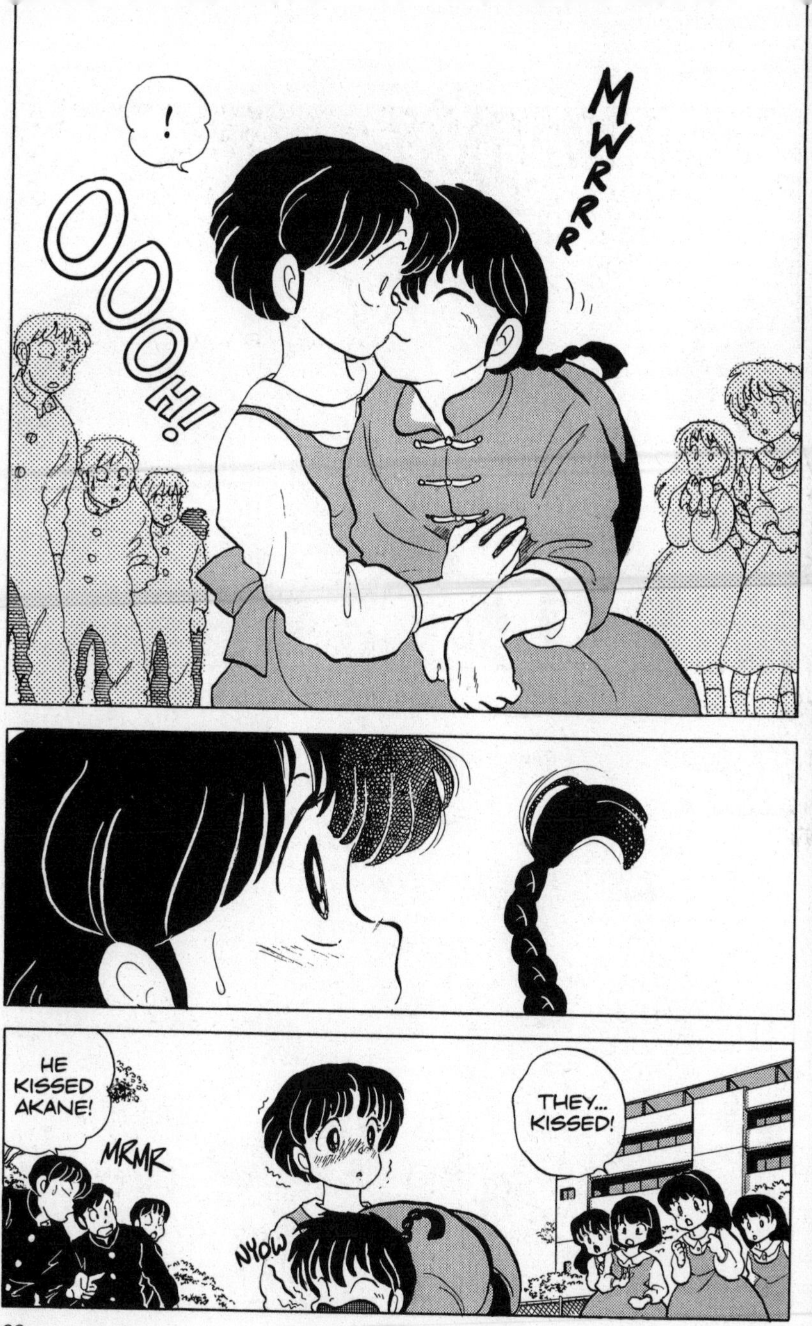
MWRRRR
!
OOOH!
THEY... KISSED!
HE KISSED AKANE!
MRMR
NYOW

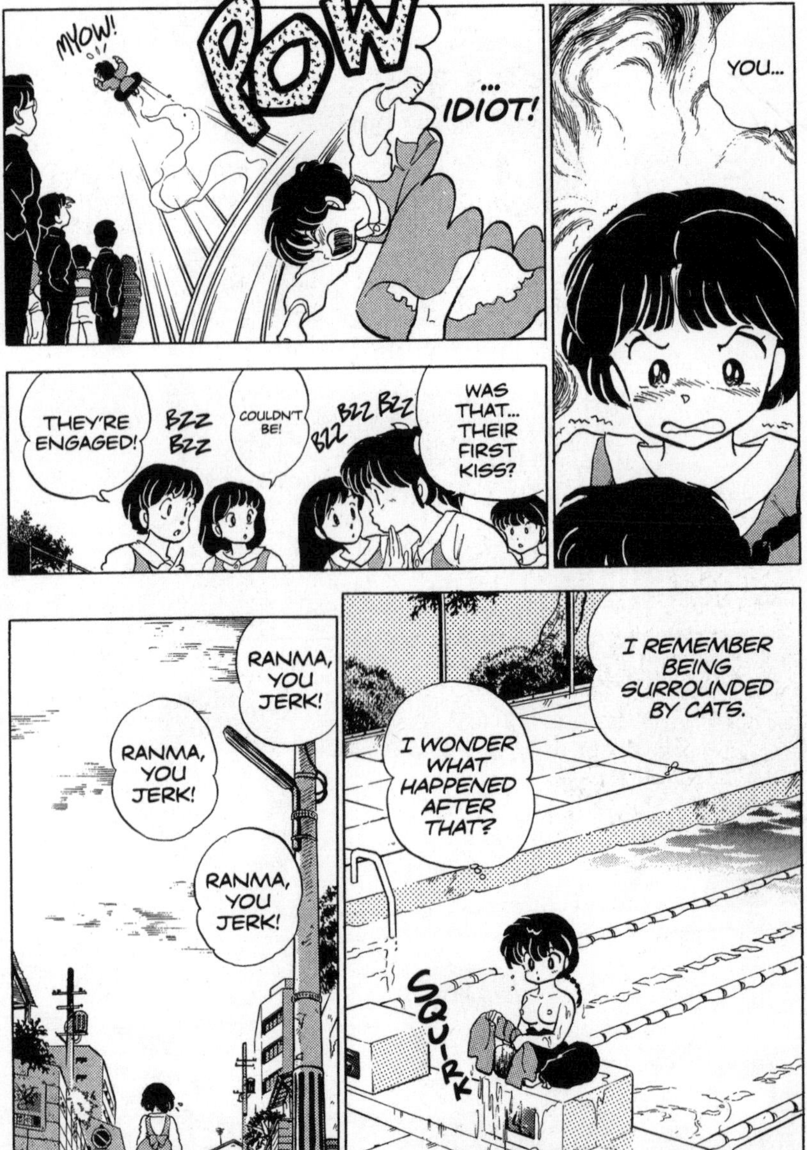
YOU...
...IDIOT!
POW
MYOW!
WAS THAT... THEIR FIRST KISS?
BZZ BZZ BZZ
COULDN'T BE!
BZZ BZZ
THEY'RE ENGAGED!
I REMEMBER BEING SURROUNDED BY CATS.
I WONDER WHAT HAPPENED AFTER THAT?
SQUIRK
RANMA, YOU JERK!
RANMA, YOU JERK!
RANMA, YOU JERK!

PART 5
YOU'D HAVE KISSED ANYBODY?

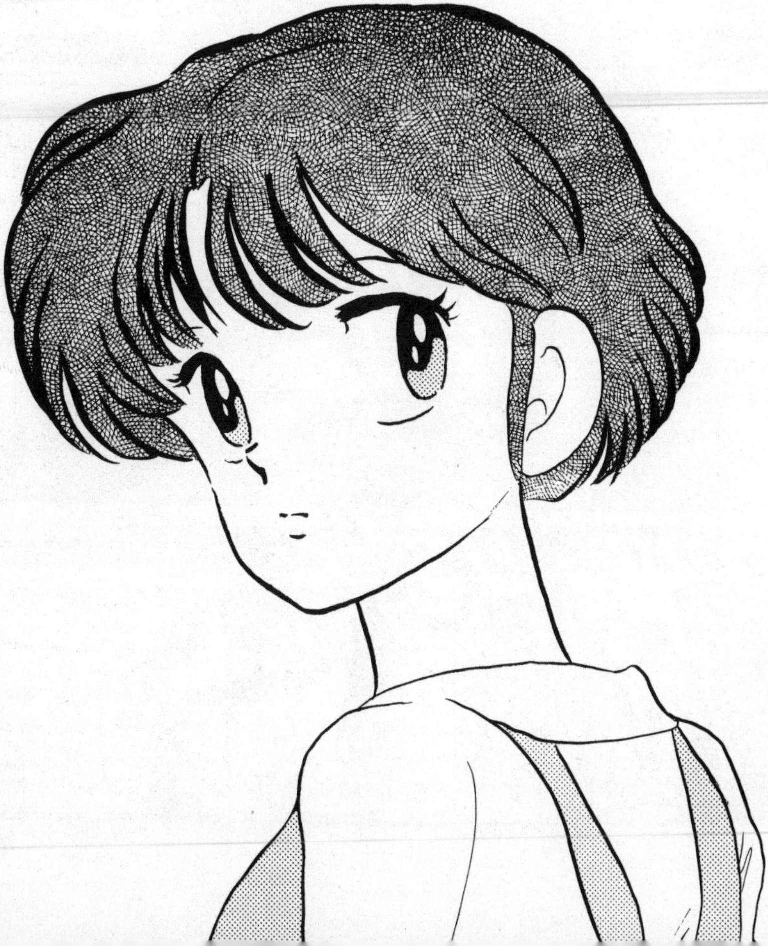

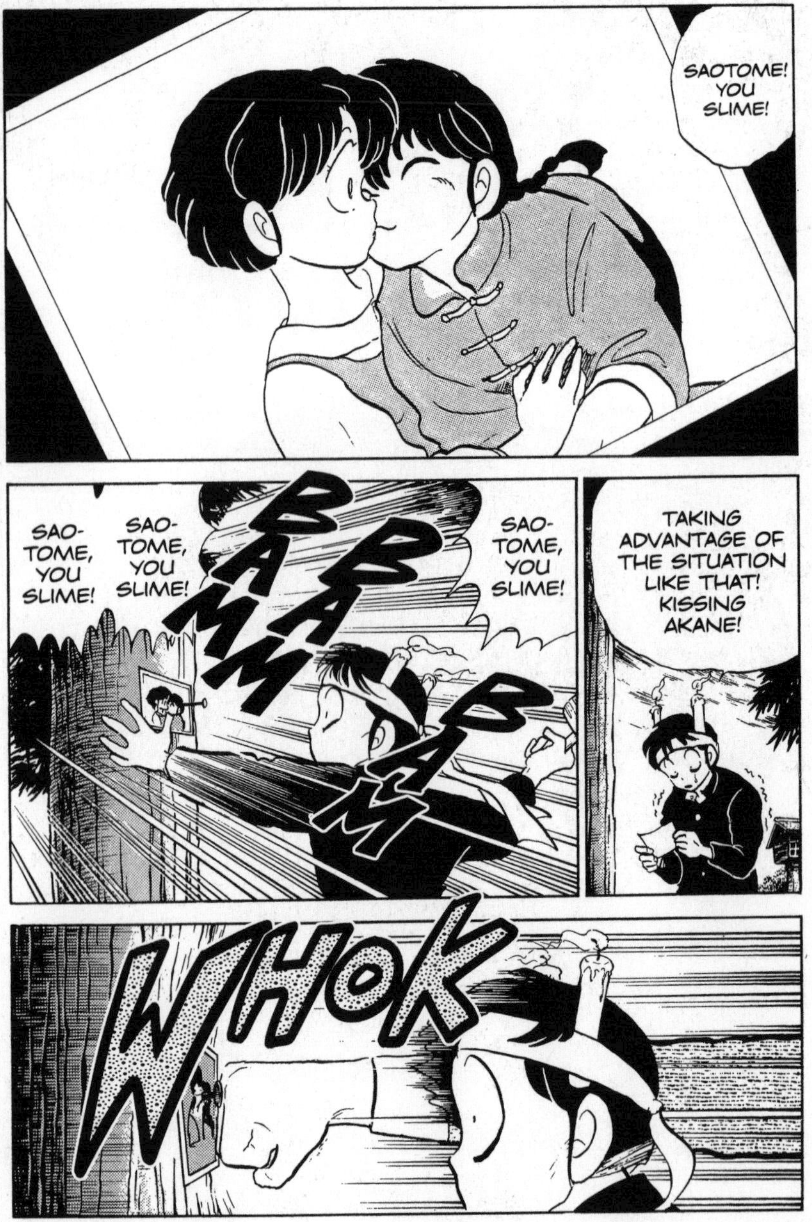
SAOTOME! YOU SLIME!
TAKING ADVANTAGE OF THE SITUATION LIKE THAT! KISSING AKANE!
SAO-TOME, YOU SLIME!
BAMM
BAMM
BAM
SAO-TOME, YOU SLIME!
SAO-TOME, YOU SLIME!
WHOK

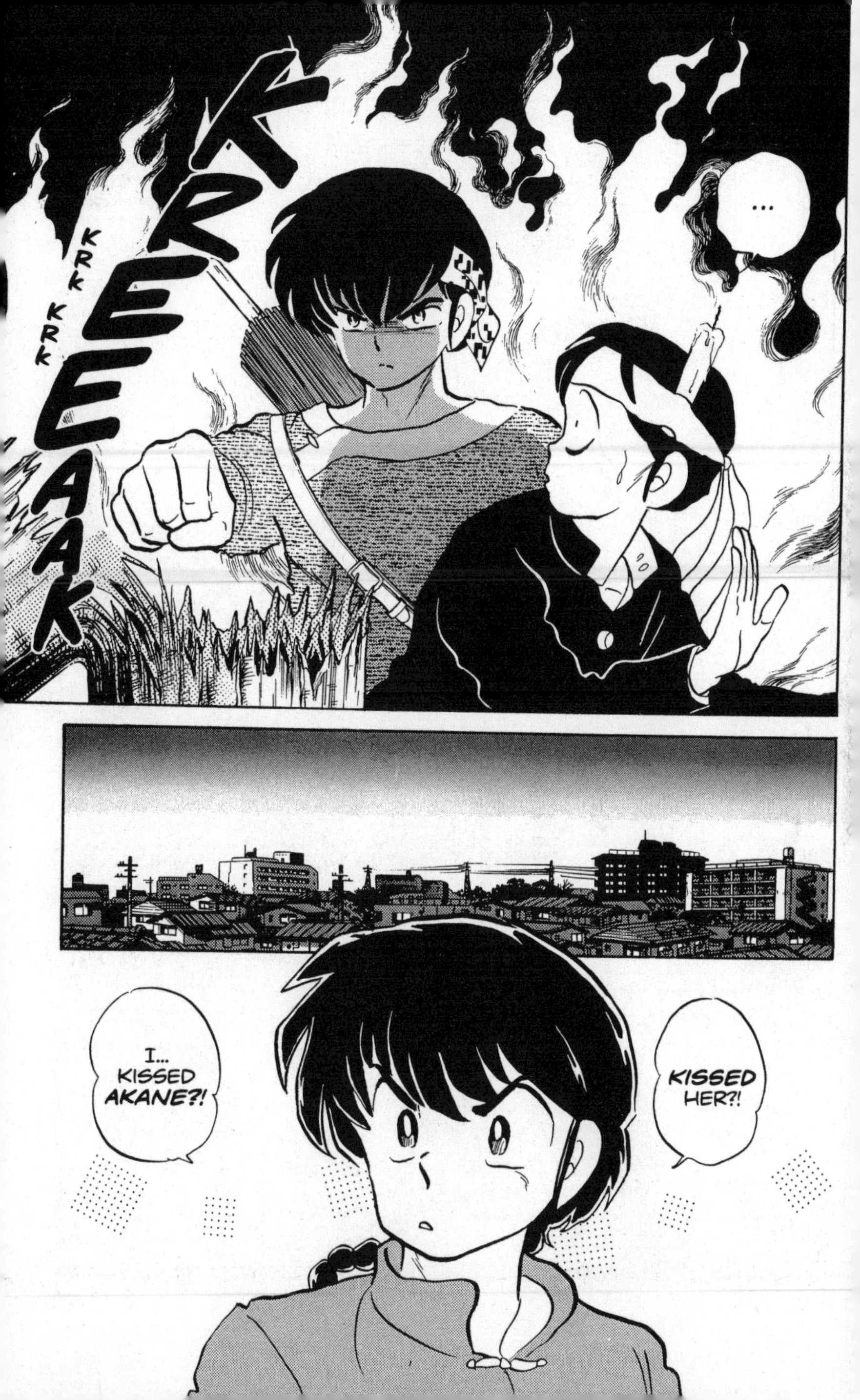
...
KREEEAAK
KRK KRK
KRK KRK
KISSED HER?!
I... KISSED AKANE?!

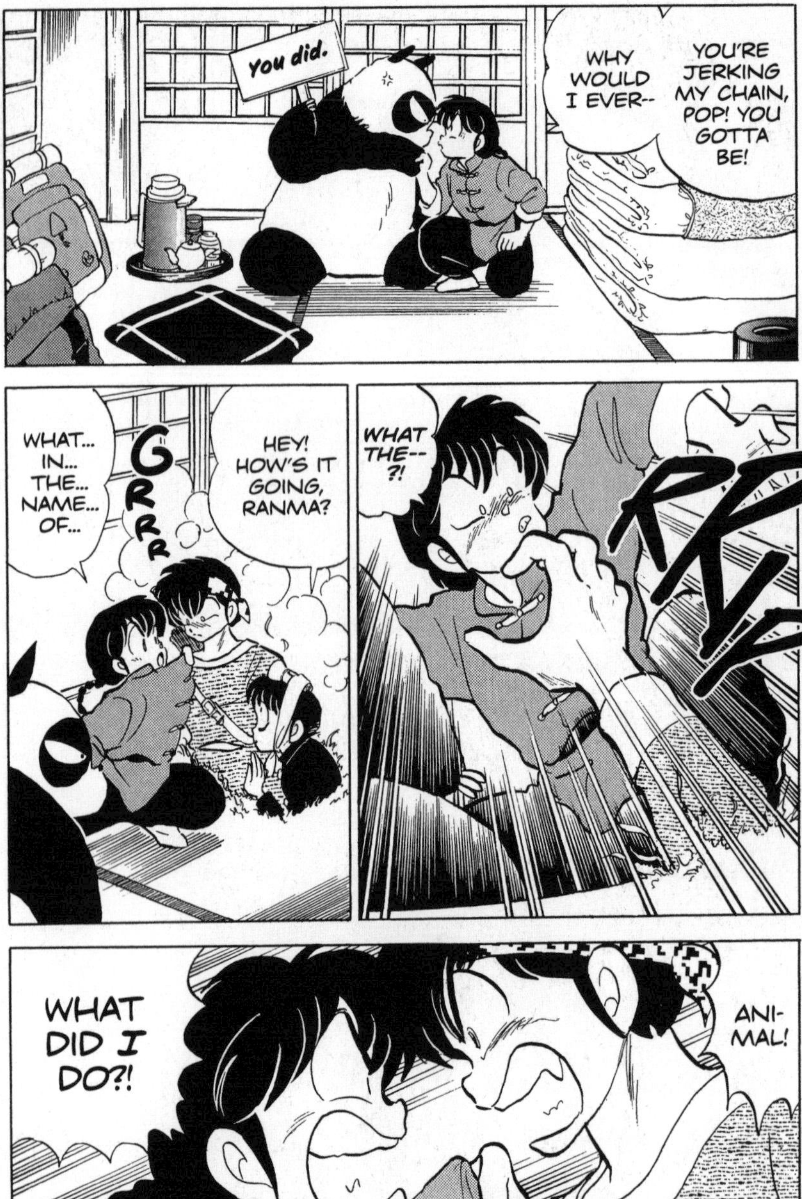
YOU'RE JERKING MY CHAIN, POP! YOU GOTTA BE!
WHY WOULD I EVER--
You did.
WHAT THE-- ?!
RRIP
HEY! HOW'S IT GOING, RANMA?
GRRR
WHAT... IN... THE... NAME... OF...
ANI-MAL!
WHAT DID I DO?!

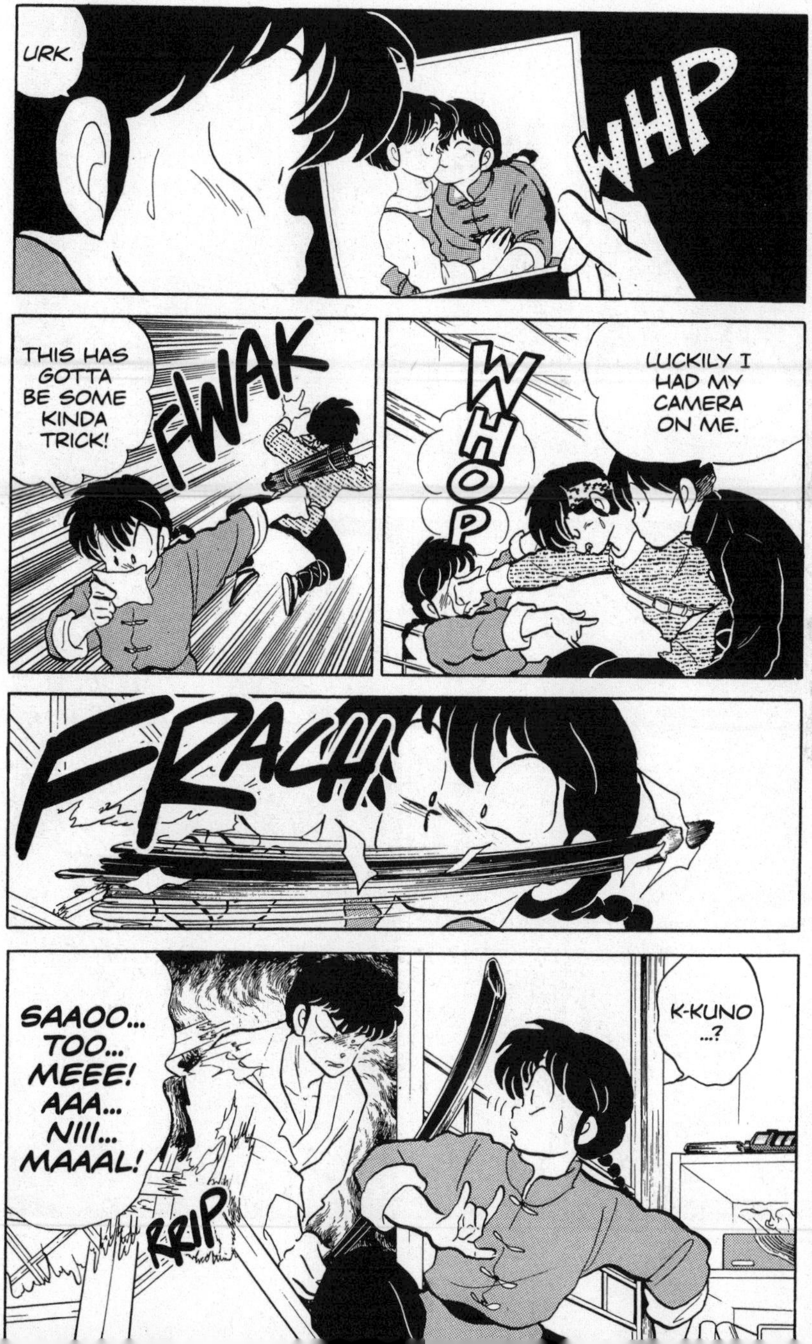
URK.
WHP
WHOP
LUCKILY I HAD MY CAMERA ON ME.
THIS HAS GOTTA BE SOME KINDA TRICK!
FWAK
FRACH
K-KUNO ...?
SAAOO... TOO... MEEE! AAA... NIII... MAAAL!
RRIP

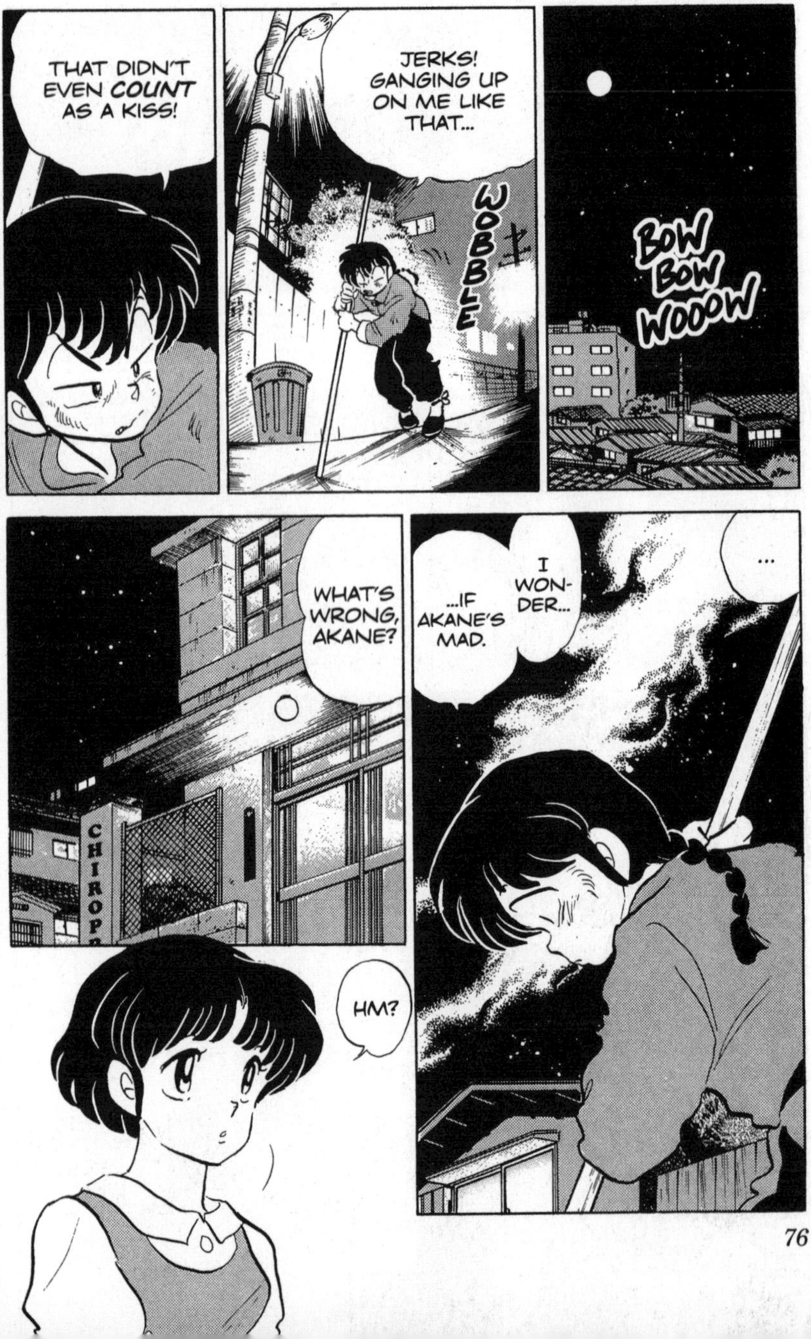
BOW BOW WOOOW
JERKS! GANGING UP ON ME LIKE THAT...
WOBBLE
THAT DIDN'T EVEN COUNT AS A KISS!
...
I WONDER...
...IF AKANE'S MAD.
WHAT'S WRONG, AKANE?
HM?

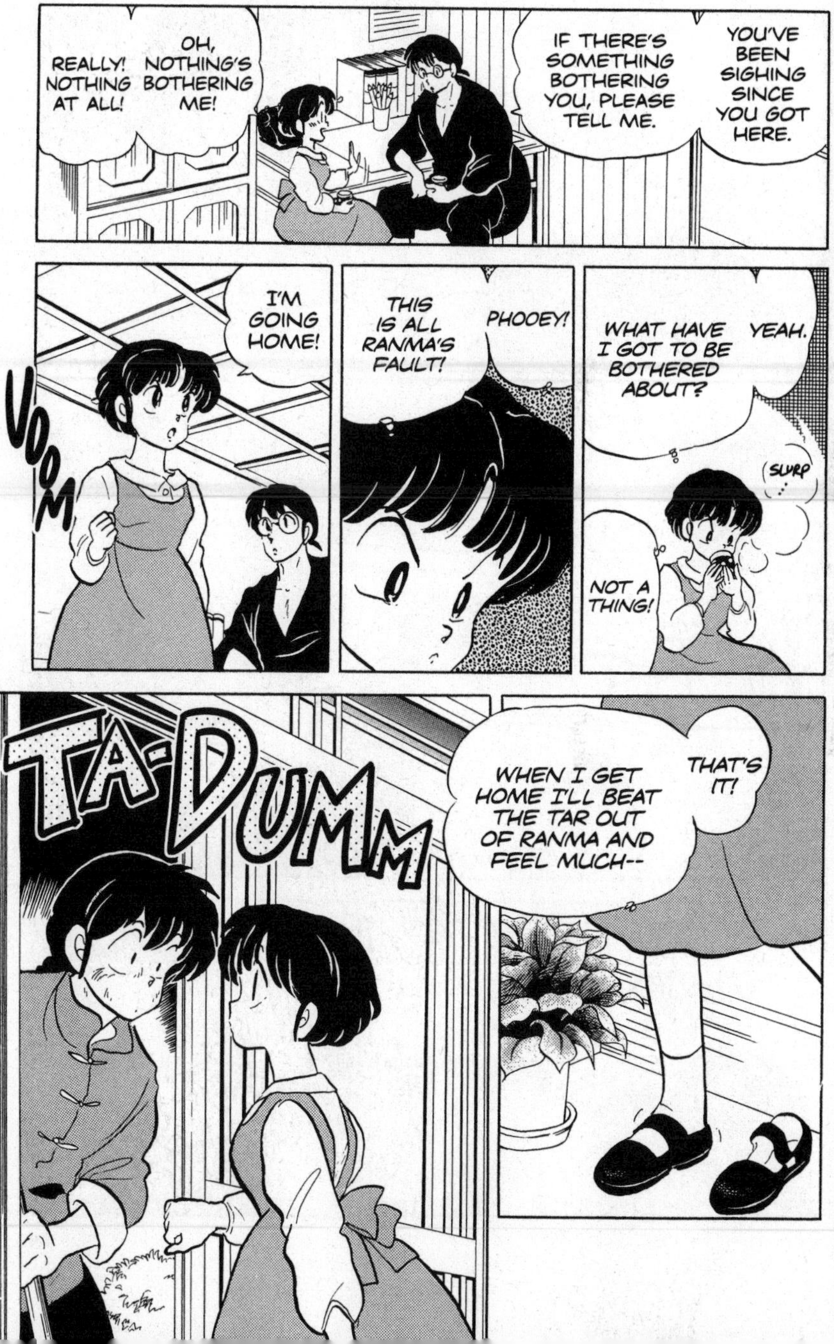
YOU'VE BEEN SIGHING SINCE YOU GOT HERE.
IF THERE'S SOMETHING BOTHERING YOU, PLEASE TELL ME.
OH, NOTHING'S BOTHERING ME!
REALLY! NOTHING AT ALL!
YEAH.
WHAT HAVE I GOT TO BE BOTHERED ABOUT?
SLURP
NOT A THING!
PHOOEY!
THIS IS ALL RANMA'S FAULT!
I'M GOING HOME!
VOOOM
THAT'S IT!
WHEN I GET HOME I'LL BEAT THE TAR OUT OF RANMA AND FEEL MUCH--
TA-DUMM

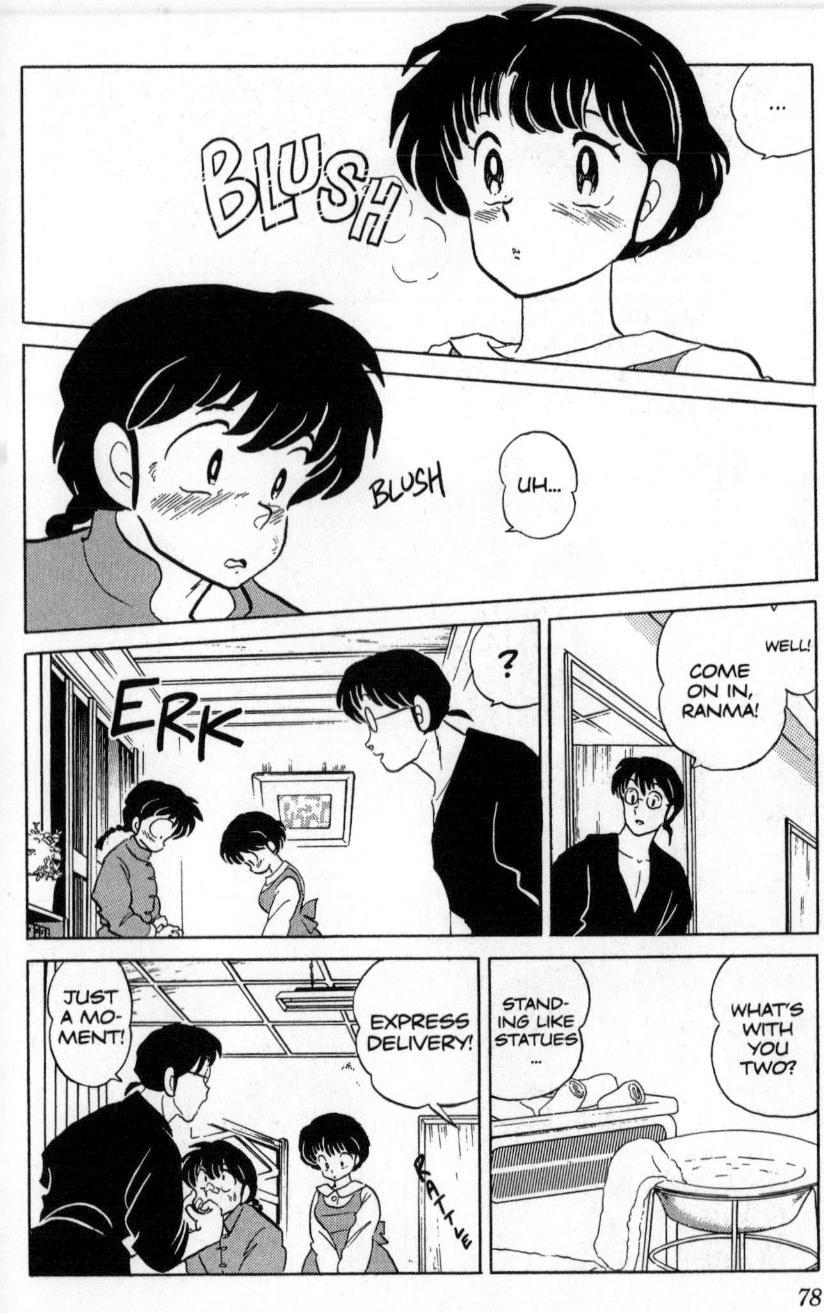
...
BLUSH
UH...
BLUSH
WELL! COME ON IN, RANMA!
?
ERK
WHAT'S WITH YOU TWO?
STAND-ING LIKE STATUES ...
EXPRESS DELIVERY!
RATTLE
JUST A MO-MENT!

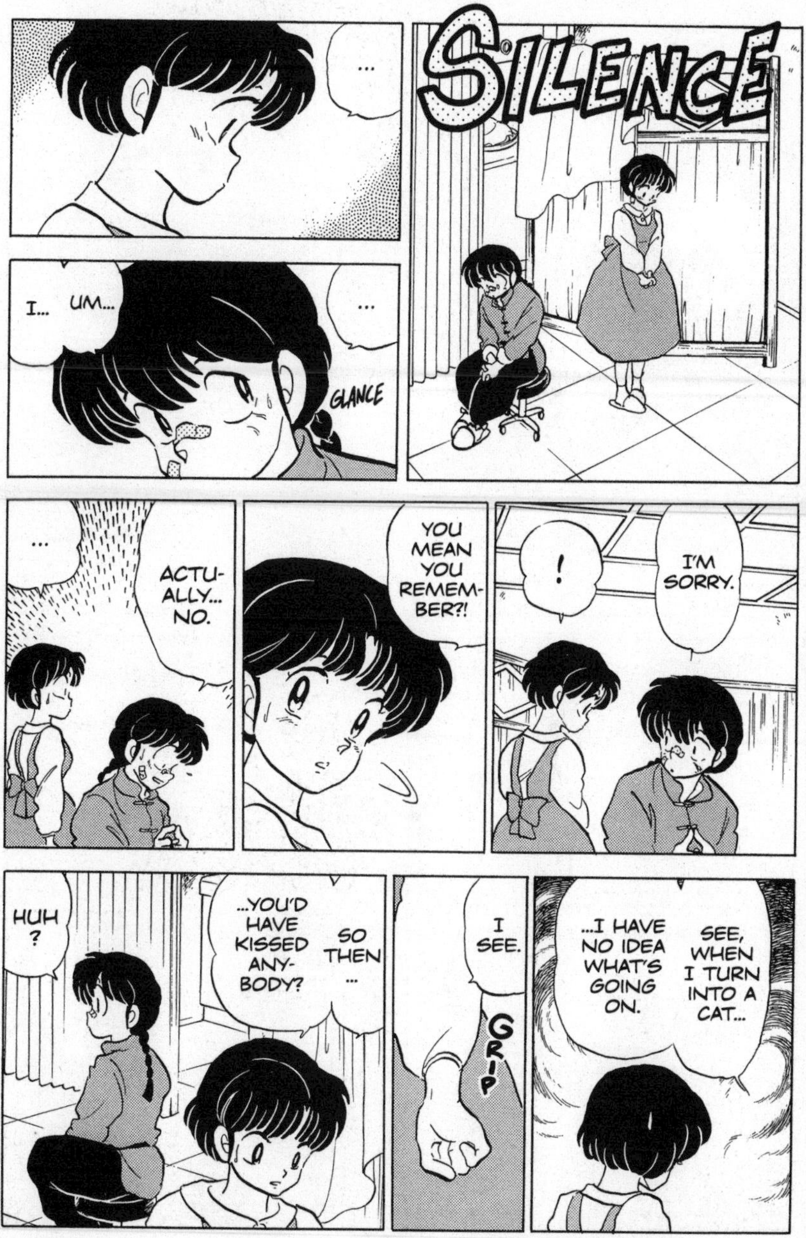
SILENCE
...
...
I... UM...
GLANCE
I'M SORRY.
!
YOU MEAN YOU REMEMBER?!
ACTUALLY... NO.
...
SEE, WHEN I TURN INTO A CAT...
...I HAVE NO IDEA WHAT'S GOING ON.
I SEE.
GRIP
SO THEN ...
...YOU'D HAVE KISSED ANYBODY?
HUH?

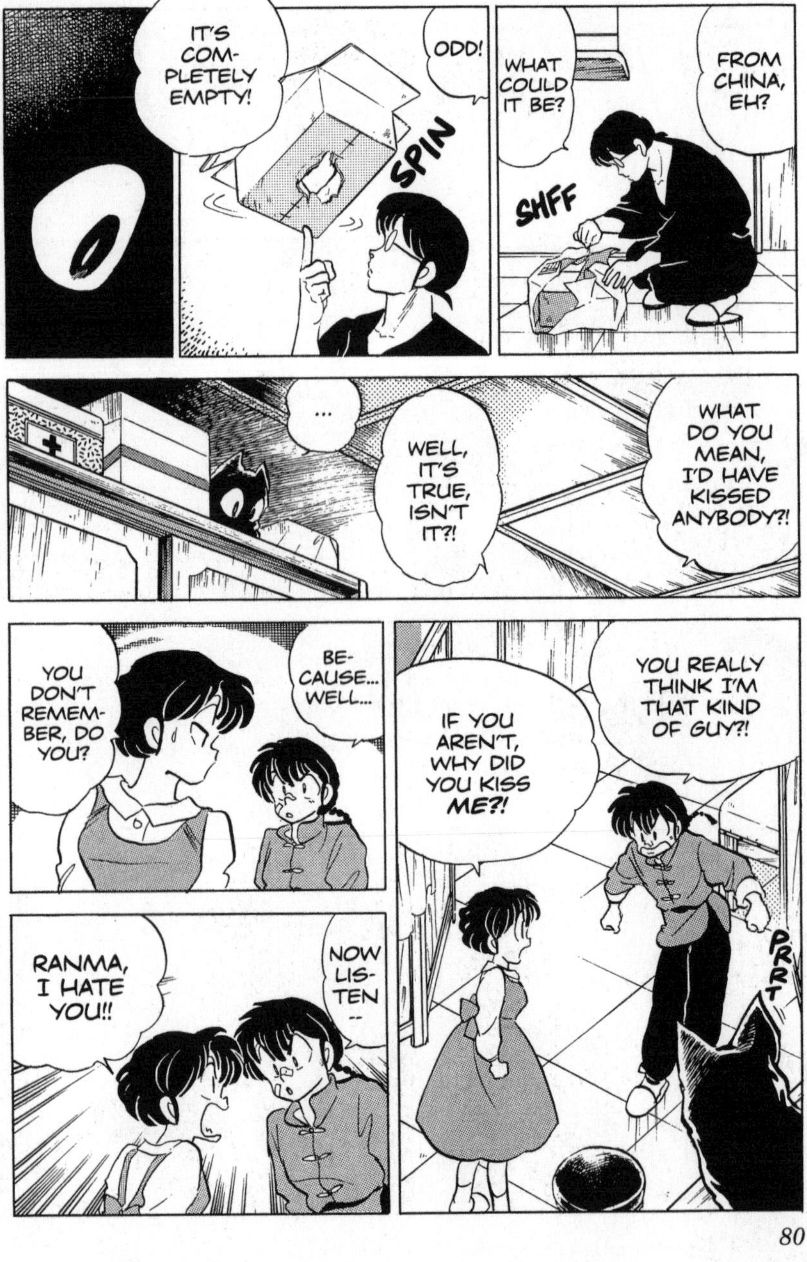
FROM CHINA, EH?
WHAT COULD IT BE?
SHFF
ODD!
SPIN
IT'S COMPLETELY EMPTY!
WHAT DO YOU MEAN, I'D HAVE KISSED ANYBODY?!
WELL, IT'S TRUE, ISN'T IT?!
...
YOU REALLY THINK I'M THAT KIND OF GUY?!
IF YOU AREN'T, WHY DID YOU KISS ME?!
PRRT
BECAUSE... WELL...
YOU DON'T REMEMBER, DO YOU?
NOW LISTEN --
RANMA, I HATE YOU!!

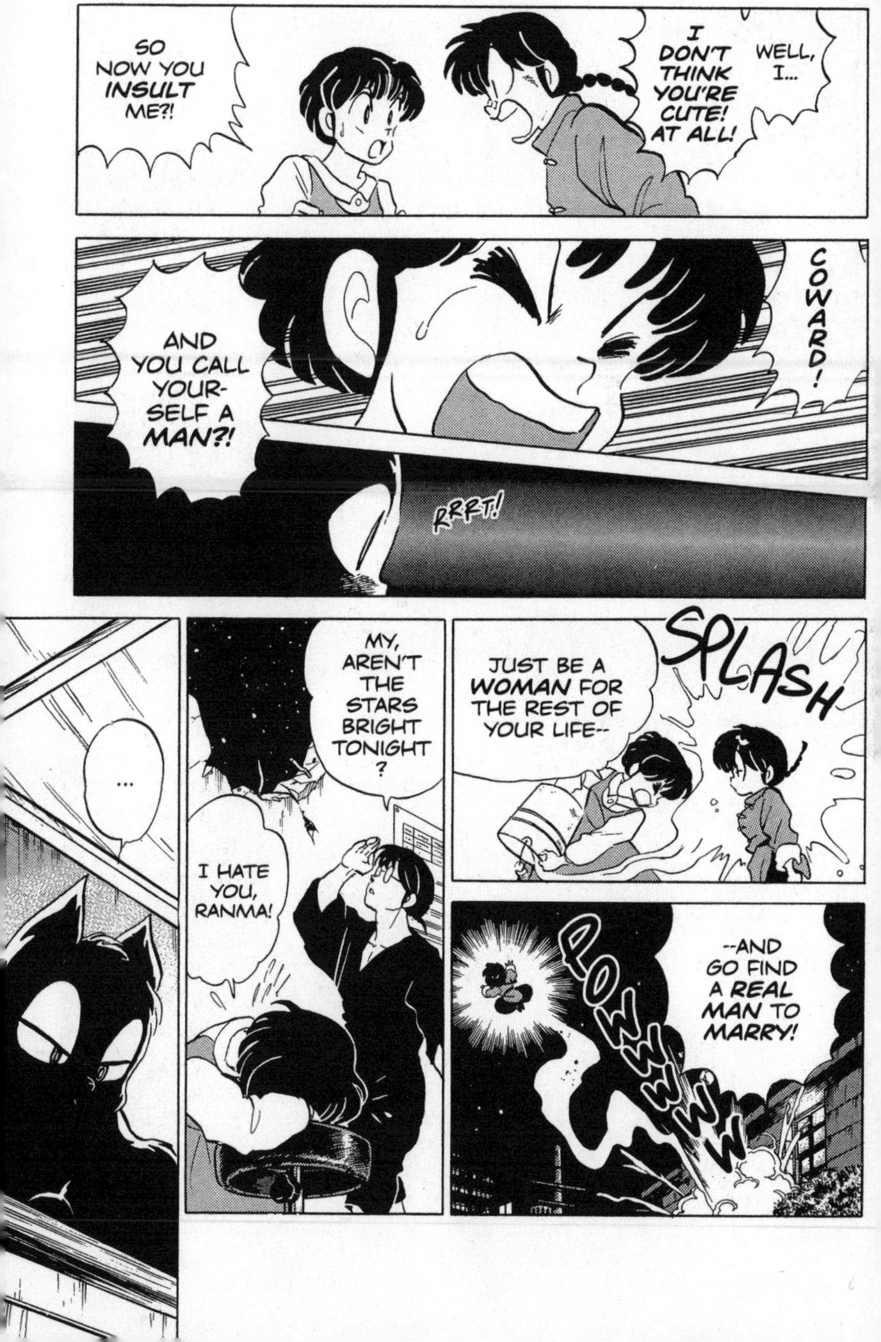
WELL, I...
I DON'T THINK YOU'RE CUTE! AT ALL!
SO NOW YOU INSULT ME?!
COWARD!
AND YOU CALL YOUR-SELF A MAN?!
RRRT!
SPLASH
JUST BE A WOMAN FOR THE REST OF YOUR LIFE--
--AND GO FIND A REAL MAN TO MARRY!
POWWWWWW
MY, AREN'T THE STARS BRIGHT TONIGHT?
I HATE YOU, RANMA!
...

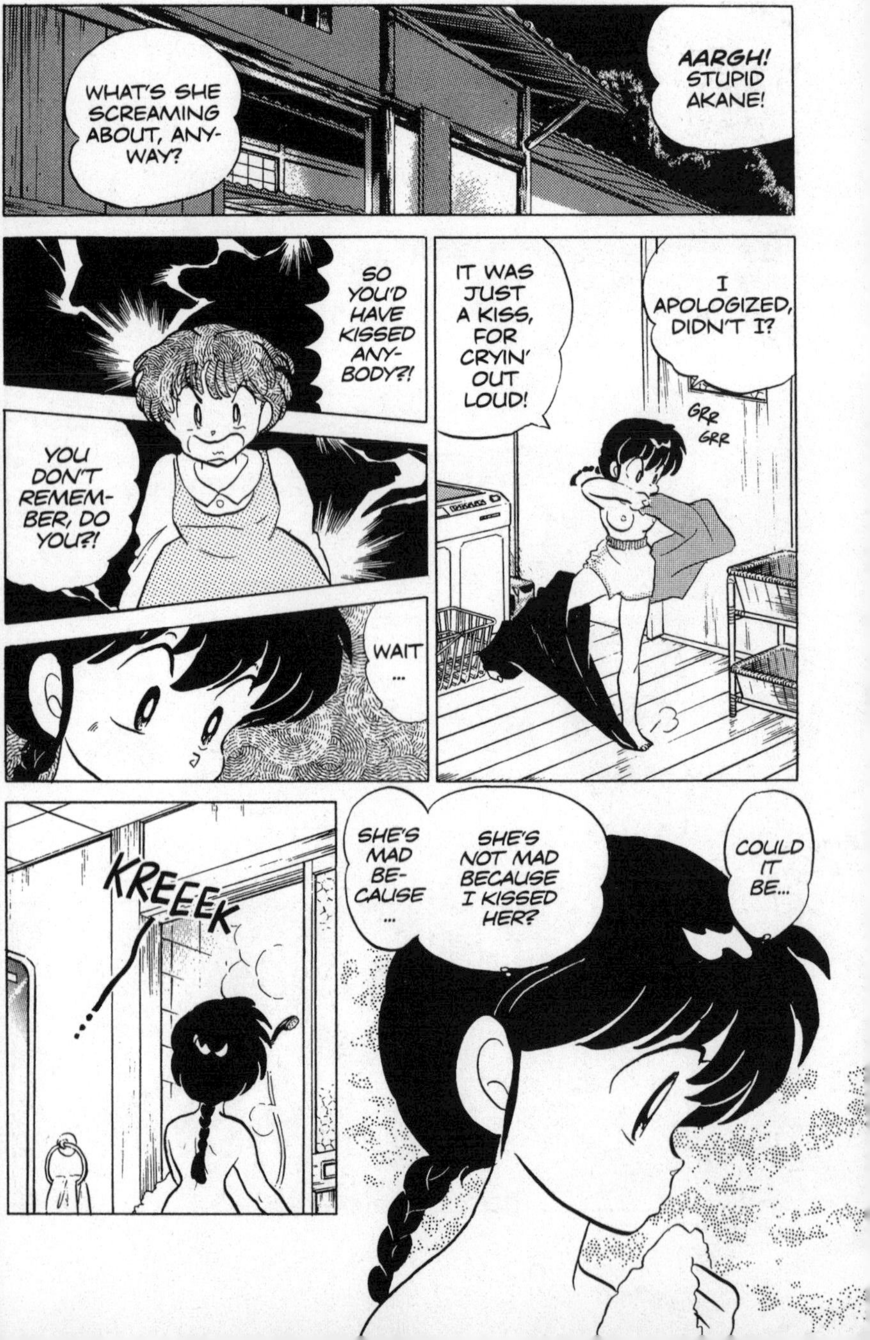
AARGH! STUPID AKANE!
WHAT'S SHE SCREAMING ABOUT, ANY-WAY?
I APOLOGIZED, DIDN'T I?
GRR GRR
IT WAS JUST A KISS, FOR CRYIN' OUT LOUD!
SO YOU'D HAVE KISSED ANY-BODY?!
YOU DON'T REMEM-BER, DO YOU?!
WAIT ...
COULD IT BE...
SHE'S NOT MAD BECAUSE I KISSED HER?
SHE'S MAD BE-CAUSE ...
KREEEK
...

NYOW

SPLAP SPLAP SPLAP

AAAAH!!

NYOW NYOW NYOW

MEW?

AAH!

AAH!

AAH!

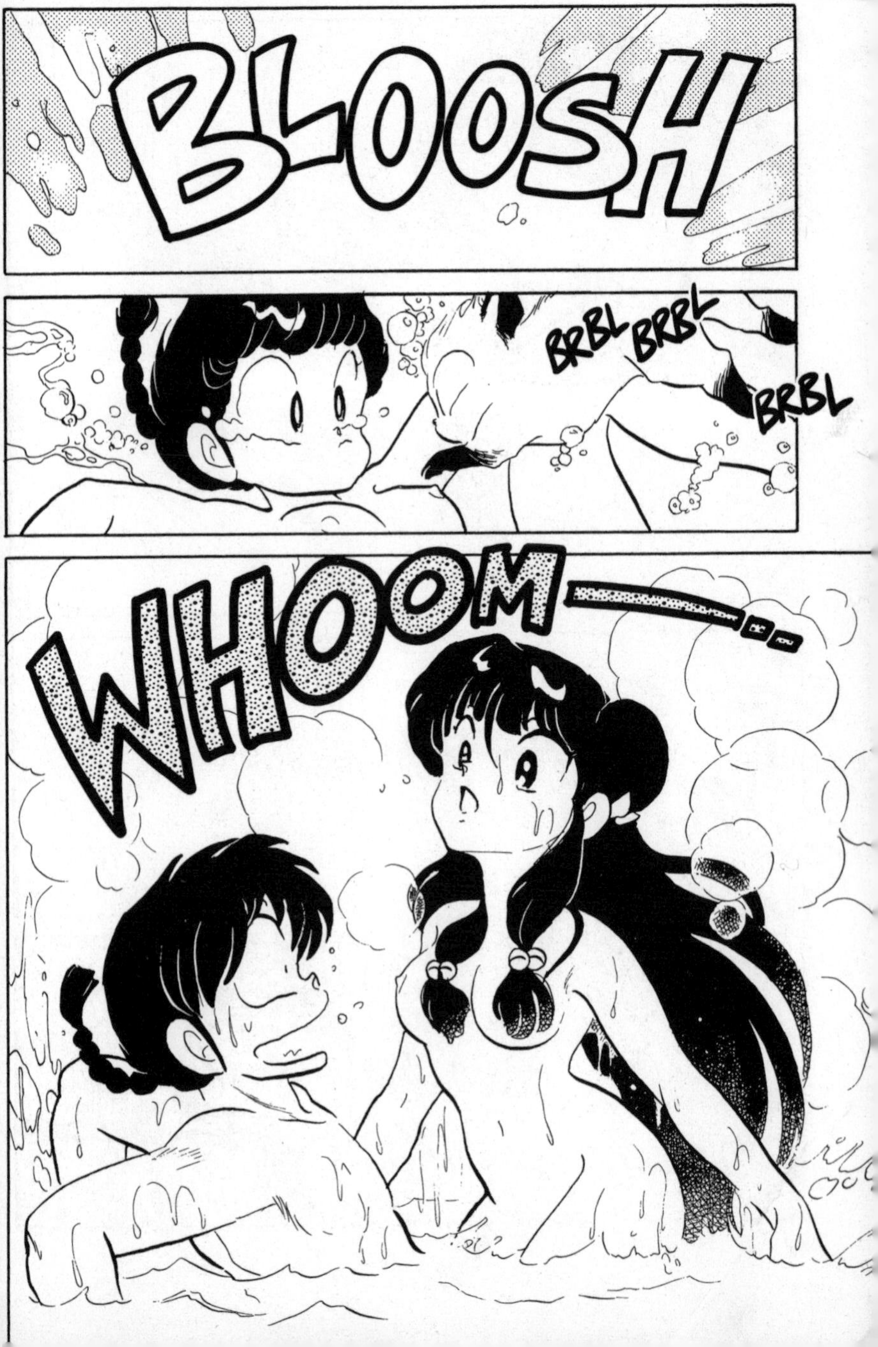
BLOOSH
BRBL BRBL
BRBL
WHOOOM—...

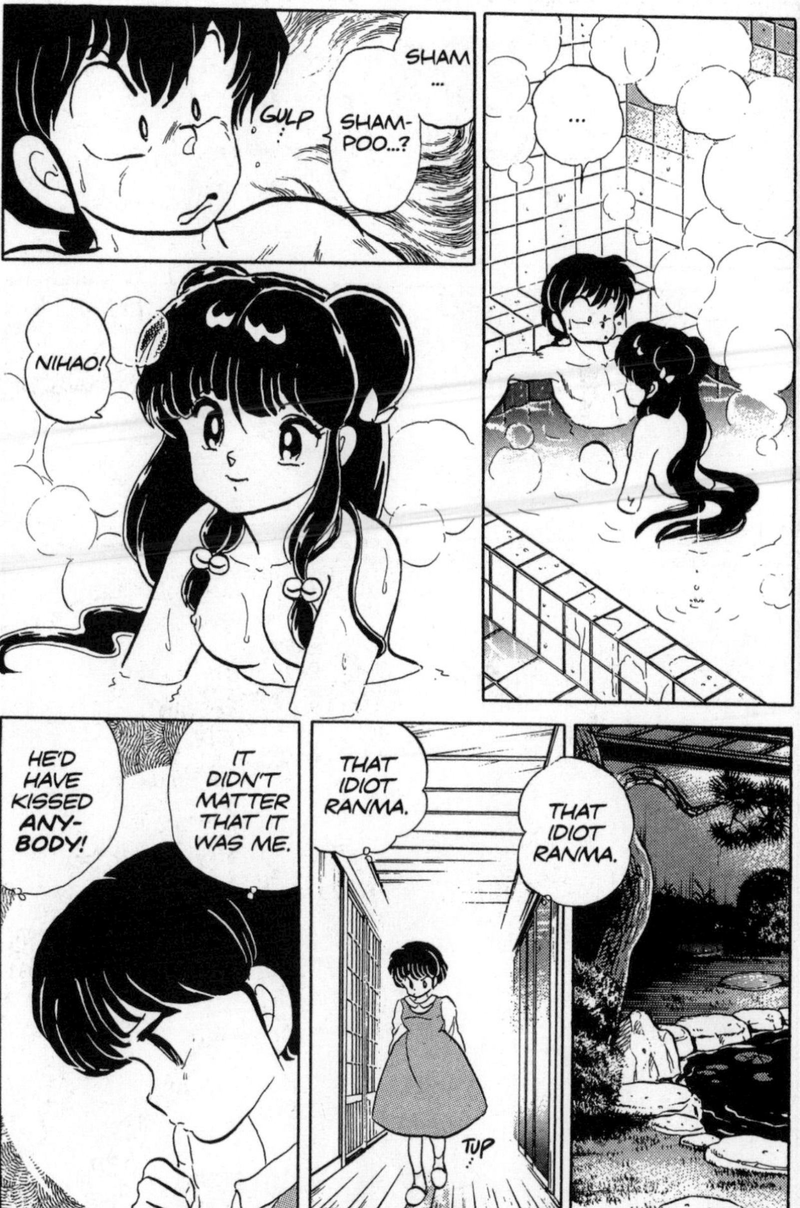
...
SHAM ... SHAMPOO...?
GULP
NIHAO!
THAT IDIOT RANMA.
THAT IDIOT RANMA.
TUP
IT DIDN'T MATTER THAT IT WAS ME.
HE'D HAVE KISSED ANYBODY!

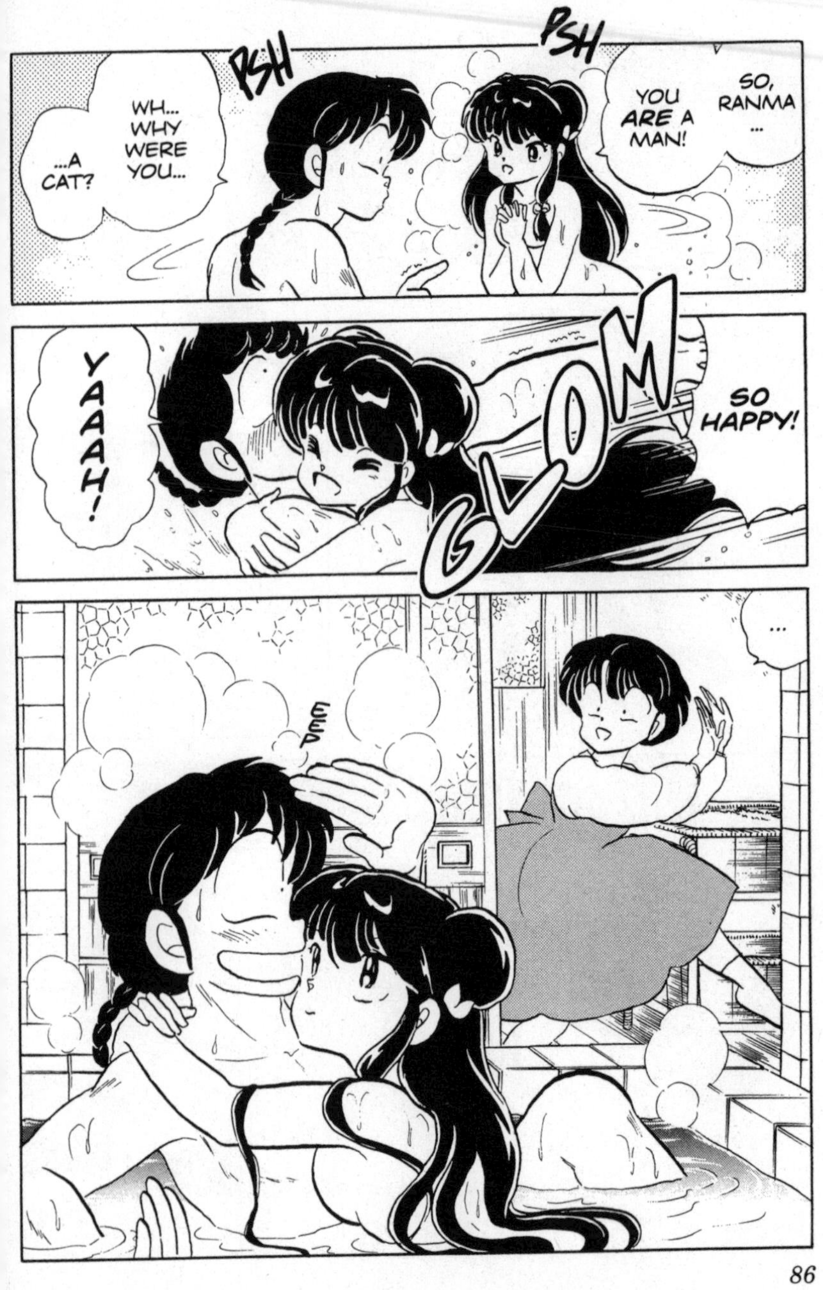
SO, RANMA ...
YOU ARE A MAN!
PSH
PSH
WH... WHY WERE YOU...
...A CAT?
SO HAPPY!
GLOM
YAAAH!
...
EEP

PART 6
SHAMPOO RIDES AGAIN

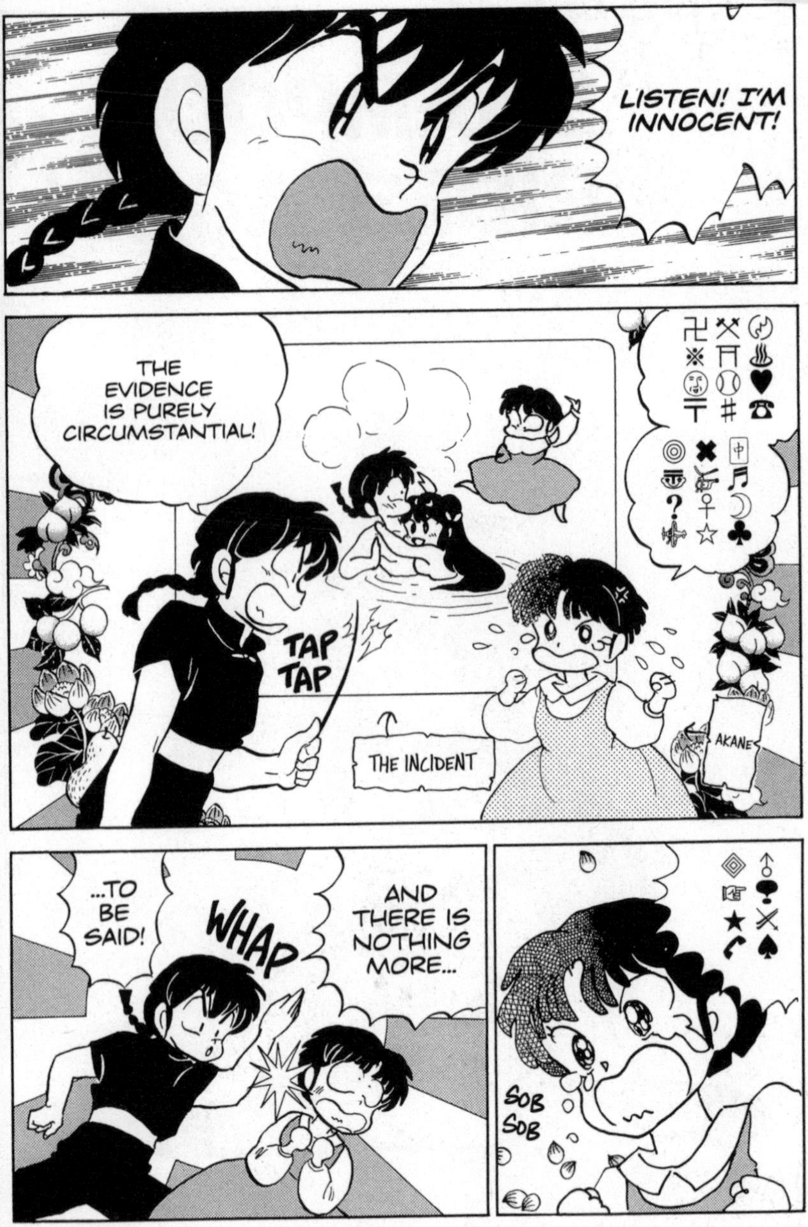
LISTEN! I'M INNOCENT!
THE EVIDENCE IS PURELY CIRCUMSTANTIAL!
TAP TAP
AKANE
THE INCIDENT
SOB SOB
AND THERE IS NOTHING MORE...
WHAP
...TO BE SAID!

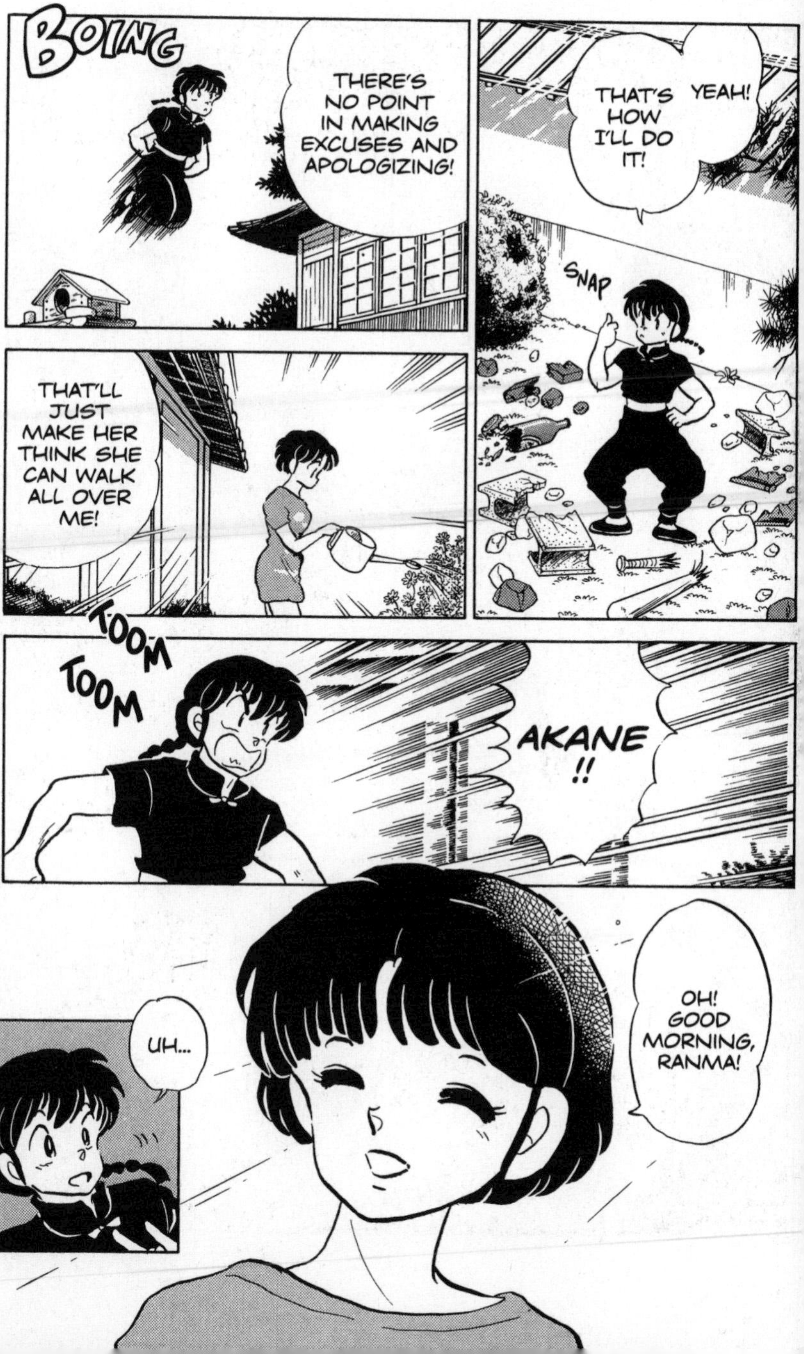
YEAH!
THAT'S HOW I'LL DO IT!
SNAP
BOING
THERE'S NO POINT IN MAKING EXCUSES AND APOLOGIZING!
THAT'LL JUST MAKE HER THINK SHE CAN WALK ALL OVER ME!
AKANE!!
TOOM
TOOM
OH! GOOD MORNING, RANMA!
UH...

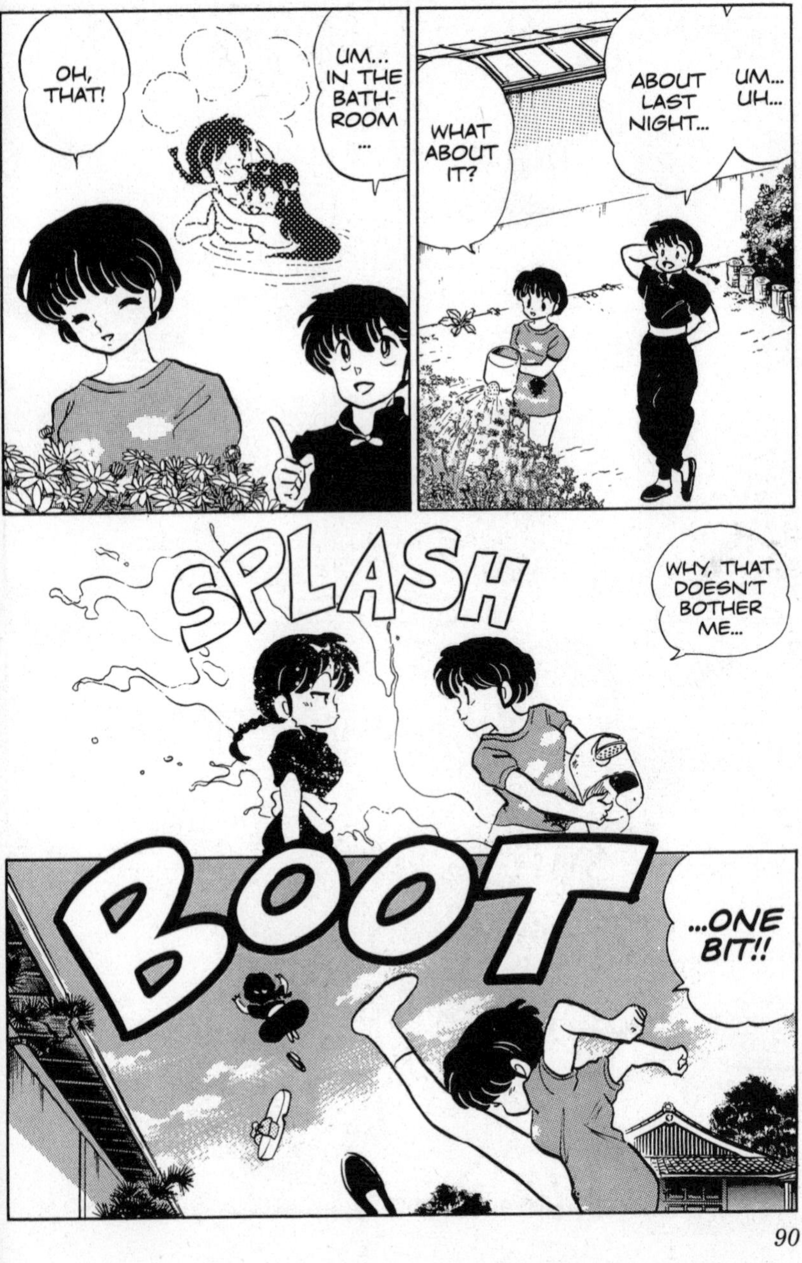
UM... UH...
ABOUT LAST NIGHT...
WHAT ABOUT IT?
UM... IN THE BATH-ROOM ...
OH, THAT!
WHY, THAT DOESN'T BOTHER ME...
SPLASH
...ONE BIT!!
BOOT

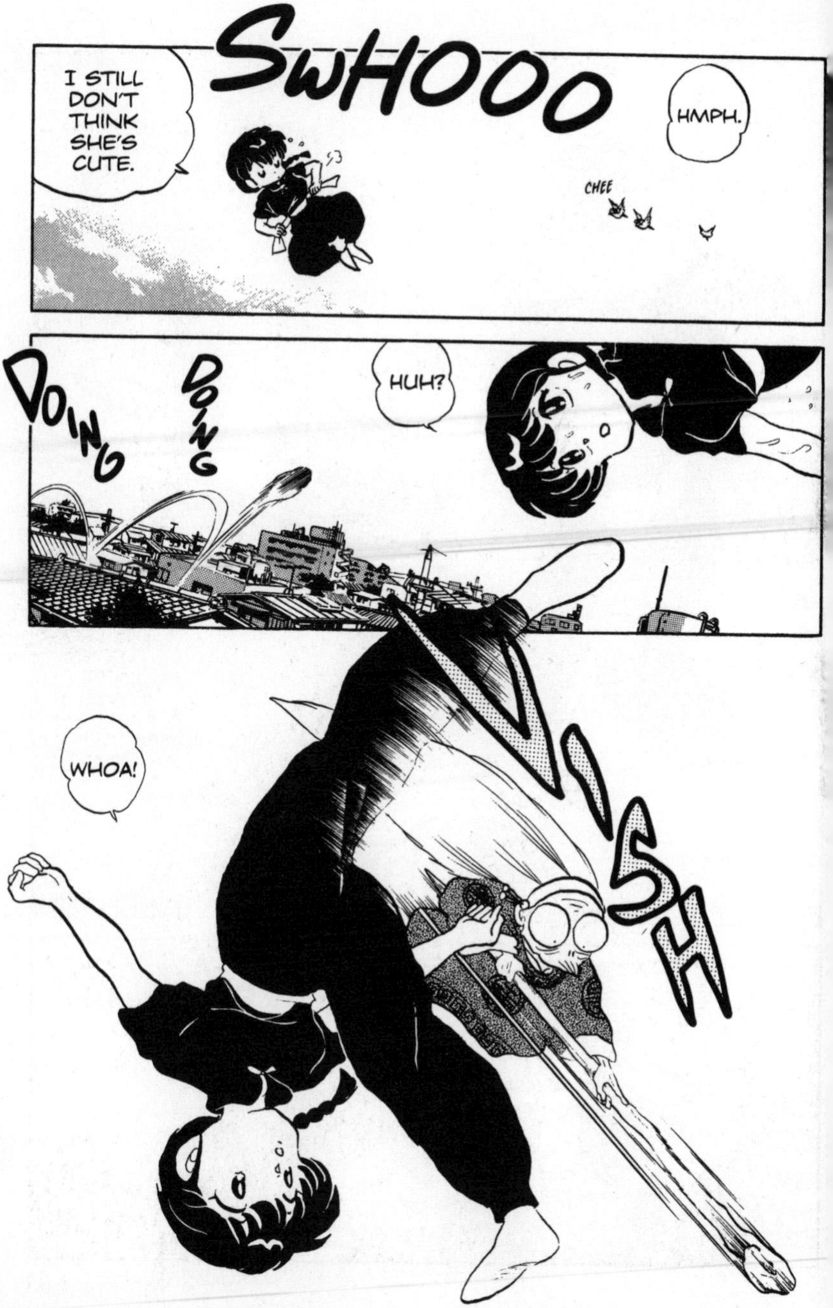
SWHOOO
HMPH.
CHEE
I STILL DON'T THINK SHE'S CUTE.
HUH?
DOING
DOING
VISHH
WHOA!

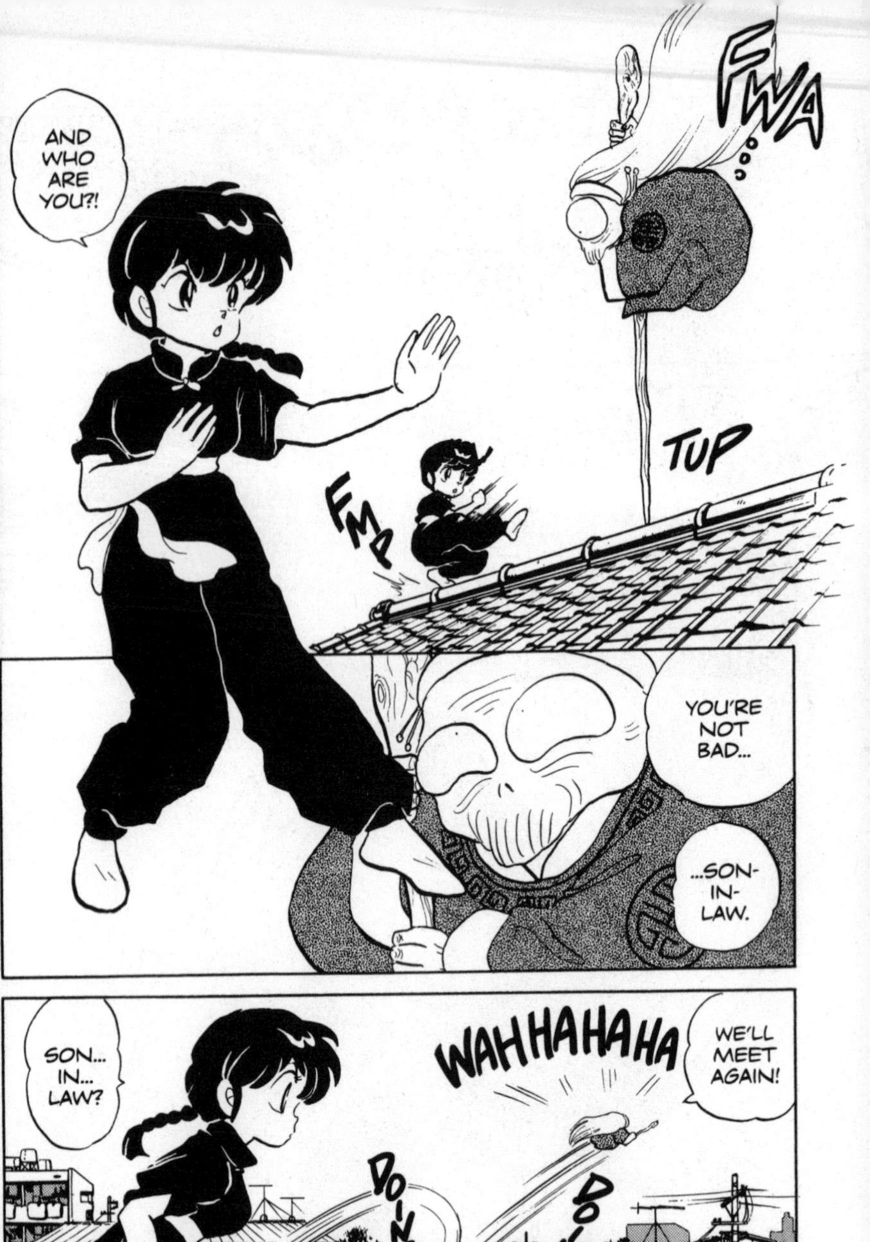
FWA
TUP
FMP
AND WHO ARE YOU?!
YOU'RE NOT BAD...
...SON-IN-LAW.
WE'LL MEET AGAIN!
WAHHAHAHA
DOING
DOING
SON... IN... LAW?

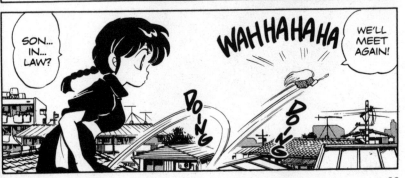

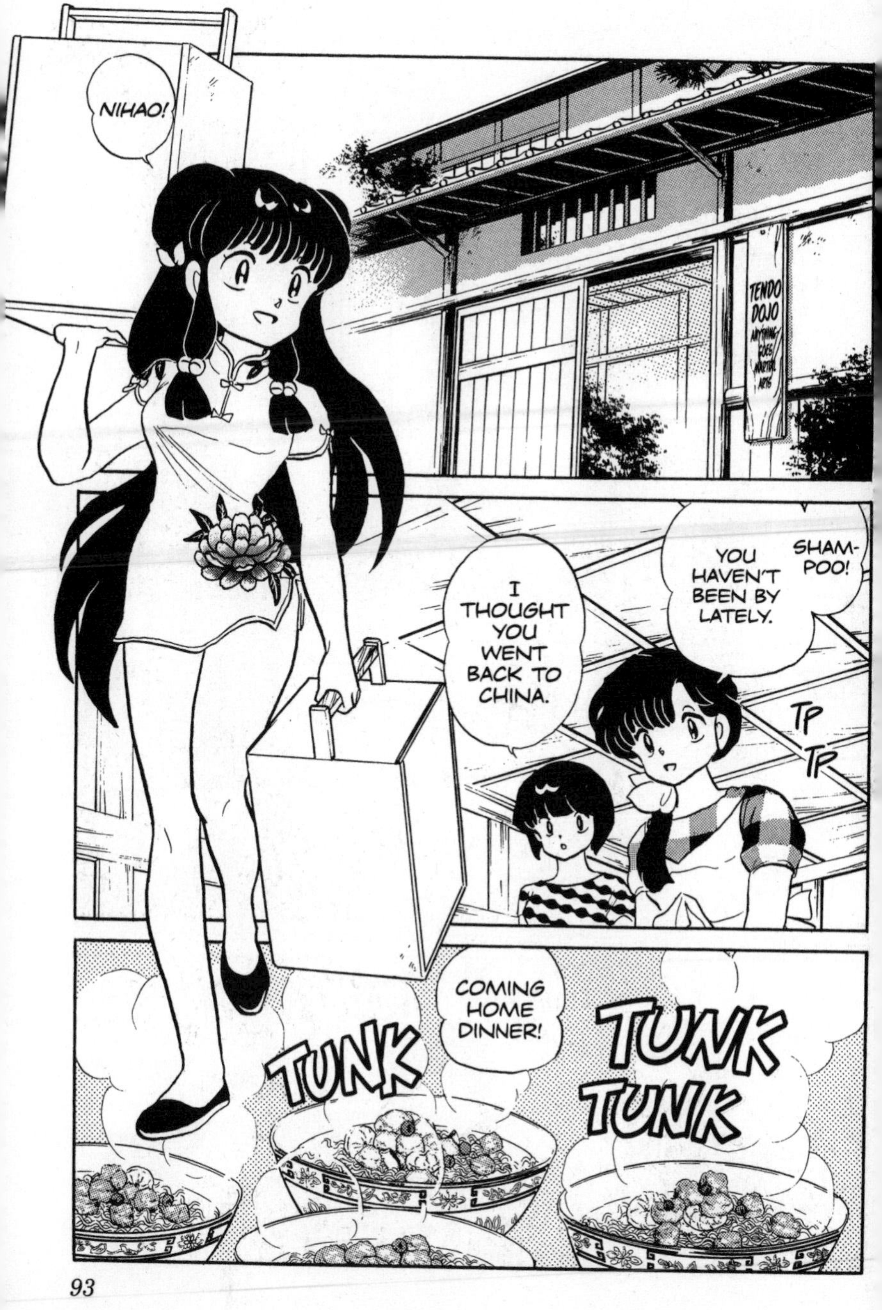
NIHAO!
TENDO DOJO ANYTHING GOES MARTIAL ARTS
SHAM-POO!
YOU HAVEN'T BEEN BY LATELY.
I THOUGHT YOU WENT BACK TO CHINA.
TP TP
TUNK TUNK
COMING HOME DINNER!
TUNK

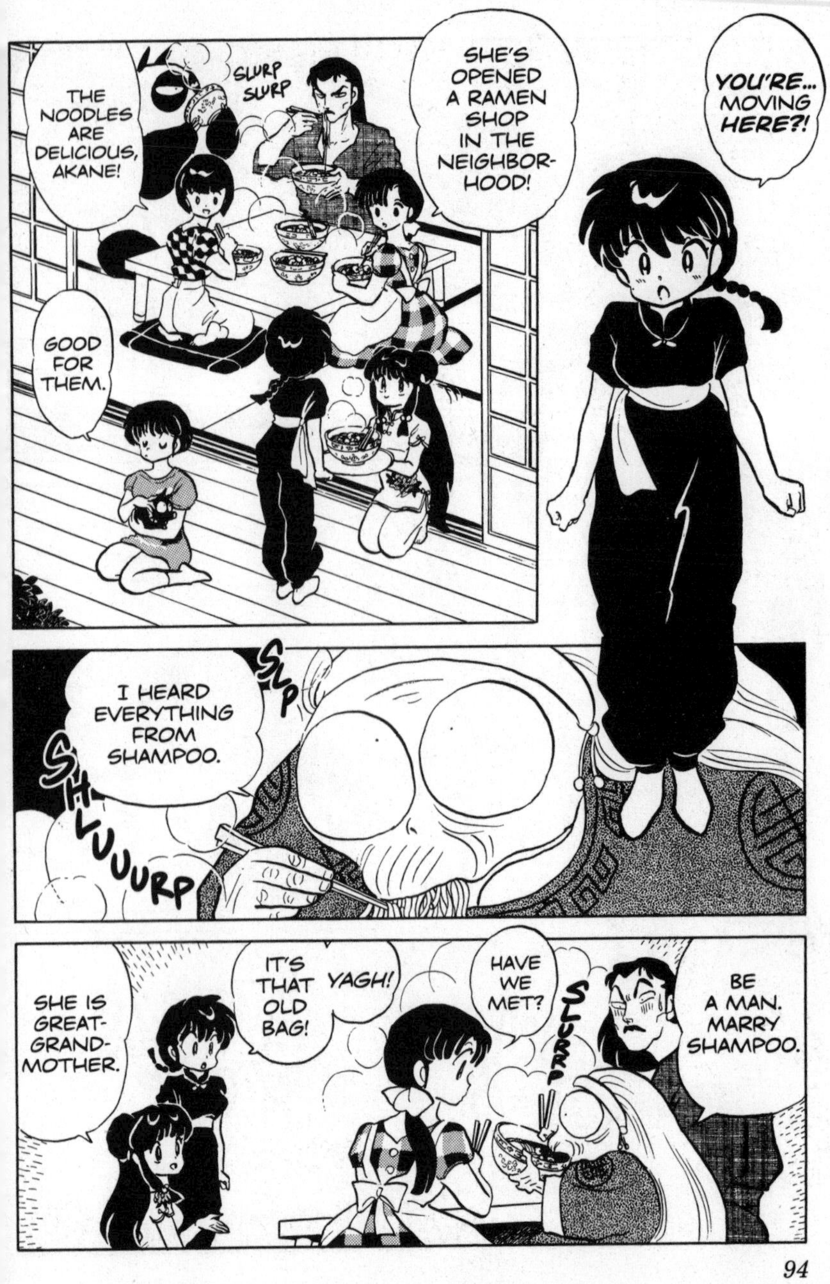
YOU'RE... MOVING HERE?!
SHE'S OPENED A RAMEN SHOP IN THE NEIGHBOR-HOOD!
SLURP SLURP
THE NOODLES ARE DELICIOUS, AKANE!
GOOD FOR THEM.
SLP
I HEARD EVERYTHING FROM SHAMPOO.
SHHLUUUURP
BE A MAN. MARRY SHAMPOO.
SLURRP
HAVE WE MET?
YAGH!
IT'S THAT OLD BAG!
SHE IS GREAT-GRANDMOTHER.

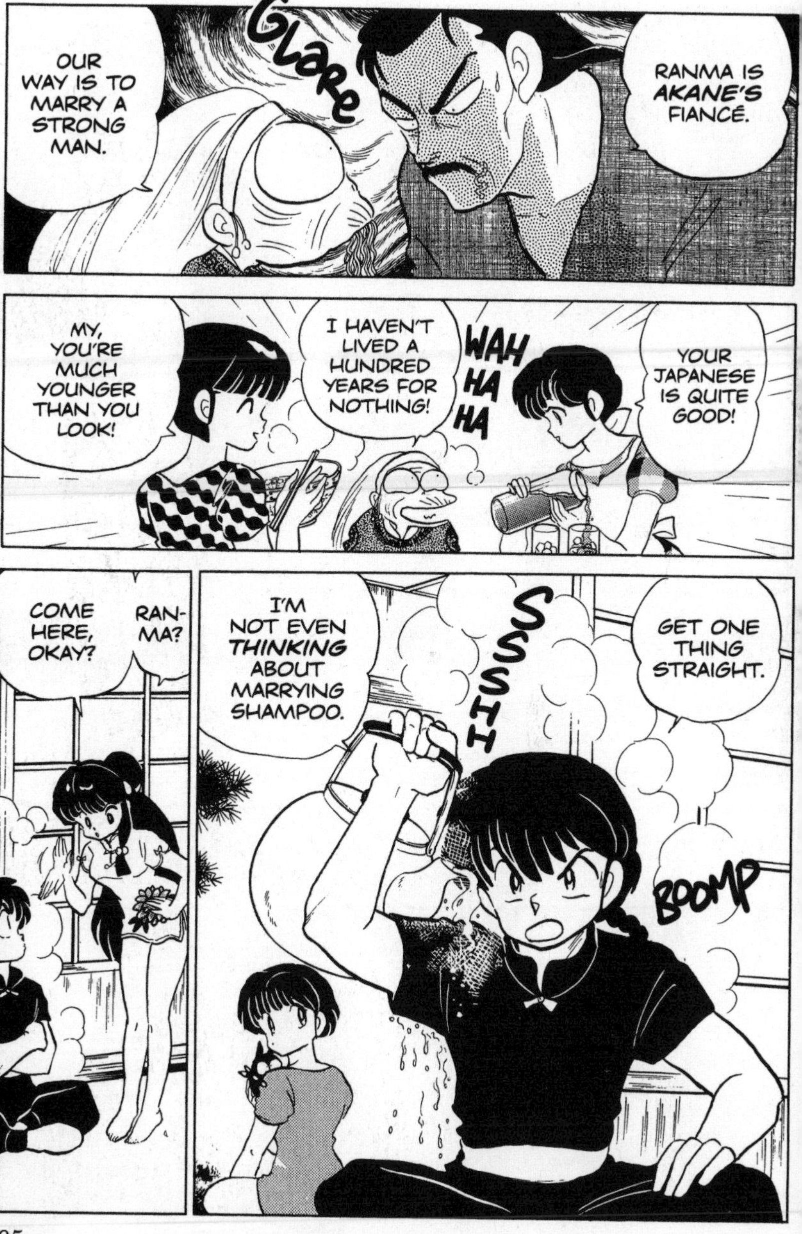
RANMA IS AKANE'S FIANCÉ.
GLARE
OUR WAY IS TO MARRY A STRONG MAN.
YOUR JAPANESE IS QUITE GOOD!
WAH HA HA
I HAVEN'T LIVED A HUNDRED YEARS FOR NOTHING!
MY, YOU'RE MUCH YOUNGER THAN YOU LOOK!
GET ONE THING STRAIGHT.
SSSHH
I'M NOT EVEN THINKING ABOUT MARRYING SHAMPOO.
BOOMP
RAN-MA?
COME HERE, OKAY?

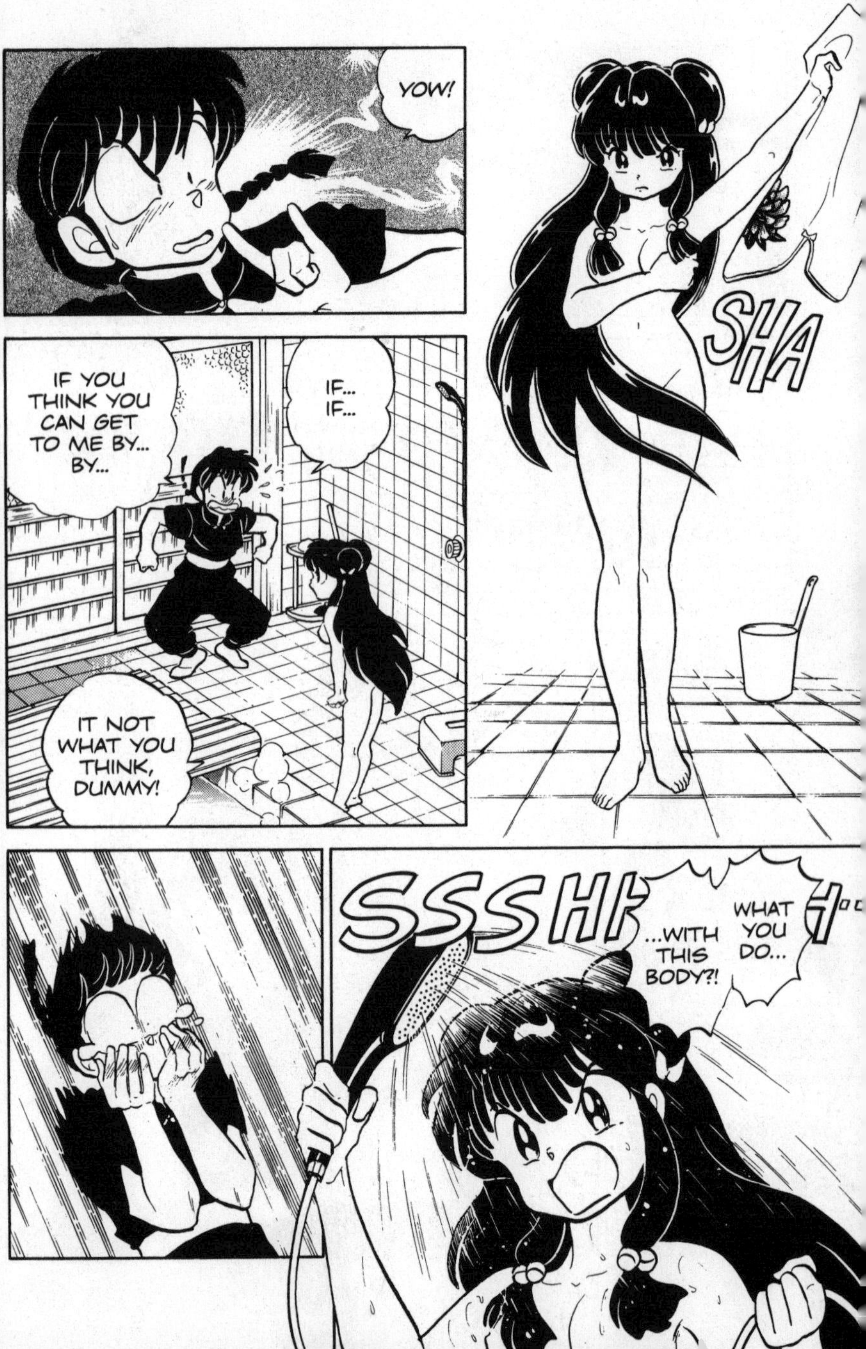
SHA
YOW!
IF... IF...
IF YOU THINK YOU CAN GET TO ME BY... BY...
IT NOT WHAT YOU THINK, DUMMY!
SSSHH
WHAT YOU DO...
...WITH THIS BODY?!

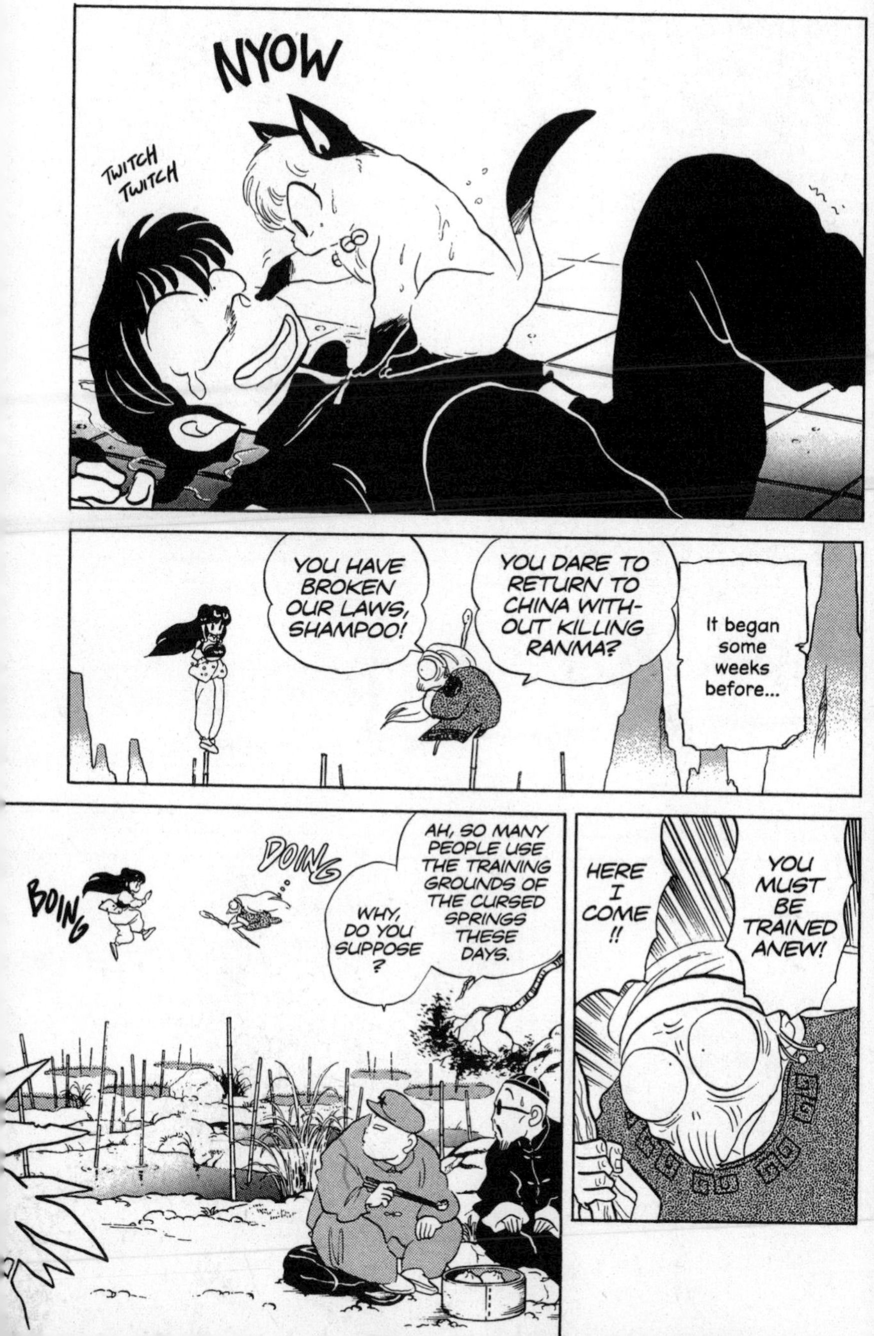
NYOW
TWITCH TWITCH
It began some weeks before...
YOU DARE TO RETURN TO CHINA WITH-OUT KILLING RANMA?
YOU HAVE BROKEN OUR LAWS, SHAMPOO!
YOU MUST BE TRAINED ANEW!
HERE I COME !!
AH, SO MANY PEOPLE USE THE TRAINING GROUNDS OF THE CURSED SPRINGS THESE DAYS.
WHY, DO YOU SUPPOSE ?
DOINGS
BOING

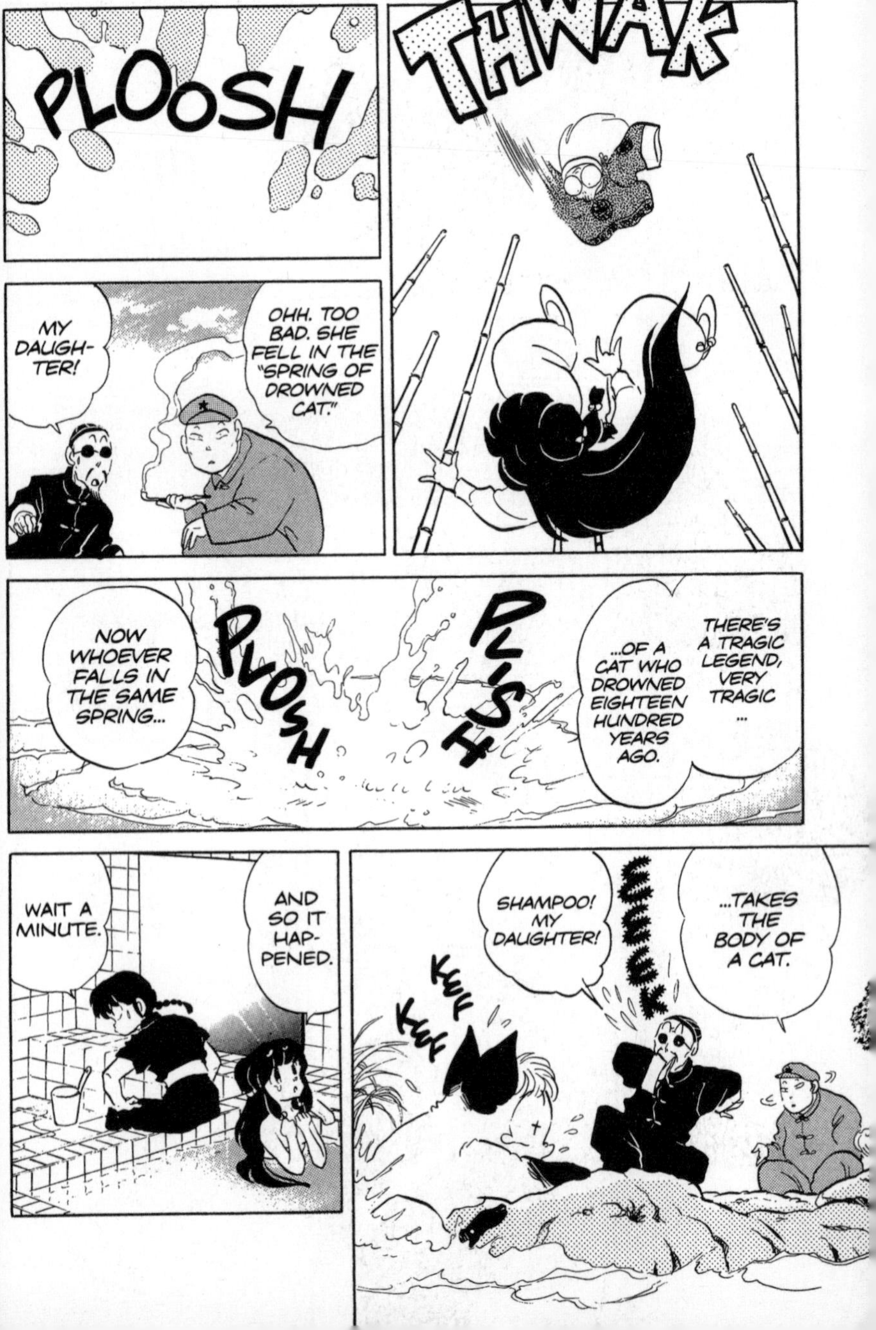
THWAK
PLOOSH
OHH. TOO BAD. SHE FELL IN THE "SPRING OF DROWNED CAT."
MY DAUGHTER!
THERE'S A TRAGIC LEGEND, VERY TRAGIC ...
...OF A CAT WHO DROWNED EIGHTEEN HUNDRED YEARS AGO.
PLISH
PLOOSH
NOW WHOEVER FALLS IN THE SAME SPRING...
...TAKES THE BODY OF A CAT.
EEEK
SHAMPOO! MY DAUGHTER!
KUFF
KUFF
AND SO IT HAP-PENED.
WAIT A MINUTE.

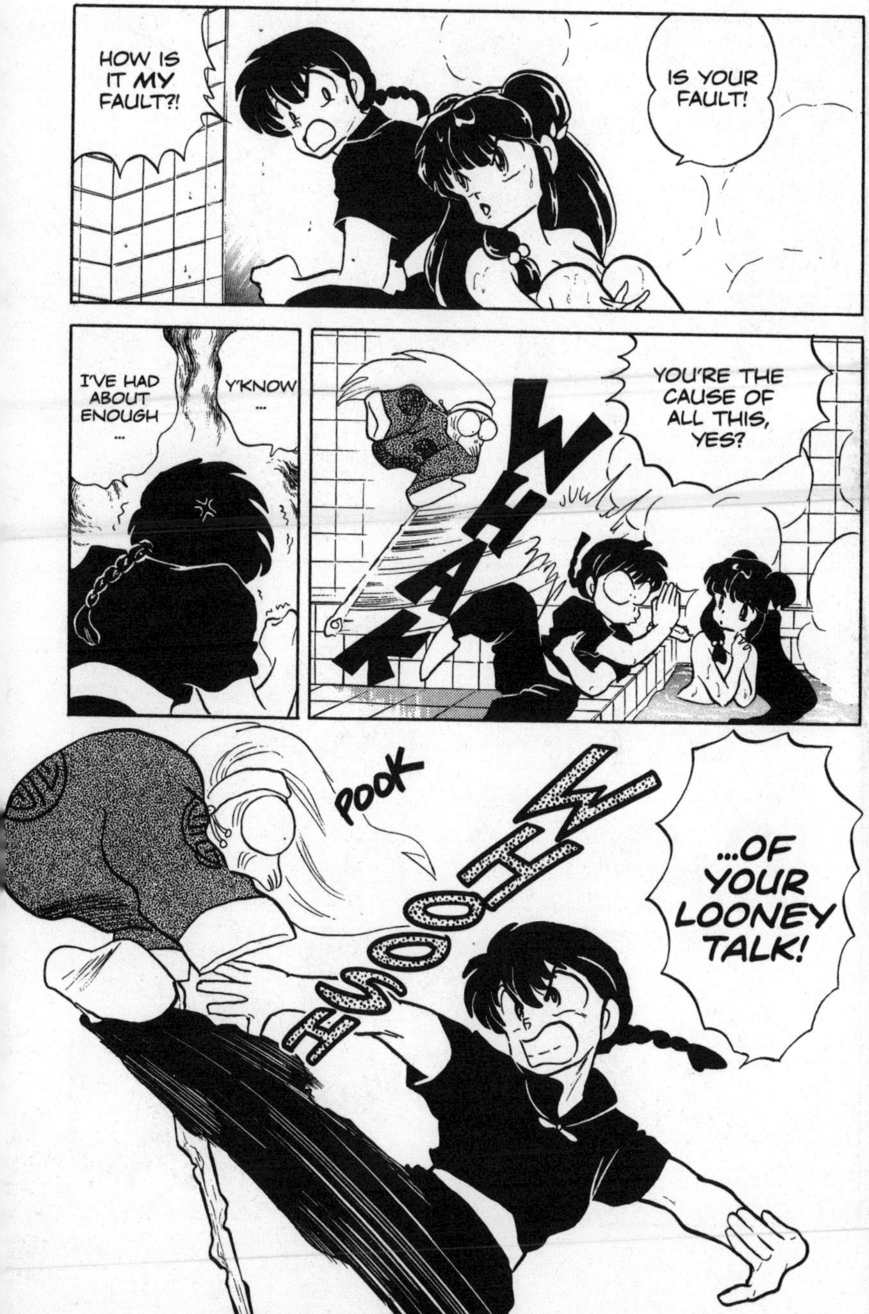
IS YOUR FAULT!
HOW IS IT MY FAULT?!
YOU'RE THE CAUSE OF ALL THIS, YES?
WHAAK
Y'KNOW ...
I'VE HAD ABOUT ENOUGH ...
...OF YOUR LOONEY TALK!
WHOOSH
POOK

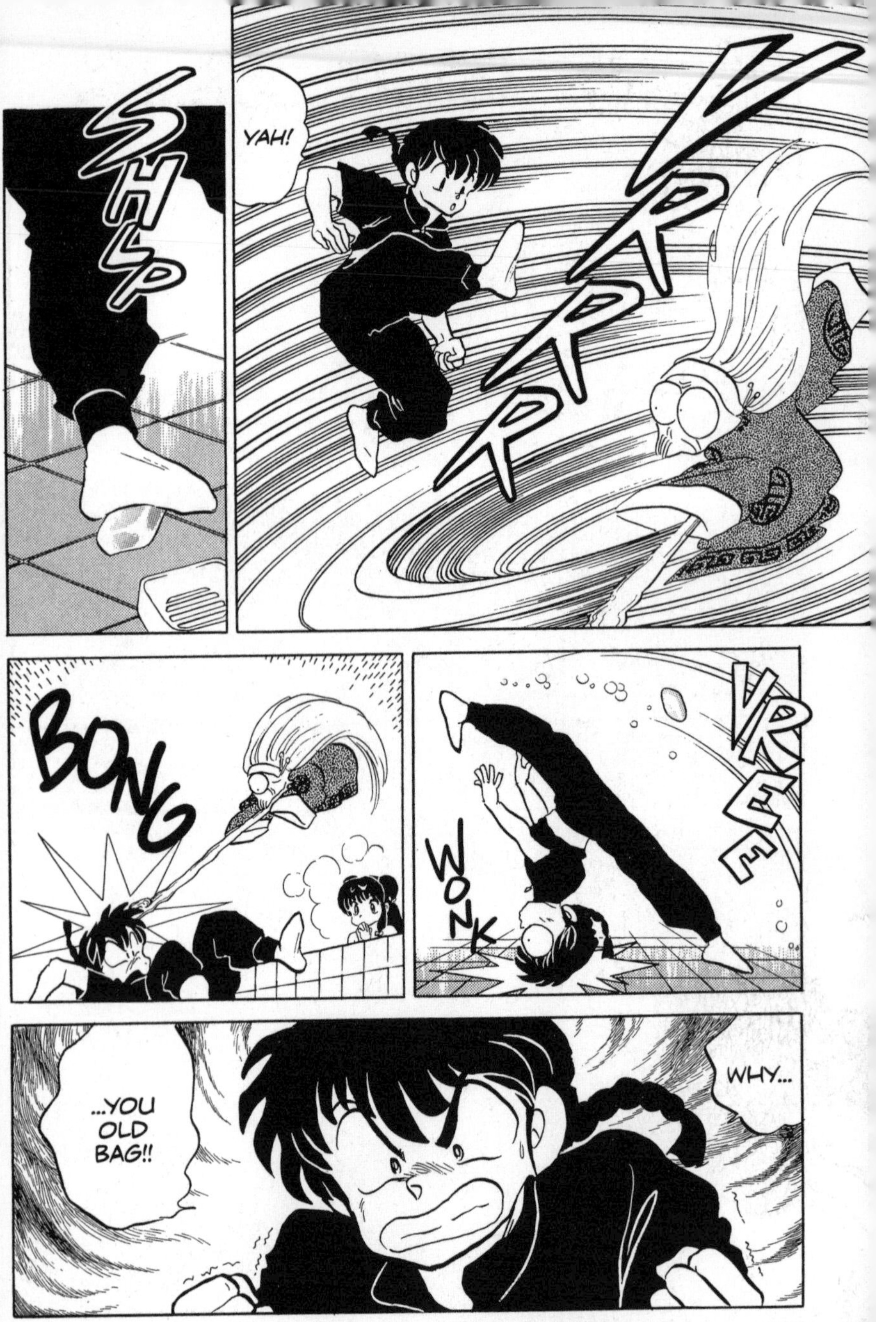

VRRRR
YAH!
SHLP
VREE
WONK
BONG
WHY...
...YOU OLD BAG!!

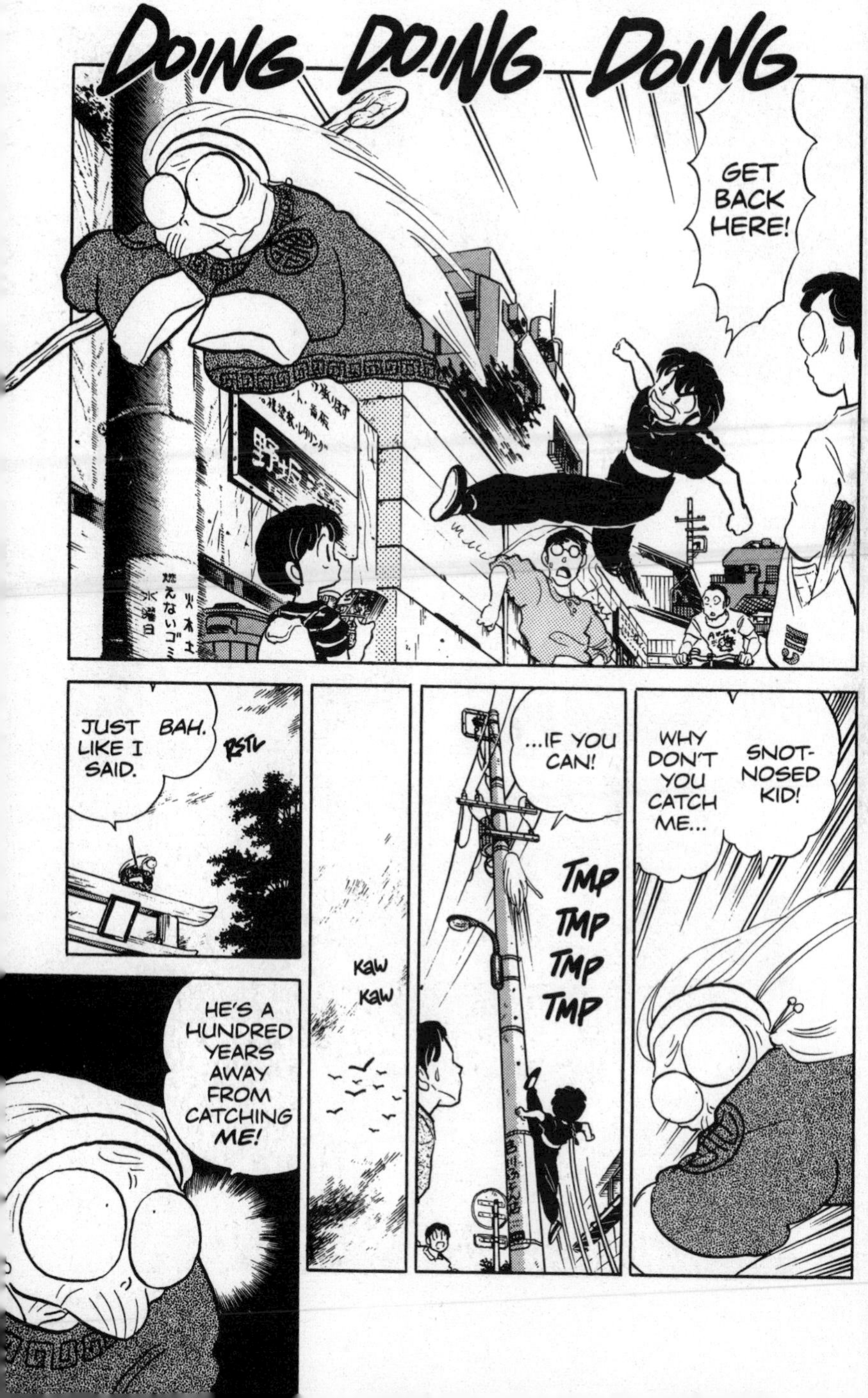
DOING DOING DOING
GET BACK HERE!
SNOT-NOSED KID!
WHY DON'T YOU CATCH ME...
...IF YOU CAN!
TMP TMP TMP TMP
KAW KAW
BAH.
JUST LIKE I SAID.
RSTL
HE'S A HUNDRED YEARS AWAY FROM CATCHING ME!

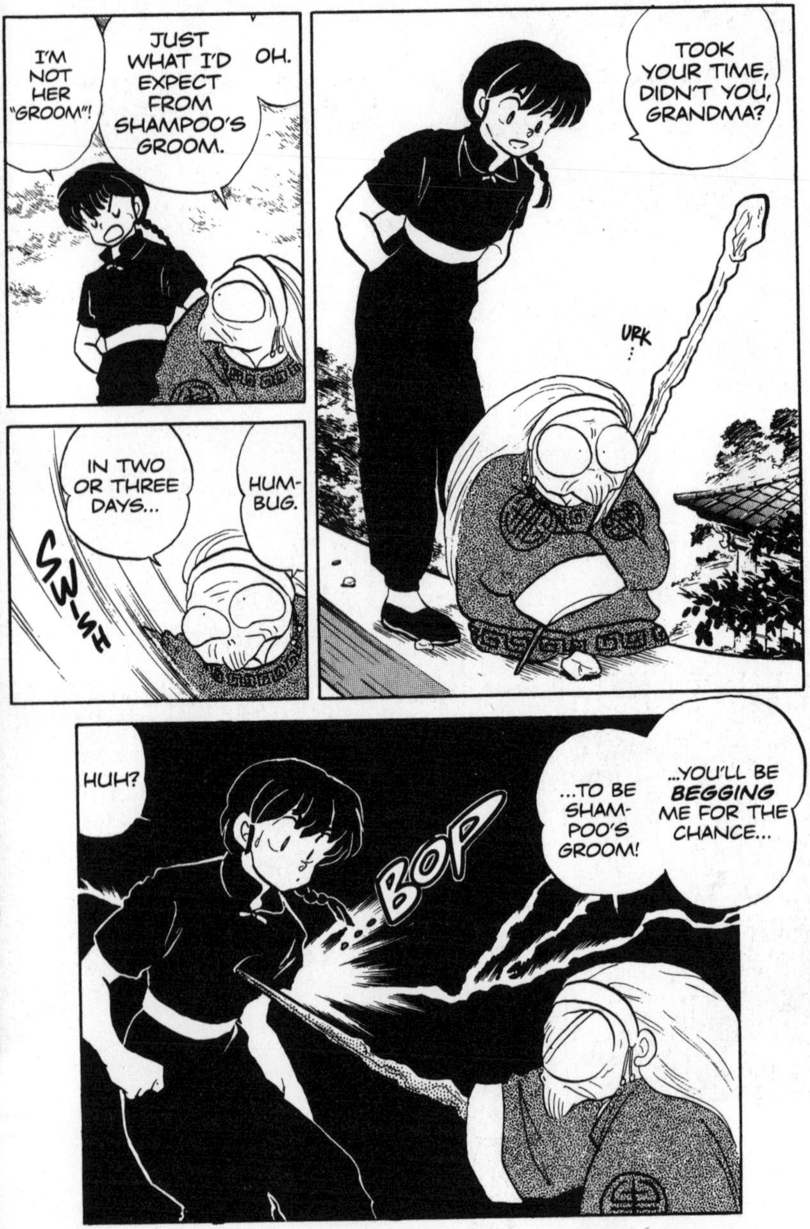
TOOK YOUR TIME, DIDN'T YOU, GRANDMA?
URK
OH.
JUST WHAT I'D EXPECT FROM SHAMPOO'S GROOM.
I'M NOT HER "GROOM"!
HUM-BUG.
IN TWO OR THREE DAYS...
SWISH
...YOU'LL BE BEGGING ME FOR THE CHANCE...
...TO BE SHAM-POO'S GROOM!
BOP
HUH?

PART 7
ATTACK OF THE WILD MOUSSE

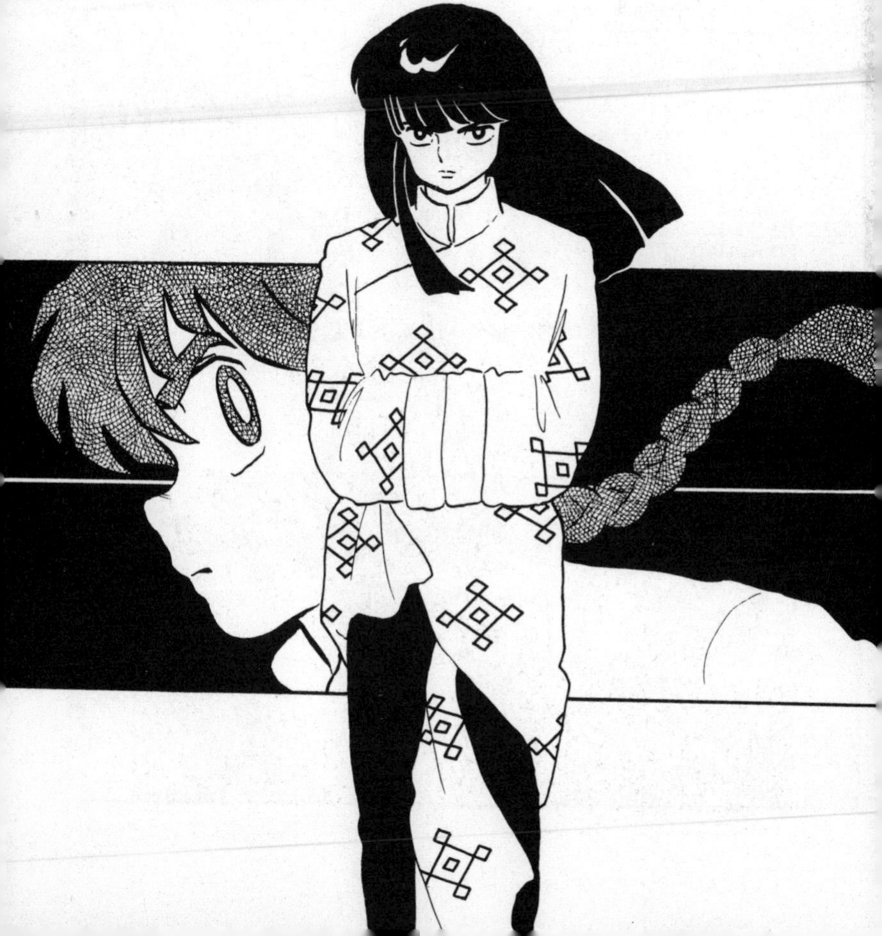

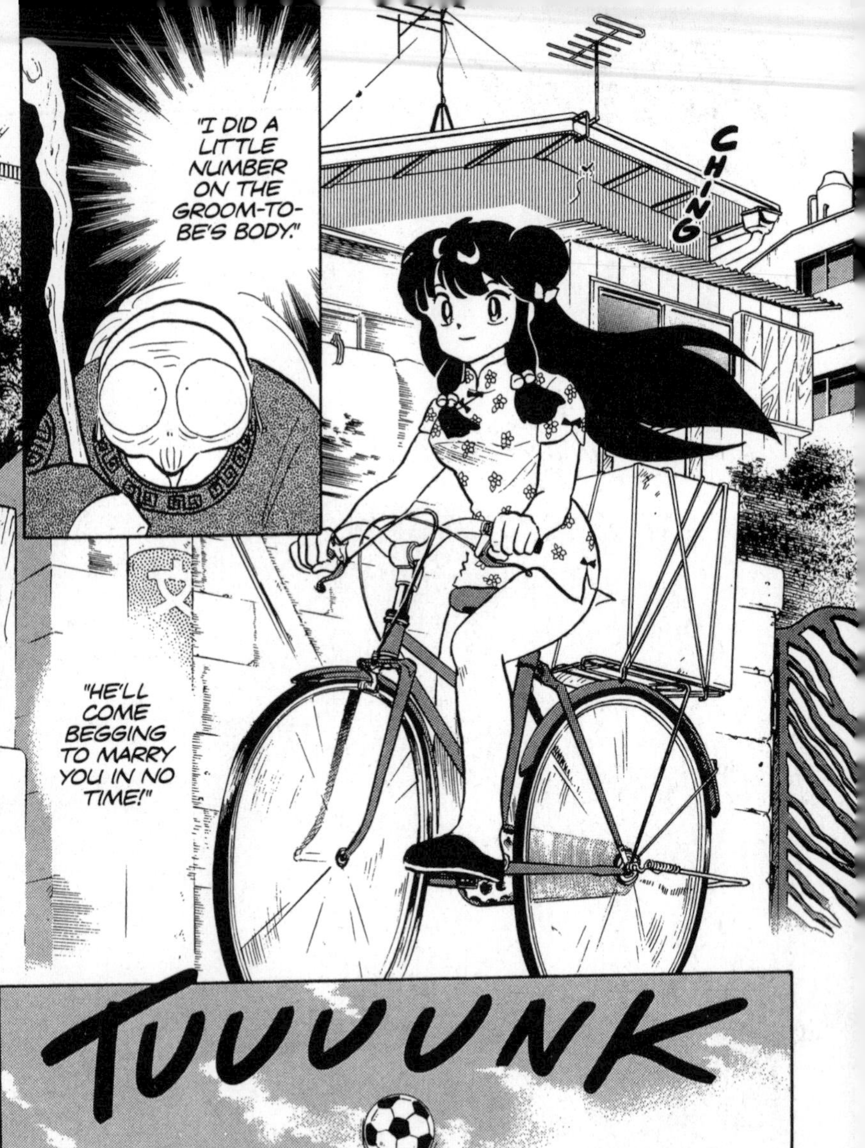
CHING
"I DID A LITTLE NUMBER ON THE GROOM-TO-BE'S BODY."
"HE'LL COME BEGGING TO MARRY YOU IN NO TIME!"
TUUUUNK
WHEE
YAY

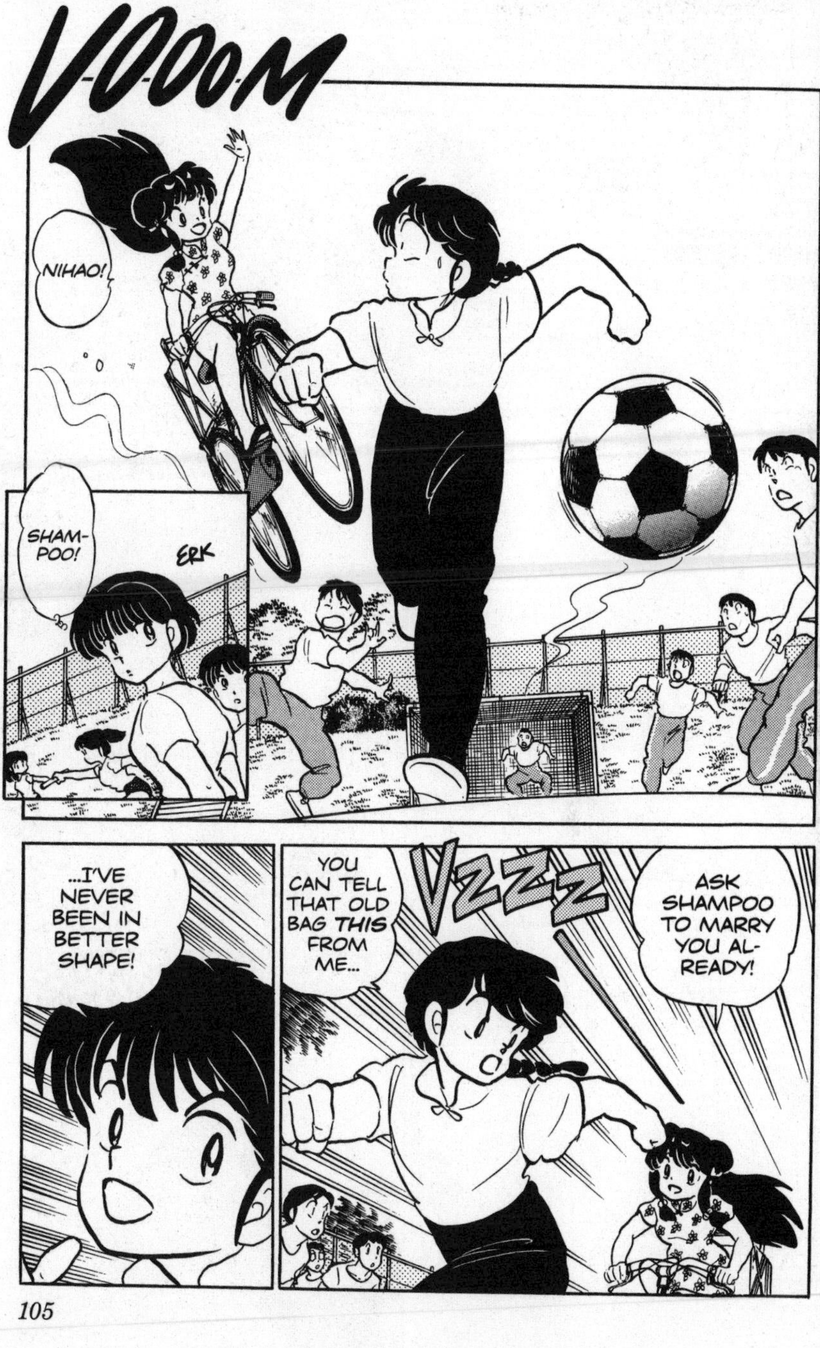
V-O-O-O-M
NIHAO!
SHAM-POO!
ERK
ASK SHAMPOO TO MARRY YOU AL-READY!
VZZZ
YOU CAN TELL THAT OLD BAG THIS FROM ME...
...I'VE NEVER BEEN IN BETTER SHAPE!

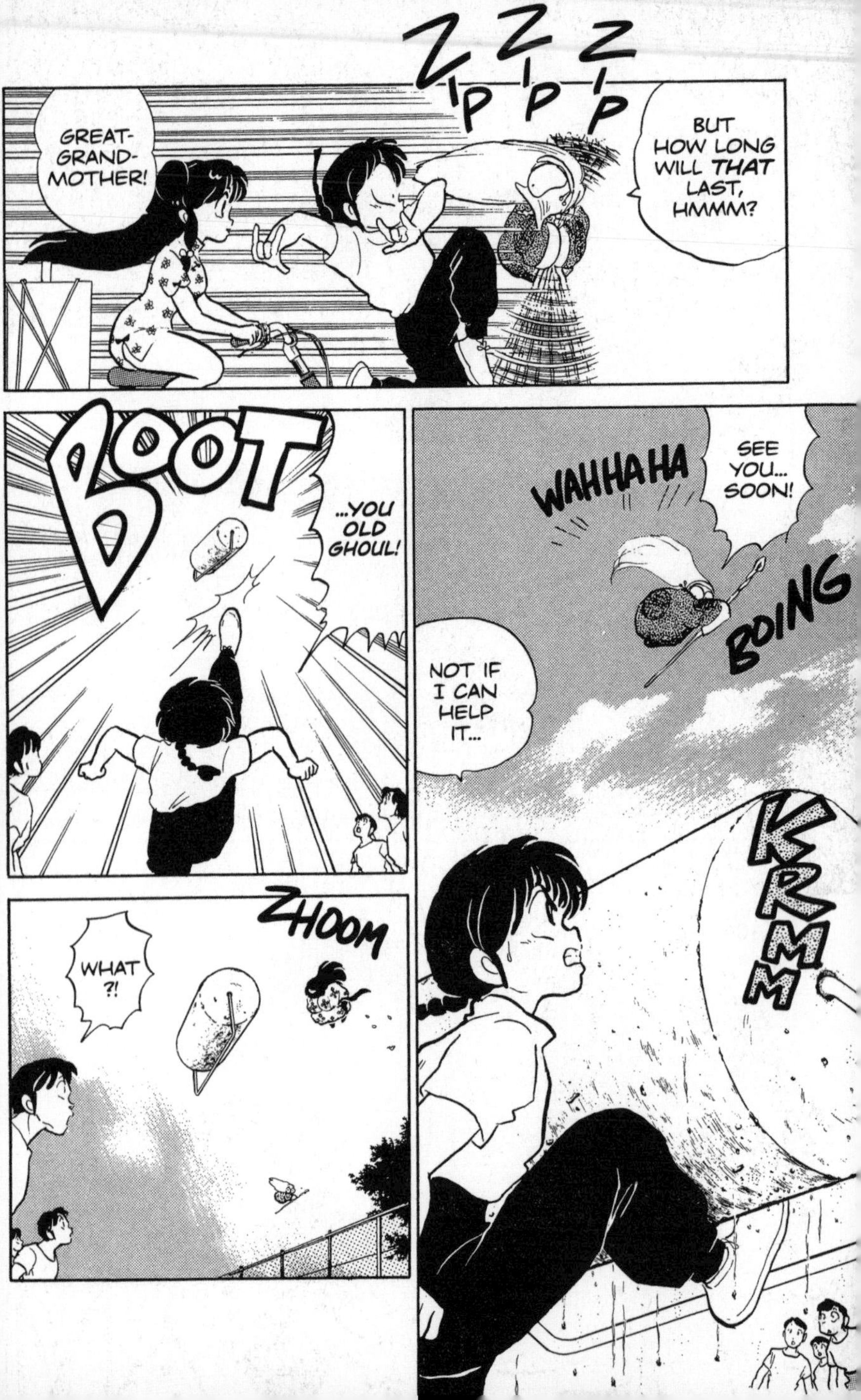
ZIP ZIP ZIP
BUT HOW LONG WILL THAT LAST, HMMM?
GREAT-GRAND-MOTHER!
SEE YOU... SOON!
WAHHAHA
BOING
NOT IF I CAN HELP IT...
KRMM
BOOT
...YOU OLD GHOUL!
ZHOOM
WHAT?!

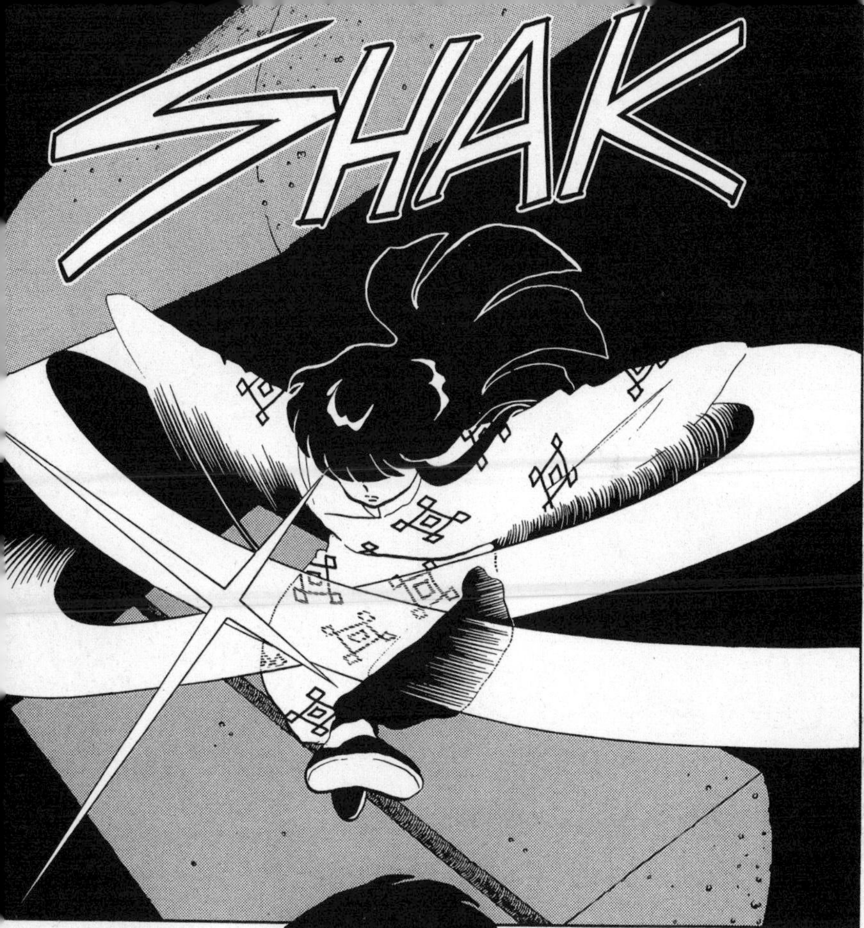
SHAK
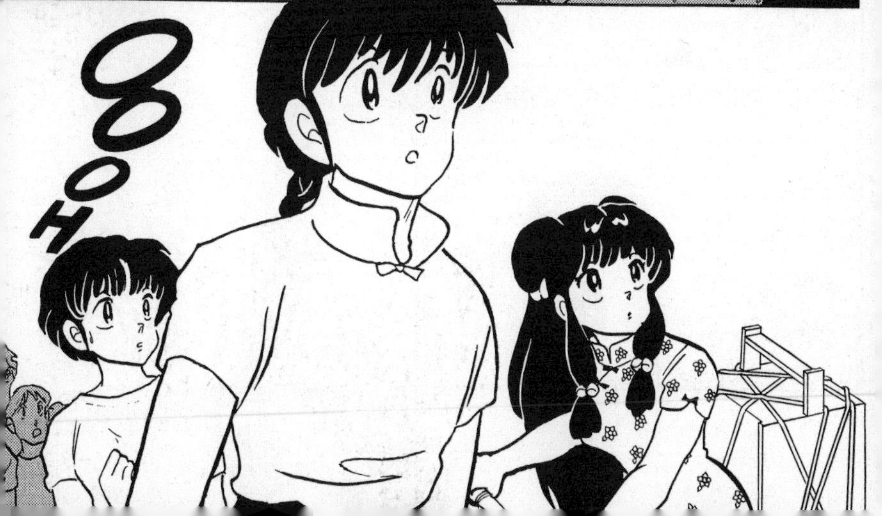
OOOH

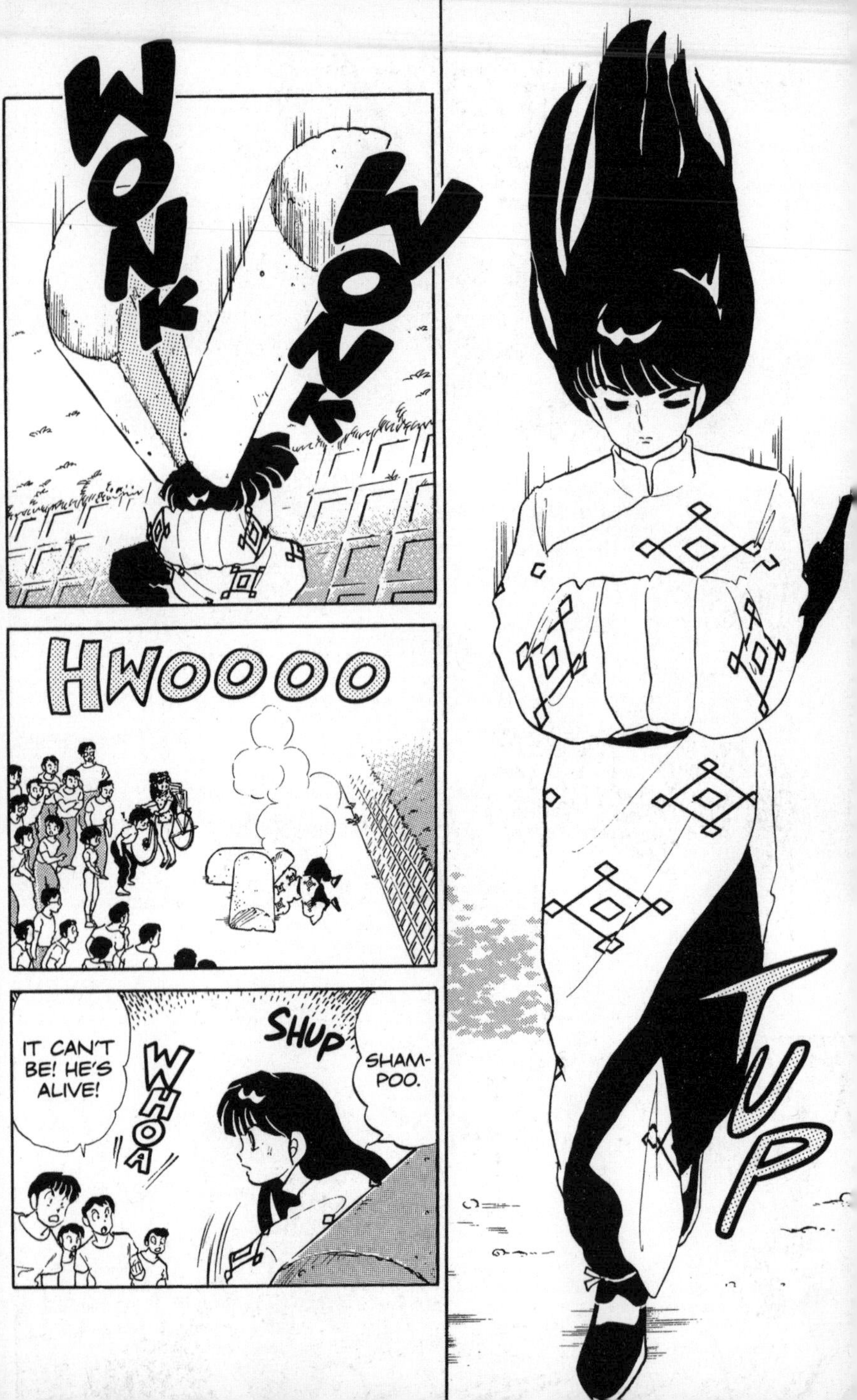
TUP
WONK
WONK
HWOOOO
SHUP
SHAM-
POO.
WHOA
IT CAN'T
BE! HE'S
ALIVE!

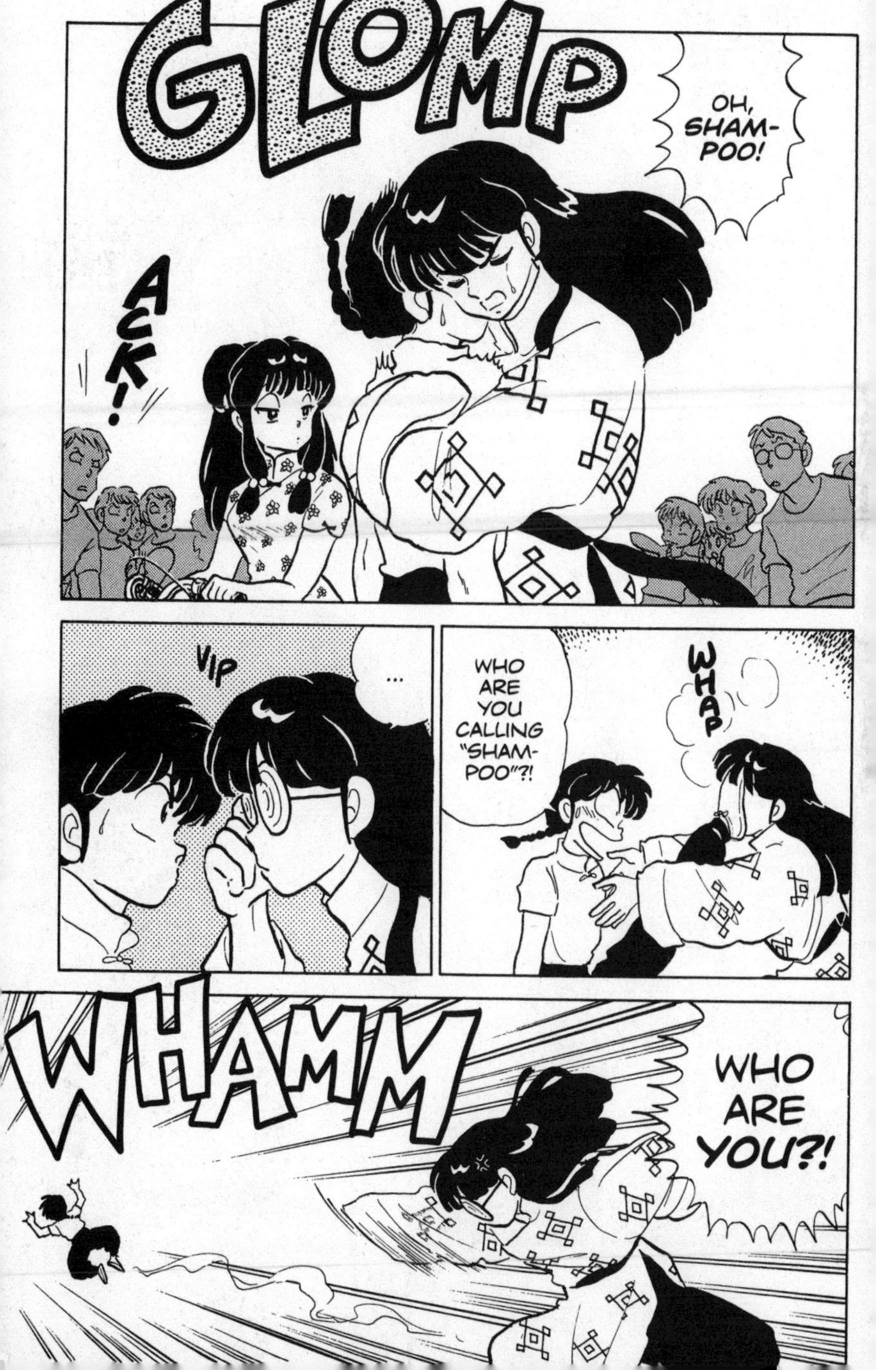
GLOMP
OH, SHAM-POO!
ACK!
WHO ARE YOU CALLING "SHAM-POO"?!
WHAP
...
VIP
WHAMM
WHO ARE YOU?!

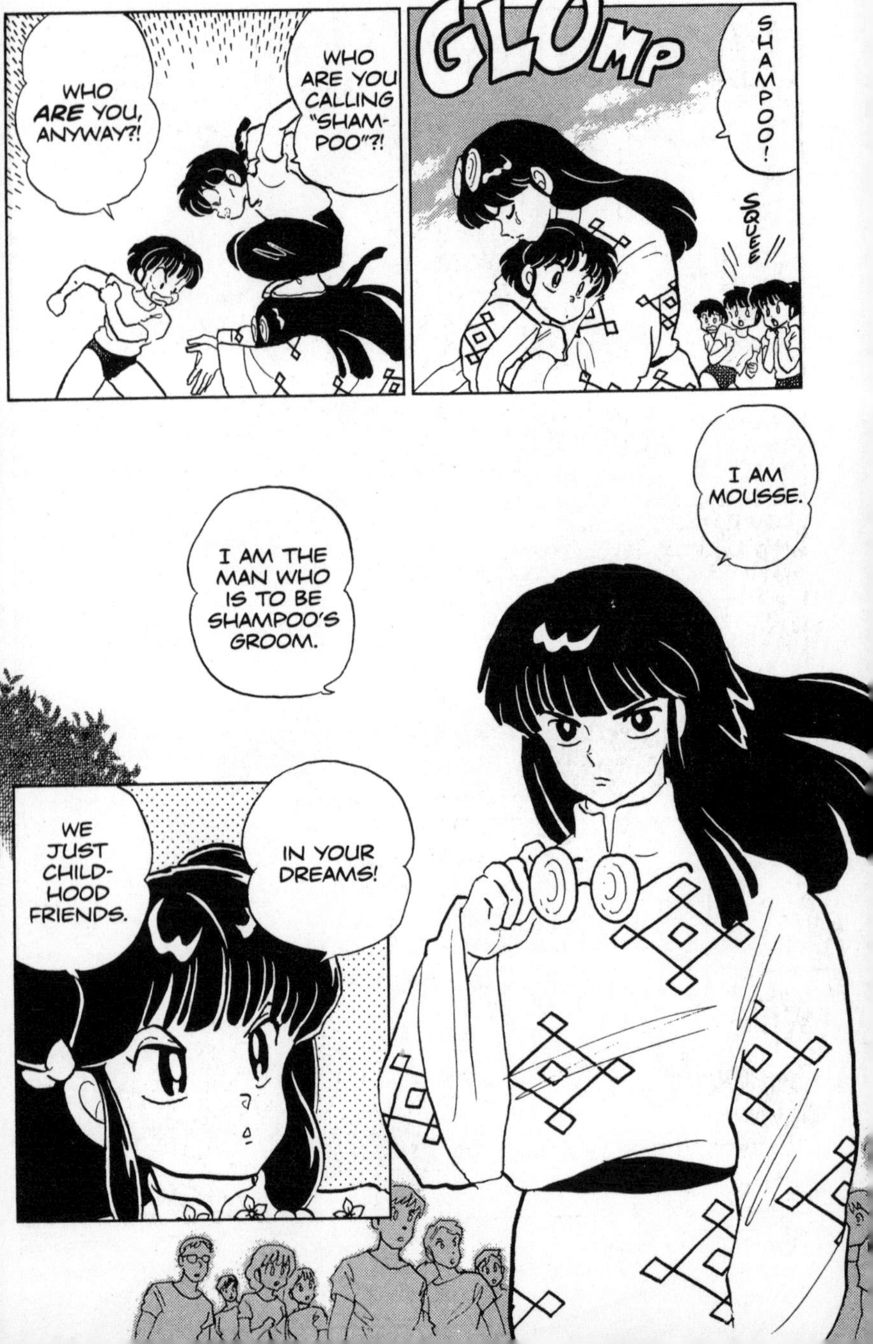
GLOMP
SHAMPOO!
SQUEE
WHO ARE YOU CALLING "SHAMPOO"?!
WHO ARE YOU, ANYWAY?!
I AM MOUSSE.
I AM THE MAN WHO IS TO BE SHAMPOO'S GROOM.
IN YOUR DREAMS!
WE JUST CHILDHOOD FRIENDS.

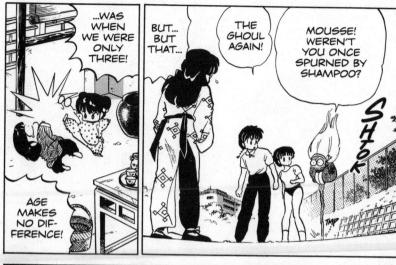

MOUSSE! WEREN'T YOU ONCE SPURNED BY SHAMPOO?
THE GHOUL AGAIN!
BUT... BUT THAT...
SHTOK
TMP
...WAS WHEN WE WERE ONLY THREE!
AGE MAKES NO DIF-FERENCE!
IT HAS BEEN DECIDED! THIS MAN IS SHAMPOO'S GROOM!
NOT IF YOU ASK ME, I'M NOT!
HAVE YOU NO EARS?! RANMA IS ENGAGED TO AKANE!
DAD, PLEASE!

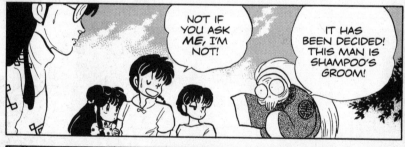

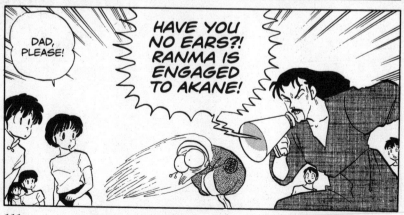

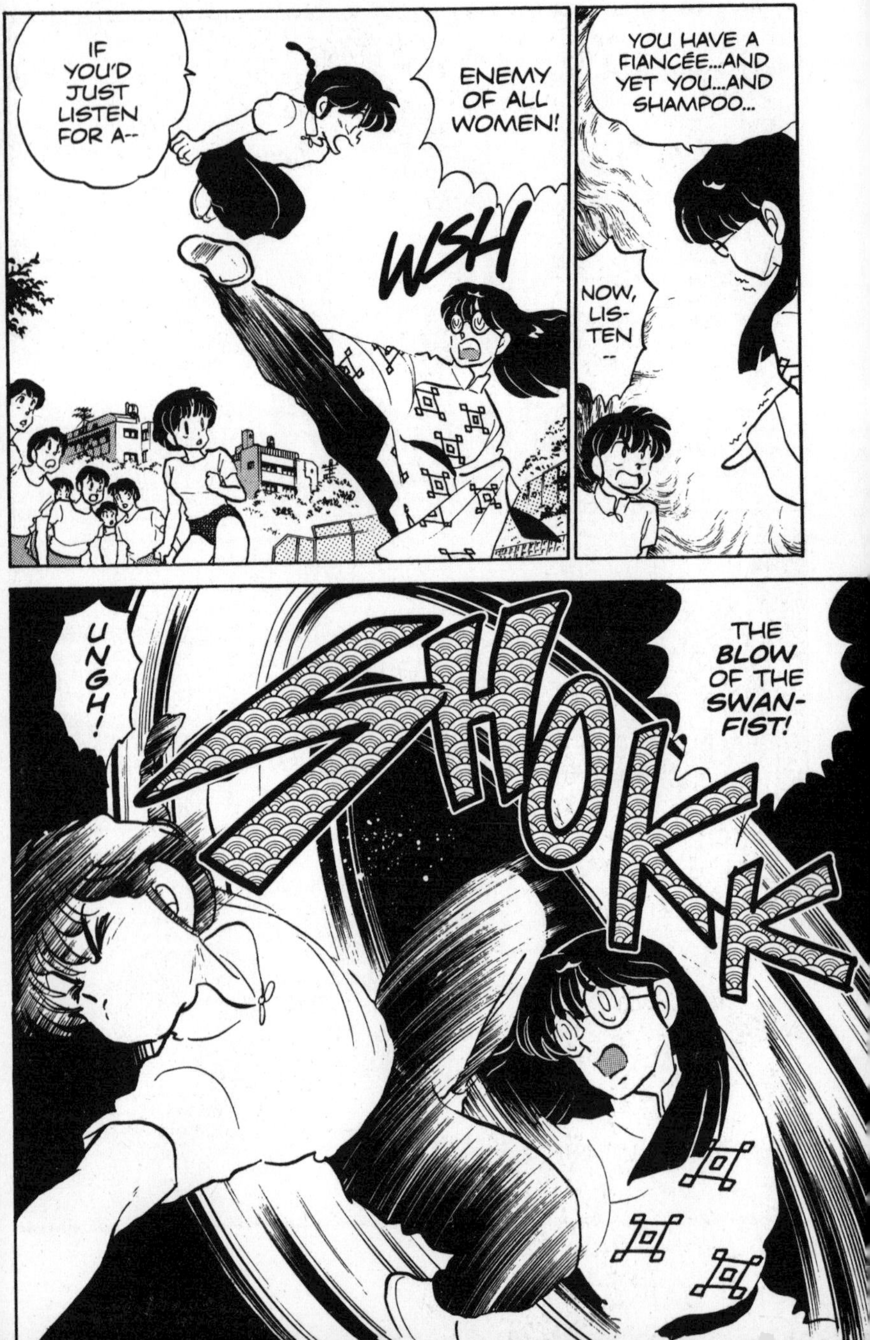
YOU HAVE A FIANCÉE...AND YET YOU...AND SHAMPOO...
NOW, LIS-TEN --
ENEMY OF ALL WOMEN!
IF YOU'D JUST LISTEN FOR A--
WSH
THE BLOW OF THE SWAN-FIST!
SHOKK
UNGH!

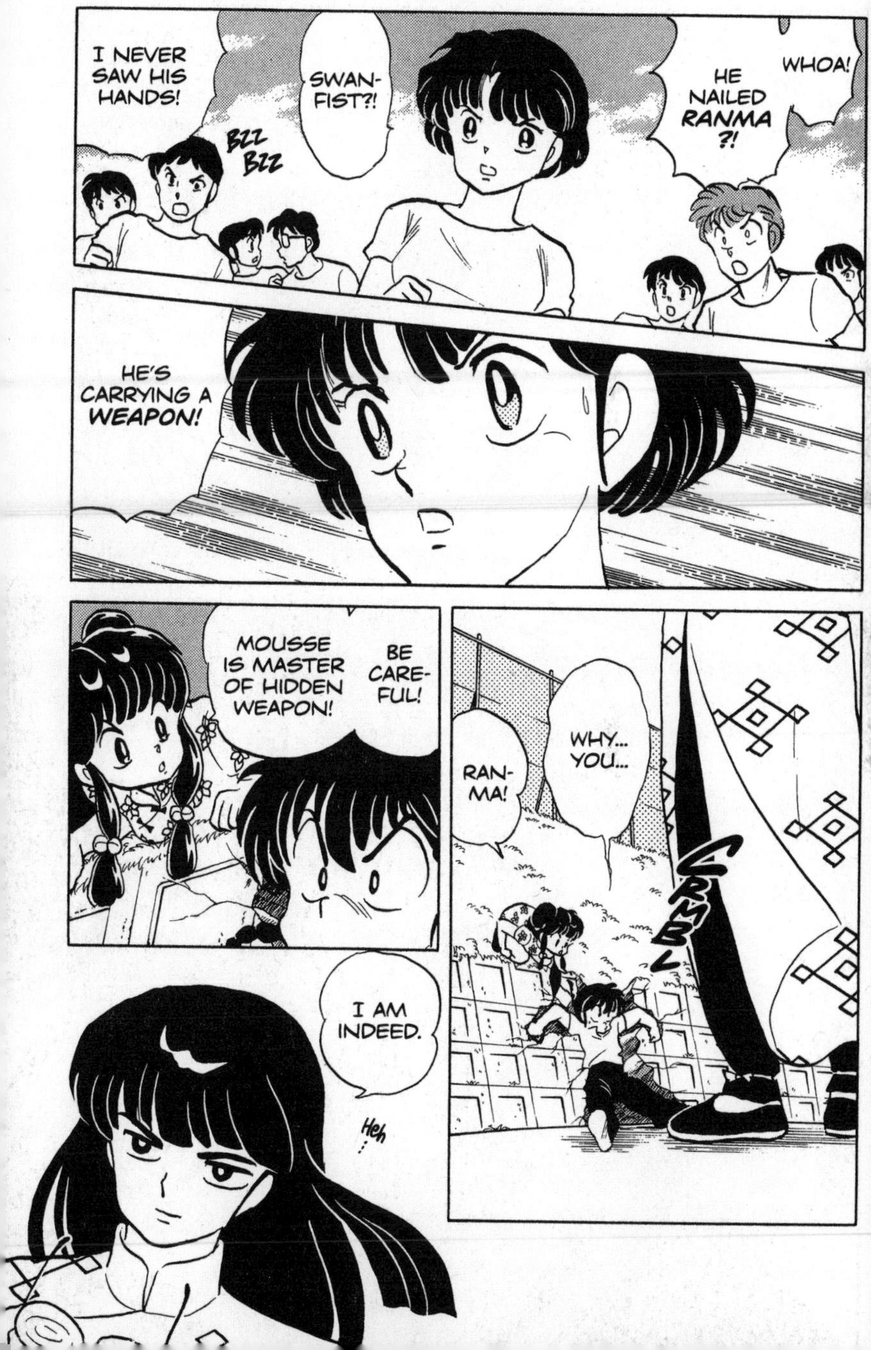
WHOA!
HE NAILED RANMA?!
SWAN-FIST?!
BZZ BZZ
I NEVER SAW HIS HANDS!
HE'S CARRYING A WEAPON!
WHY... YOU...
RAN-MA!
CRMBL
BE CARE-FUL!
MOUSSE IS MASTER OF HIDDEN WEAPON!
I AM INDEED.
Heh...

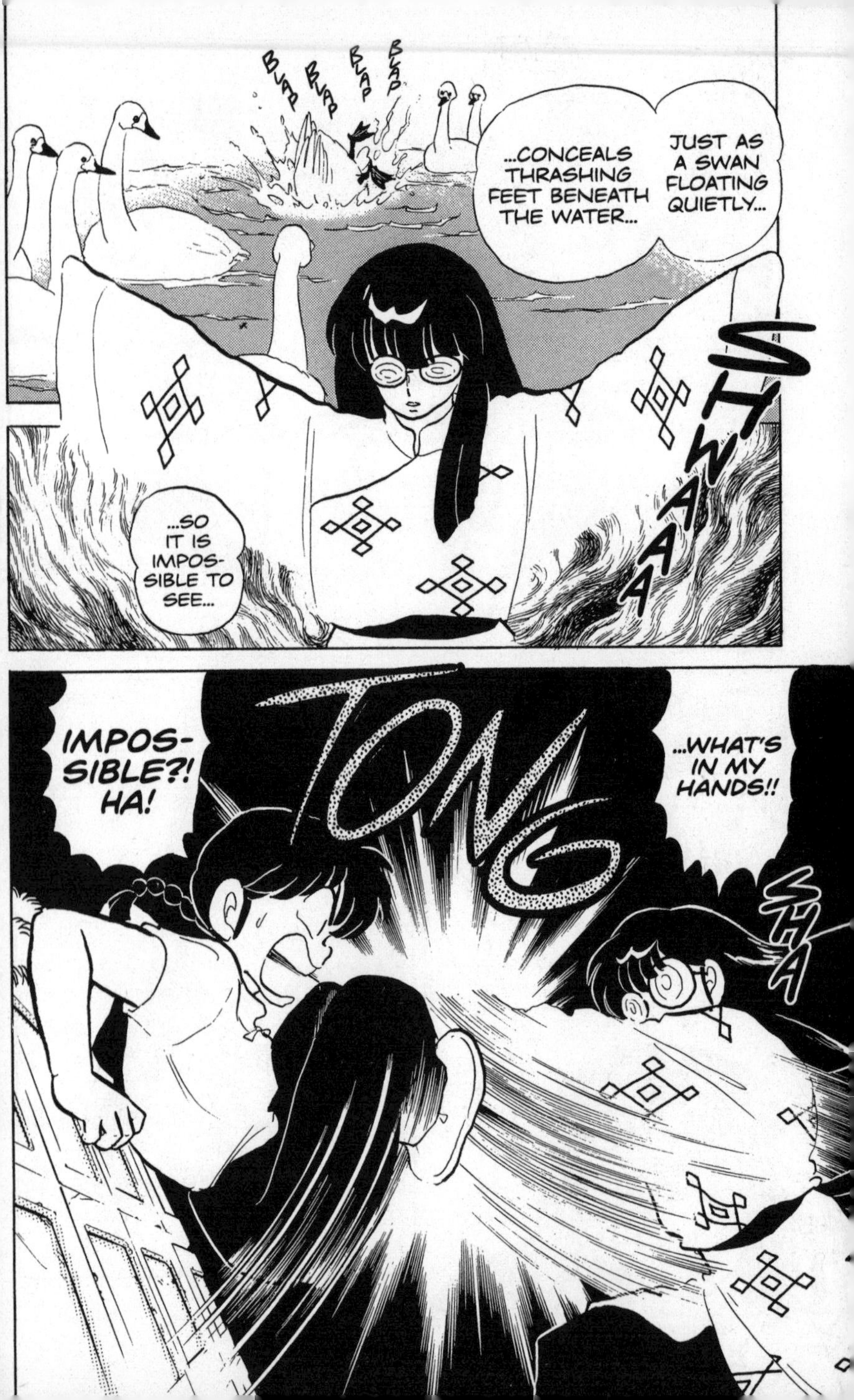
BLAP
BLAP
BLAP
BLAP
JUST AS A SWAN FLOATING QUIETLY...
...CONCEALS THRASHING FEET BENEATH THE WATER...
SHWAAAA
...SO IT IS IMPOSSIBLE TO SEE...
...WHAT'S IN MY HANDS!!
TONG
SHA
IMPOSSIBLE?! HA!

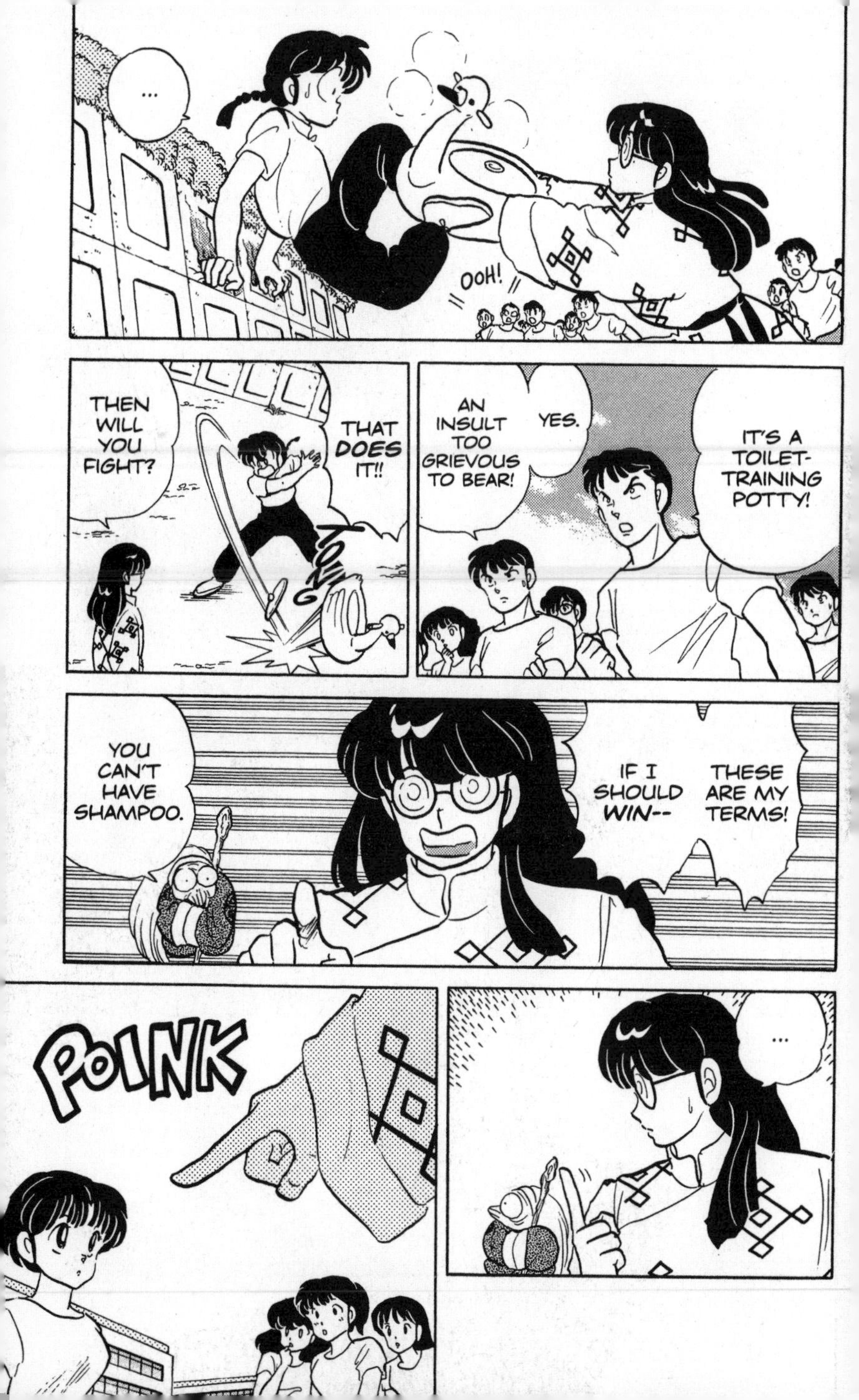
...
OOH!
IT'S A TOILET-TRAINING POTTY!
YES.
AN INSULT TOO GRIEVOUS TO BEAR!
THAT **DOES** IT!!
THEN WILL YOU FIGHT?
THESE ARE MY TERMS!
IF I SHOULD **WIN**--
YOU CAN'T HAVE SHAMPOO.
...
POINK

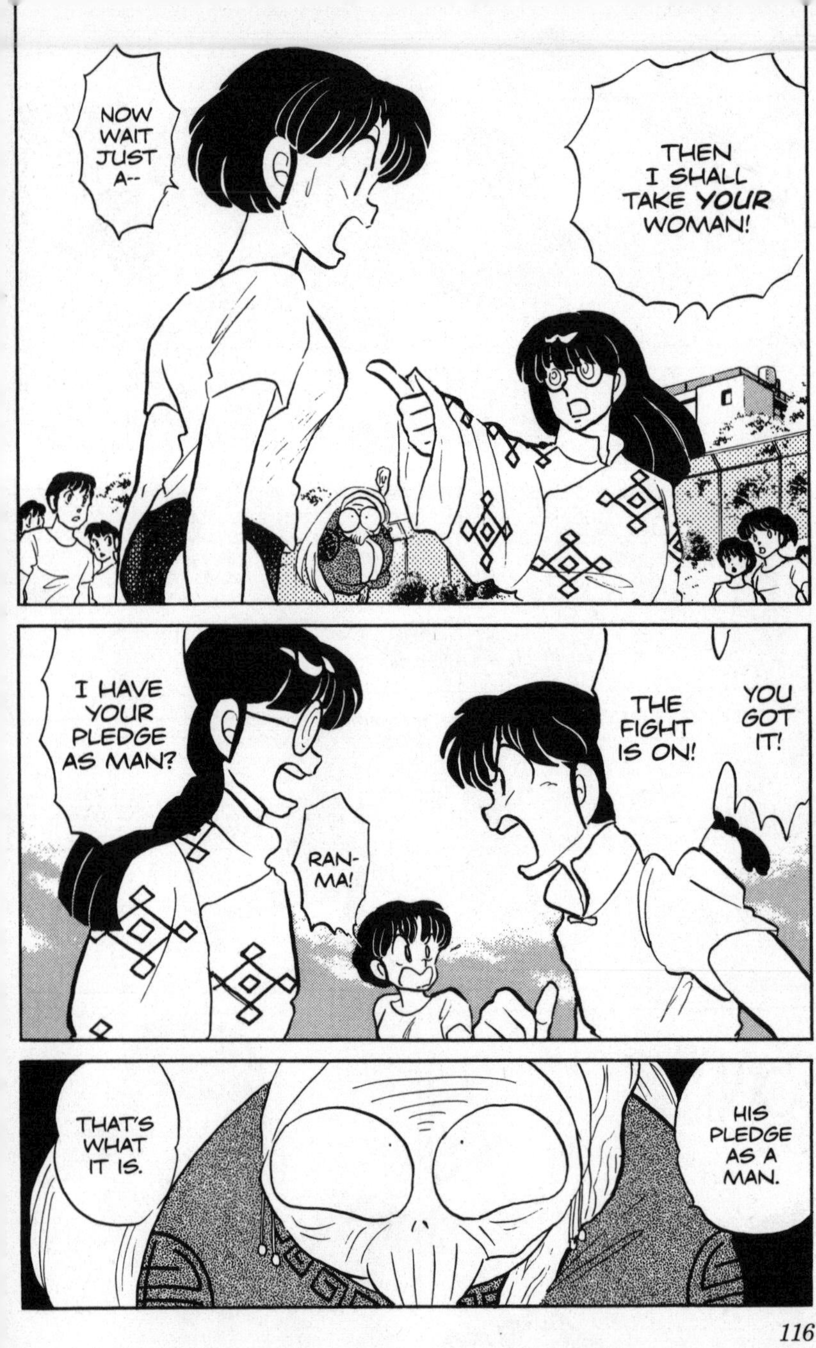
THEN I SHALL TAKE YOUR WOMAN!
NOW WAIT JUST A--
YOU GOT IT!
THE FIGHT IS ON!
I HAVE YOUR PLEDGE AS MAN?
RAN-MA!
HIS PLEDGE AS A MAN.
THAT'S WHAT IT IS.

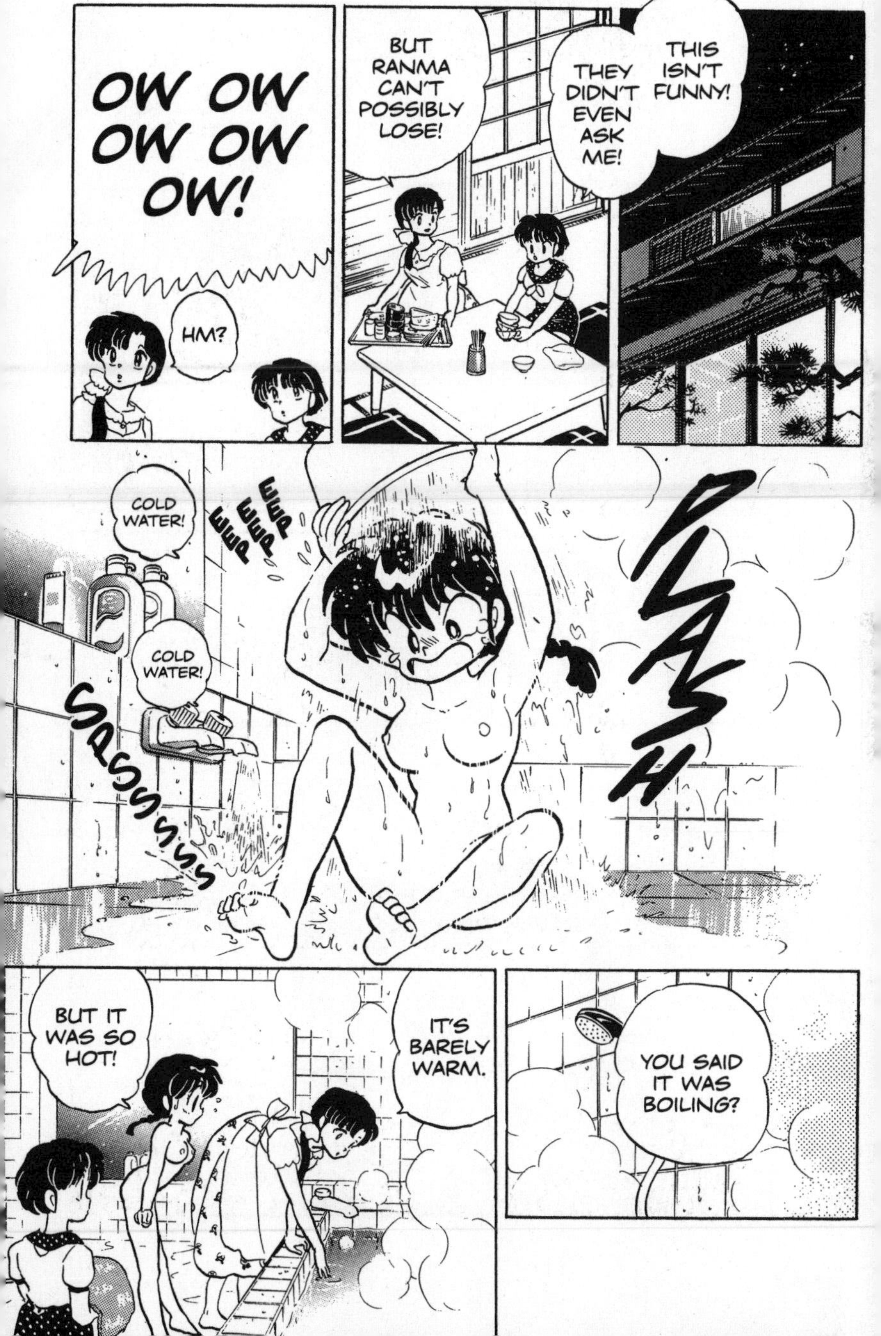
THIS ISN'T FUNNY!
THEY DIDN'T EVEN ASK ME!
BUT RANMA CAN'T POSSIBLY LOSE!
OW OW OW OW OW!
HM?
PLASH
WEEP WEEP WEEP
COLD WATER!
COLD WATER!
SPSSSSSSS
YOU SAID IT WAS BOILING?
IT'S BARELY WARM.
BUT IT WAS SO HOT!

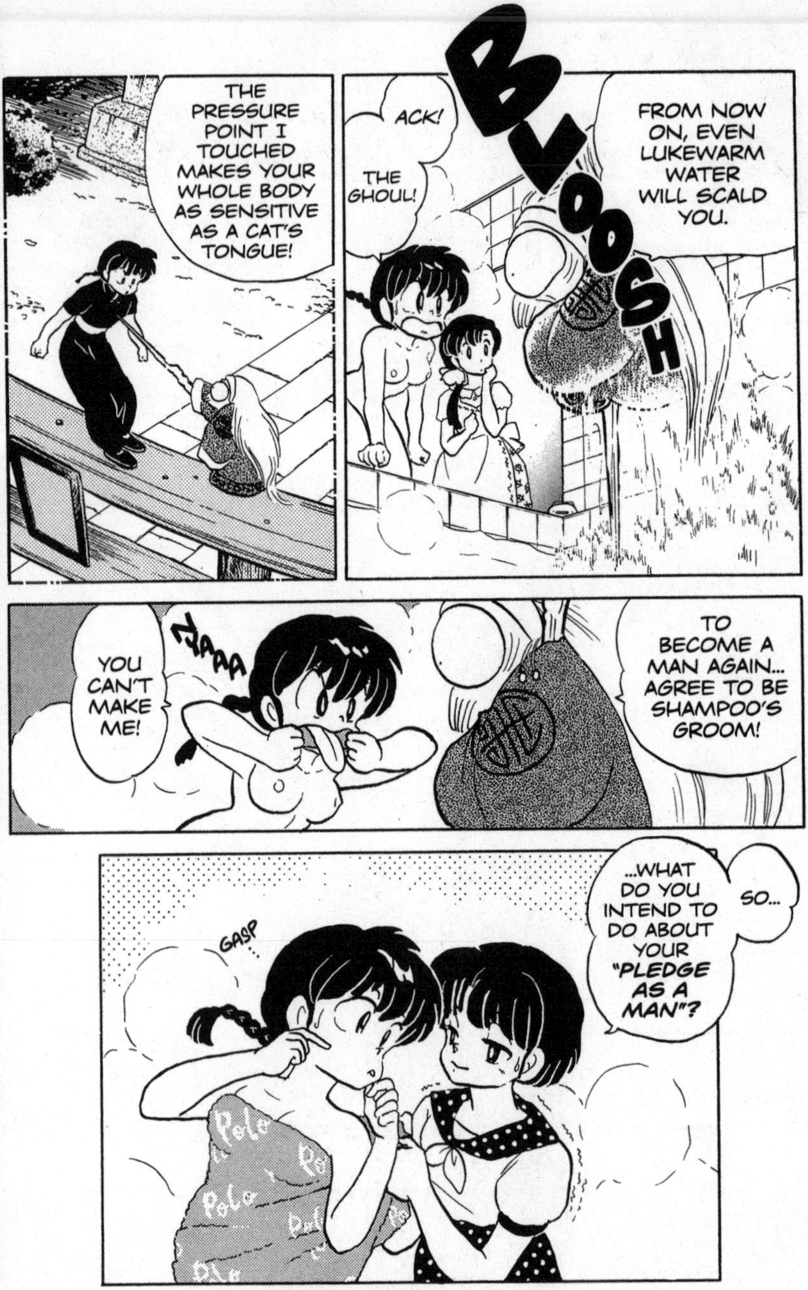
BLOOSH
FROM NOW ON, EVEN LUKEWARM WATER WILL SCALD YOU.
ACK!
THE GHOUL!
THE PRESSURE POINT I TOUCHED MAKES YOUR WHOLE BODY AS SENSITIVE AS A CAT'S TONGUE!
TO BECOME A MAN AGAIN... AGREE TO BE SHAMPOO'S GROOM!
YOU CAN'T MAKE ME!
SO...
...WHAT DO YOU INTEND TO DO ABOUT YOUR "PLEDGE AS A MAN"?
GASP...

PART 8
THE MARTIAL ARTS MAGIC SHOW

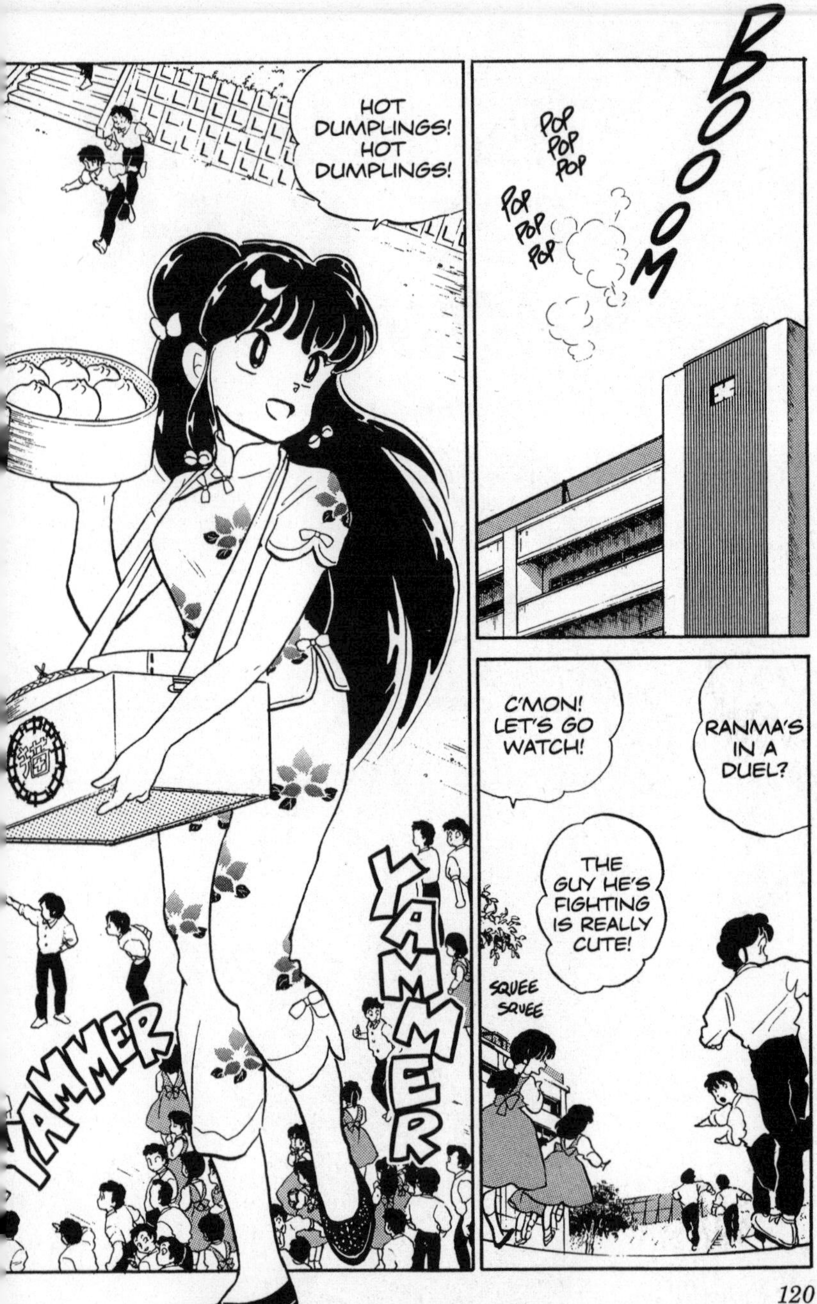
BOOOOM
POP POP POP
POP POP POP
RANMA'S IN A DUEL?
C'MON! LET'S GO WATCH!
THE GUY HE'S FIGHTING IS REALLY CUTE!
SQUEE SQUEE
HOT DUMPLINGS! HOT DUMPLINGS!
YAMMER
YAMMER

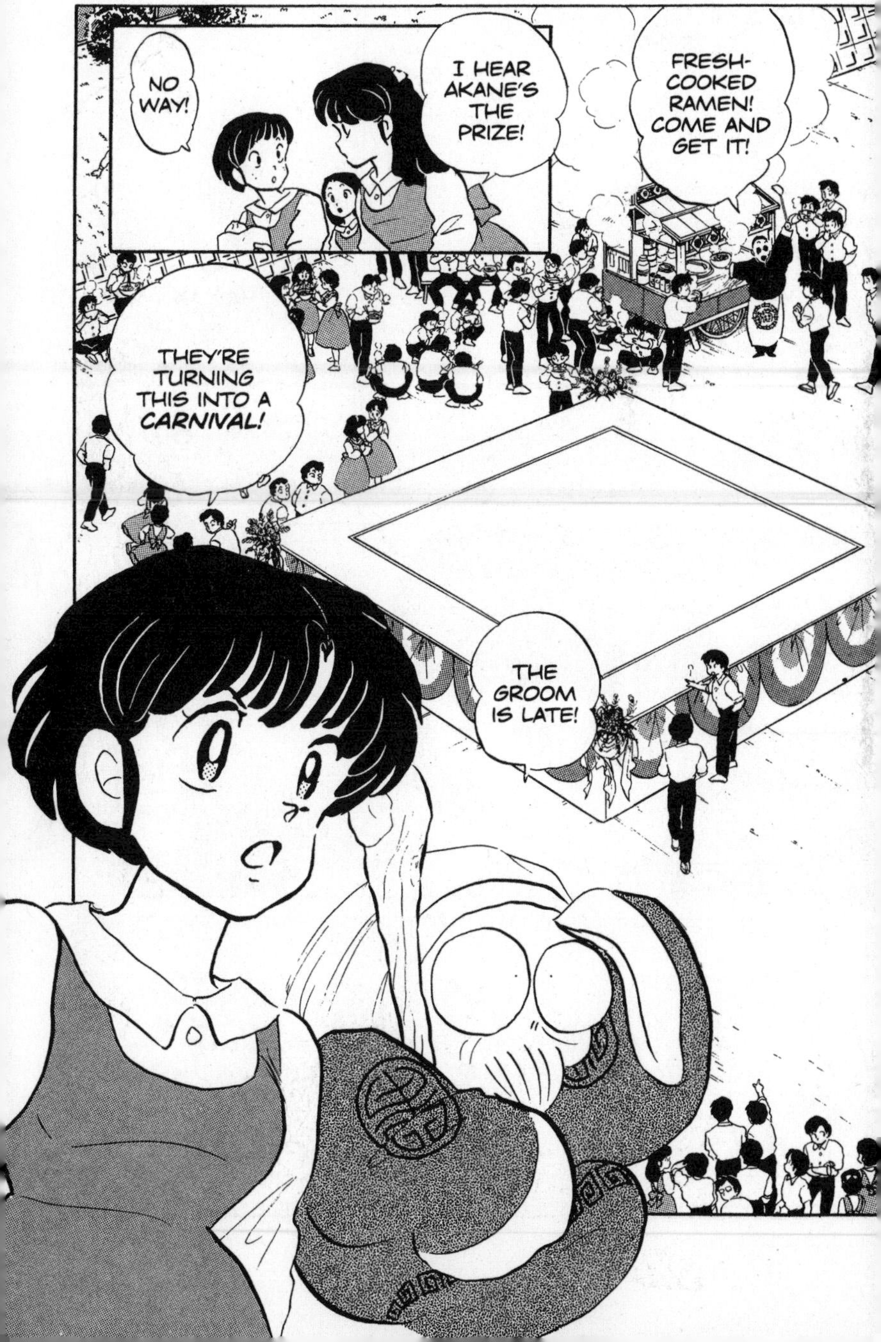
FRESH-COOKED RAMEN! COME AND GET IT!
I HEAR AKANE'S THE PRIZE!
NO WAY!
THEY'RE TURNING THIS INTO A CARNIVAL!
THE GROOM IS LATE!

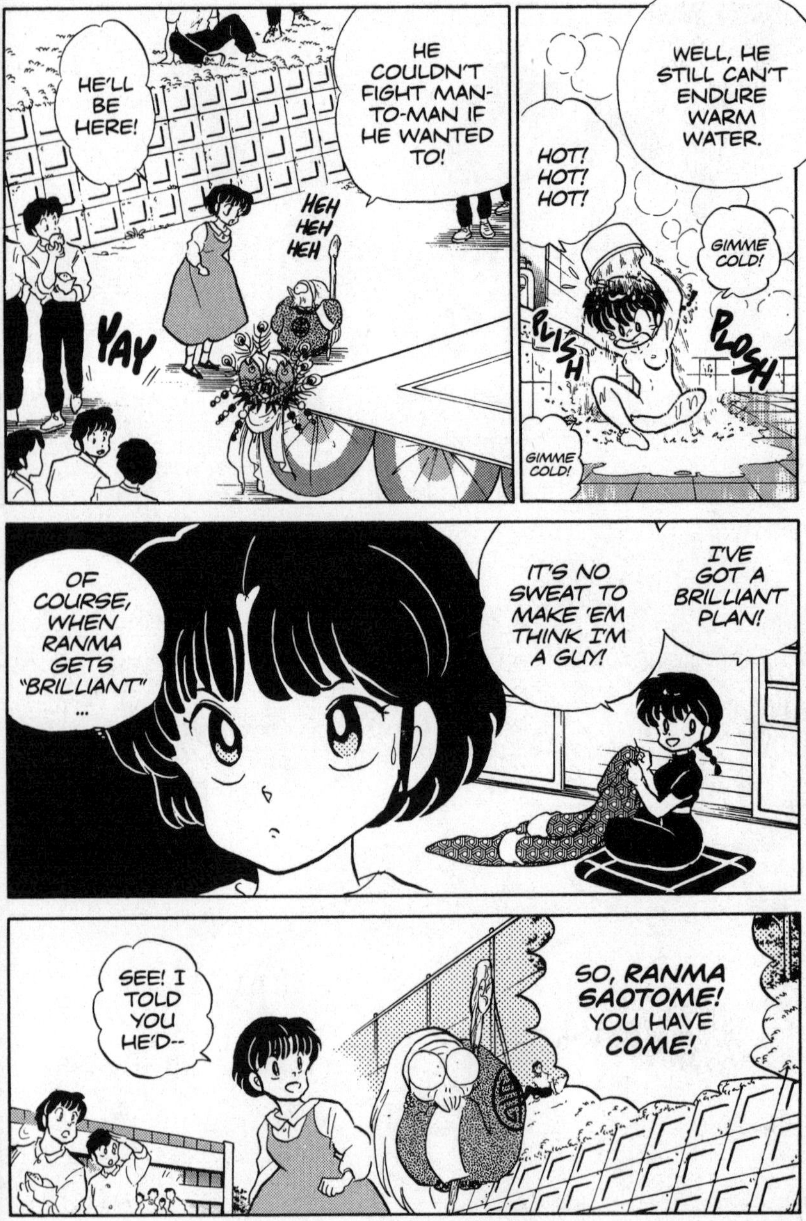
WELL, HE STILL CAN'T ENDURE WARM WATER.
HOT! HOT! HOT!
GIMME COLD!
PLOSH
PLISH
GIMME COLD!
HE COULDN'T FIGHT MAN-TO-MAN IF HE WANTED TO!
HEH HEH HEH
HE'LL BE HERE!
YAY
I'VE GOT A BRILLIANT PLAN!
IT'S NO SWEAT TO MAKE 'EM THINK I'M A GUY!
OF COURSE, WHEN RANMA GETS "BRILLIANT" ...
SO, RANMA SAOTOME! YOU HAVE COME!
SEE! I TOLD YOU HE'D--

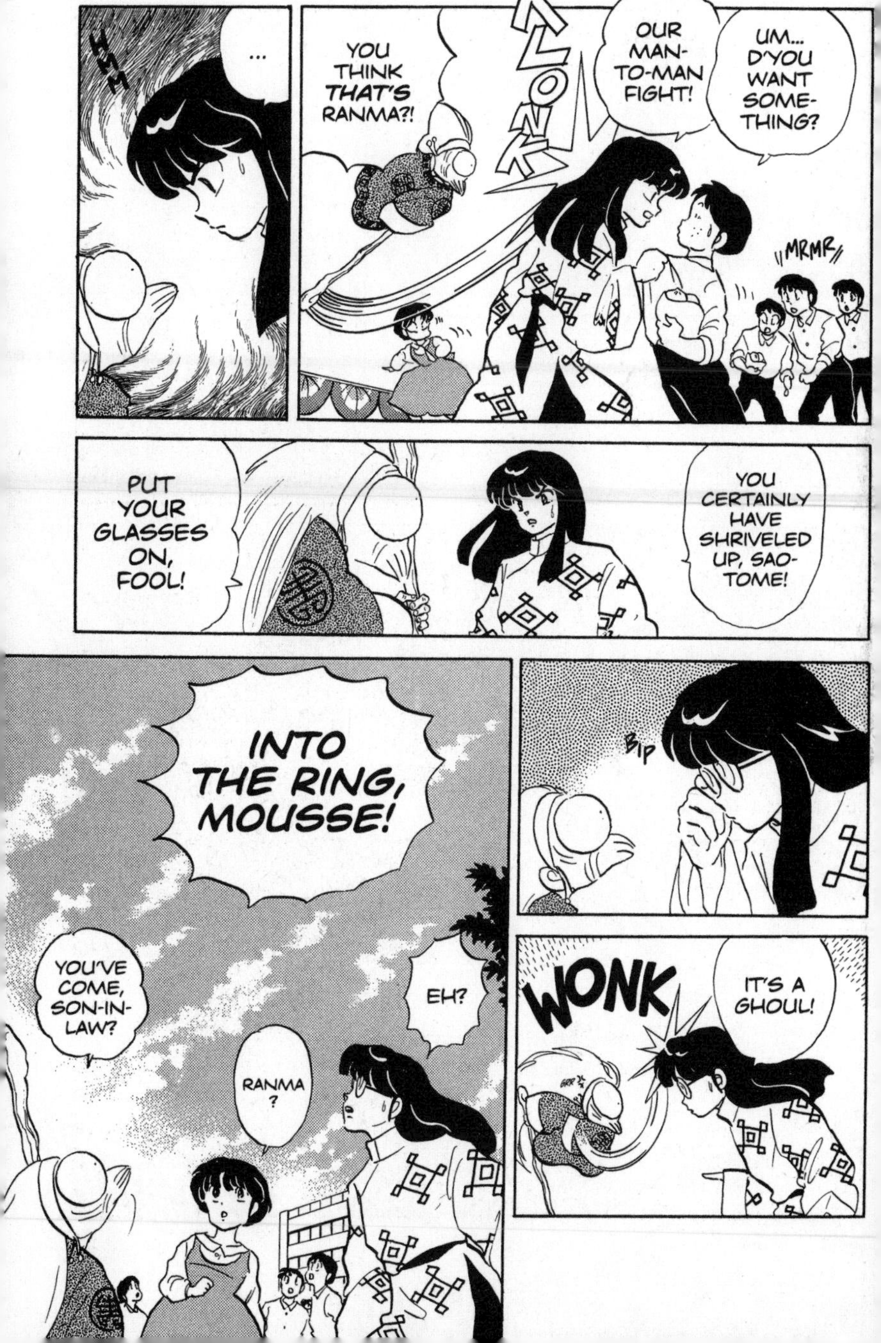
UM... D'YOU WANT SOME-THING?
OUR MAN-TO-MAN FIGHT!
KLONK
YOU THINK THAT'S RANMA?!
MRMR
HMM
...
YOU CERTAINLY HAVE SHRIVELED UP, SAO-TOME!
PUT YOUR GLASSES ON, FOOL!
BIP
IT'S A GHOUL!
WONK
INTO THE RING, MOUSSE!
EH?
YOU'VE COME, SON-IN-LAW?
RANMA ?

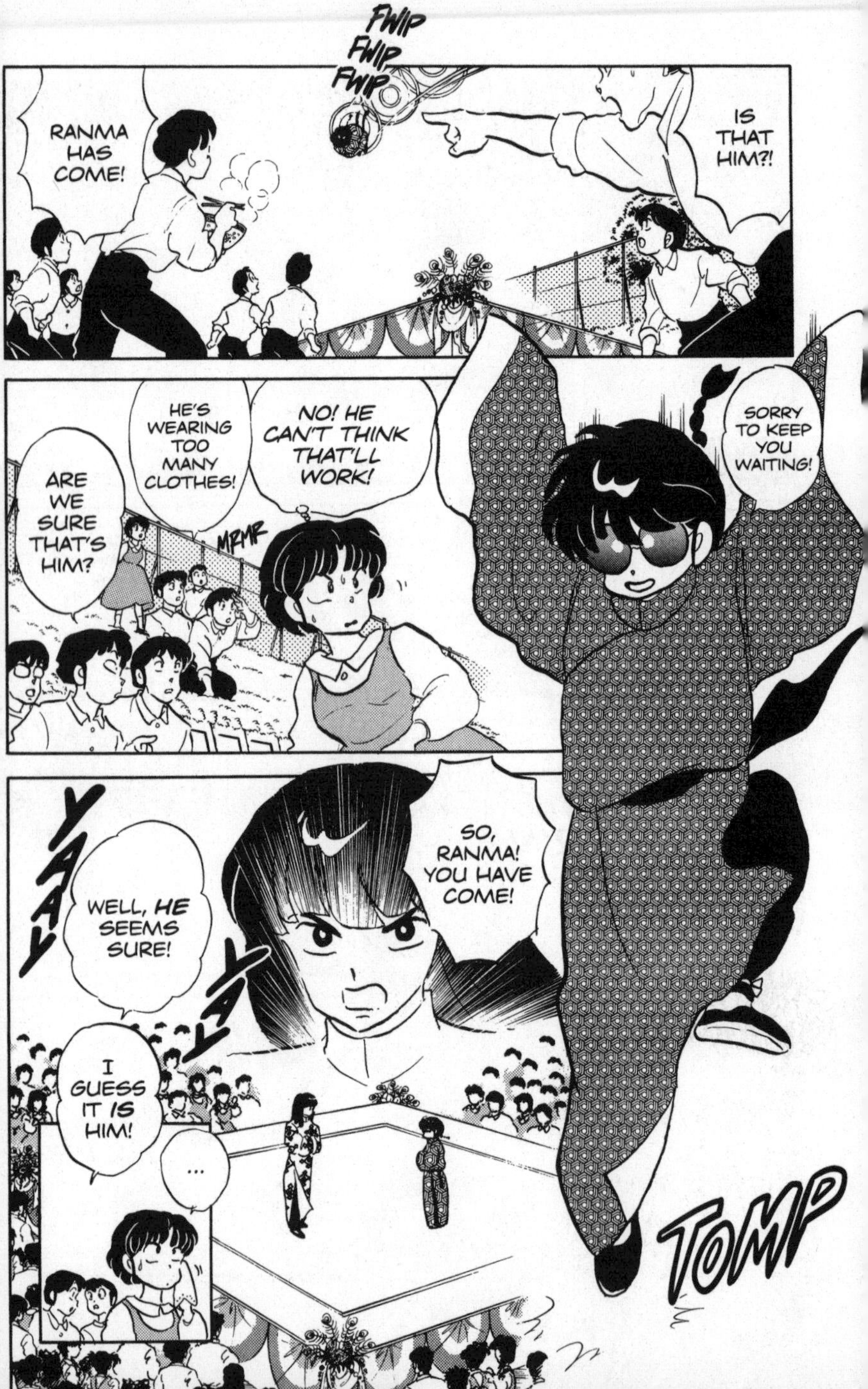
FWIP FWIP FWIP
IS THAT HIM?!
RANMA HAS COME!
SORRY TO KEEP YOU WAITING!
NO! HE CAN'T THINK THAT'LL WORK!
HE'S WEARING TOO MANY CLOTHES!
MRMR
ARE WE SURE THAT'S HIM?
TOMP
SO, RANMA! YOU HAVE COME!
YAY
YAY
WELL, HE SEEMS SURE!
I GUESS IT IS HIM!
...

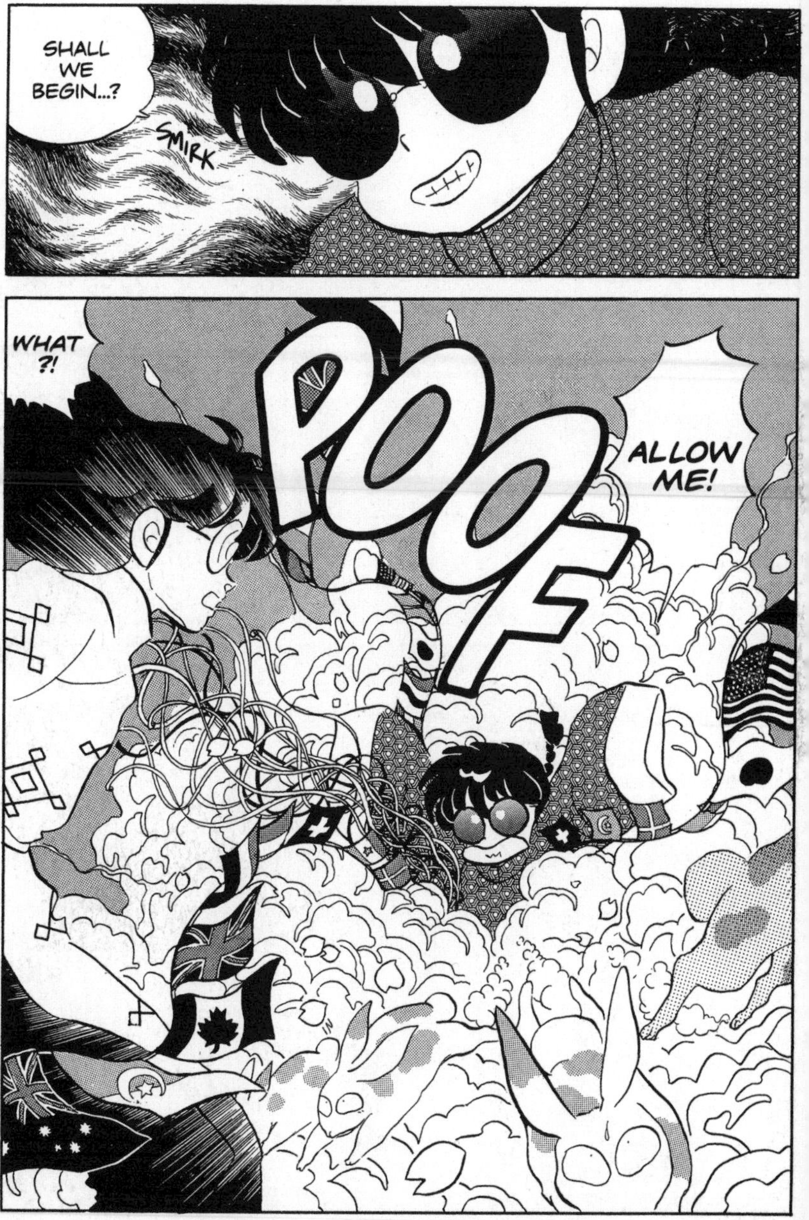
SHALL WE BEGIN...?
SMIRK
ALLOW ME!
POOF
WHAT ?!

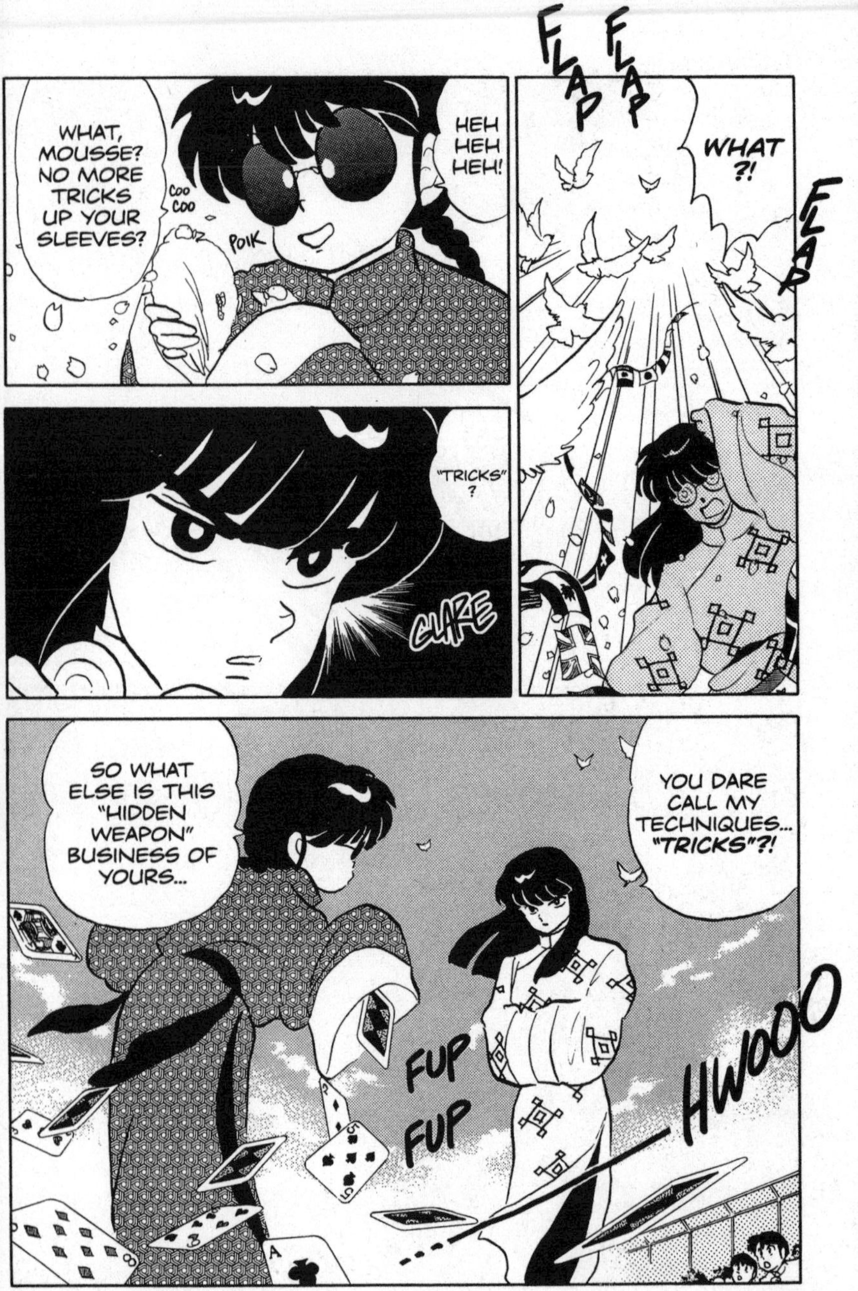

FLAP FLAP
WHAT ?!
FLAP
HEH HEH HEH!
WHAT, MOUSSE? NO MORE TRICKS UP YOUR SLEEVES?
COO COO
POIK
"TRICKS" ?
GLARE
YOU DARE CALL MY TECHNIQUES... "TRICKS"?!
SO WHAT ELSE IS THIS "HIDDEN WEAPON" BUSINESS OF YOURS...
FUP FUP
HWOOO

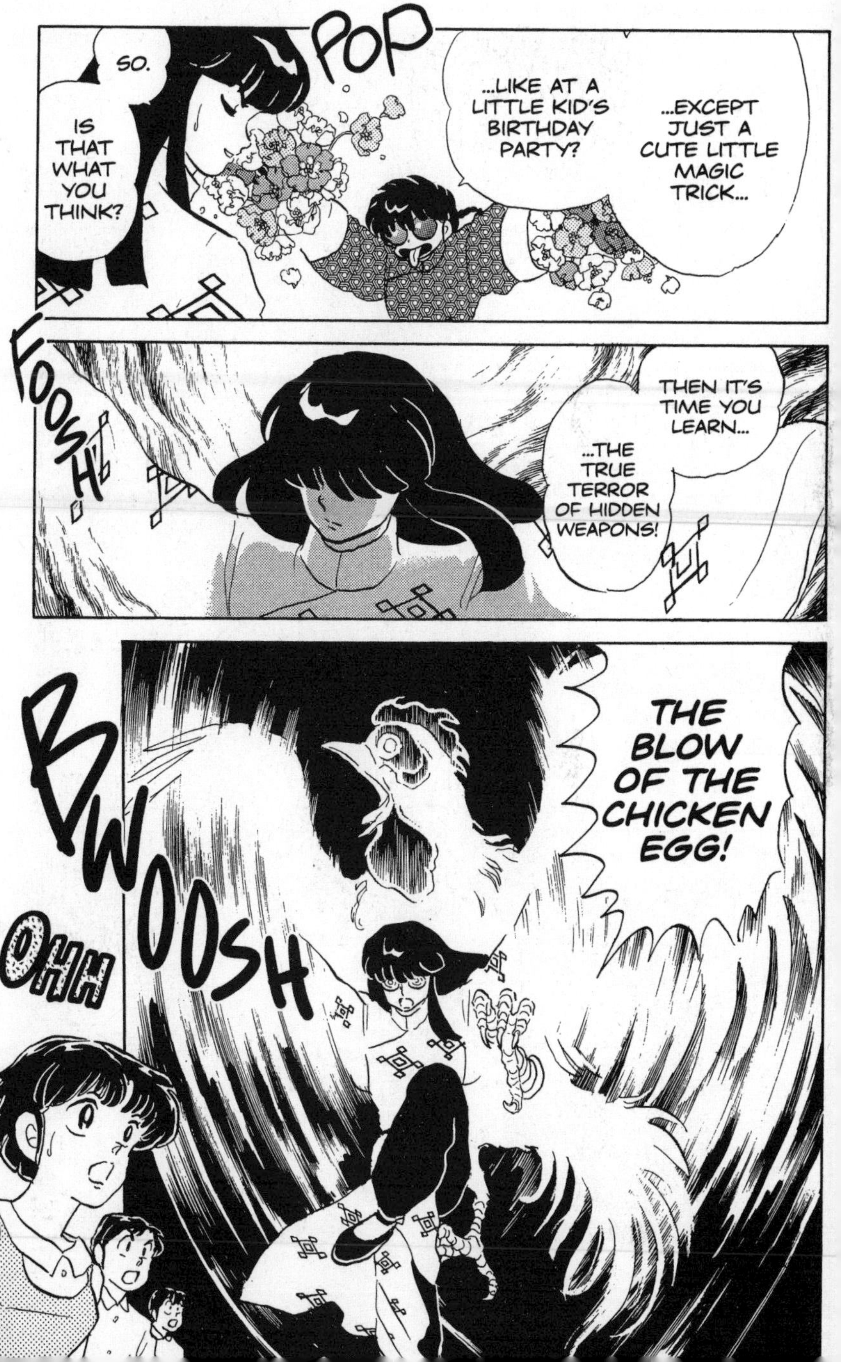
...EXCEPT JUST A CUTE LITTLE MAGIC TRICK...
...LIKE AT A LITTLE KID'S BIRTHDAY PARTY?
POP
SO.
IS THAT WHAT YOU THINK?
THEN IT'S TIME YOU LEARN...
...THE TRUE TERROR OF HIDDEN WEAPONS!
FOOSH
THE BLOW OF THE CHICKEN EGG!
BWOOSH
OHH

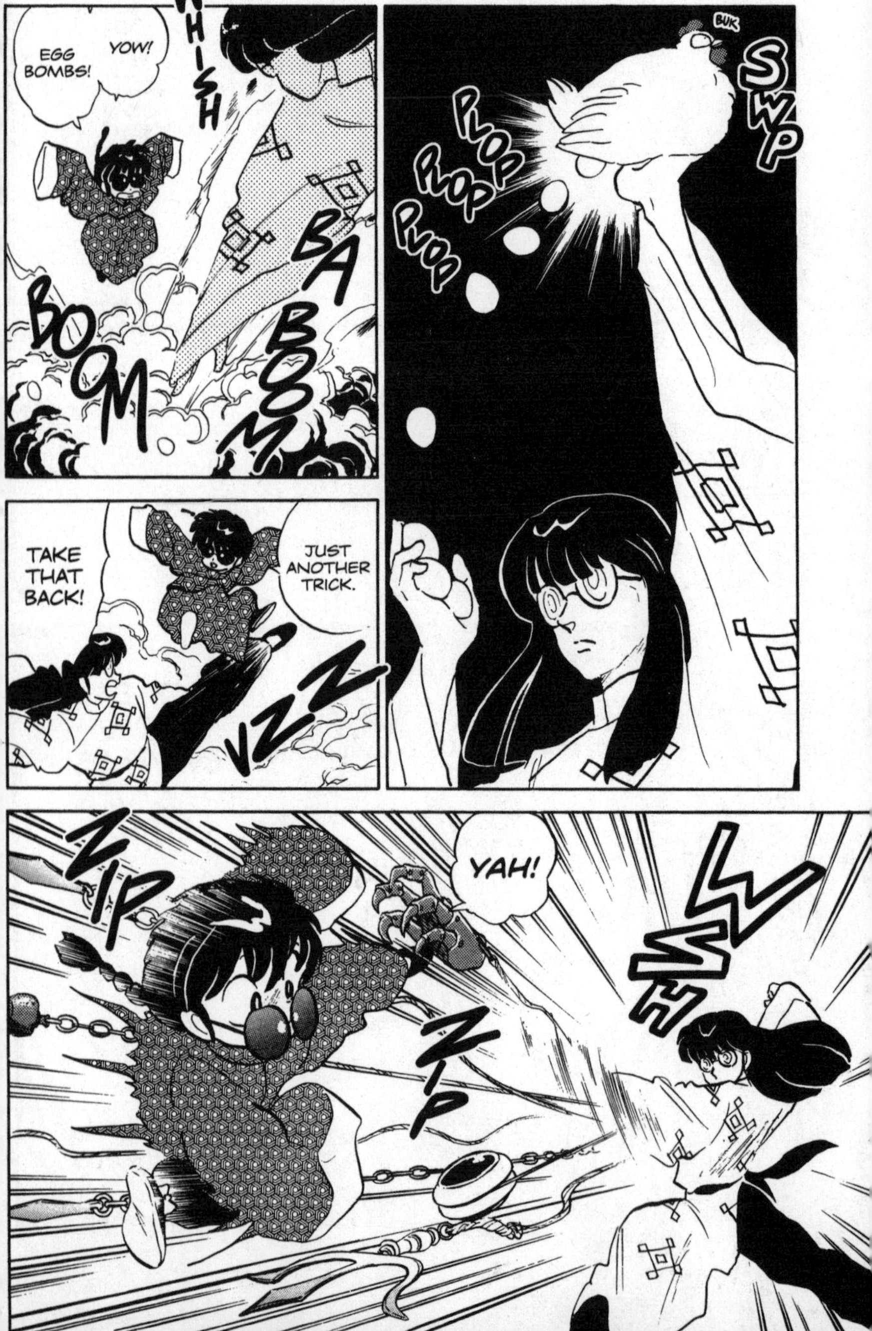
BUK
SWP
PLOP PLOP PLOP
WHISH
YOW!
EGG BOMBS!
BA BOOM
BOOM
JUST ANOTHER TRICK.
TAKE THAT BACK!
VZZZ
YAH!
WSH
ZIP
ZIP

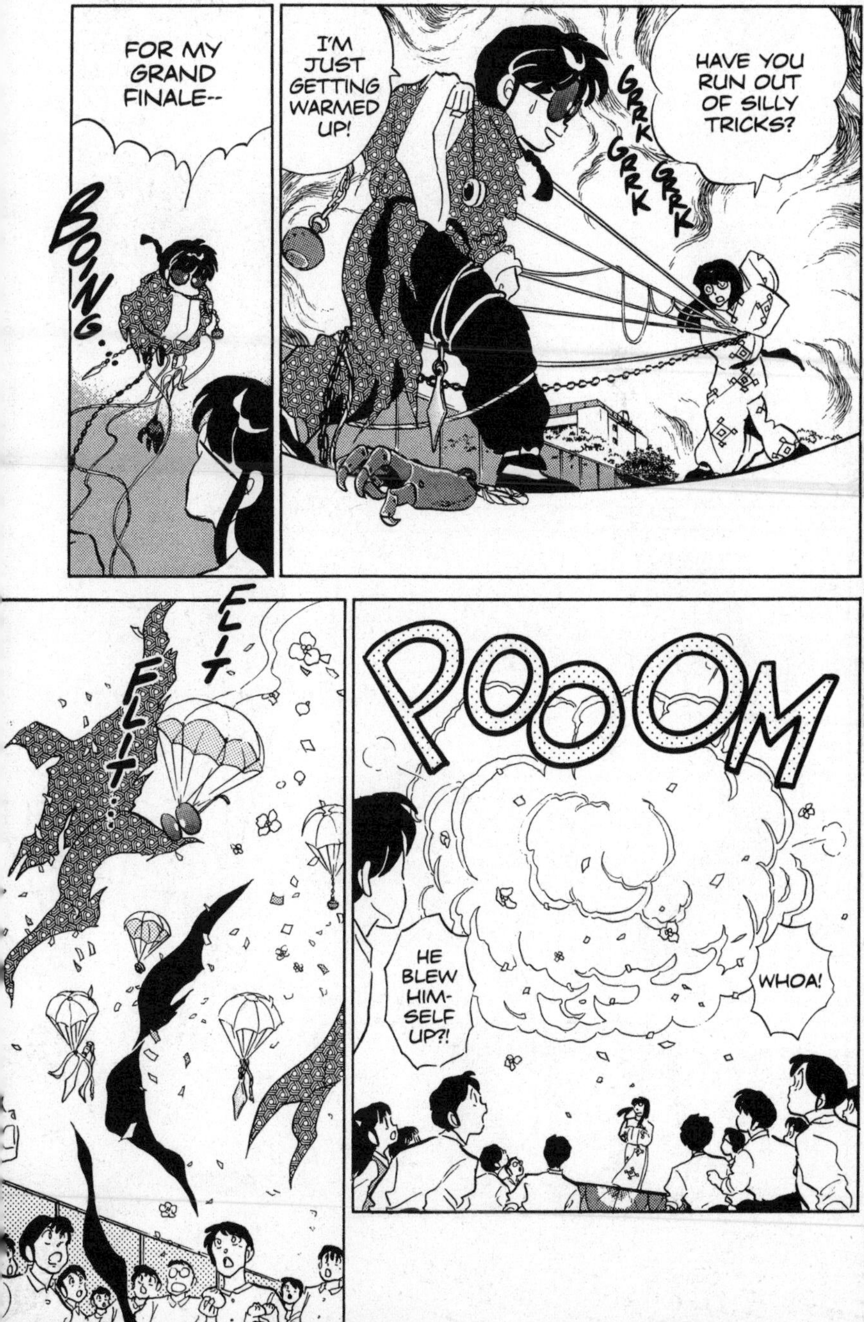
HAVE YOU RUN OUT OF SILLY TRICKS?
GRRK GRRK GRRK
I'M JUST GETTING WARMED UP!
FOR MY GRAND FINALE--
BOING...
POOOM
WHOA!
HE BLEW HIM-SELF UP?!
FLIT
FLIT...

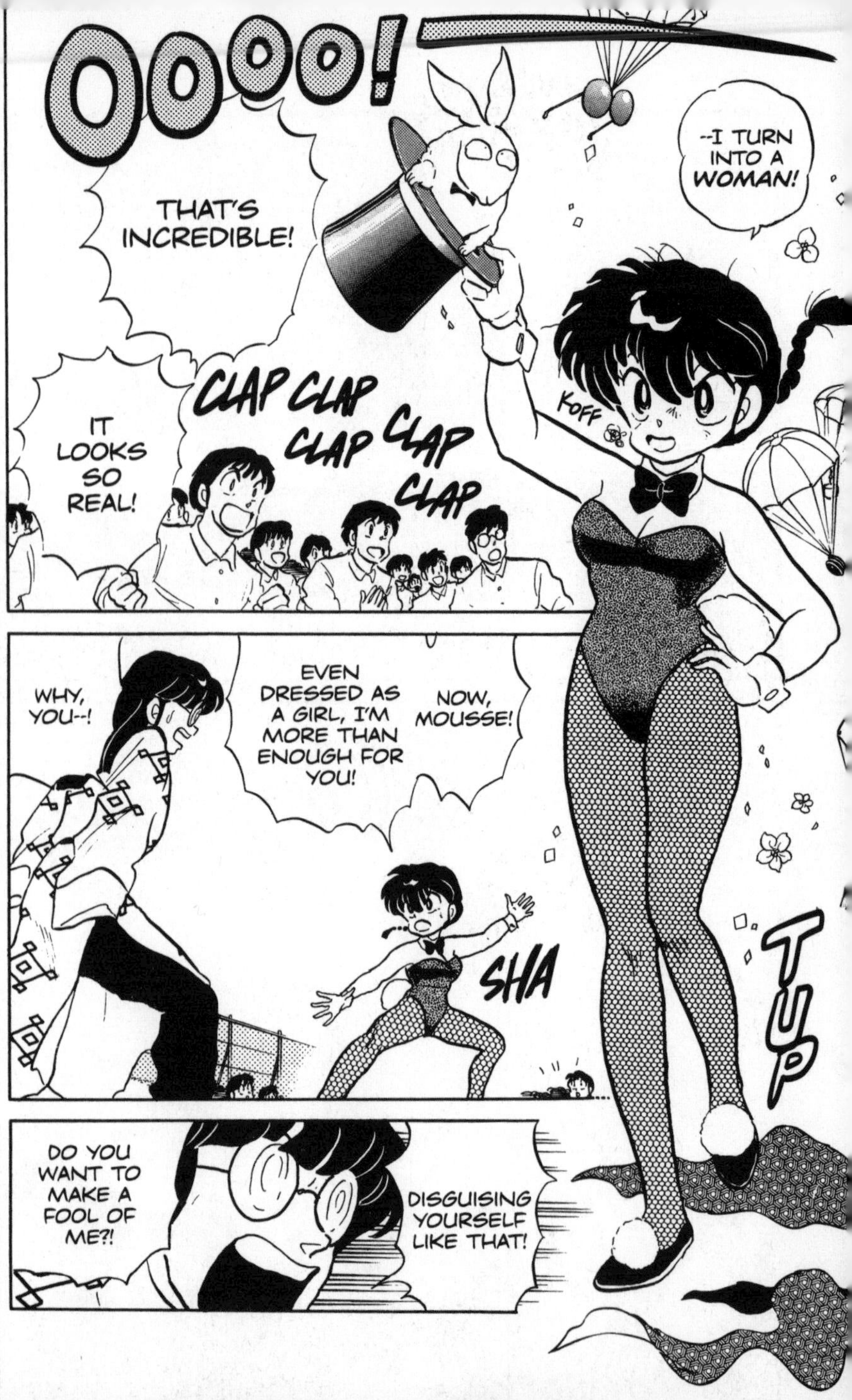
--I TURN INTO A WOMAN!
KOFF
TUP
OOOOO!
THAT'S INCREDIBLE!
CLAP CLAP CLAP CLAP CLAP
IT LOOKS SO REAL!
NOW, MOUSSE!
EVEN DRESSED AS A GIRL, I'M MORE THAN ENOUGH FOR YOU!
WHY, YOU--!
SHA
DISGUISING YOURSELF LIKE THAT!
DO YOU WANT TO MAKE A FOOL OF ME?!

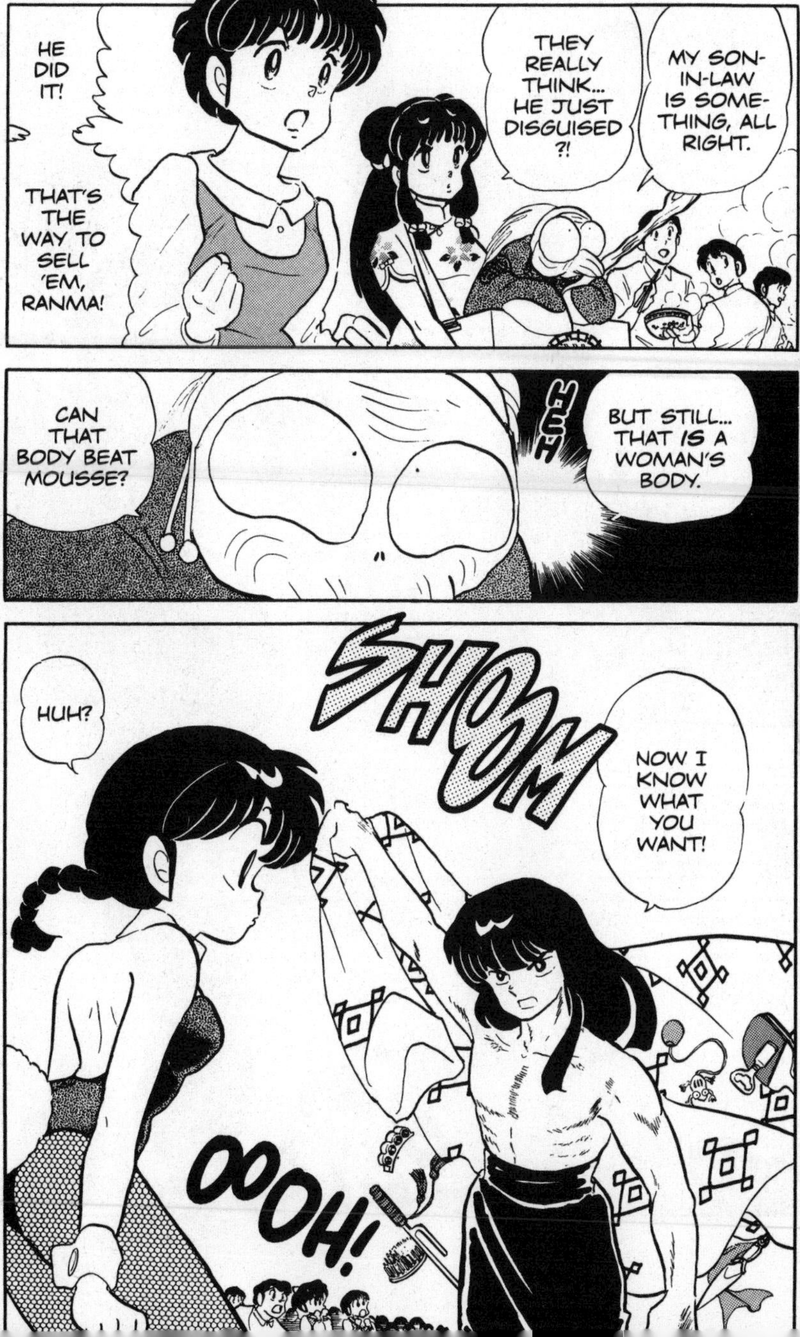
MY SON-IN-LAW IS SOMETHING, ALL RIGHT.
THEY REALLY THINK... HE JUST DISGUISED ?!
HE DID IT!
THAT'S THE WAY TO SELL 'EM, RANMA!
HEH
BUT STILL... THAT IS A WOMAN'S BODY.
CAN THAT BODY BEAT MOUSSE?
SHOOM
NOW I KNOW WHAT YOU WANT!
HUH?
OOOH!

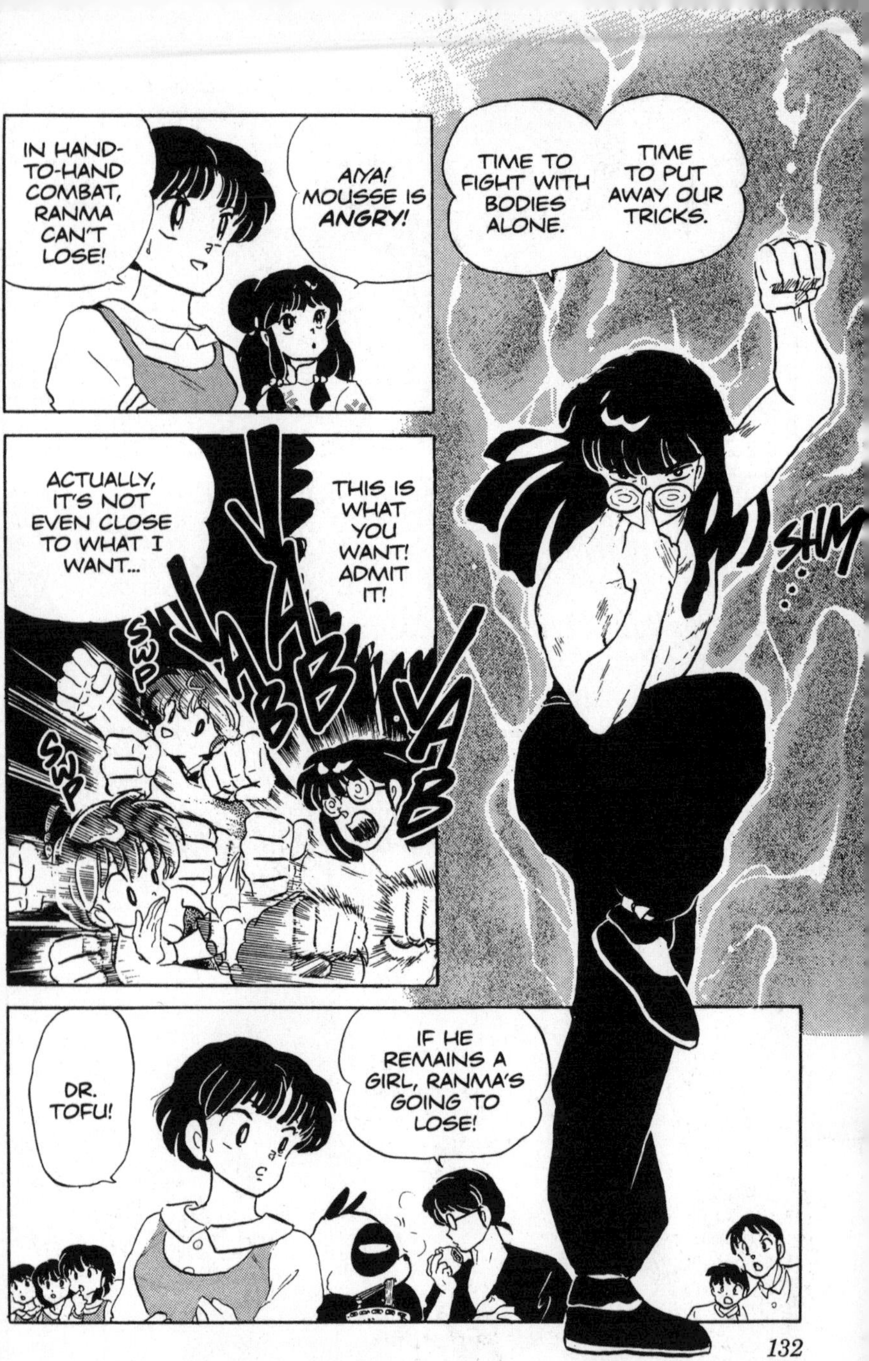

SHUM
TIME TO PUT AWAY OUR TRICKS.
TIME TO FIGHT WITH BODIES ALONE.
AIYA! MOUSSE IS ANGRY!
IN HAND-TO-HAND COMBAT, RANMA CAN'T LOSE!
JABB
JABB
THIS IS WHAT YOU WANT! ADMIT IT!
SWP
SWP
ACTUALLY, IT'S NOT EVEN CLOSE TO WHAT I WANT...
IF HE REMAINS A GIRL, RANMA'S GOING TO LOSE!
DR. TOFU!

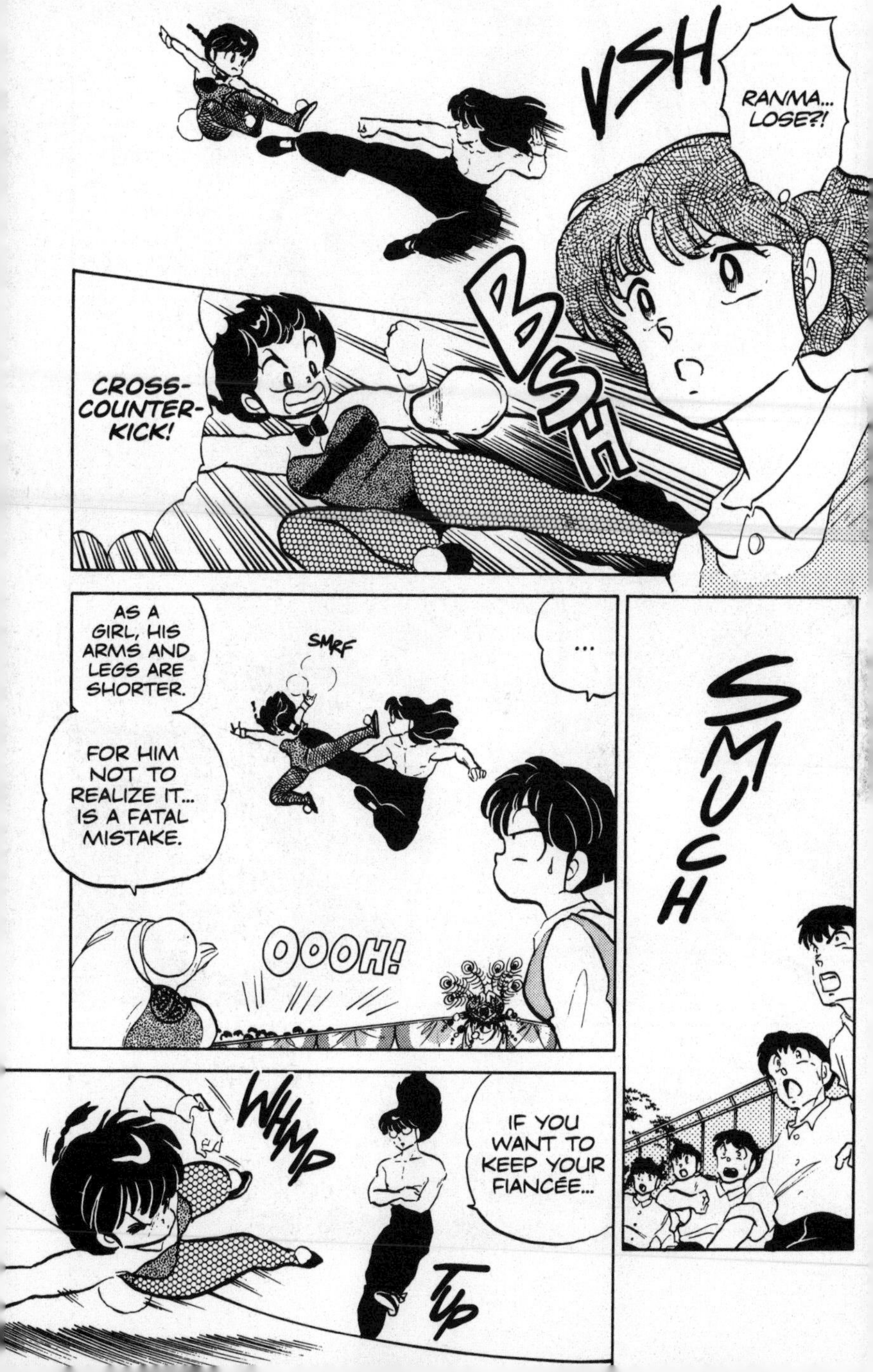
RANMA... LOSE?!
VSH
BASH
CROSS-COUNTER-KICK!
SMUCH
...
AS A GIRL, HIS ARMS AND LEGS ARE SHORTER.
FOR HIM NOT TO REALIZE IT... IS A FATAL MISTAKE.
SMRF
OOOH!
IF YOU WANT TO KEEP YOUR FIANCÉE...
WHMP
TUP

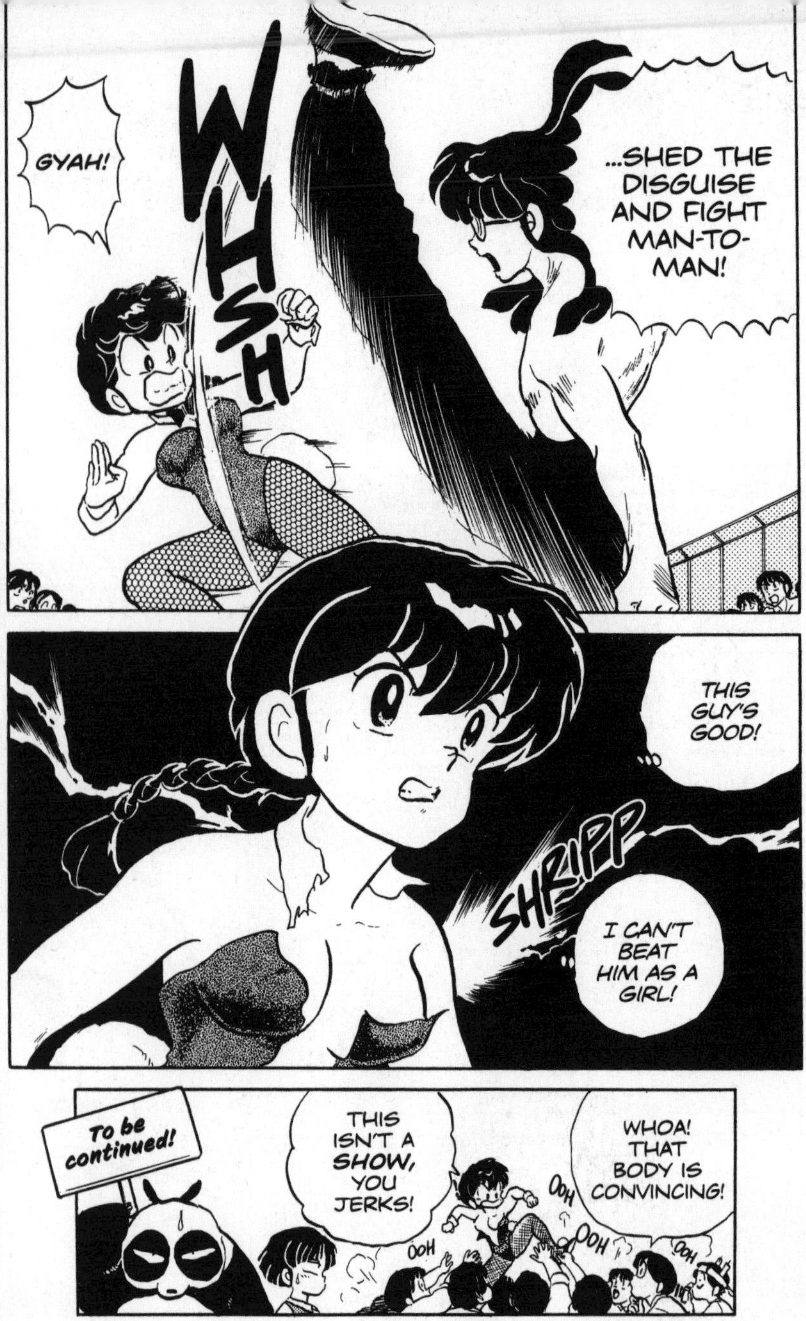
...SHED THE DISGUISE AND FIGHT MAN-TO-MAN!
WHSH
GYAH!
THIS GUY'S GOOD!
SHRIPP
I CAN'T BEAT HIM AS A GIRL!
WHOA! THAT BODY IS CONVINCING!
OOH
OOH
OOH
OOH
THIS ISN'T A SHOW, YOU JERKS!
OOH
To be continued!

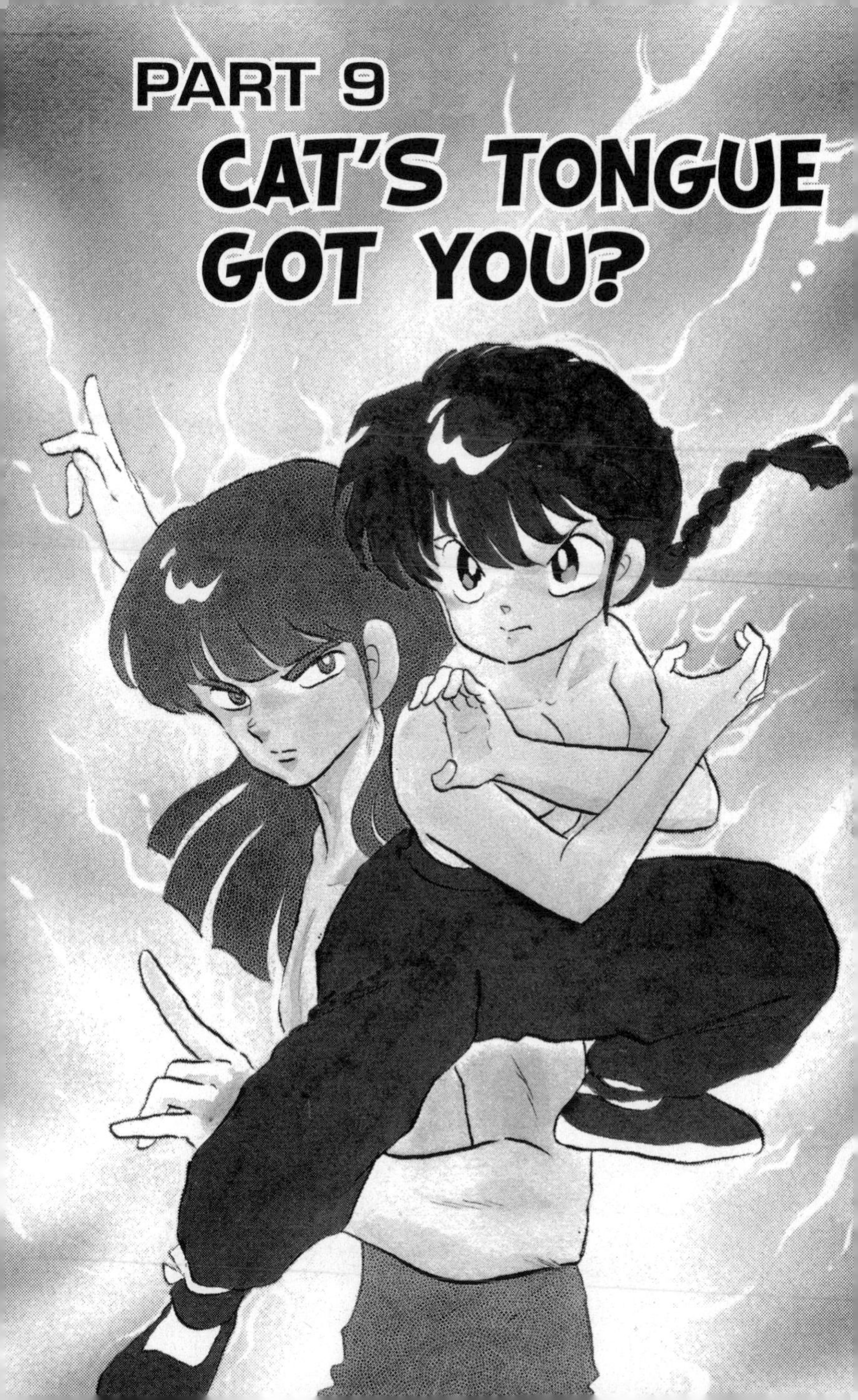
PART 9
CAT'S TONGUE GOT YOU?

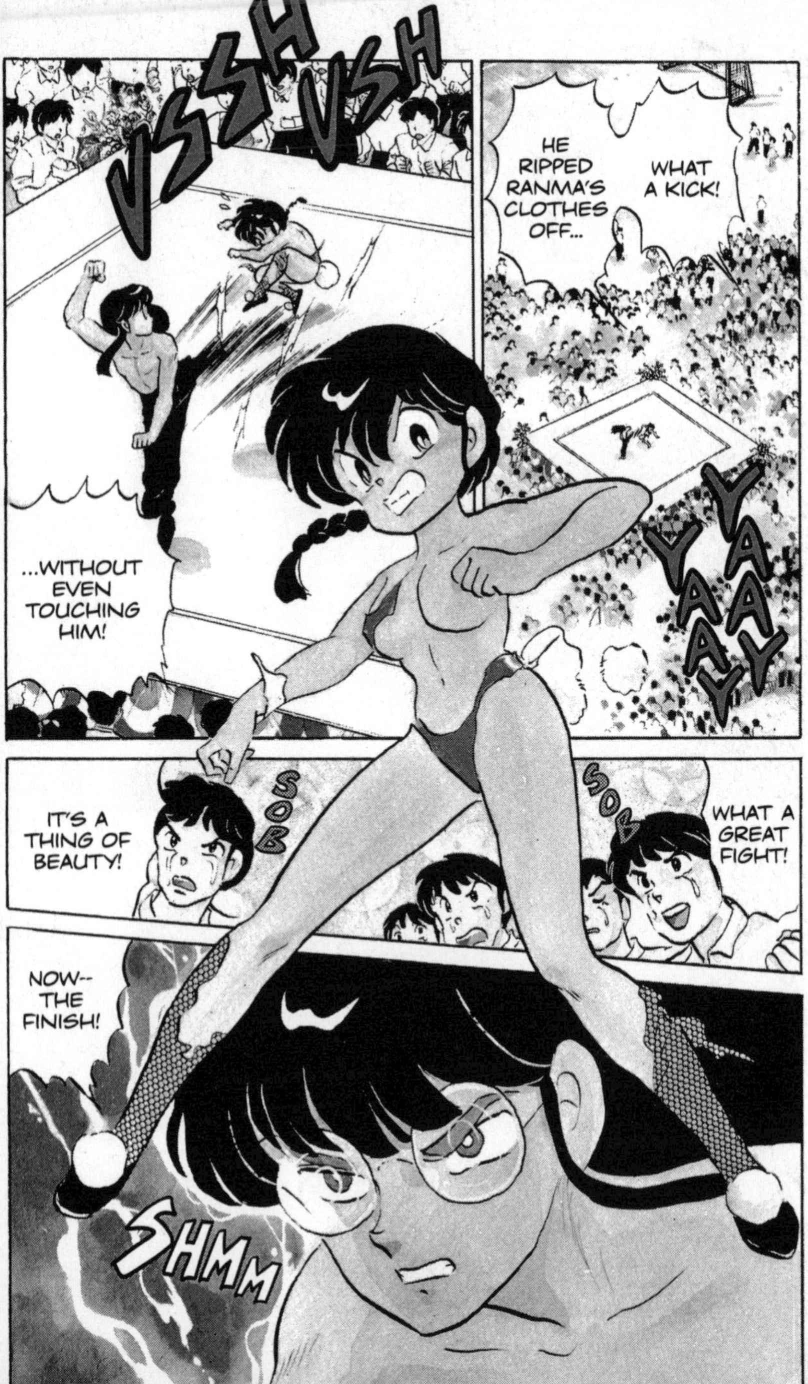
WHAT A KICK!
HE RIPPED RANMA'S CLOTHES OFF...
YAAAY
VSSH VSH
...WITHOUT EVEN TOUCHING HIM!
WHAT A GREAT FIGHT!
SOB
SOB
IT'S A THING OF BEAUTY!
NOW-- THE FINISH!
SHMM

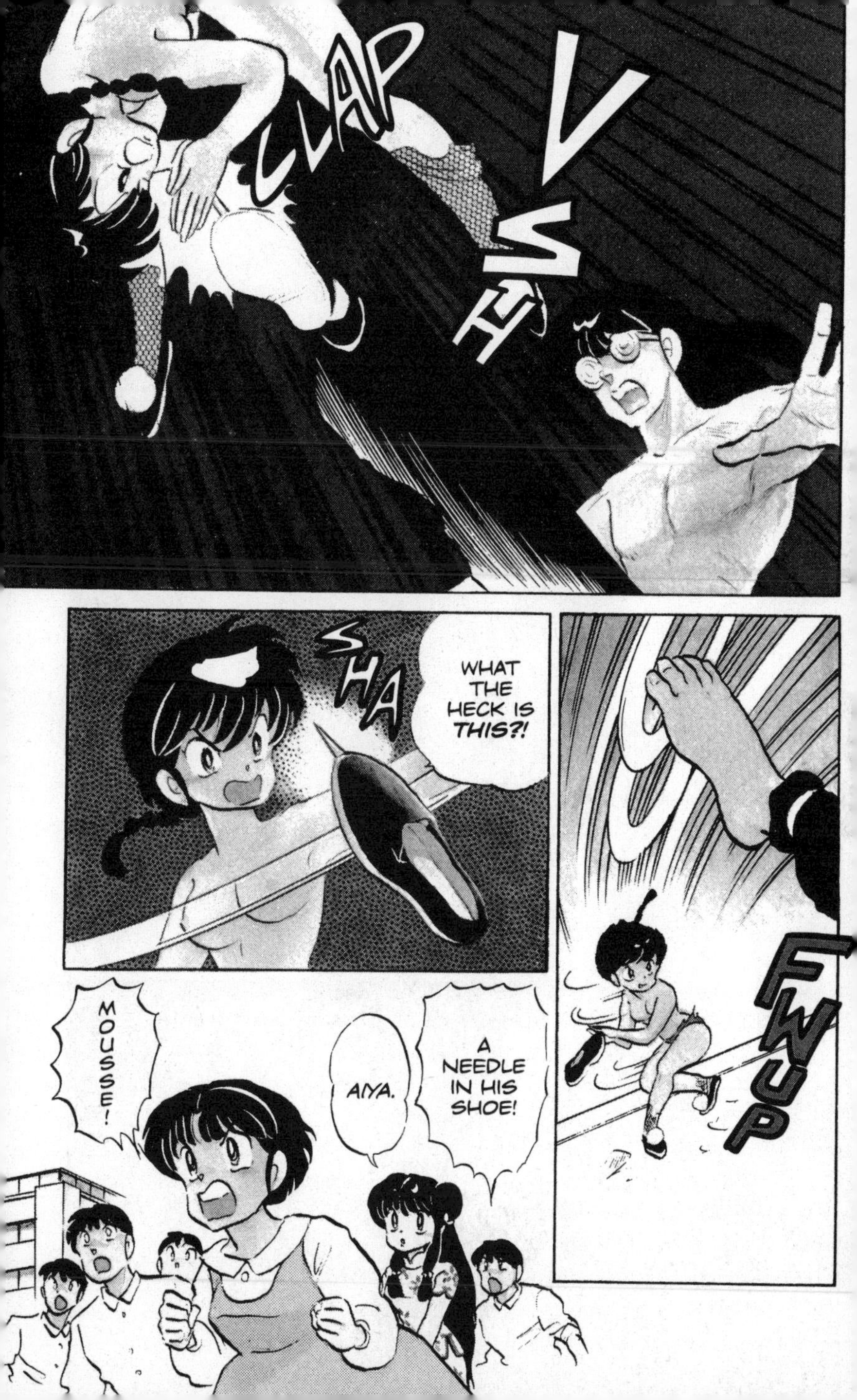
CLAP
FWUP
SHA
WHAT THE HECK IS THIS?!
A NEEDLE IN HIS SHOE!
AIYA.
MOUSSE!

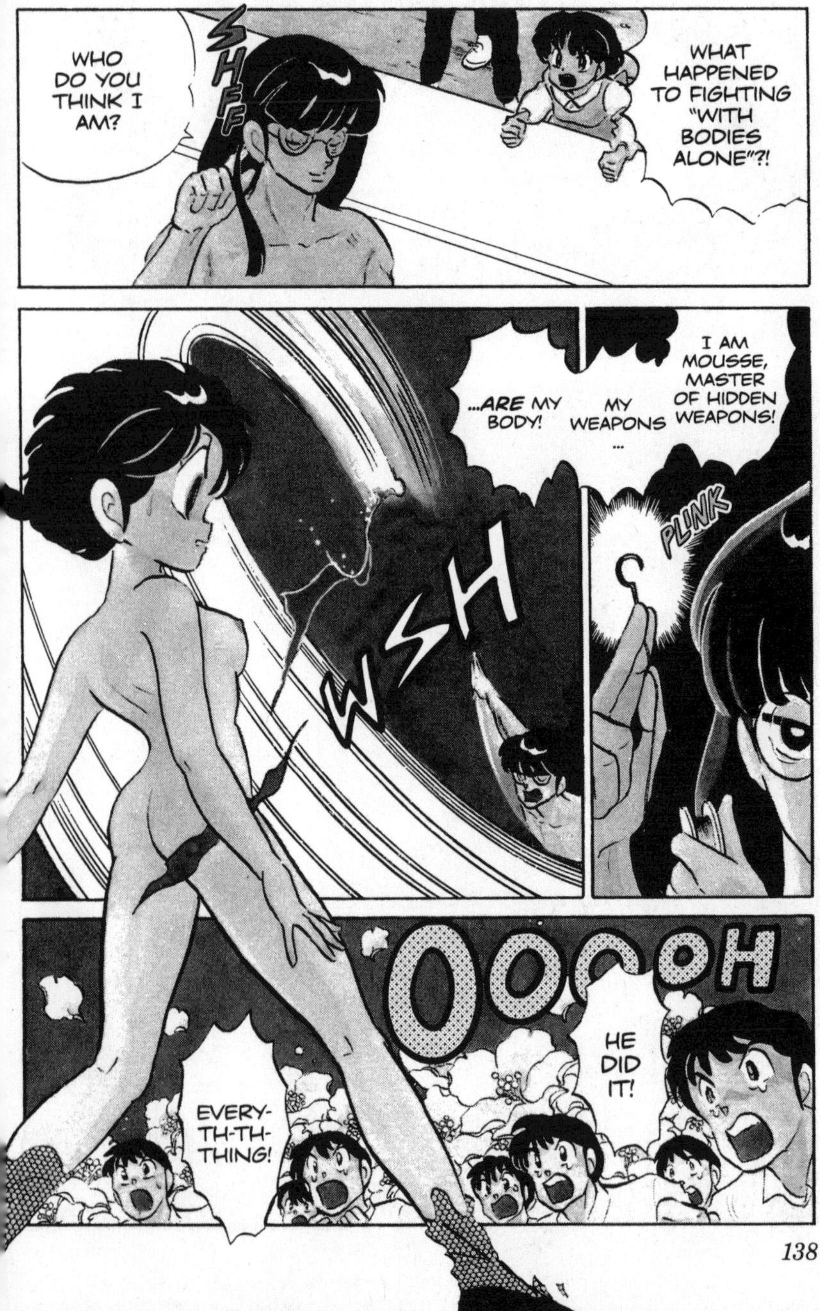
WHAT HAPPENED TO FIGHTING "WITH BODIES ALONE"?!
SHFF
WHO DO YOU THINK I AM?
I AM MOUSSE, MASTER OF HIDDEN WEAPONS!
MY WEAPONS ...
...ARE MY BODY!
PLINK
WSH
OOOOH
HE DID IT!
EVERY-TH-TH-THING!

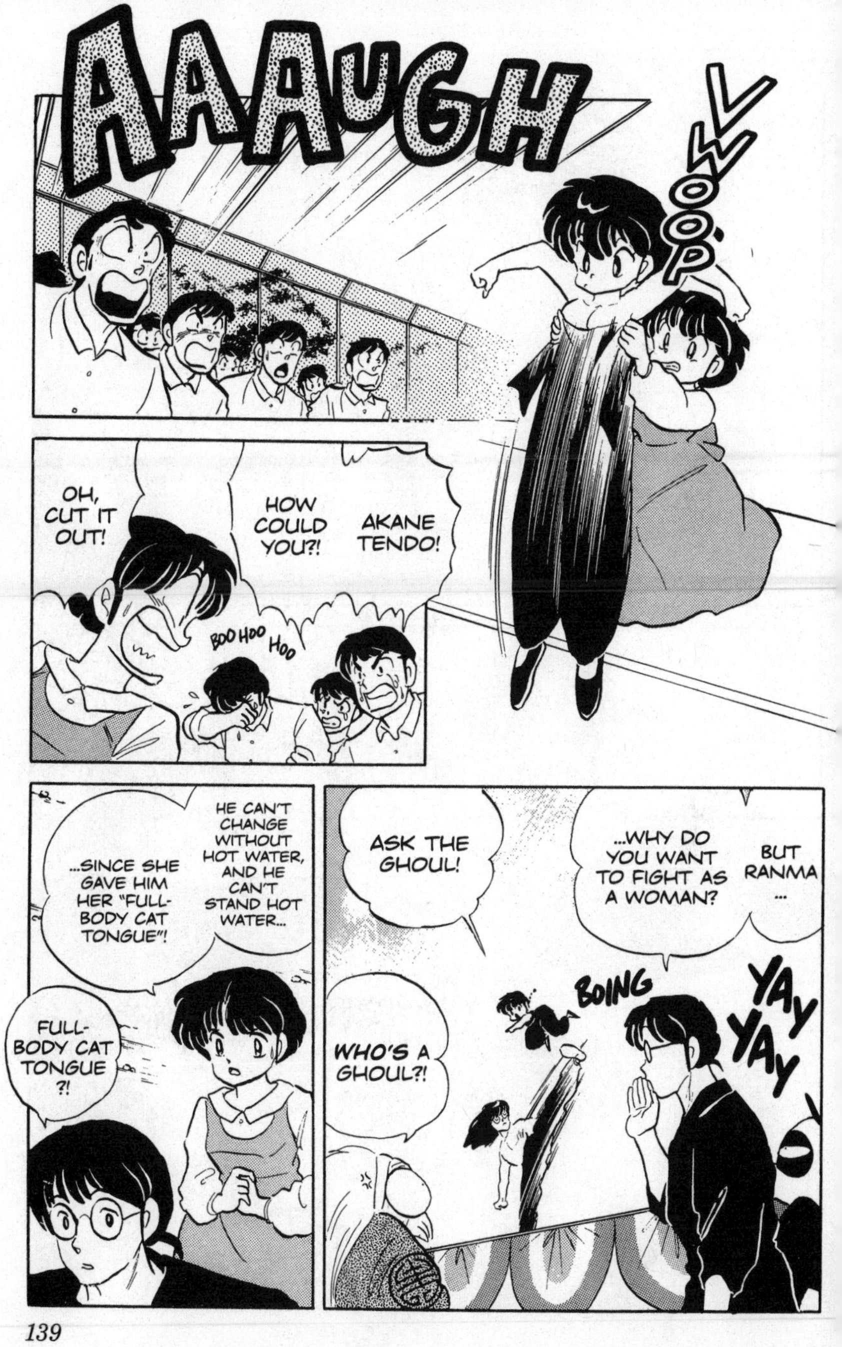
WOOP
AAAUGH
AKANE TENDO!
HOW COULD YOU?!
OH, CUT IT OUT!
BOO HOO HOO
BUT RANMA ...
...WHY DO YOU WANT TO FIGHT AS A WOMAN?
ASK THE GHOUL!
YAY YAY
BOING
WHO'S A GHOUL?!
HE CAN'T CHANGE WITHOUT HOT WATER, AND HE CAN'T STAND HOT WATER...
...SINCE SHE GAVE HIM HER "FULL-BODY CAT TONGUE"!
FULL-BODY CAT TONGUE ?!

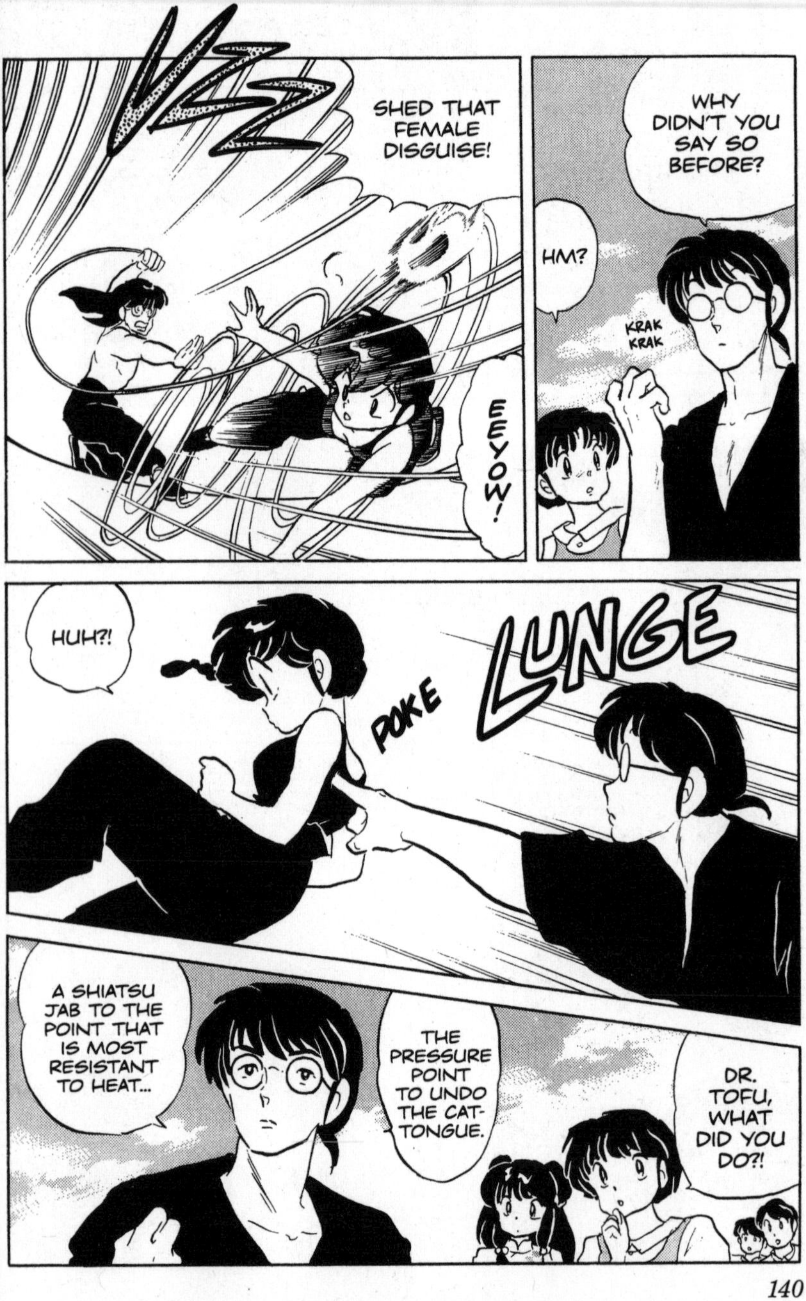
WHY DIDN'T YOU SAY SO BEFORE?
HM?
KRAK KRAK
VSZ
SHED THAT FEMALE DISGUISE!
EEYOW!
LUNGE
POKE
HUH?!
DR. TOFU, WHAT DID YOU DO?!
THE PRESSURE POINT TO UNDO THE CAT-TONGUE.
A SHIATSU JAB TO THE POINT THAT IS MOST RESISTANT TO HEAT...

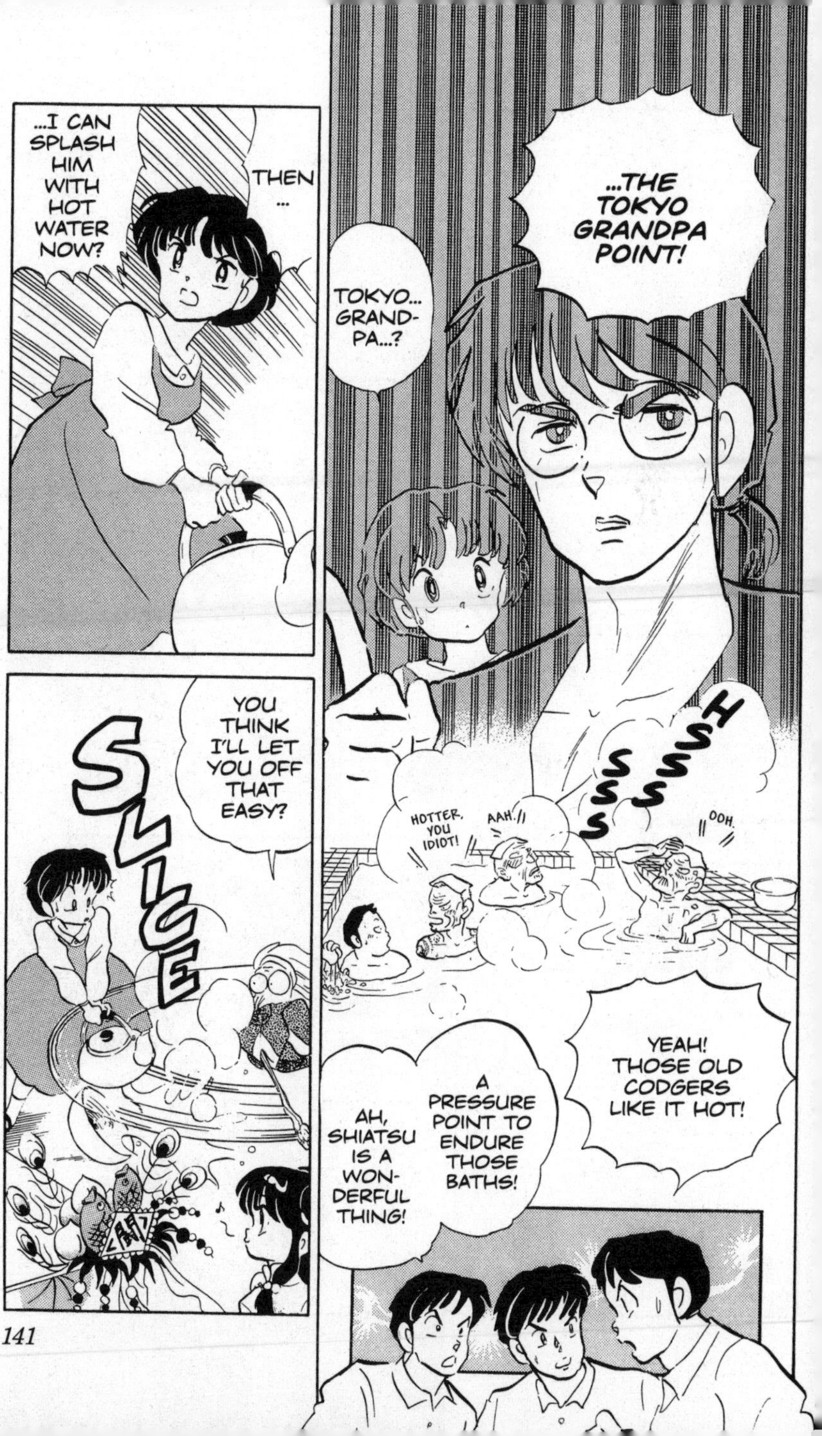
...THE TOKYO GRANDPA POINT!
TOKYO... GRAND-PA...?
HSSSSSSSH
HOTTER, YOU IDIOT!
AAH.
OOH.
YEAH! THOSE OLD CODGERS LIKE IT HOT!
A PRESSURE POINT TO ENDURE THOSE BATHS!
AH, SHIATSU IS A WON-DERFUL THING!
THEN...
...I CAN SPLASH HIM WITH HOT WATER NOW?
YOU THINK I'LL LET YOU OFF THAT EASY?
SLICE

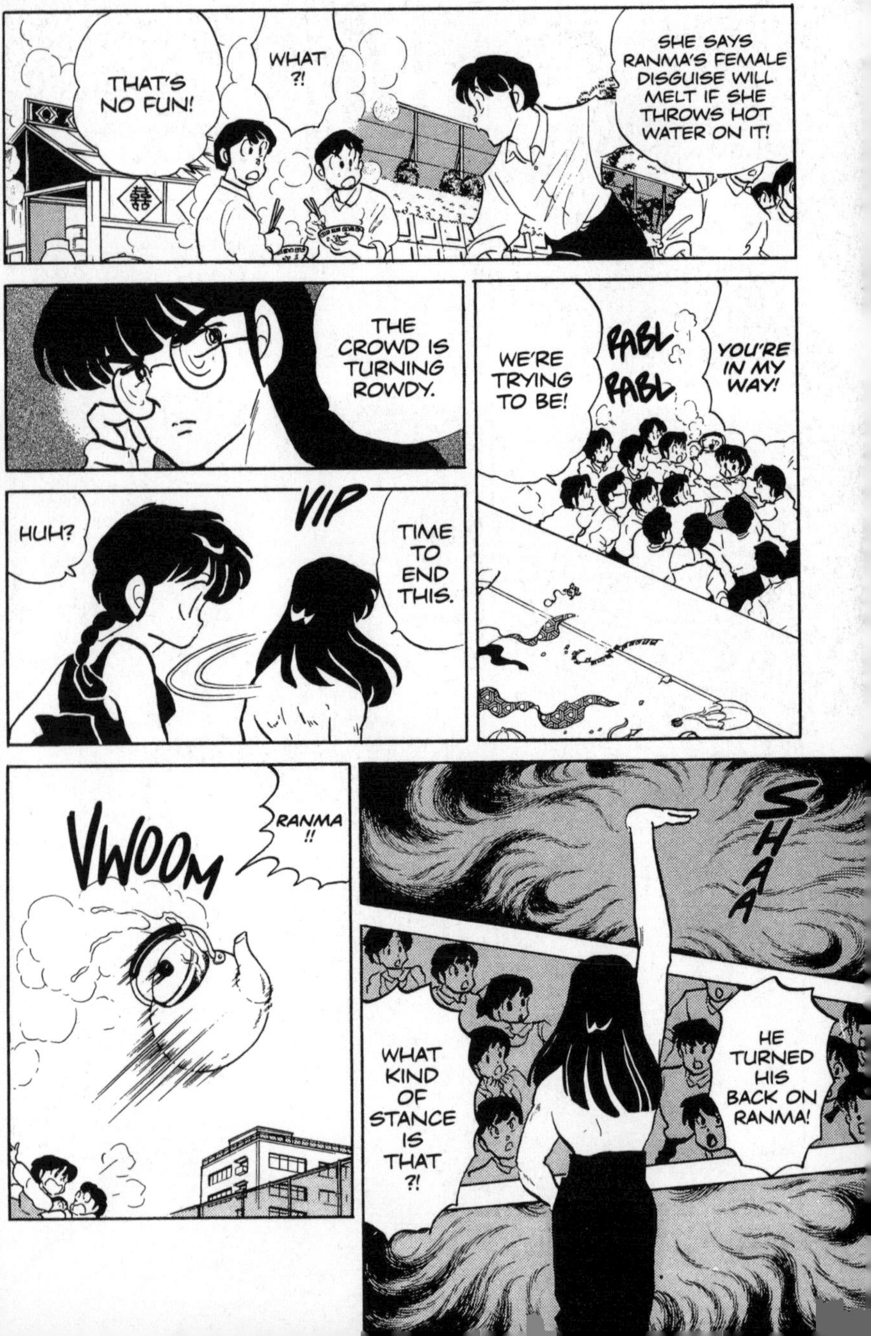
SHE SAYS RANMA'S FEMALE DISGUISE WILL MELT IF SHE THROWS HOT WATER ON IT!
WHAT ?!
THAT'S NO FUN!
YOU'RE IN MY WAY!
RABL
RABL
WE'RE TRYING TO BE!
THE CROWD IS TURNING ROWDY.
VIP
TIME TO END THIS.
HUH?
SHAA
HE TURNED HIS BACK ON RANMA!
WHAT KIND OF STANCE IS THAT ?!
RANMA !!
VWOOM

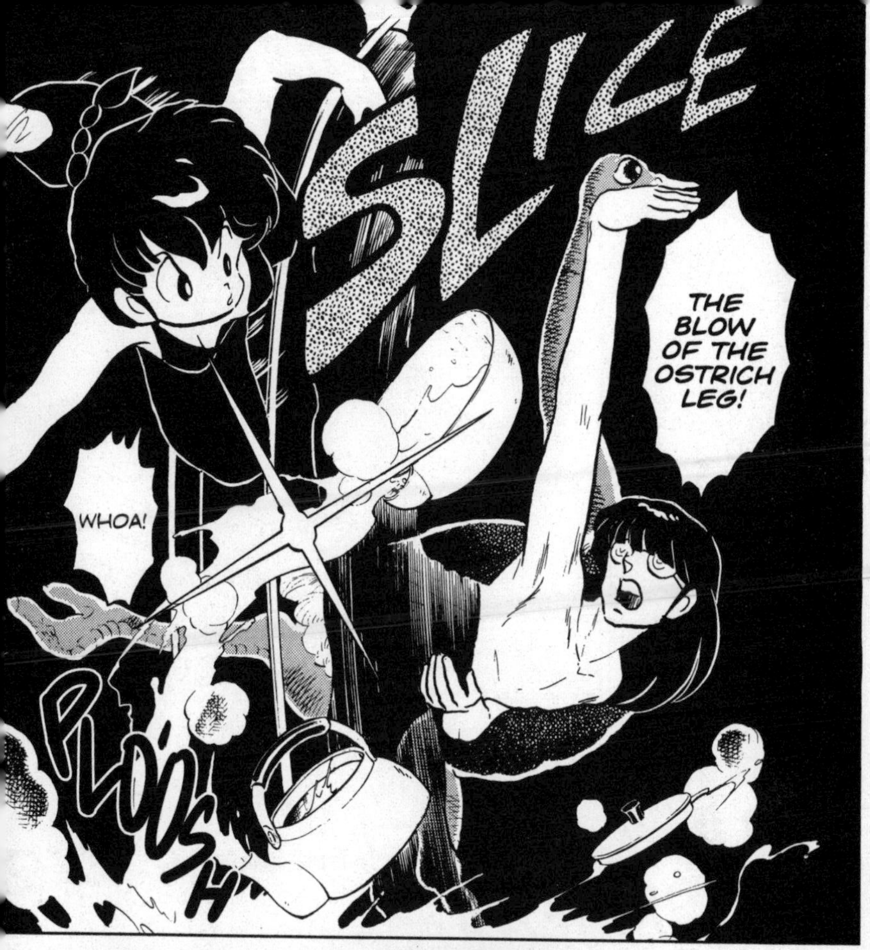
SLICE
THE BLOW OF THE OSTRICH LEG!
WHOA!
PLOOSH

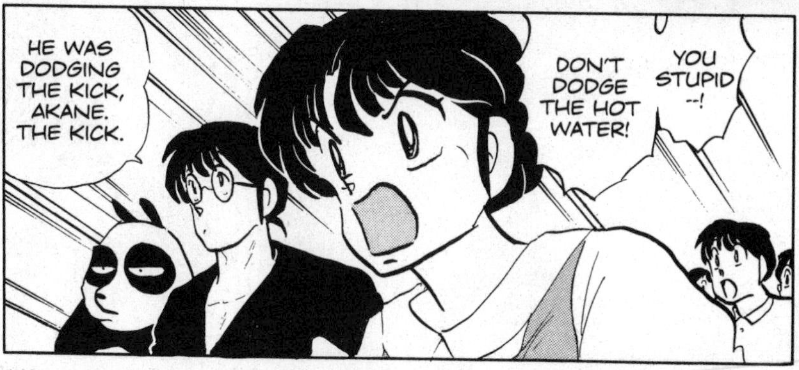
YOU STUPID --!
DON'T DODGE THE HOT WATER!
HE WAS DODGING THE KICK, AKANE. THE KICK.

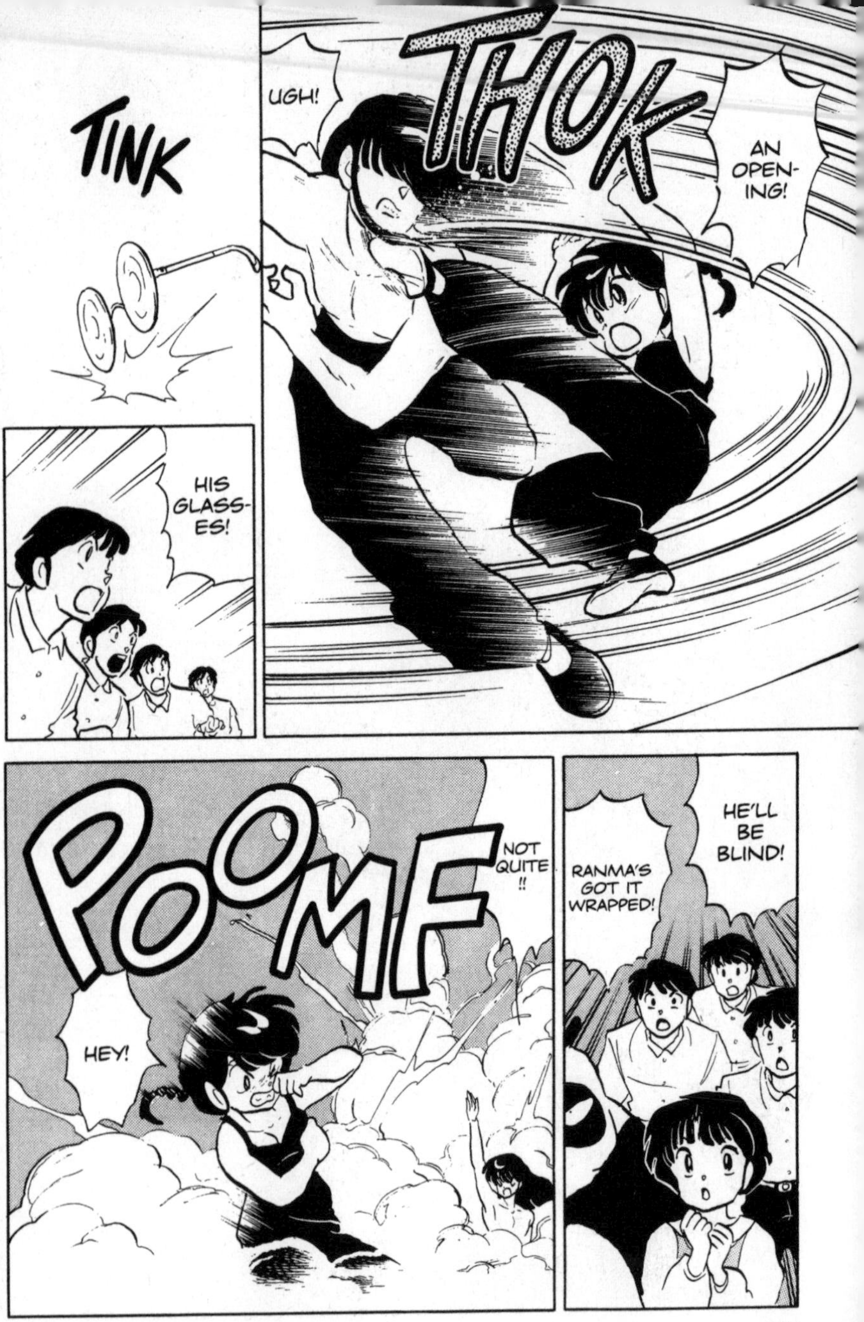
AN OPENING!
THOK
UGH!
TINK
HIS GLASSES!
HE'LL BE BLIND!
RANMA'S GOT IT WRAPPED!
NOT QUITE !!
POOMF
HEY!

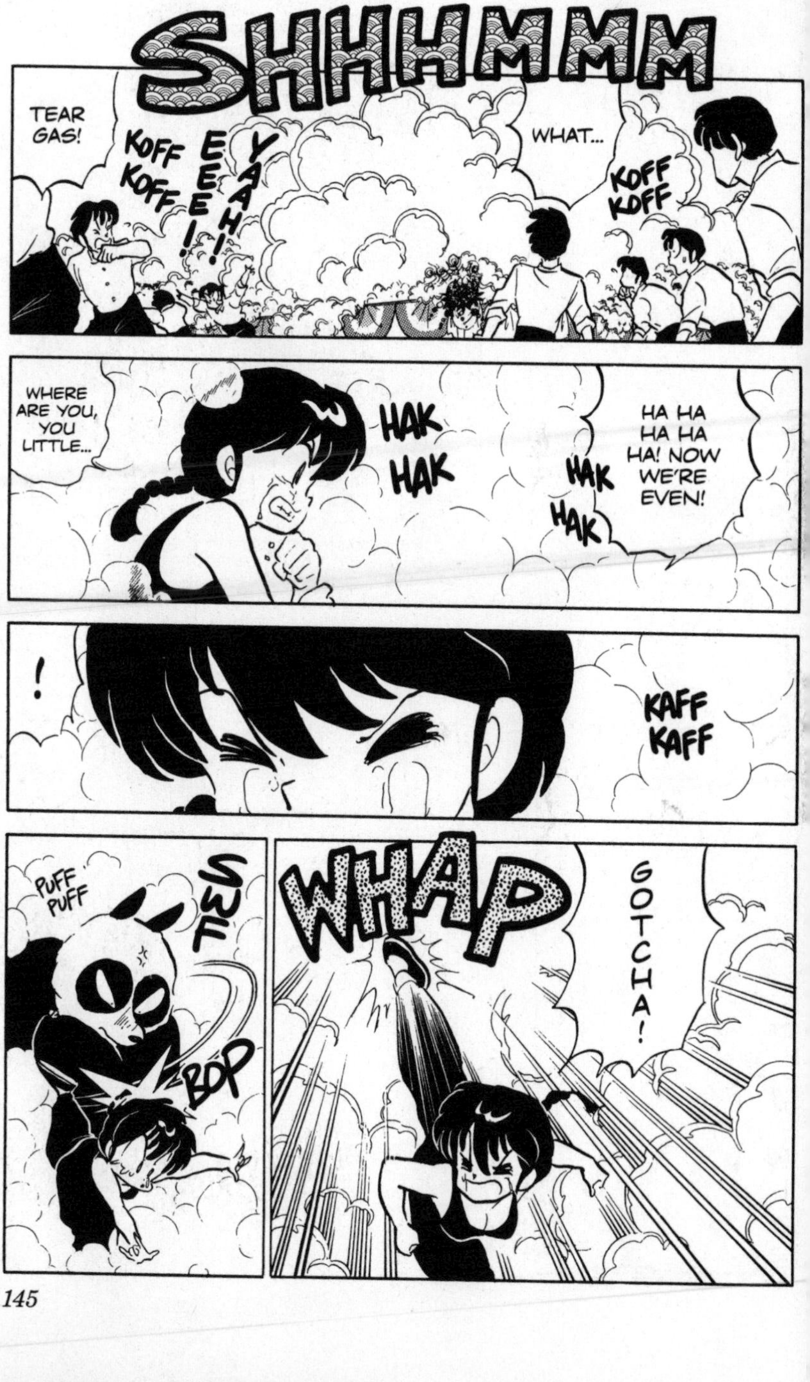
SHHHMMMM
WHAT...
KOFF KOFF
YAAAH!!
EEEE!!
KOFF KOFF
TEAR GAS!
HA HA HA HA HA! NOW WE'RE EVEN!
HAK HAK
HAK HAK
WHERE ARE YOU, YOU LITTLE...
KAFF KAFF
!
GOTCHA!
WHAP
SWF
PUFF PUFF
BOP

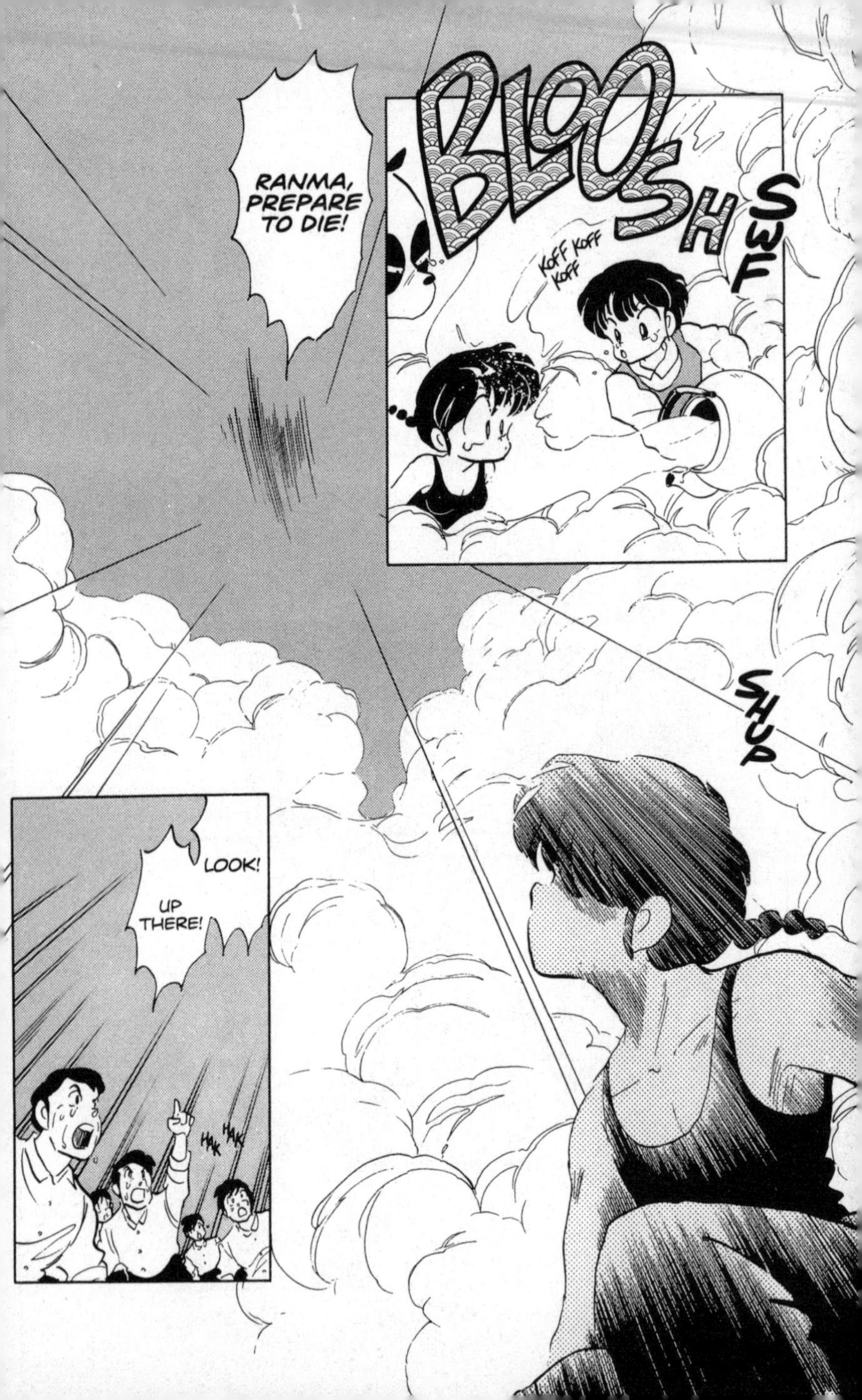
BLOOSH
SWF
KOFF KOFF KOFF
RANMA, PREPARE TO DIE!
SHUP
LOOK!
UP THERE!
HAK HAK

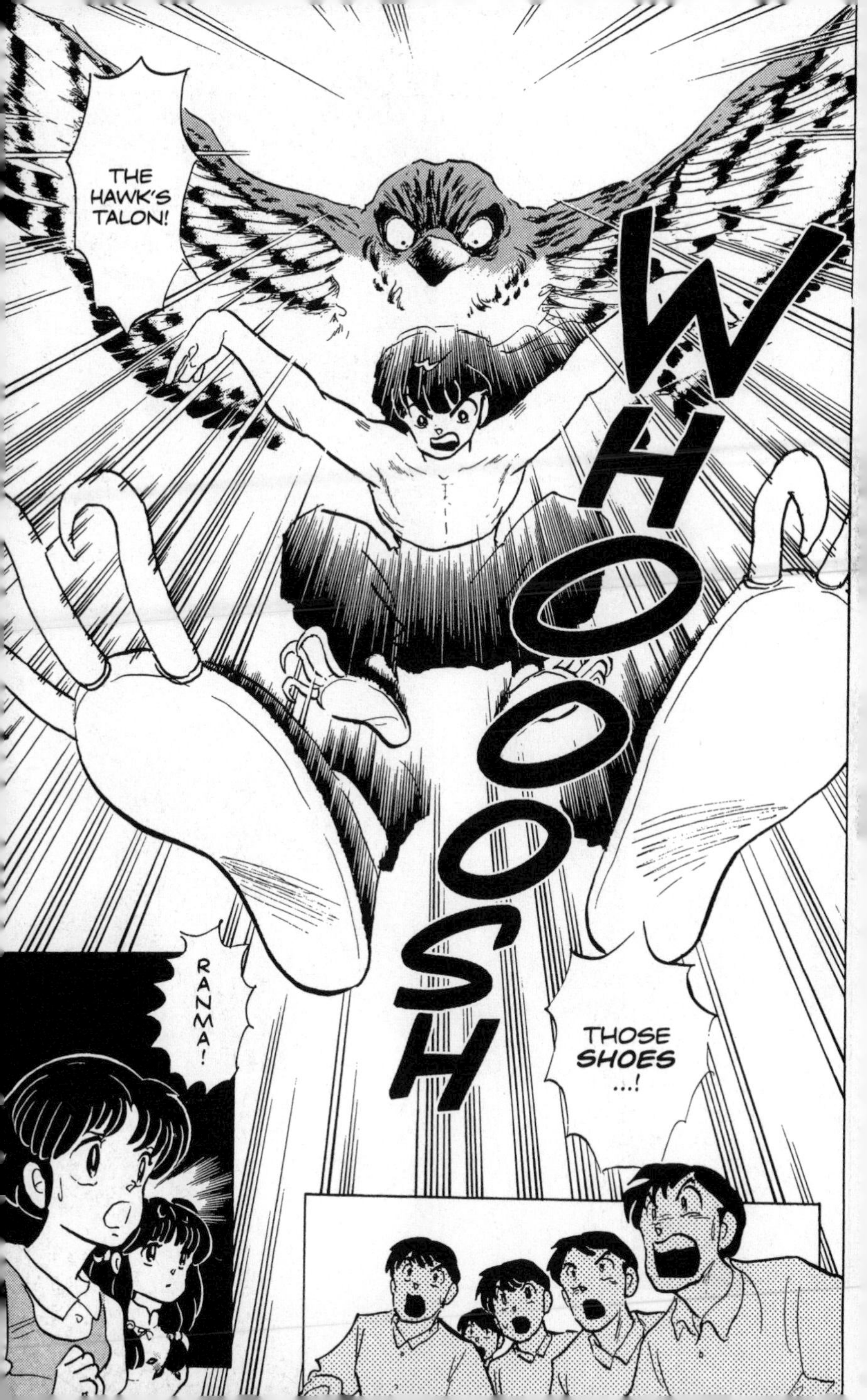
THE HAWK'S TALON!
WHOOOOSH
THOSE SHOES ...!
RANMA!

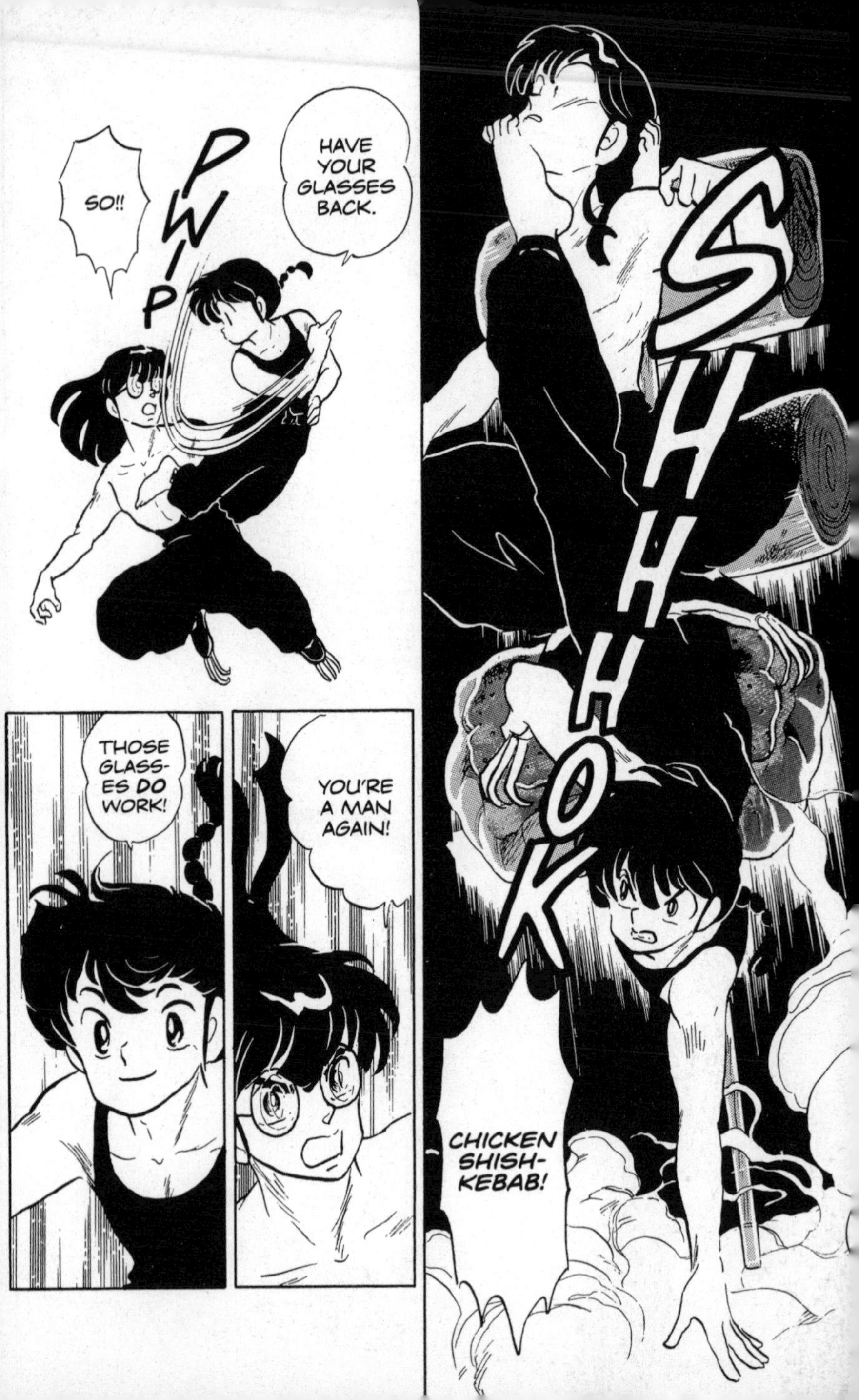
SHHHHOOK
CHICKEN SHISH-KEBAB!
HAVE YOUR GLASSES BACK.
PWIP
SO!!
YOU'RE A MAN AGAIN!
THOSE GLASS-ES DO WORK!

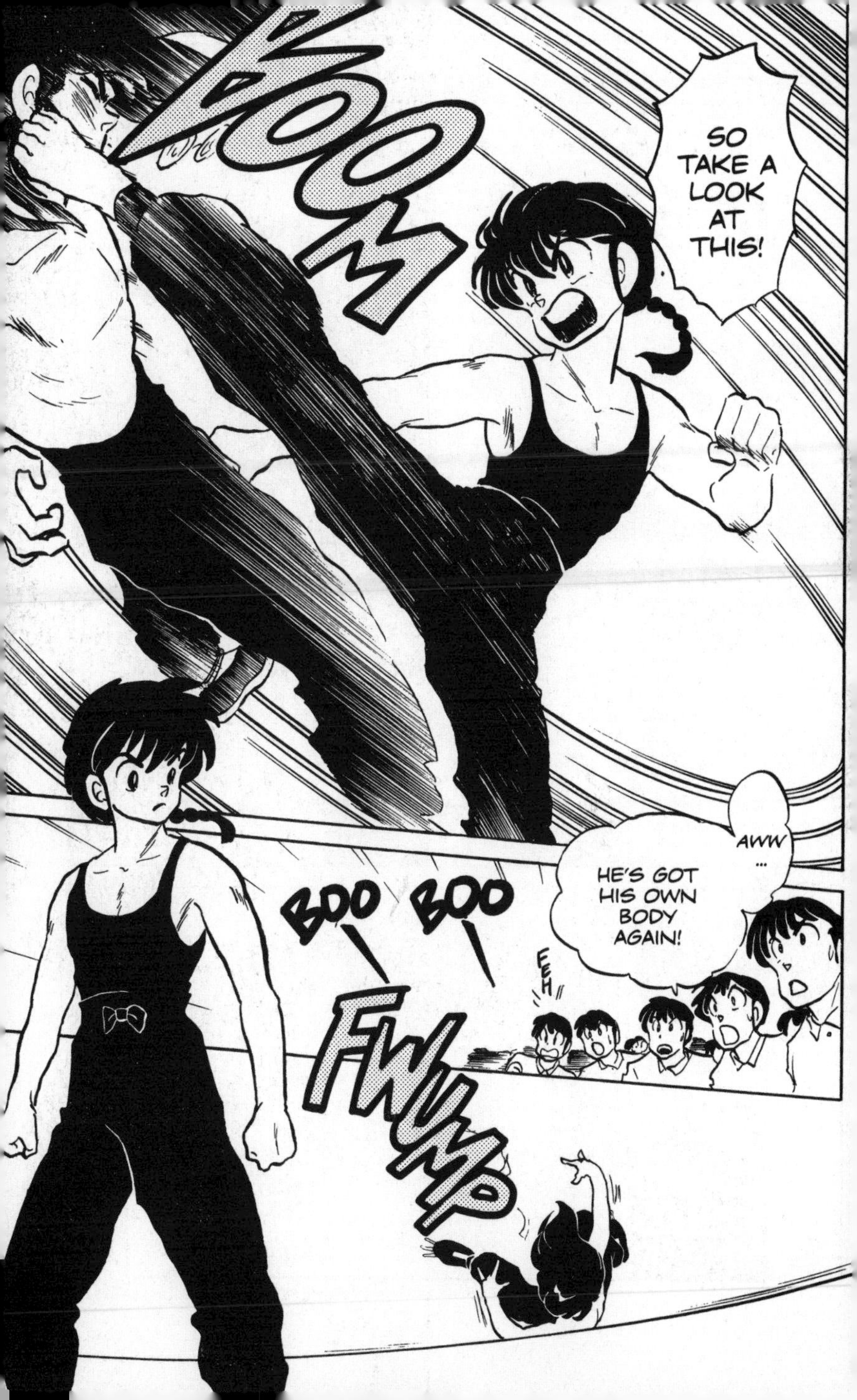
SO TAKE A LOOK AT THIS!
VOOM
AWW ...
HE'S GOT HIS OWN BODY AGAIN!
EEH
BOO BOO
FWUMP

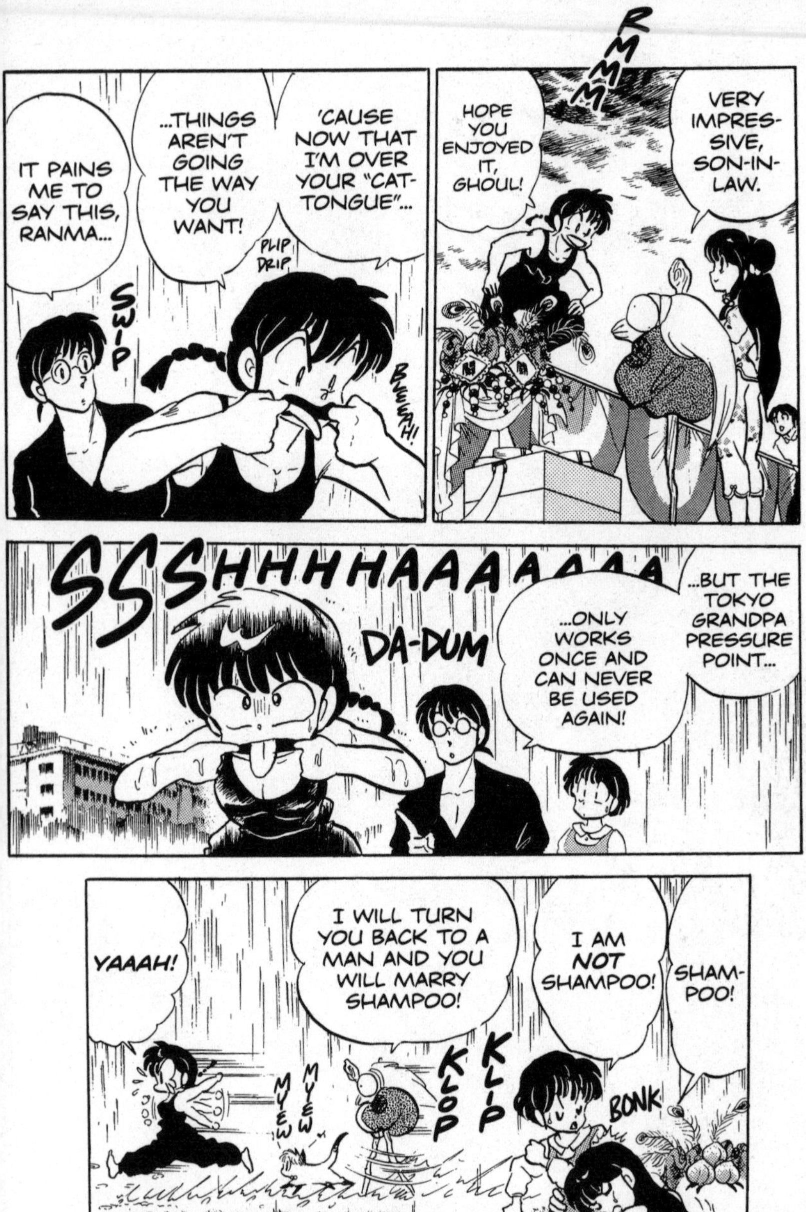
RMMMM
VERY IMPRESSIVE, SON-IN-LAW.
HOPE YOU ENJOYED IT, GHOUL!
'CAUSE NOW THAT I'M OVER YOUR "CAT-TONGUE"...
...THINGS AREN'T GOING THE WAY YOU WANT!
PLIP DRIP
IT PAINS ME TO SAY THIS, RANMA...
BLEEAH!
SWIP
...BUT THE TOKYO GRANDPA PRESSURE POINT...
...ONLY WORKS ONCE AND CAN NEVER BE USED AGAIN!
SSSHHHHAAAAAAAA
DA-DUM
SHAM-POO!
I AM **NOT** SHAMPOO!
BONK
KLIP
KLOP
I WILL TURN YOU BACK TO A MAN AND YOU WILL MARRY SHAMPOO!
MYEW MYEW
MYEW
YAAAH!

PART 10

THE PHOENIX PILL

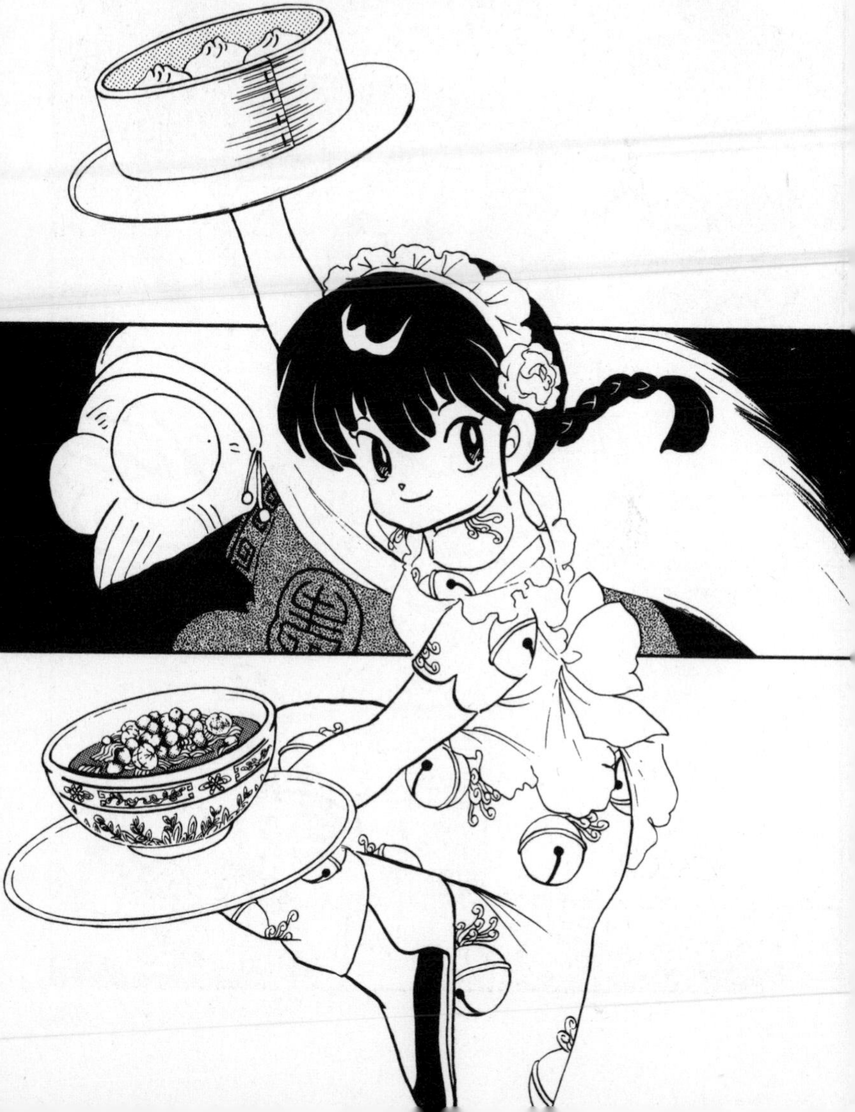

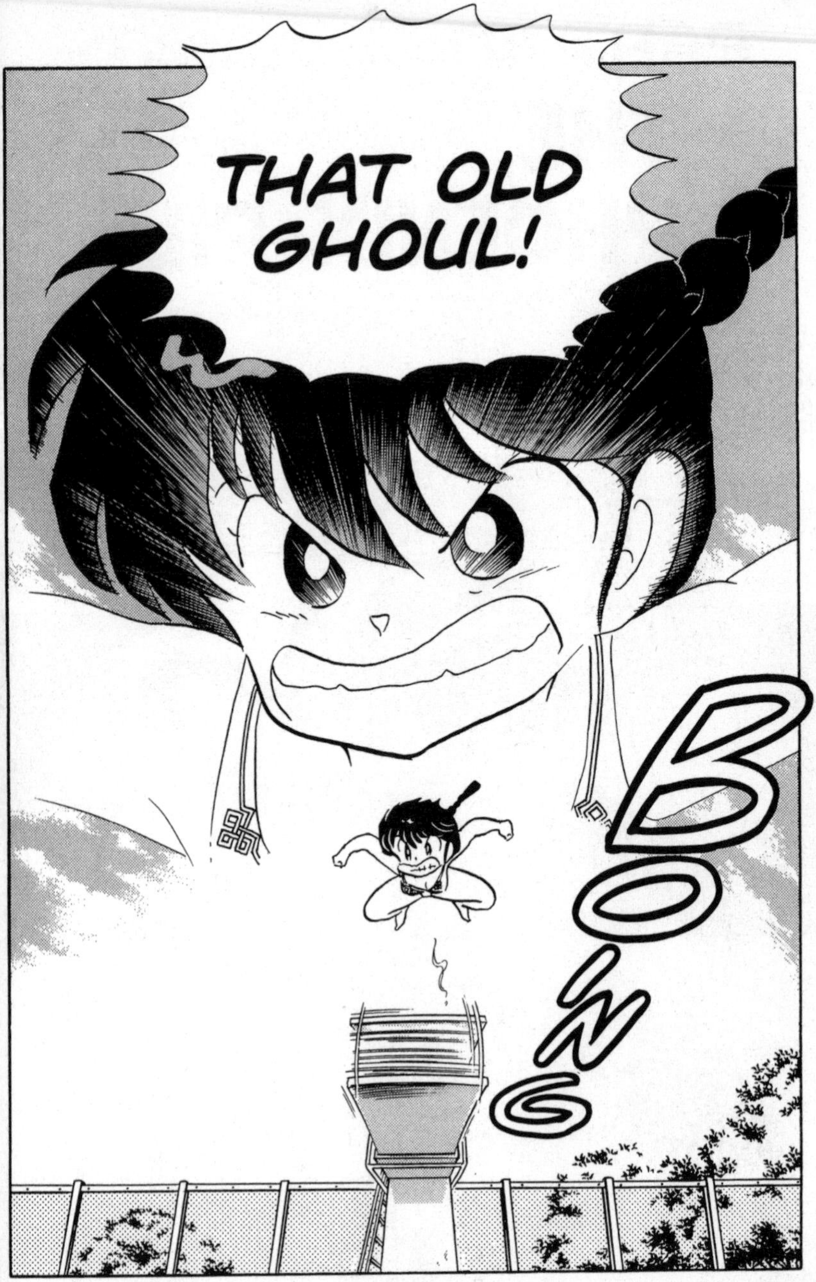
THAT OLD GHOUL!
BOING

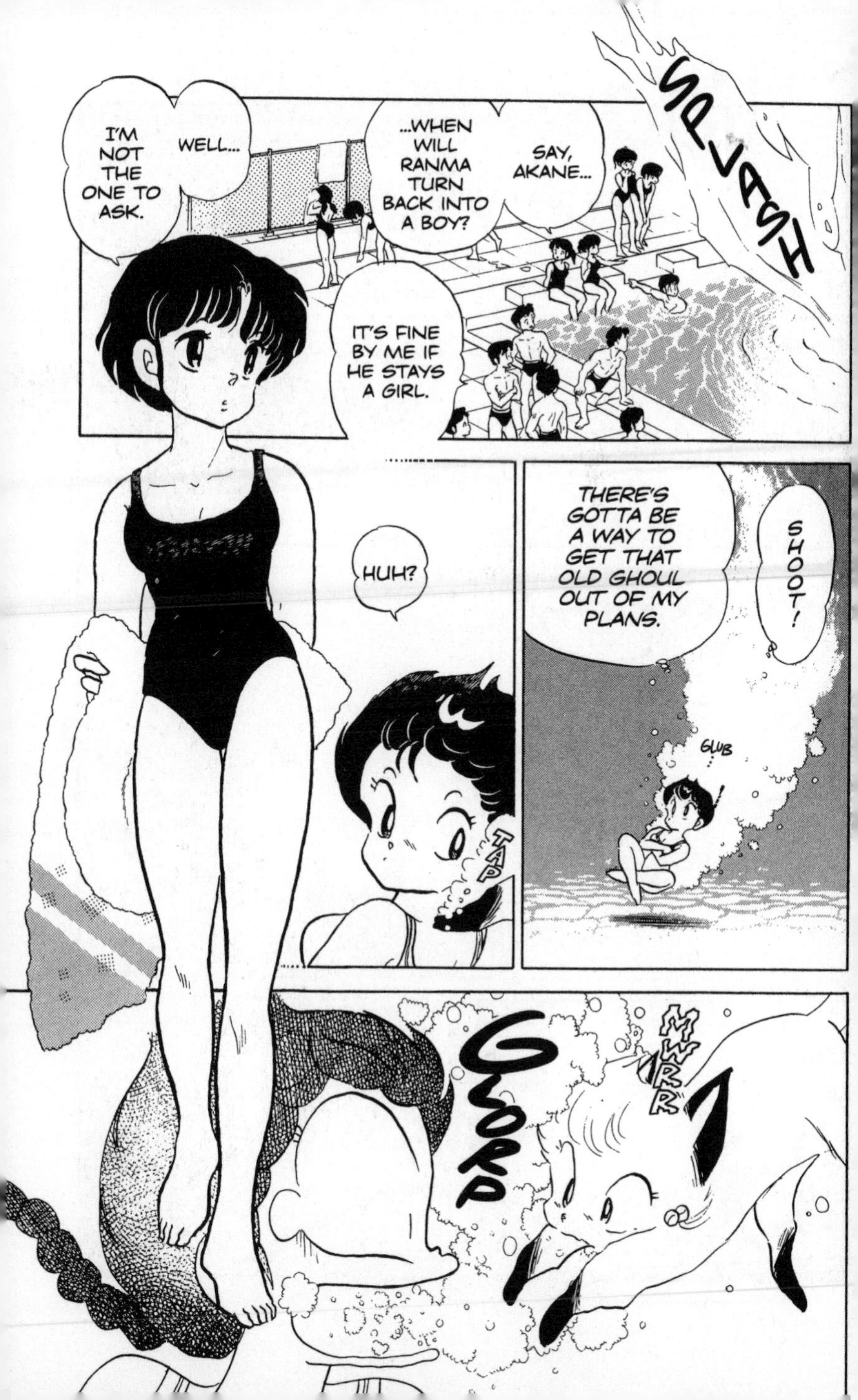
SPLASH
SAY, AKANE...
...WHEN WILL RANMA TURN BACK INTO A BOY?
WELL...
I'M NOT THE ONE TO ASK.
IT'S FINE BY ME IF HE STAYS A GIRL.
SHOOT!
THERE'S GOTTA BE A WAY TO GET THAT OLD GHOUL OUT OF MY PLANS.
GLUB
HUH?
TAP
MWRR
GLORP

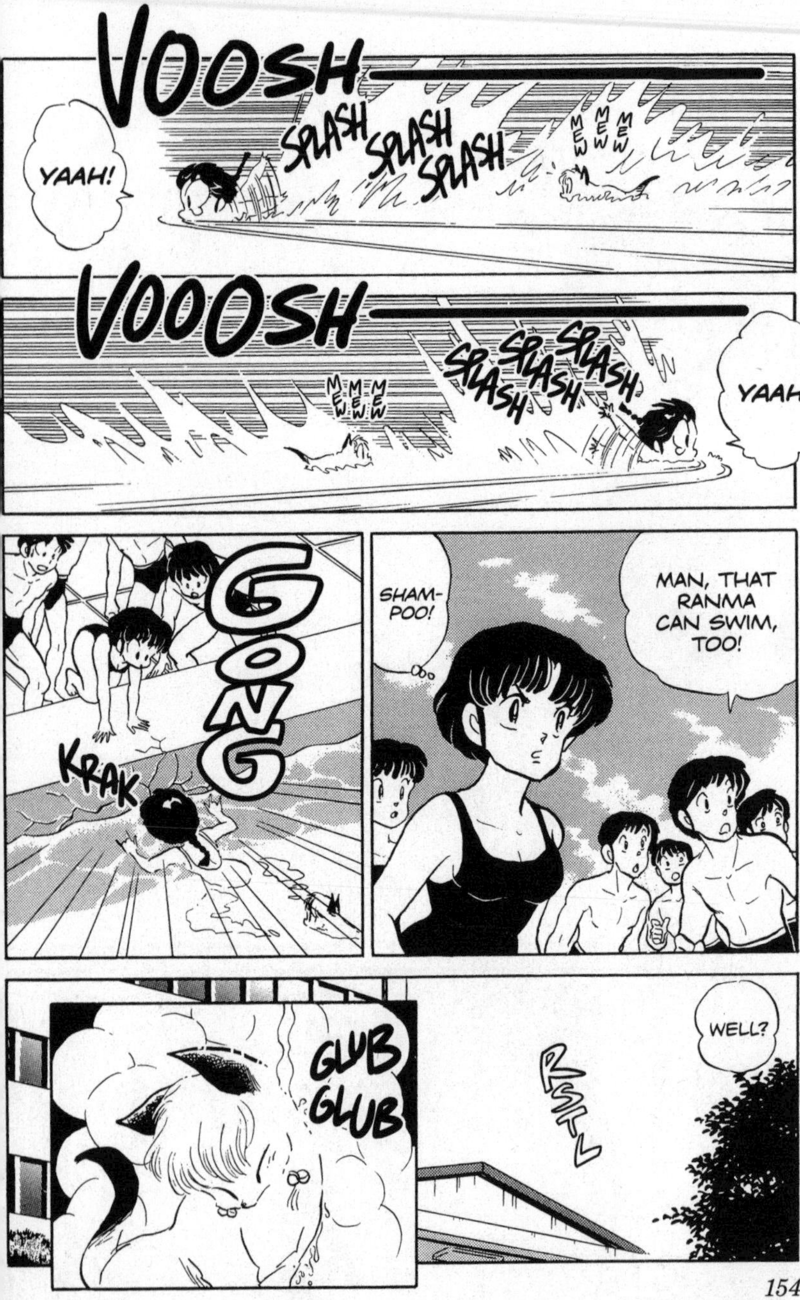
VOOSH
SPLASH SPLASH SPLASH
MEW MEW MEW
YAAH!
VOOOSH
YAAH!
SPLASH SPLASH SPLASH
MEW MEW MEW
MAN, THAT RANMA CAN SWIM, TOO!
SHAM-POO!
GONG
KRAK
WELL?
RSTL
GLUB GLUB

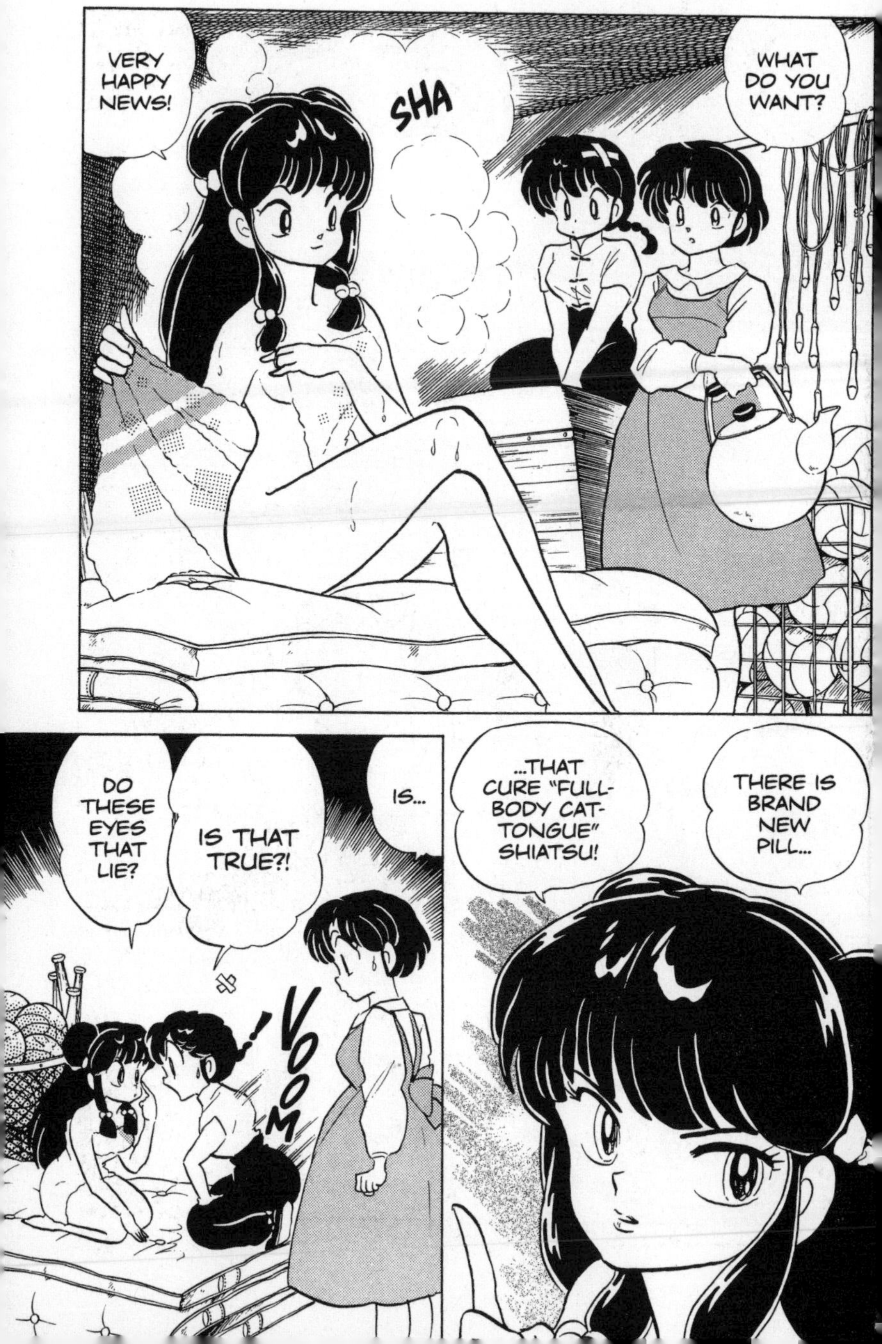
WHAT DO YOU WANT?
SHA
VERY HAPPY NEWS!
THERE IS BRAND NEW PILL...
...THAT CURE "FULL-BODY CAT-TONGUE" SHIATSU!
IS...
IS THAT TRUE?!
!
VOOOM
DO THESE EYES THAT LIE?

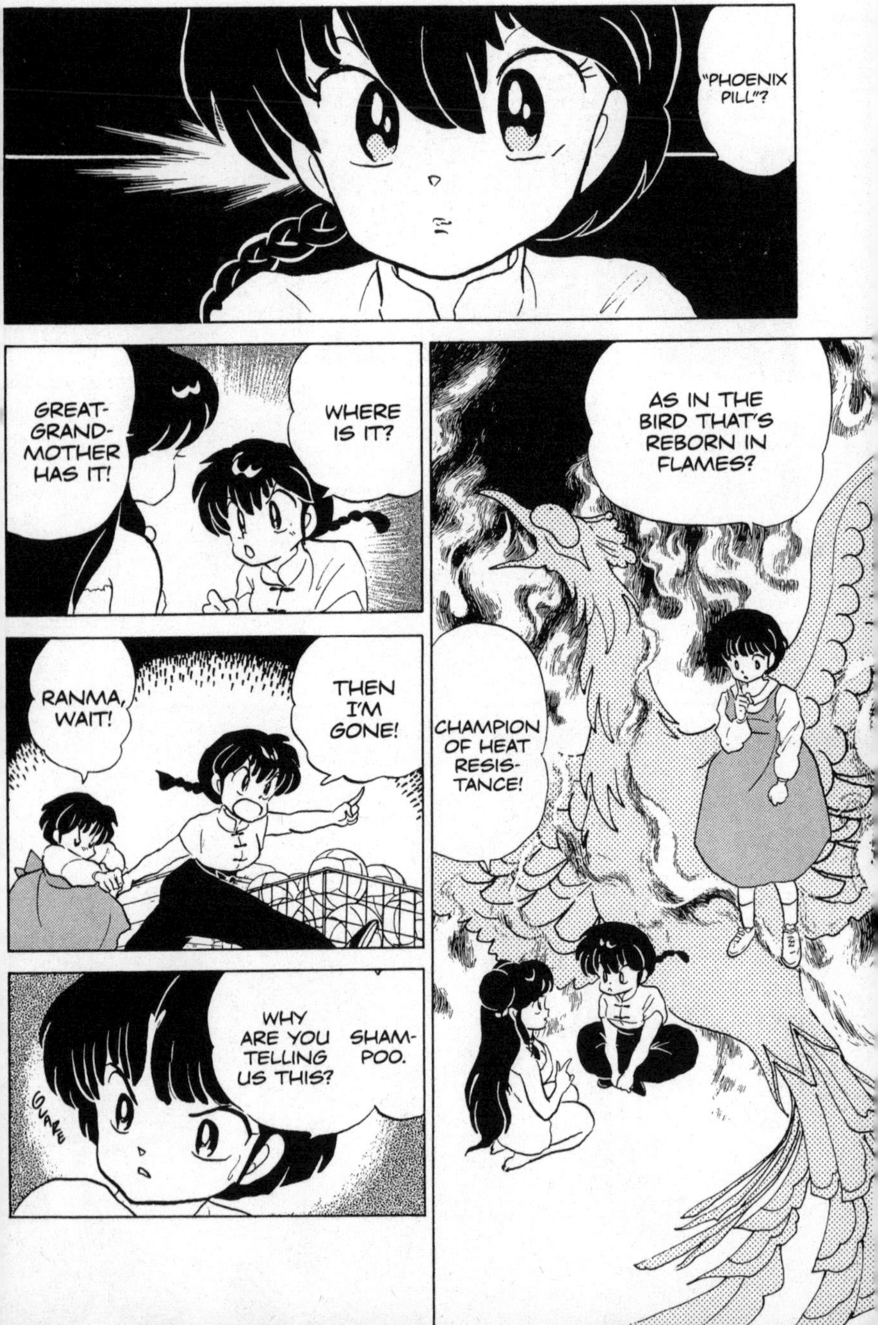
"PHOENIX PILL"?
AS IN THE BIRD THAT'S REBORN IN FLAMES?
CHAMPION OF HEAT RESISTANCE!
WHERE IS IT?
GREAT-GRANDMOTHER HAS IT!
THEN I'M GONE!
RANMA, WAIT!
SHAMPOO.
WHY ARE YOU TELLING US THIS?

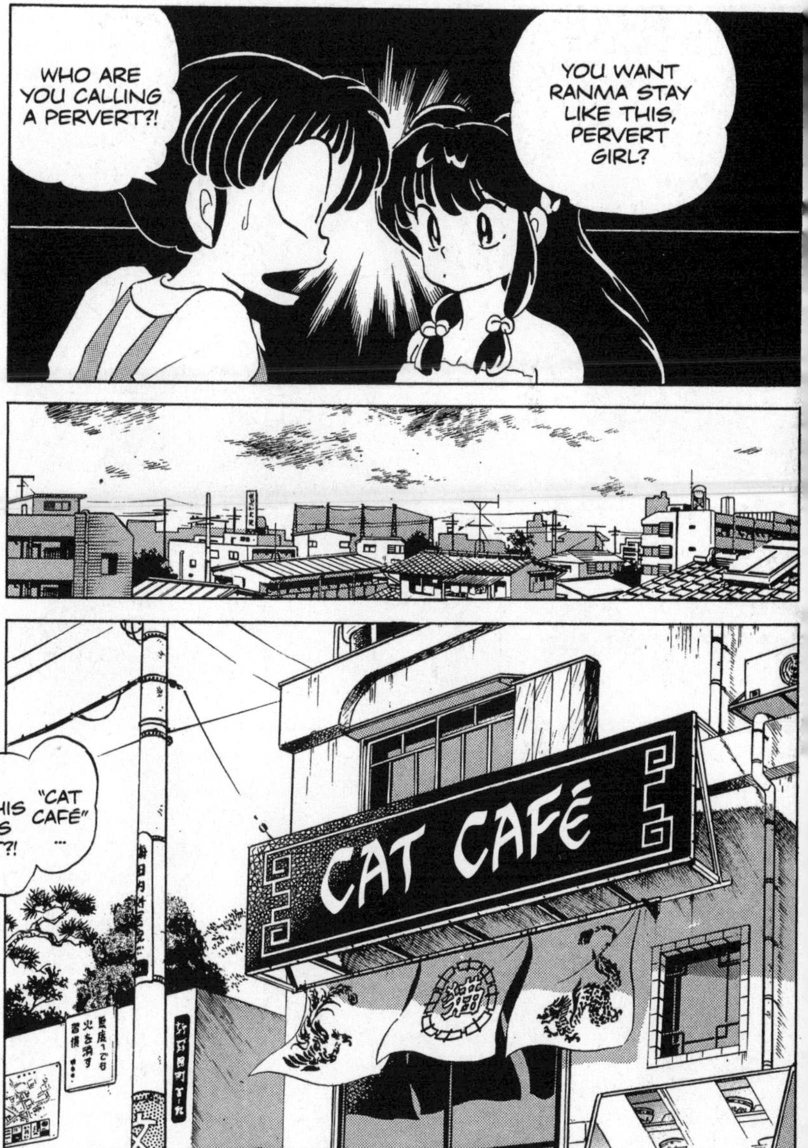
YOU WANT RANMA STAY LIKE THIS, PERVERT GIRL?
WHO ARE YOU CALLING A PERVERT?!
THIS IS IT?! "CAT CAFÉ" ...
CAT CAFÉ

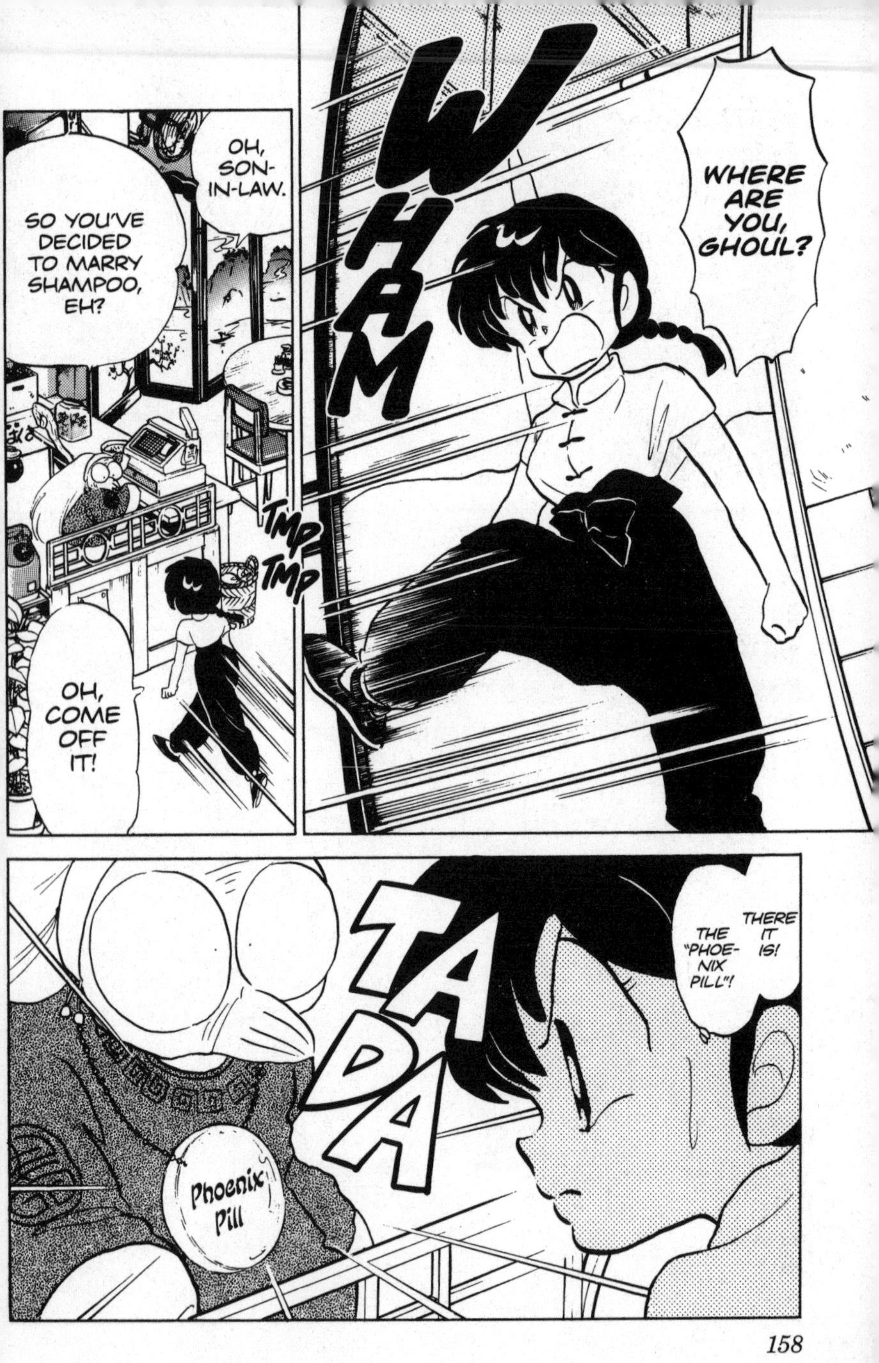
WHERE ARE YOU, GHOUL?
WHAM
OH, SON-IN-LAW.
SO YOU'VE DECIDED TO MARRY SHAMPOO, EH?
TMP TMP
OH, COME OFF IT!
THERE IT IS!
THE "PHOENIX PILL"!
TA DA
Phoenix Pill

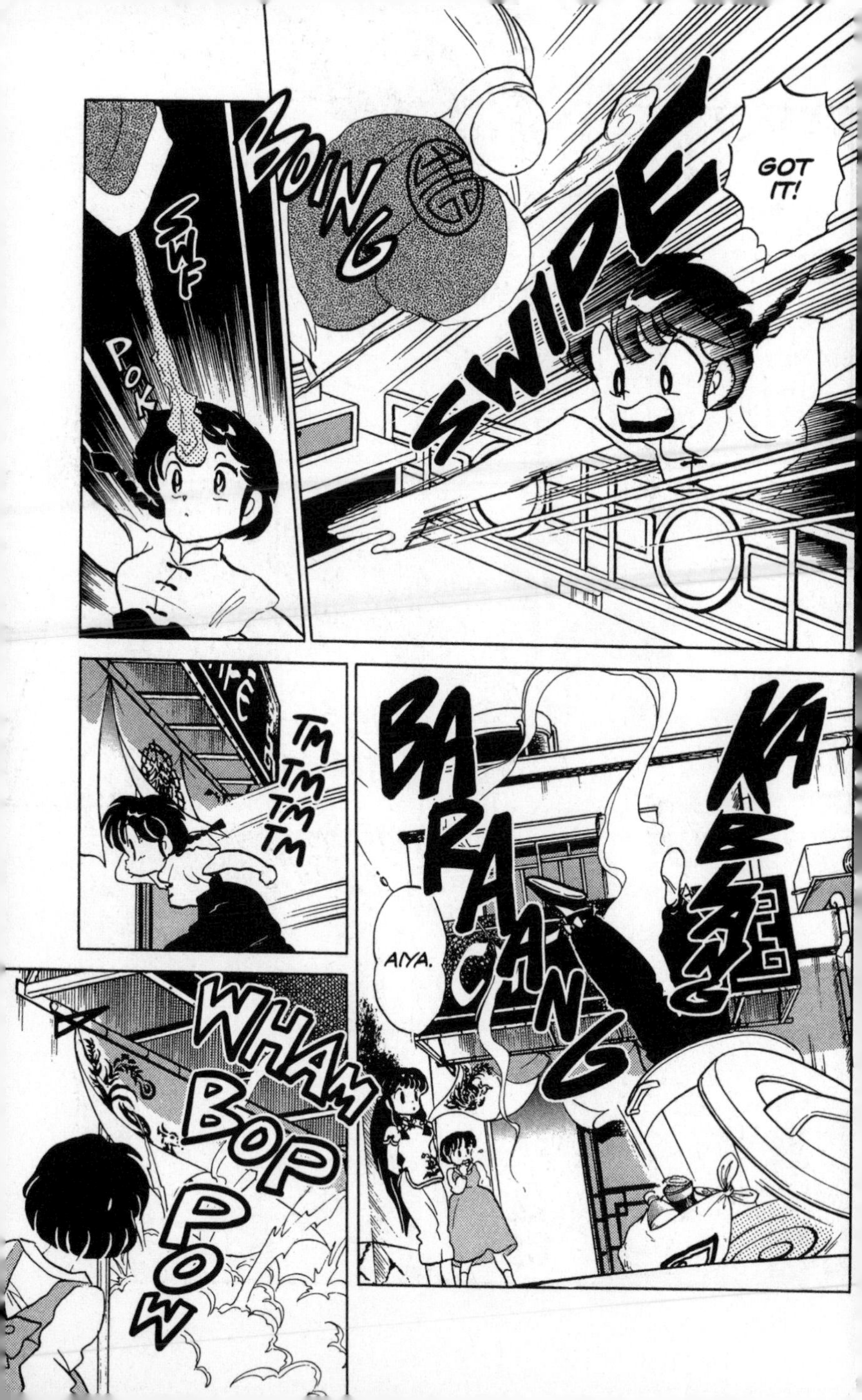
GOT IT!
SWIPE!
BOING
SWF
POK
AIYA.
BA
RA
CANG
TM TM TM TM
WHAM
BOP
POW

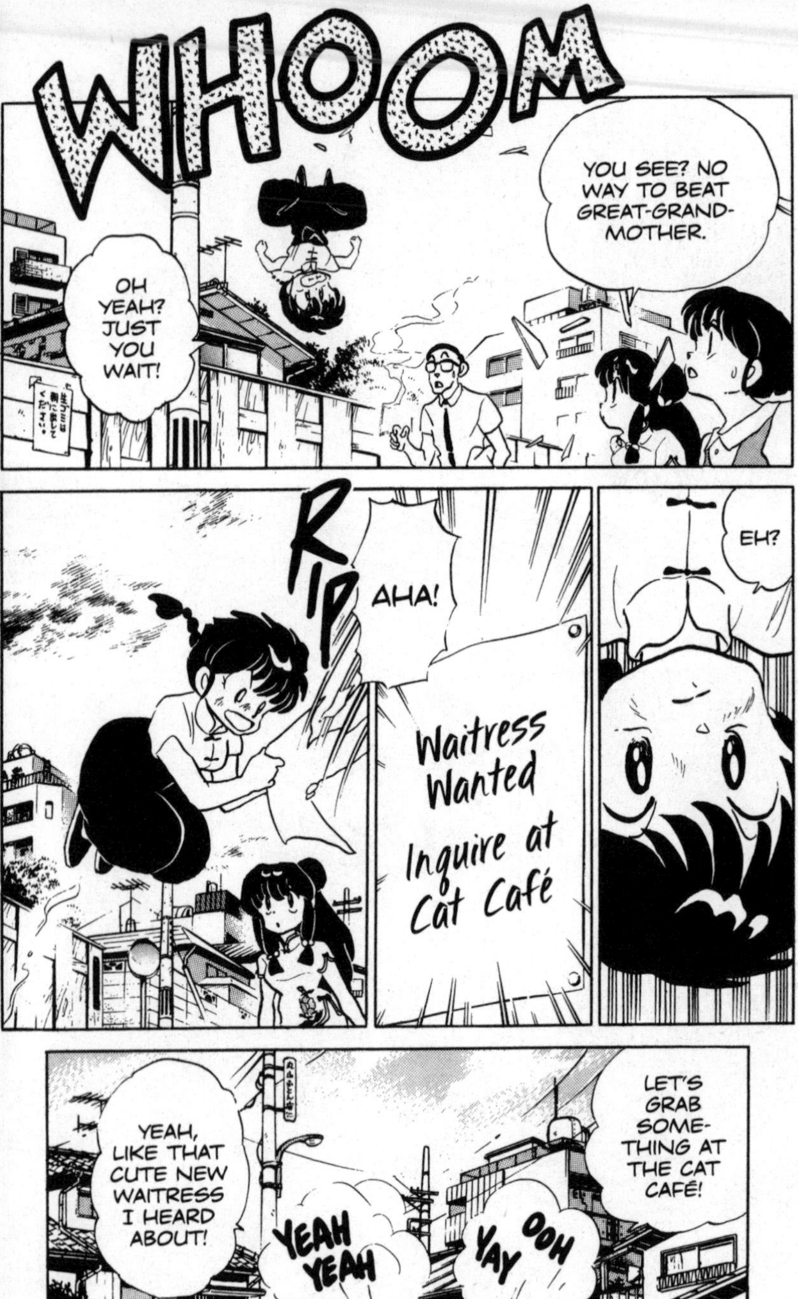
WHOOM
YOU SEE? NO WAY TO BEAT GREAT-GRAND-MOTHER.
OH YEAH? JUST YOU WAIT!
EH?
Waitress Wanted Inquire at Cat Café
RIP
AHA!
LET'S GRAB SOME-THING AT THE CAT CAFÉ!
OOH YAY
YEAH YEAH
YEAH, LIKE THAT CUTE NEW WAITRESS I HEARD ABOUT!

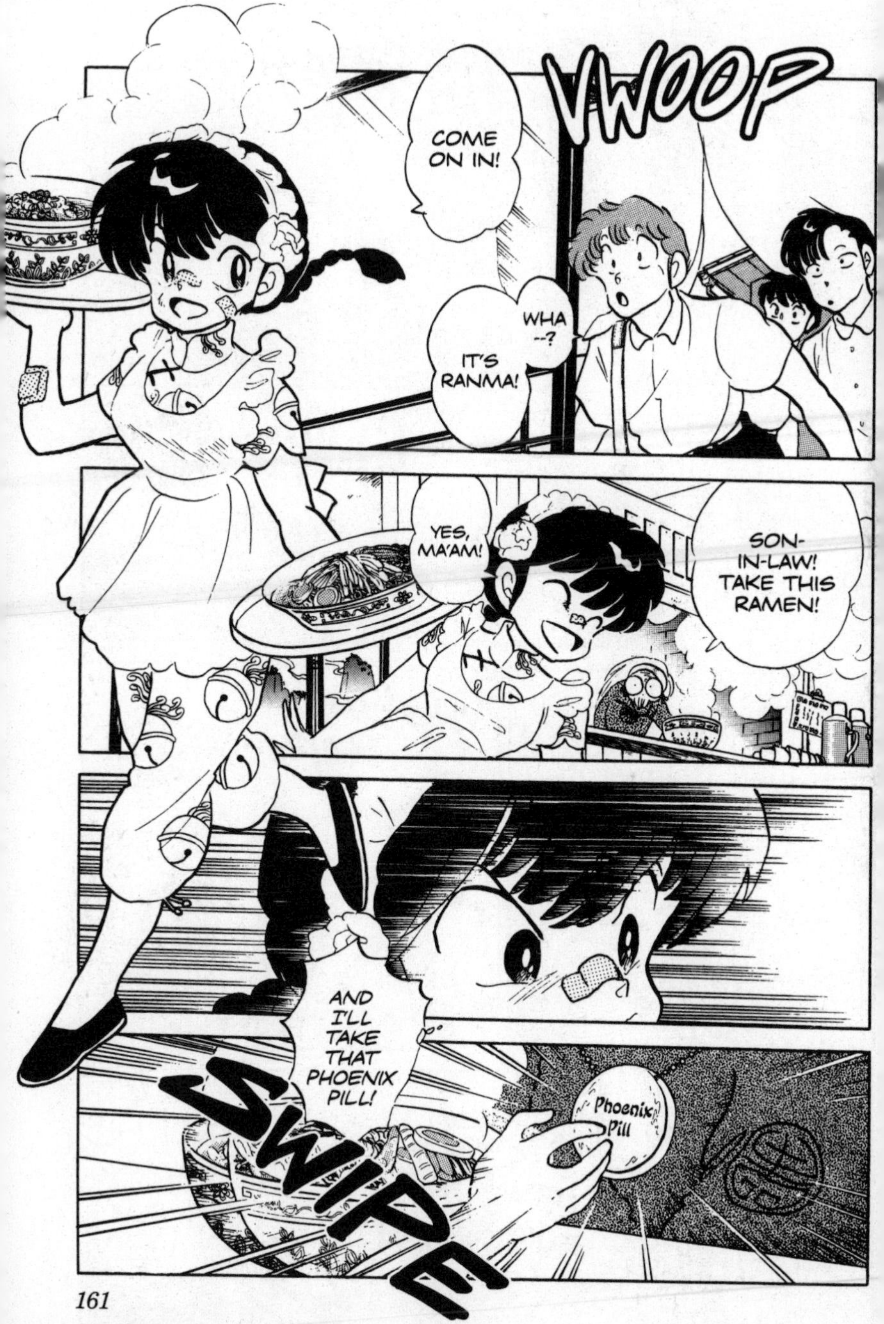
VWOOP
COME ON IN!
WHA --?
IT'S RANMA!
SON-IN-LAW! TAKE THIS RAMEN!
YES, MA'AM!
AND I'LL TAKE THAT PHOENIX PILL!
Phoenix Pill
SWIPE

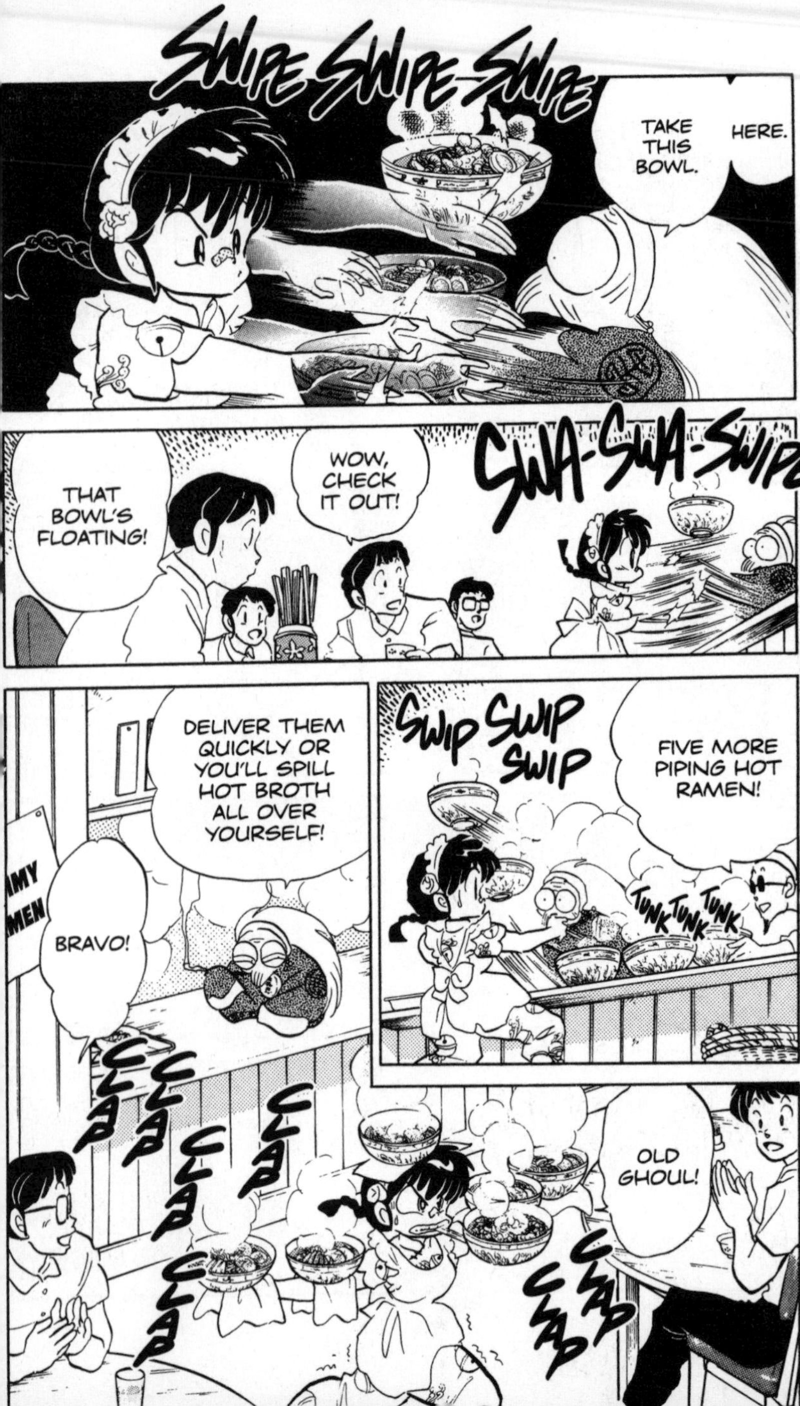
SWIPE SWIPE SWIPE
TAKE THIS BOWL. HERE.
SWA-SWA-SWIPE
WOW, CHECK IT OUT!
THAT BOWL'S FLOATING!
FIVE MORE PIPING HOT RAMEN!
SWIP SWIP SWIP
TUNK TUNK TUNK
DELIVER THEM QUICKLY OR YOU'LL SPILL HOT BROTH ALL OVER YOURSELF!
BRAVO!
OLD GHOUL!
CLAP CLAP CLAP
CLAP CLAP CLAP CLAP CLAP

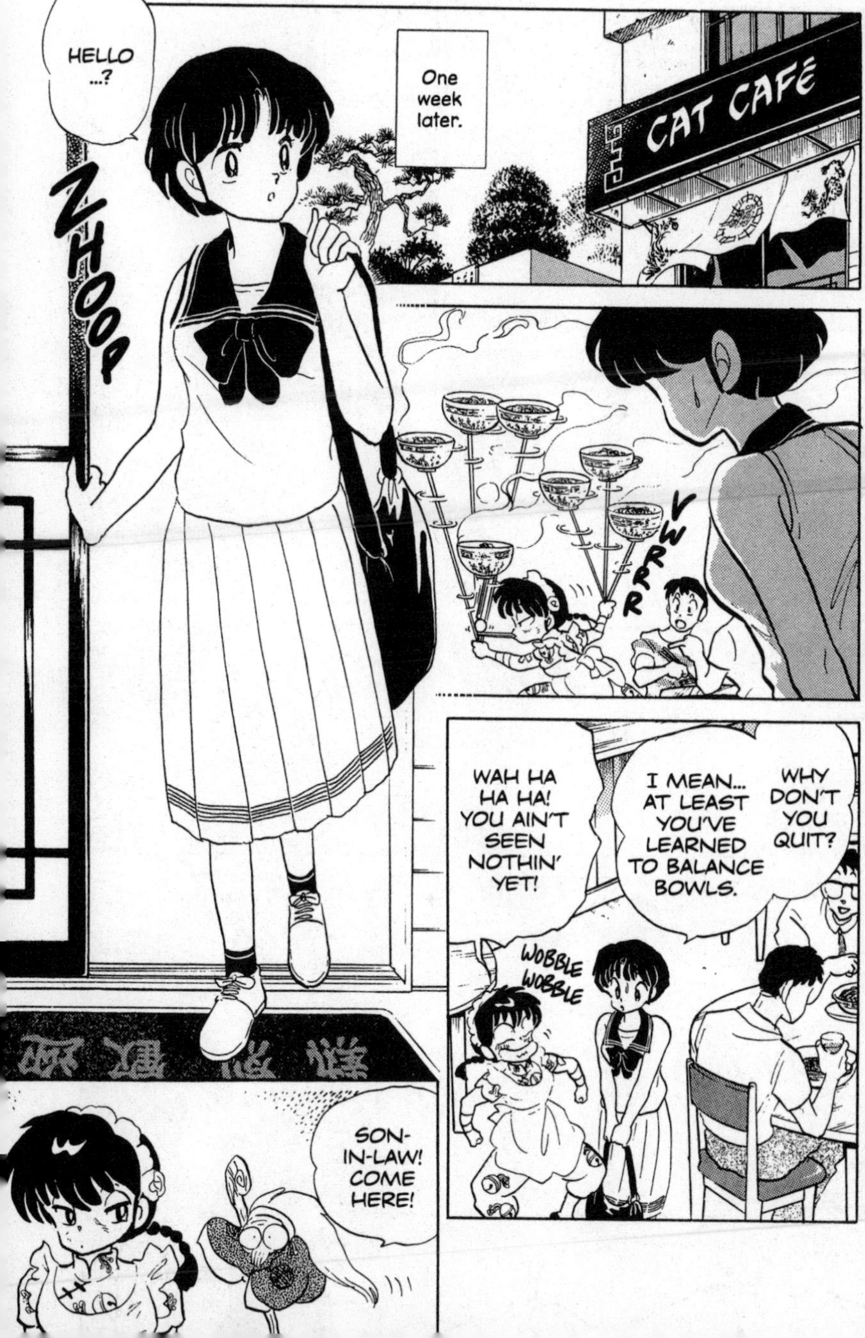
One week later.
CAT CAFÉ
VWRRR
WHY DON'T YOU QUIT?
I MEAN... AT LEAST YOU'VE LEARNED TO BALANCE BOWLS.
WAH HA HA HA! YOU AIN'T SEEN NOTHIN' YET!
WOBBLE WOBBLE
HELLO ...?
ZHOOOP
SON-IN-LAW! COME HERE!

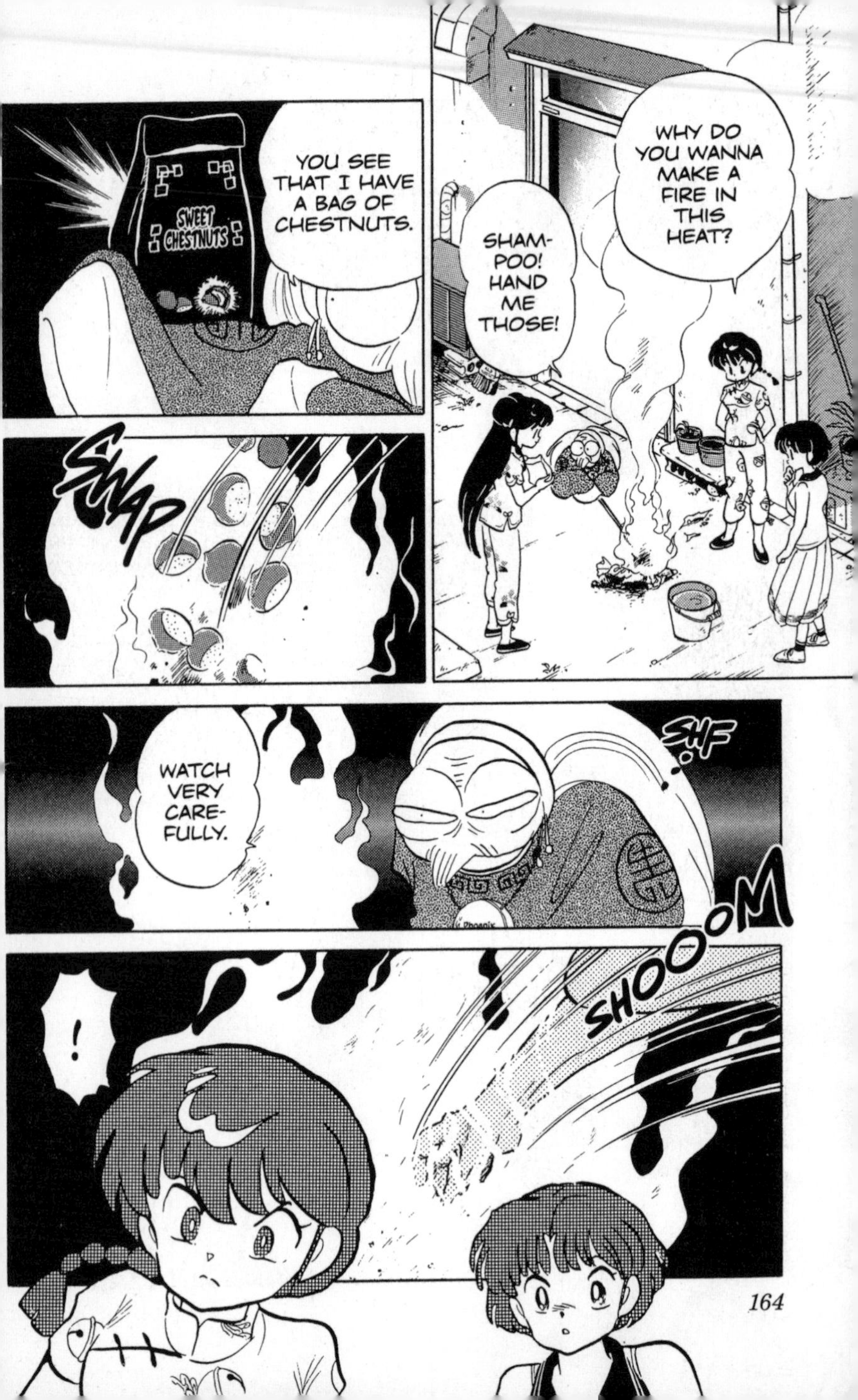
WHY DO YOU WANNA MAKE A FIRE IN THIS HEAT?
SHAM-POO! HAND ME THOSE!
YOU SEE THAT I HAVE A BAG OF CHESTNUTS.
SWEET CHESTNUTS
SWAP
SHF
WATCH VERY CARE-FULLY.
SHOOOOM
!

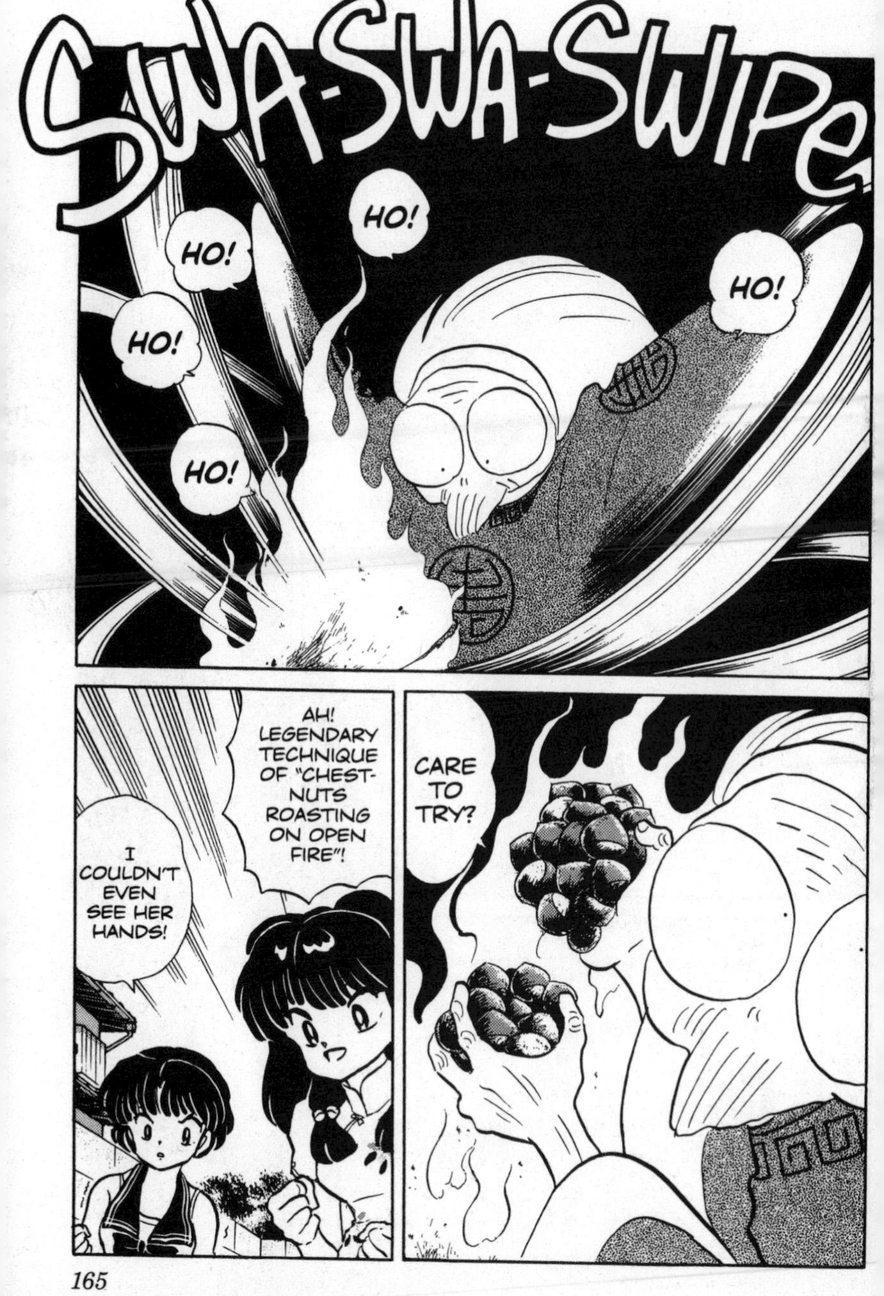
SWA-SWA-SWIPE
HO!
HO!
HO!
HO!
HO!
CARE TO TRY?
AH! LEGENDARY TECHNIQUE OF "CHESTNUTS ROASTING ON OPEN FIRE"!
I COULDN'T EVEN SEE HER HANDS!

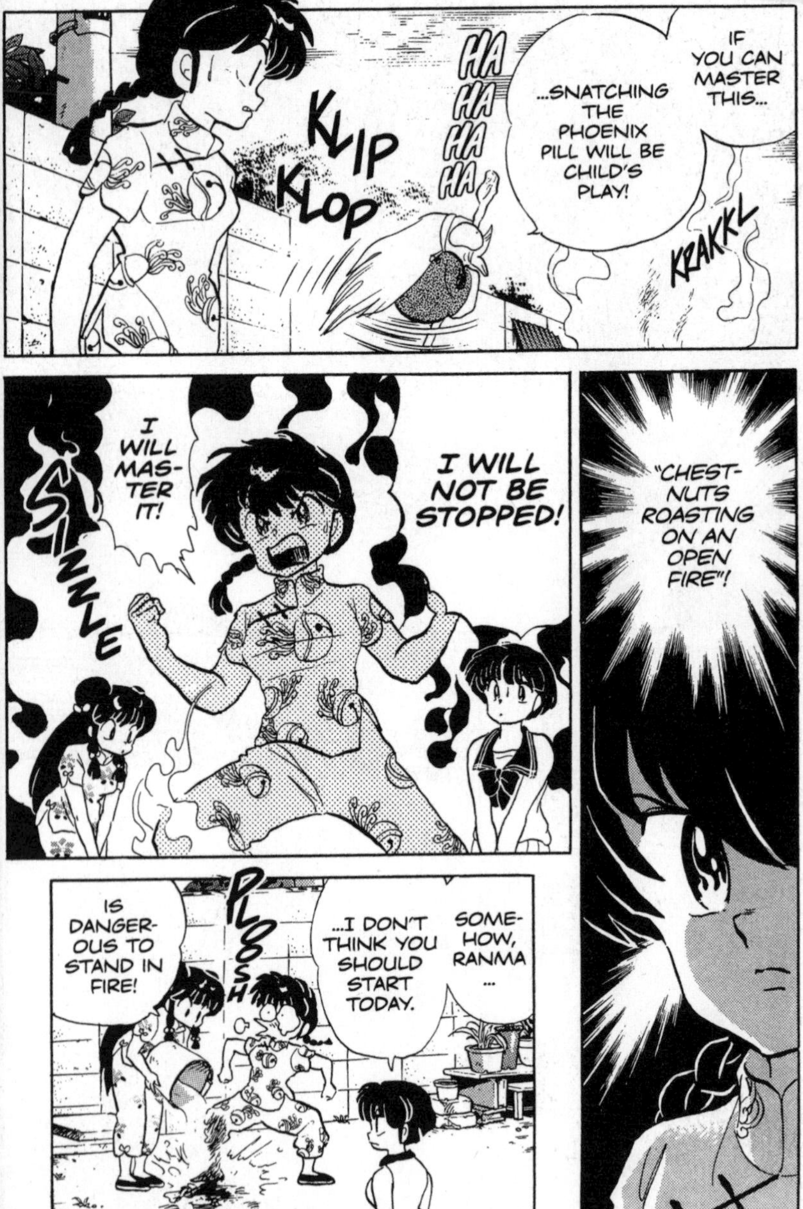
IF YOU CAN MASTER THIS...
...SNATCHING THE PHOENIX PILL WILL BE CHILD'S PLAY!
KRAKKL
HA HA HA HA
KLIP KLOP
"CHEST-NUTS ROASTING ON AN OPEN FIRE"!
I WILL NOT BE STOPPED!
I WILL MAS-TER IT!
SIZZLE
SOME-HOW, RANMA ...
...I DON'T THINK YOU SHOULD START TODAY.
PLOOSH
IS DANGER-OUS TO STAND IN FIRE!

PART 11
ALL'S FAIR AT THE FAIR

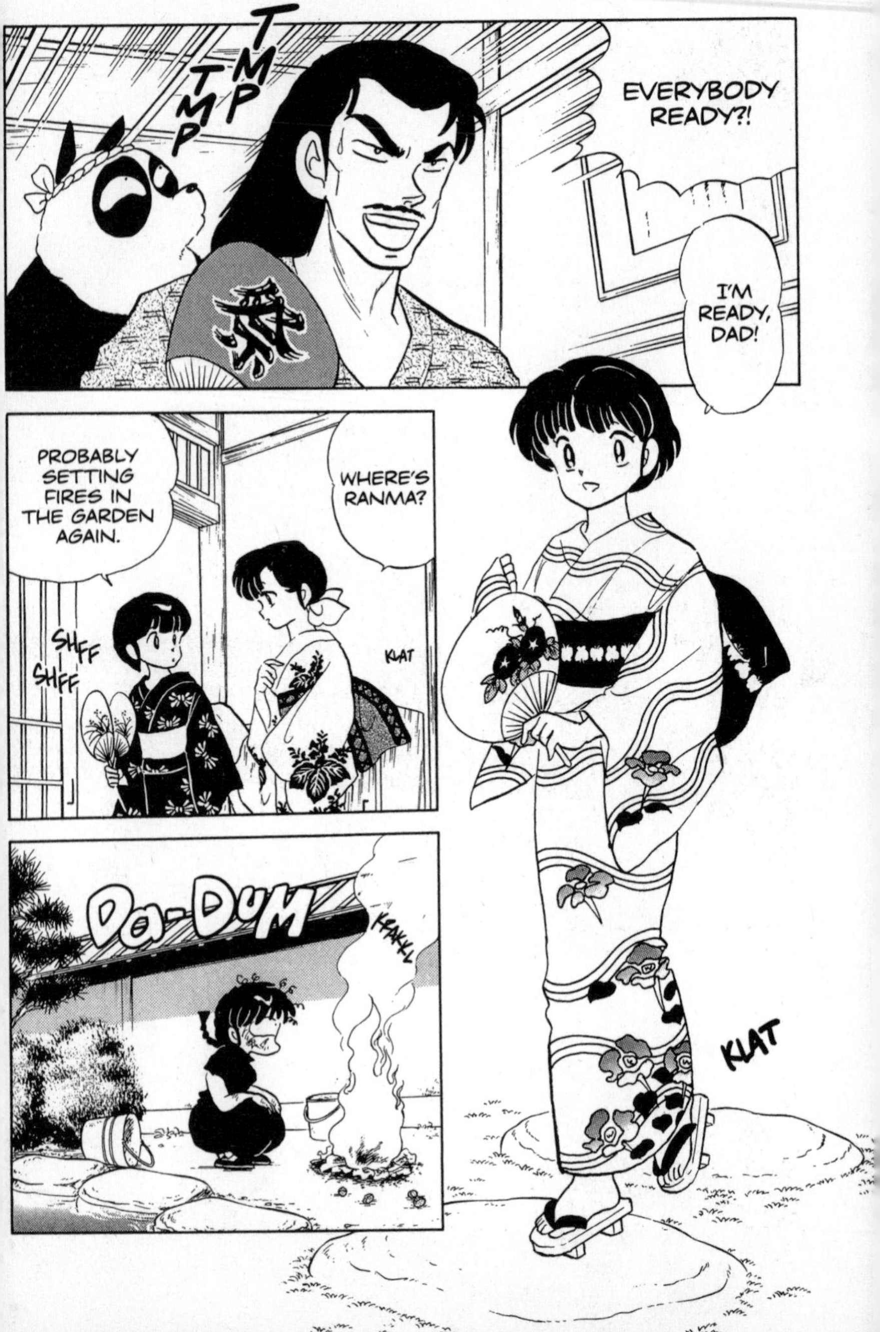
EVERYBODY READY?!
TMP TMP
I'M READY, DAD!
KLAT
WHERE'S RANMA?
PROBABLY SETTING FIRES IN THE GARDEN AGAIN.
KLAT
SHFF SHFF
KRAKKL
DA-DUM

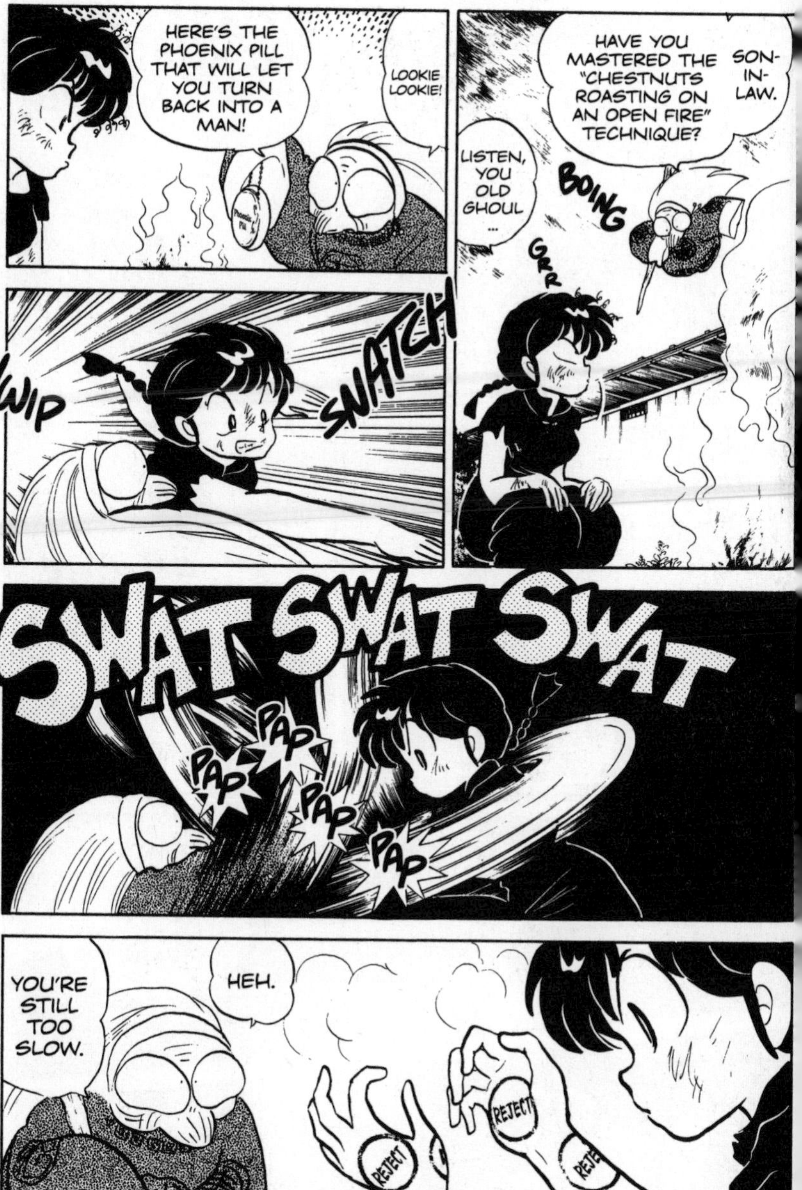
SON-IN-LAW.
HAVE YOU MASTERED THE "CHESTNUTS ROASTING ON AN OPEN FIRE" TECHNIQUE?
BOING
LISTEN, YOU OLD GHOUL ...
GRR
LOOKIE LOOKIE!
HERE'S THE PHOENIX PILL THAT WILL LET YOU TURN BACK INTO A MAN!
SWATCH
VWIP
SWAT SWAT SWAT
PAP
PAP
PAP
PAP
HEH.
YOU'RE STILL TOO SLOW.
REJECT
REJECT
REJE

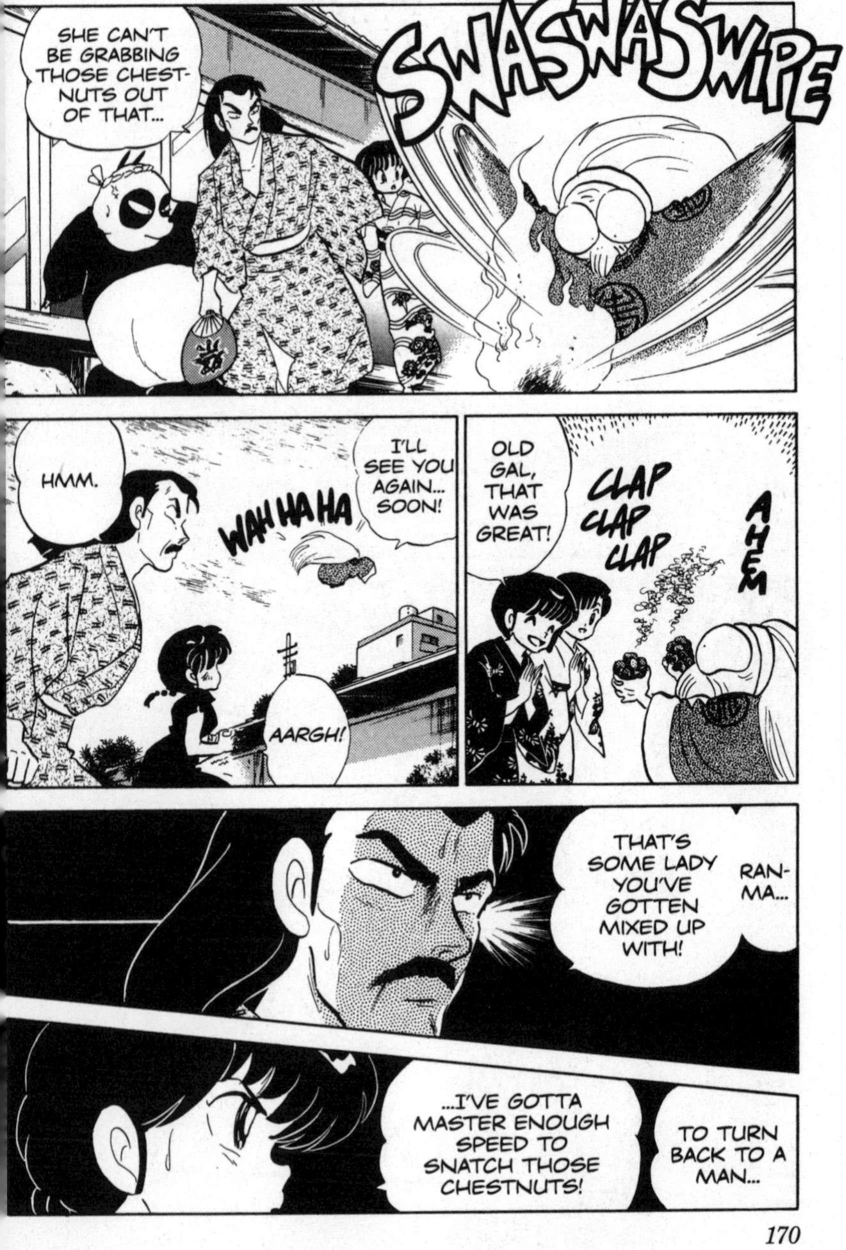
SWASWASWIPE
SHE CAN'T BE GRABBING THOSE CHESTNUTS OUT OF THAT...
OLD GAL, THAT WAS GREAT!
CLAP CLAP CLAP
AHEM
I'LL SEE YOU AGAIN... SOON!
WAH HA HA
HMM.
AARGH!
RAN-MA...
THAT'S SOME LADY YOU'VE GOTTEN MIXED UP WITH!
TO TURN BACK TO A MAN...
...I'VE GOTTA MASTER ENOUGH SPEED TO SNATCH THOSE CHESTNUTS!

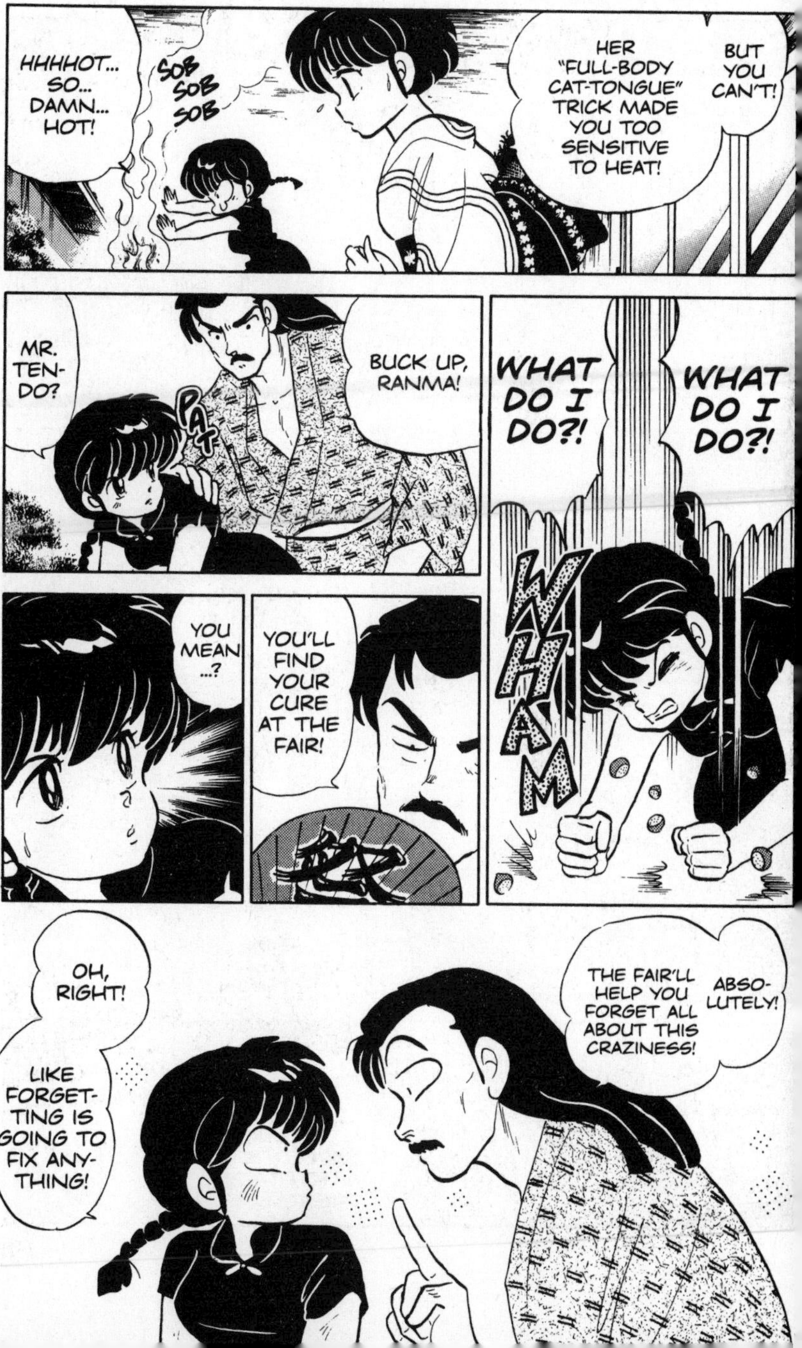
BUT YOU CAN'T!
HER "FULL-BODY CAT-TONGUE" TRICK MADE YOU TOO SENSITIVE TO HEAT!
SOB SOB SOB
HHHHOT... SO... DAMN... HOT!
WHAT DO I DO?!
WHAT DO I DO?!
WHAM
BUCK UP, RANMA!
PAT
MR. TEN-DO?
YOU'LL FIND YOUR CURE AT THE FAIR!
YOU MEAN ...?
ABSO-LUTELY!
THE FAIR'LL HELP YOU FORGET ALL ABOUT THIS CRAZINESS!
OH, RIGHT!
LIKE FORGET-TING IS GOING TO FIX ANY-THING!

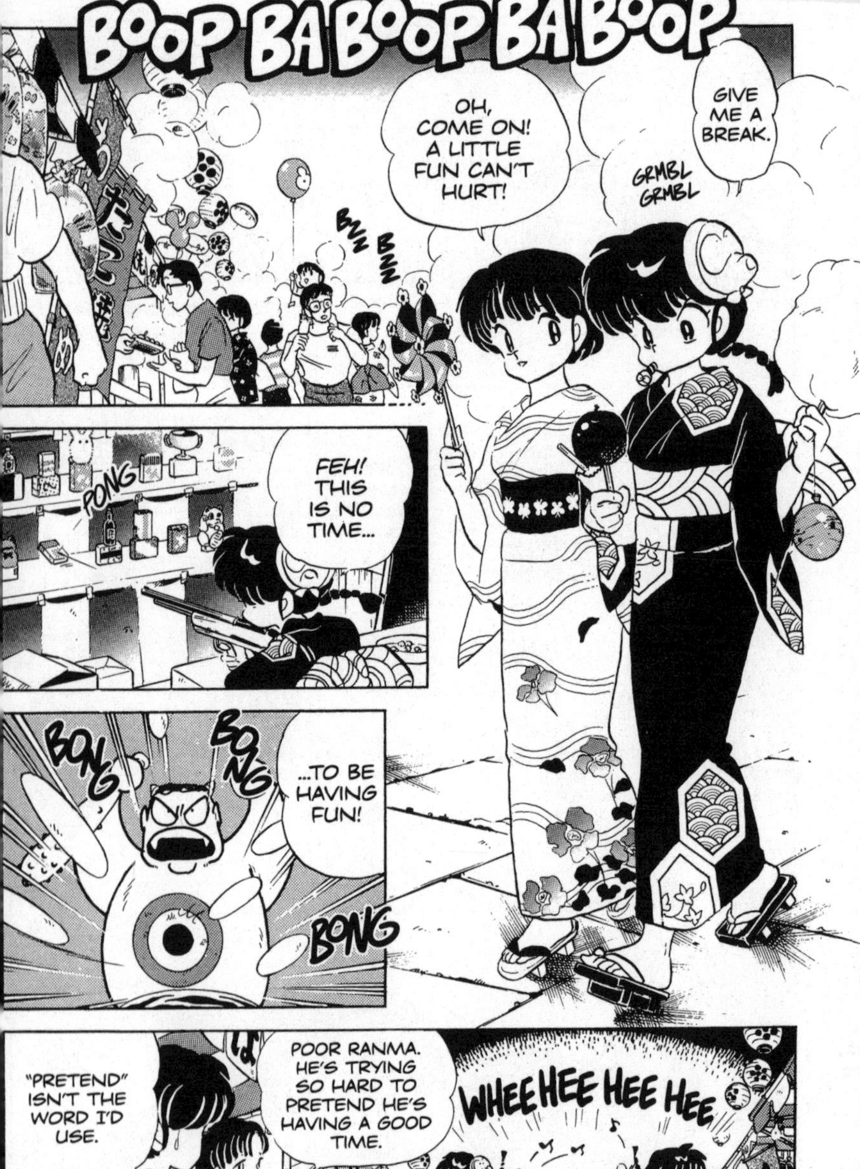

BOOP BA BOOP BA BOOP
GIVE ME A BREAK.
GRMBL GRMBL
OH, COME ON! A LITTLE FUN CAN'T HURT!
BZZ BZZ
FEH! THIS IS NO TIME...
PONG
...TO BE HAVING FUN!
BONG
BONG
BONG
WHEE HEE HEE HEE
POOR RANMA. HE'S TRYING SO HARD TO PRETEND HE'S HAVING A GOOD TIME.
"PRETEND" ISN'T THE WORD I'D USE.

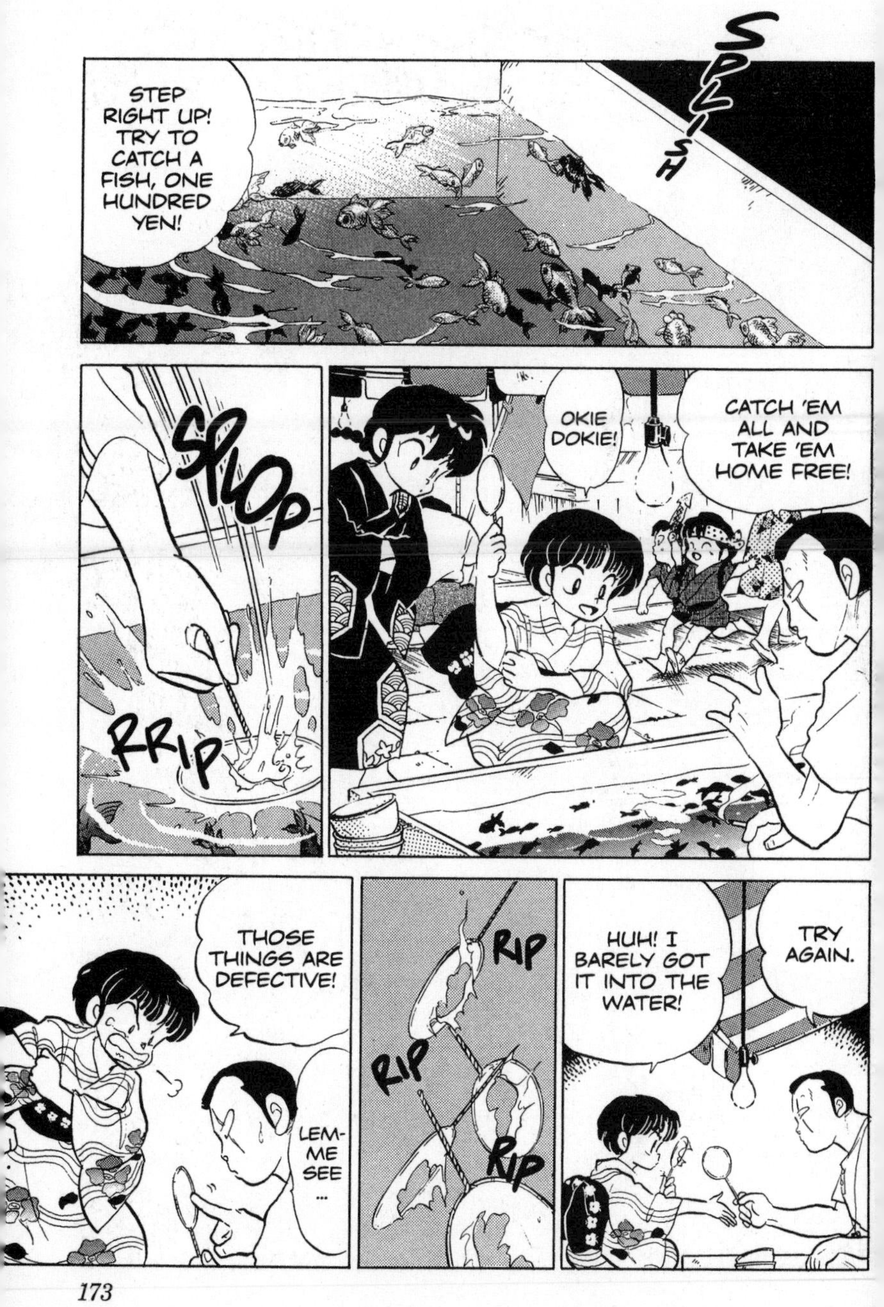
SPLISH
STEP RIGHT UP! TRY TO CATCH A FISH, ONE HUNDRED YEN!
CATCH 'EM ALL AND TAKE 'EM HOME FREE!
OKIE DOKIE!
SPLOP
RRIP
TRY AGAIN.
HUH! I BARELY GOT IT INTO THE WATER!
RIP
RIP
RIP
THOSE THINGS ARE DEFECTIVE!
LEM-ME SEE ...

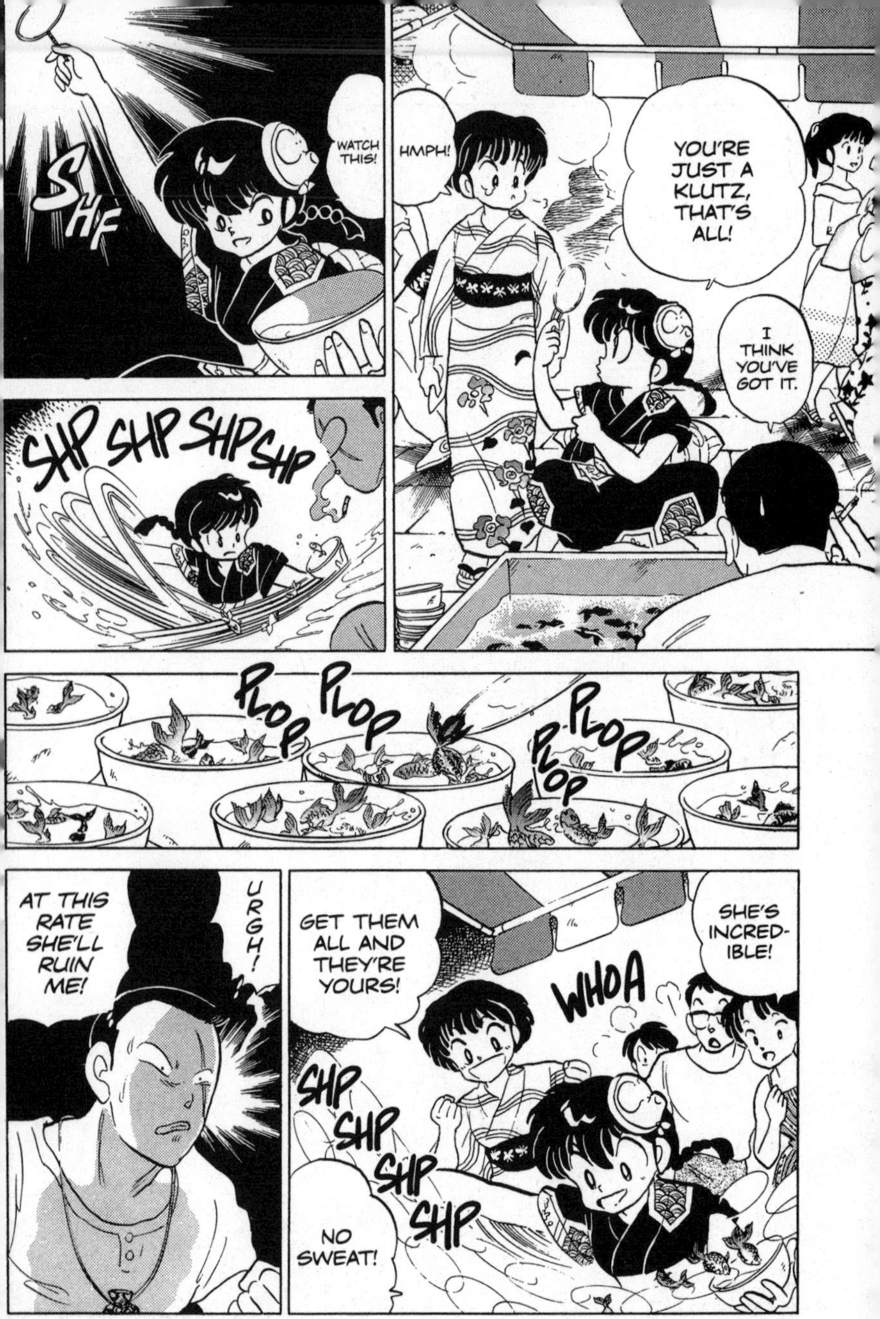
YOU'RE JUST A KLUTZ, THAT'S ALL!
HMPH!
I THINK YOU'VE GOT IT.
WATCH THIS!
SHF
SHP SHP SHP SHP
PLOP
PLOP
PLOP
PLOP
SHE'S INCREDIBLE!
WHOA
GET THEM ALL AND THEY'RE YOURS!
SHP SHP SHP SHP
NO SWEAT!
URGH!
AT THIS RATE SHE'LL RUIN ME!

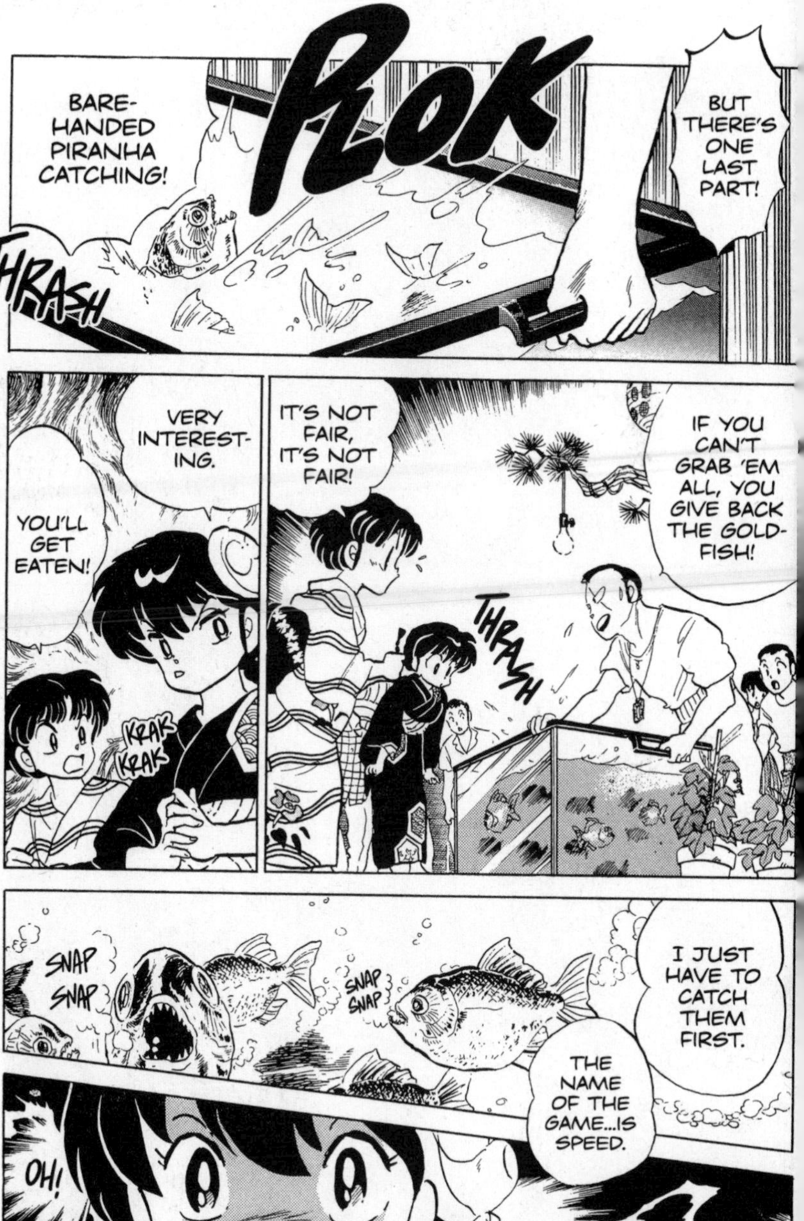
BUT THERE'S ONE LAST PART!
POK
BARE-HANDED PIRANHA CATCHING!
THRASH
IF YOU CAN'T GRAB 'EM ALL, YOU GIVE BACK THE GOLD-FISH!
IT'S NOT FAIR, IT'S NOT FAIR!
THRASH
VERY INTEREST-ING.
YOU'LL GET EATEN!
KRAK KRAK
I JUST HAVE TO CATCH THEM FIRST.
SNAP SNAP
SNAP SNAP
THE NAME OF THE GAME...IS SPEED.
OH!

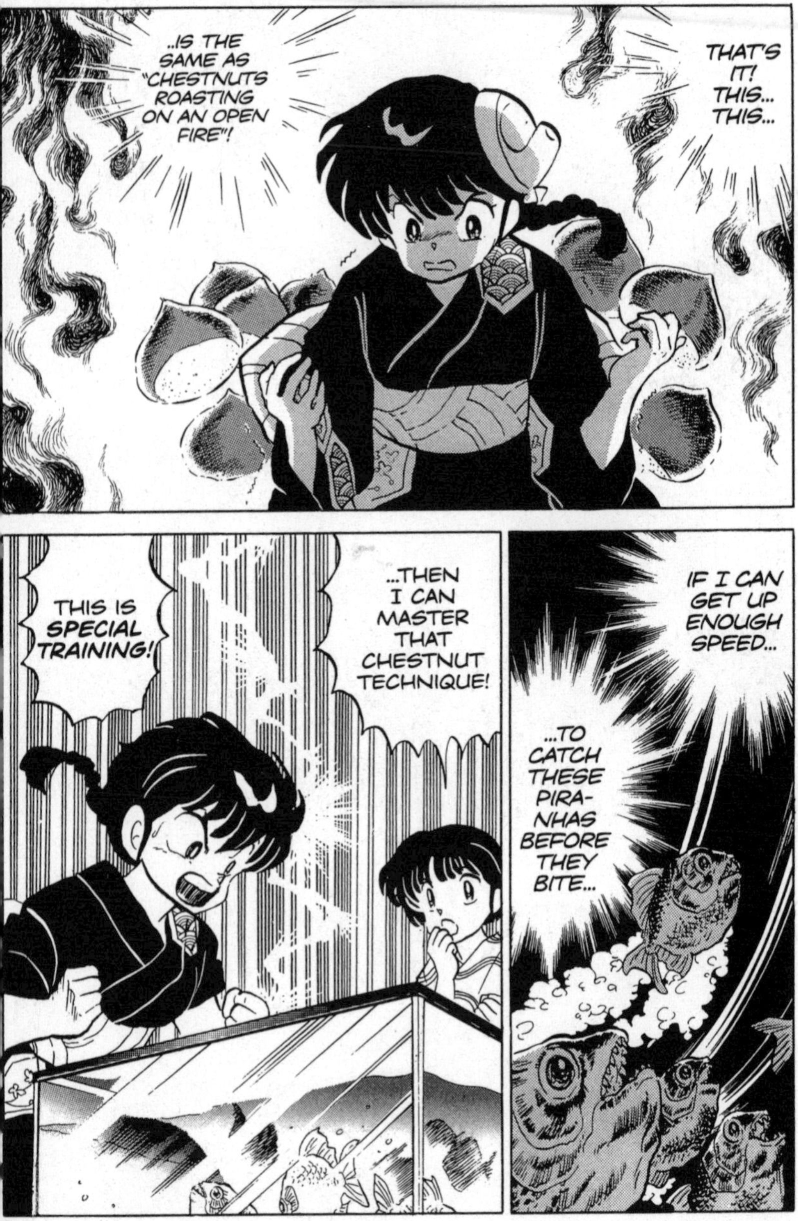
THAT'S IT! THIS... THIS...
..IS THE SAME AS "CHESTNUTS ROASTING ON AN OPEN FIRE"!
IF I CAN GET UP ENOUGH SPEED...
...TO CATCH THESE PIRA-NHAS BEFORE THEY BITE...
...THEN I CAN MASTER THAT CHESTNUT TECHNIQUE!
THIS IS SPECIAL TRAINING!

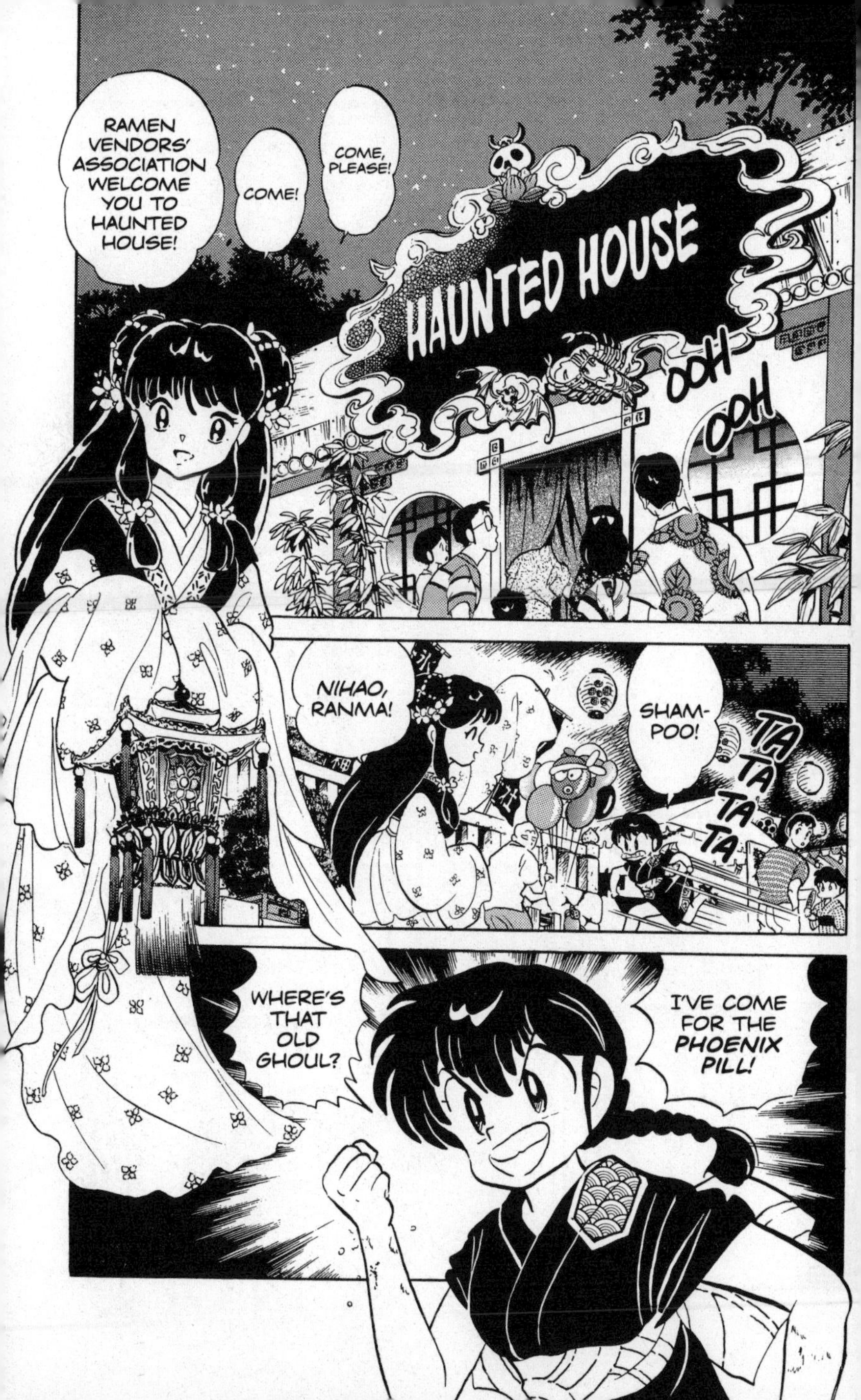
COME, PLEASE!
COME!
RAMEN VENDORS' ASSOCIATION WELCOME YOU TO HAUNTED HOUSE!
HAUNTED HOUSE
OOH
OOH
TA TA TA TA
SHAM-POO!
NIHAO, RANMA!
I'VE COME FOR THE PHOENIX PILL!
WHERE'S THAT OLD GHOUL?

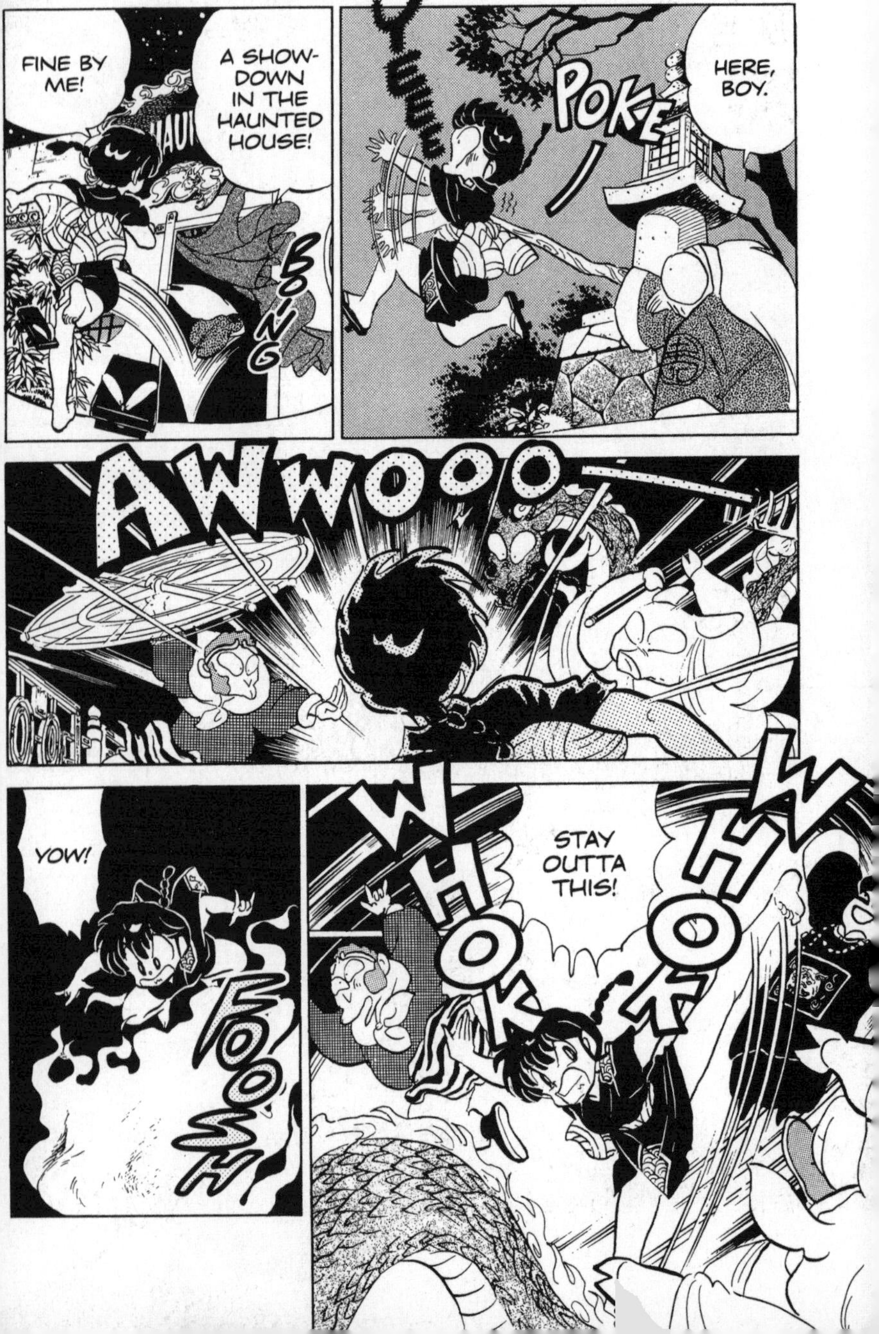
HERE, BOY.
POKE
YEEE
A SHOW-DOWN IN THE HAUNTED HOUSE!
FINE BY ME!
BOING
AWWOOO
WHOK
STAY OUTTA THIS!
WHOK
YOW!
FOOOSH

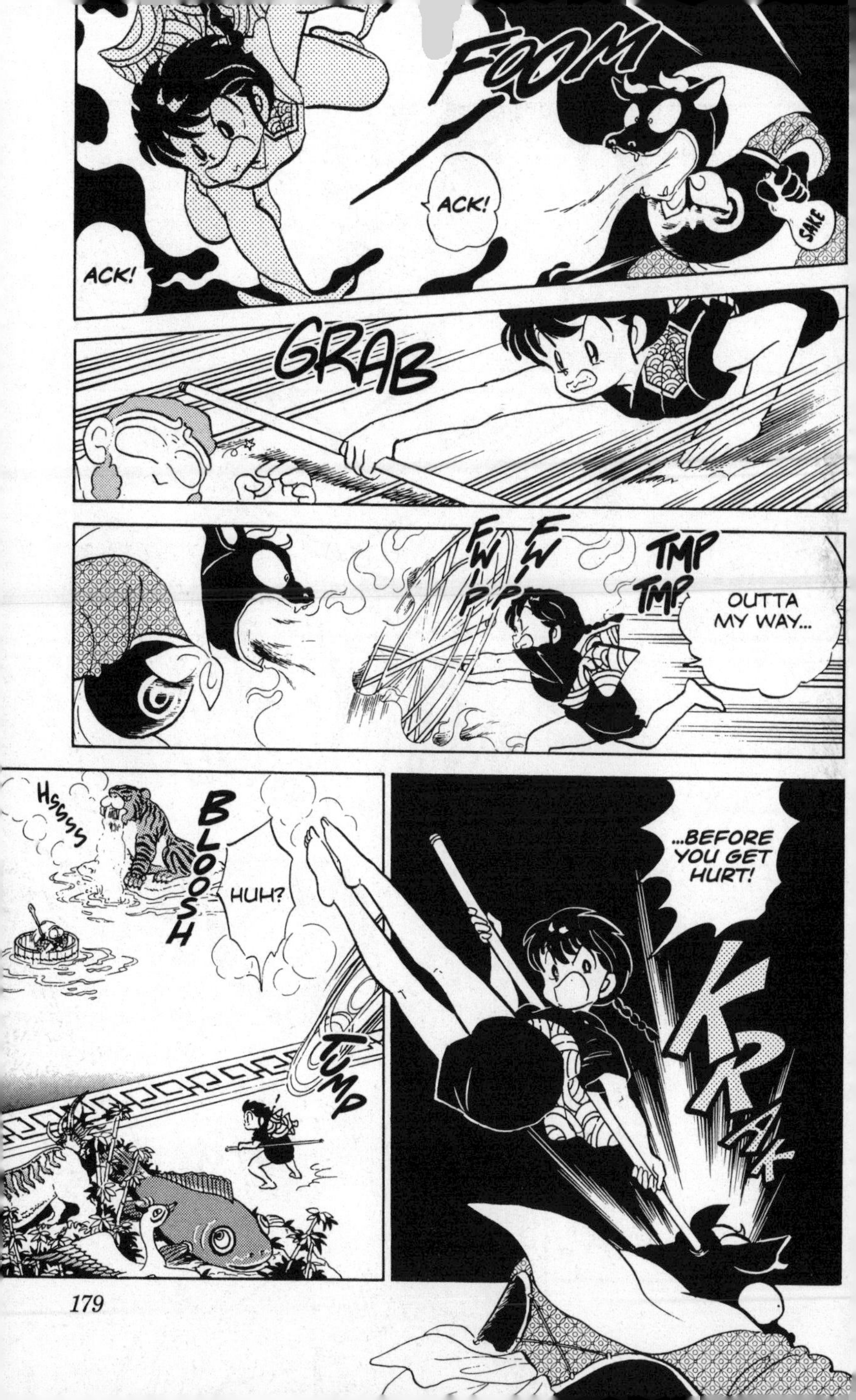
FOOM
SAKE
ACK!
ACK!
GRAB
OUTTA MY WAY...
TMP TMP
FWIP
FWIP
...BEFORE YOU GET HURT!
KRAK
BLOOOSH
HUH?
Hsssss
TUMP

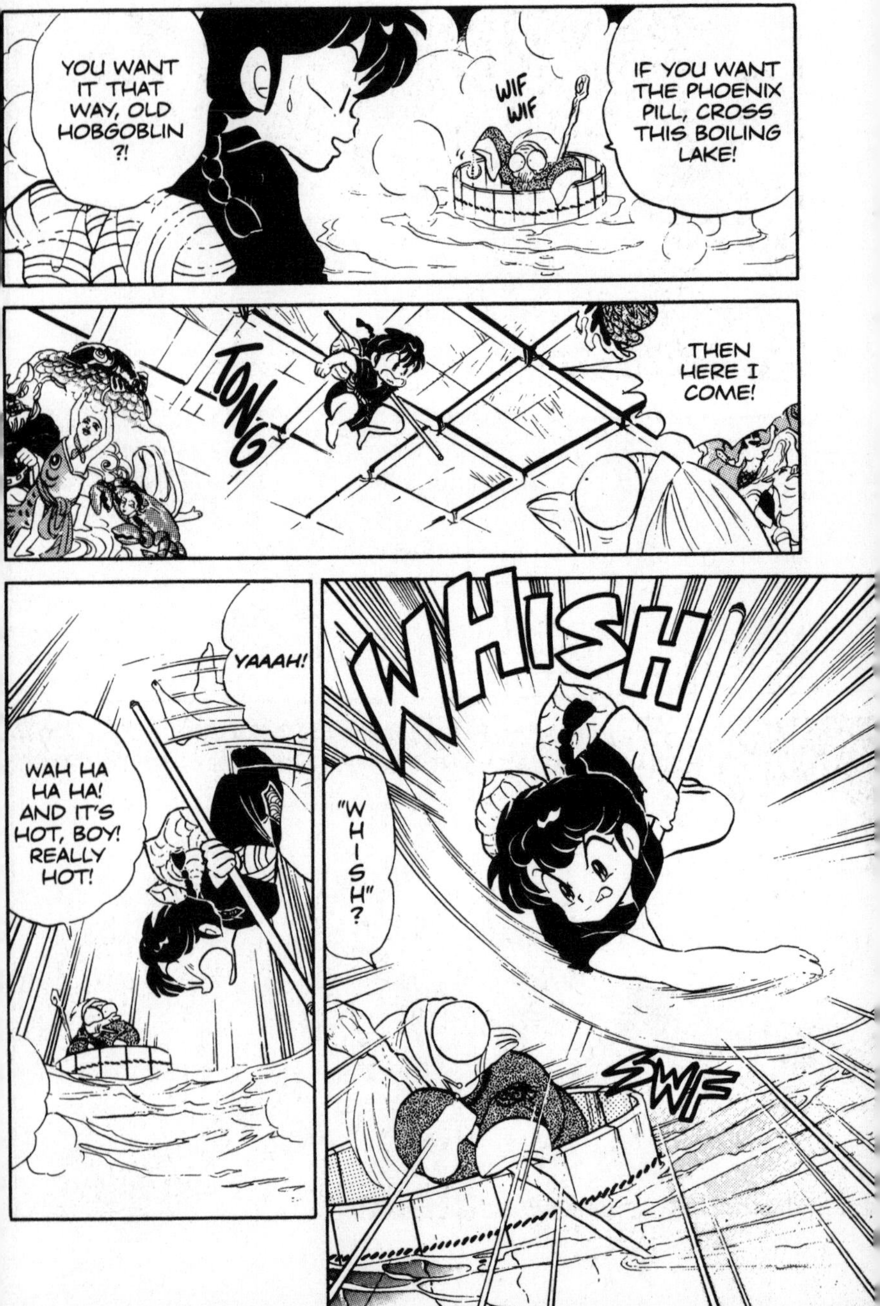
IF YOU WANT THE PHOENIX PILL, CROSS THIS BOILING LAKE!
WIF WIF
YOU WANT IT THAT WAY, OLD HOBGOBLIN ?!
THEN HERE I COME!
TONG
WHISH
"WHISH"?
SWF
YAAAH!
WAH HA HA HA! AND IT'S HOT, BOY! REALLY HOT!

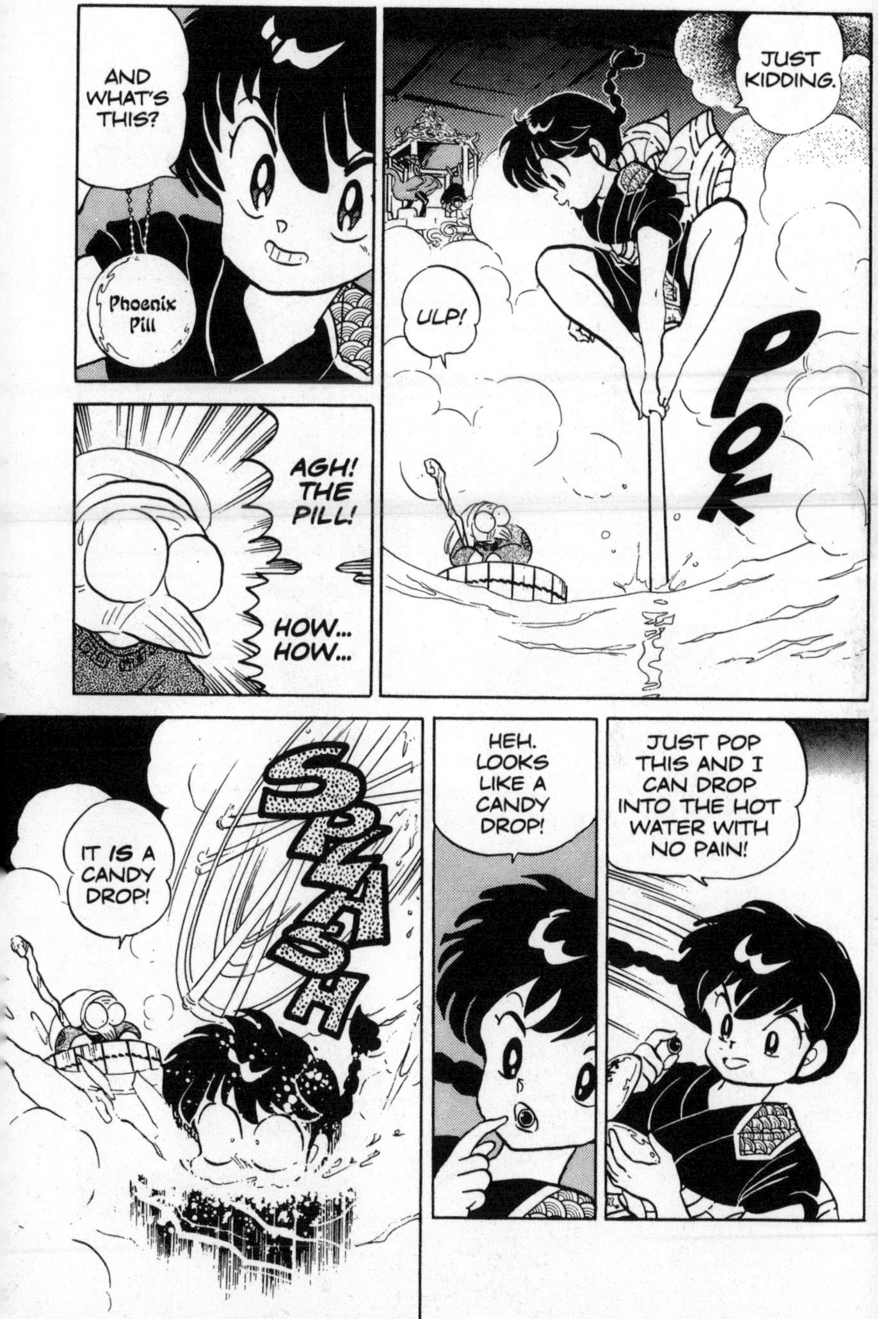
JUST KIDDING.
ULP!
POK
AND WHAT'S THIS?
Phoenix Pill
AGH! THE PILL!
HOW... HOW...
JUST POP THIS AND I CAN DROP INTO THE HOT WATER WITH NO PAIN!
HEH. LOOKS LIKE A CANDY DROP!
IT IS A CANDY DROP!
SPLASH

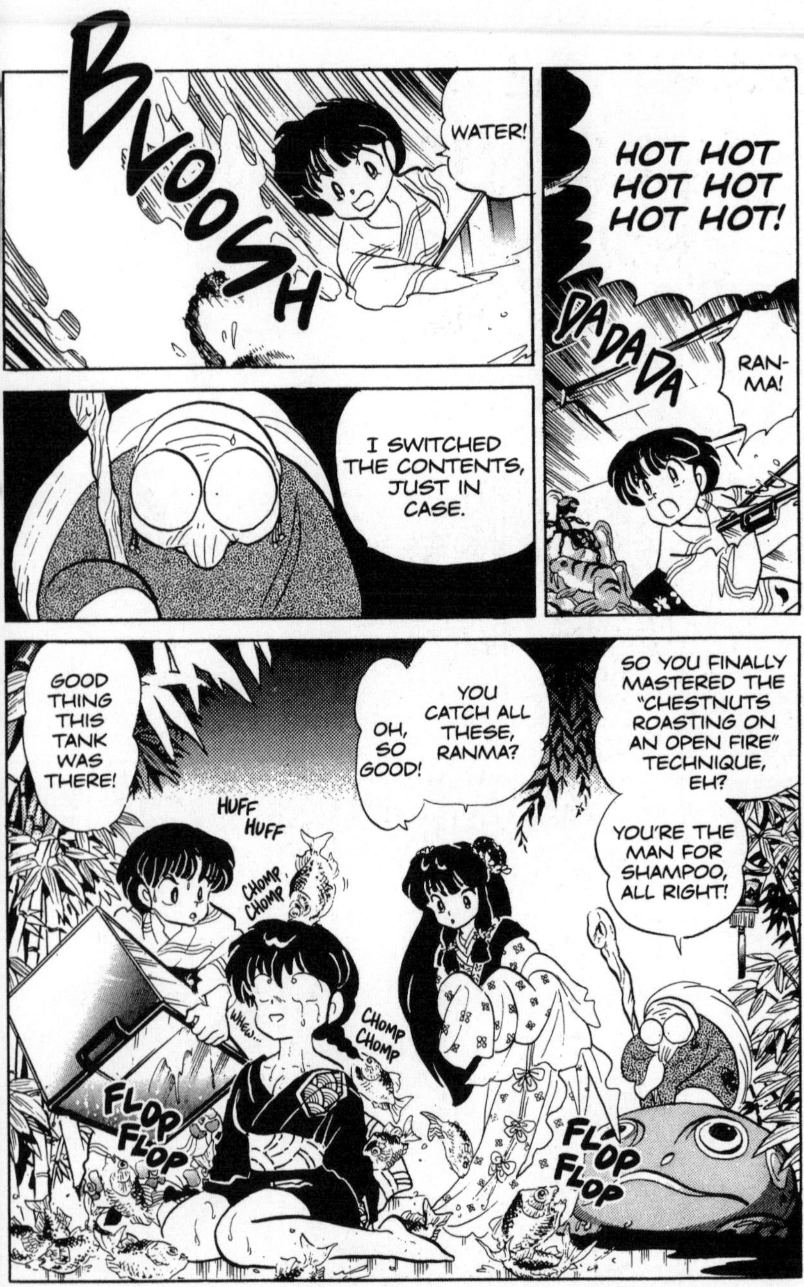
HOT HOT HOT HOT HOT HOT!
BVOOSH
WATER!
DADADA
RAN-MA!
I SWITCHED THE CONTENTS, JUST IN CASE.
SO YOU FINALLY MASTERED THE "CHESTNUTS ROASTING ON AN OPEN FIRE" TECHNIQUE, EH?
YOU'RE THE MAN FOR SHAMPOO, ALL RIGHT!
YOU CATCH ALL THESE, RANMA?
OH, SO GOOD!
GOOD THING THIS TANK WAS THERE!
HUFF HUFF
CHOMP CHOMP
WHEW...
CHOMP CHOMP
FLOP FLOP
FLOP FLOP

PART 12
WAR OF THE MELONS

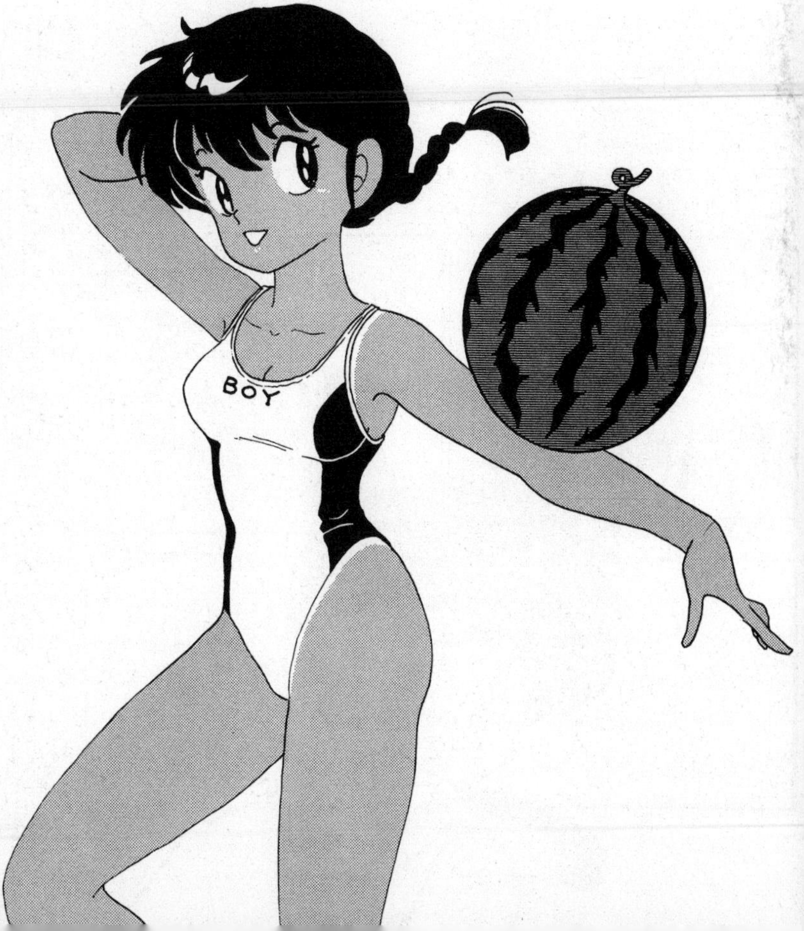
BOY

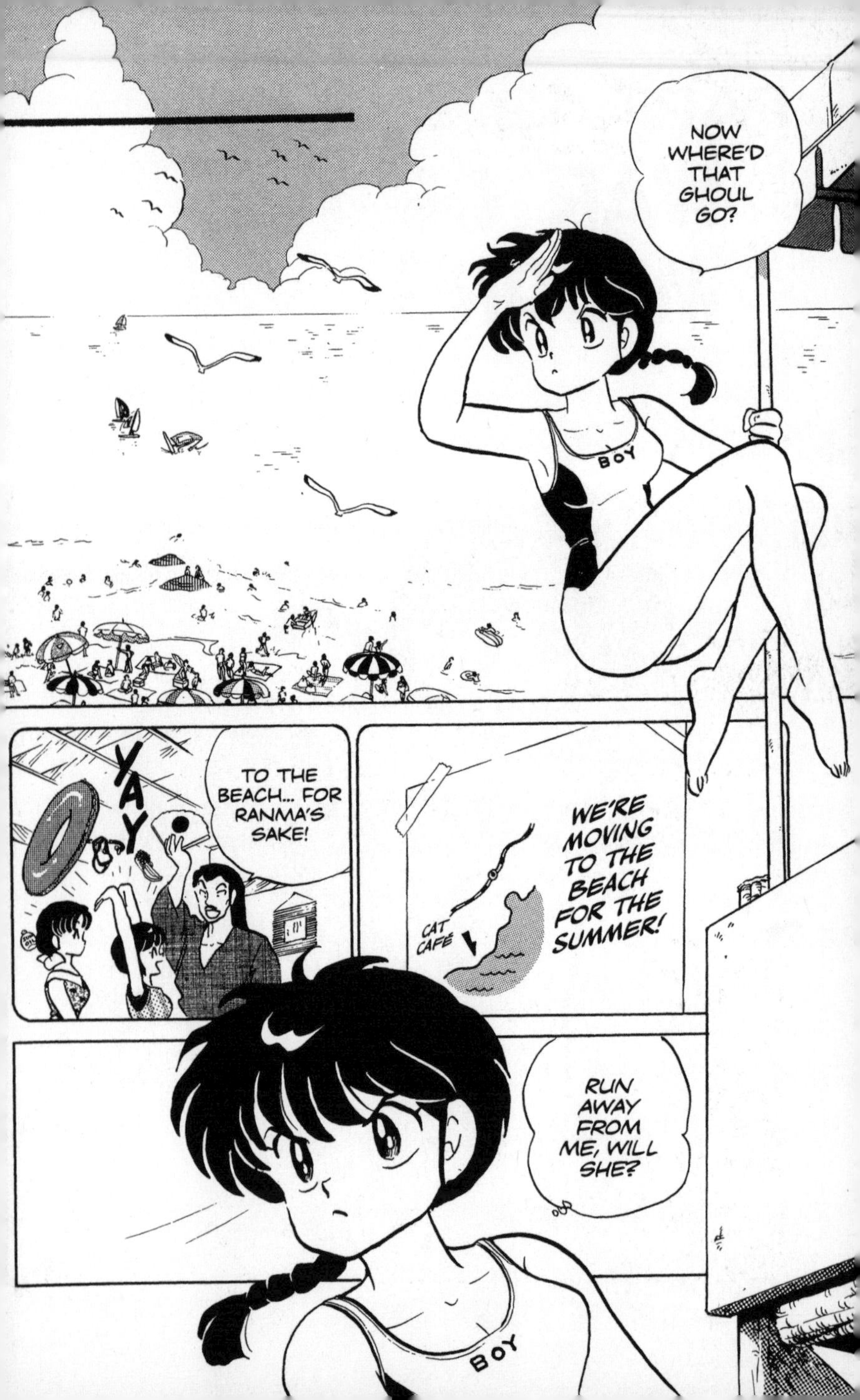
NOW WHERE'D THAT GHOUL GO?
BOY
CAT CAFÉ
WE'RE MOVING TO THE BEACH FOR THE SUMMER!
YAY
TO THE BEACH... FOR RANMA'S SAKE!
RUN AWAY FROM ME, WILL SHE?
BOY

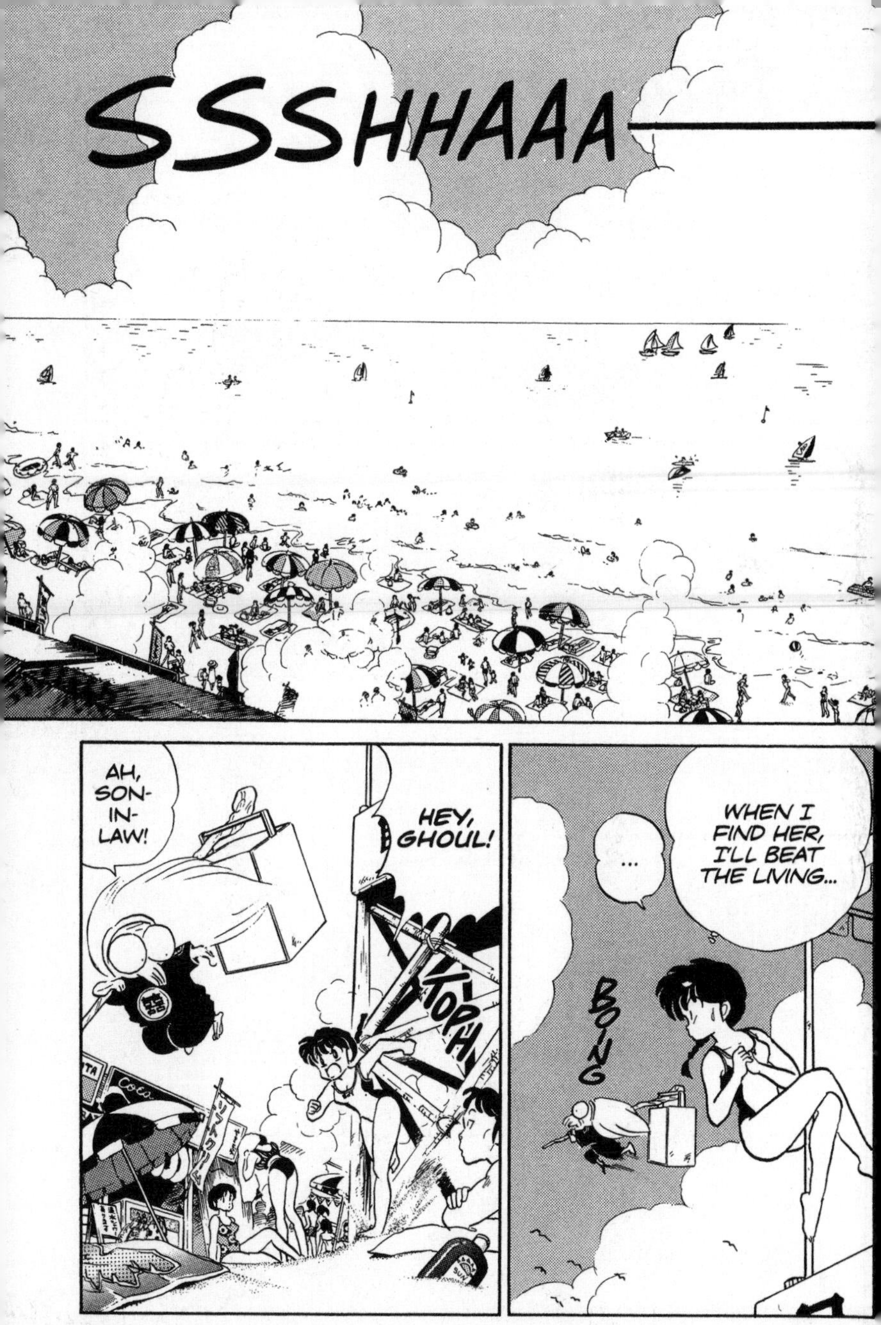
SSSHHAAA
WHEN I FIND HER, I'LL BEAT THE LIVING...
...
BOING
HEY, GHOUL!
AH, SON-IN-LAW!
KTOPH

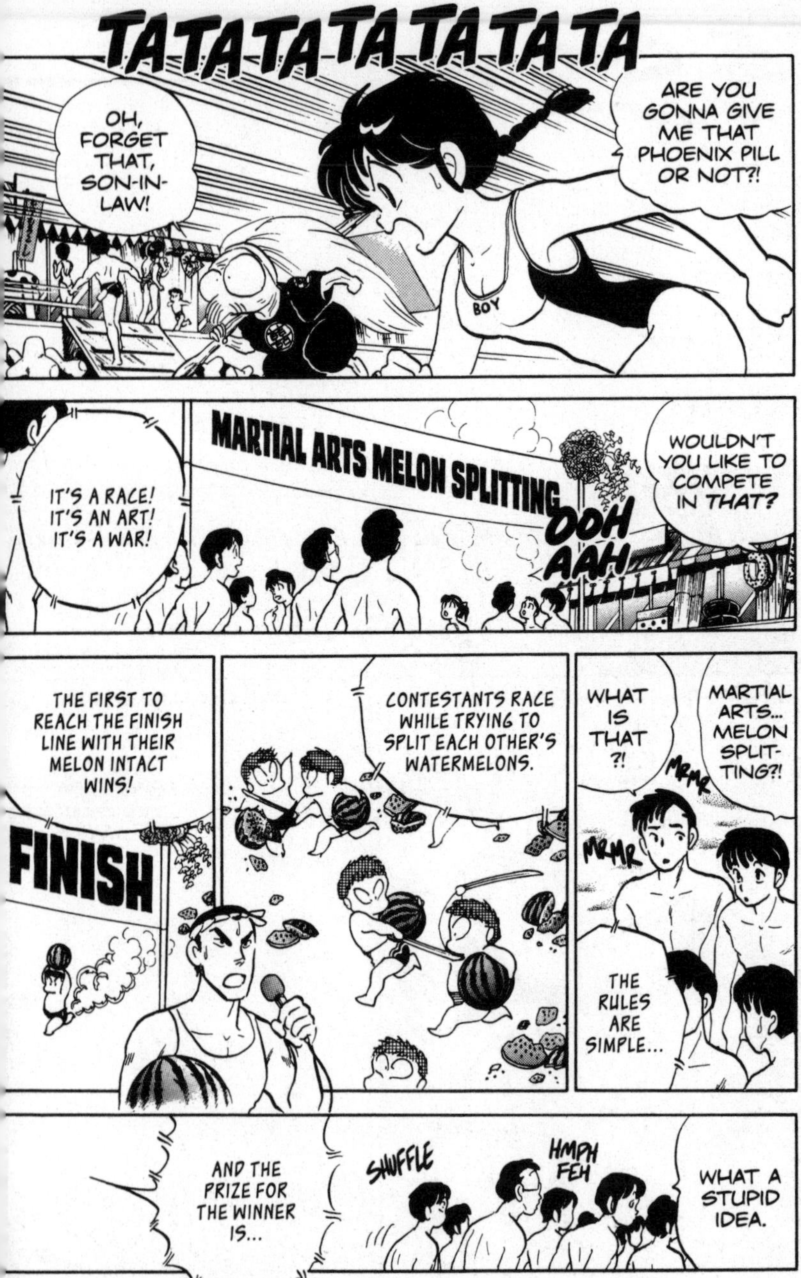
TA TA TA TA TA TA TA TA
ARE YOU GONNA GIVE ME THAT PHOENIX PILL OR NOT?!
BOY
OH, FORGET THAT, SON-IN-LAW!
WOULDN'T YOU LIKE TO COMPETE IN *THAT?*
MARTIAL ARTS MELON SPLITTING
OOH AAH
IT'S A RACE! IT'S AN ART! IT'S A WAR!
MARTIAL ARTS... MELON SPLIT-TING?!
WHAT IS THAT?!
MRMR
MRMR
THE RULES ARE SIMPLE...
CONTESTANTS RACE WHILE TRYING TO SPLIT EACH OTHER'S WATERMELONS.
THE FIRST TO REACH THE FINISH LINE WITH THEIR MELON INTACT WINS!
FINISH
WHAT A STUPID IDEA.
HMPH FEH
SHUFFLE
AND THE PRIZE FOR THE WINNER IS...

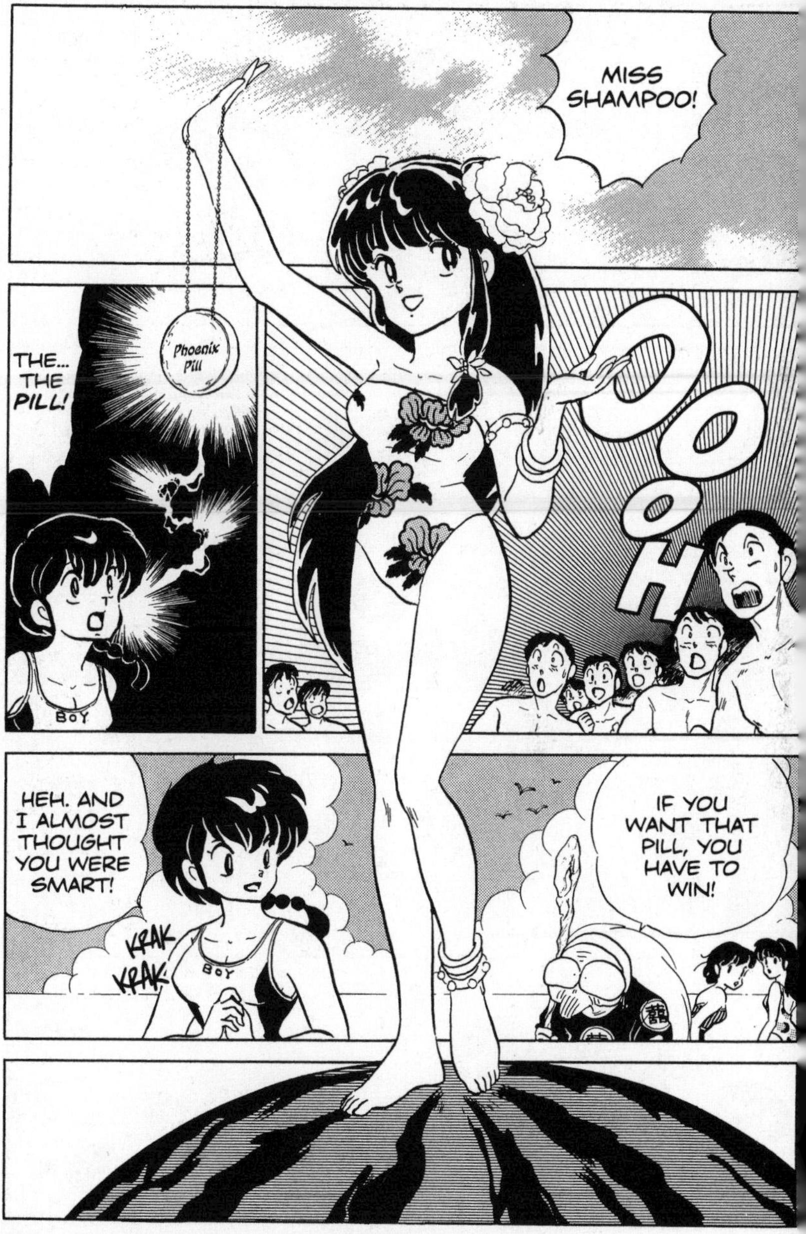
MISS SHAMPOO!
OOOOH
Phoenix Pill
THE... THE PILL!
BOY
IF YOU WANT THAT PILL, YOU HAVE TO WIN!
HEH. AND I ALMOST THOUGHT YOU WERE SMART!
KRAK KRAK
BOY

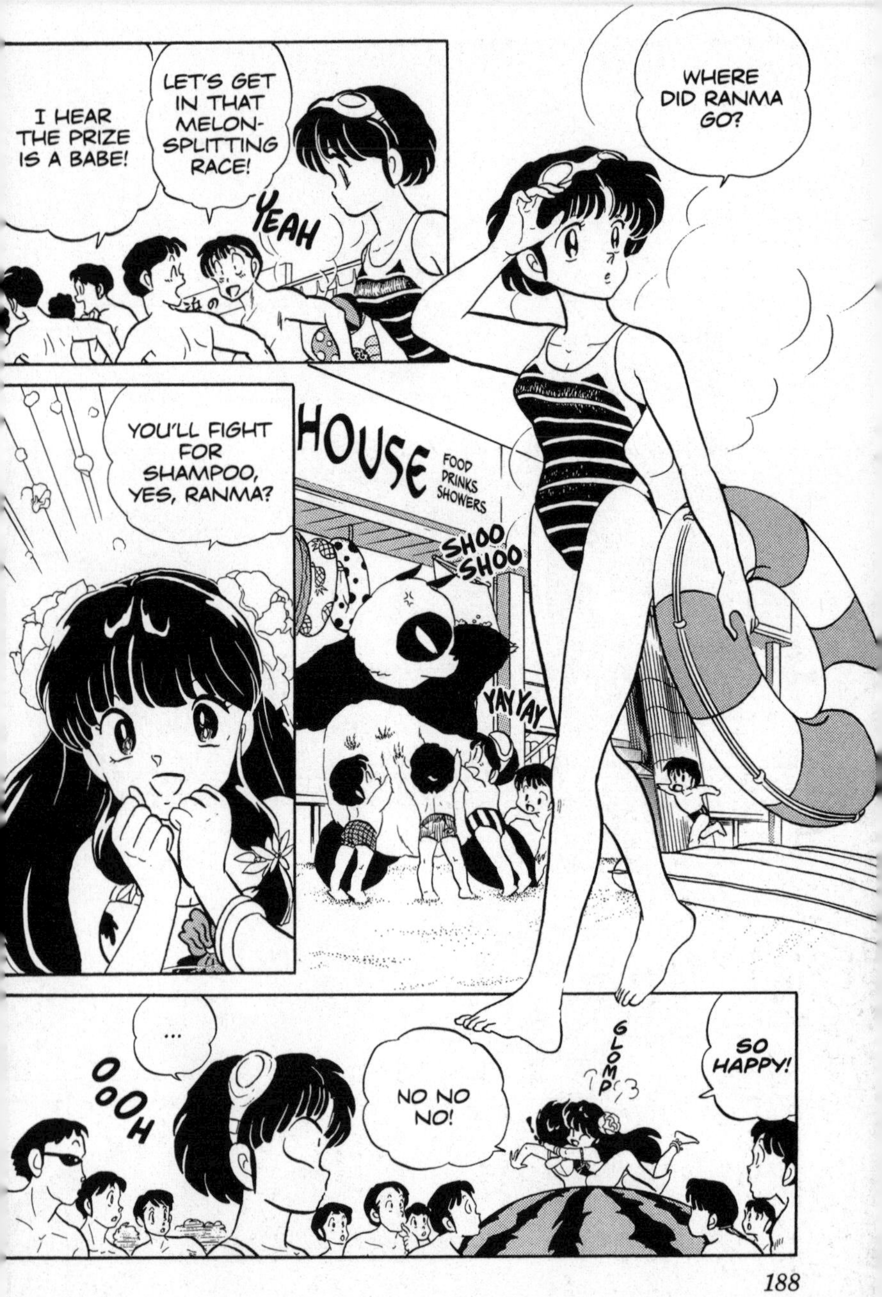
WHERE DID RANMA GO?
HOUSE
FOOD DRINKS SHOWERS
SHOO SHOO
YAYYAY
YEAH
LET'S GET IN THAT MELON-SPLITTING RACE!
I HEAR THE PRIZE IS A BABE!
YOU'LL FIGHT FOR SHAMPOO, YES, RANMA?
SO HAPPY!
GLOMP
NO NO NO!
...
OOOH

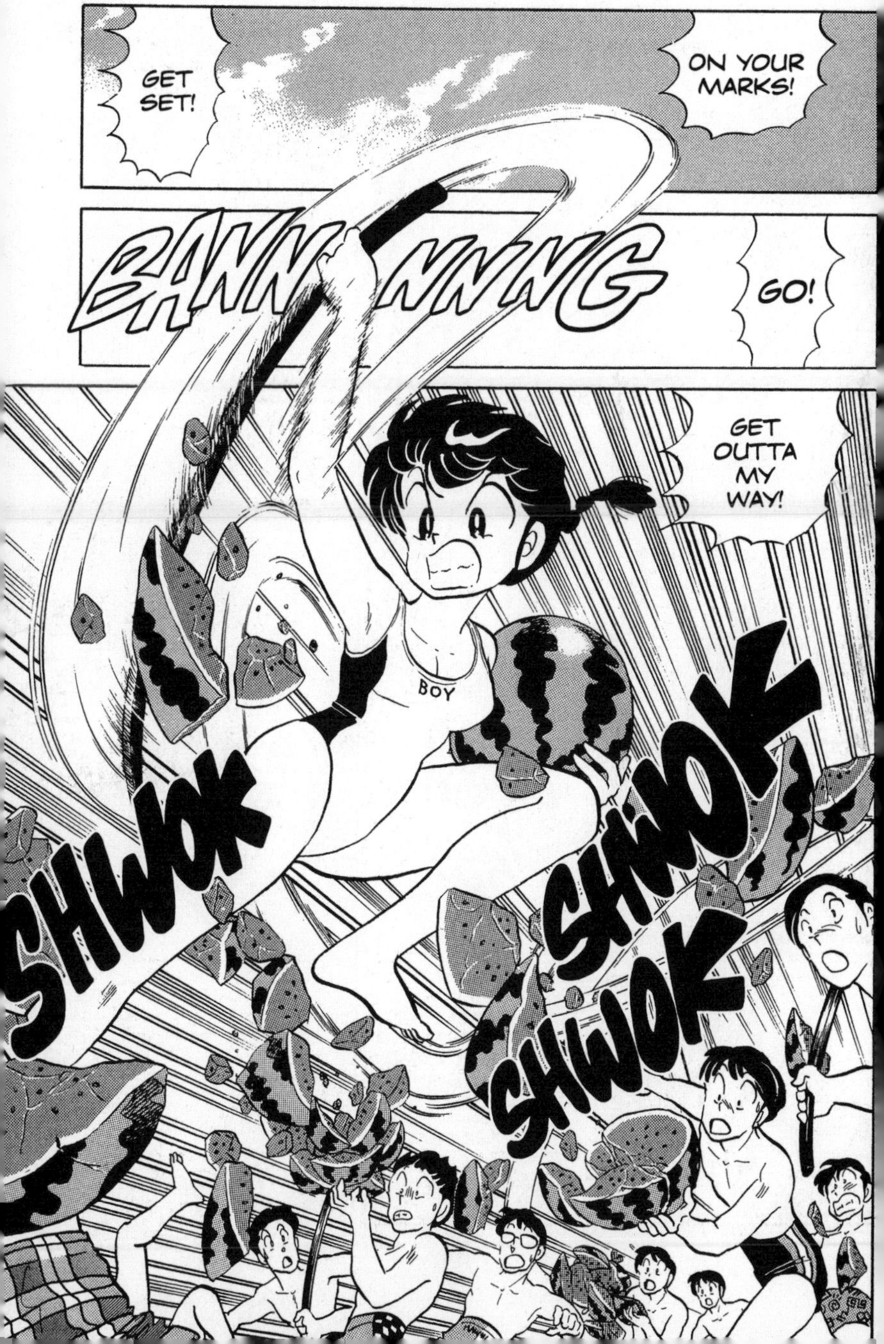
ON YOUR MARKS!
GET SET!
GO!
BANNNNNNG
GET OUTTA MY WAY!
SHWOK
SHWOK
SHWOK

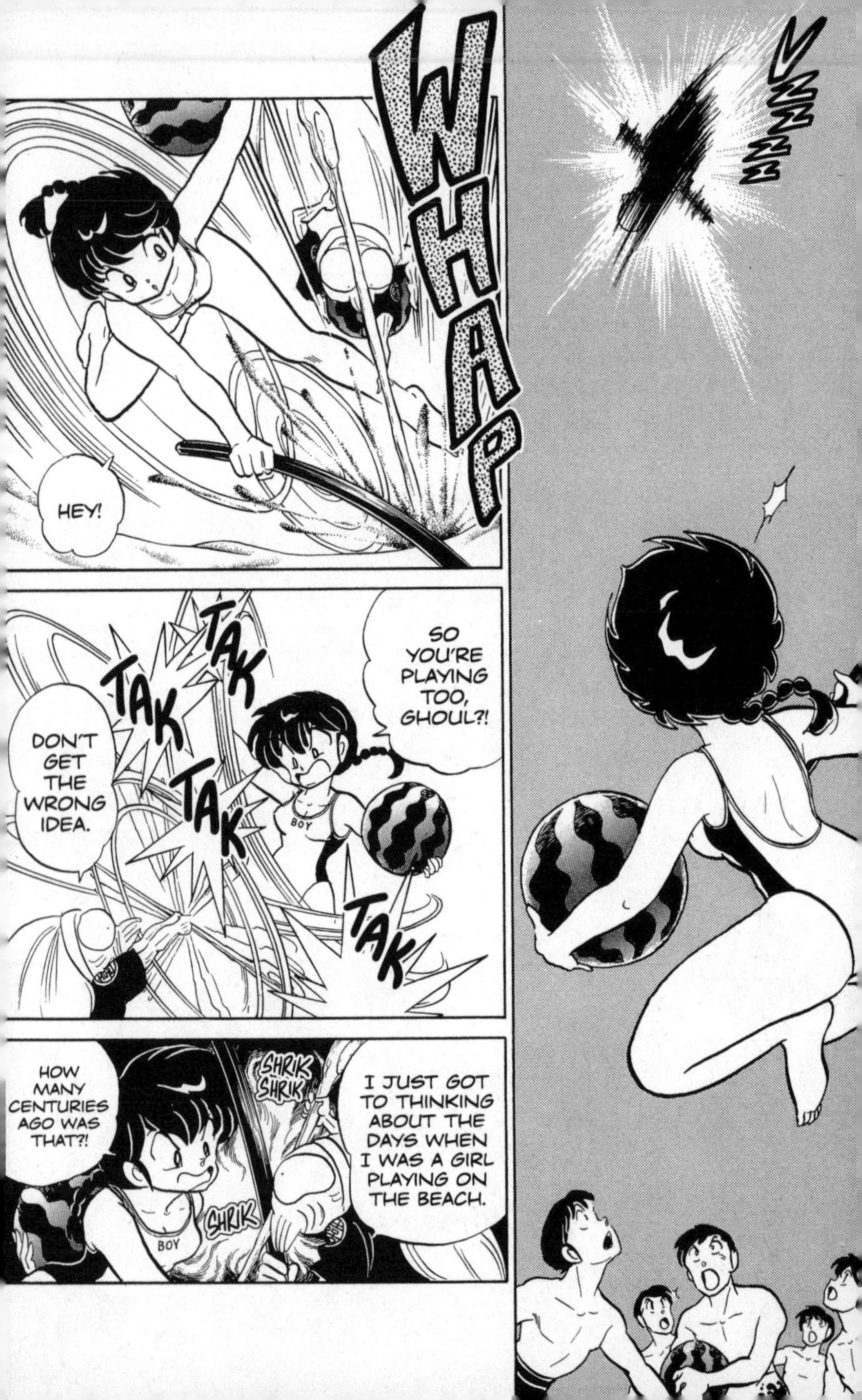
WHAP
HEY!
SO YOU'RE PLAYING TOO, GHOUL?!
TAK
TAK
TAK
TAK
BOY
DON'T GET THE WRONG IDEA.
I JUST GOT TO THINKING ABOUT THE DAYS WHEN I WAS A GIRL PLAYING ON THE BEACH.
SHRIK SHRIK
SHRIK
HOW MANY CENTURIES AGO WAS THAT?!
BOY

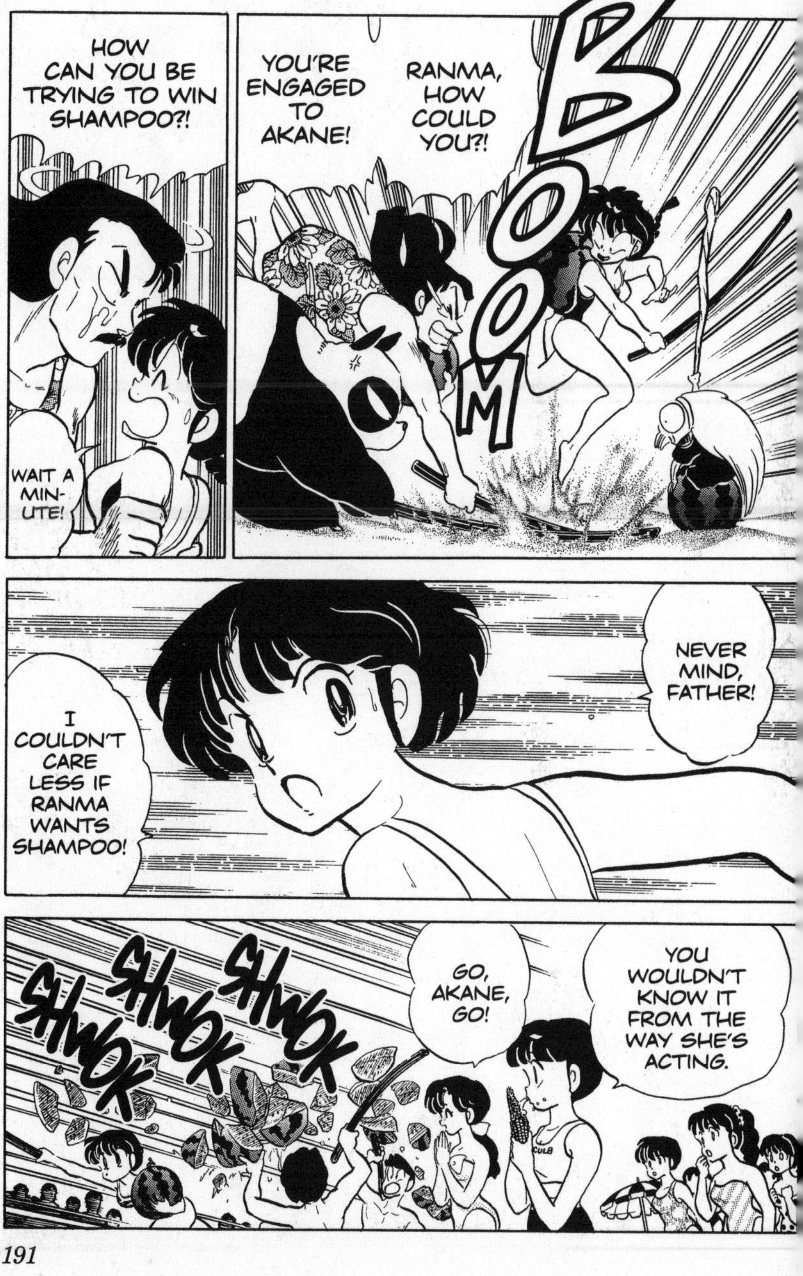
RANMA, HOW COULD YOU?!
YOU'RE ENGAGED TO AKANE!
BOOM
HOW CAN YOU BE TRYING TO WIN SHAMPOO?!
WAIT A MIN-UTE!
NEVER MIND, FATHER!
I COULDN'T CARE LESS IF RANMA WANTS SHAMPOO!
YOU WOULDN'T KNOW IT FROM THE WAY SHE'S ACTING.
GO, AKANE, GO!
SHWOK
SHWOK
SHWOK
SHWOK

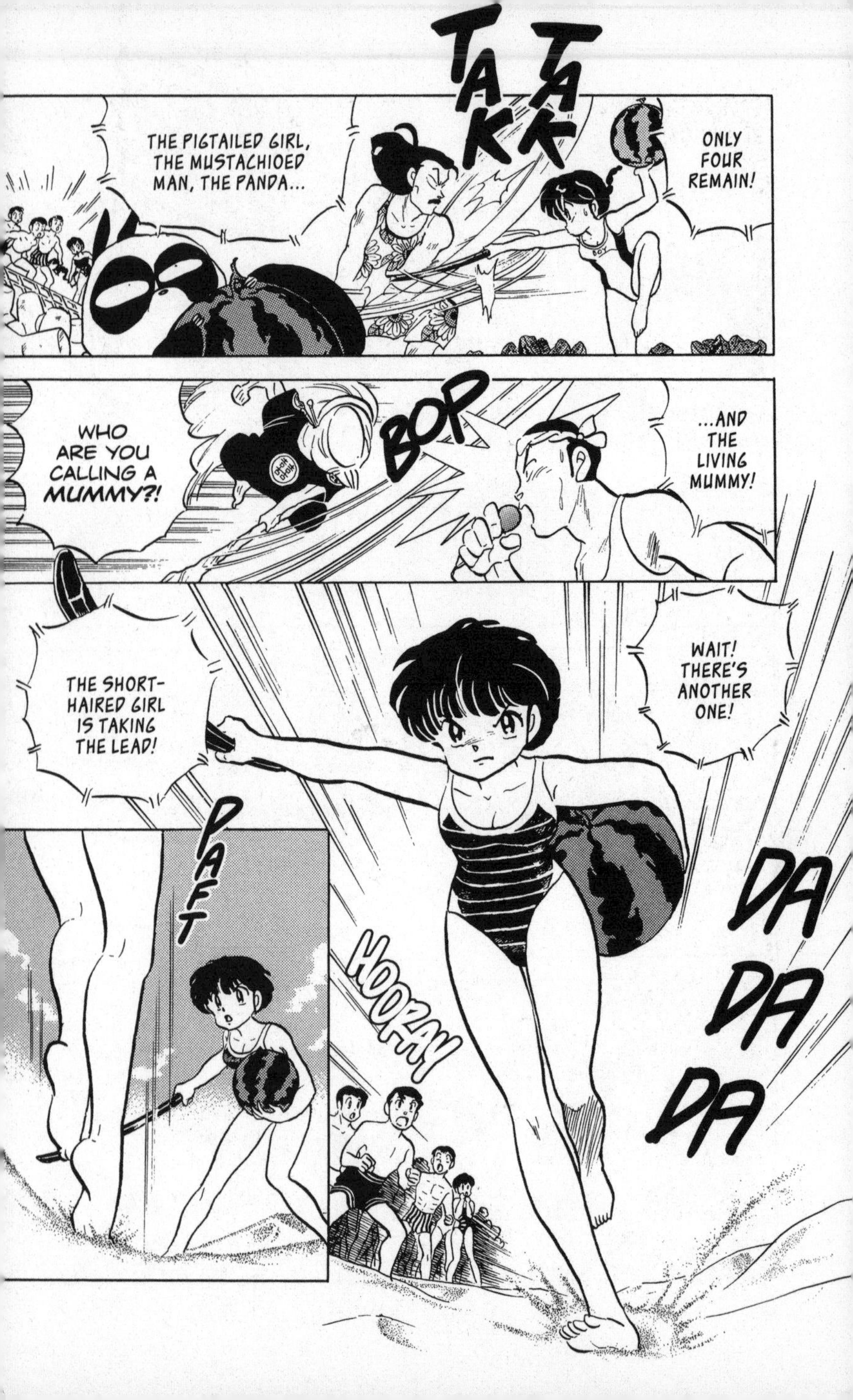
TAKK TAKK
ONLY FOUR REMAIN!
THE PIGTAILED GIRL, THE MUSTACHIOED MAN, THE PANDA...
...AND THE LIVING MUMMY!
BOP
WHO ARE YOU CALLING A MUMMY?!
WAIT! THERE'S ANOTHER ONE!
THE SHORT-HAIRED GIRL IS TAKING THE LEAD!
DA DA DA
HOORAY
PAFT

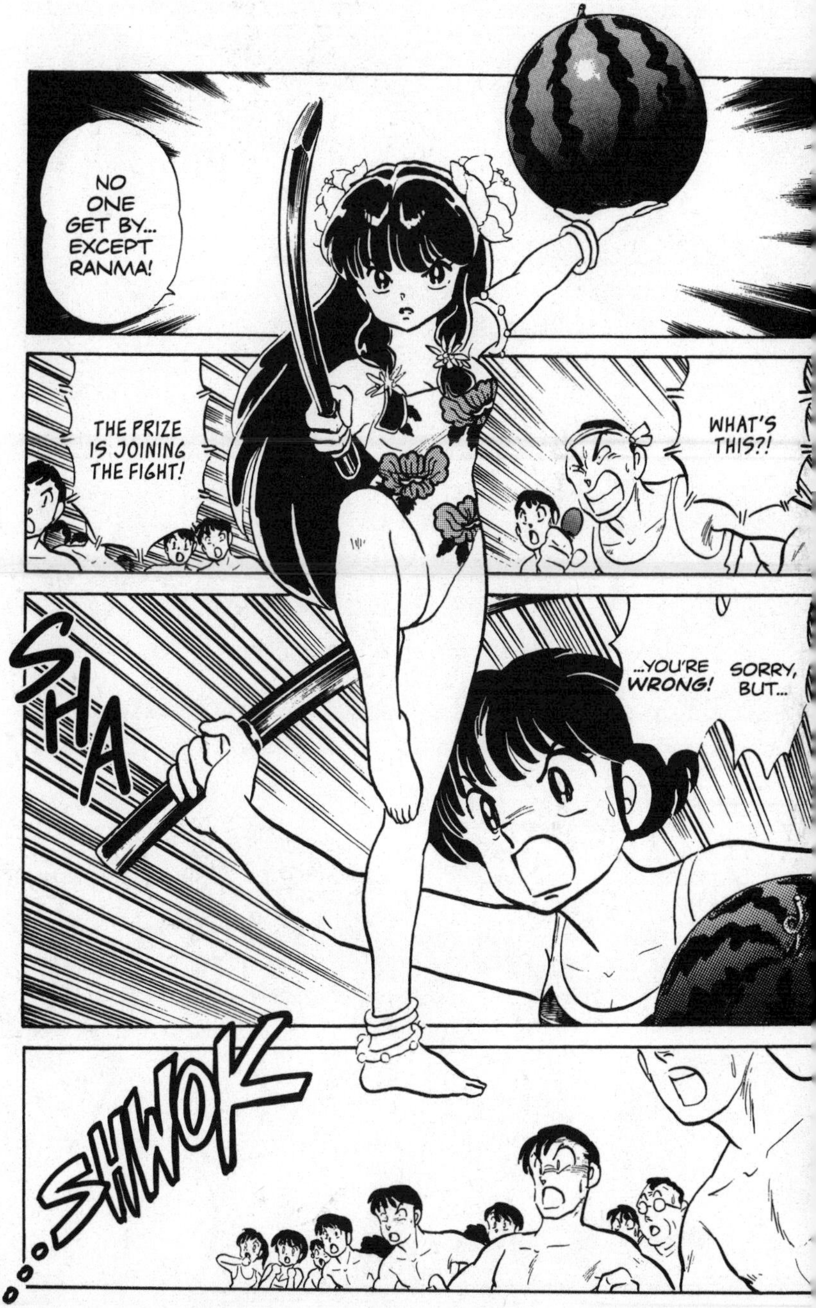
NO ONE GET BY... EXCEPT RANMA!
WHAT'S THIS?!
THE PRIZE IS JOINING THE FIGHT!
SORRY, BUT...
...YOU'RE WRONG!
SHA
...SHWOK

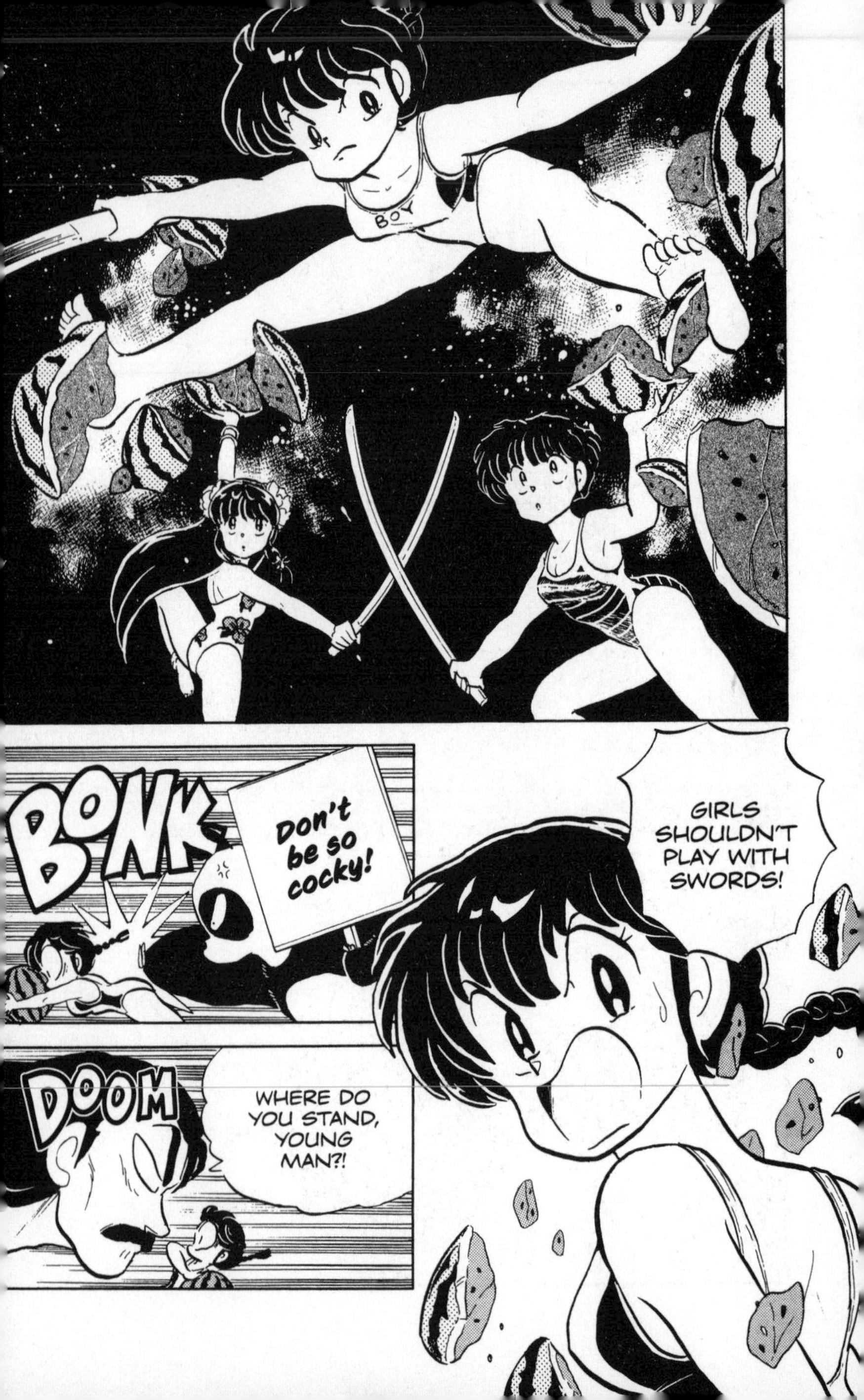
GIRLS SHOULDN'T PLAY WITH SWORDS!
BONK
Don't be so cocky!
DOOM
WHERE DO YOU STAND, YOUNG MAN?!

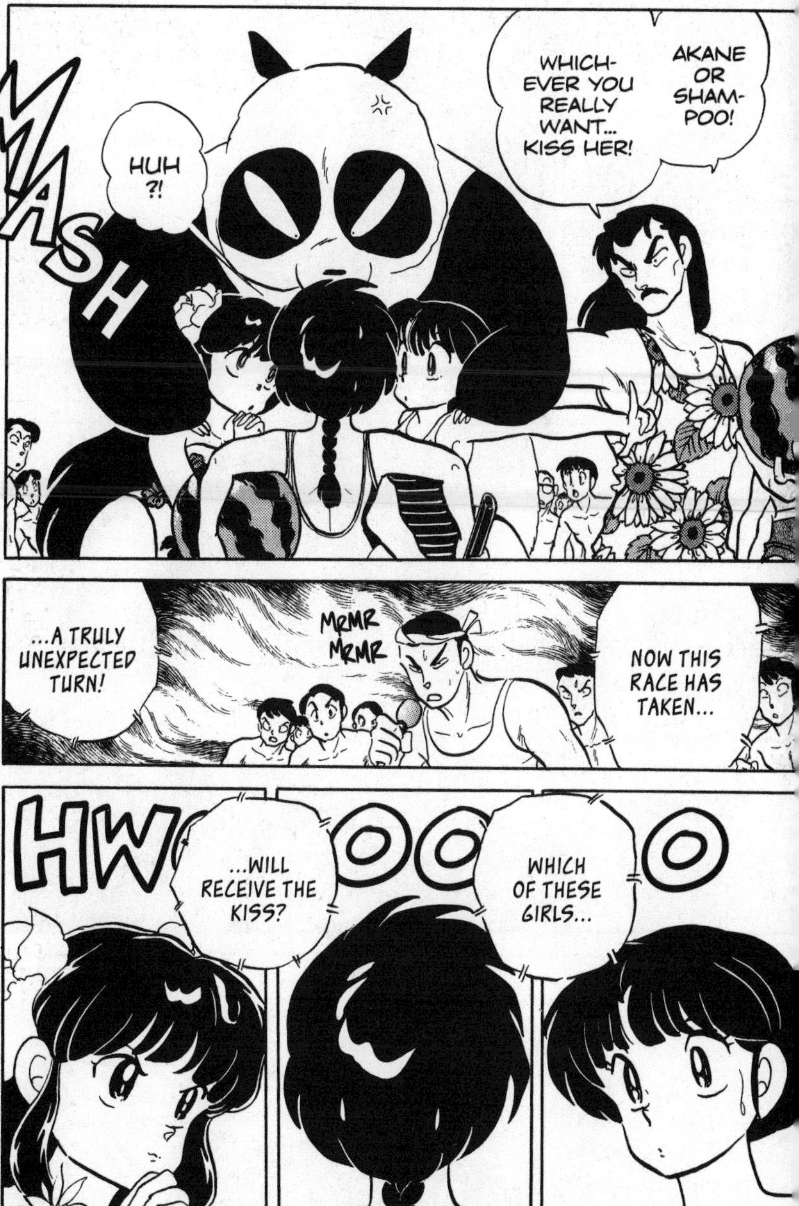
AKANE OR SHAM-POO!
WHICH-EVER YOU REALLY WANT... KISS HER!
HUH ?!
MASH
NOW THIS RACE HAS TAKEN...
MRMR MRMR
...A TRULY UNEXPECTED TURN!
WHICH OF THESE GIRLS...
HWOOOO
...WILL RECEIVE THE KISS?

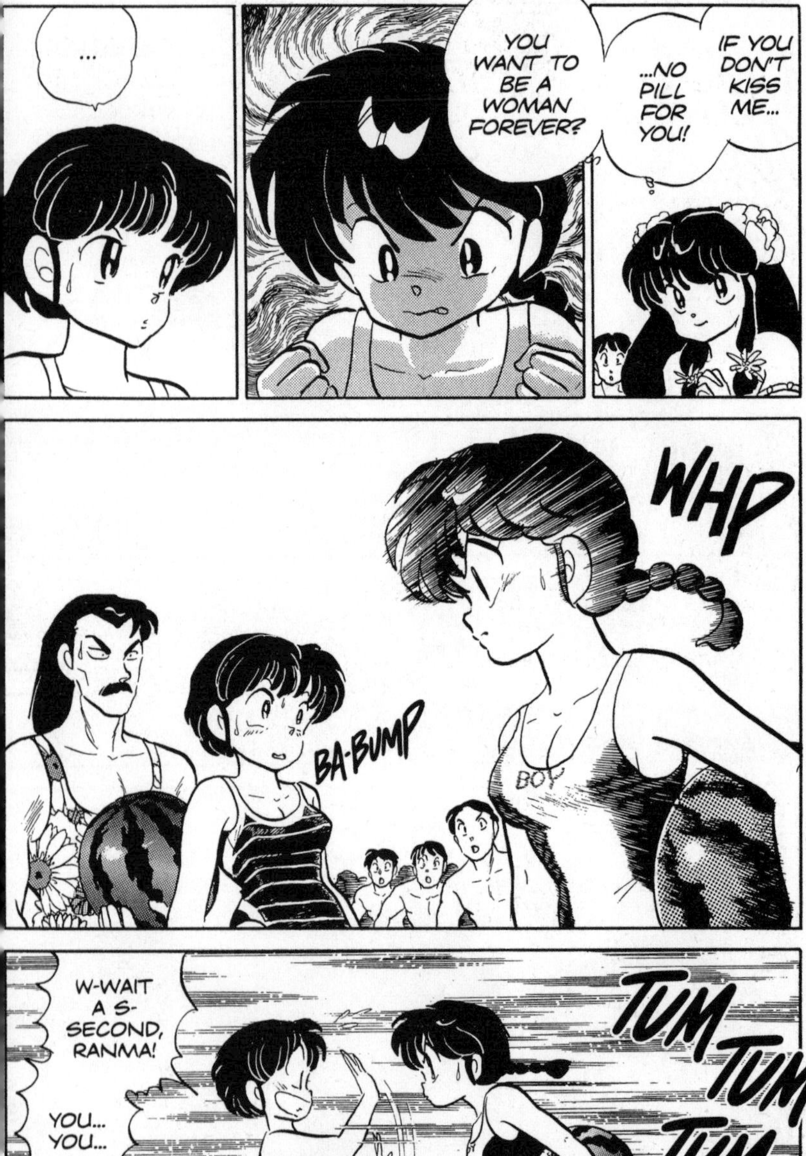
IF YOU DON'T KISS ME...
...NO PILL FOR YOU!
YOU WANT TO BE A WOMAN FOREVER?
...
WHP
BOY
BA-BUMP
TUM TUM TUM
W-WAIT A S-SECOND, RANMA!
YOU... YOU...

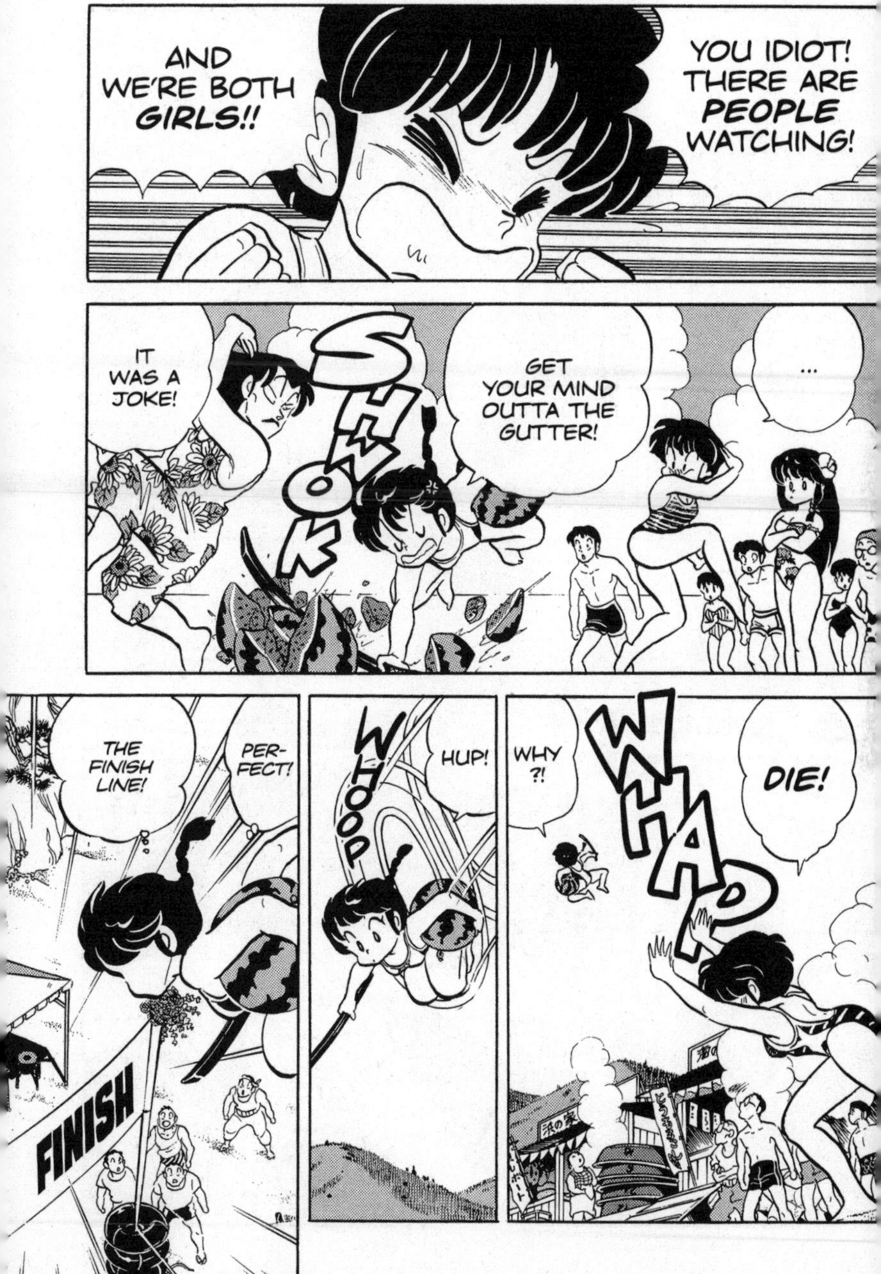
YOU IDIOT! THERE ARE PEOPLE WATCHING!
AND WE'RE BOTH GIRLS!!
...
GET YOUR MIND OUTTA THE GUTTER!
SHWOK
IT WAS A JOKE!
DIE!
WHAP
WHY ?!
HUP!
WHOOP
PER- FECT!
THE FINISH LINE!
FINISH

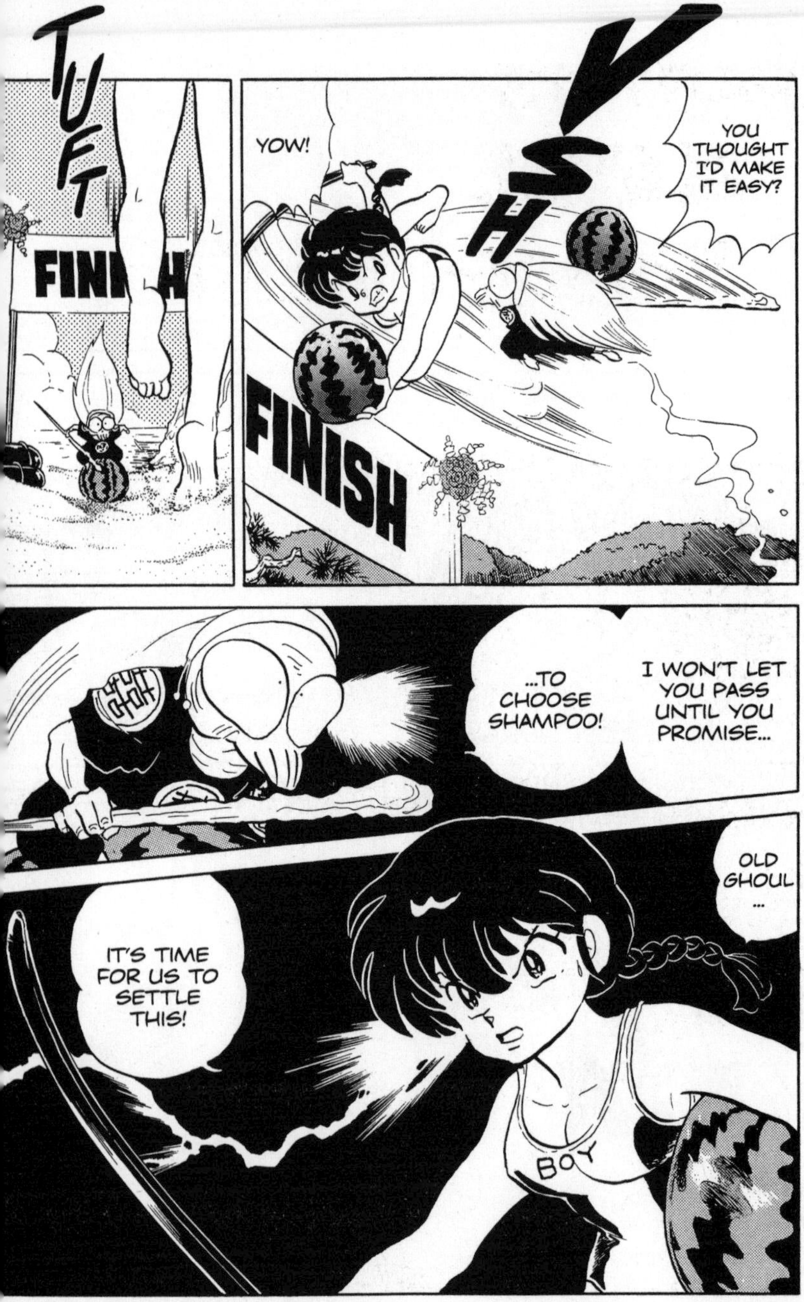

YOU THOUGHT I'D MAKE IT EASY?
VSHH
YOW!
FINISH
TUFT
FINISH
I WON'T LET YOU PASS UNTIL YOU PROMISE...
...TO CHOOSE SHAMPOO!
OLD GHOUL ...
IT'S TIME FOR US TO SETTLE THIS!
BOY

PART 13

NAVAL ENGAGEMENT

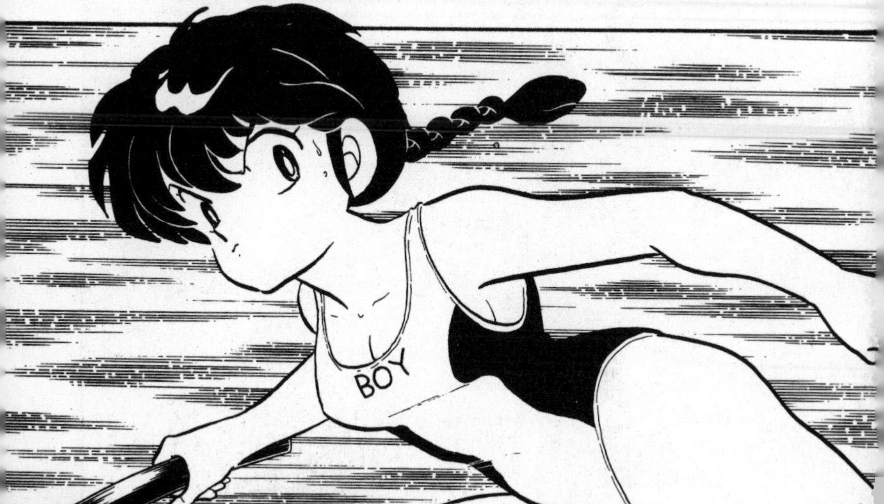
BOY

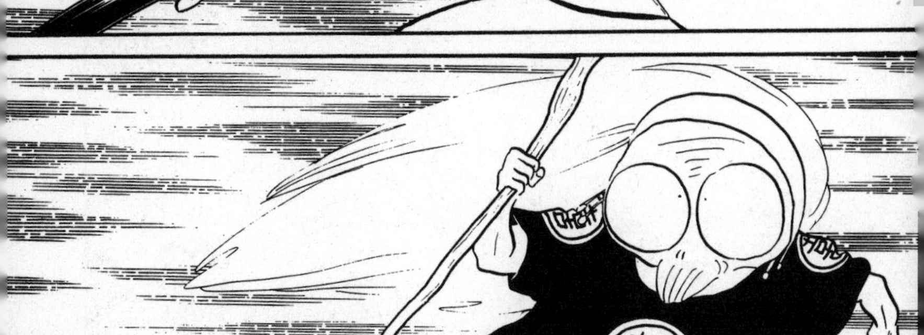

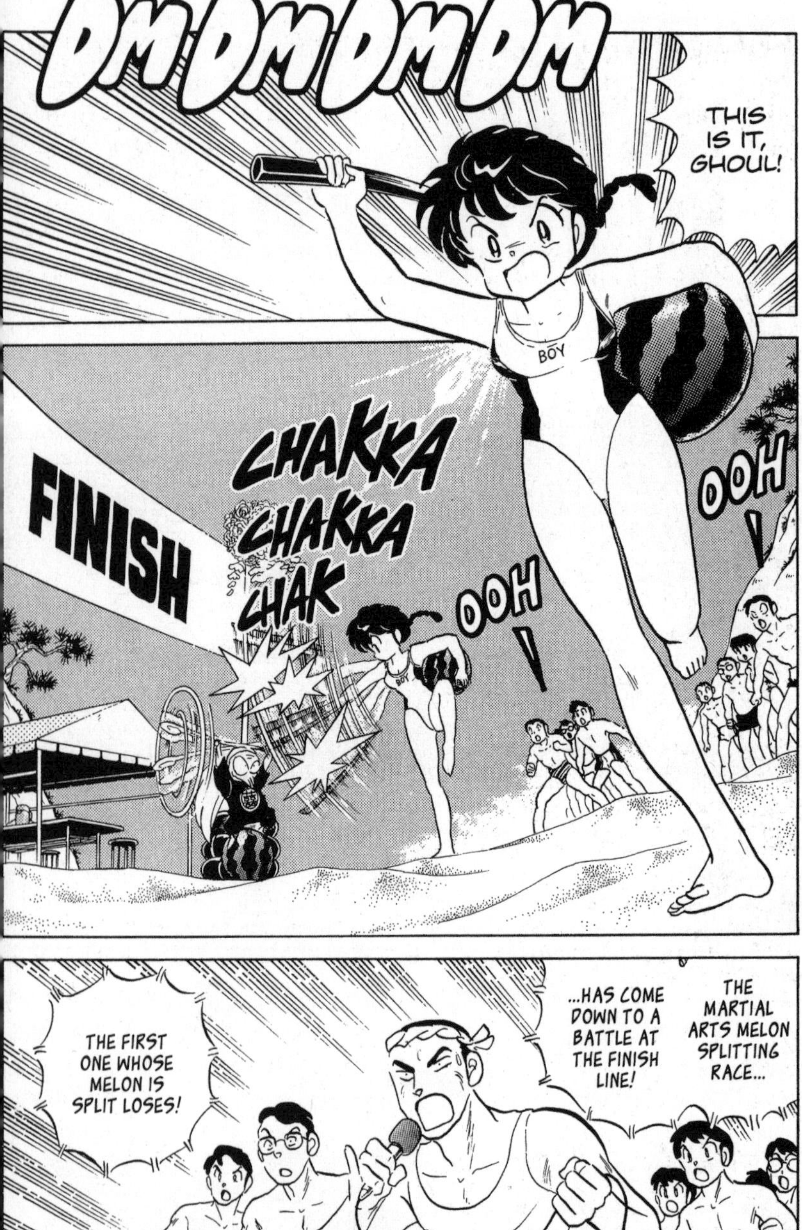
DM DM DM DM DM
THIS IS IT, GHOUL!
BOY
OOH
OOH
CHAKKA CHAKKA CHAK
FINISH
THE MARTIAL ARTS MELON SPLITTING RACE...
...HAS COME DOWN TO A BATTLE AT THE FINISH LINE!
THE FIRST ONE WHOSE MELON IS SPLIT LOSES!

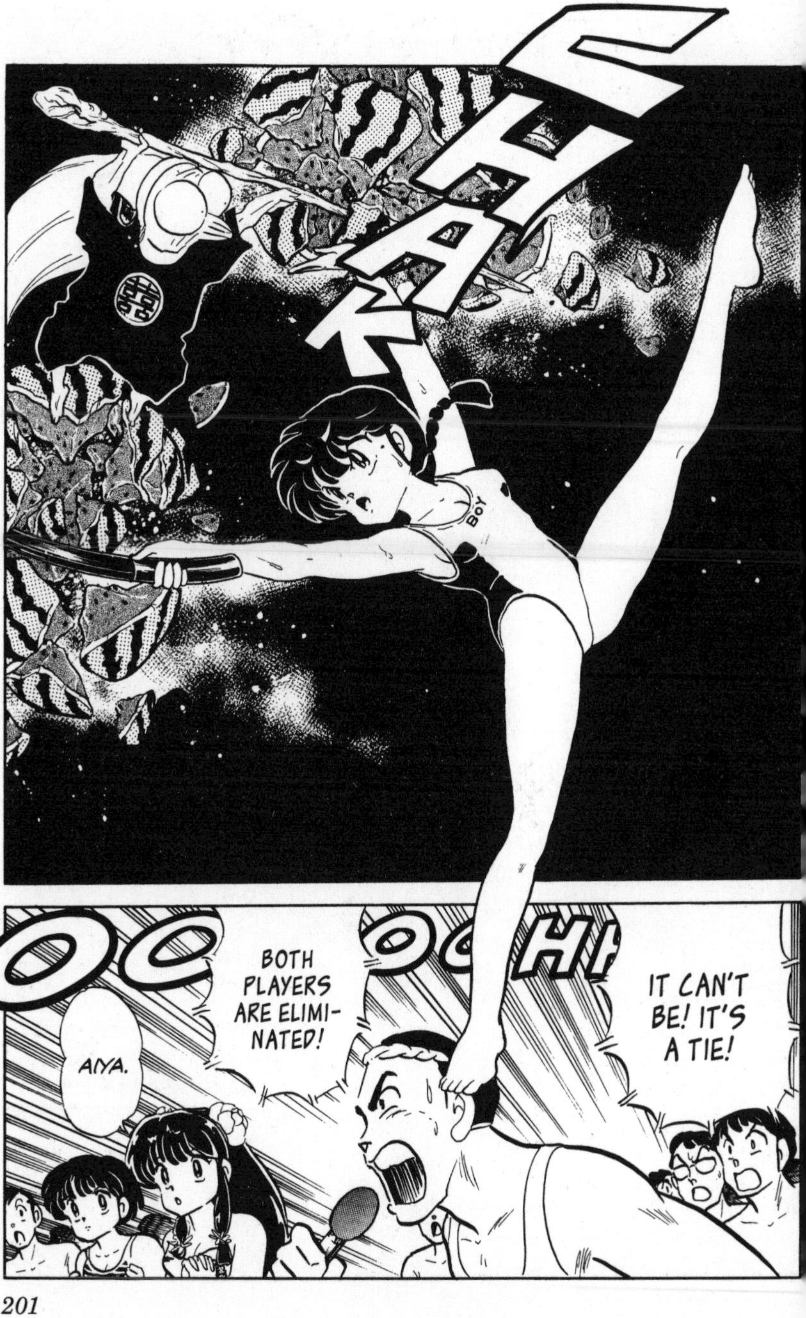
CHAAK
OOOOH
IT CAN'T BE! IT'S A TIE!
BOTH PLAYERS ARE ELIMI-NATED!
AIYA.

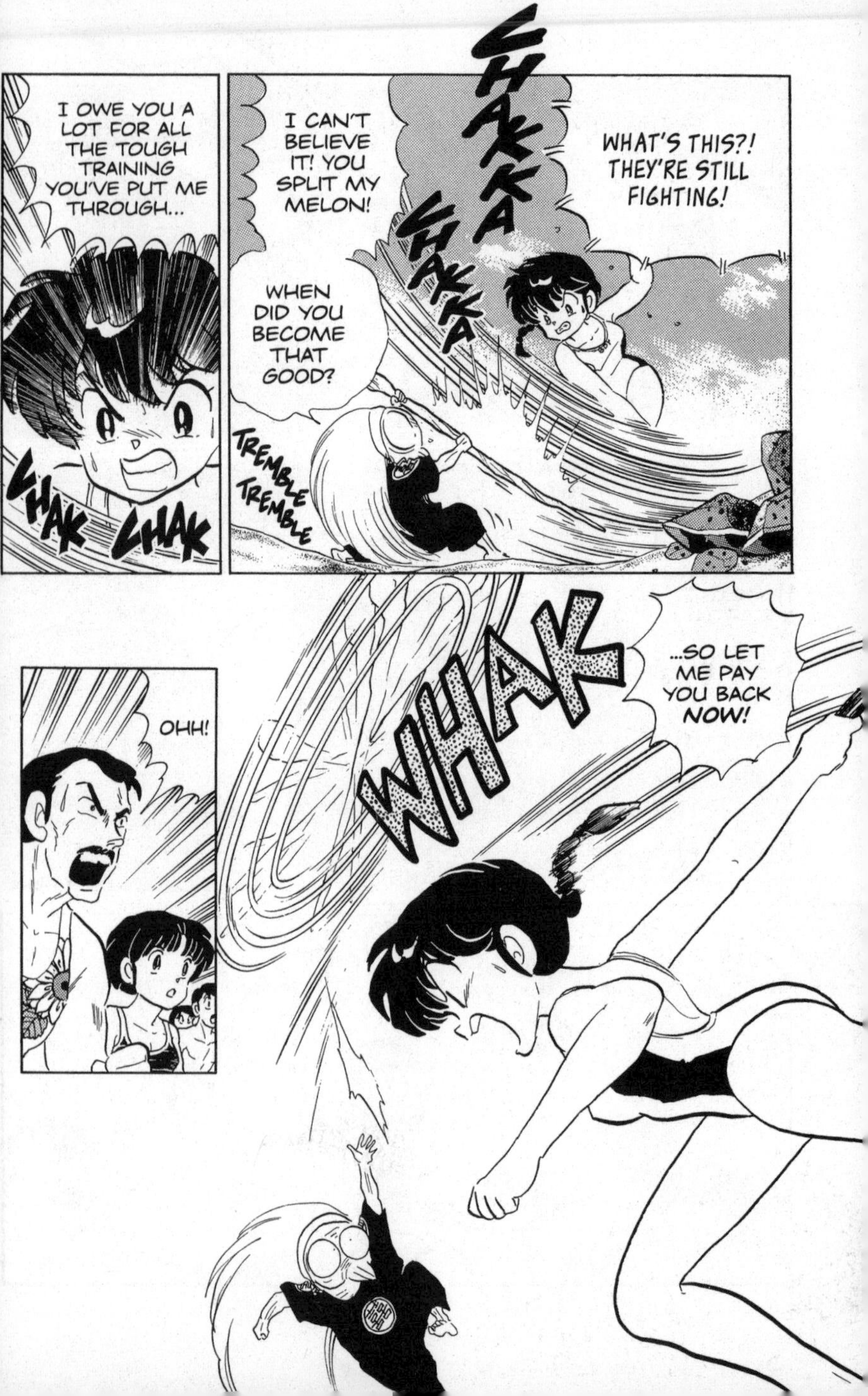
CHAKA
CHAKA
WHAT'S THIS?! THEY'RE STILL FIGHTING!
I CAN'T BELIEVE IT! YOU SPLIT MY MELON!
WHEN DID YOU BECOME THAT GOOD?
TREMBLE TREMBLE
I OWE YOU A LOT FOR ALL THE TOUGH TRAINING YOU'VE PUT ME THROUGH...
WHAK CHAK
...SO LET ME PAY YOU BACK **NOW!**
WHAK
OHH!

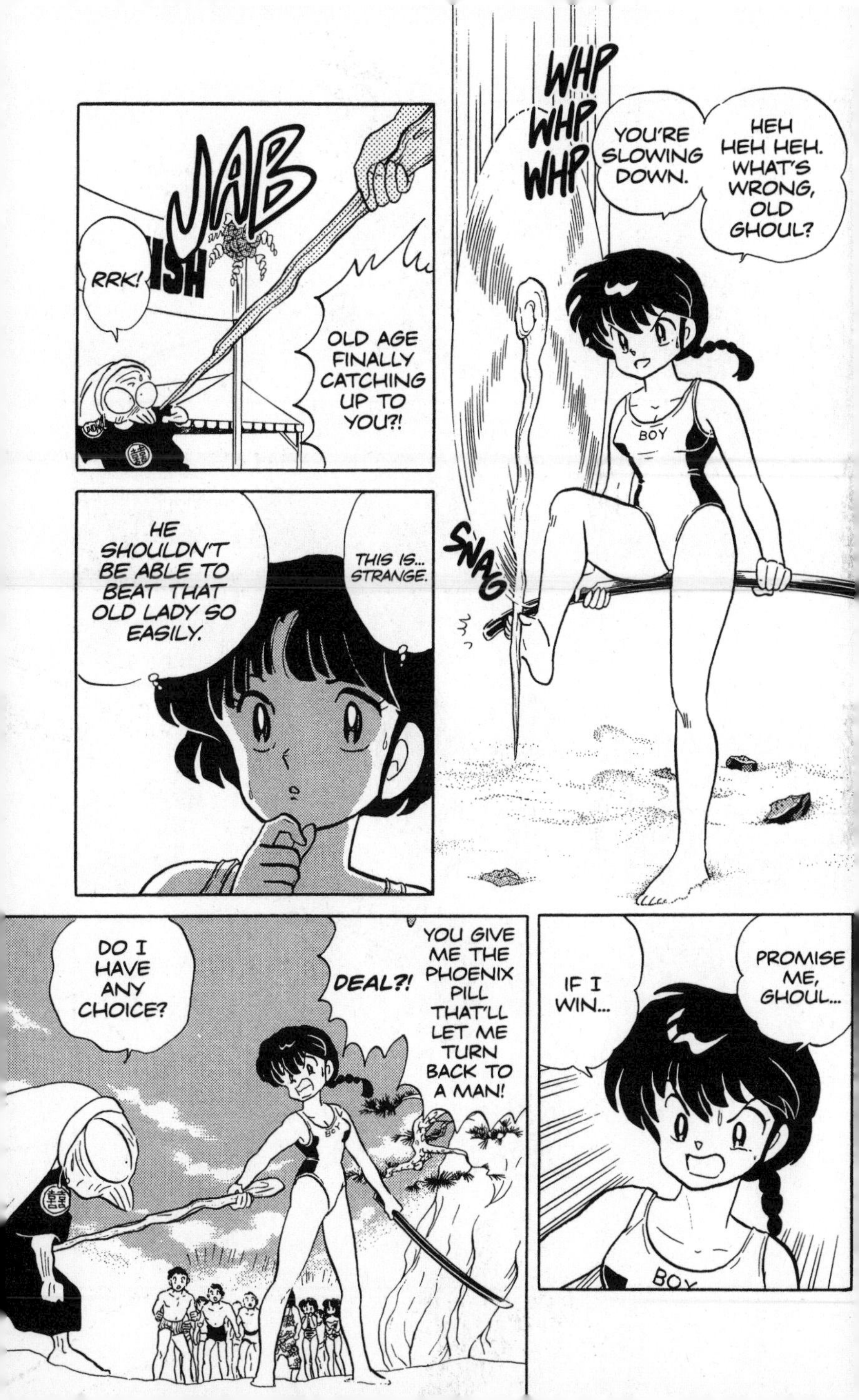
HEH HEH HEH. WHAT'S WRONG, OLD GHOUL?
YOU'RE SLOWING DOWN.
WHP WHP WHP
SNAG
JAB
OLD AGE FINALLY CATCHING UP TO YOU?!
RRK!
THIS IS... STRANGE.
HE SHOULDN'T BE ABLE TO BEAT THAT OLD LADY SO EASILY.
PROMISE ME, GHOUL...
IF I WIN...
BOY
YOU GIVE ME THE PHOENIX PILL THAT'LL LET ME TURN BACK TO A MAN!
DEAL?!
DO I HAVE ANY CHOICE?

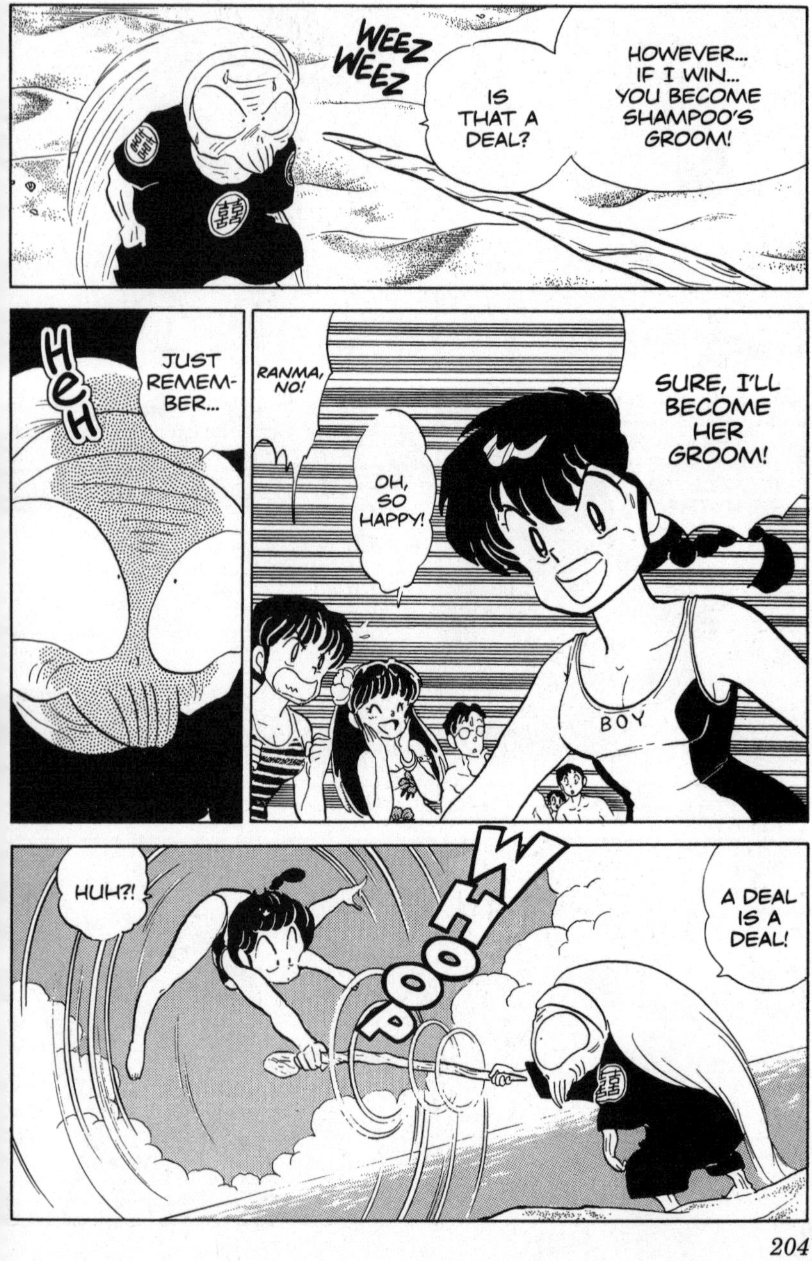
HOWEVER... IF I WIN... YOU BECOME SHAMPOO'S GROOM!
IS THAT A DEAL?
WEEZ WEEZ
SURE, I'LL BECOME HER GROOM!
RANMA, NO!
OH, SO HAPPY!
BOY
JUST REMEMBER...
HEH
A DEAL IS A DEAL!
WHOOP
HUH?!

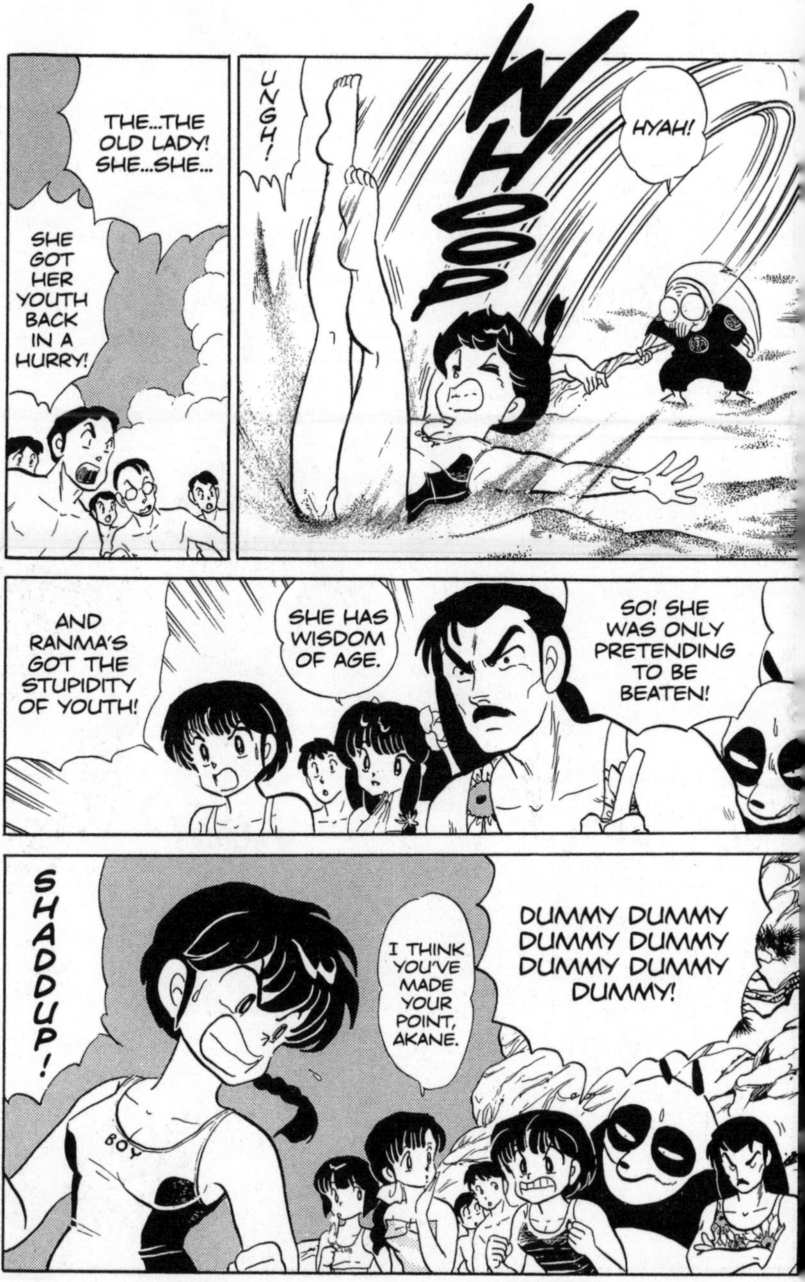
WHOOOP
HYAH!
UNGH!
THE...THE OLD LADY! SHE...SHE...
SHE GOT HER YOUTH BACK IN A HURRY!
SO! SHE WAS ONLY PRETENDING TO BE BEATEN!
SHE HAS WISDOM OF AGE.
AND RANMA'S GOT THE STUPIDITY OF YOUTH!
DUMMY DUMMY DUMMY DUMMY DUMMY DUMMY DUMMY!
I THINK YOU'VE MADE YOUR POINT, AKANE.
SHADDUP!
BOY

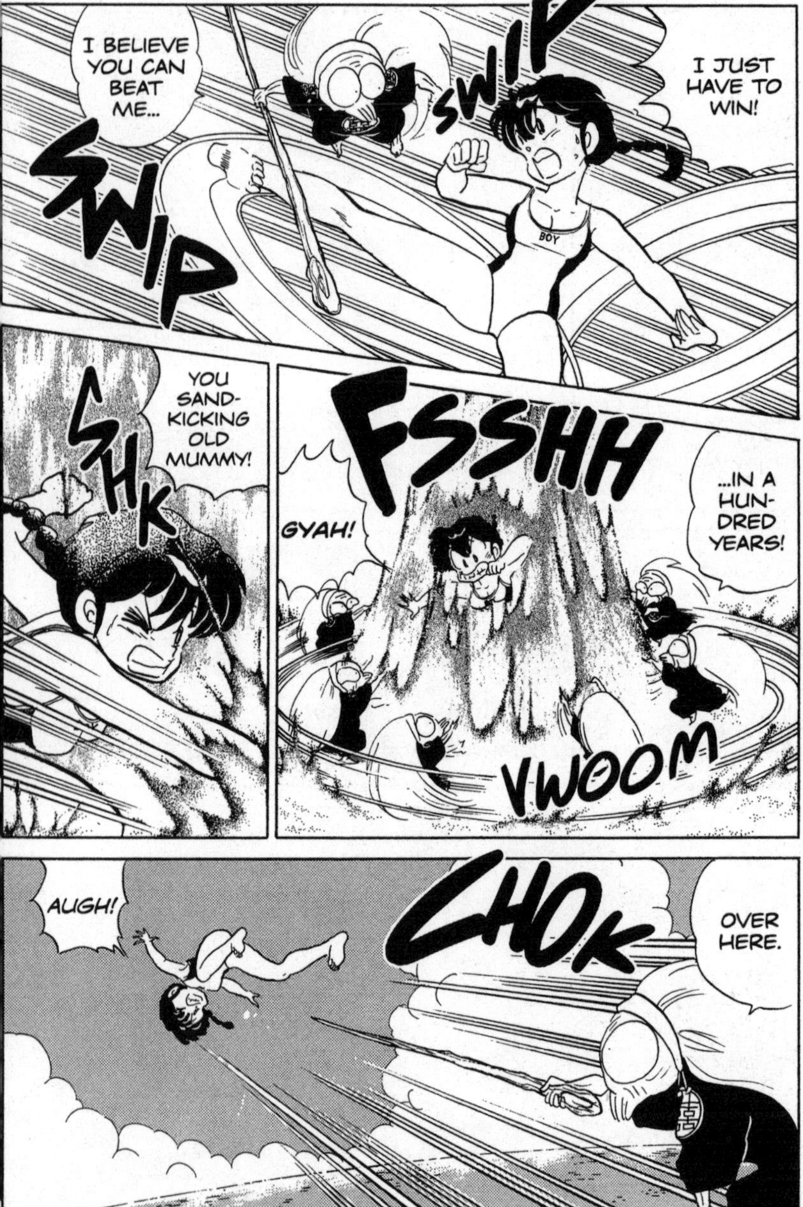
I JUST HAVE TO WIN!
SWIP
I BELIEVE YOU CAN BEAT ME...
SWIP
...IN A HUN-DRED YEARS!
FSSHH
GYAH!
VWOOM
YOU SAND-KICKING OLD MUMMY!
SHK
OVER HERE.
CHOK
AUGH!

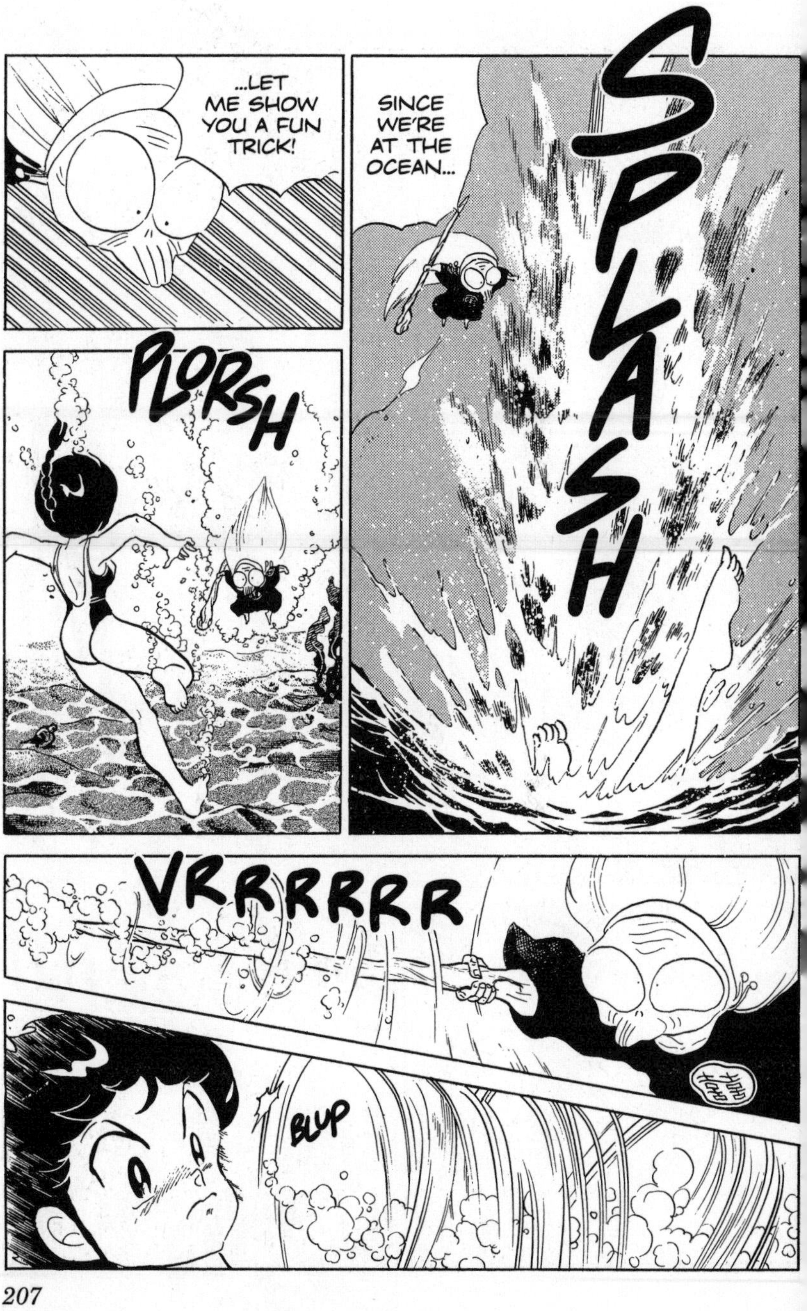
SINCE WE'RE AT THE OCEAN...
SPLASH
...LET ME SHOW YOU A FUN TRICK!
PLORSH
VRRRRRR
BLUP

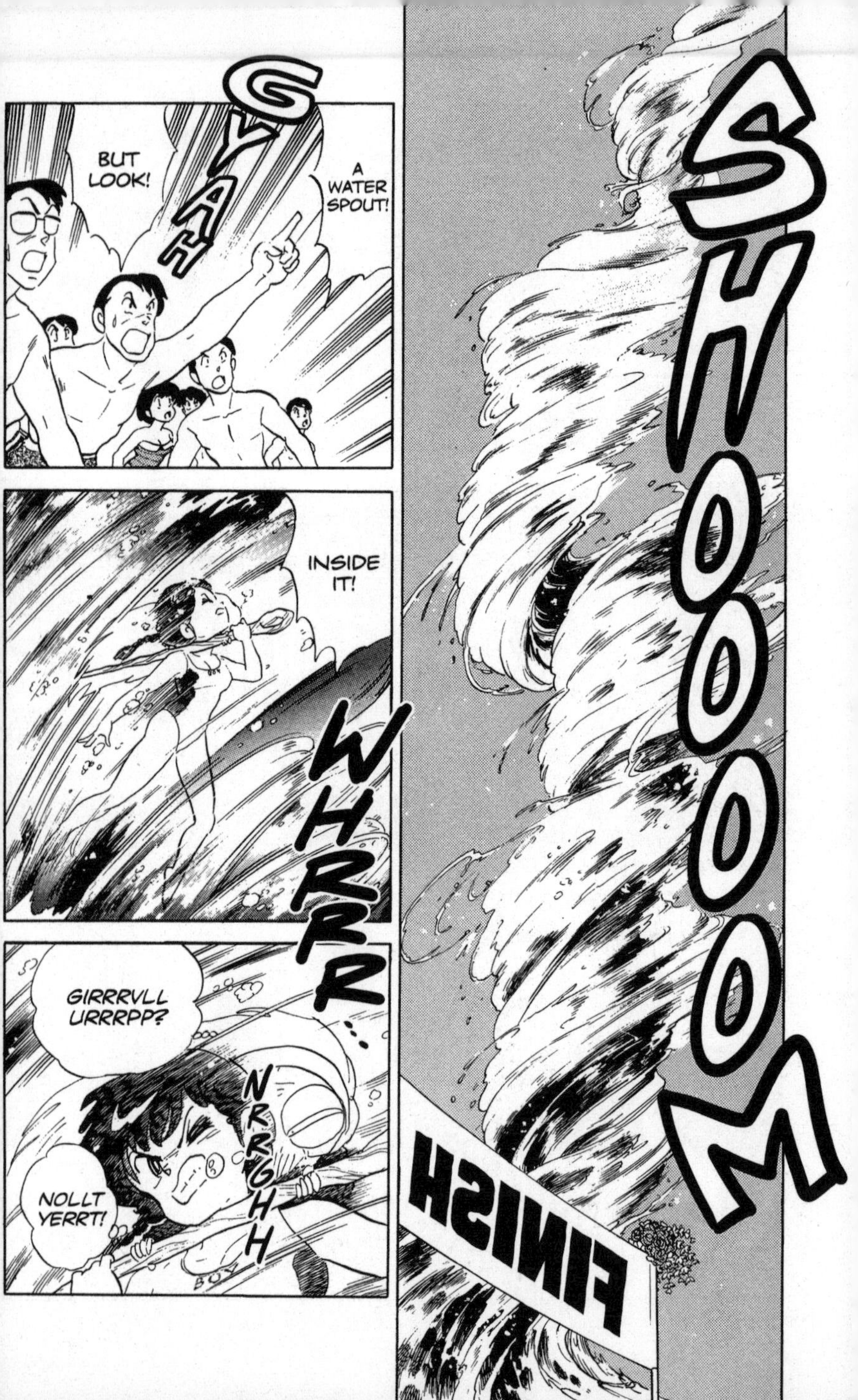
SHOOOOM
FINISH
GYAAH
A WATER SPOUT!
BUT LOOK!
INSIDE IT!
WHRRR...
GIRRRVLL URRRPP?
NRRGHH
NOLLT YERRT!

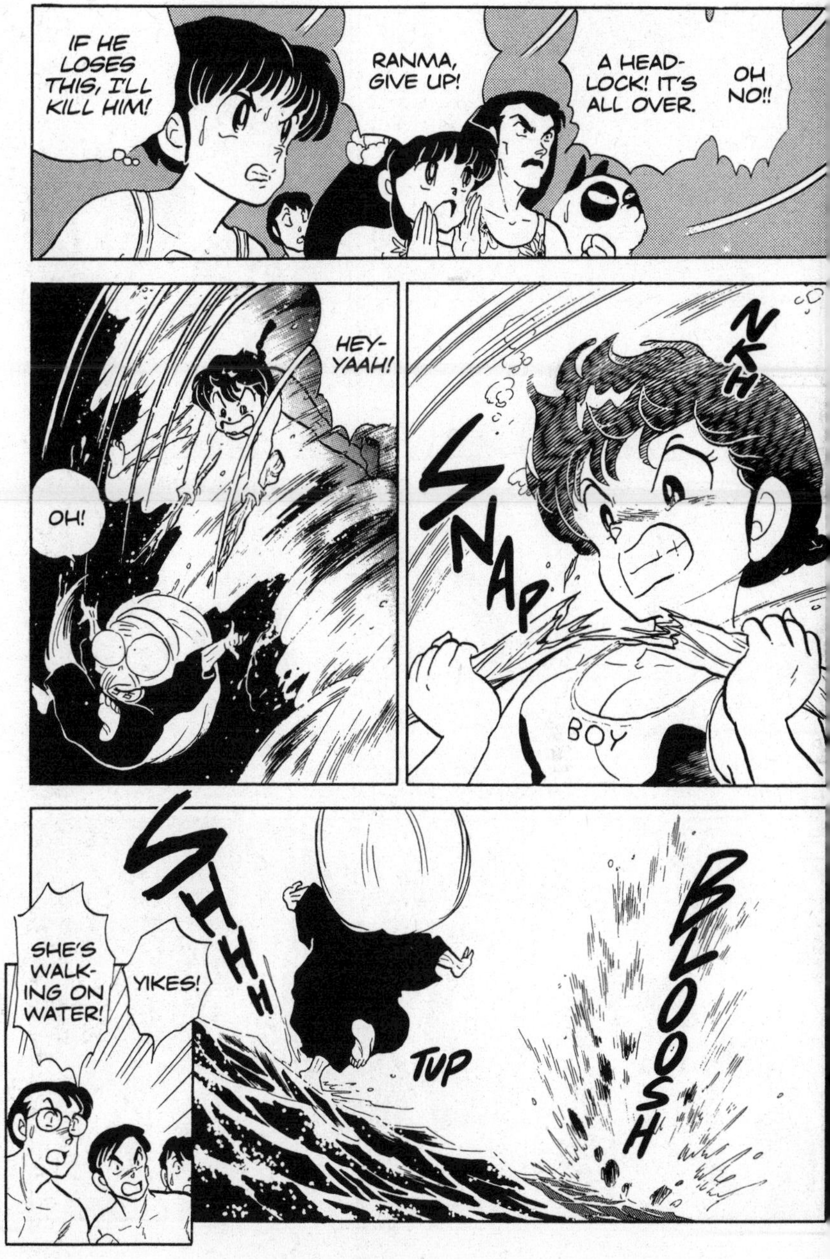
OH NO!!
A HEAD-LOCK! IT'S ALL OVER.
RANMA, GIVE UP!
IF HE LOSES THIS, I'LL KILL HIM!
NKH
SNAP
BOY
HEY-YAAH!
OH!
BLOOOSH
TUP
SHHHH
YIKES!
SHE'S WALKING ON WATER!

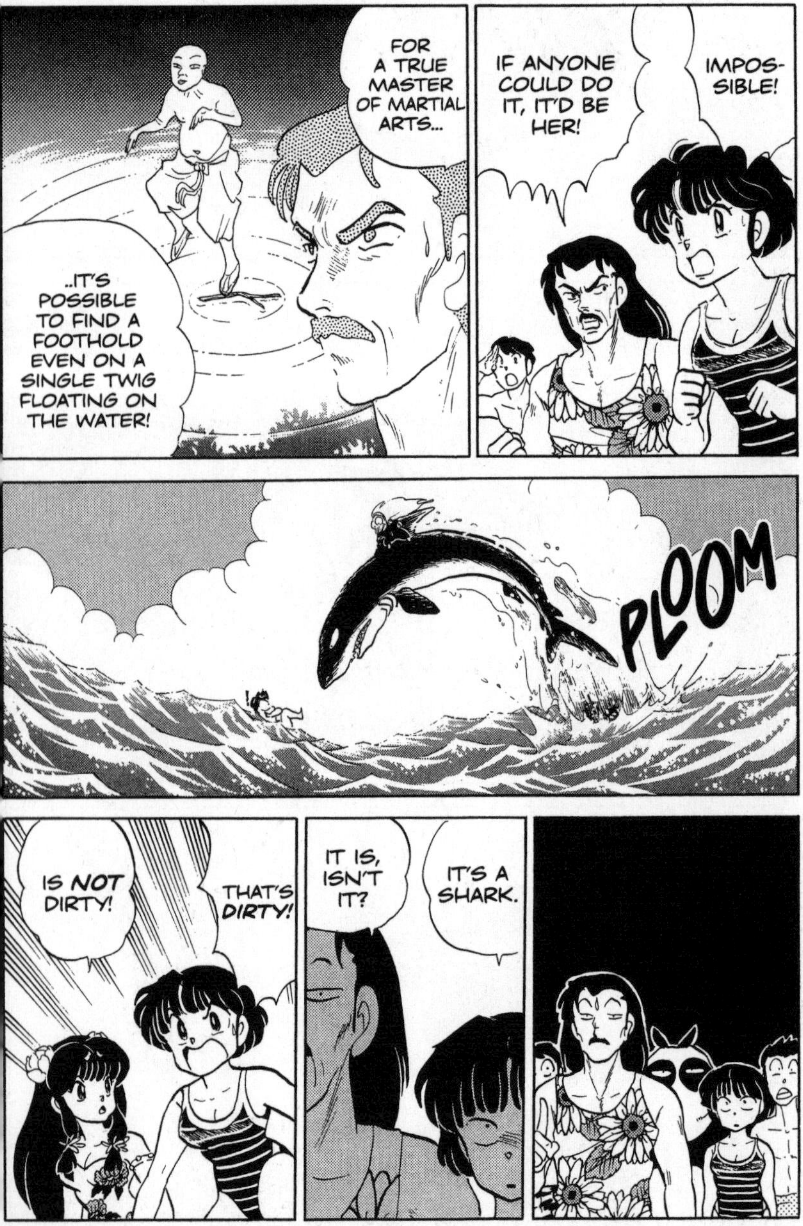
IMPOS-SIBLE!
IF ANYONE COULD DO IT, IT'D BE HER!
FOR A TRUE MASTER OF MARTIAL ARTS...
..IT'S POSSIBLE TO FIND A FOOTHOLD EVEN ON A SINGLE TWIG FLOATING ON THE WATER!
PLOOM
IT'S A SHARK.
IT IS, ISN'T IT?
THAT'S *DIRTY!*
IS ***NOT*** DIRTY!

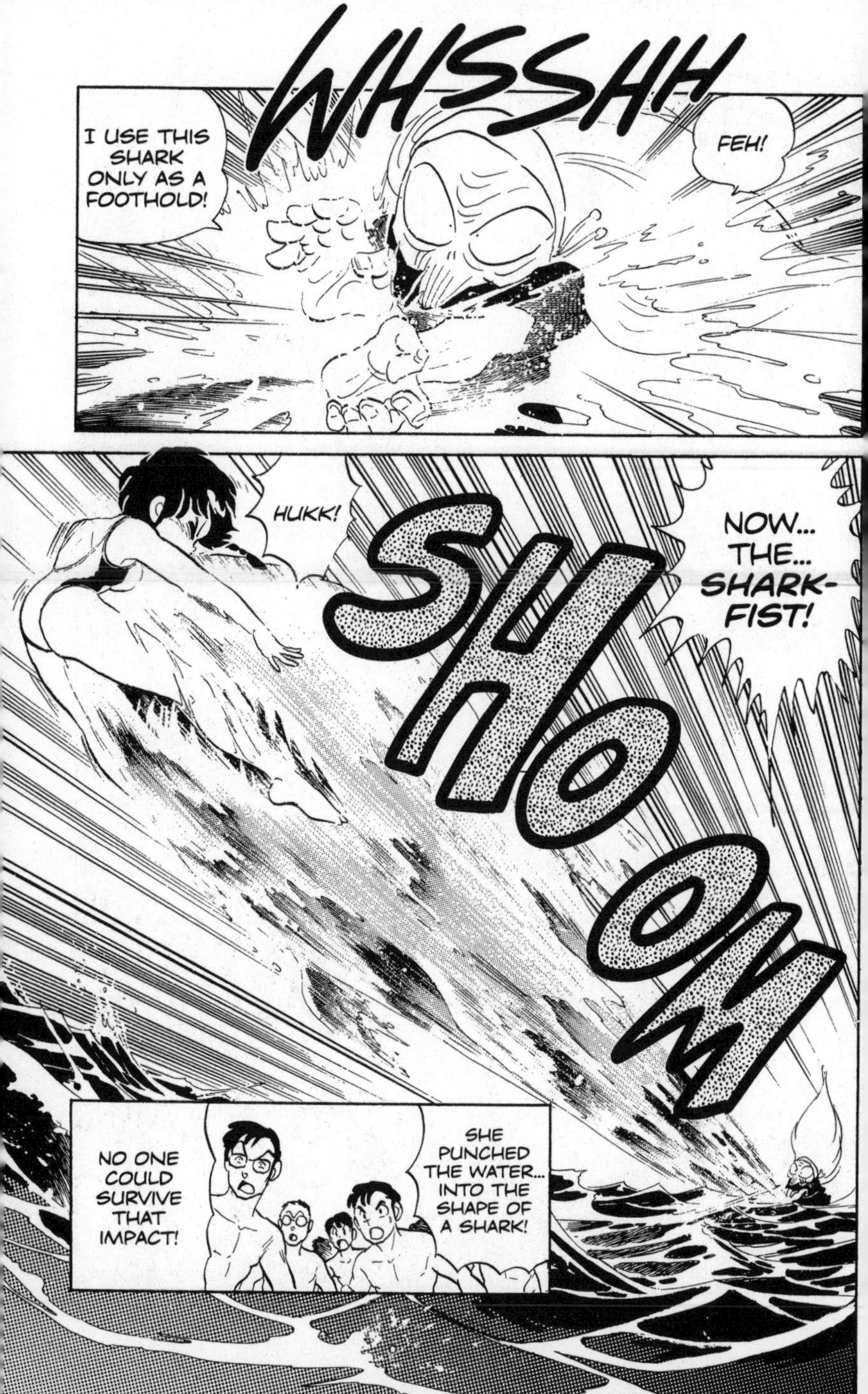
WHSSHH
FEH!
I USE THIS SHARK ONLY AS A FOOTHOLD!
NOW... THE... SHARK-FIST!
SHOOM
HUKK!
SHE PUNCHED THE WATER... INTO THE SHAPE OF A SHARK!
NO ONE COULD SURVIVE THAT IMPACT!

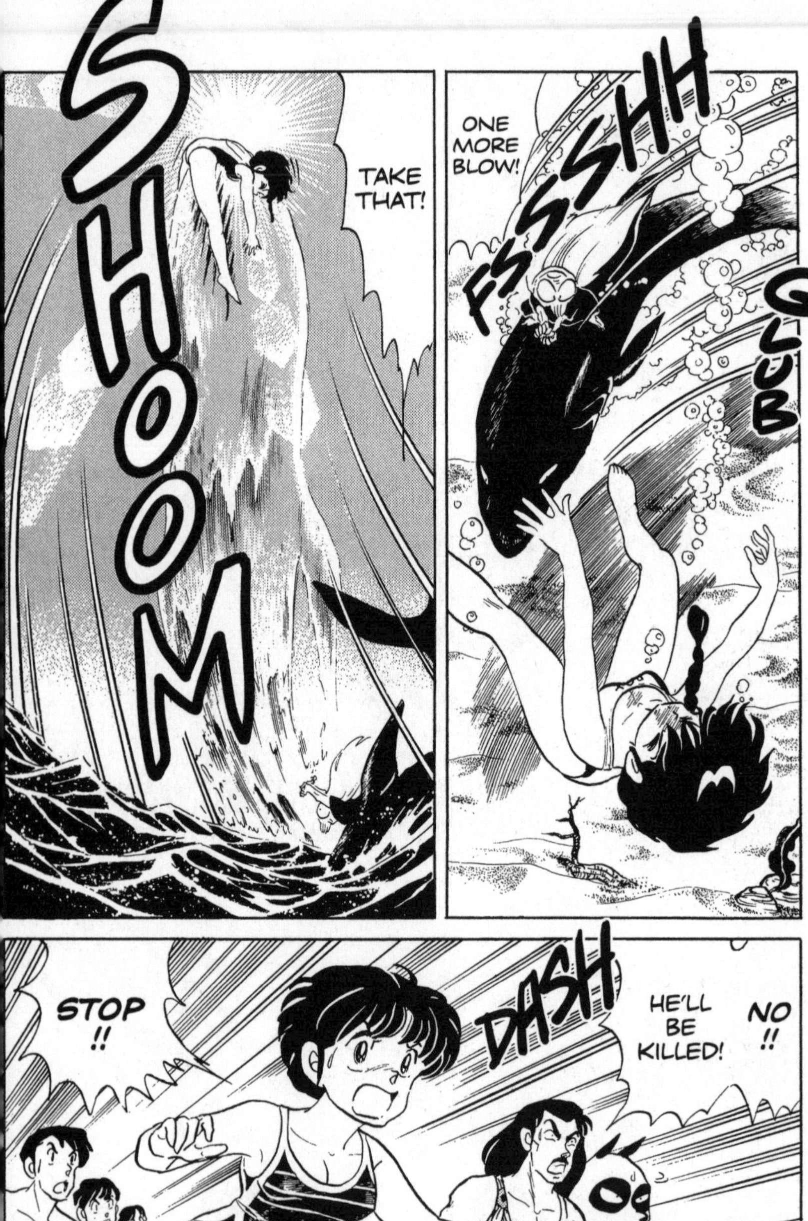
ONE MORE BLOW!
FSSSHH
GLUB
TAKE THAT!
SHOOM
NO !!
HE'LL BE KILLED!
DASH
STOP !!

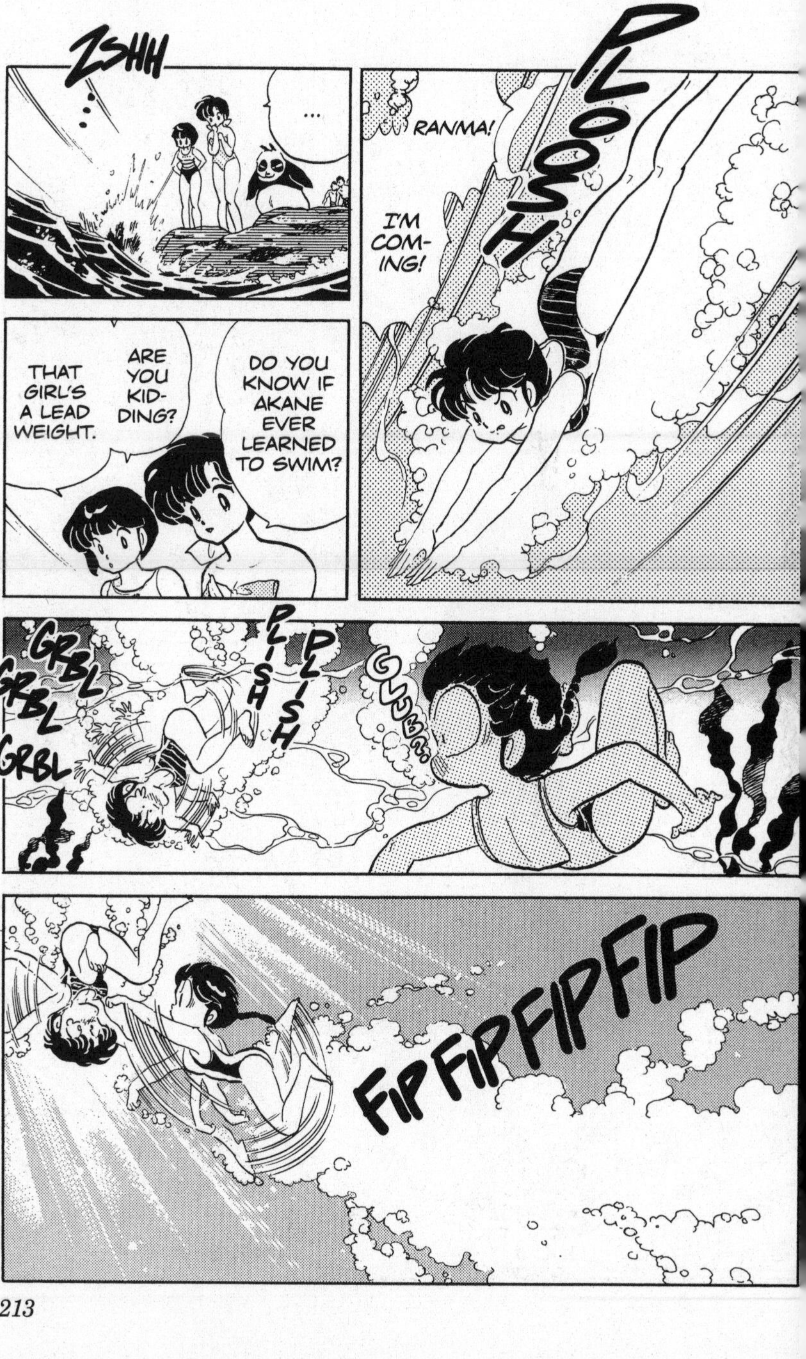
PLOOSH
RANMA!
I'M COMING!
ZSHH
...
...
DO YOU KNOW IF AKANE EVER LEARNED TO SWIM?
ARE YOU KIDDING?
THAT GIRL'S A LEAD WEIGHT.
GLUB?
PLISH PLISH
GRBL GRBL GRBL
FIP FIP FIP FIP FIP

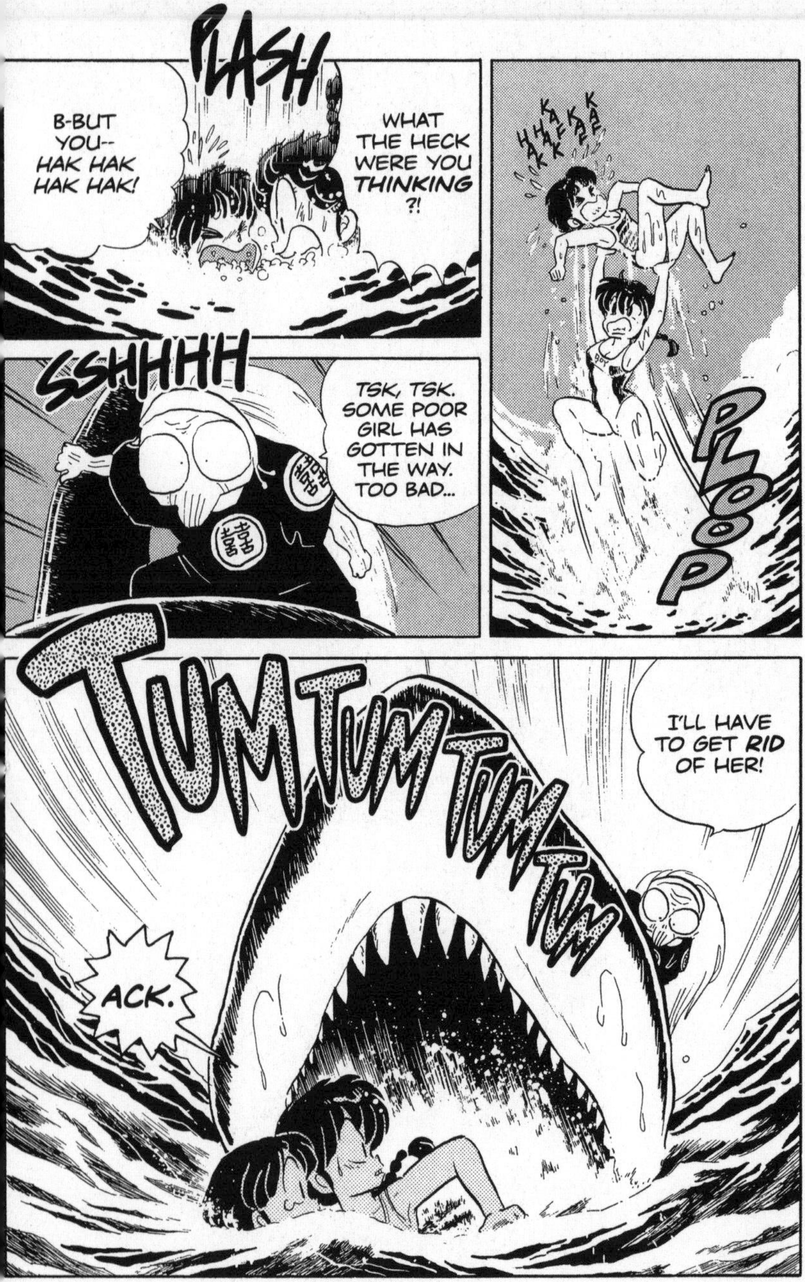
HAK HAK
PLOOP
PLASH
WHAT THE HECK WERE YOU THINKING ?!
B-BUT YOU-- HAK HAK HAK HAK!
SSHHHH
TSK, TSK. SOME POOR GIRL HAS GOTTEN IN THE WAY. TOO BAD...
I'LL HAVE TO GET RID OF HER!
TUM TUM TUM TUM
ACK.

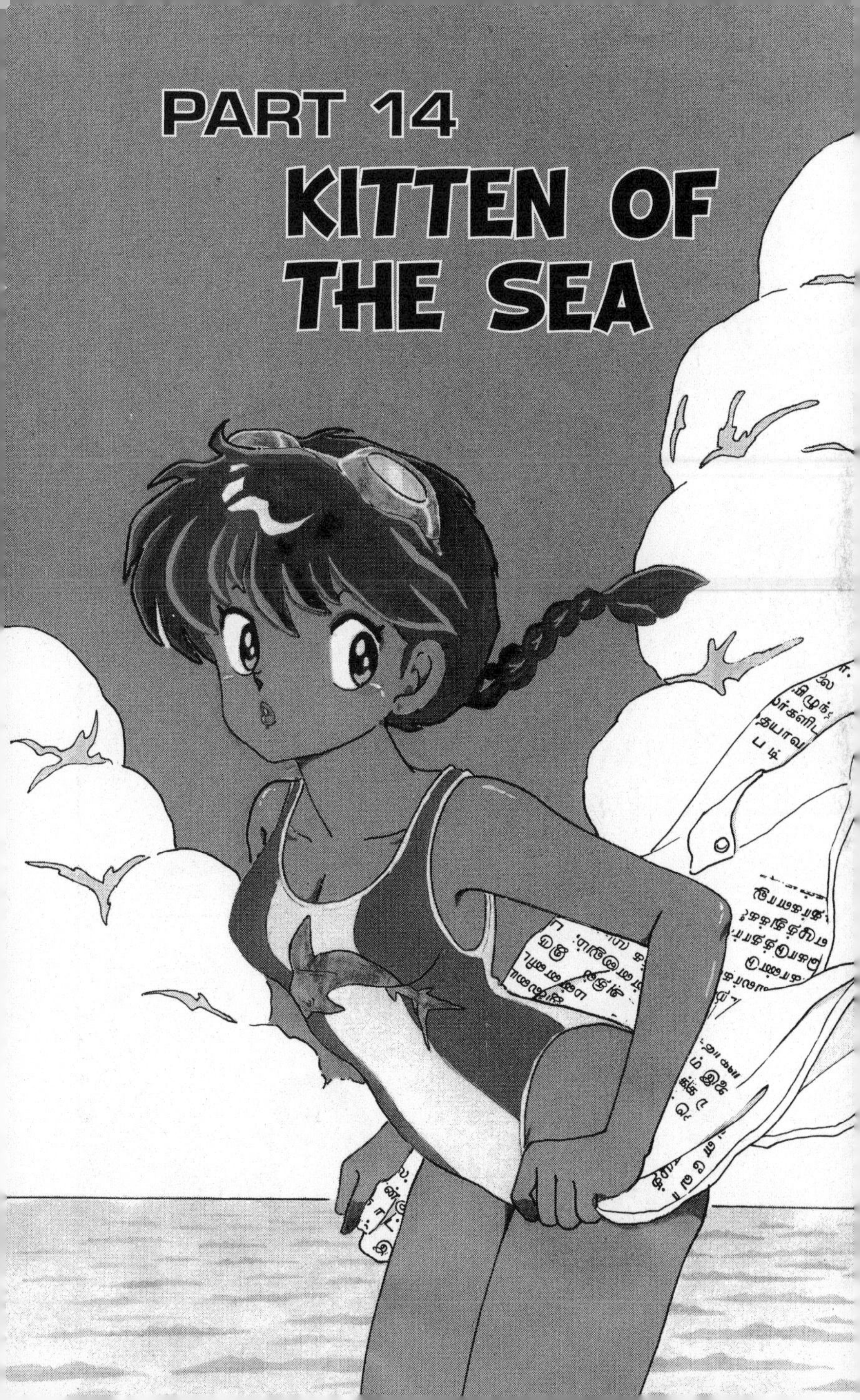
PART 14
KITTEN OF THE SEA

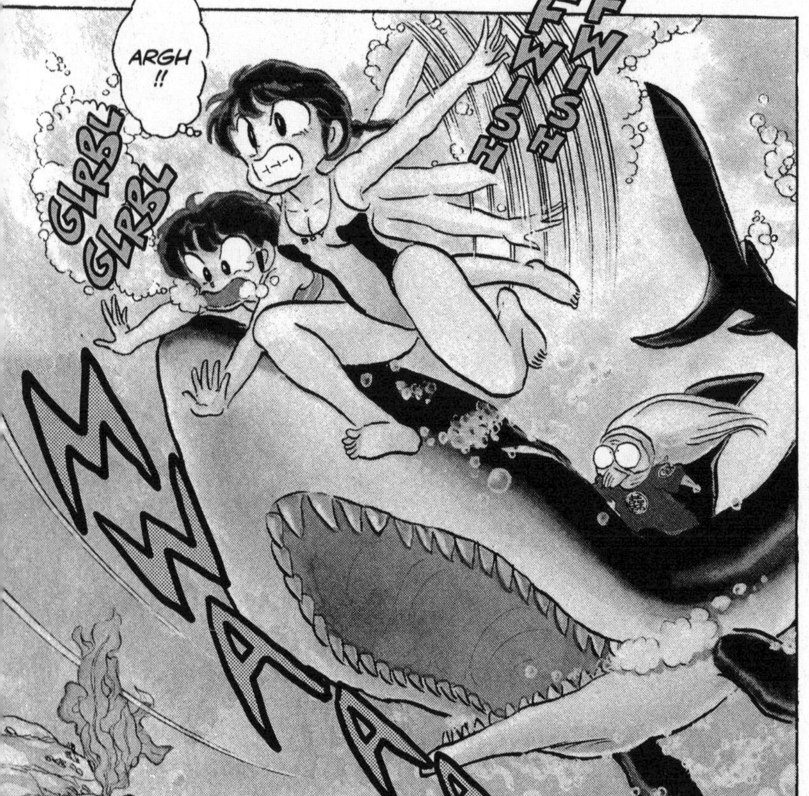
FWISH
FWISH
ARGH!!
GLRBL GLRBL
MWAAAA

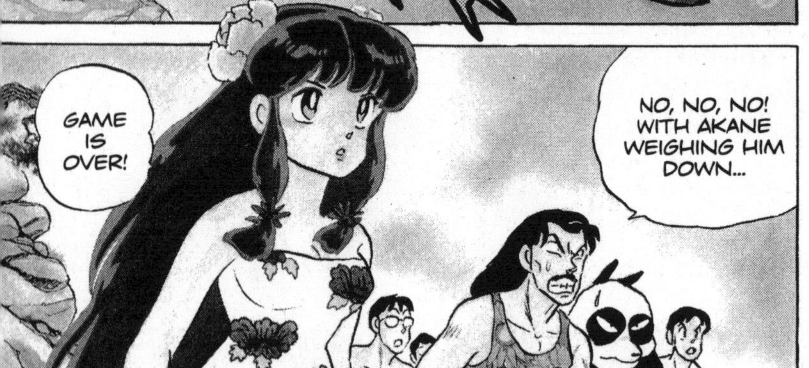
NO, NO, NO! WITH AKANE WEIGHING HIM DOWN...
GAME IS OVER!

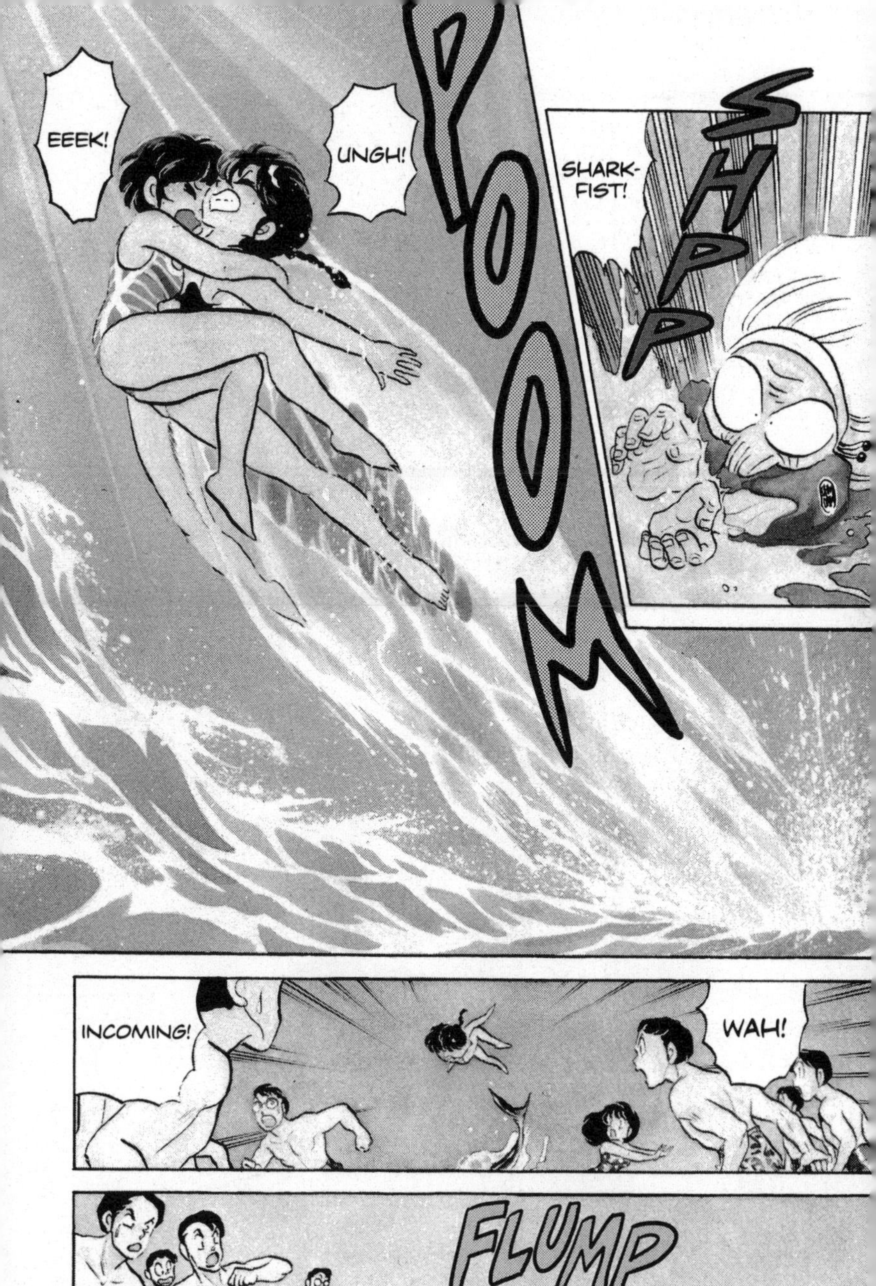
SHARK-FIST!
SHPP
UNGH!
EEEK!
OOOM
WAH!
INCOMING!
FLUMP

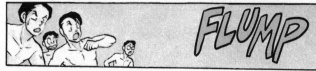

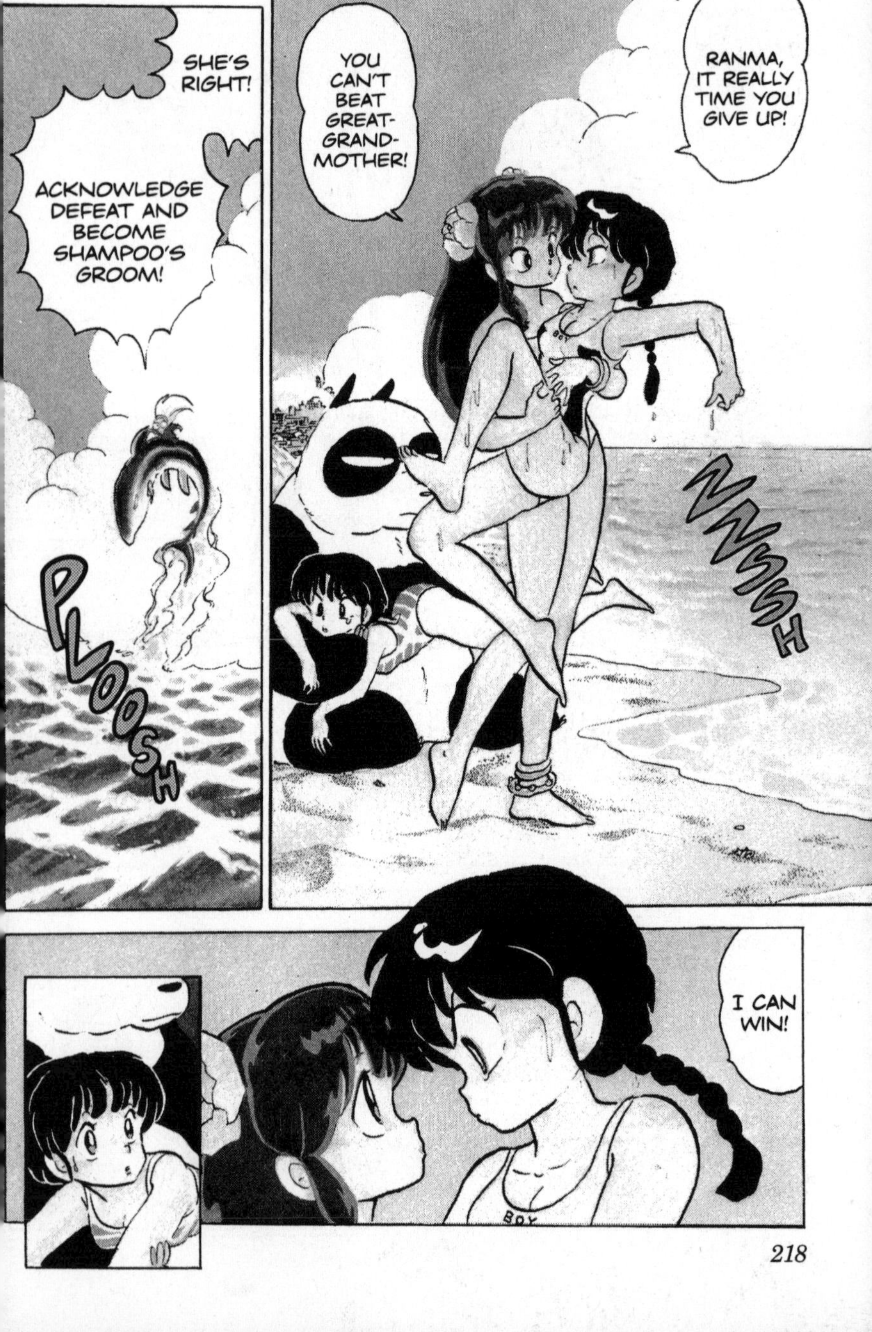
RANMA, IT REALLY TIME YOU GIVE UP!
YOU CAN'T BEAT GREAT-GRANDMOTHER!
NNSSH
SHE'S RIGHT!
ACKNOWLEDGE DEFEAT AND BECOME SHAMPOO'S GROOM!
PLOOSH
I CAN WIN!

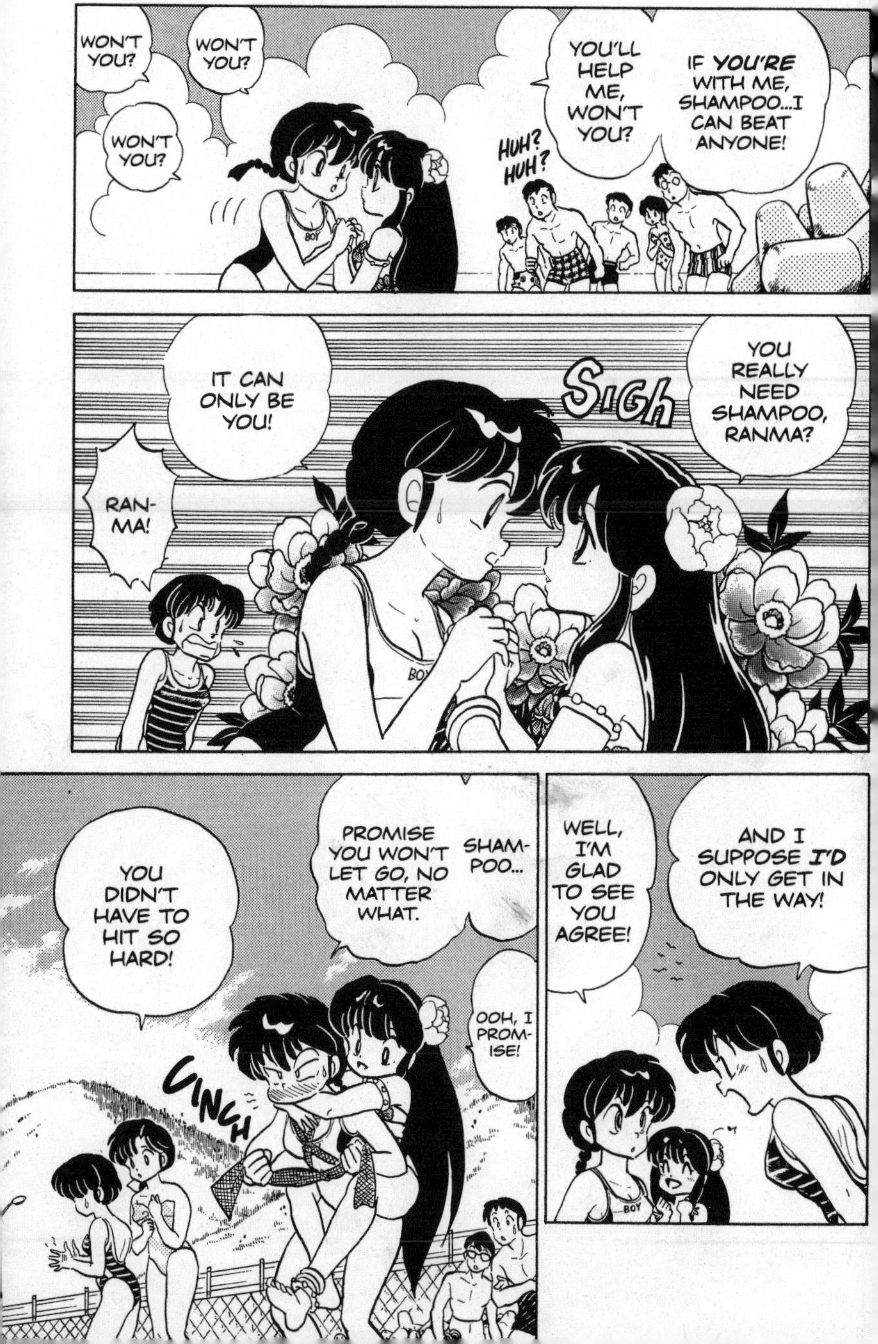
IF YOU'RE WITH ME, SHAMPOO...I CAN BEAT ANYONE!
YOU'LL HELP ME, WON'T YOU?
HUH? HUH?
WON'T YOU?
WON'T YOU?
WON'T YOU?
YOU REALLY NEED SHAMPOO, RANMA?
SIGH
IT CAN ONLY BE YOU!
RAN-MA!
AND I SUPPOSE I'D ONLY GET IN THE WAY!
WELL, I'M GLAD TO SEE YOU AGREE!
SHAM-POO...
PROMISE YOU WON'T LET GO, NO MATTER WHAT.
OOH, I PROMISE!
YOU DIDN'T HAVE TO HIT SO HARD!
CINCH

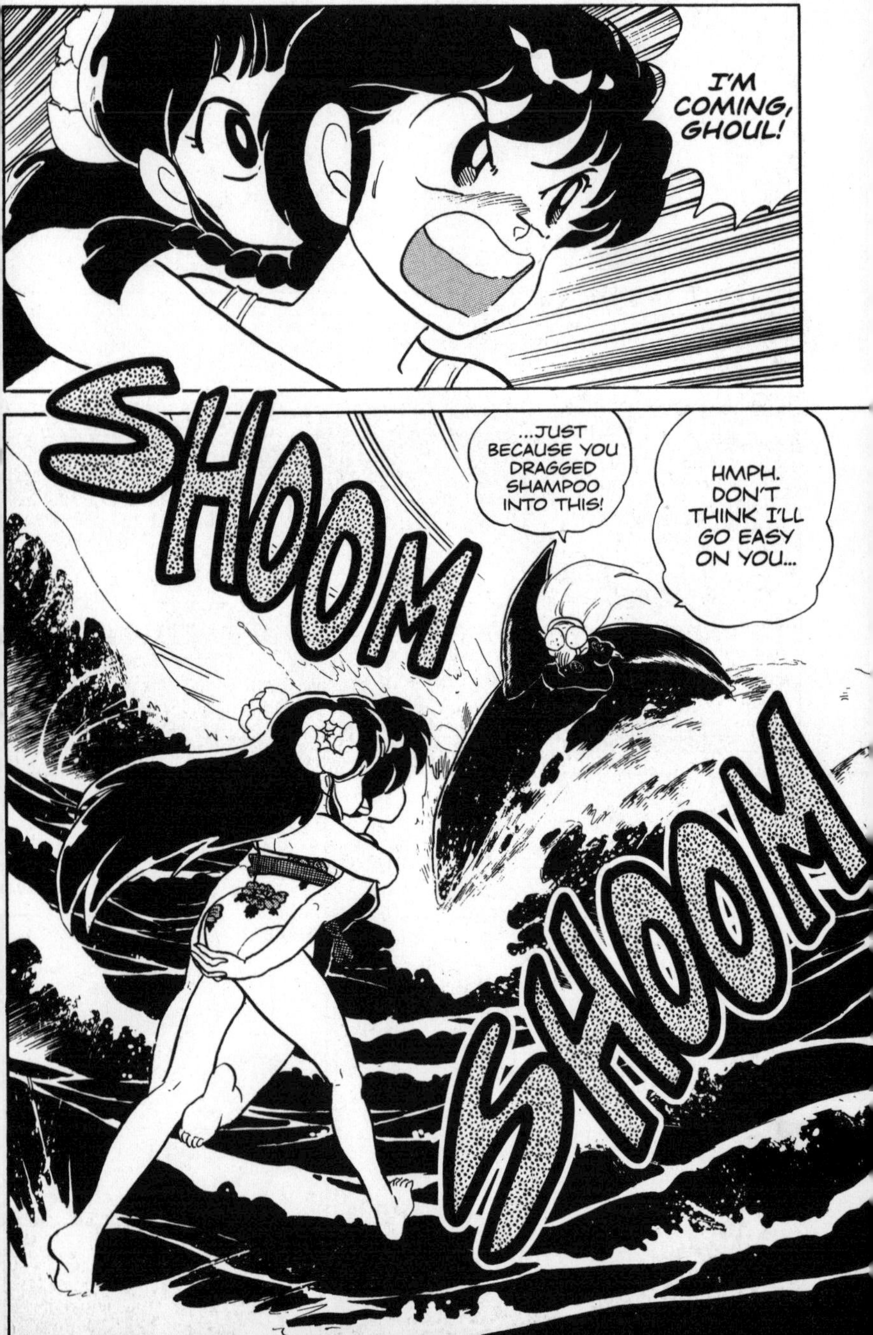
I'M COMING, GHOUL!
HMPH. DON'T THINK I'LL GO EASY ON YOU...
...JUST BECAUSE YOU DRAGGED SHAMPOO INTO THIS!
SHOOM
SHOOM

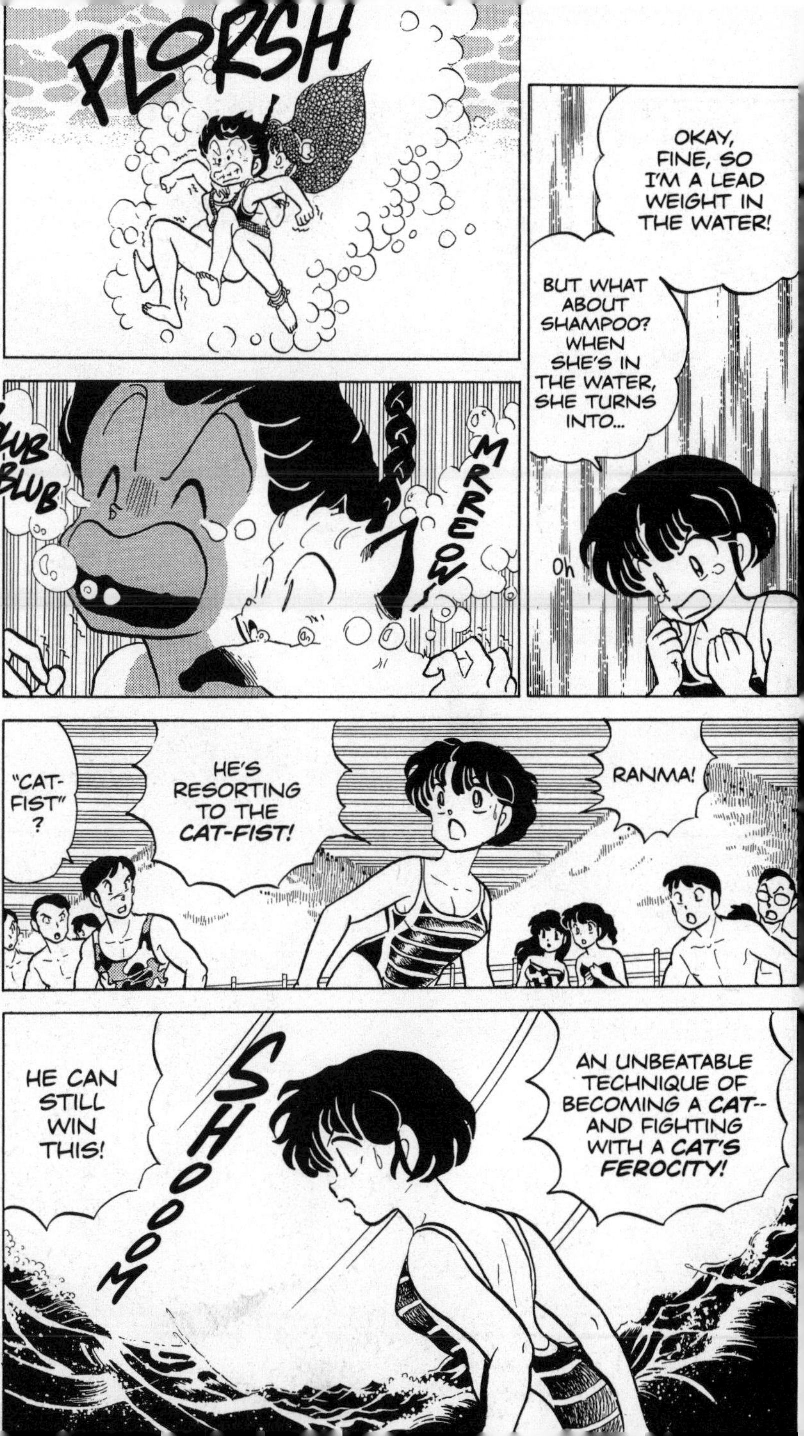
OKAY, FINE, SO I'M A LEAD WEIGHT IN THE WATER!
BUT WHAT ABOUT SHAMPOO? WHEN SHE'S IN THE WATER, SHE TURNS INTO...
Oh
PLORSH
MRREOW
BLUB BLUB
RANMA!
HE'S RESORTING TO THE CAT-FIST!
"CAT-FIST"?
AN UNBEATABLE TECHNIQUE OF BECOMING A CAT-- AND FIGHTING WITH A CAT'S FEROCITY!
SHOOOOOM
HE CAN STILL WIN THIS!

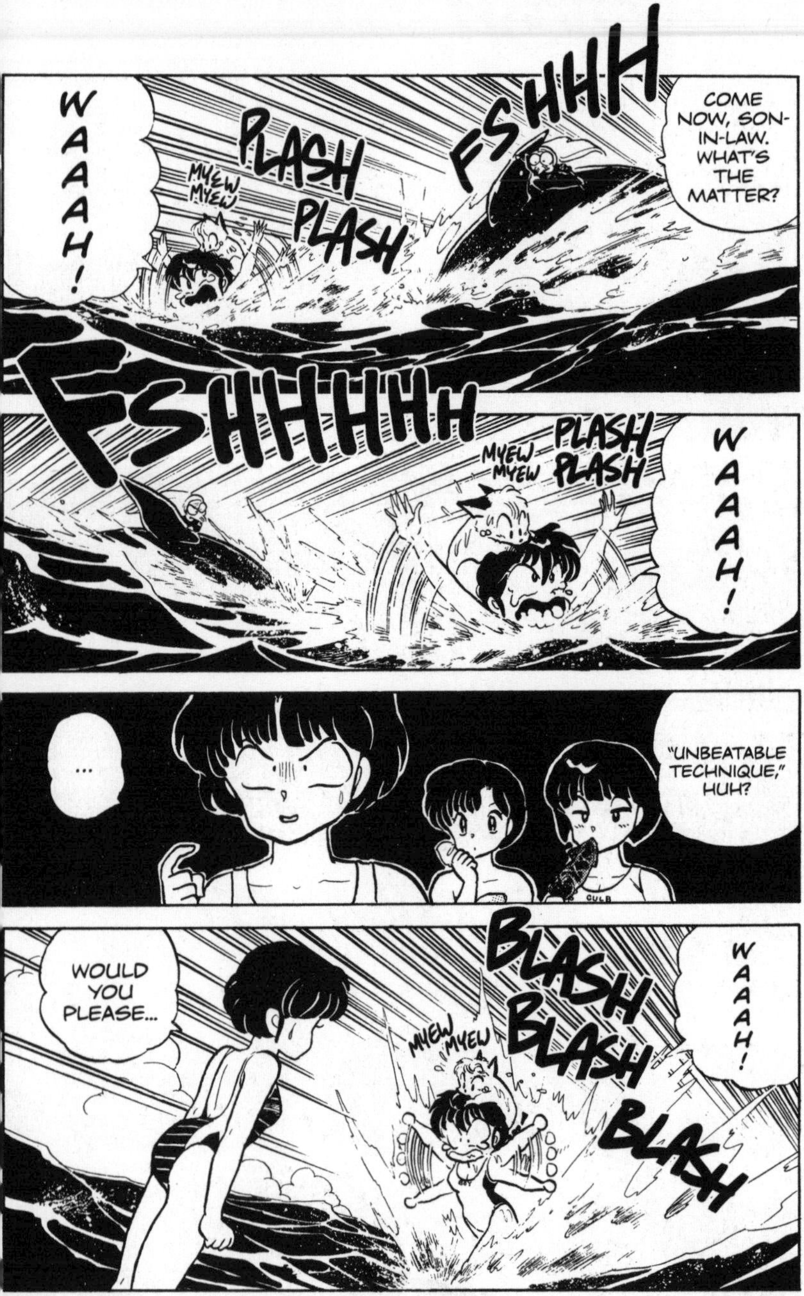
COME NOW, SON-IN-LAW. WHAT'S THE MATTER?
FSHHH
PLASH PLASH
MYEW MYEW
WAAAAH!
FSHHHHHH
WAAAAH!
PLASH PLASH
MYEW MYEW
"UNBEATABLE TECHNIQUE," HUH?
...
WAAAH!
BLASH BLASH BLASH
MYEW MYEW
WOULD YOU PLEASE...

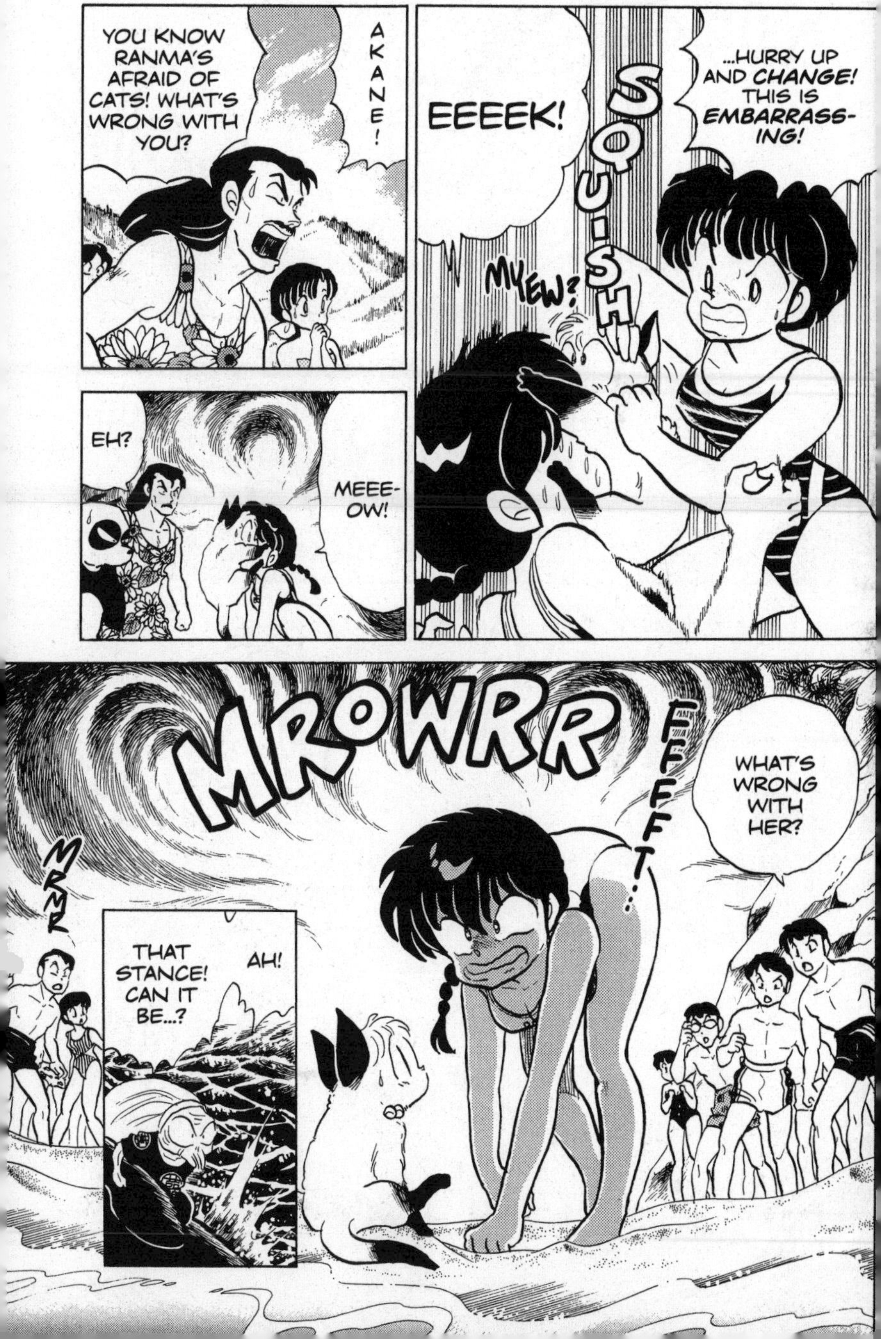
...HURRY UP AND CHANGE! THIS IS EMBARRASS-ING!
SQUISH
EEEEK!
MYEW?
AKANE!
YOU KNOW RANMA'S AFRAID OF CATS! WHAT'S WRONG WITH YOU?
MEEE-OW!
EH?
WHAT'S WRONG WITH HER?
FFFFFT...
MROWRR
AH!
THAT STANCE! CAN IT BE...?
MRMR

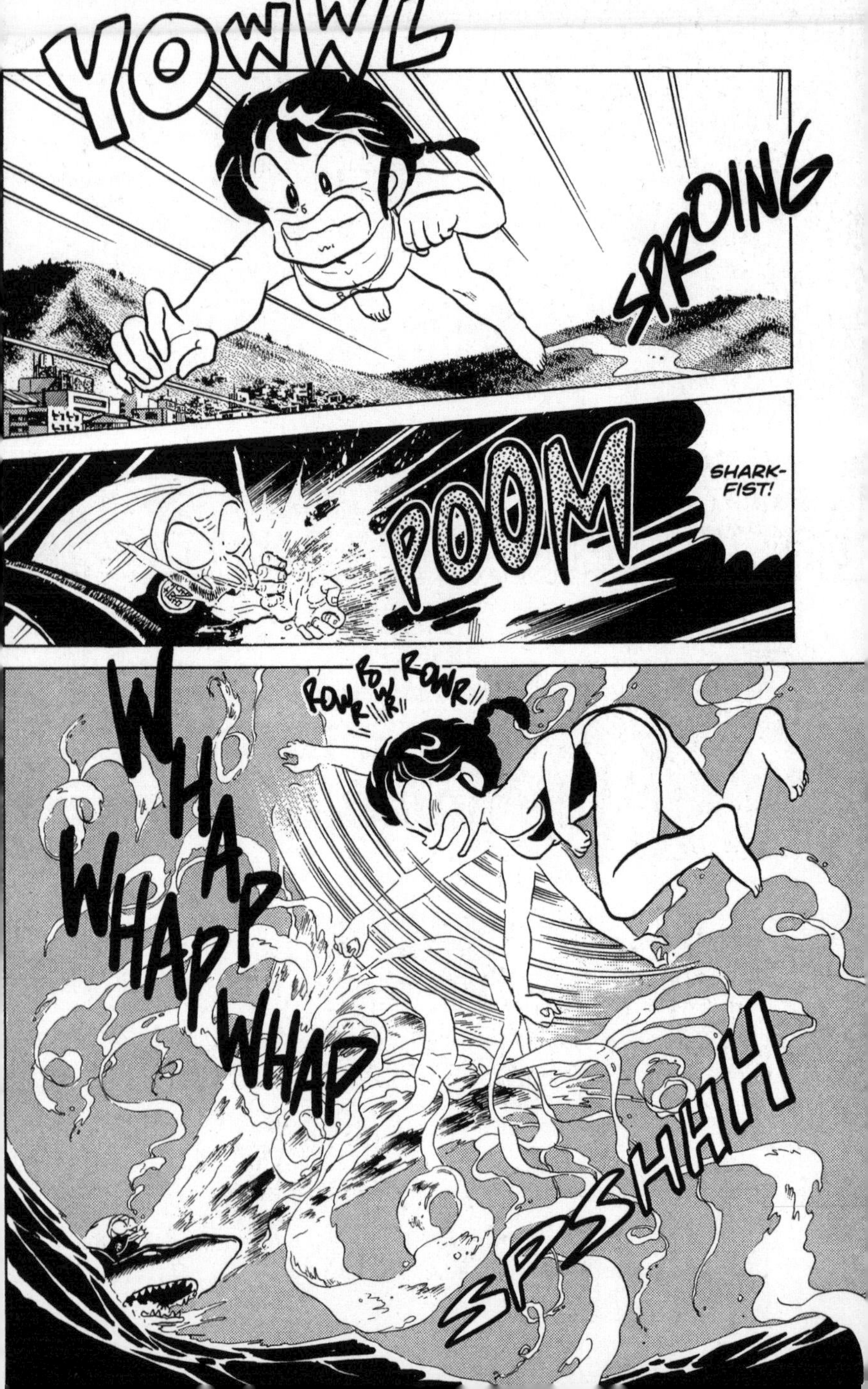
YOWWL
SPROING
SHARK-FIST!
POOM
ROWR ROWR ROWR
WHAP WHAP WHAP
SPSHHHH

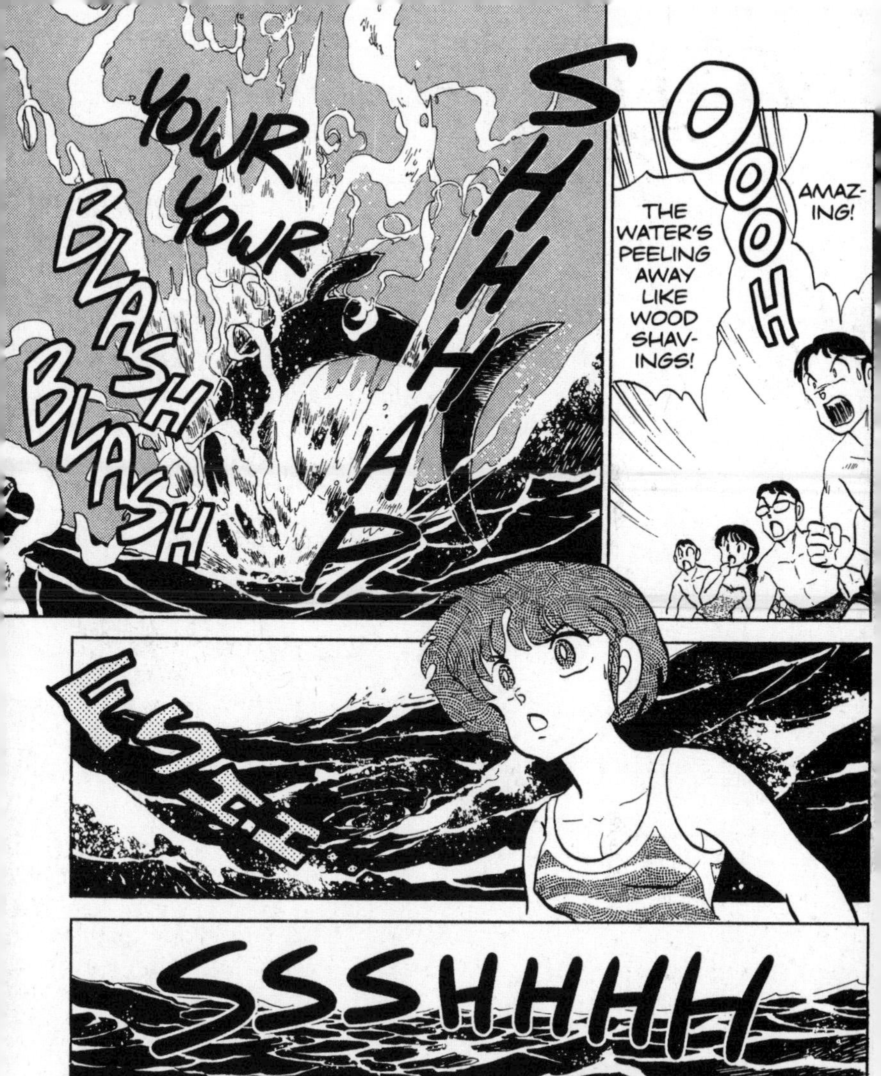
SOOOH
AMAZ-
ING!
THE WATER'S PEELING AWAY LIKE WOOD SHAV-INGS!
SHHHAP
YOWR YOWR
BLASH BLASH
SSSHHHH
SO...SO QUIET!
WHAT HAPPENED OUT THERE?

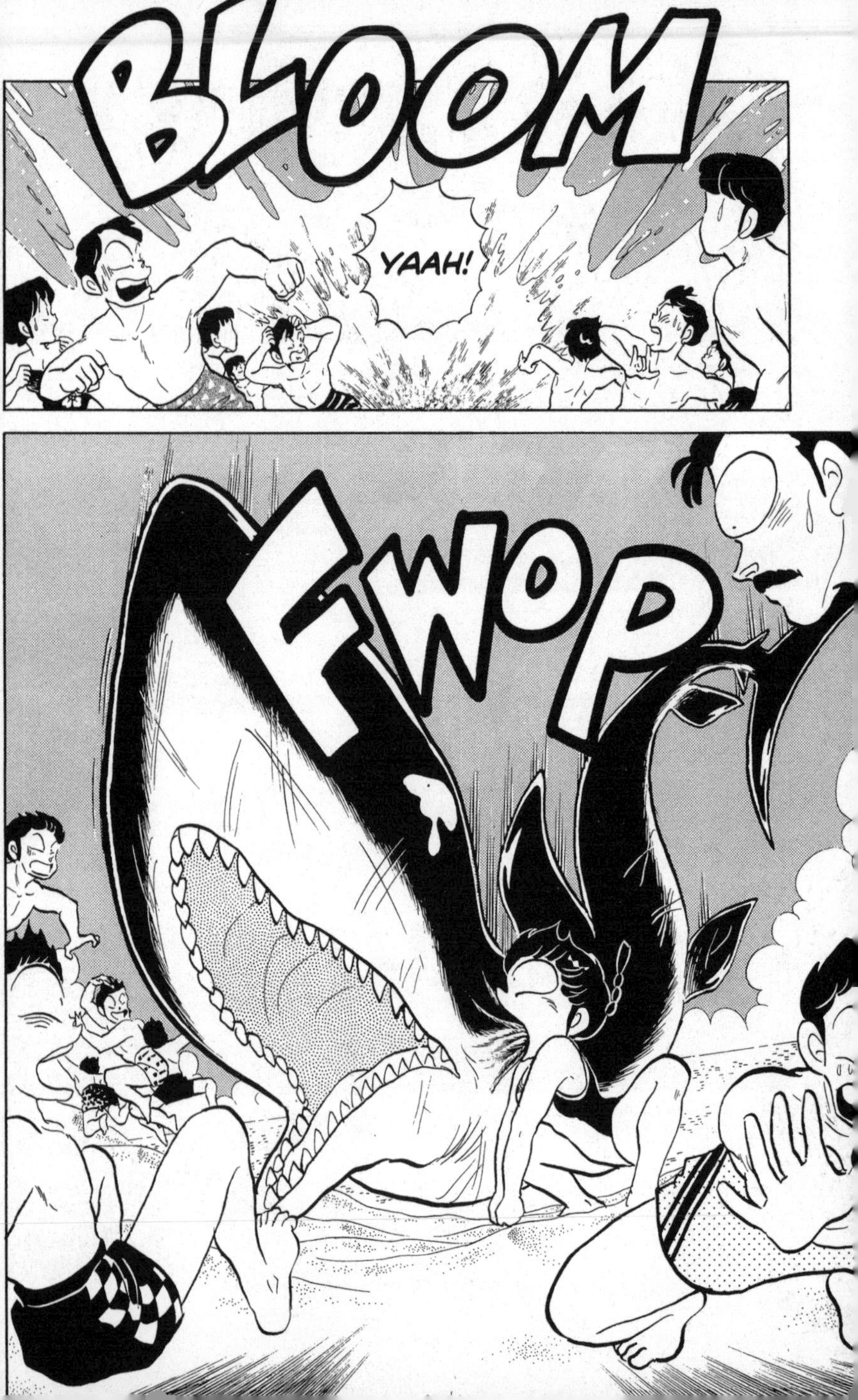
BLOOM
YAAH!
FWOP

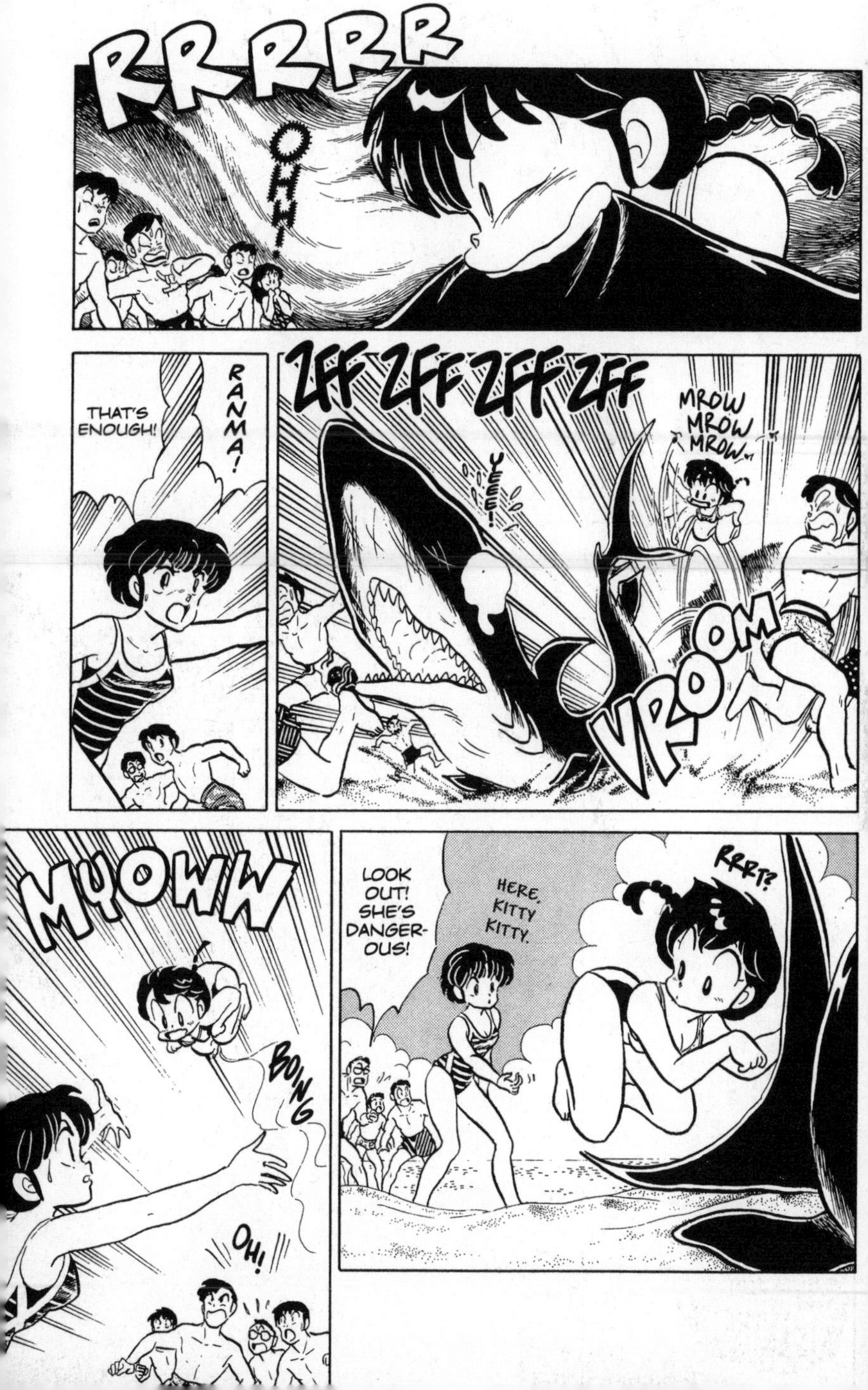
RRRRR
OHHH!
ZFF ZFF ZFF ZFF
MROW MROW MROW
YEEE!
VROOM
RANMA!
THAT'S ENOUGH!
RRRT?
HERE, KITTY KITTY.
LOOK OUT! SHE'S DANGER-OUS!
MYOWW
BOING
OH!

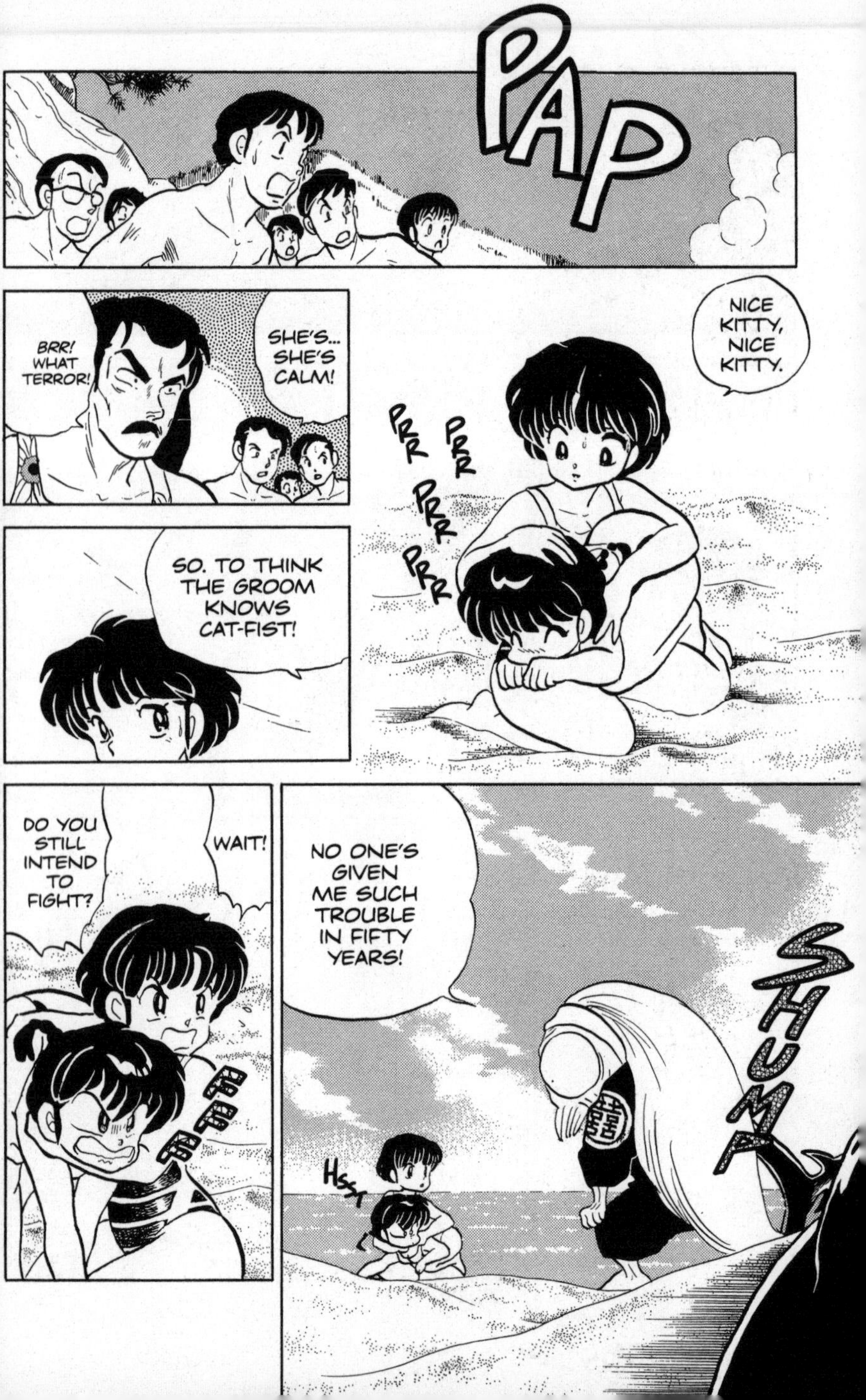
PAP
NICE KITTY, NICE KITTY.
PRR PRR PRR PRR
SHE'S... SHE'S CALM!
BRR! WHAT TERROR!
SO. TO THINK THE GROOM KNOWS CAT-FIST!
NO ONE'S GIVEN ME SUCH TROUBLE IN FIFTY YEARS!
SHUMA
HSSS
WAIT!
DO YOU STILL INTEND TO FIGHT?

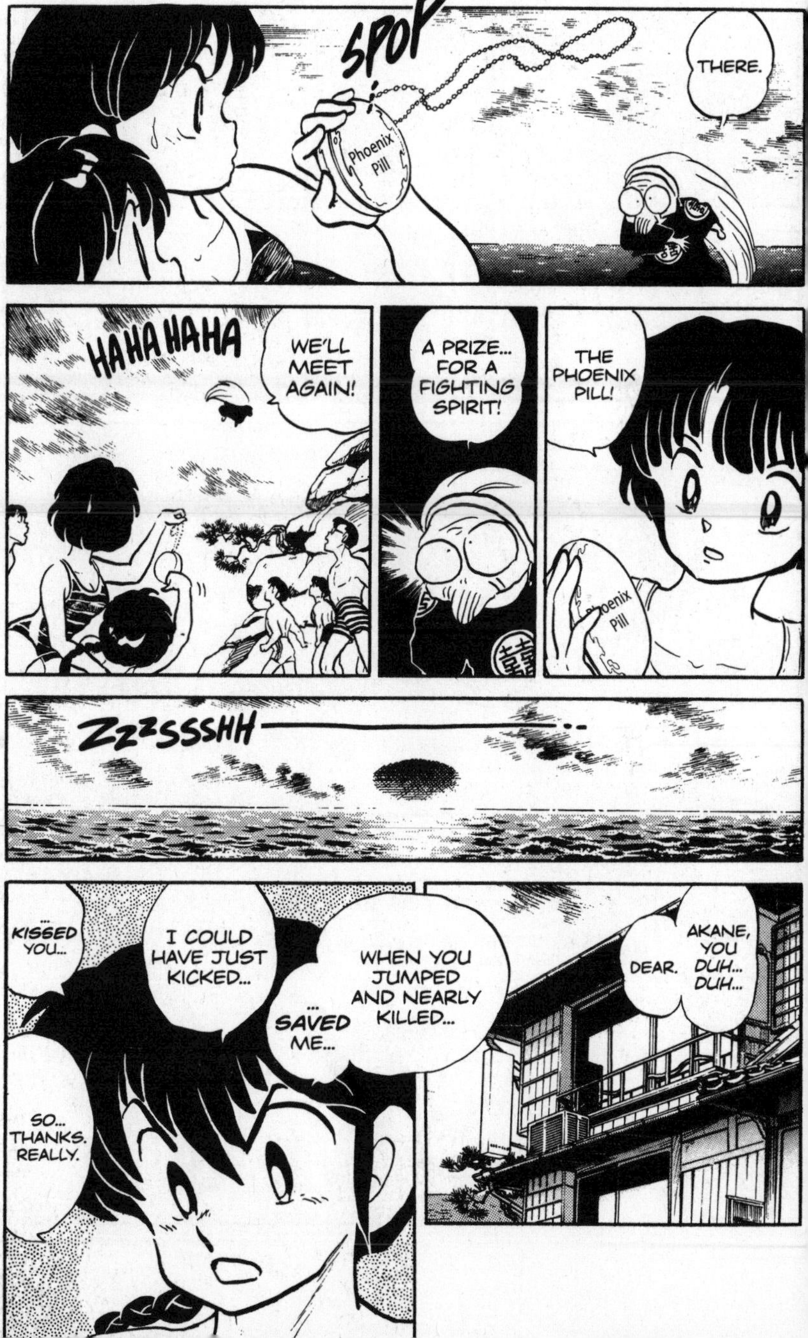
THERE.
SPOP
Phoenix Pill
THE PHOENIX PILL!
Phoenix Pill
A PRIZE... FOR A FIGHTING SPIRIT!
WE'LL MEET AGAIN!
HAHAHAHA
ZZZSSSHH
AKANE, YOU DUH... DUH...
DEAR.
WHEN YOU JUMPED AND NEARLY KILLED...
...SAVED ME...
I COULD HAVE JUST KICKED...
...KISSED YOU...
SO... THANKS. REALLY.

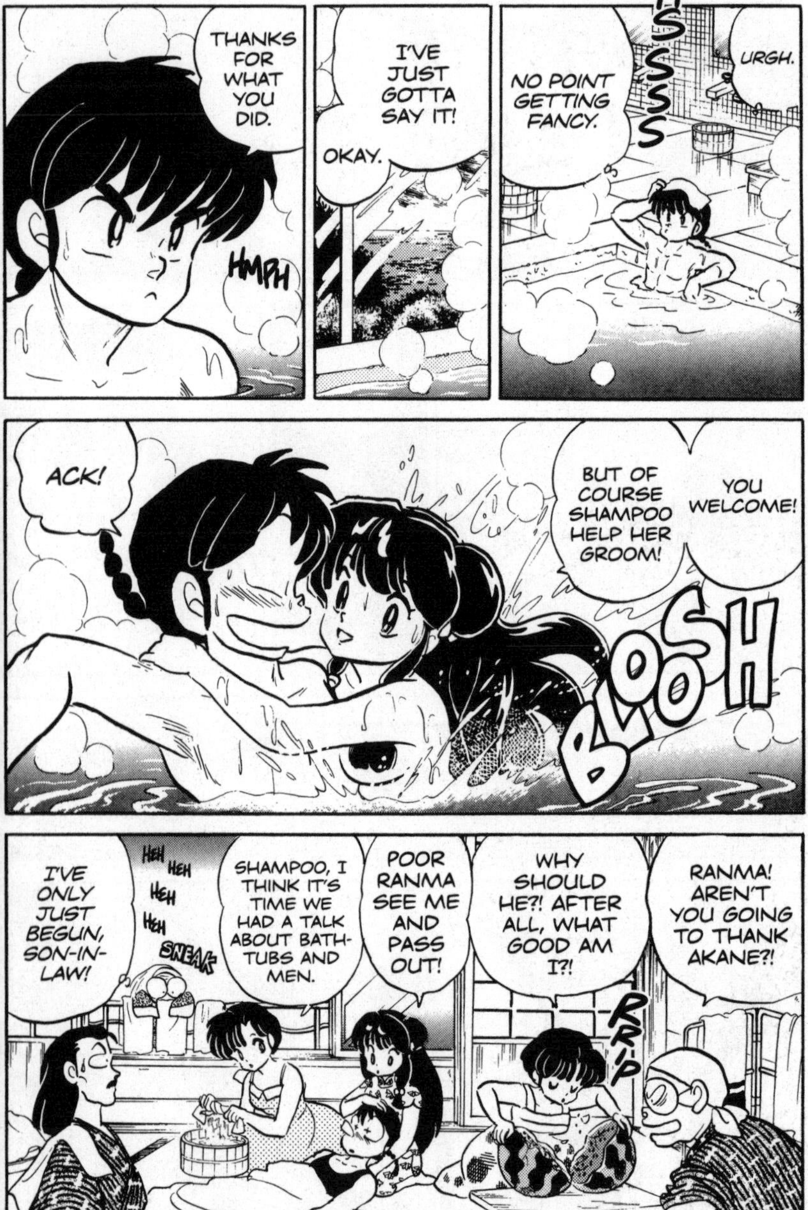
URGH.
HSSSS
NO POINT GETTING FANCY.
I'VE JUST GOTTA SAY IT!
OKAY.
THANKS FOR WHAT YOU DID.
HMPH
YOU WELCOME!
BUT OF COURSE SHAMPOO HELP HER GROOM!
BLOOSH
ACK!
RANMA! AREN'T YOU GOING TO THANK AKANE?!
WHY SHOULD HE?! AFTER ALL, WHAT GOOD AM I?!
RRIP
POOR RANMA SEE ME AND PASS OUT!
SHAMPOO, I THINK IT'S TIME WE HAD A TALK ABOUT BATH-TUBS AND MEN.
HEH HEH HEH HEH
SNEAK
I'VE ONLY JUST BEGUN, SON-IN-LAW!

PART 15
CARE TO JOIN ME?

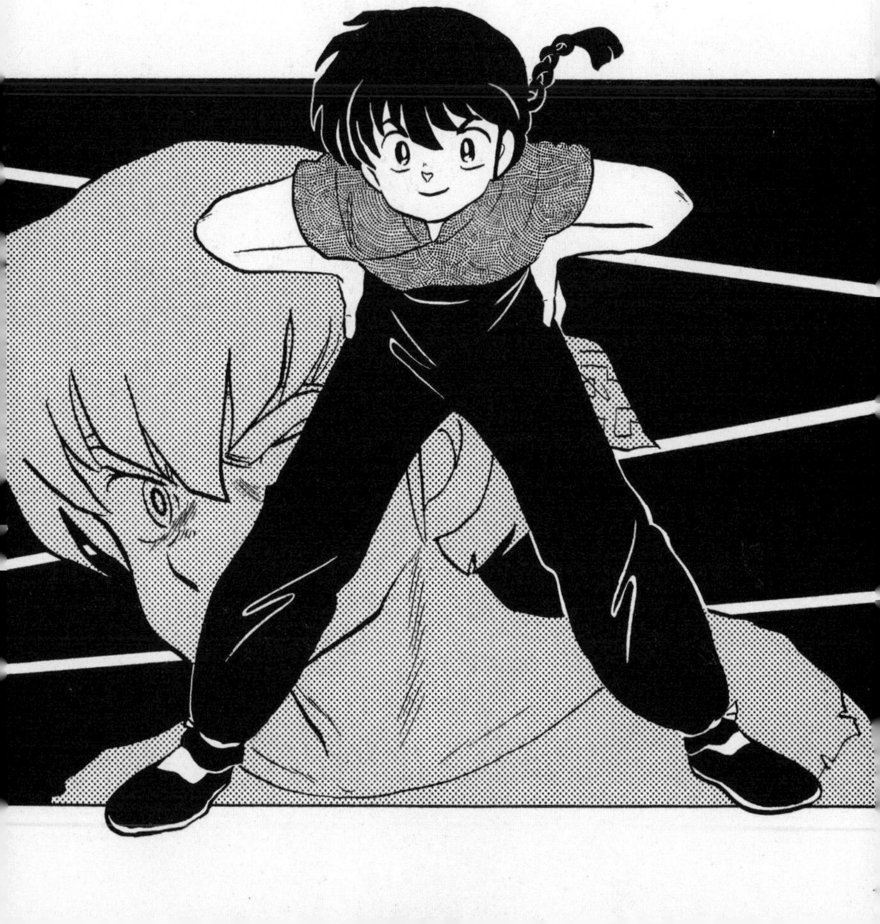

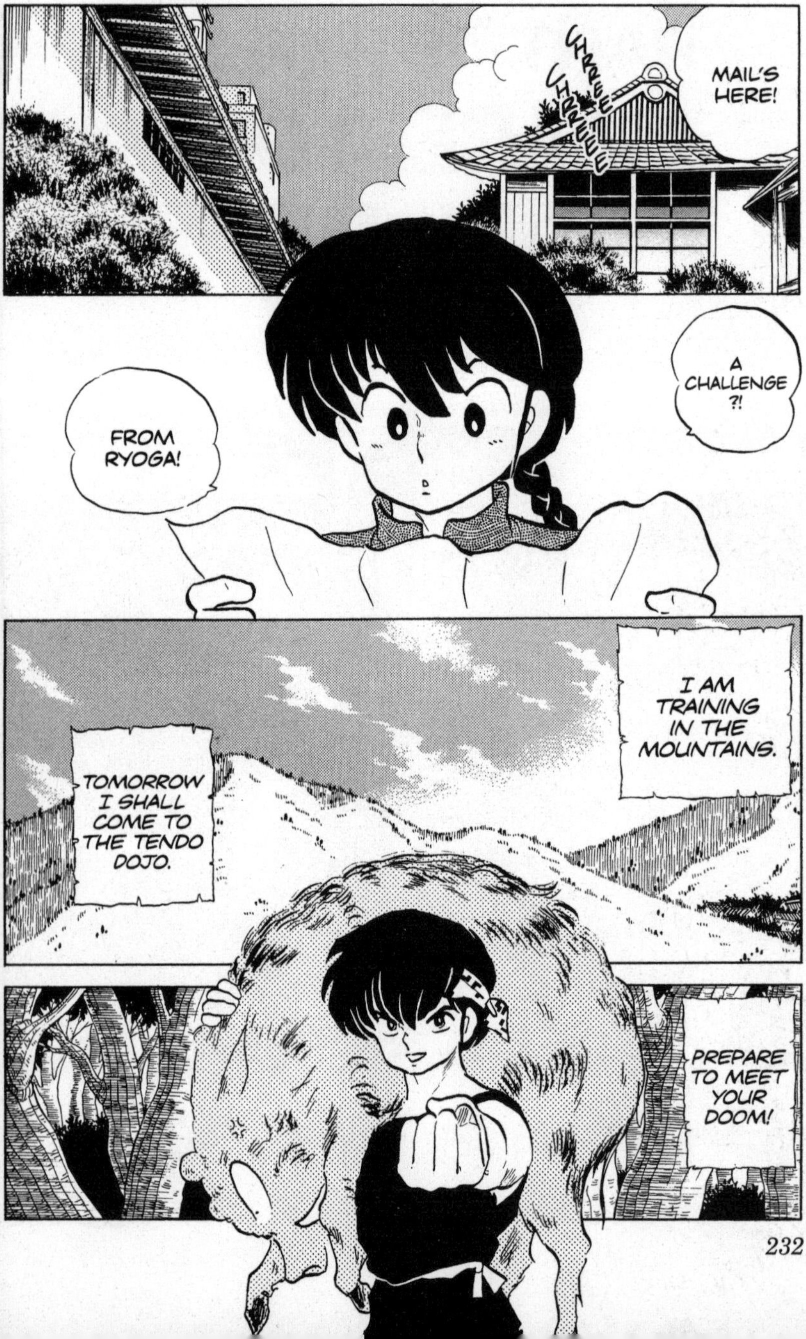
MAIL'S HERE!
CHRREEE CHRREEE
A CHALLENGE?!
FROM RYOGA!
I AM TRAINING IN THE MOUNTAINS.
TOMORROW I SHALL COME TO THE TENDO DOJO.
PREPARE TO MEET YOUR DOOM!

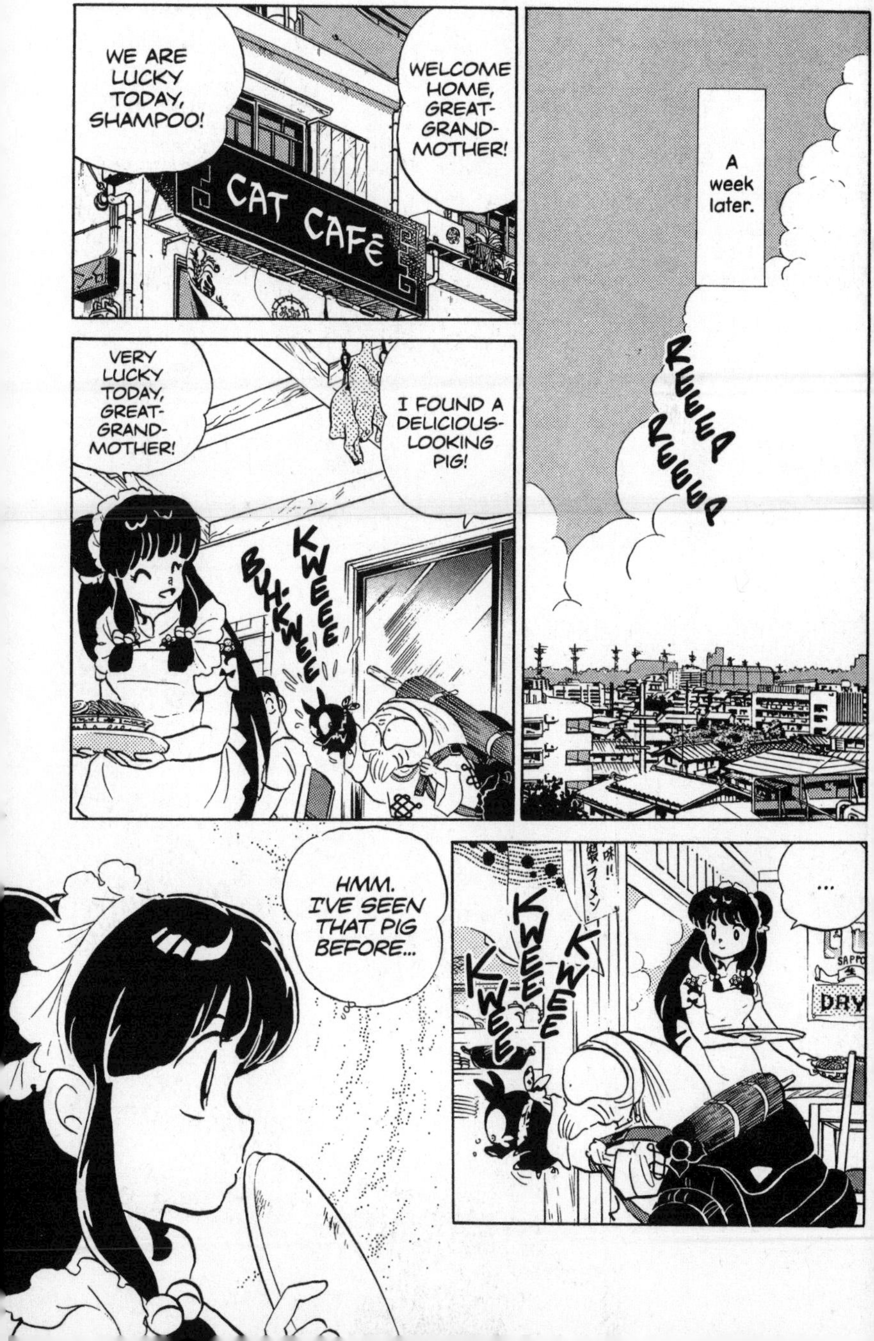
A week later.
REEEEP REEEEP
CAT CAFÉ
WELCOME HOME, GREAT-GRANDMOTHER!
WE ARE LUCKY TODAY, SHAMPOO!
I FOUND A DELICIOUS-LOOKING PIG!
VERY LUCKY TODAY, GREAT-GRANDMOTHER!
KWEEE
BUHKWEEE
...
KWEEE
KWEEE
KWEEE
HMM. I'VE SEEN THAT PIG BEFORE...

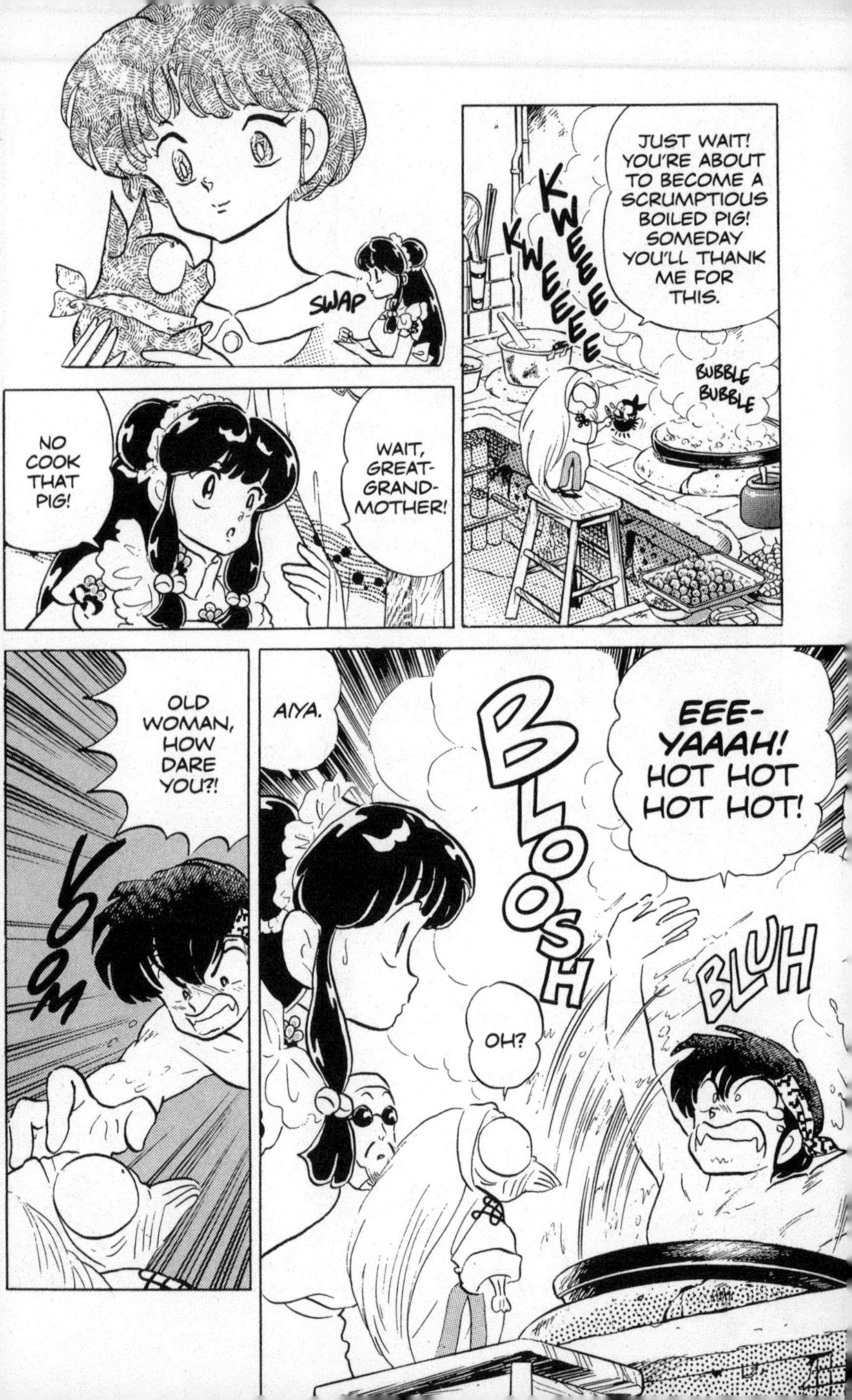
JUST WAIT! YOU'RE ABOUT TO BECOME A SCRUMPTIOUS BOILED PIG! SOMEDAY YOU'LL THANK ME FOR THIS.
KWEEEE
KWEEEEE
BUBBLE BUBBLE
SWAP
WAIT, GREAT-GRANDMOTHER!
NO COOK THAT PIG!
EEE-YAAAH! HOT HOT HOT HOT!
BLOOSH
AIYA.
BLUH
OH?
OLD WOMAN, HOW DARE YOU?!
VOOM

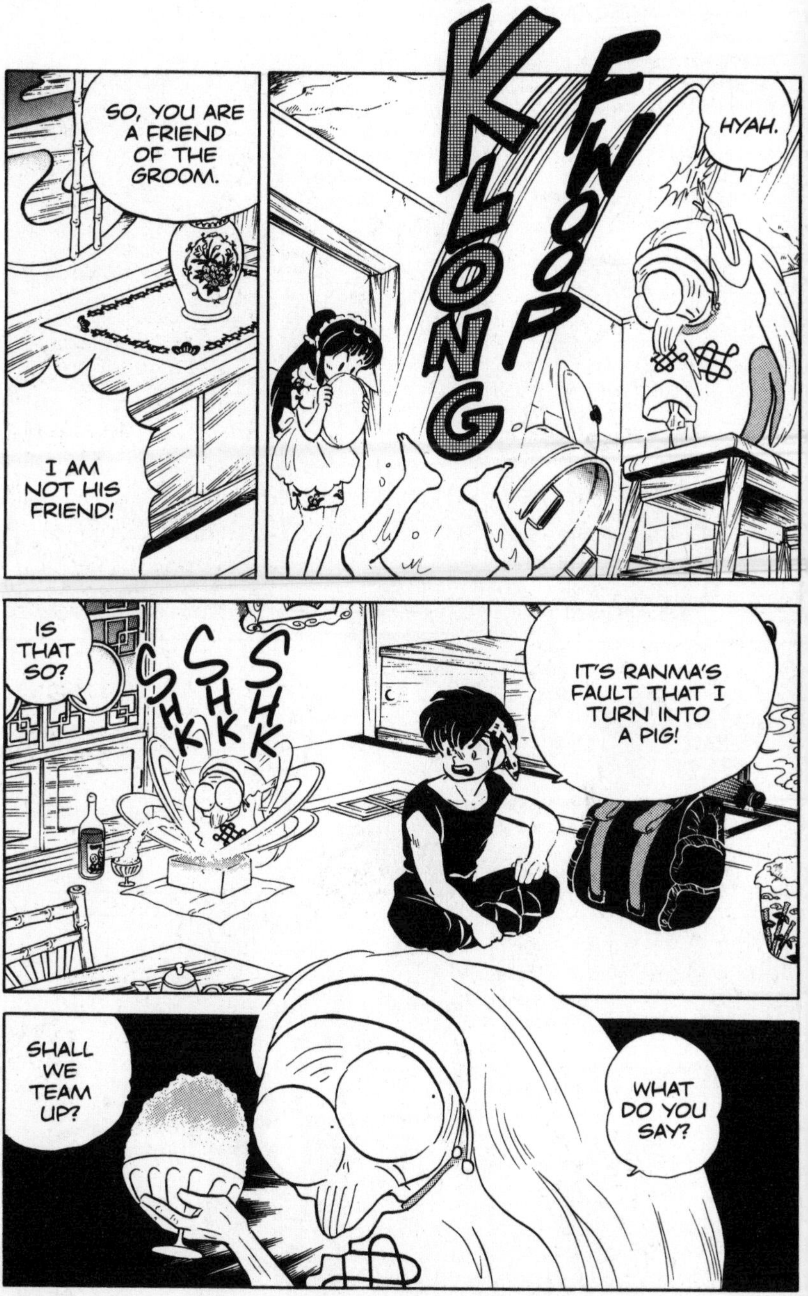
HYAH.
FWOOP
KLLONG
SO, YOU ARE A FRIEND OF THE GROOM.
I AM NOT HIS FRIEND!
IT'S RANMA'S FAULT THAT I TURN INTO A PIG!
IS THAT SO?
SHK SHK SHK
SHALL WE TEAM UP?
WHAT DO YOU SAY?

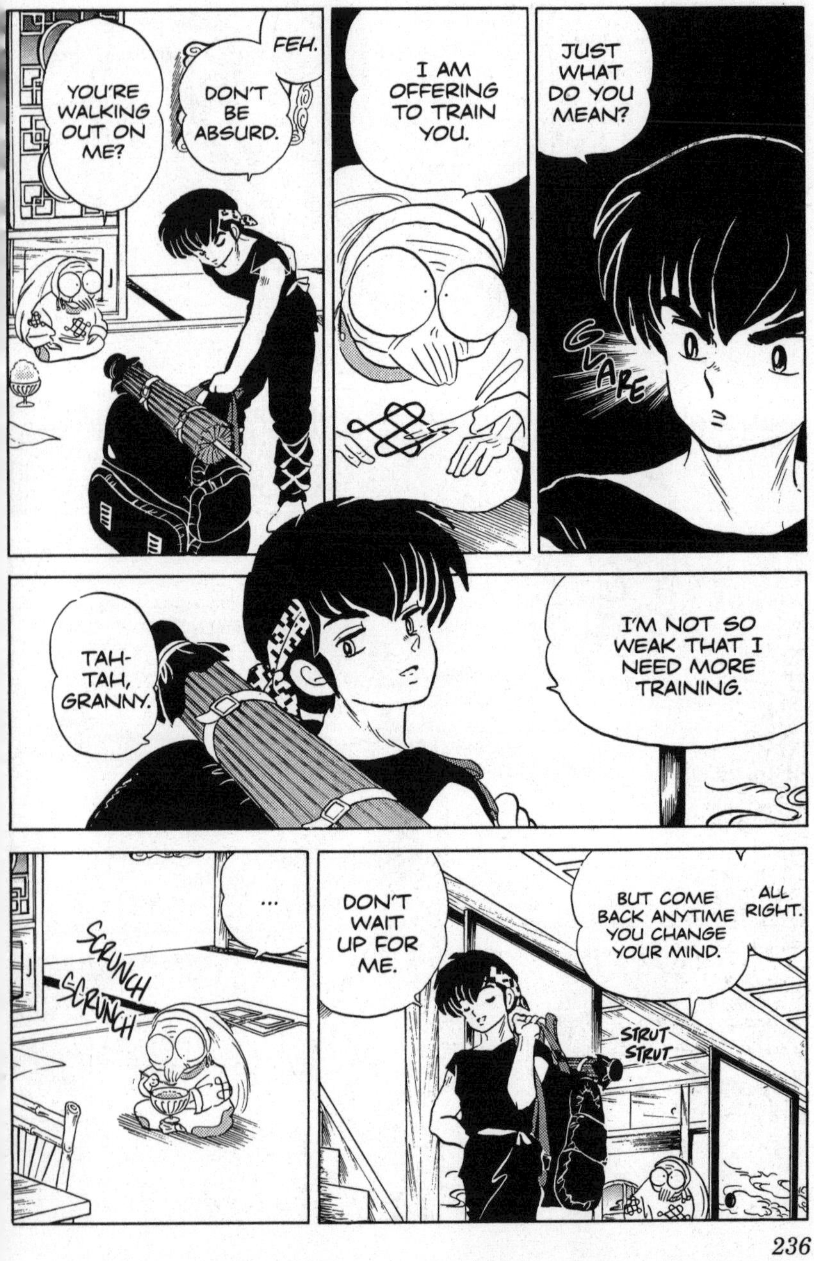

JUST WHAT DO YOU MEAN?
GLARE
I AM OFFERING TO TRAIN YOU.
FEH.
DON'T BE ABSURD.
YOU'RE WALKING OUT ON ME?
I'M NOT SO WEAK THAT I NEED MORE TRAINING.
TAH-TAH, GRANNY.
ALL RIGHT.
BUT COME BACK ANYTIME YOU CHANGE YOUR MIND.
STRUT STRUT
DON'T WAIT UP FOR ME.
...
SCRUNCH SCRUNCH

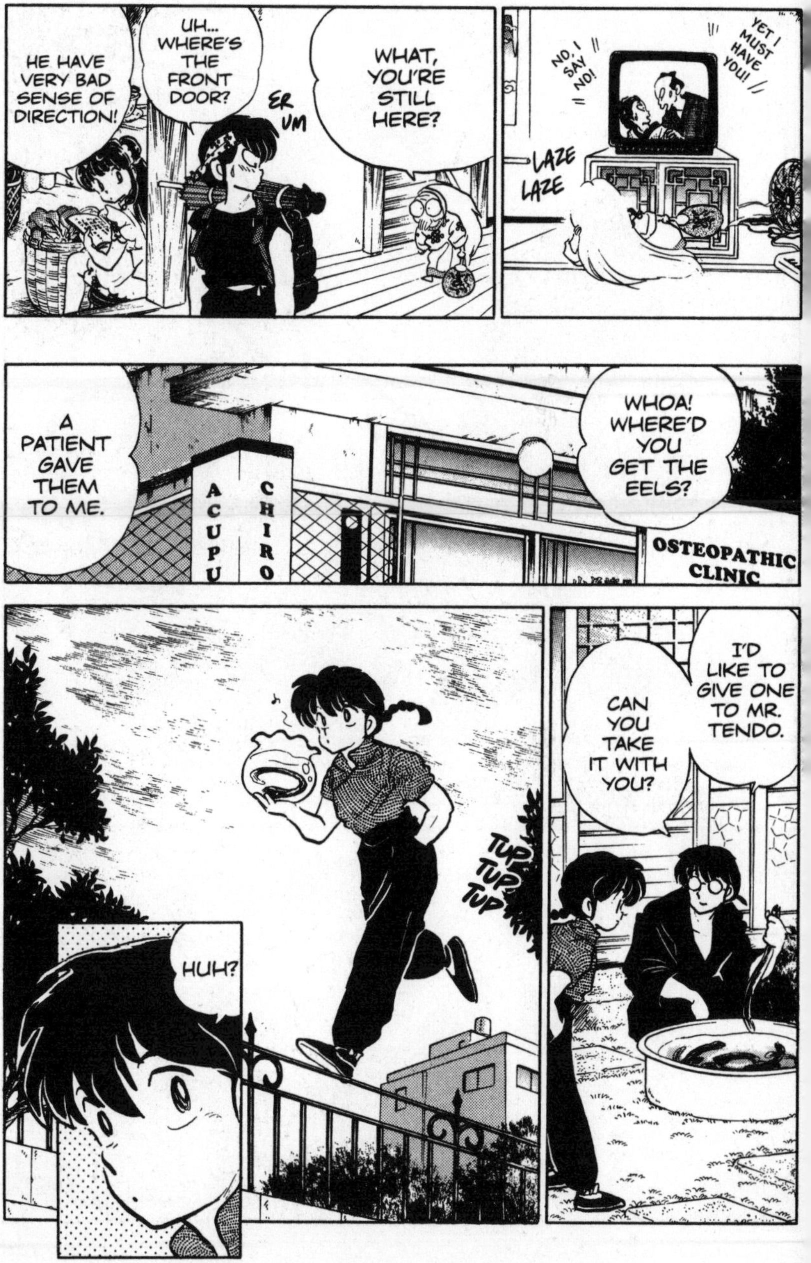
YET I MUST HAVE YOU!!
NO, I SAY NO!
LAZE LAZE
WHAT, YOU'RE STILL HERE?
ER UM
UH... WHERE'S THE FRONT DOOR?
HE HAVE VERY BAD SENSE OF DIRECTION!
WHOA! WHERE'D YOU GET THE EELS?
OSTEOPATHIC CLINIC
CHIRO
ACUPU
A PATIENT GAVE THEM TO ME.
I'D LIKE TO GIVE ONE TO MR. TENDO.
CAN YOU TAKE IT WITH YOU?
TUP TUP TUP
HUH?

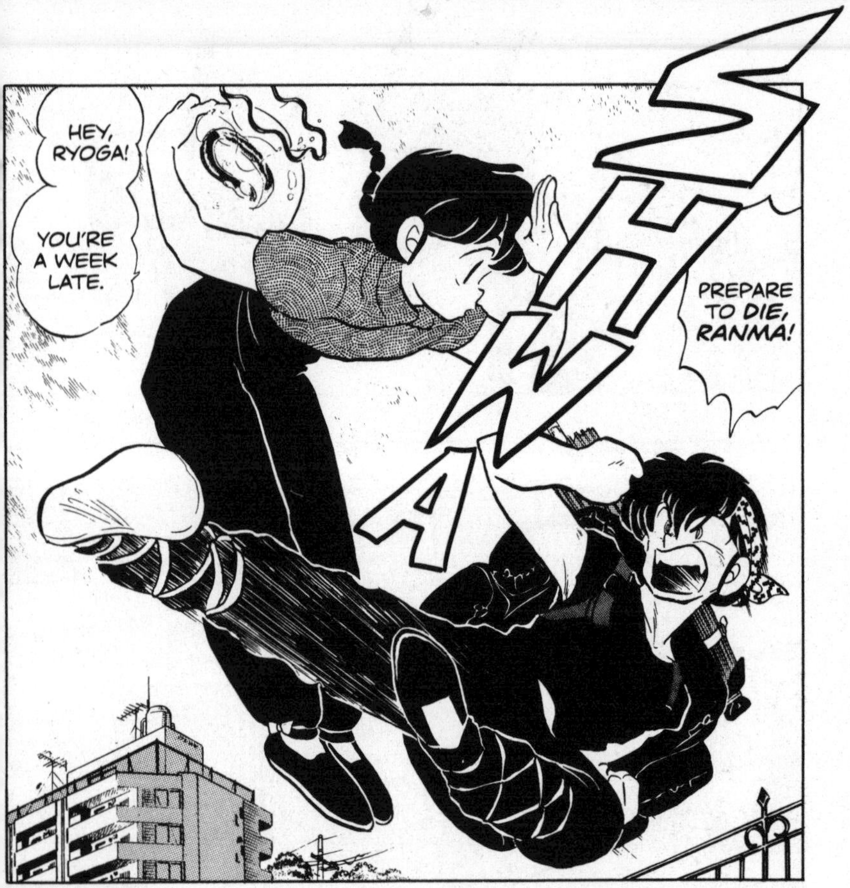
SHWA
PREPARE TO DIE, RANMA!
HEY, RYOGA!
YOU'RE A WEEK LATE.

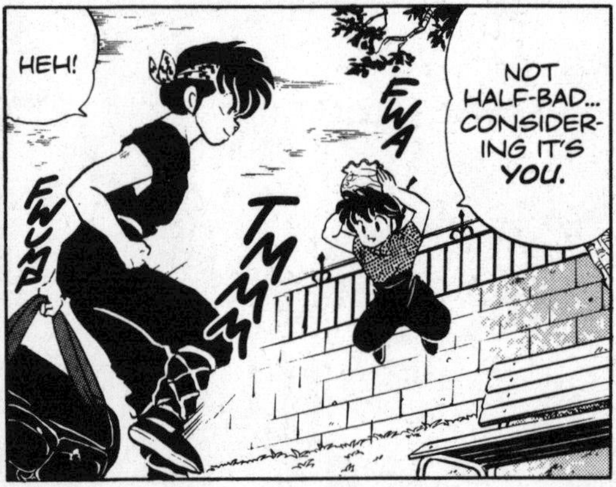
NOT HALF-BAD... CONSIDER-ING IT'S YOU.
FWA
HEH!
TMMM
FWUMP

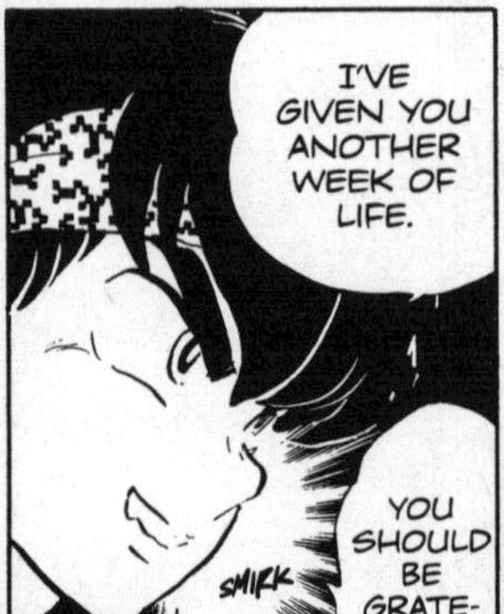
I'VE GIVEN YOU ANOTHER WEEK OF LIFE.
YOU SHOULD BE GRATE-FUL!
SMIRK

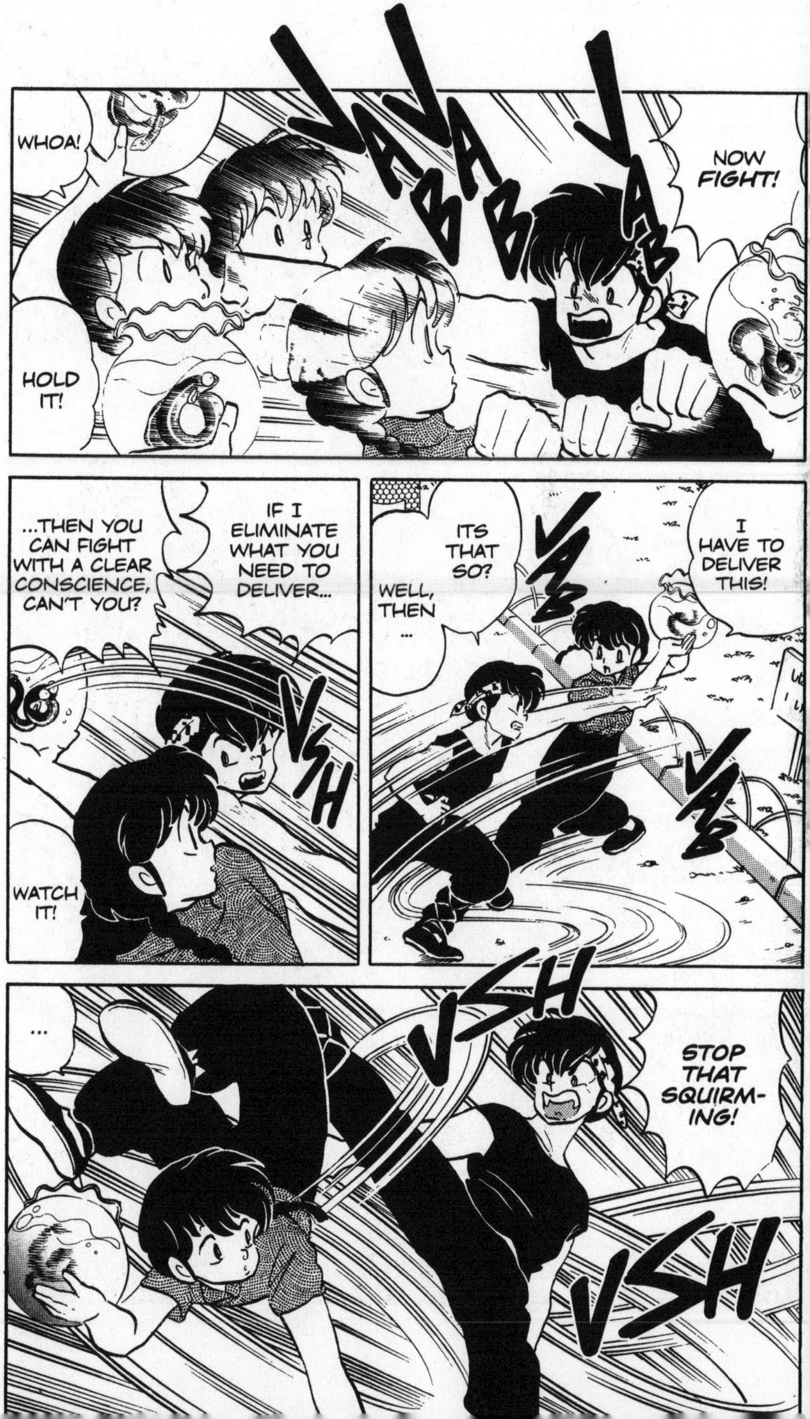
NOW FIGHT!
JAB JAB JAB
JAB
WHOA!
HOLD IT!
I HAVE TO DELIVER THIS!
ITS THAT SO?
WELL, THEN ...
JAB
JAB
IF I ELIMINATE WHAT YOU NEED TO DELIVER...
...THEN YOU CAN FIGHT WITH A CLEAR CONSCIENCE, CAN'T YOU?
VSH
WATCH IT!
STOP THAT SQUIRM-ING!
VSH
VSH
...

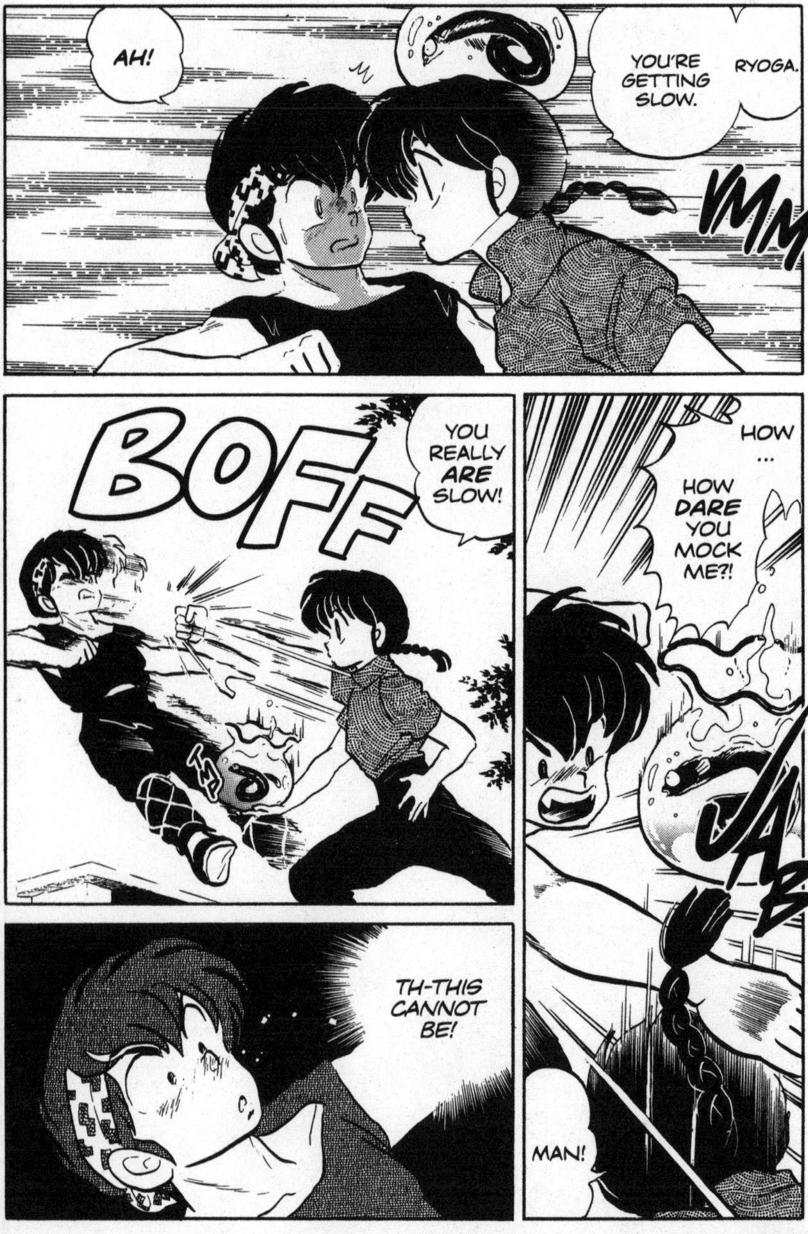

YOU'RE GETTING SLOW. RYOGA.
VMM
AH!
HOW ... HOW DARE YOU MOCK ME?!
JAB
MAN!
YOU REALLY ARE SLOW!
BOFF
TH-THIS CANNOT BE!

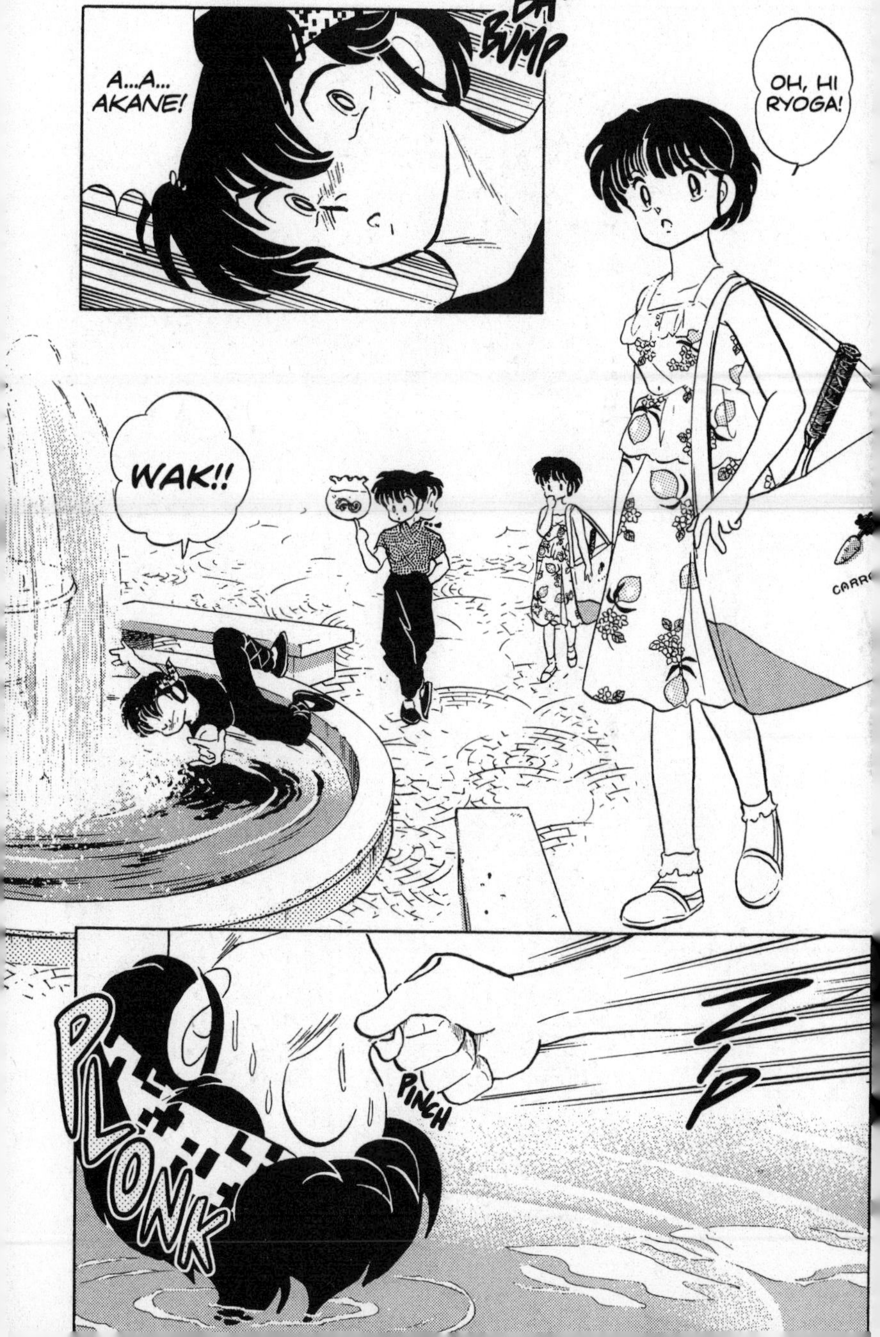
OH, HI RYOGA!
BA-BUMP
A...A... AKANE!
WAK!!
ZIP
PINCH
PLONK

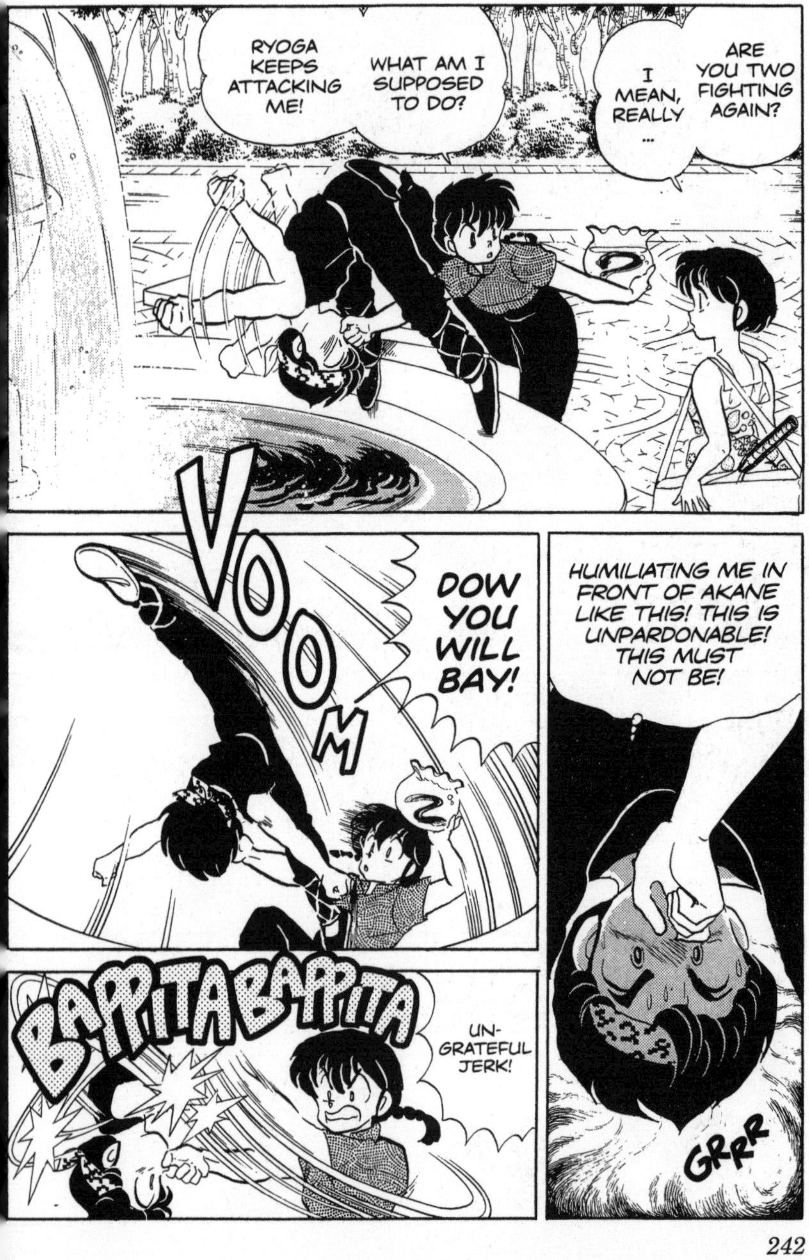
ARE YOU TWO FIGHTING AGAIN?
I MEAN, REALLY ...
WHAT AM I SUPPOSED TO DO?
RYOGA KEEPS ATTACKING ME!
HUMILIATING ME IN FRONT OF AKANE LIKE THIS! THIS IS UNPARDONABLE! THIS MUST NOT BE!
GRRR
VOOM
DOW YOU WILL BAY!
BAPPITABAPPITA
UN-GRATEFUL JERK!

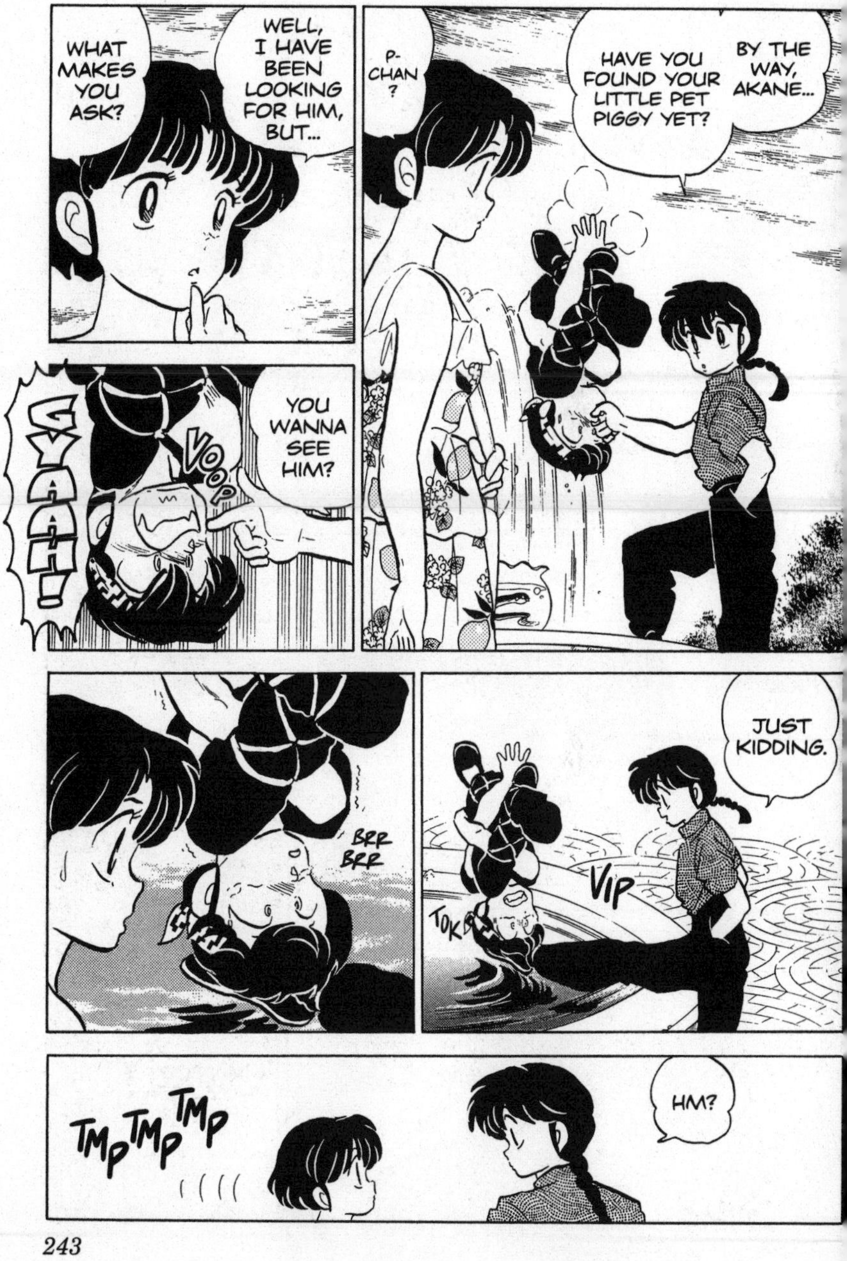
BY THE WAY, AKANE...
HAVE YOU FOUND YOUR LITTLE PET PIGGY YET?
P-CHAN?
WELL, I HAVE BEEN LOOKING FOR HIM, BUT...
WHAT MAKES YOU ASK?
YOU WANNA SEE HIM?
VOOP
GYAAH!
JUST KIDDING.
VIP
TOK
BRR BRR
HM?
TMP TMP TMP

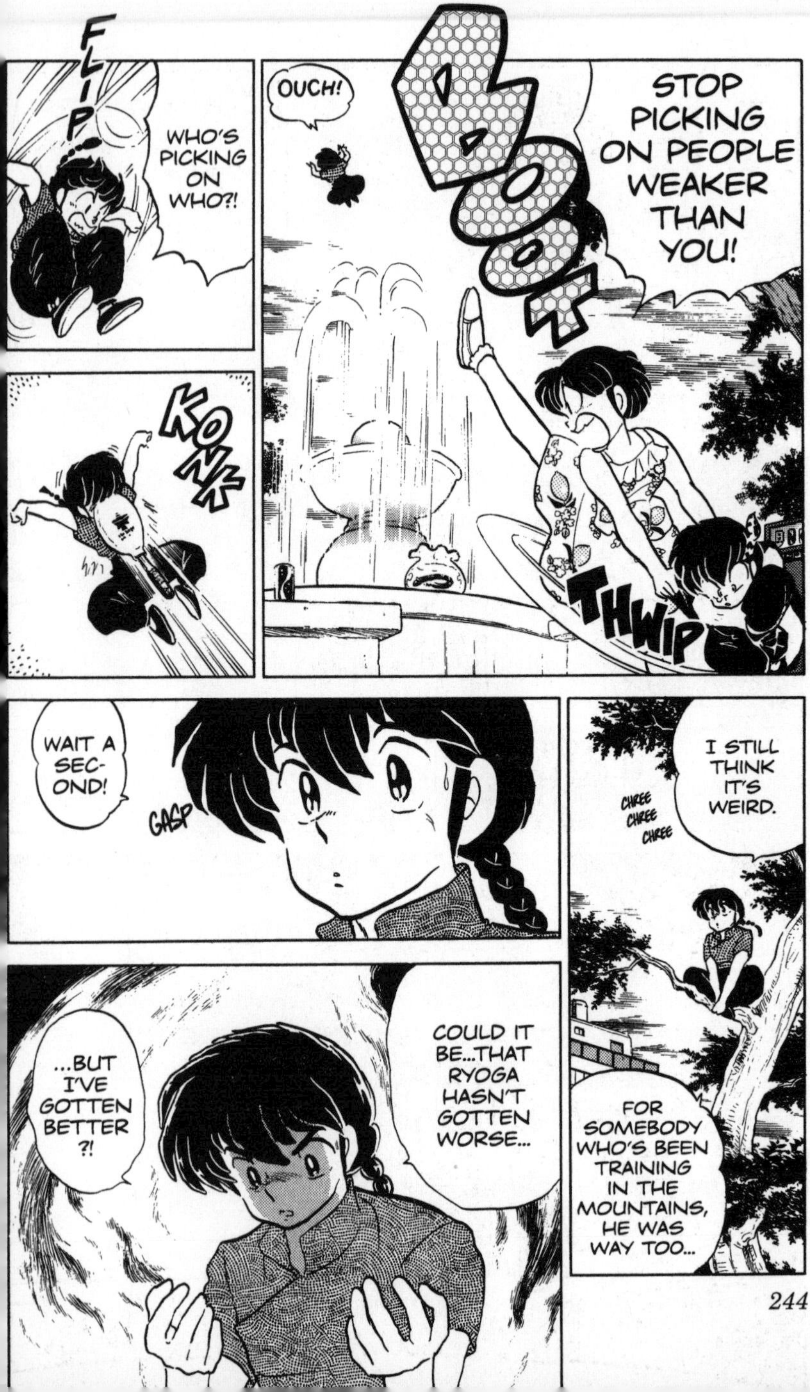
STOP PICKING ON PEOPLE WEAKER THAN YOU!
DOOOK
OUCH!
THWIP
FLIP
WHO'S PICKING ON WHO?!
KONK
I STILL THINK IT'S WEIRD.
CHREE CHREE CHREE
FOR SOMEBODY WHO'S BEEN TRAINING IN THE MOUNTAINS, HE WAS WAY TOO...
WAIT A SEC- OND!
GASP
COULD IT BE...THAT RYOGA HASN'T GOTTEN WORSE...
...BUT I'VE GOTTEN BETTER?!

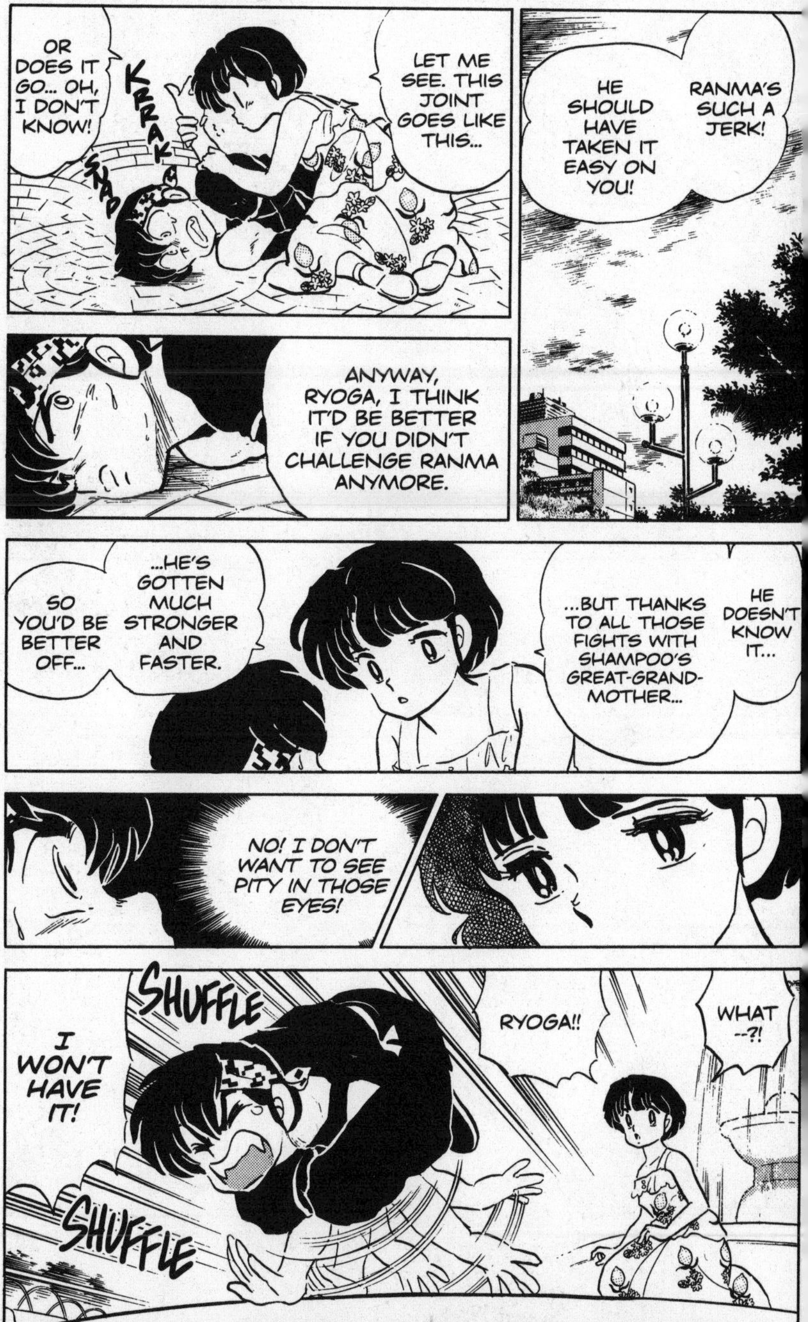
RANMA'S SUCH A JERK!
HE SHOULD HAVE TAKEN IT EASY ON YOU!
LET ME SEE. THIS JOINT GOES LIKE THIS...
KRRAK
SNAP
OR DOES IT GO... OH, I DON'T KNOW!
ANYWAY, RYOGA, I THINK IT'D BE BETTER IF YOU DIDN'T CHALLENGE RANMA ANYMORE.
HE DOESN'T KNOW IT...
...BUT THANKS TO ALL THOSE FIGHTS WITH SHAMPOO'S GREAT-GRAND-MOTHER...
...HE'S GOTTEN MUCH STRONGER AND FASTER.
SO YOU'D BE BETTER OFF...
NO! I DON'T WANT TO SEE PITY IN THOSE EYES!
WHAT--?!
RYOGA!!
SHUFFLE
I WON'T HAVE IT!
SHUFFLE

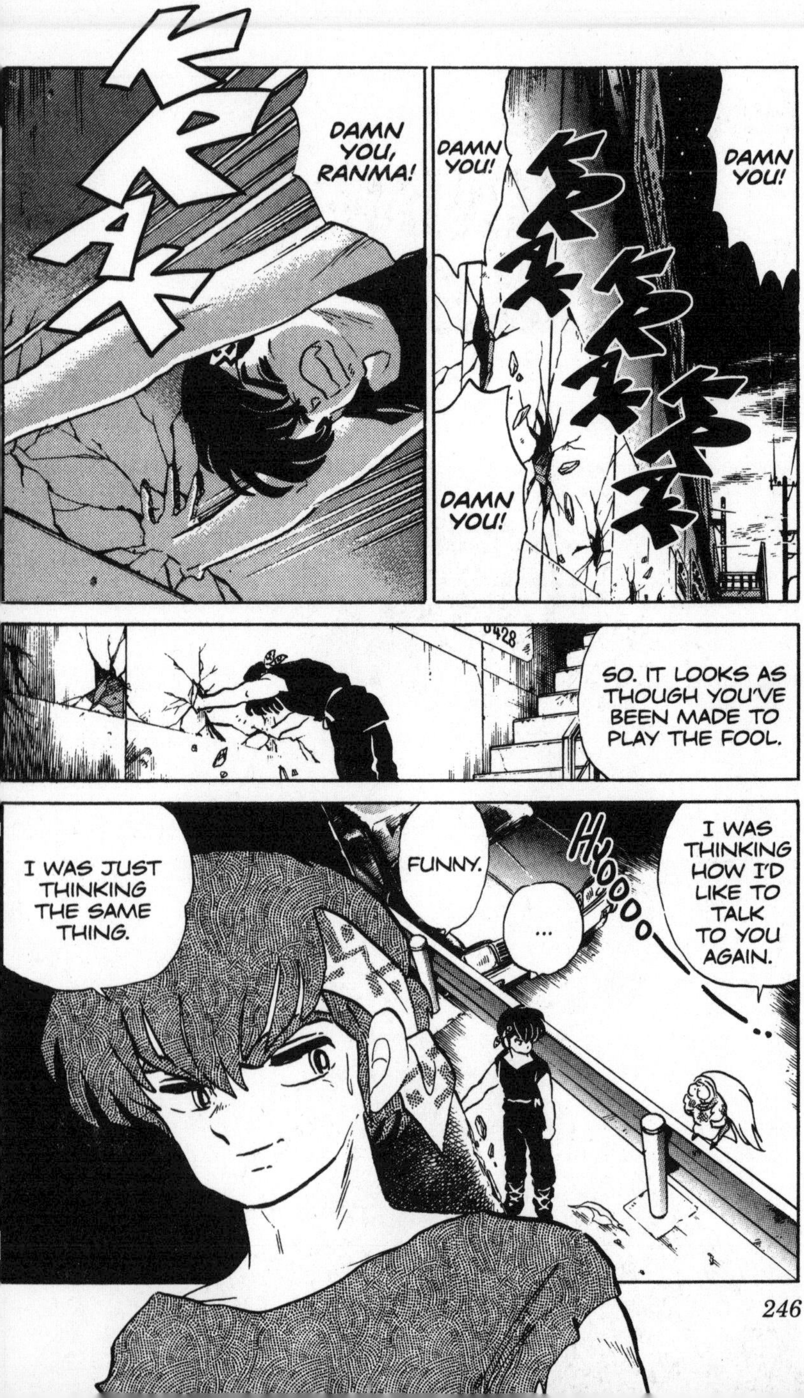
DAMN YOU!
KRAKKKKK
DAMN YOU!
DAMN YOU!
KRAK
DAMN YOU, RANMA!
SO. IT LOOKS AS THOUGH YOU'VE BEEN MADE TO PLAY THE FOOL.
I WAS THINKING HOW I'D LIKE TO TALK TO YOU AGAIN.
HYOOOOO—...
...
FUNNY.
I WAS JUST THINKING THE SAME THING.

PART 16
TRAINING MEALS

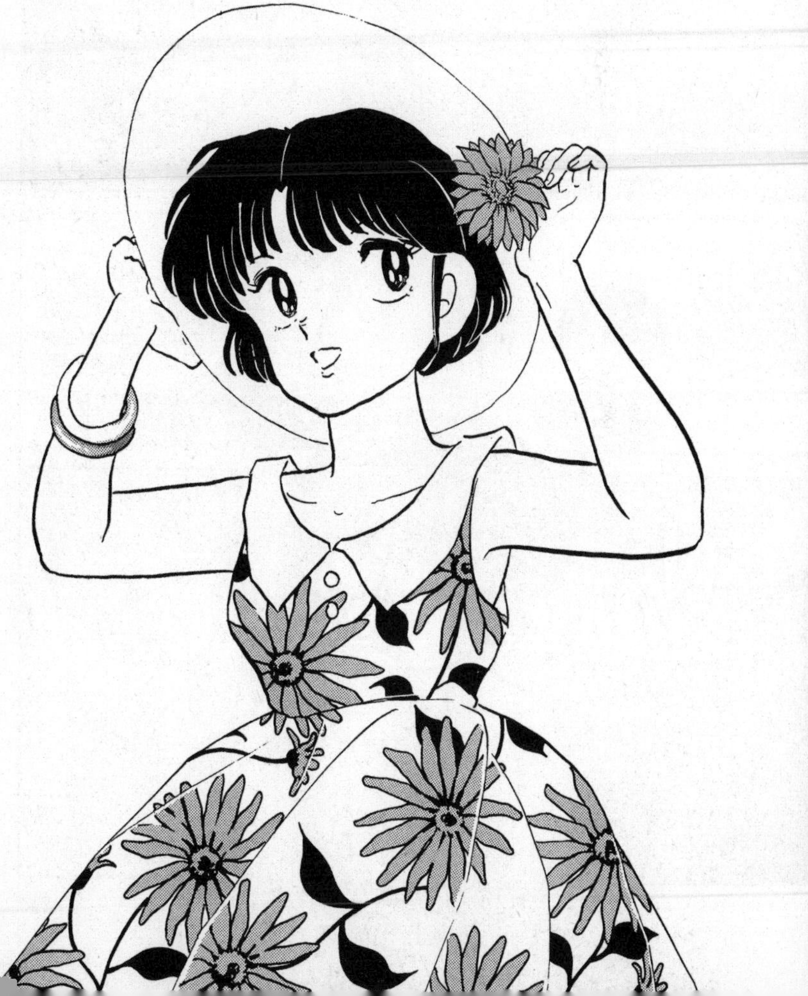

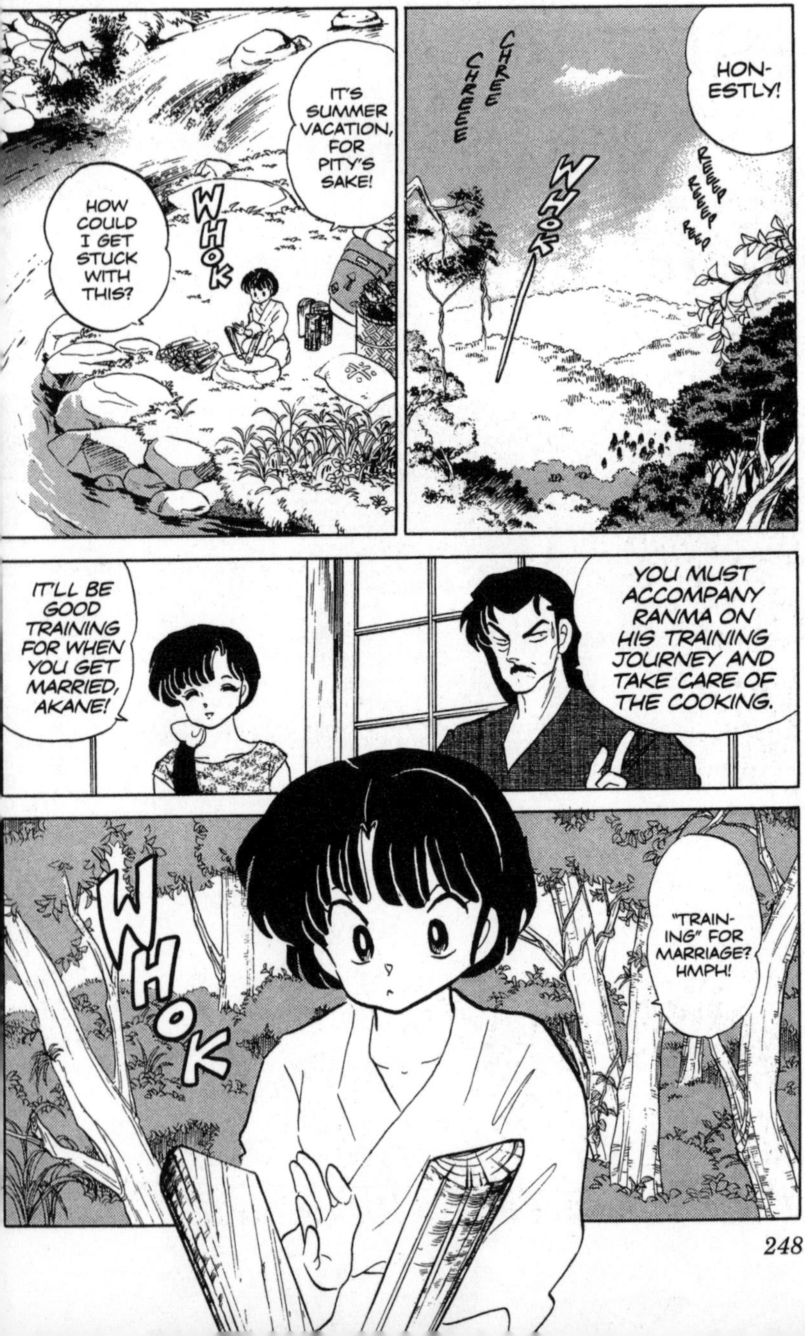
HON-
ESTLY!
CHREE
CHREEE
WHOK
IT'S SUMMER VACATION, FOR PITY'S SAKE!
WHOK
HOW COULD I GET STUCK WITH THIS?
YOU MUST ACCOMPANY RANMA ON HIS TRAINING JOURNEY AND TAKE CARE OF THE COOKING.
IT'LL BE GOOD TRAINING FOR WHEN YOU GET MARRIED, AKANE!
"TRAIN-
ING" FOR MARRIAGE? HMPH!
WHOK

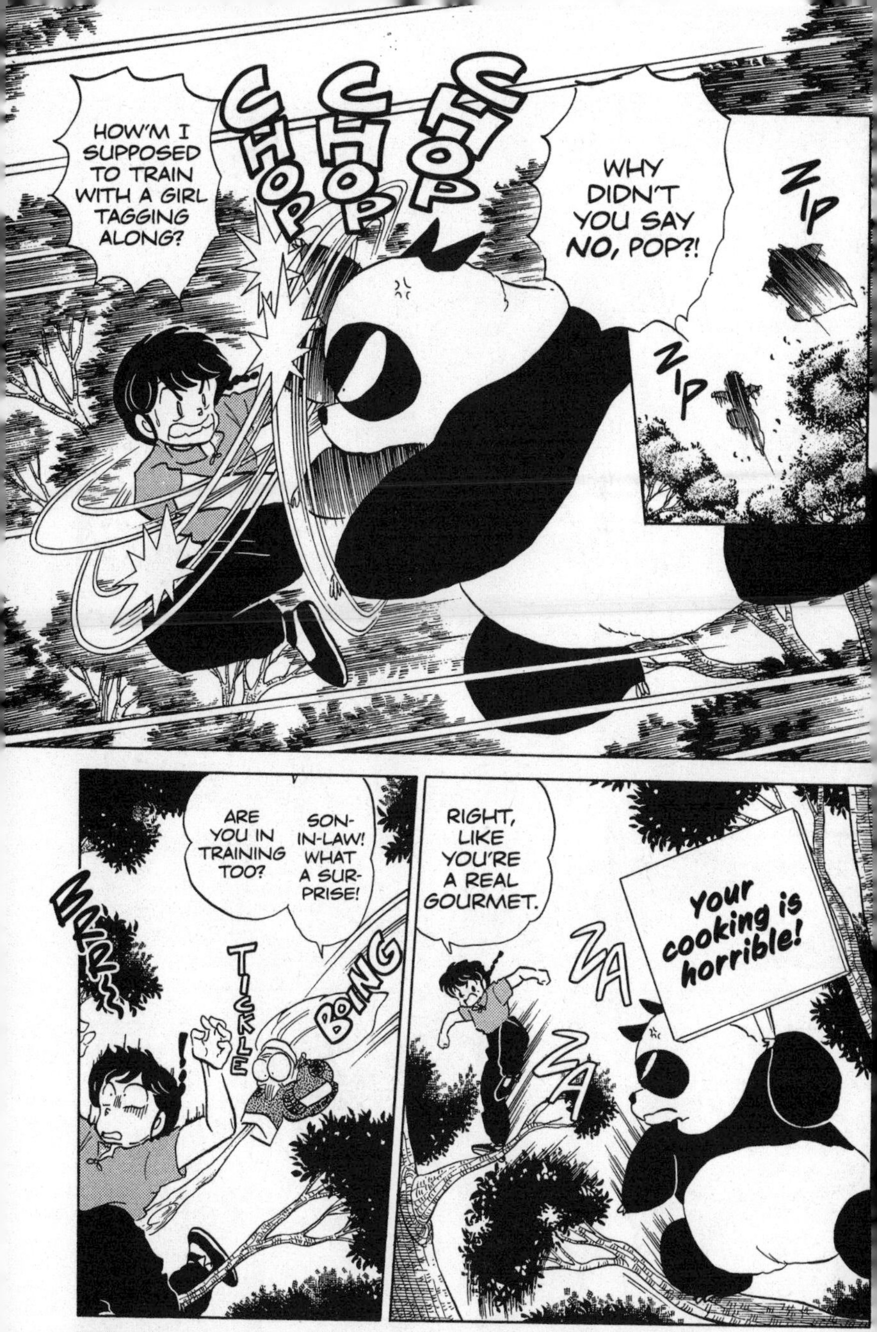
ZIP
ZIP
WHY DIDN'T YOU SAY NO, POP?!
CHOP CHOP CHOP
HOW'M I SUPPOSED TO TRAIN WITH A GIRL TAGGING ALONG?
Your cooking is horrible!
ZA
ZA
RIGHT, LIKE YOU'RE A REAL GOURMET.
SON-IN-LAW! WHAT A SUR-PRISE!
ARE YOU IN TRAINING TOO?
BOING
TICKLE

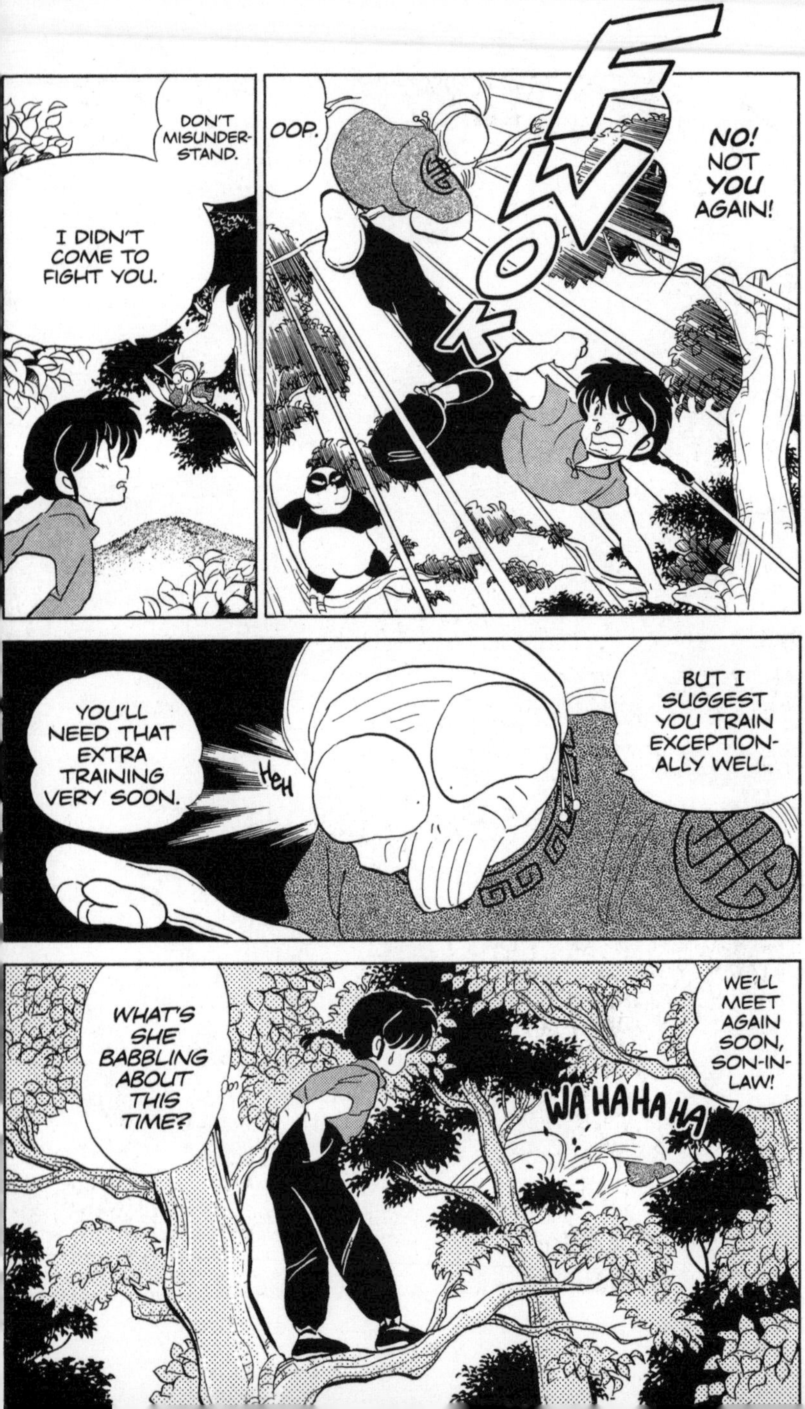
NO! NOT YOU AGAIN!
FWOOK
OOP.
DON'T MISUNDER-STAND.
I DIDN'T COME TO FIGHT YOU.
BUT I SUGGEST YOU TRAIN EXCEPTION-ALLY WELL.
HEH
YOU'LL NEED THAT EXTRA TRAINING VERY SOON.
WE'LL MEET AGAIN SOON, SON-IN-LAW!
WA HA HA HA
WHAT'S SHE BABBLING ABOUT THIS TIME?

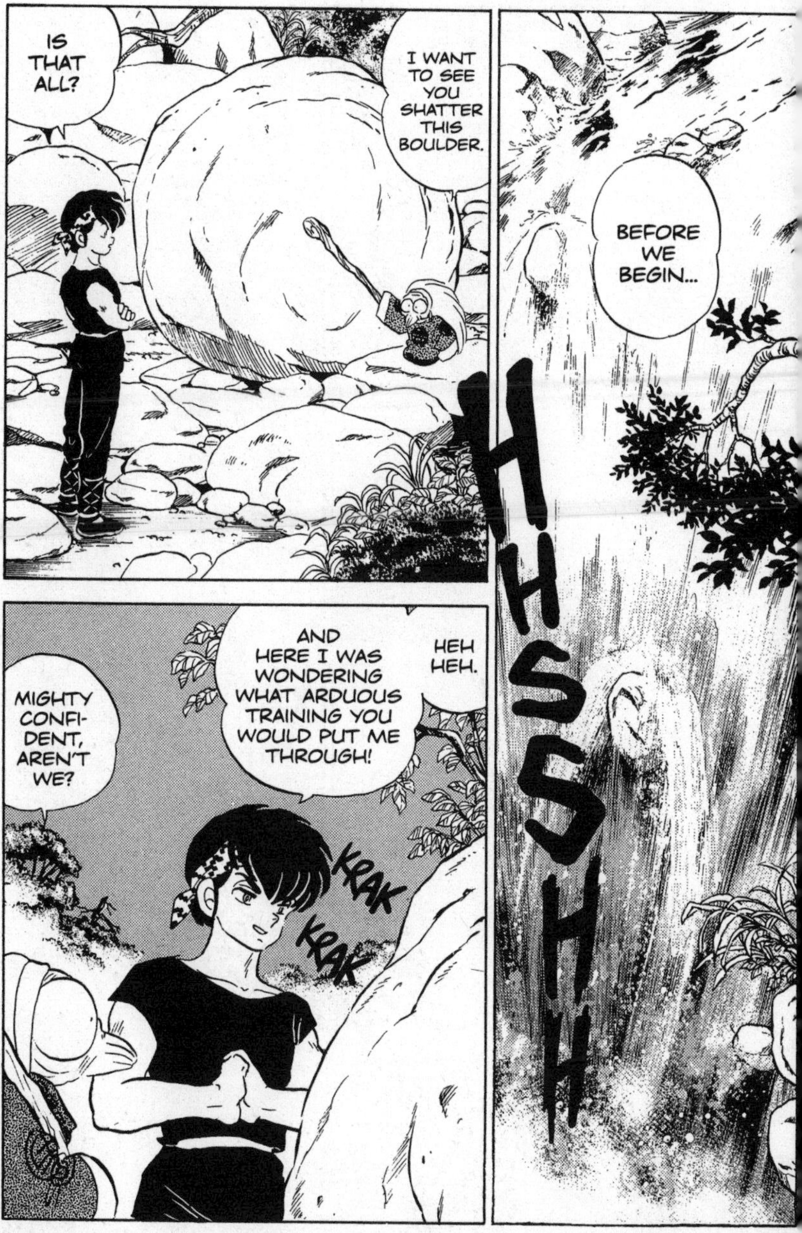
BEFORE WE BEGIN...
HHSSHH
I WANT TO SEE YOU SHATTER THIS BOULDER.
IS THAT ALL?
HEH HEH.
AND HERE I WAS WONDERING WHAT ARDUOUS TRAINING YOU WOULD PUT ME THROUGH!
MIGHTY CONFI-DENT, AREN'T WE?
KRAK
KRAK

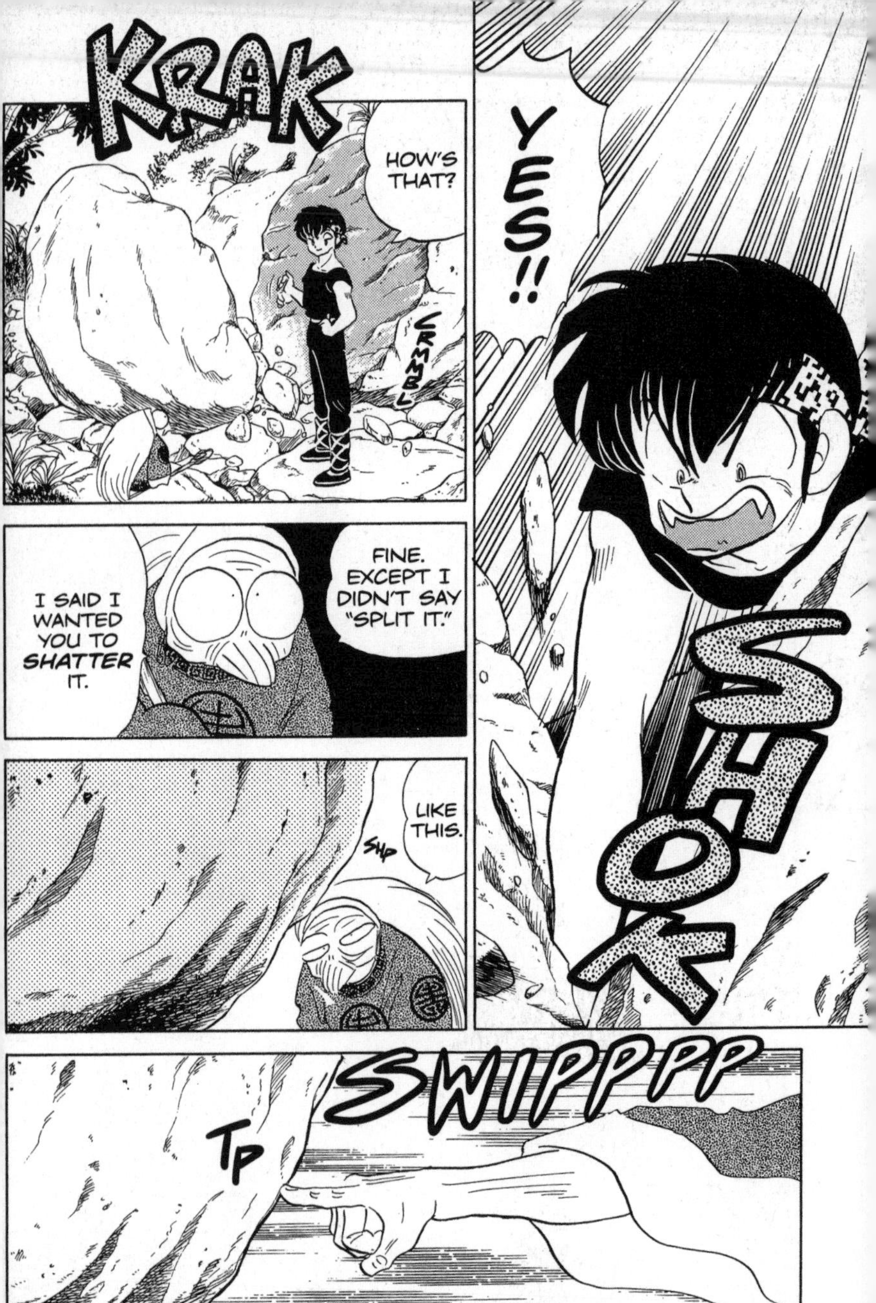
YES!!
SHOOK
KRAK
HOW'S THAT?
CRMMBL
FINE. EXCEPT I DIDN'T SAY "SPLIT IT."
I SAID I WANTED YOU TO SHATTER IT.
LIKE THIS.
SHP
SWIPPPP
TP

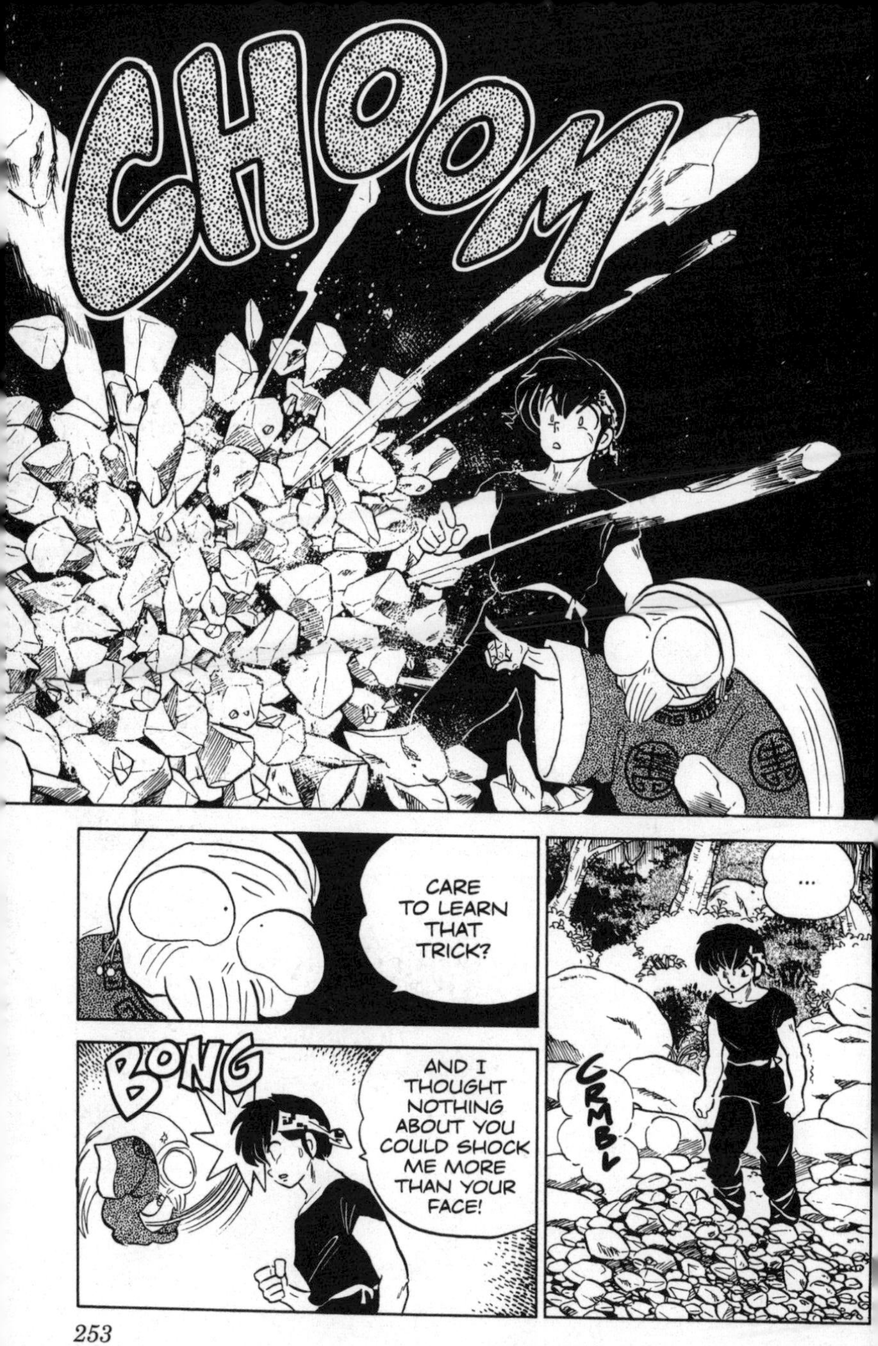
CHOOM
...
CRMBL
CARE TO LEARN THAT TRICK?
BONG
AND I THOUGHT NOTHING ABOUT YOU COULD SHOCK ME MORE THAN YOUR FACE!

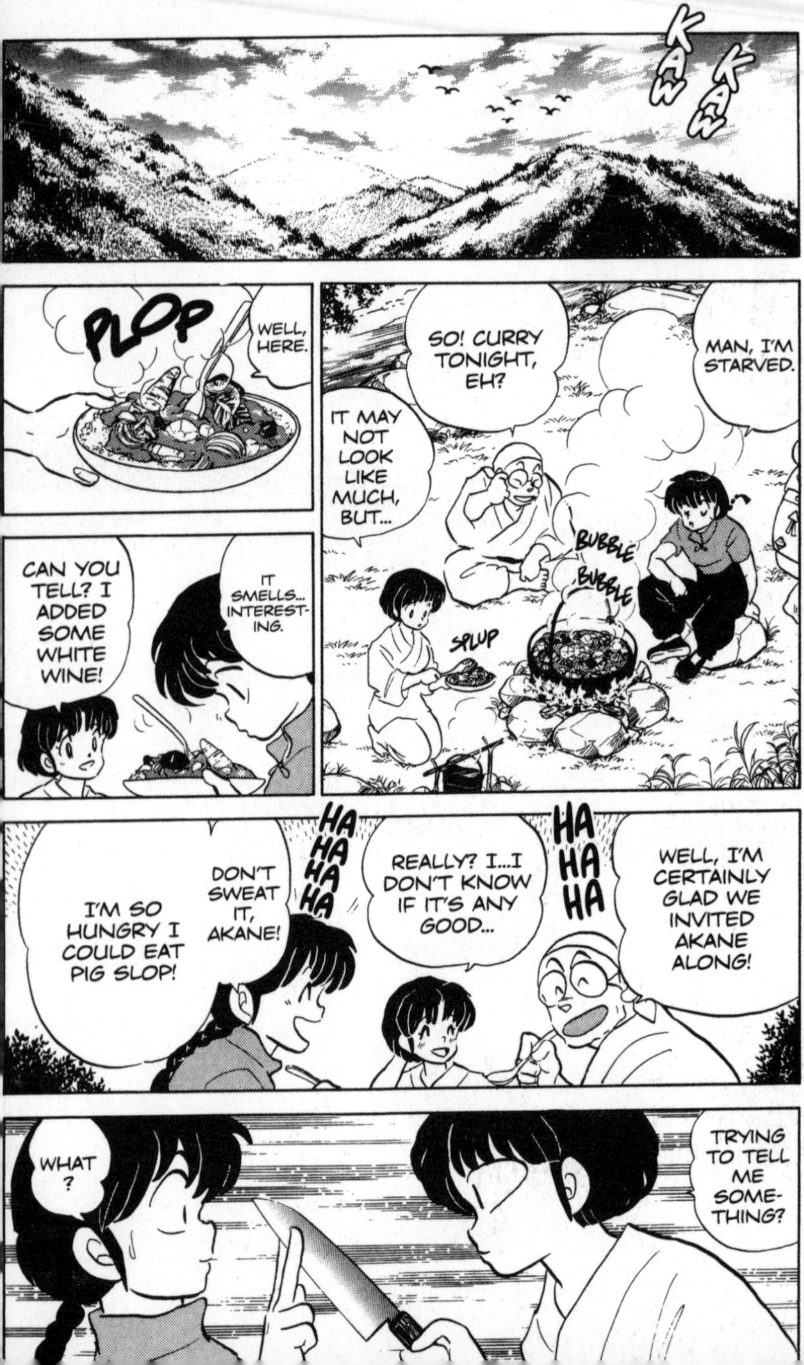
KAW KAW
MAN, I'M STARVED.
SO! CURRY TONIGHT, EH?
IT MAY NOT LOOK LIKE MUCH, BUT...
BUBBLE
BUBBLE
SPLUP
WELL, HERE.
PLOP
IT SMELLS... INTERESTING.
CAN YOU TELL? I ADDED SOME WHITE WINE!
WELL, I'M CERTAINLY GLAD WE INVITED AKANE ALONG!
HA HA HA
REALLY? I...I DON'T KNOW IF IT'S ANY GOOD...
HA HA HA HA
DON'T SWEAT IT, AKANE!
I'M SO HUNGRY I COULD EAT PIG SLOP!
TRYING TO TELL ME SOMETHING?
WHAT?

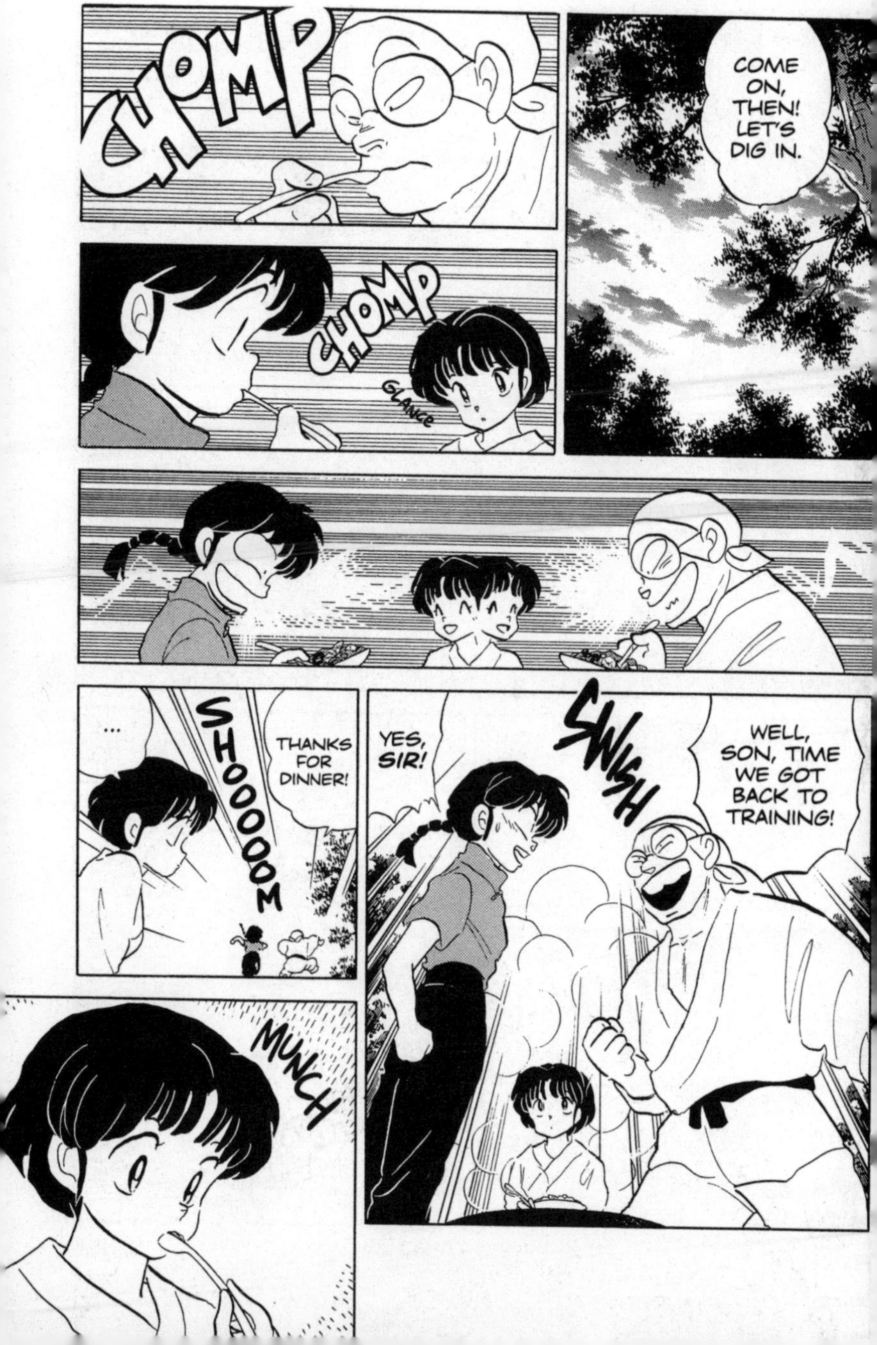
COME ON, THEN! LET'S DIG IN.
CHOMP
CHOMP
GLANCE
WELL, SON, TIME WE GOT BACK TO TRAINING!
SWISH
YES, SIR!
THANKS FOR DINNER!
SHOOOOOOM
...
MUNCH

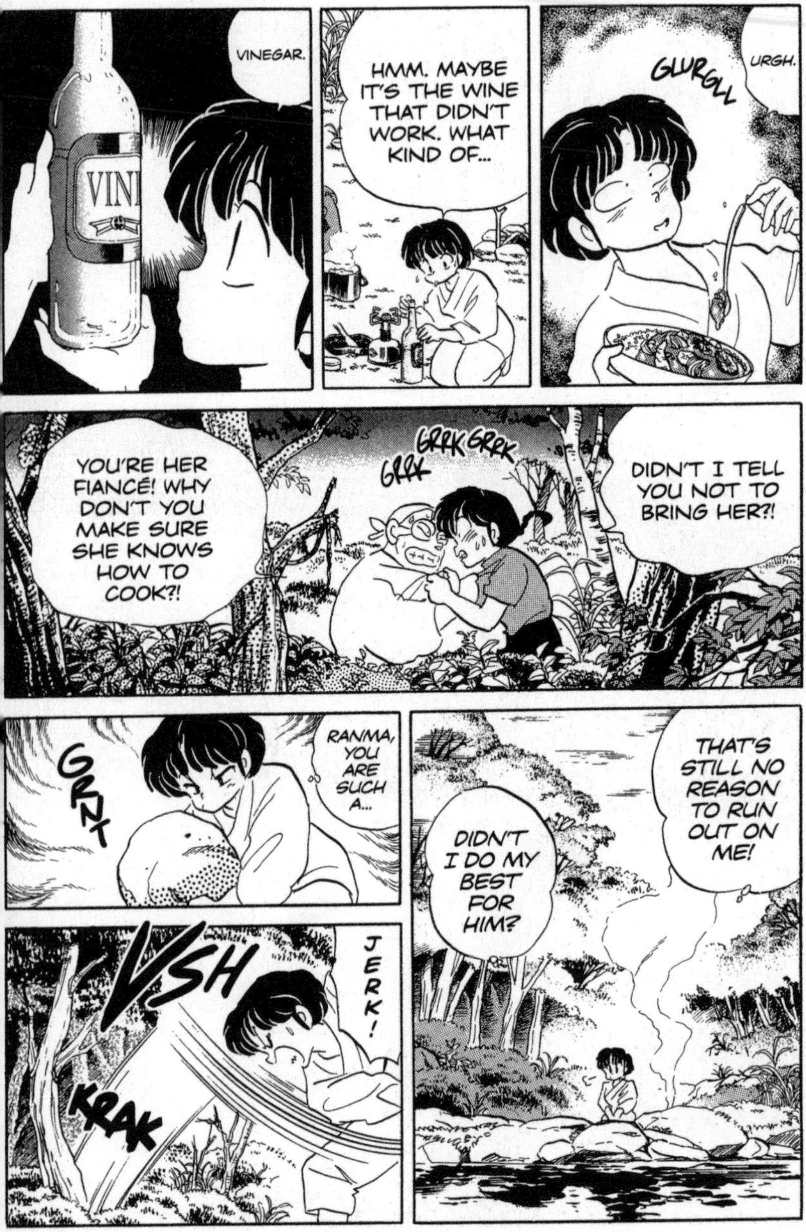
GLURGLL
URGH.
HMM. MAYBE IT'S THE WINE THAT DIDN'T WORK. WHAT KIND OF...
VINEGAR.
DIDN'T I TELL YOU NOT TO BRING HER?!
GRRK GRRK GRRK
YOU'RE HER FIANCÉ! WHY DON'T YOU MAKE SURE SHE KNOWS HOW TO COOK?!
THAT'S STILL NO REASON TO RUN OUT ON ME!
DIDN'T I DO MY BEST FOR HIM?
RANMA, YOU ARE SUCH A...
GRNT
JERK!
VSH
KRAK

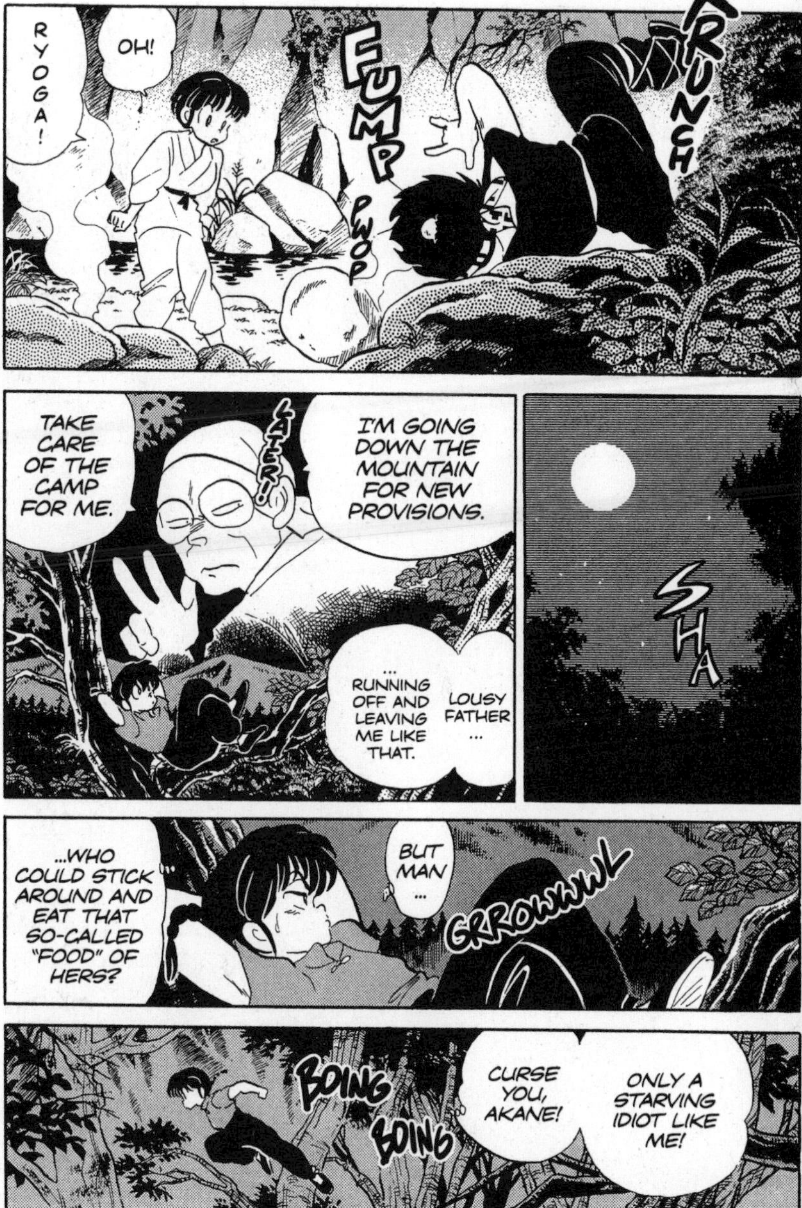
KRUNCH
FUMP
PWOP
OH!
RYOGA!
SHA
I'M GOING DOWN THE MOUNTAIN FOR NEW PROVISIONS.
LATER!
TAKE CARE OF THE CAMP FOR ME.
LOUSY FATHER ...
... RUNNING OFF AND LEAVING ME LIKE THAT.
GRROWWWL
BUT MAN ...
...WHO COULD STICK AROUND AND EAT THAT SO-CALLED "FOOD" OF HERS?
ONLY A STARVING IDIOT LIKE ME!
CURSE YOU, AKANE!
BOING
BOING

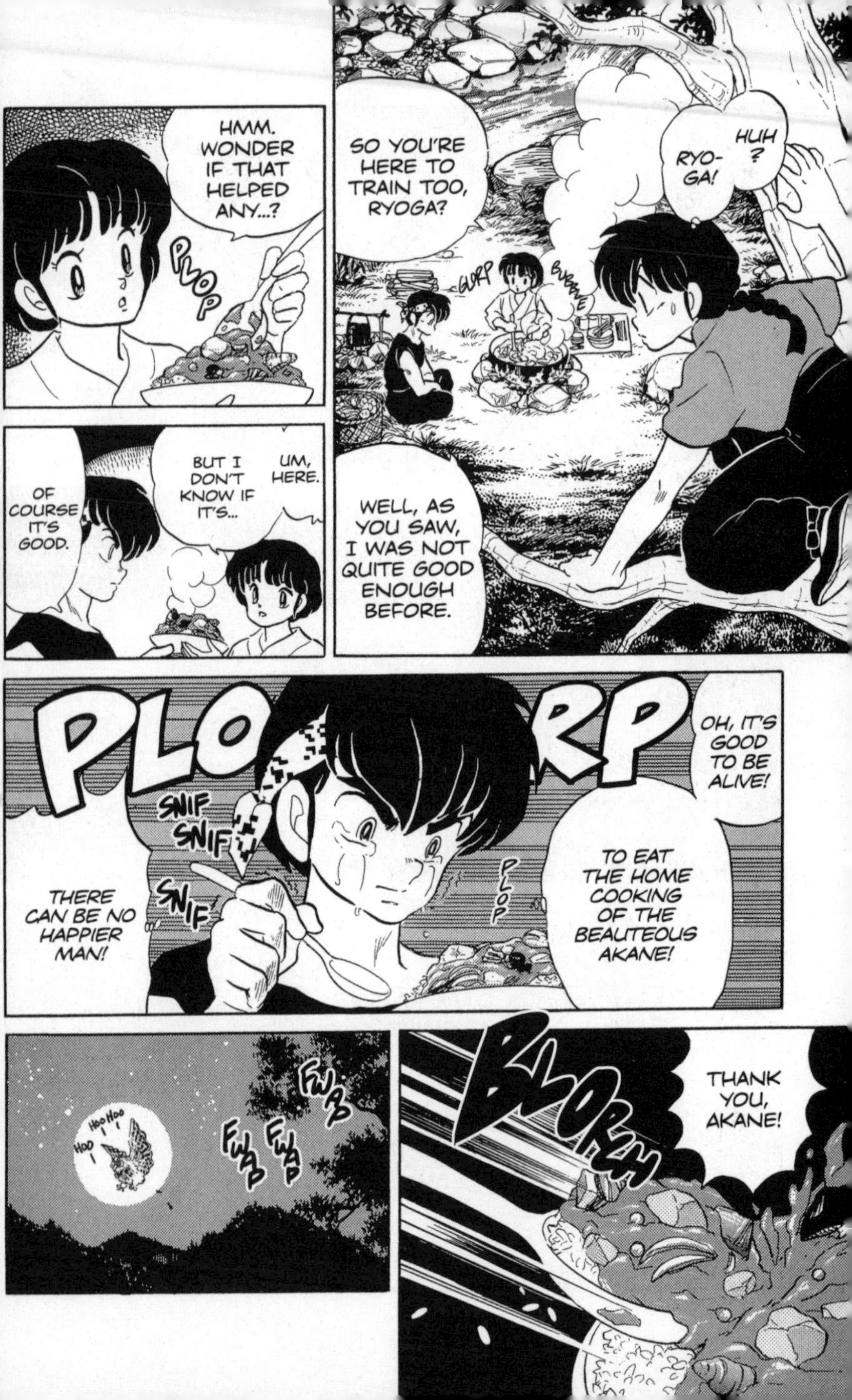
HUH ?
RYOGA!
BUBBLE
GLORP
SO YOU'RE HERE TO TRAIN TOO, RYOGA?
WELL, AS YOU SAW, I WAS NOT QUITE GOOD ENOUGH BEFORE.
HMM. WONDER IF THAT HELPED ANY...?
PLOP
UM, HERE.
BUT I DON'T KNOW IF IT'S...
OF COURSE IT'S GOOD.
PLORP
OH, IT'S GOOD TO BE ALIVE!
TO EAT THE HOME COOKING OF THE BEAUTEOUS AKANE!
PLOP
SNIF
SNIF
SNIF
THERE CAN BE NO HAPPIER MAN!
THANK YOU, AKANE!
FWAP
FWAP
FWAP
HOO HOO
HOO

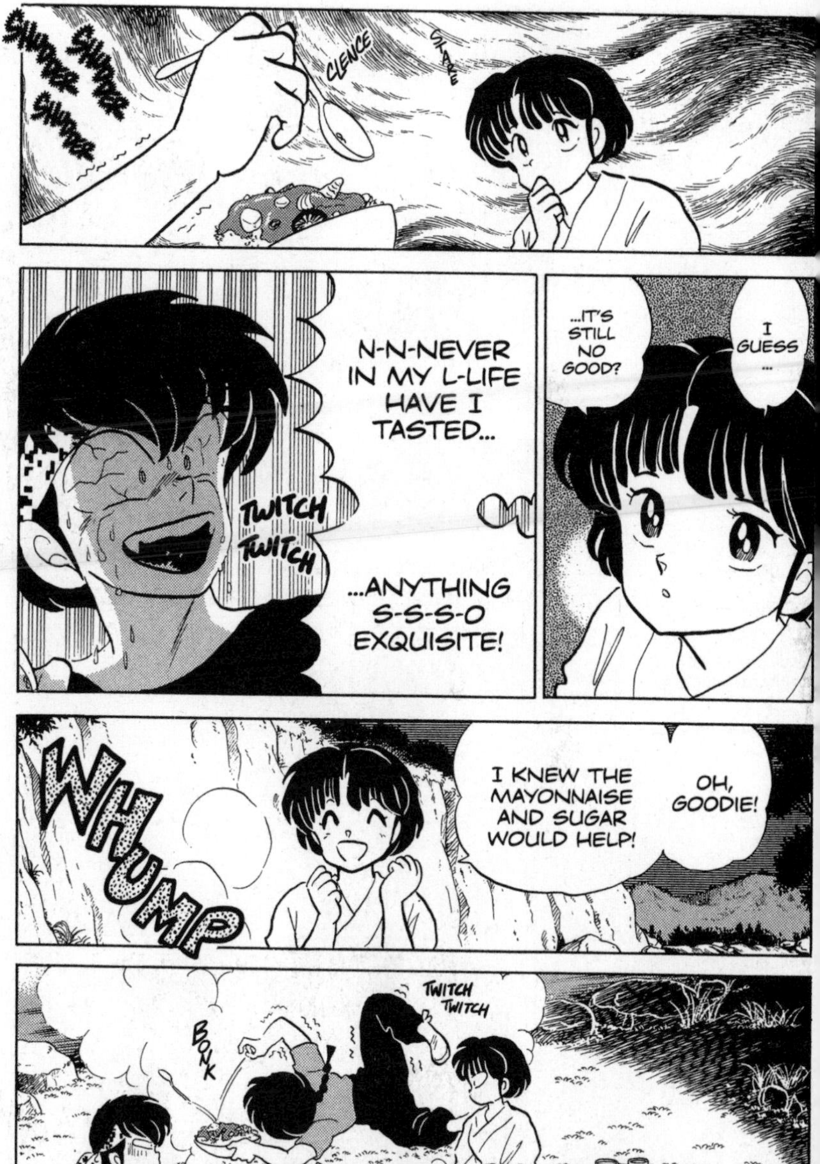
STARE
CLENCE
SHUDDER SHUDDER SHUDDER SHUDDER
I GUESS ...
...IT'S STILL NO GOOD?
N-N-NEVER IN MY L-LIFE HAVE I TASTED...
TWITCH TWITCH
...ANYTHING S-S-S-O EXQUISITE!
OH, GOODIE!
I KNEW THE MAYONNAISE AND SUGAR WOULD HELP!
WHUMP
TWITCH TWITCH
BONK

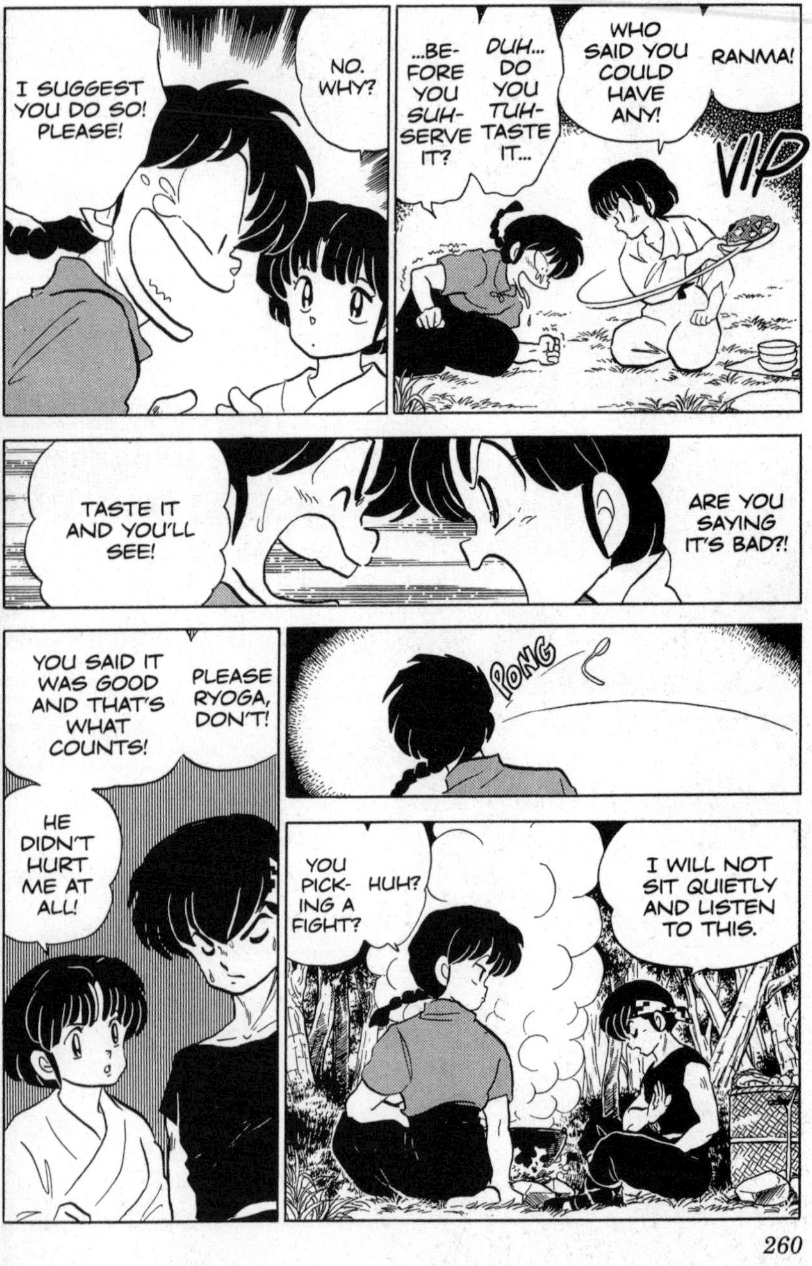
RANMA!
WHO SAID YOU COULD HAVE ANY!
VIP
DUH... DO YOU TUH-TASTE IT...
...BE-FORE YOU SUH-SERVE IT?
NO. WHY?
I SUGGEST YOU DO SO! PLEASE!
ARE YOU SAYING IT'S BAD?!
TASTE IT AND YOU'LL SEE!
PONG
I WILL NOT SIT QUIETLY AND LISTEN TO THIS.
HUH?
YOU PICK-ING A FIGHT?
PLEASE RYOGA, DON'T!
YOU SAID IT WAS GOOD AND THAT'S WHAT COUNTS!
HE DIDN'T HURT ME AT ALL!

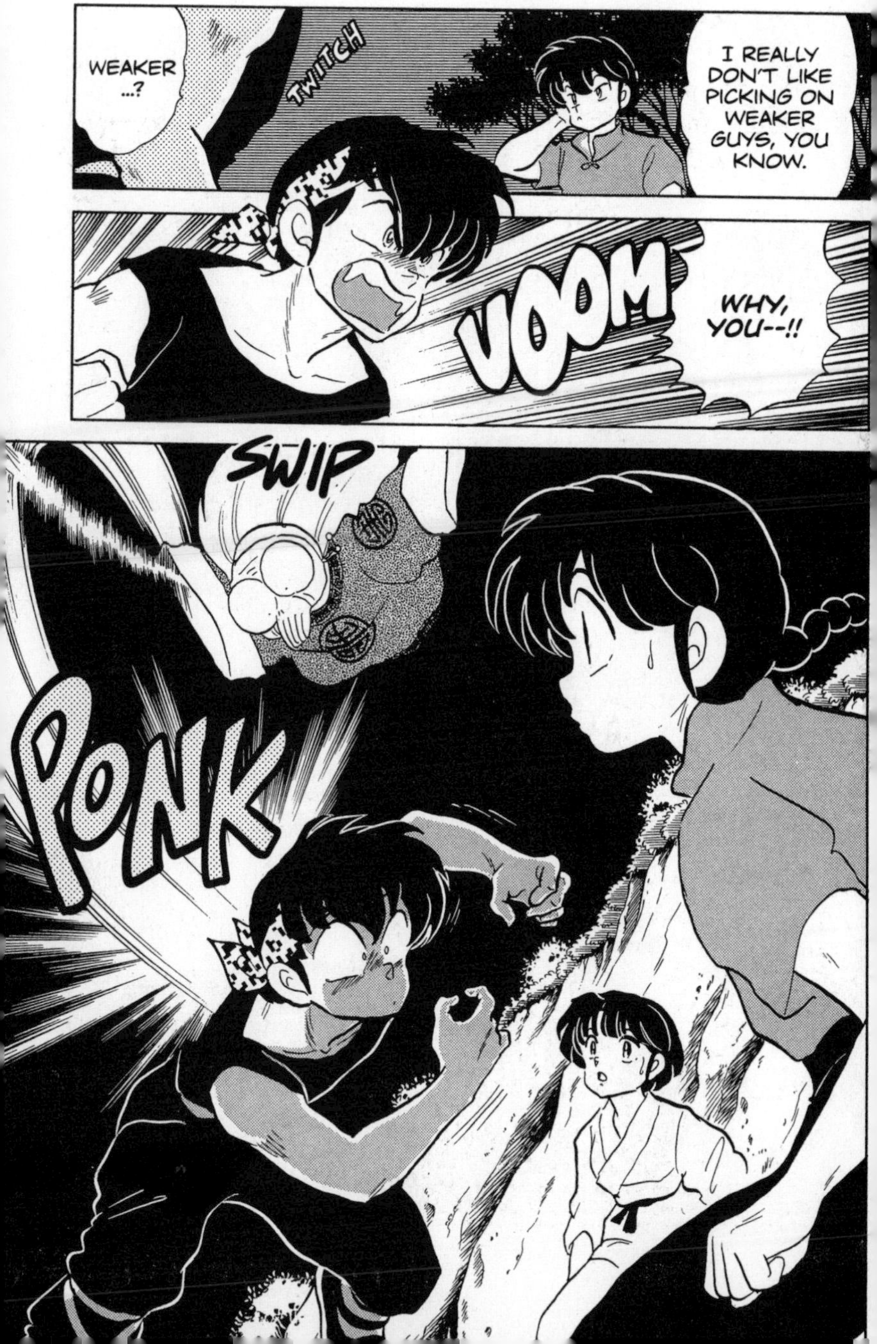
I REALLY DON'T LIKE PICKING ON WEAKER GUYS, YOU KNOW.
TWITCH
WEAKER ...?
WHY, YOU--!!
VOOM
SWIP
PONK

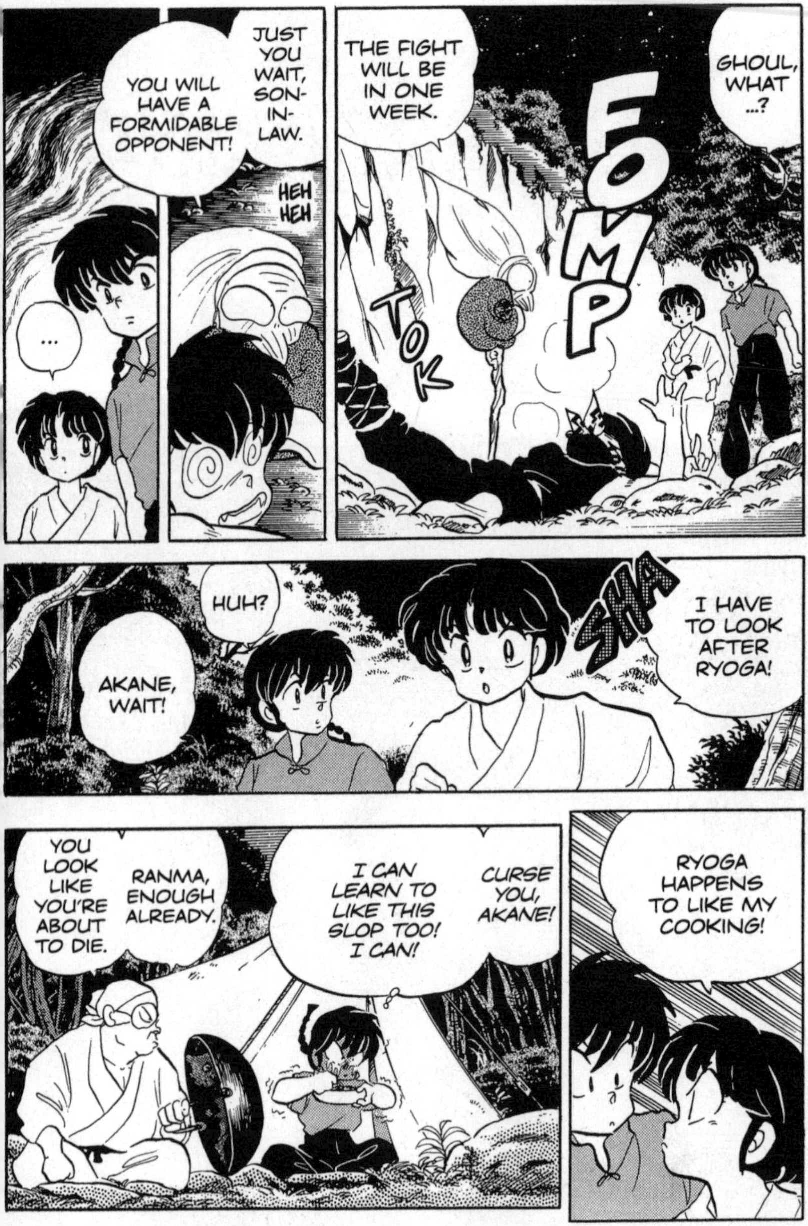
GHOUL, WHAT ...?
FOMP
THE FIGHT WILL BE IN ONE WEEK.
TOK
JUST YOU WAIT, SON-IN-LAW.
HEH HEH
YOU WILL HAVE A FORMIDABLE OPPONENT!
...
I HAVE TO LOOK AFTER RYOGA!
SHA
HUH?
AKANE, WAIT!
RYOGA HAPPENS TO LIKE MY COOKING!
CURSE YOU, AKANE!
I CAN LEARN TO LIKE THIS SLOP TOO! I CAN!
RANMA, ENOUGH ALREADY.
YOU LOOK LIKE YOU'RE ABOUT TO DIE.

PART 17
THE BREAKING POINT

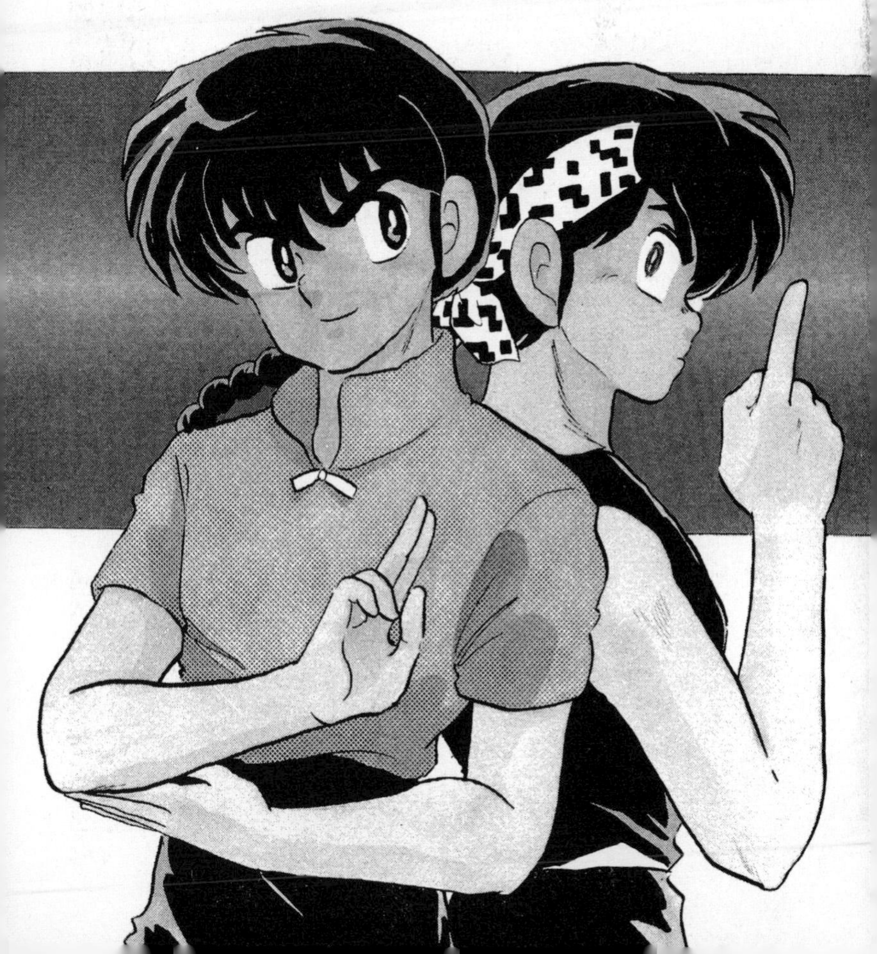

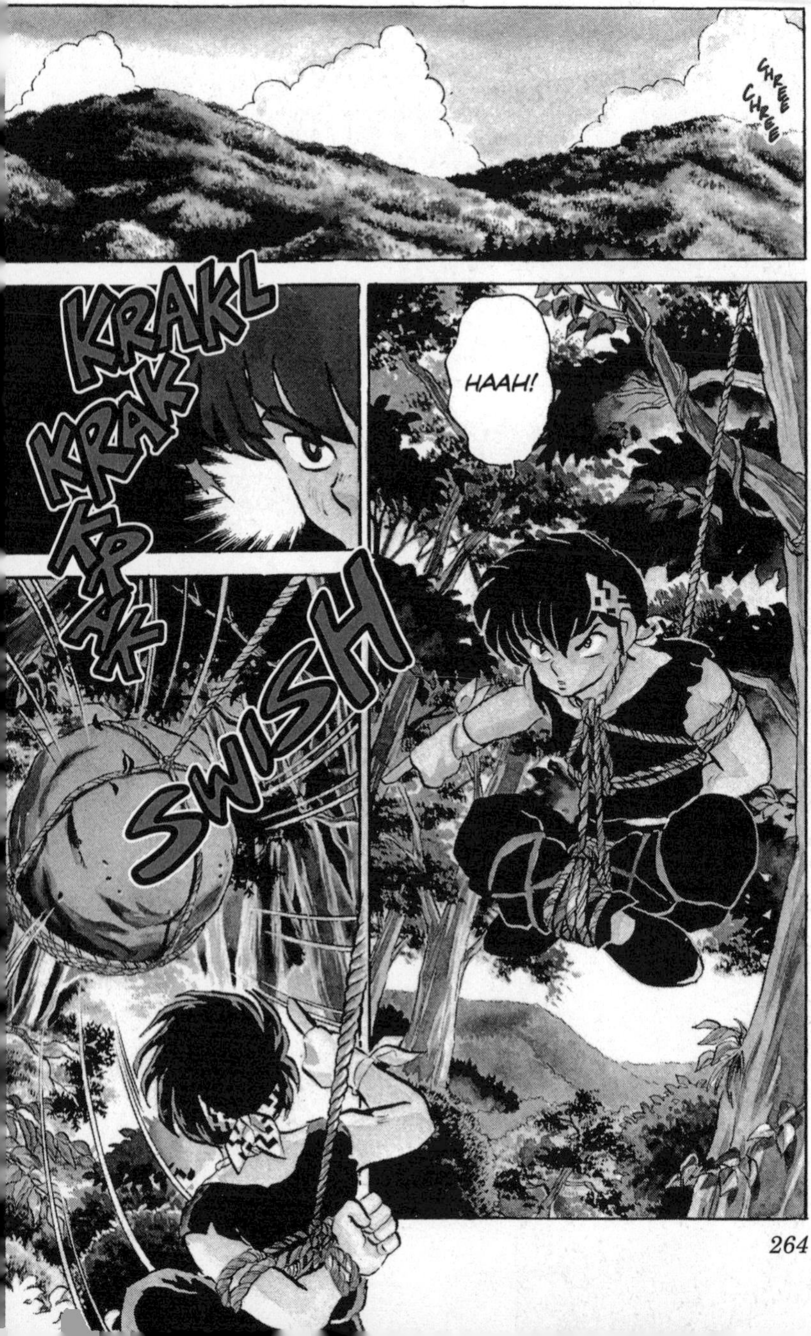
CHREE CHREE
HAAH!
KRAKL
KRAK
KRAK
SWISH

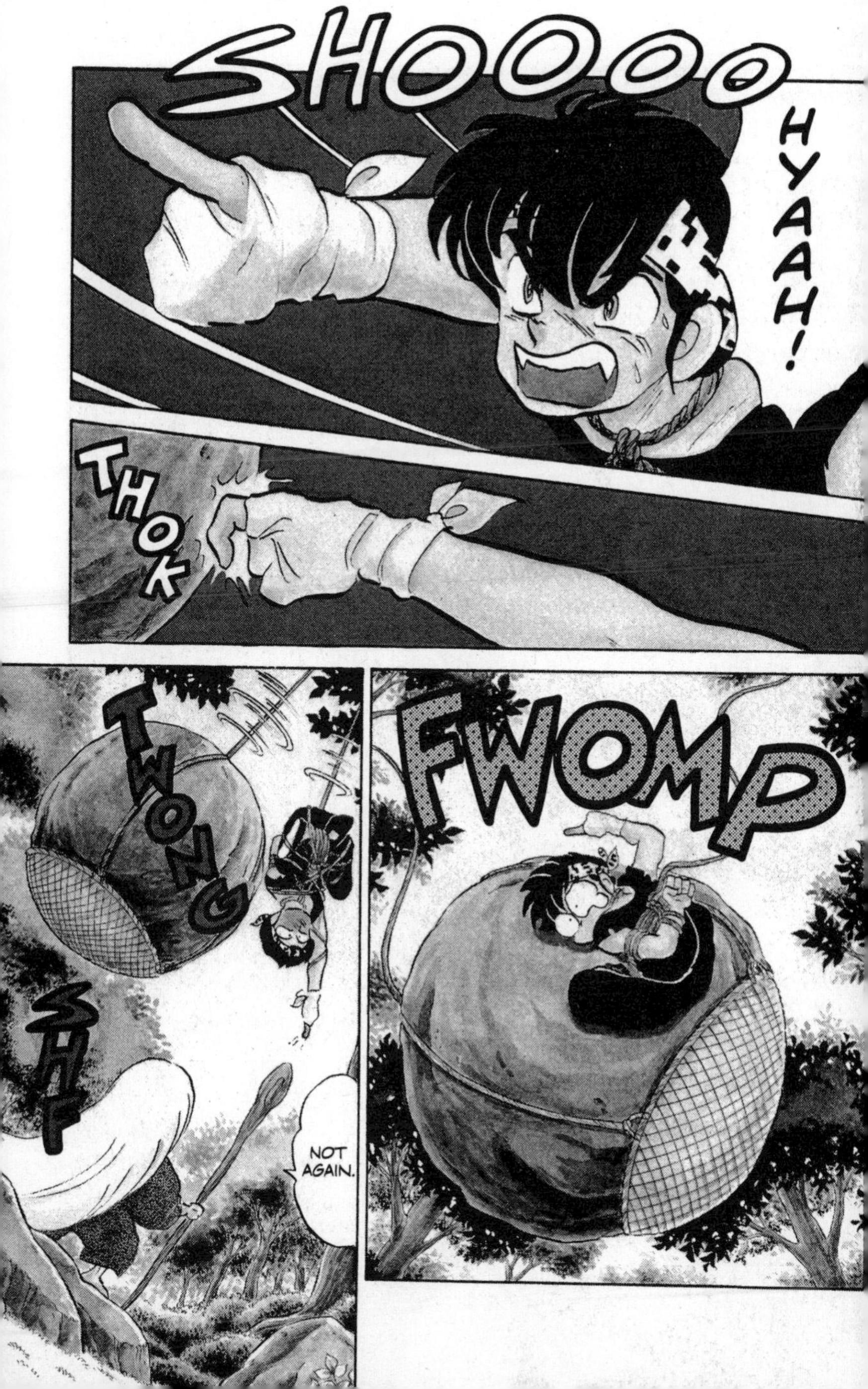
SHOOOO
HYAAAH!
THOK
FWOMP
TWONG
SHF
NOT AGAIN.

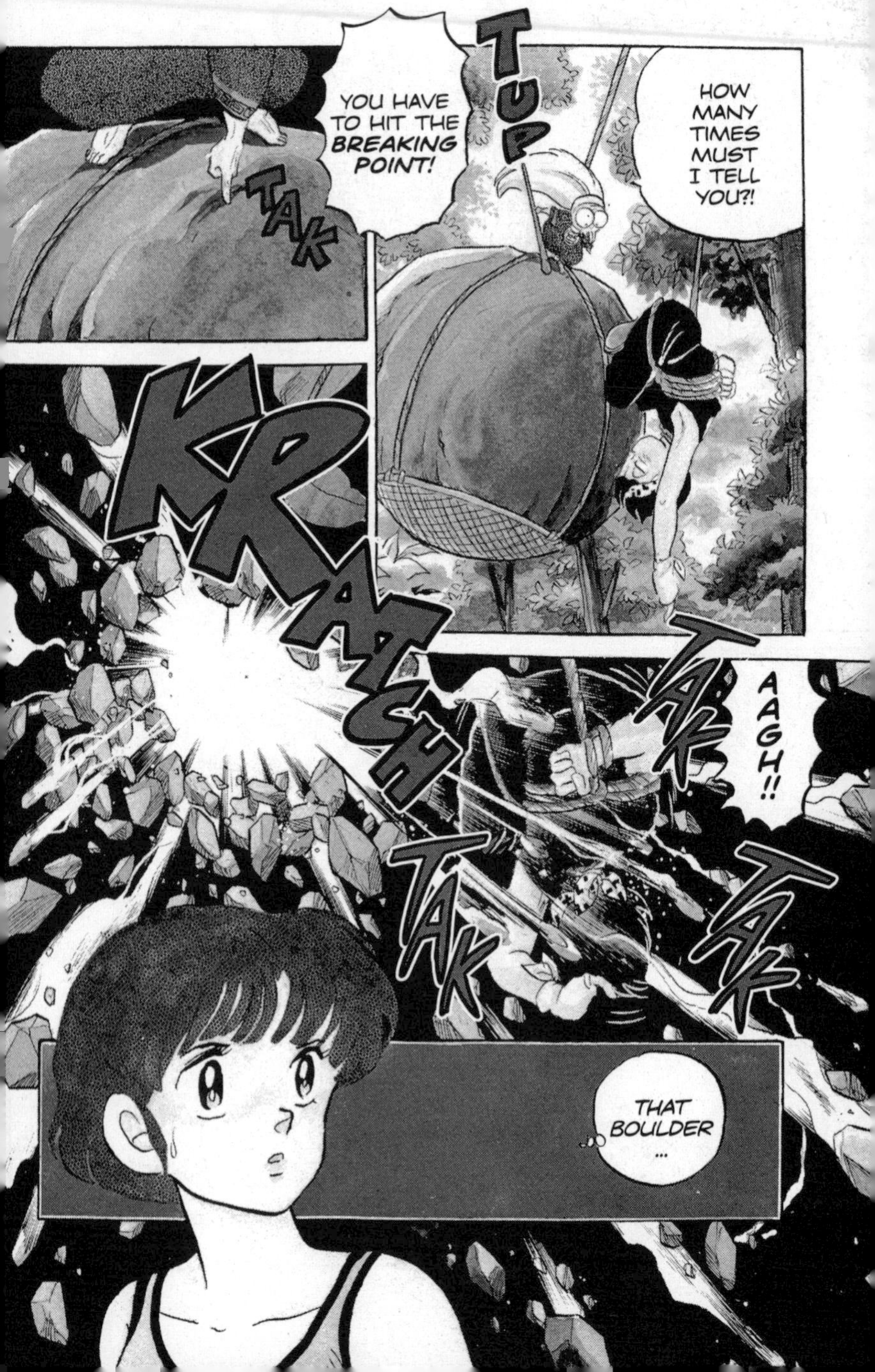
TUP
HOW MANY TIMES MUST I TELL YOU?!
YOU HAVE TO HIT THE BREAKING POINT!
TAK
KRATCH
AAGH!!
TAK
TAK
TAK
THAT BOULDER ...

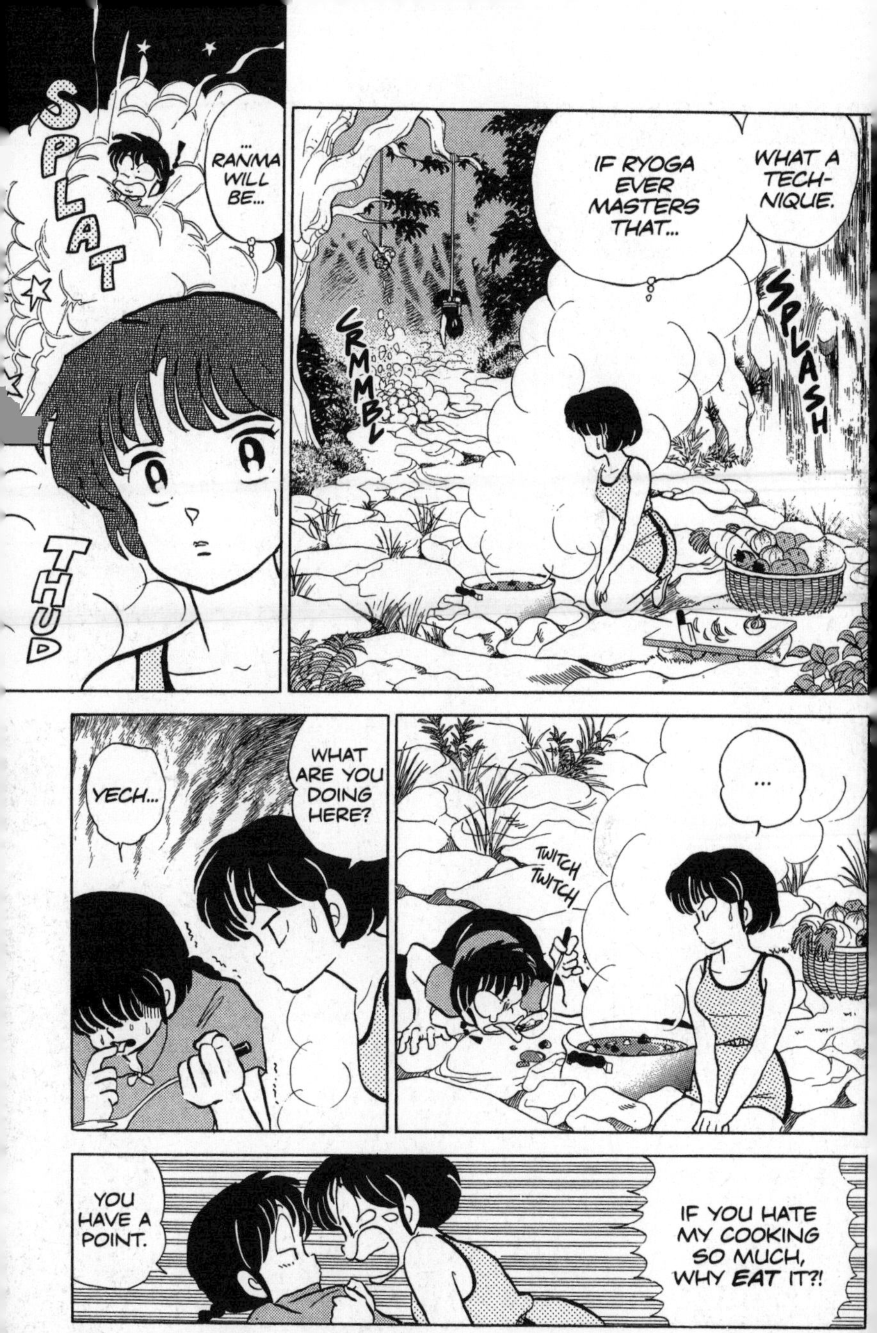
WHAT A TECH-NIQUE.
IF RYOGA EVER MASTERS THAT...
SPLASH
CRMMBL
...RANMA WILL BE...
SPLAT
THUD
...
TWITCH TWITCH
WHAT ARE YOU DOING HERE?
YECH...
IF YOU HATE MY COOKING SO MUCH, WHY **EAT** IT?!
YOU HAVE A POINT.

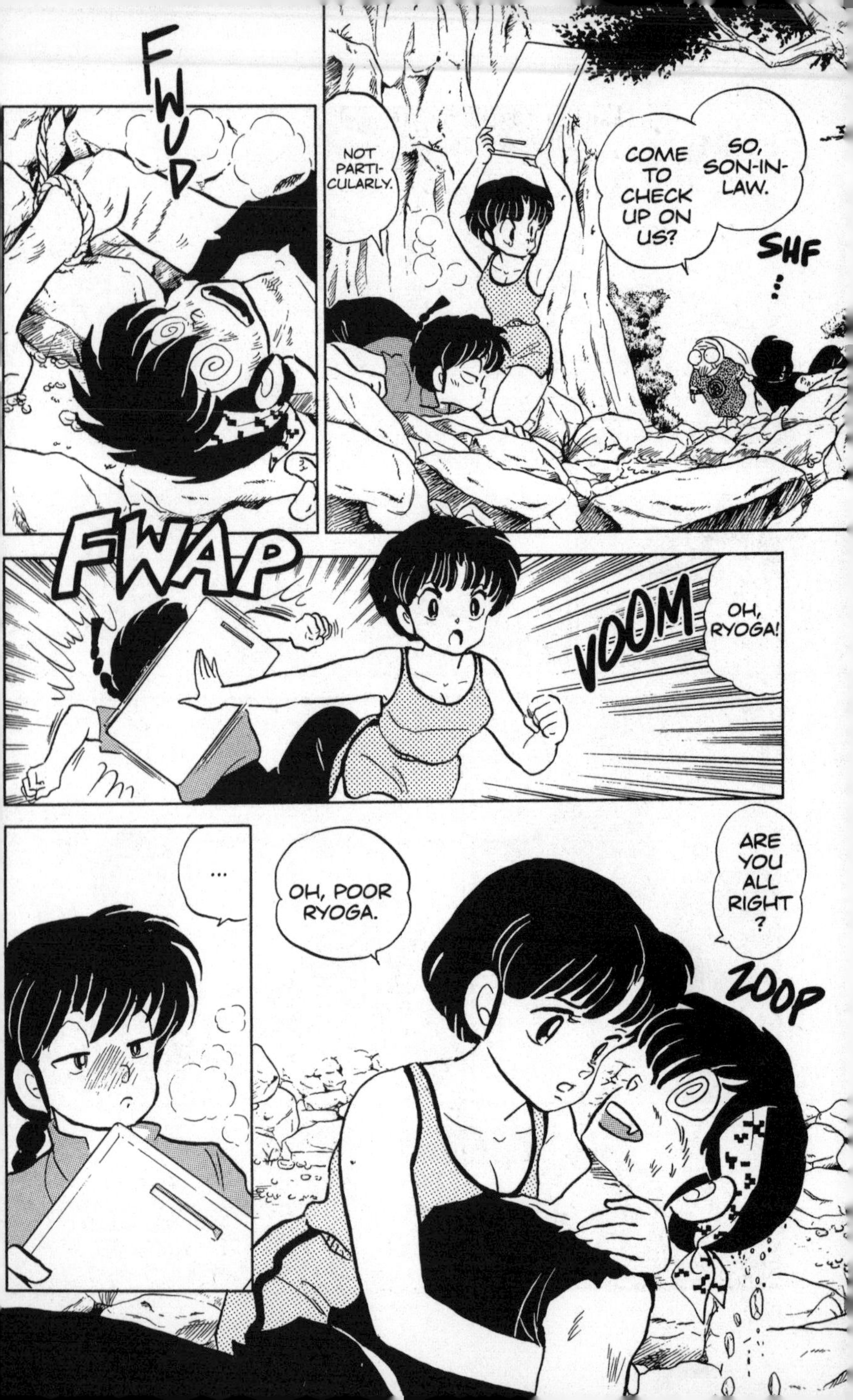
SO, SON-IN-LAW.
COME TO CHECK UP ON US?
SHF
NOT PARTICULARLY.
FWUD
OH, RYOGA!
VOOM
FWAP
ARE YOU ALL RIGHT?
ZOOP
OH, POOR RYOGA.
...

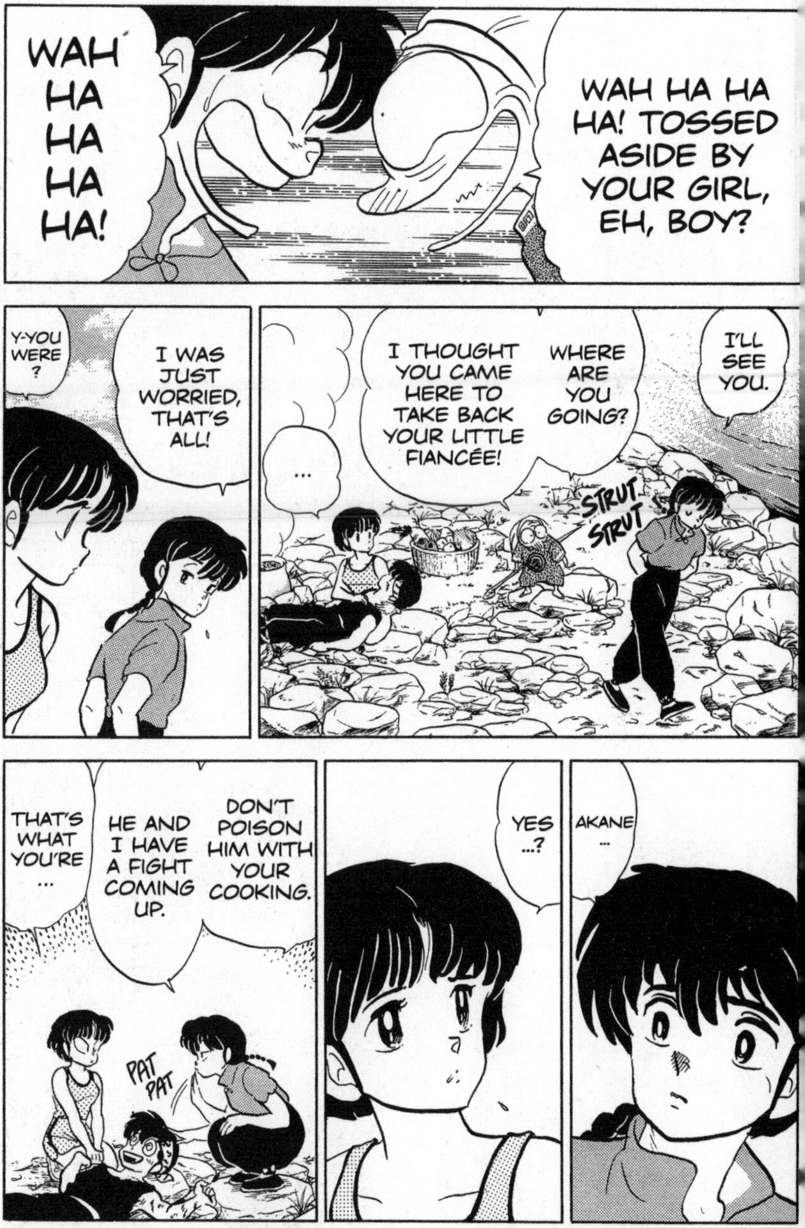
WAH HA HA HA! TOSSED ASIDE BY YOUR GIRL, EH, BOY?
WAH HA HA HA HA!
I'LL SEE YOU.
WHERE ARE YOU GOING?
I THOUGHT YOU CAME HERE TO TAKE BACK YOUR LITTLE FIANCÉE!
STRUT STRUT
...
I WAS JUST WORRIED, THAT'S ALL!
Y-YOU WERE ?
AKANE ...
YES ...?
DON'T POISON HIM WITH YOUR COOKING.
HE AND I HAVE A FIGHT COMING UP.
THAT'S WHAT YOU'RE ...
PAT PAT

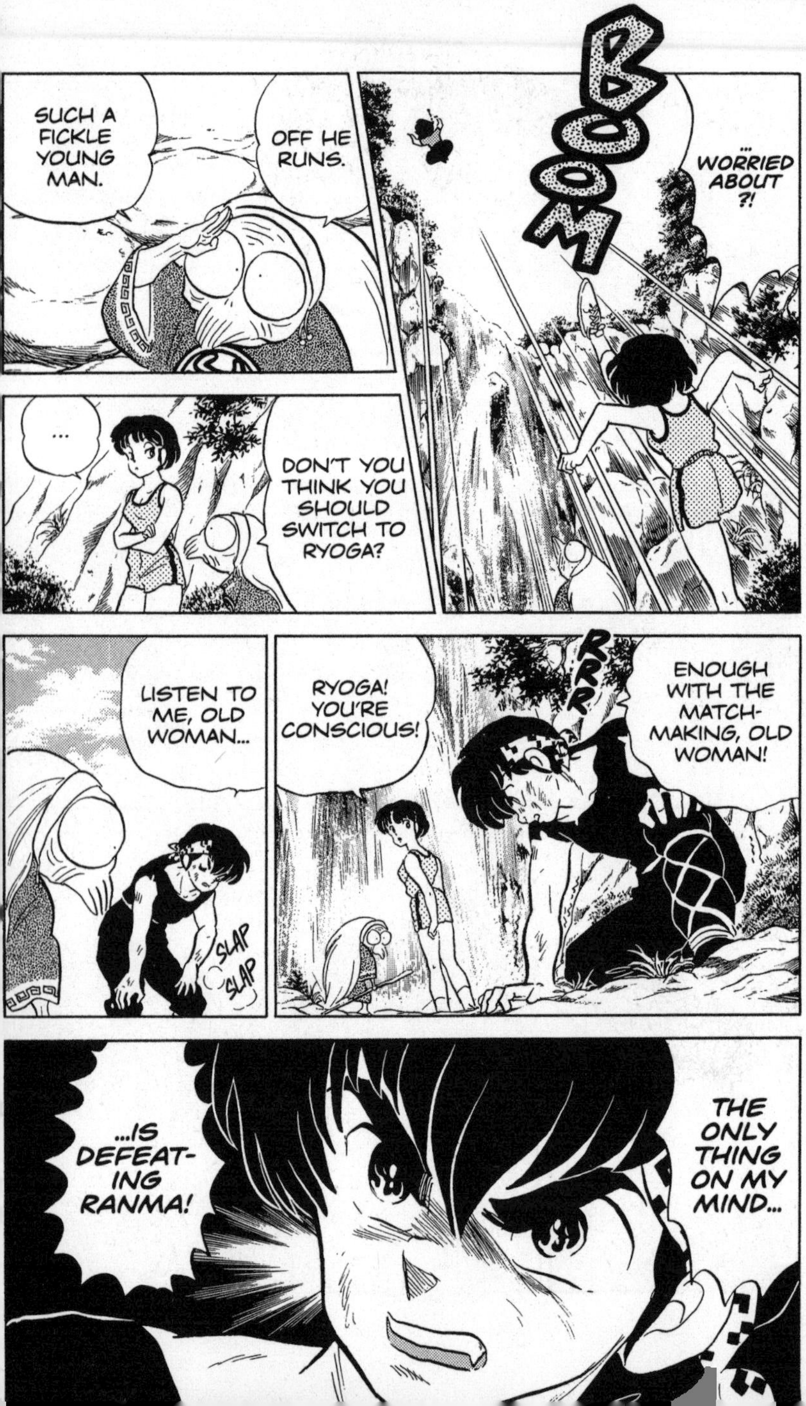

... WORRIED ABOUT ?!
BOOM
OFF HE RUNS.
SUCH A FICKLE YOUNG MAN.
DON'T YOU THINK YOU SHOULD SWITCH TO RYOGA?
...
RRR
ENOUGH WITH THE MATCH-MAKING, OLD WOMAN!
RYOGA! YOU'RE CONSCIOUS!
LISTEN TO ME, OLD WOMAN...
SLAP
SLAP
THE ONLY THING ON MY MIND...
...IS DEFEATING RANMA!

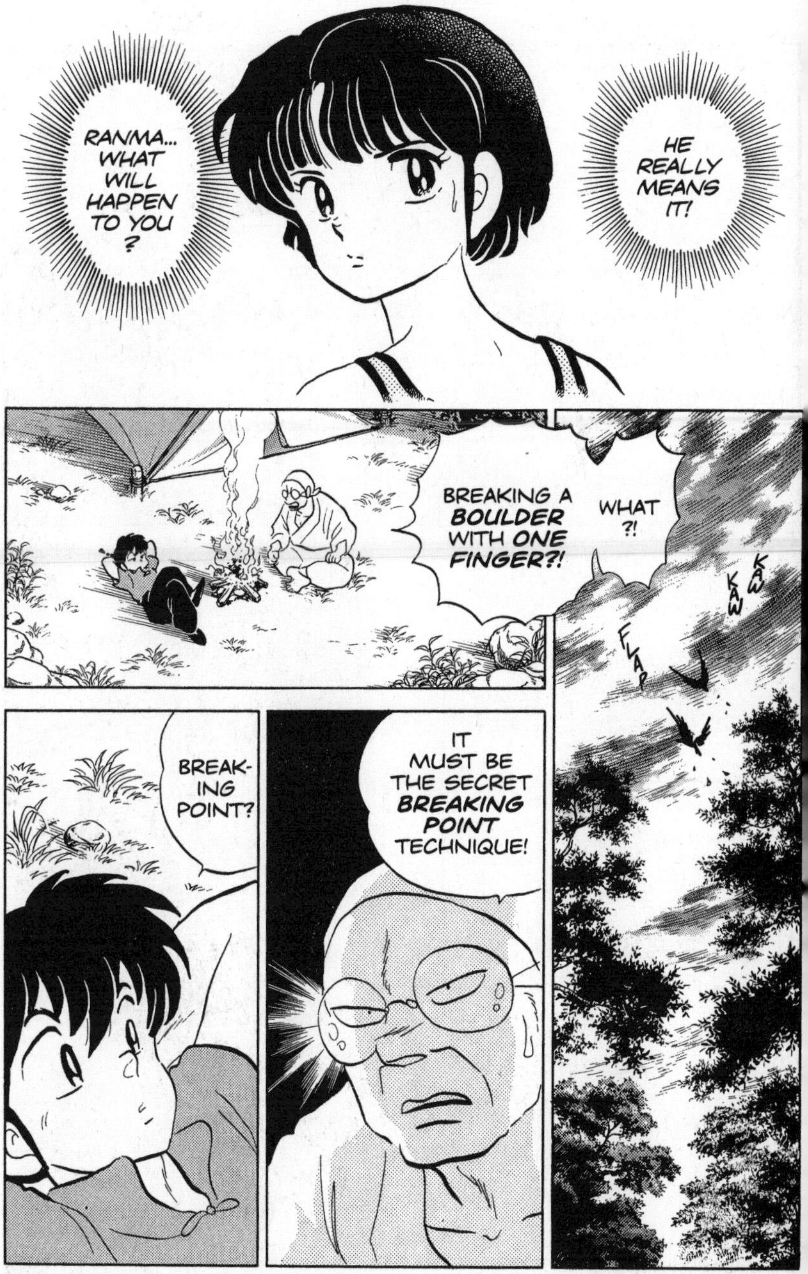
HE REALLY MEANS IT!
RANMA... WHAT WILL HAPPEN TO YOU?
WHAT?!
KAW KAW
FLAP
BREAKING A **BOULDER** WITH **ONE FINGER?!**
IT MUST BE THE SECRET **BREAKING POINT** TECHNIQUE!
BREAK-ING POINT?

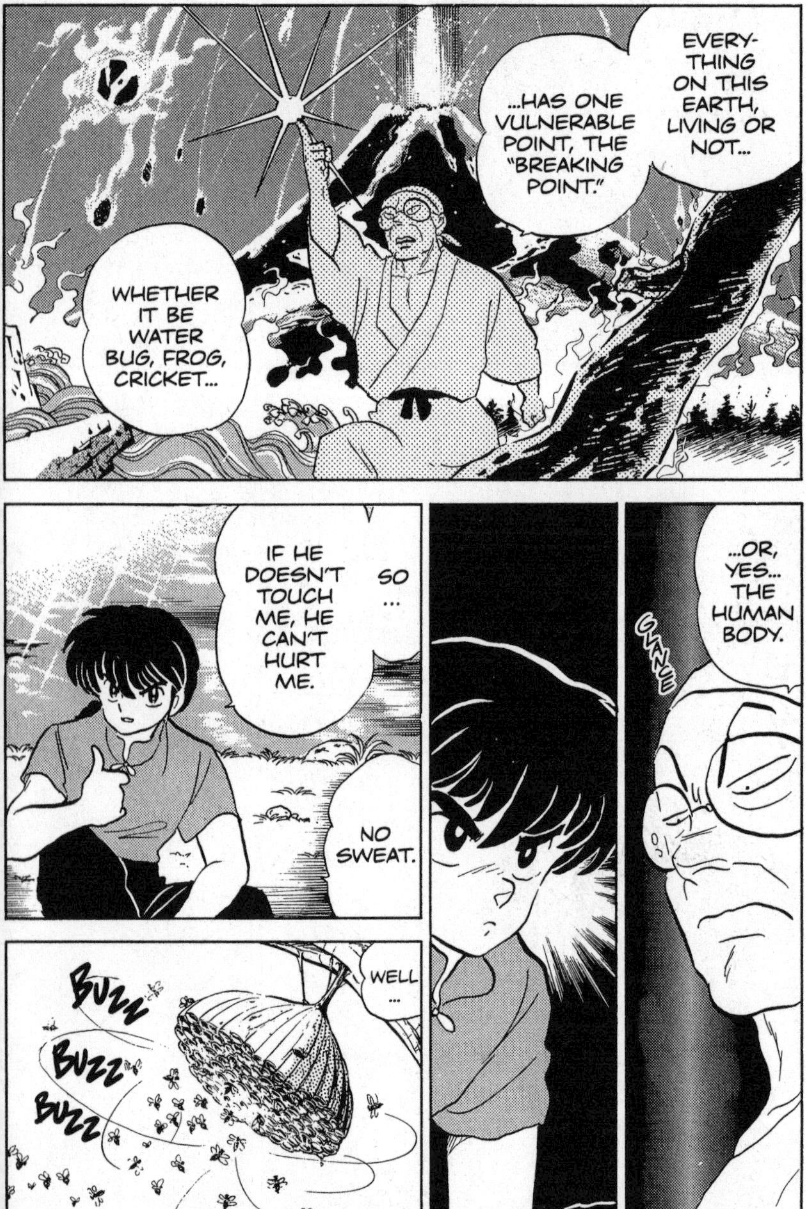
EVERYTHING ON THIS EARTH, LIVING OR NOT...
...HAS ONE VULNERABLE POINT, THE "BREAKING POINT."
WHETHER IT BE WATER BUG, FROG, CRICKET...
...OR, YES... THE HUMAN BODY.
GLANCE
SO ...
IF HE DOESN'T TOUCH ME, HE CAN'T HURT ME.
NO SWEAT.
WELL ...
BUZZ
BUZZ
BUZZ

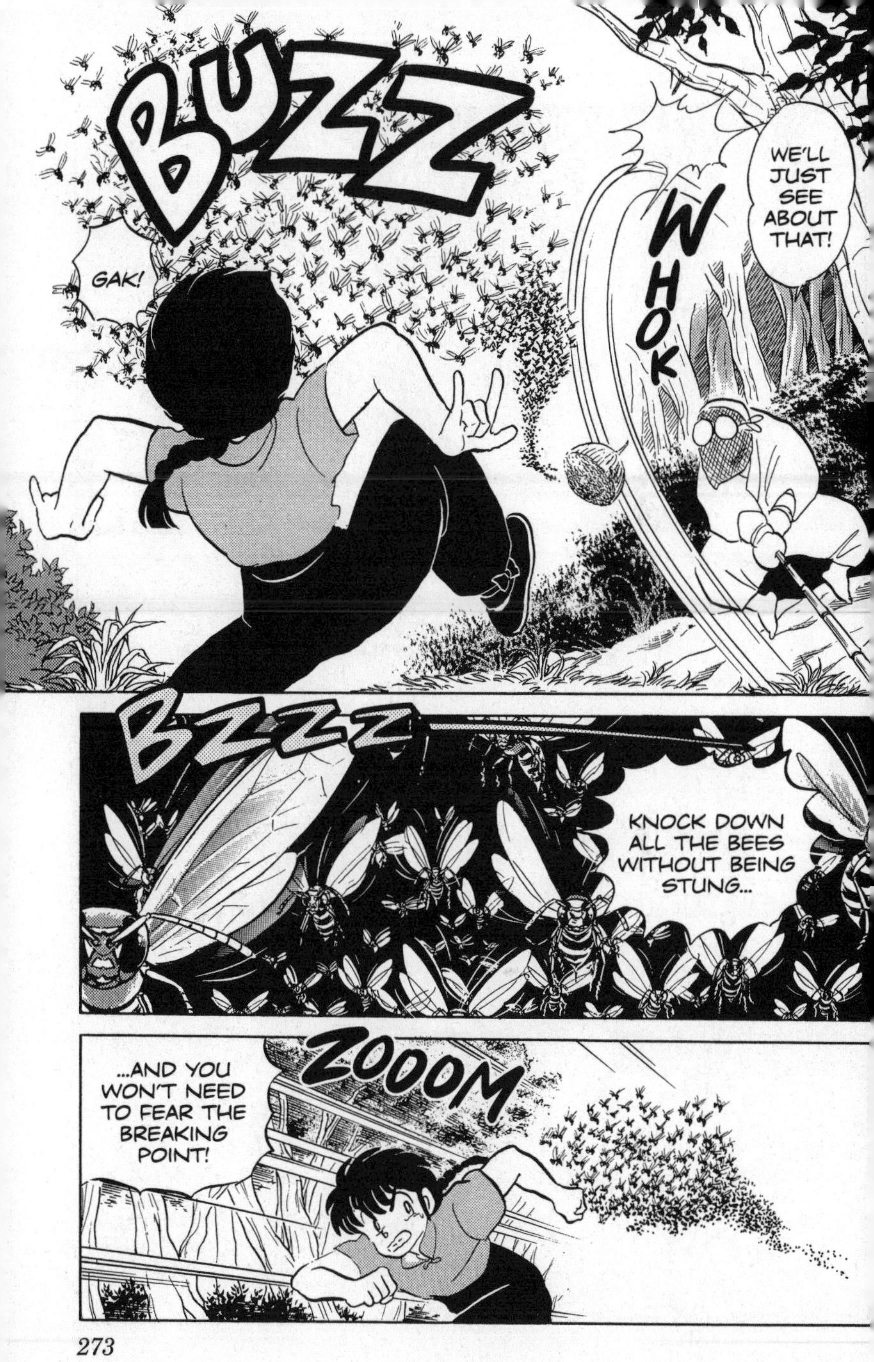
WE'LL JUST SEE ABOUT THAT!
WHOK
BUZZ
GAK!
BZZZ
KNOCK DOWN ALL THE BEES WITHOUT BEING STUNG...
ZOOOM
...AND YOU WON'T NEED TO FEAR THE BREAKING POINT!

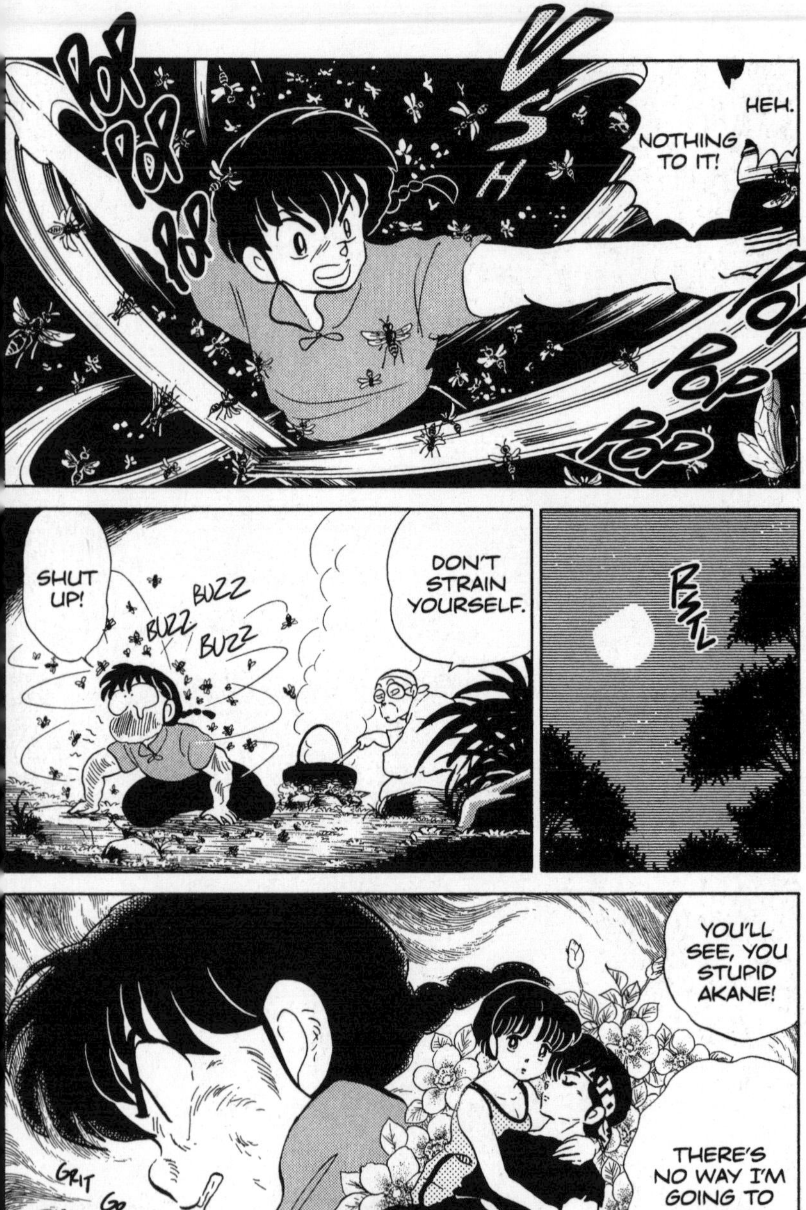
HEH.
NOTHING TO IT!
POP POP POP
VSH
POP POP POP
RSTL
DON'T STRAIN YOURSELF.
BUZZ
BUZZ
BUZZ
SHUT UP!
YOU'LL SEE, YOU STUPID AKANE!
THERE'S NO WAY I'M GOING TO LOSE!
GRIT
GRIT
GRIT

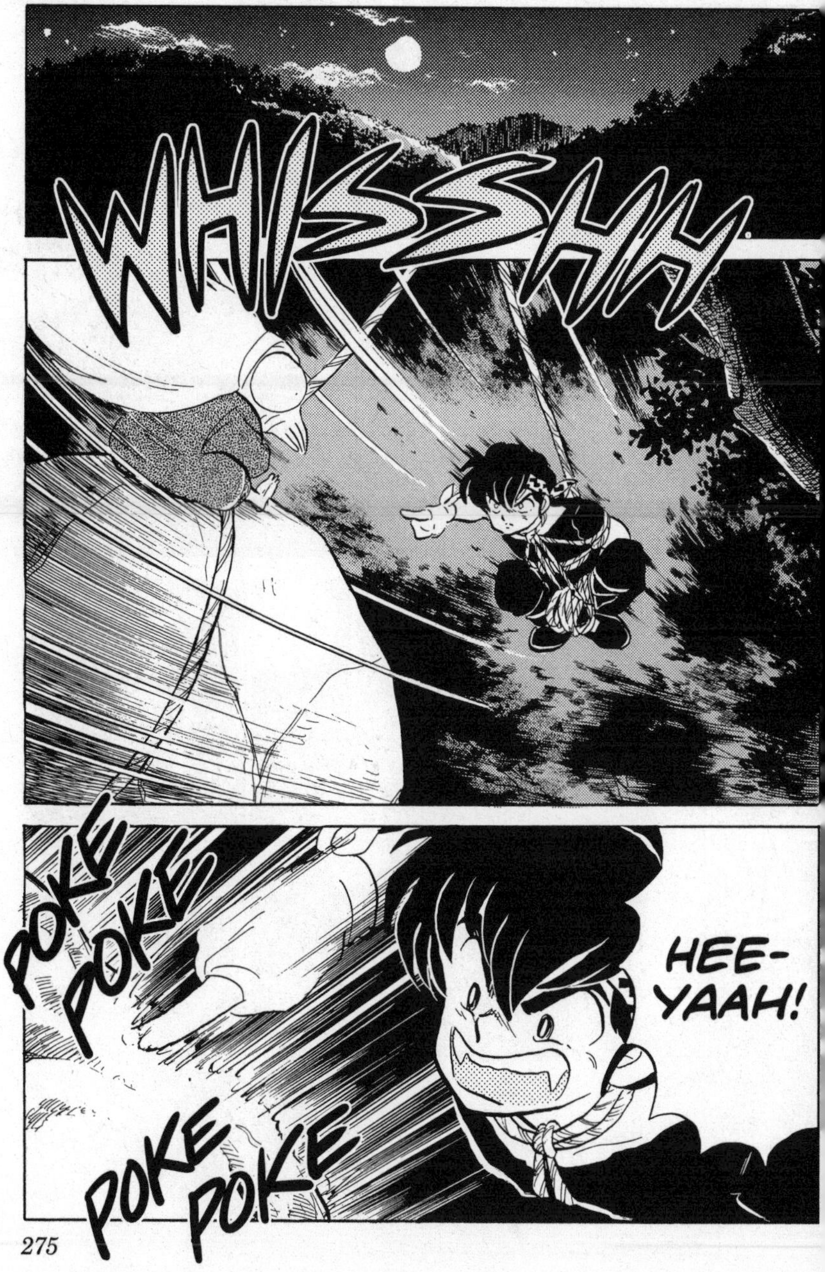
WHISSHH
HEE-YAAH!
POKE POKE
POKE POKE

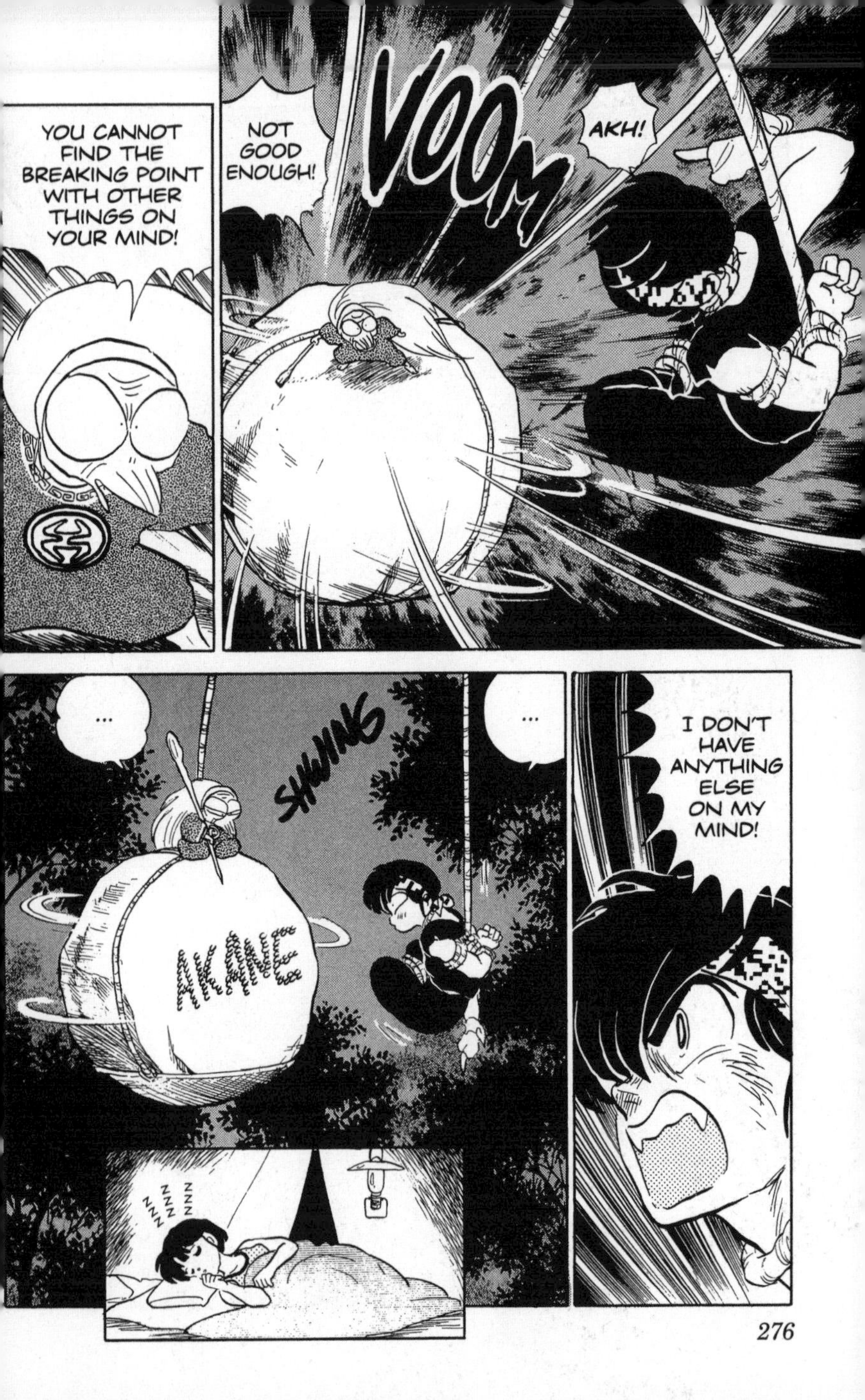
AKH!
VOOM
NOT GOOD ENOUGH!
YOU CANNOT FIND THE BREAKING POINT WITH OTHER THINGS ON YOUR MIND!
I DON'T HAVE ANYTHING ELSE ON MY MIND!
...
SHWING
...
AKANE
Z Z Z Z Z Z Z Z Z

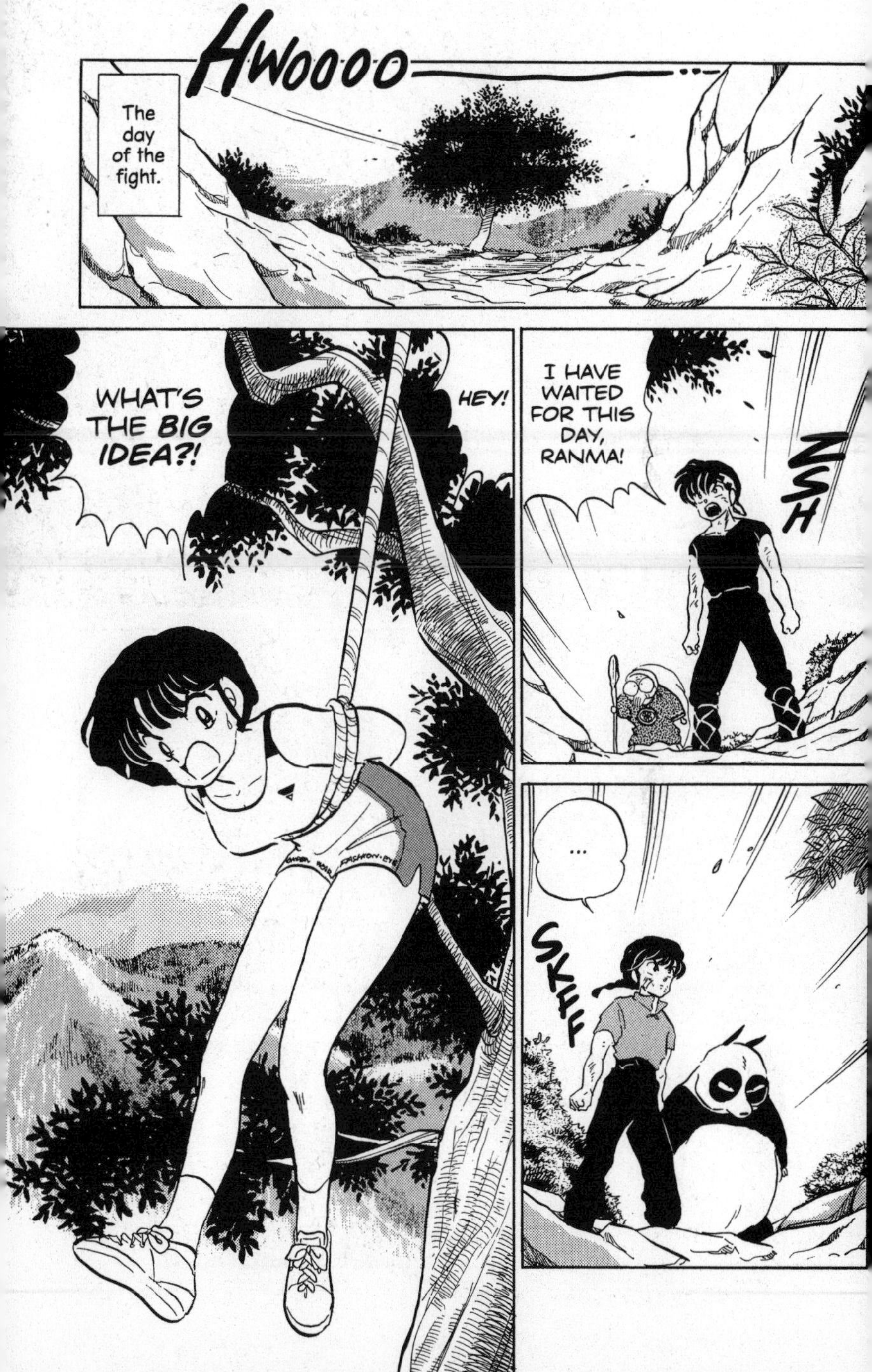
HWOOOO
The day of the fight.
I HAVE WAITED FOR THIS DAY, RANMA!
ZSH
...
SKFF
HEY!
WHAT'S THE BIG IDEA?!

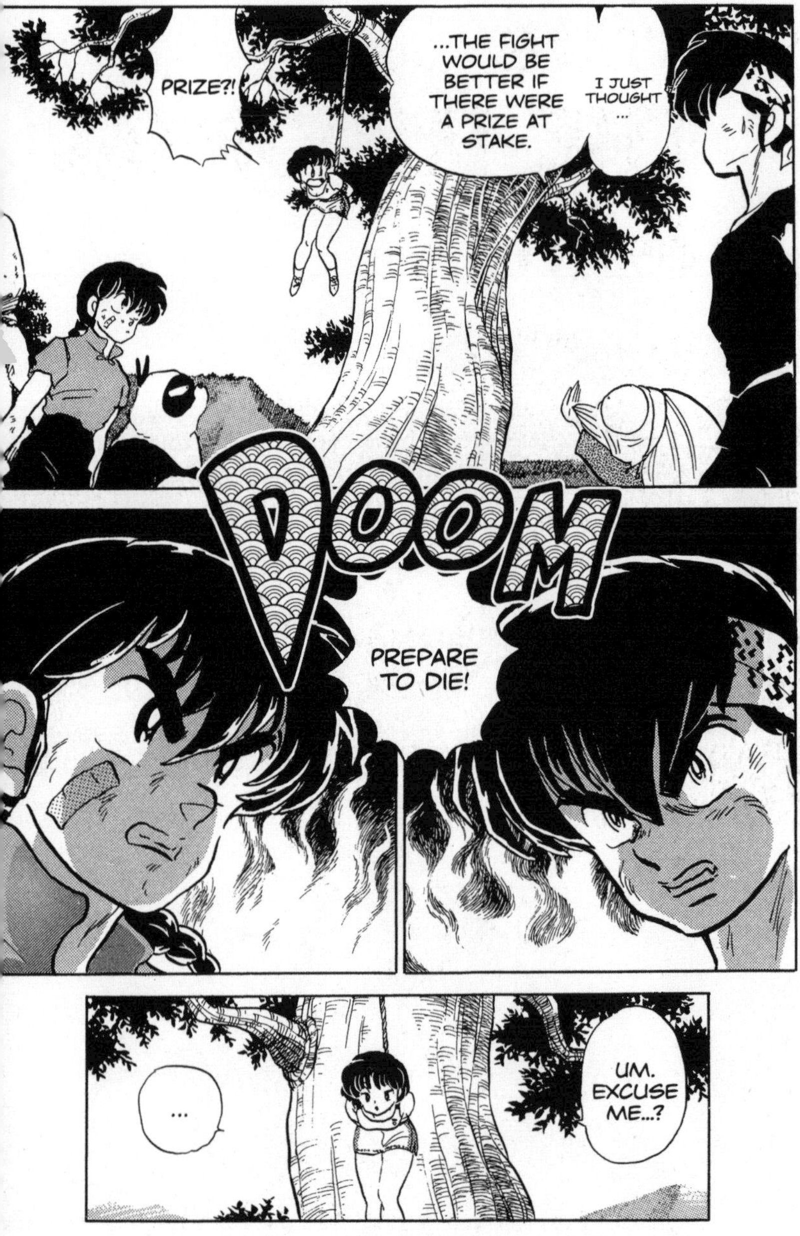
I JUST THOUGHT ...
...THE FIGHT WOULD BE BETTER IF THERE WERE A PRIZE AT STAKE.
PRIZE?!
DOOM
PREPARE TO DIE!
UM. EXCUSE ME...?
...

PART 18
THE IMMORTAL MAN

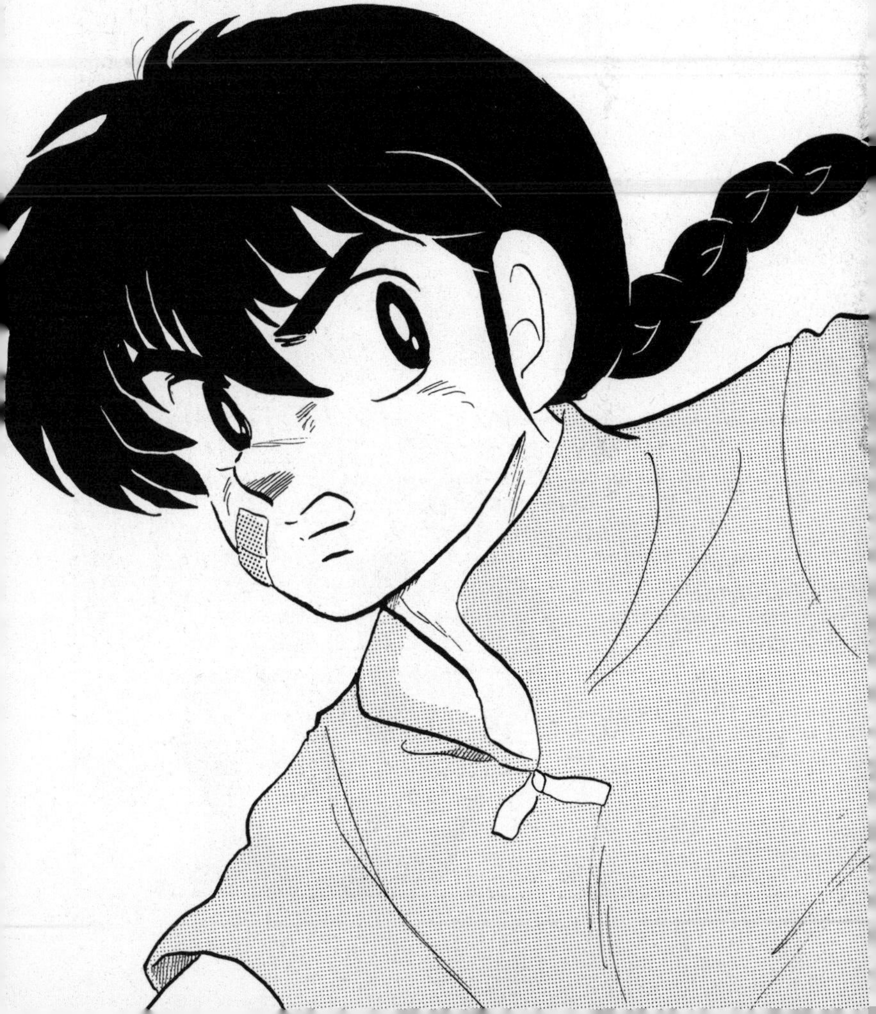

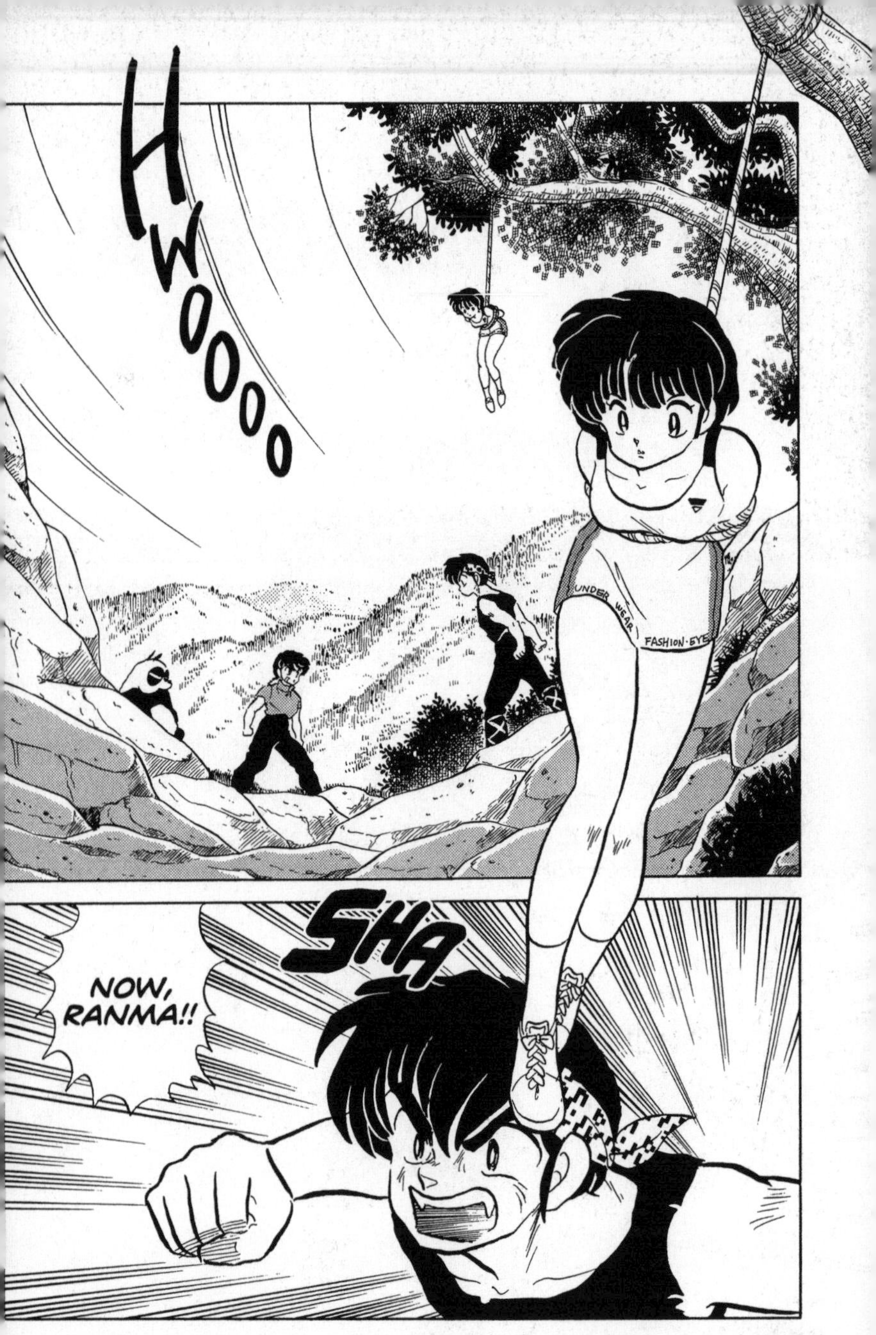
HWOOOOO
UNDER WEAR
FASHION·EYE
SHA
NOW, RANMA!!

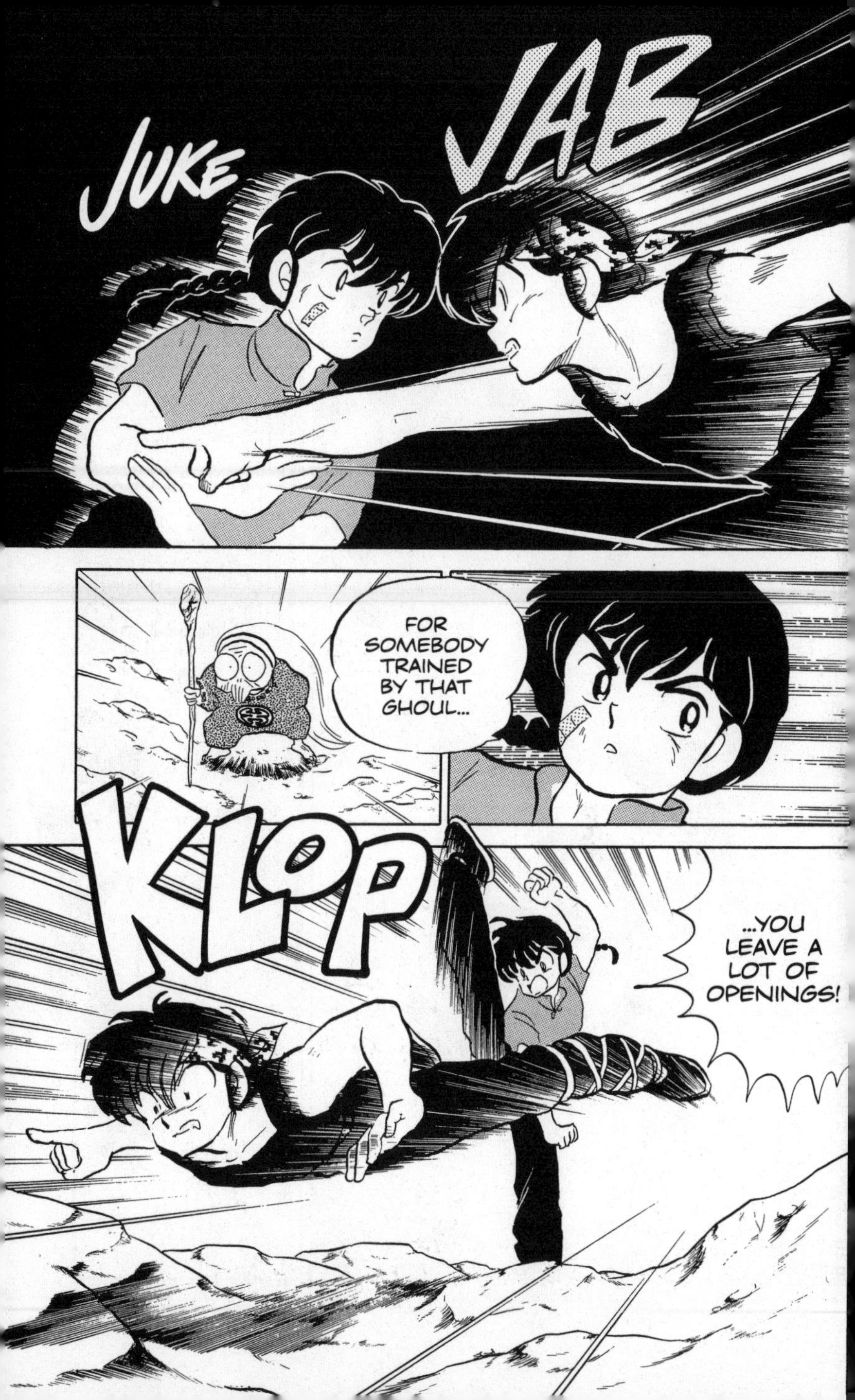
JAB
JUKE
FOR SOMEBODY TRAINED BY THAT GHOUL...
KLOP
...YOU LEAVE A LOT OF OPENINGS!

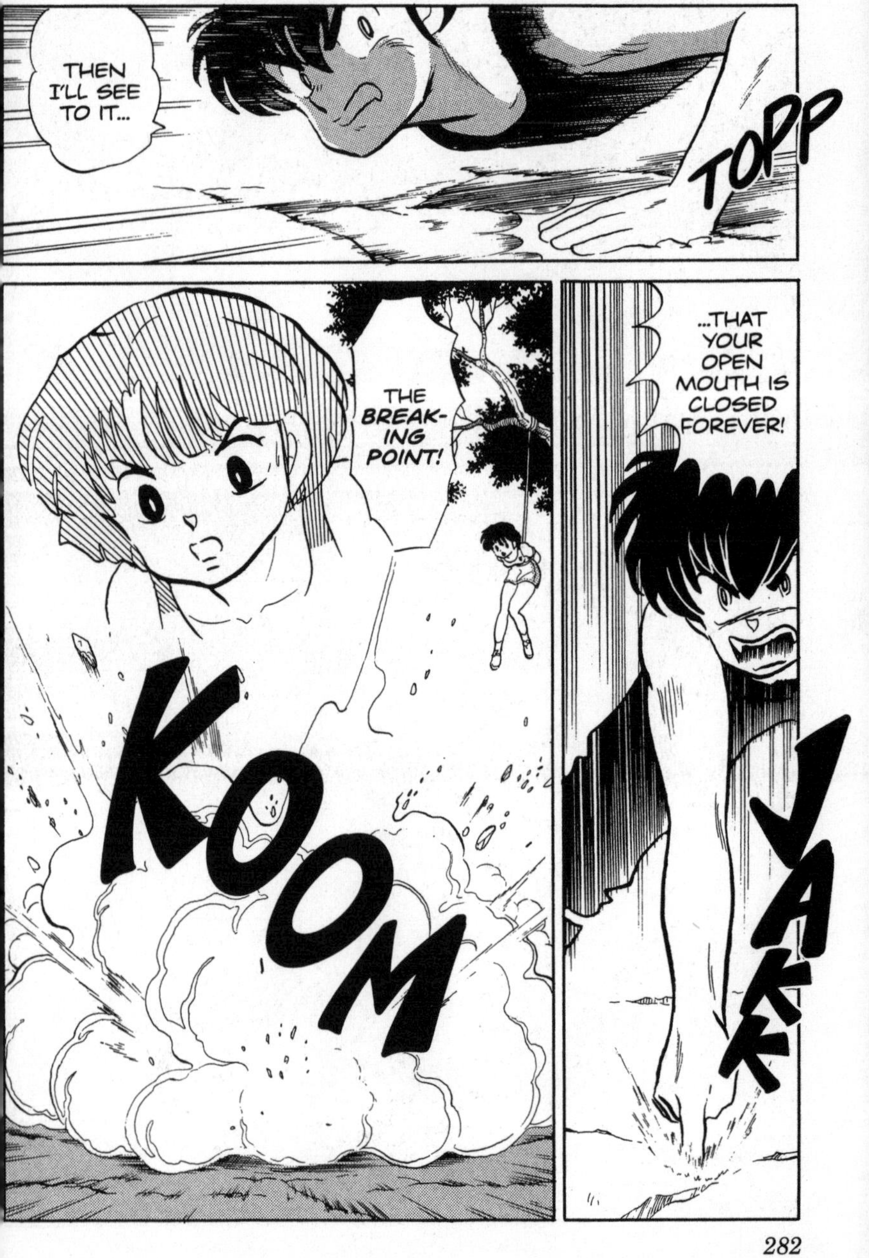
THEN I'LL SEE TO IT...
TOPP
...THAT YOUR OPEN MOUTH IS CLOSED FOREVER!
YAKK
THE BREAKING POINT!
KOOM

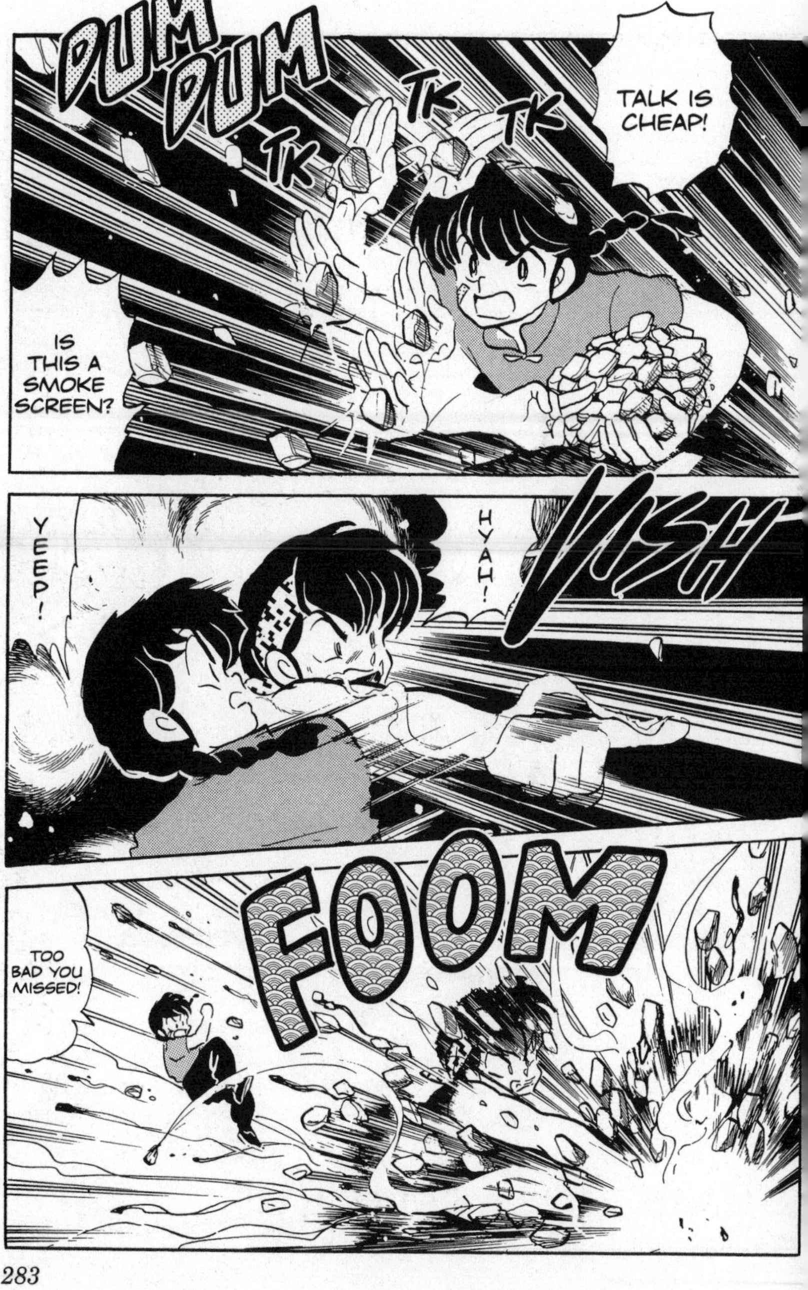
TALK IS CHEAP!
DUM DUM
TK TK TK
IS THIS A SMOKE SCREEN?
VISH
HYAH!
YEEP!
FOOM
TOO BAD YOU MISSED!

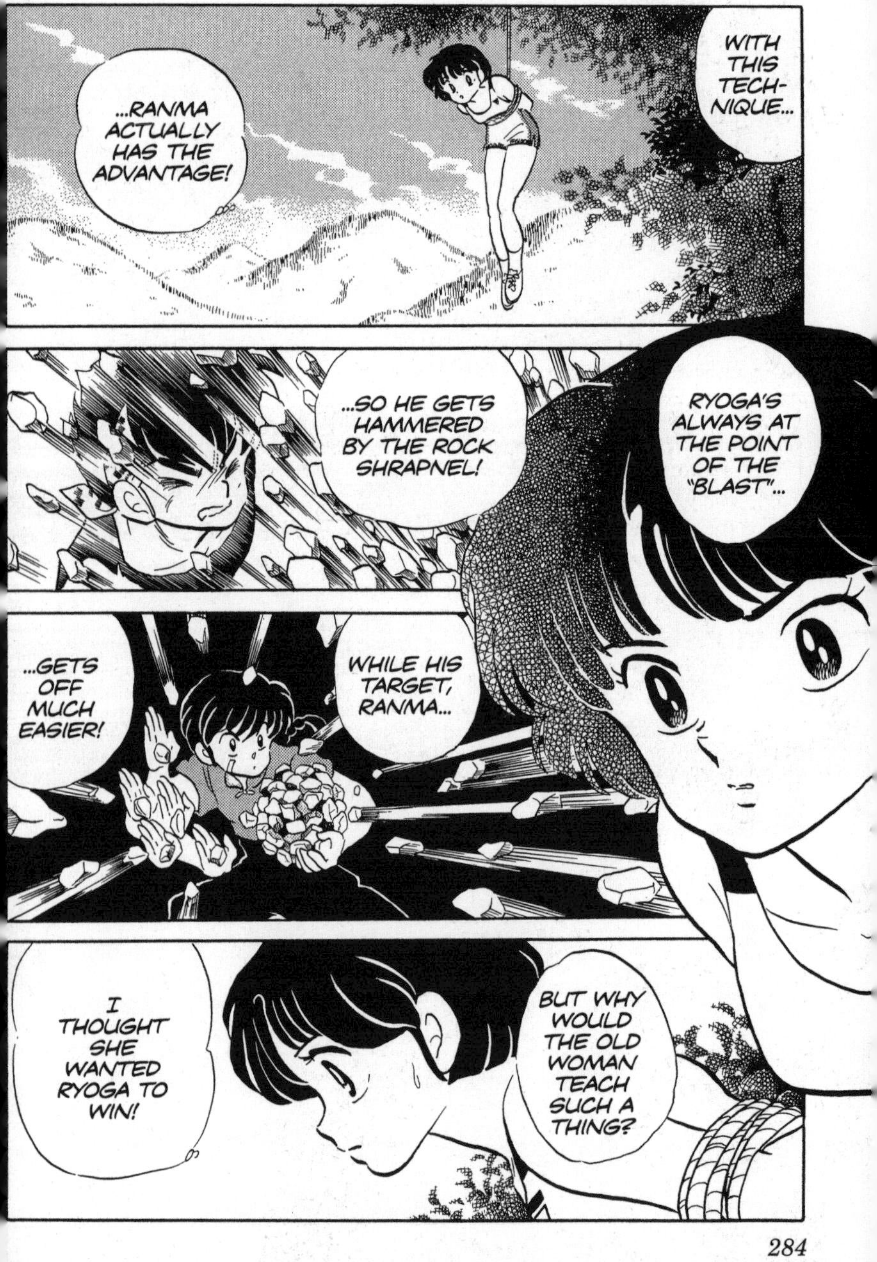
WITH THIS TECH-NIQUE...
...RANMA ACTUALLY HAS THE ADVANTAGE!
RYOGA'S ALWAYS AT THE POINT OF THE "BLAST"...
...SO HE GETS HAMMERED BY THE ROCK SHRAPNEL!
WHILE HIS TARGET, RANMA...
...GETS OFF MUCH EASIER!
BUT WHY WOULD THE OLD WOMAN TEACH SUCH A THING?
I THOUGHT SHE WANTED RYOGA TO WIN!

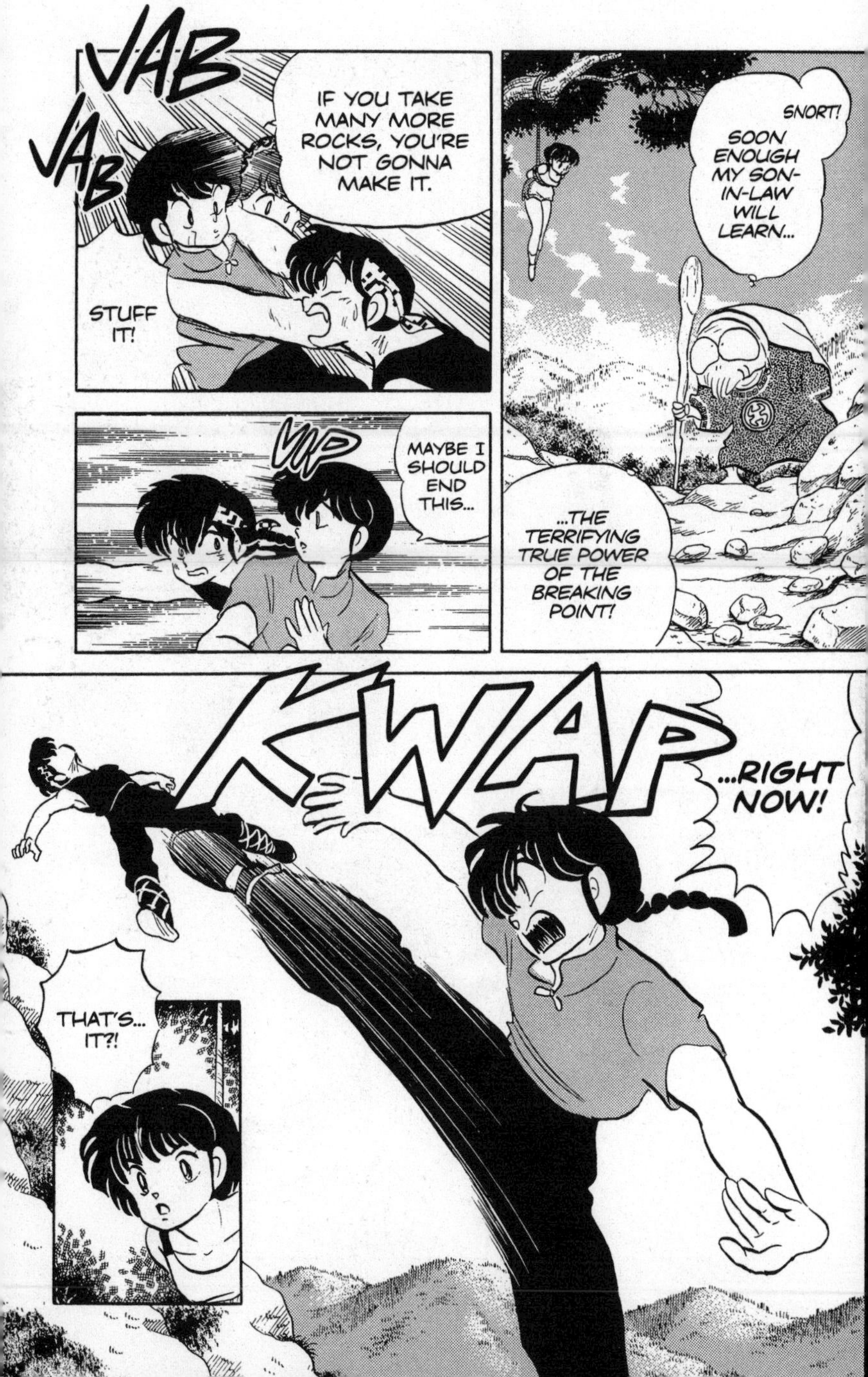
SNORT!
SOON ENOUGH MY SON-IN-LAW WILL LEARN...
...THE TERRIFYING TRUE POWER OF THE BREAKING POINT!
IF YOU TAKE MANY MORE ROCKS, YOU'RE NOT GONNA MAKE IT.
JAB
JAB
STUFF IT!
MAYBE I SHOULD END THIS...
VIP
...RIGHT NOW!
KWAP
THAT'S... IT?!

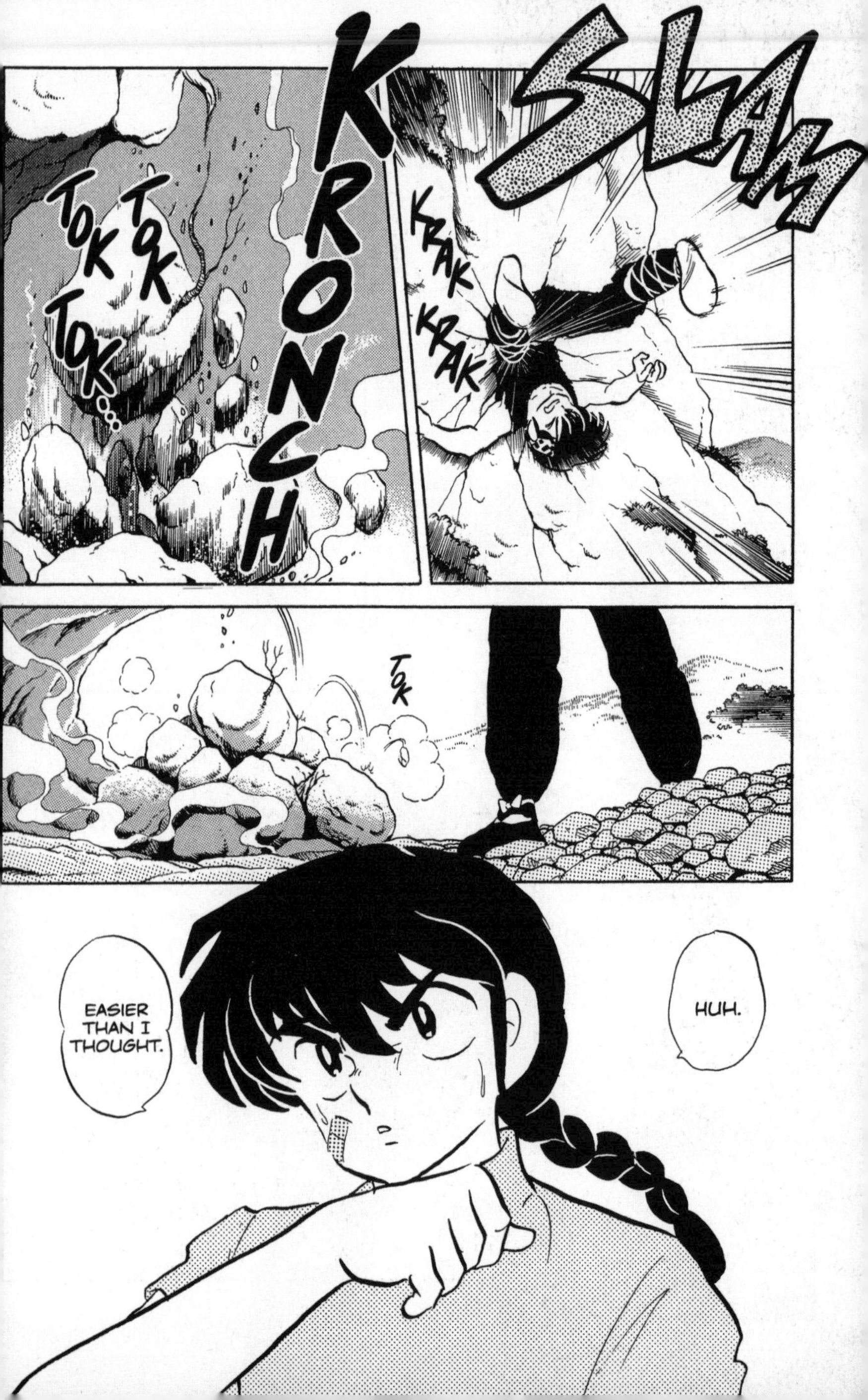
SLAM
KRAK KRAK KRAK
KRONCH
TOK TOK TOK TOK...
TOK
HUH.
EASIER THAN I THOUGHT.

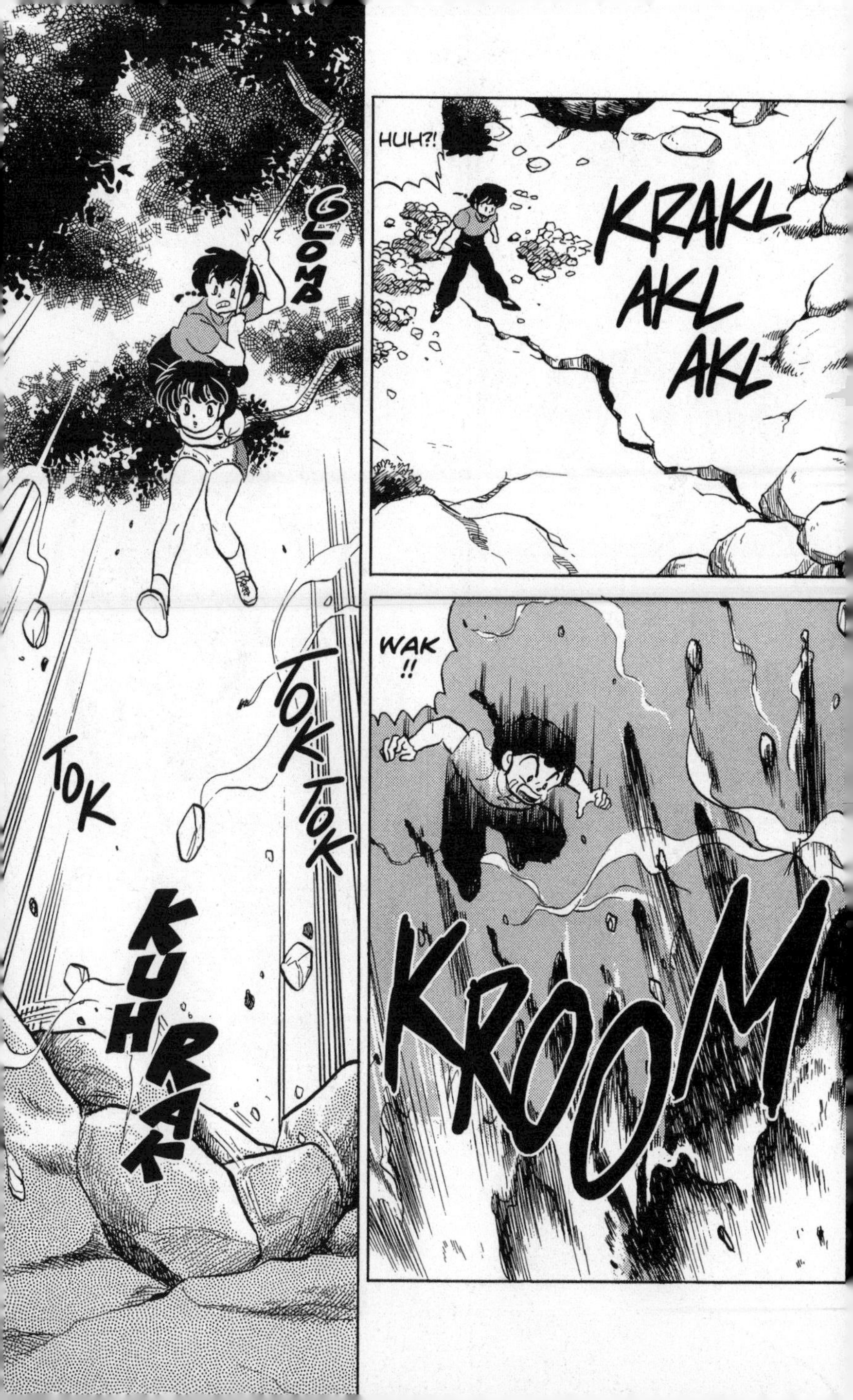
HUH?!
KRAKL AKL AKL
WAK!!
KROOM
GLOMP
TOK TOK
TOK
KUHRAK

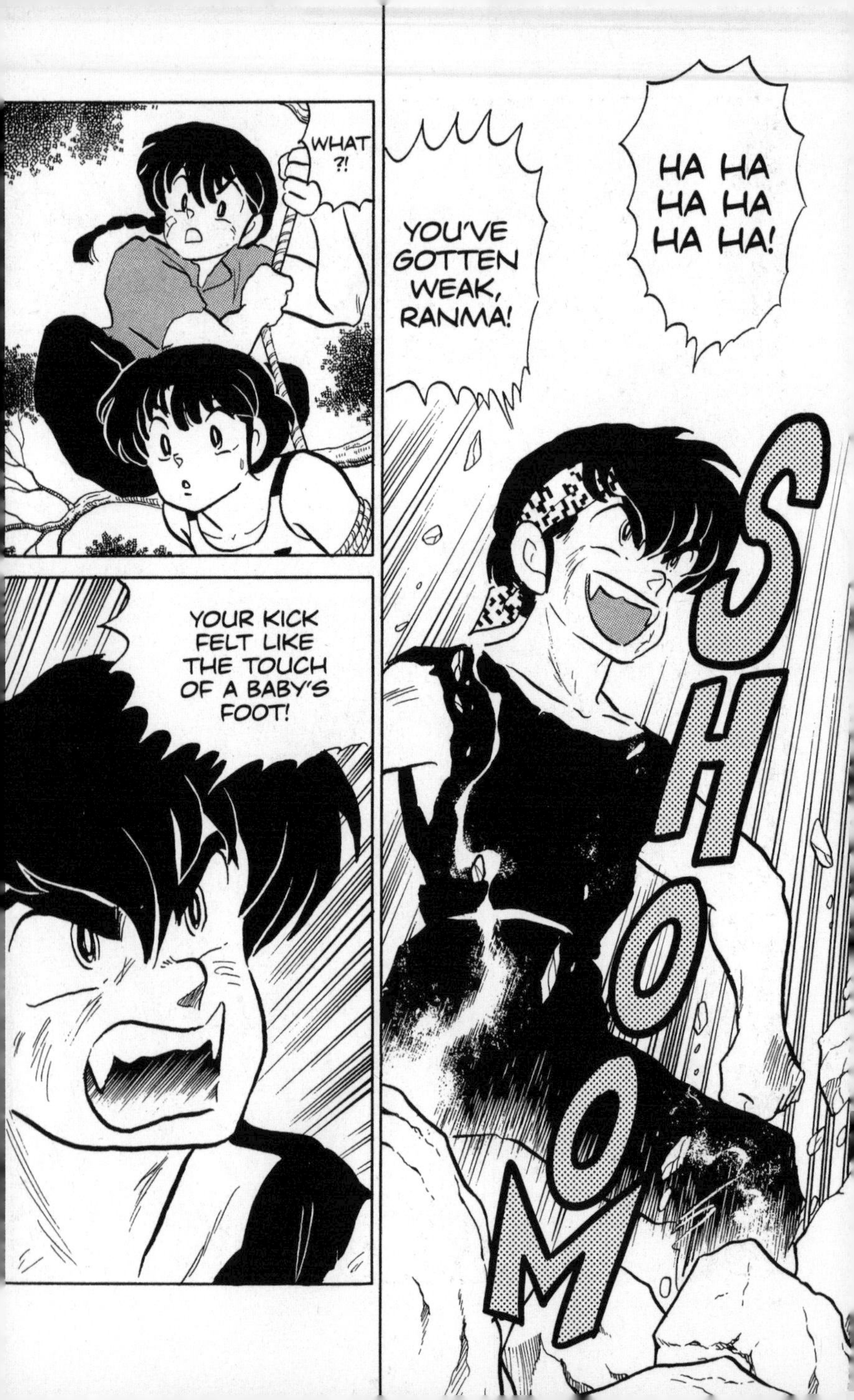
HA HA HA HA HA HA!
YOU'VE GOTTEN WEAK, RANMA!
SHOOM
WHAT ?!
YOUR KICK FELT LIKE THE TOUCH OF A BABY'S FOOT!

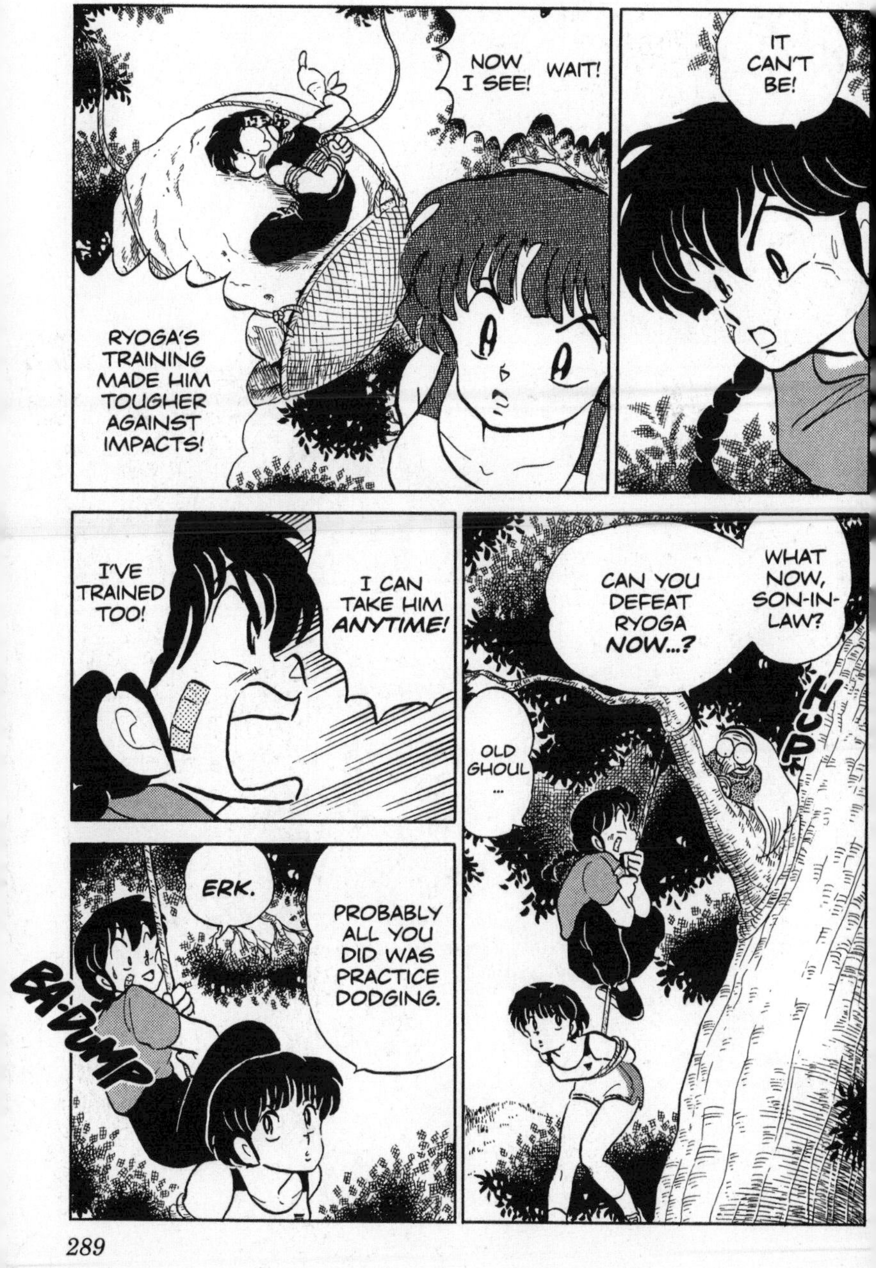
IT CAN'T BE!
WAIT!
NOW I SEE!
RYOGA'S TRAINING MADE HIM TOUGHER AGAINST IMPACTS!
WHAT NOW, SON-IN-LAW?
CAN YOU DEFEAT RYOGA NOW...?
HUP
OLD GHOUL ...
I CAN TAKE HIM ANYTIME!
I'VE TRAINED TOO!
PROBABLY ALL YOU DID WAS PRACTICE DODGING.
ERK.
BA-DUMP

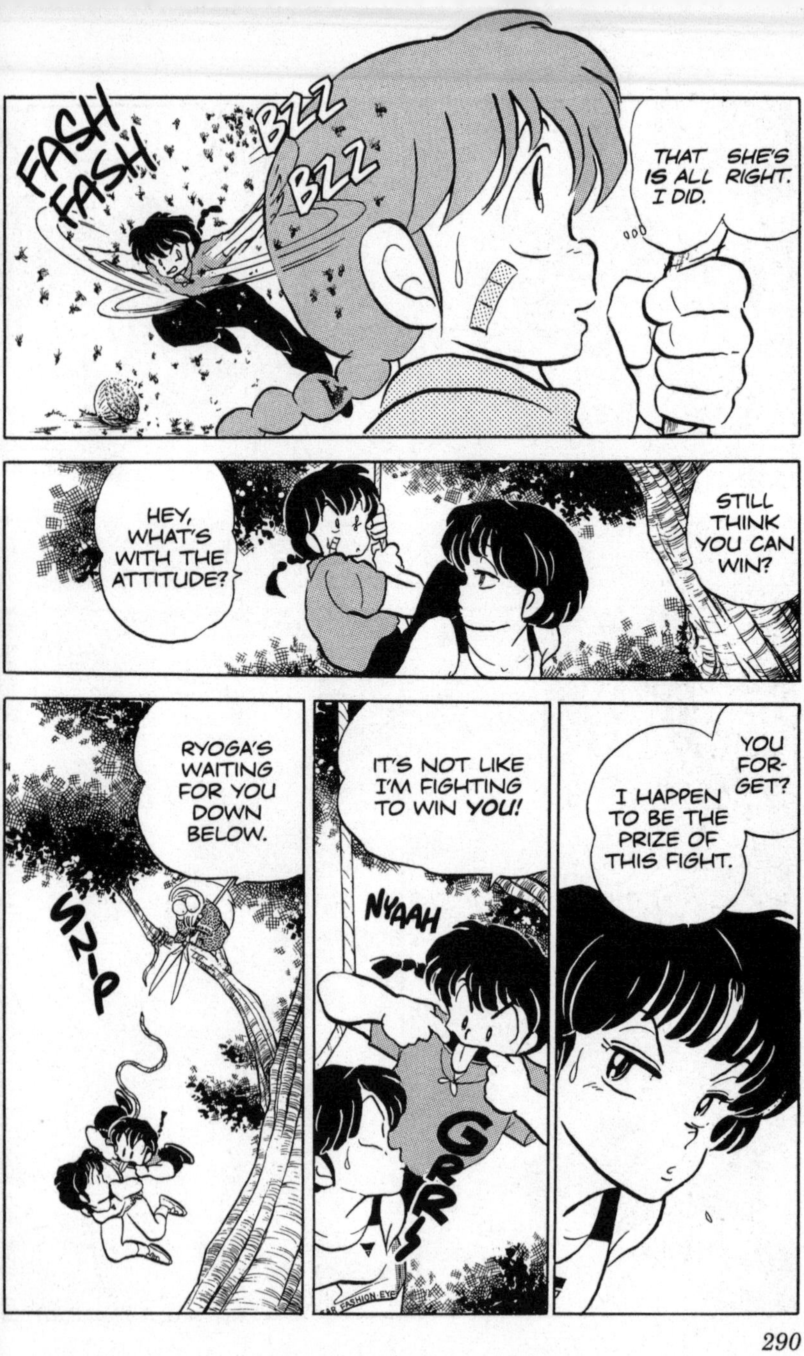
SHE'S RIGHT.
THAT IS ALL I DID.
BZZ BZZ
FASH FASH
STILL THINK YOU CAN WIN?
HEY, WHAT'S WITH THE ATTITUDE?
YOU FORGET?
I HAPPEN TO BE THE PRIZE OF THIS FIGHT.
IT'S NOT LIKE I'M FIGHTING TO WIN YOU!
NYAAH
GRRS
RYOGA'S WAITING FOR YOU DOWN BELOW.
SNIP

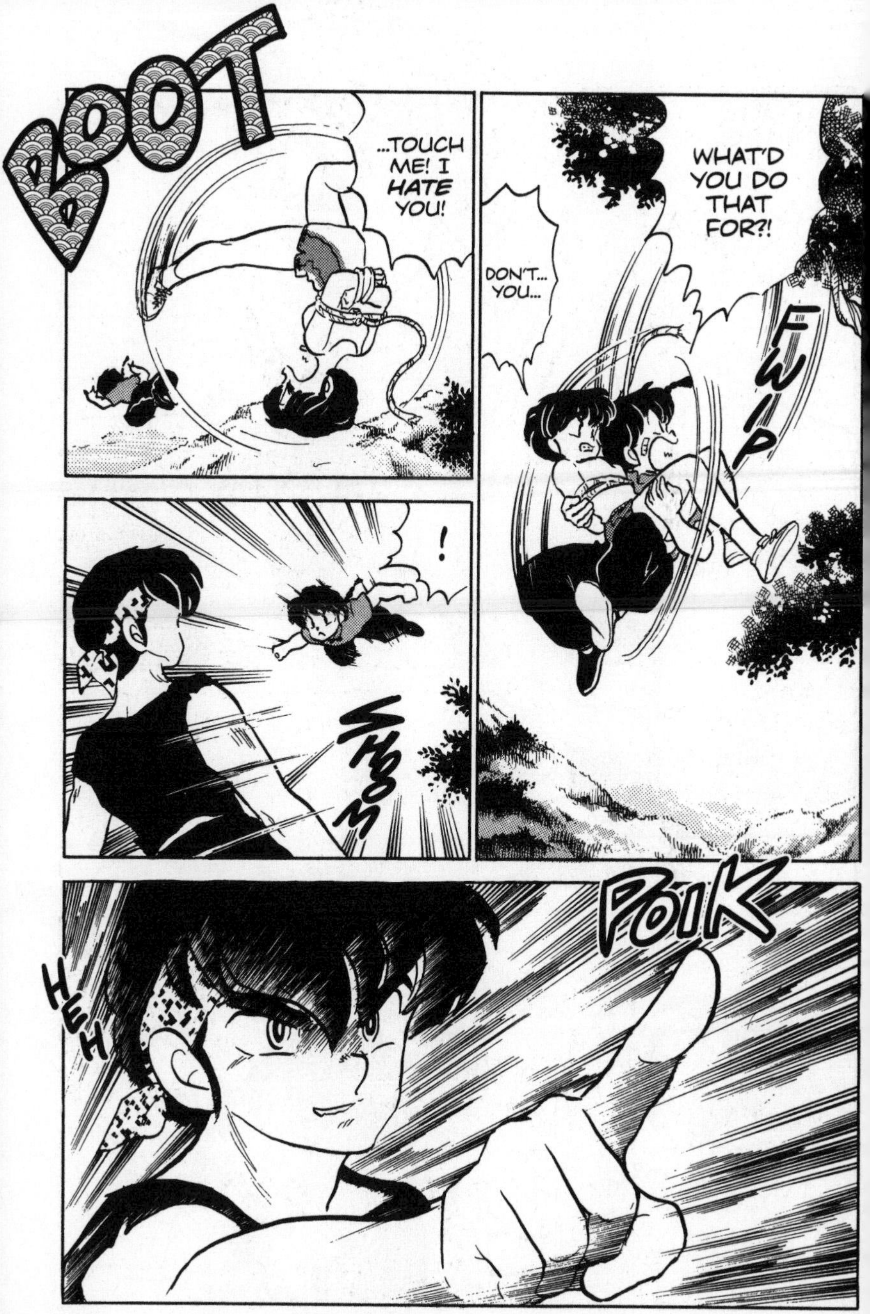
WHAT'D YOU DO THAT FOR?!
DON'T... YOU...
FWIP
BOOT
...TOUCH ME! I HATE YOU!
!
SHOOM
POIK
HEH

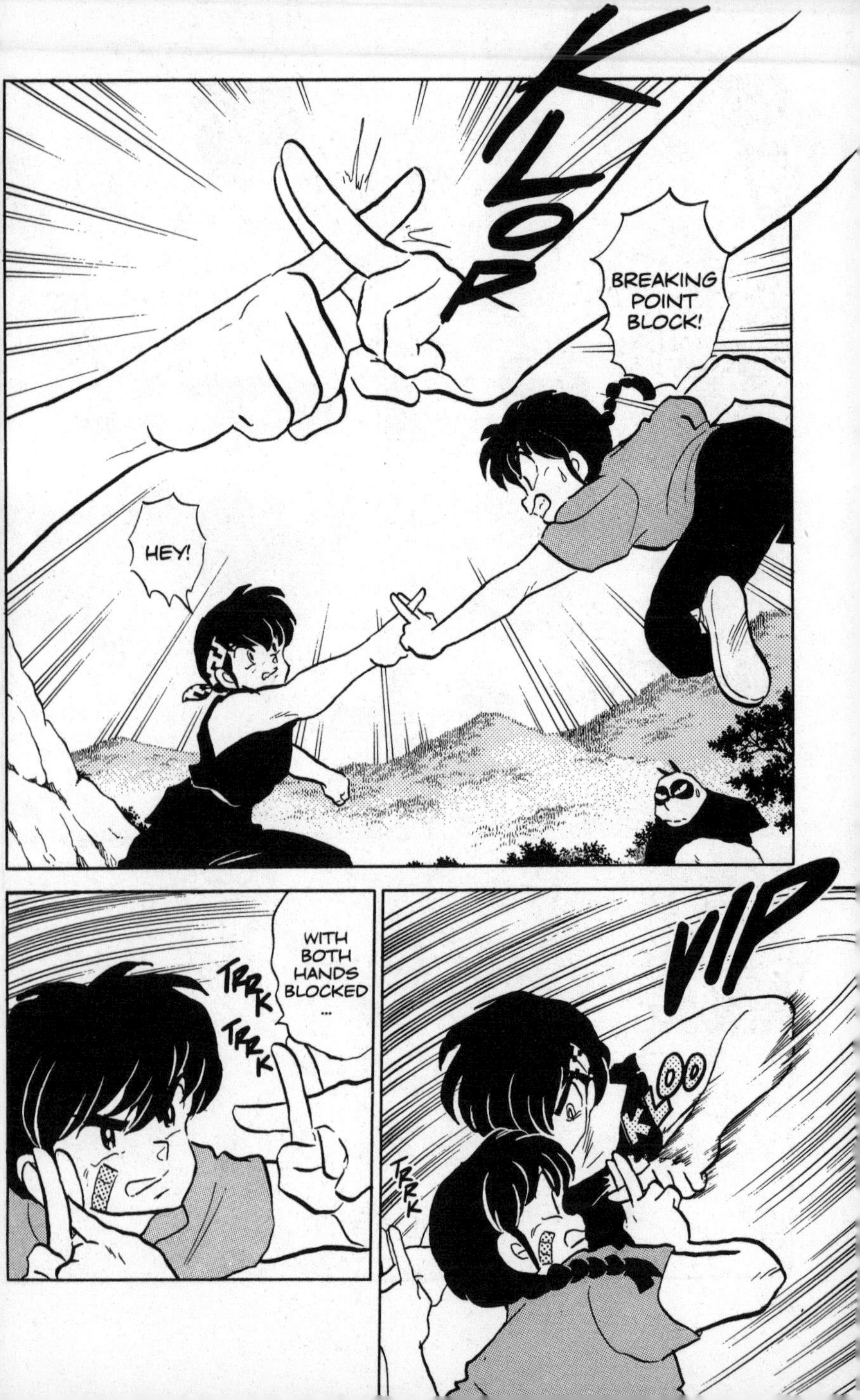
KLOP
BREAKING POINT BLOCK!
HEY!
VIP
KLOO
TRRK
WITH BOTH HANDS BLOCKED ...
TRRK
TRRK

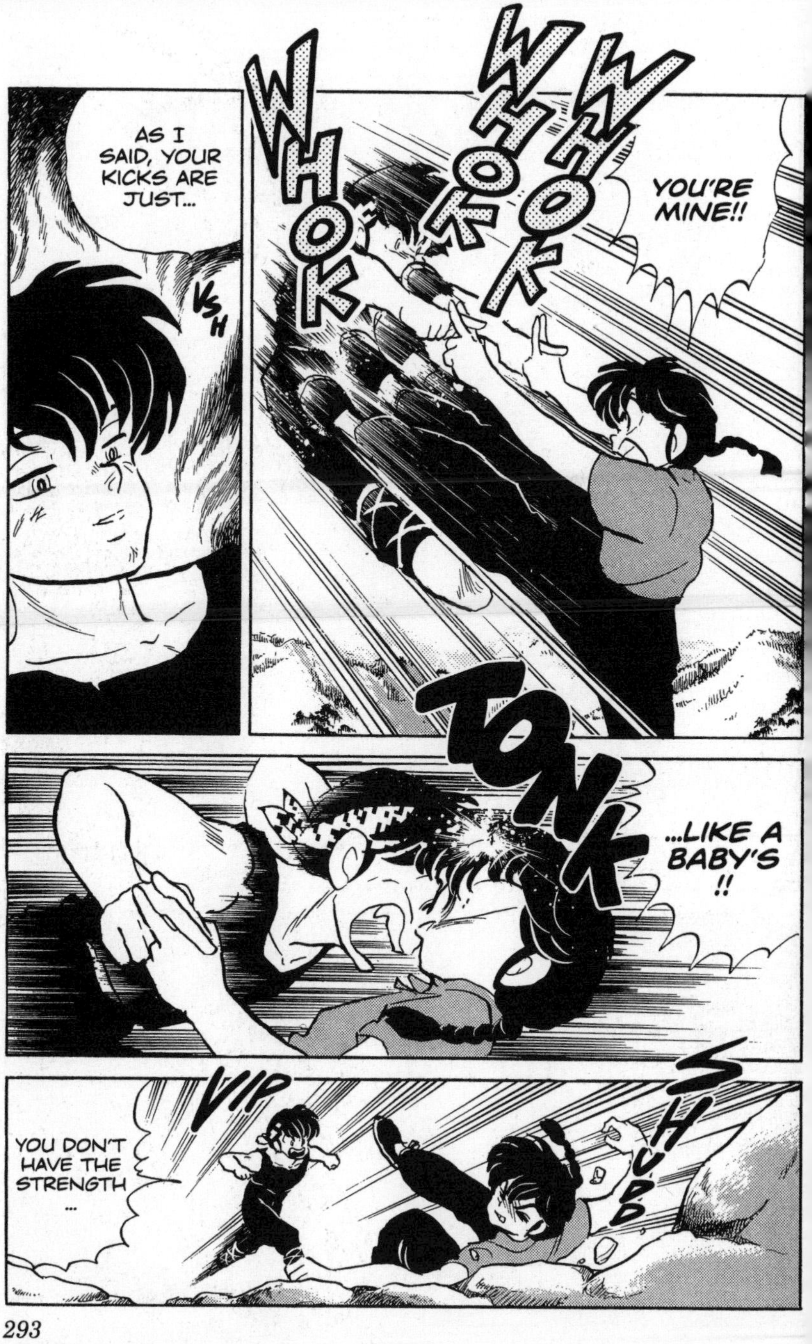
WHOK
WHOK
WHOK
YOU'RE MINE!!
AS I SAID, YOUR KICKS ARE JUST...
VSH
TONK
...LIKE A BABY'S !!
SHUDD
VIP
YOU DON'T HAVE THE STRENGTH ...

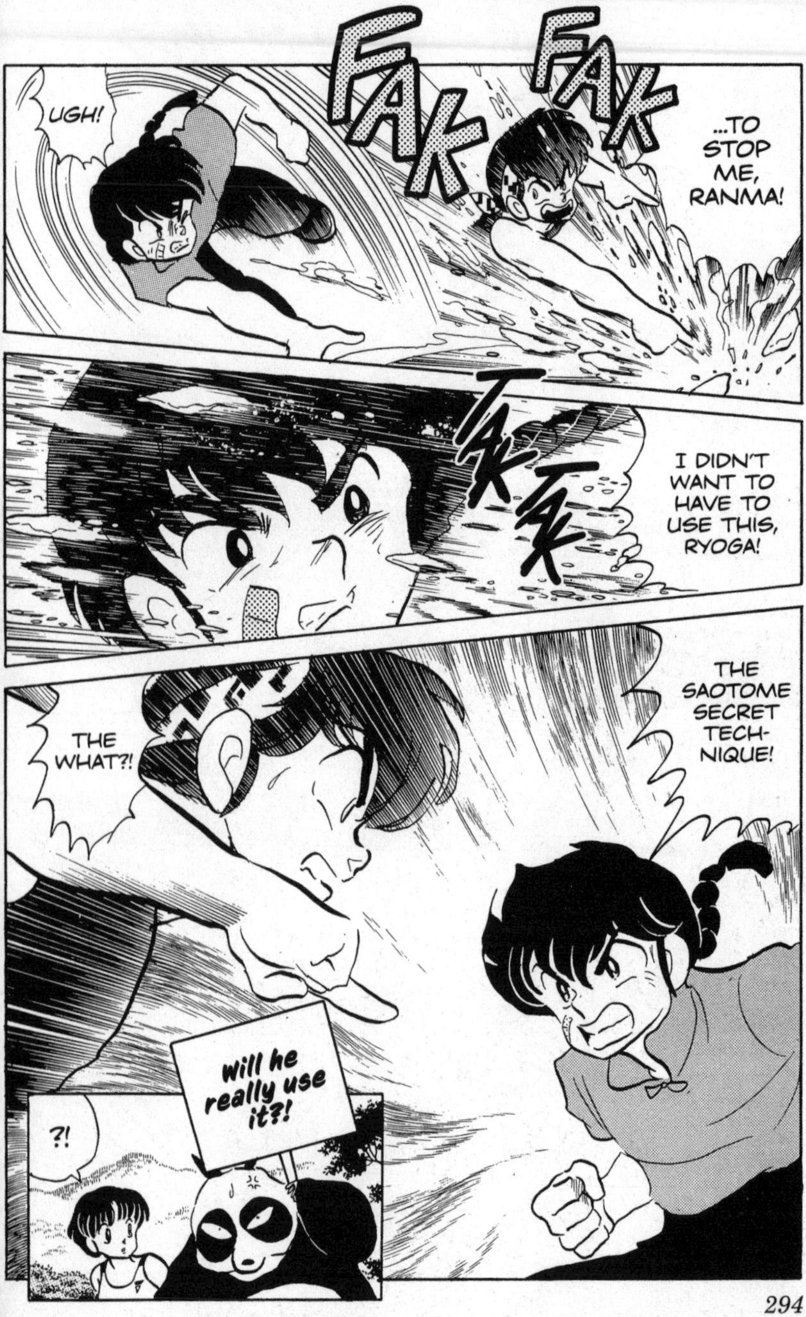
FAK FAK
...TO STOP ME, RANMA!
UGH!
TAK TAK
I DIDN'T WANT TO HAVE TO USE THIS, RYOGA!
THE SAOTOME SECRET TECH-NIQUE!
THE WHAT?!
will he really use it?!
?!

PART 19
FAST BREAK

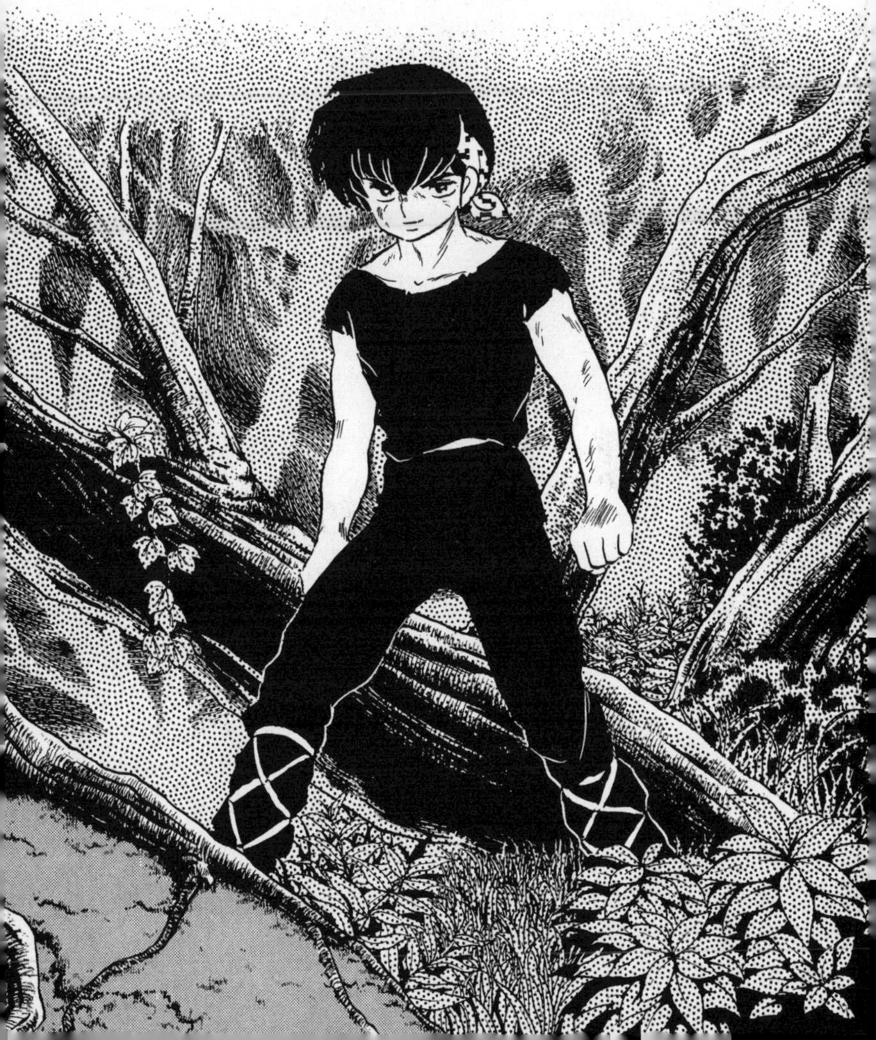

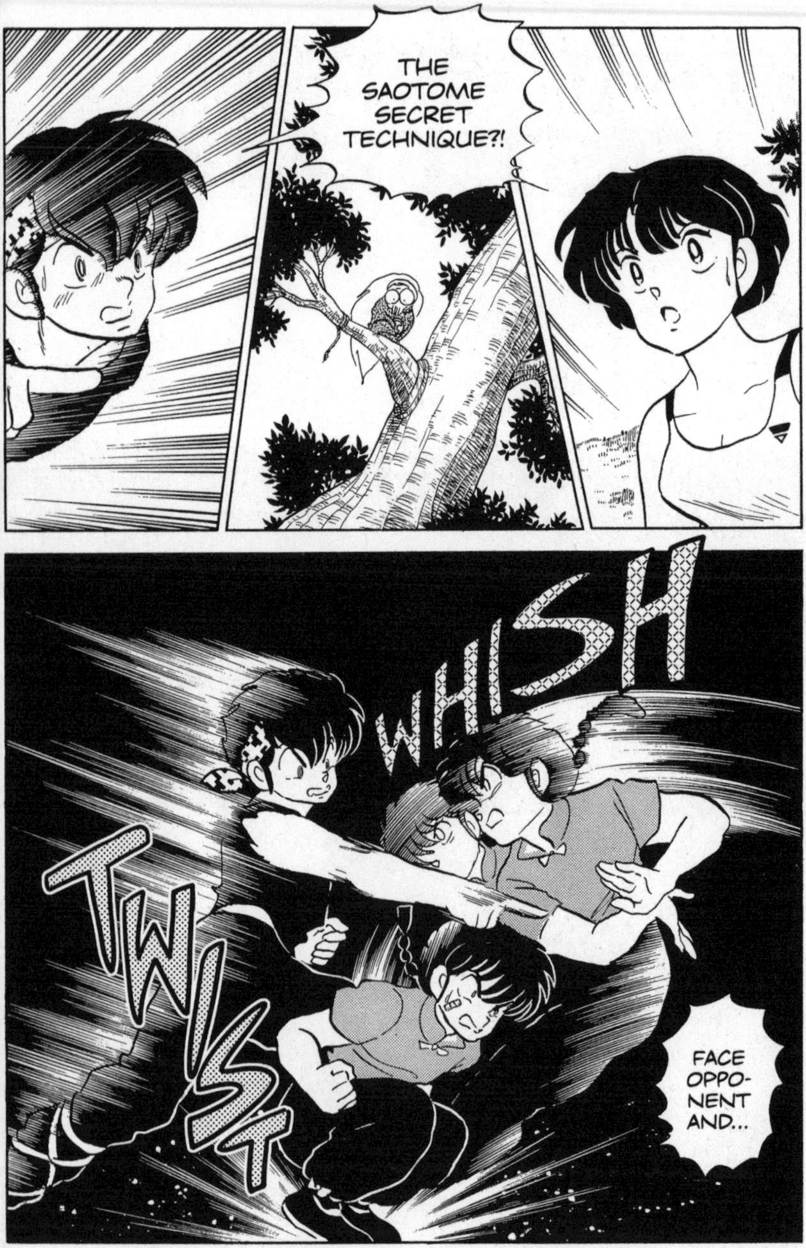
THE SAOTOME SECRET TECHNIQUE?!
WHISH
TWIST
FACE OPPO-NENT AND...

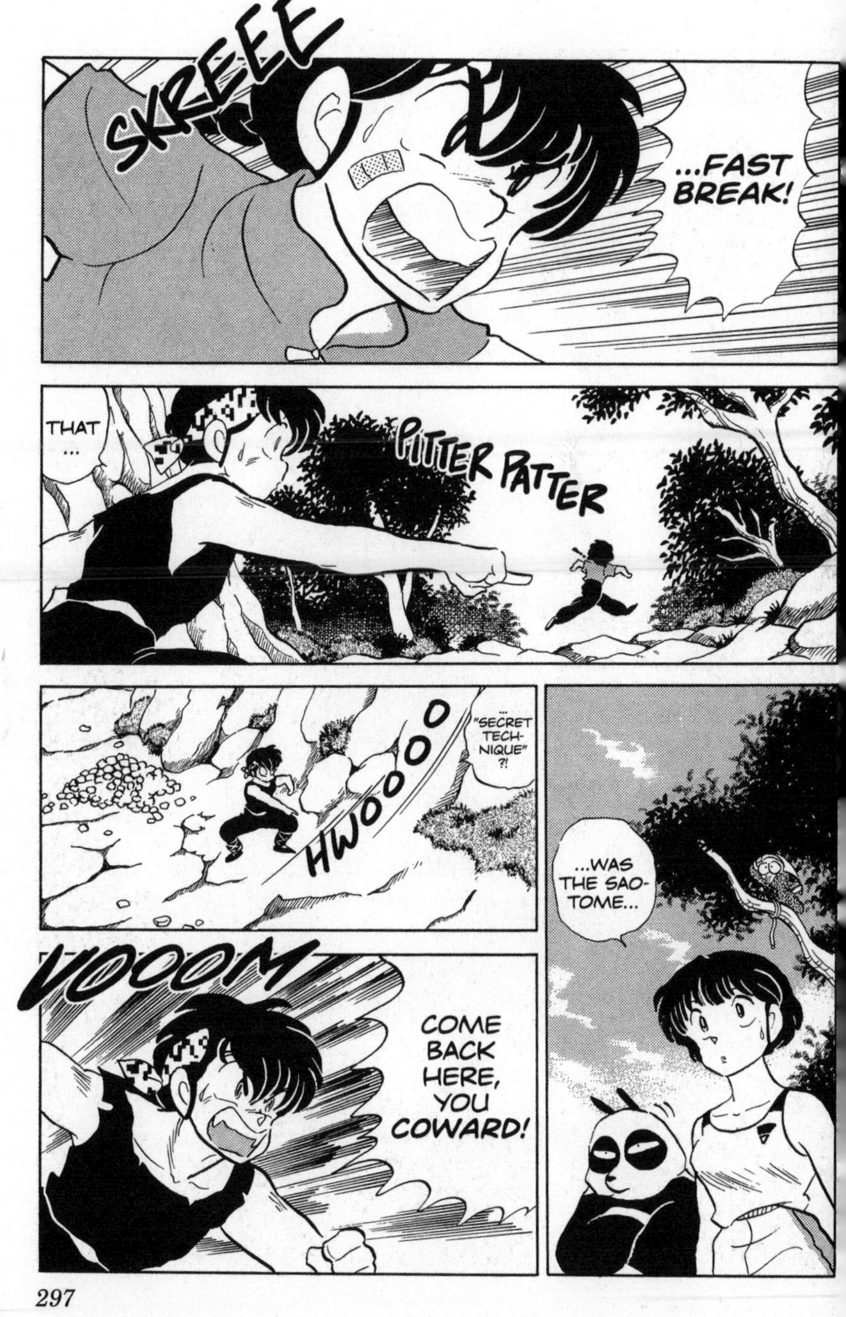
SKREEE
...FAST BREAK!
PITTER PATTER
THAT ...
...WAS THE SAO-TOME...
HWOOOOO
... "SECRET TECH-NIQUE" ?!
VOOOM
COME BACK HERE, YOU COWARD!

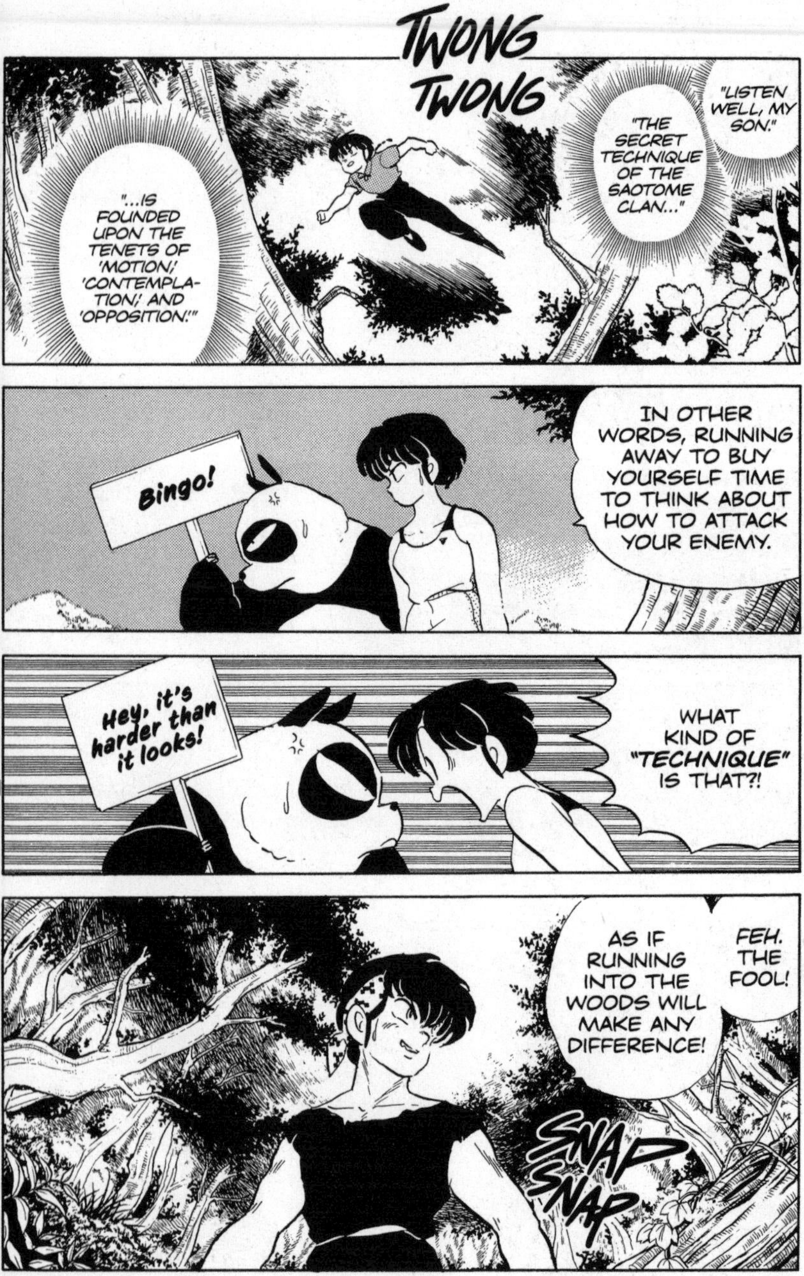
TWONG TWONG
"LISTEN WELL, MY SON."
"THE SECRET TECHNIQUE OF THE SAOTOME CLAN..."
"...IS FOUNDED UPON THE TENETS OF 'MOTION,' 'CONTEMPLATION,' AND 'OPPOSITION.'"
IN OTHER WORDS, RUNNING AWAY TO BUY YOURSELF TIME TO THINK ABOUT HOW TO ATTACK YOUR ENEMY.
Bingo!
WHAT KIND OF "TECHNIQUE" IS THAT?!
Hey, it's harder than it looks!
FEH. THE FOOL!
AS IF RUNNING INTO THE WOODS WILL MAKE ANY DIFFERENCE!
SNAP SNAP

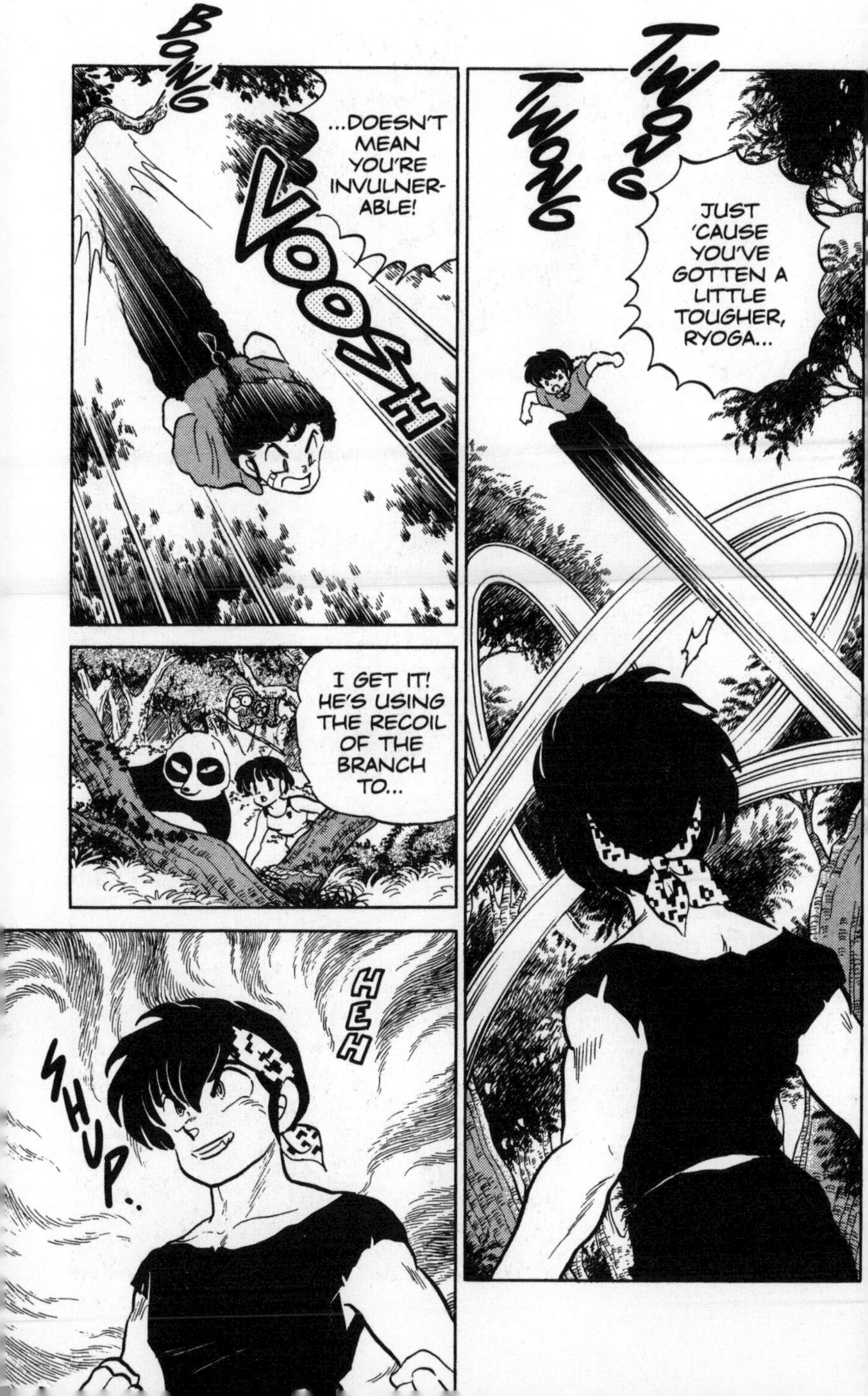
TWONG
TWONG
JUST 'CAUSE YOU'VE GOTTEN A LITTLE TOUGHER, RYOGA...
BOING
...DOESN'T MEAN YOU'RE INVULNER-ABLE!
VOOSH
I GET IT! HE'S USING THE RECOIL OF THE BRANCH TO...
HEH
SHUP..

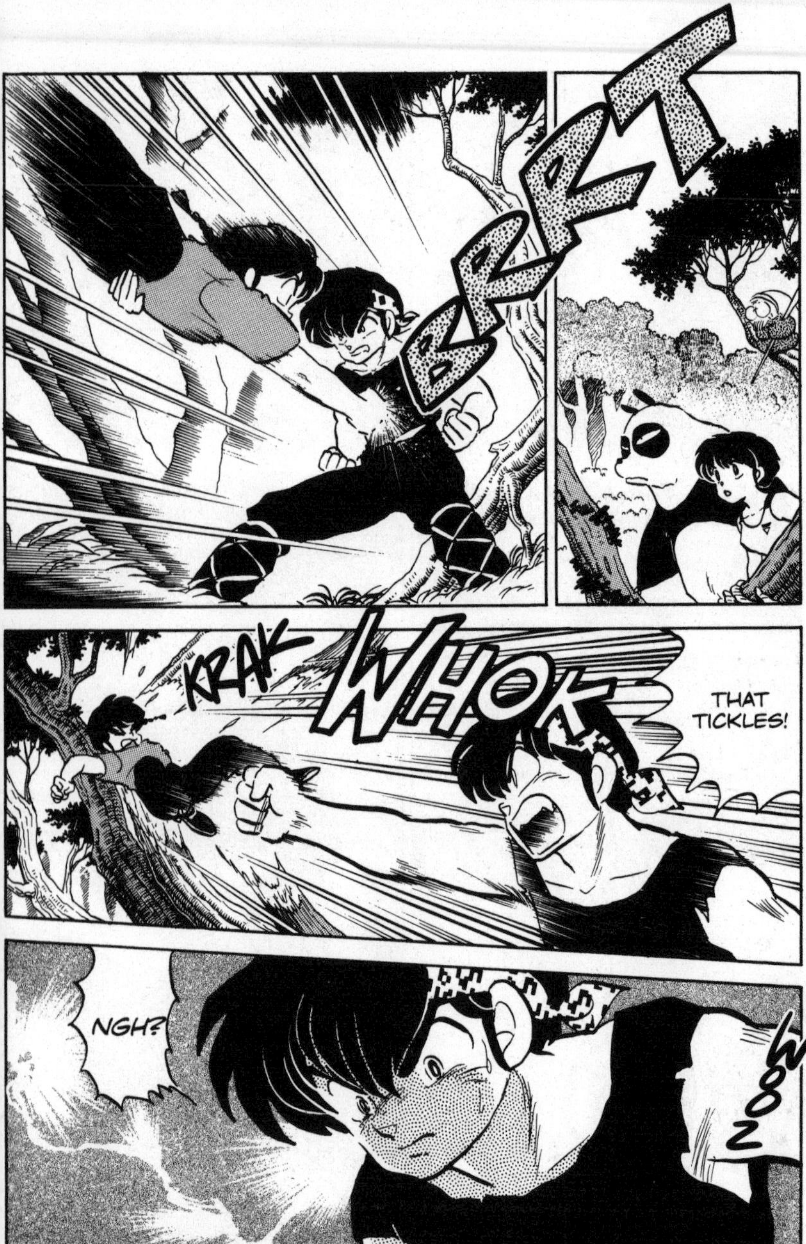
BRRPT
KRAK
WHOK
THAT TICKLES!
NGH?
WOOZ

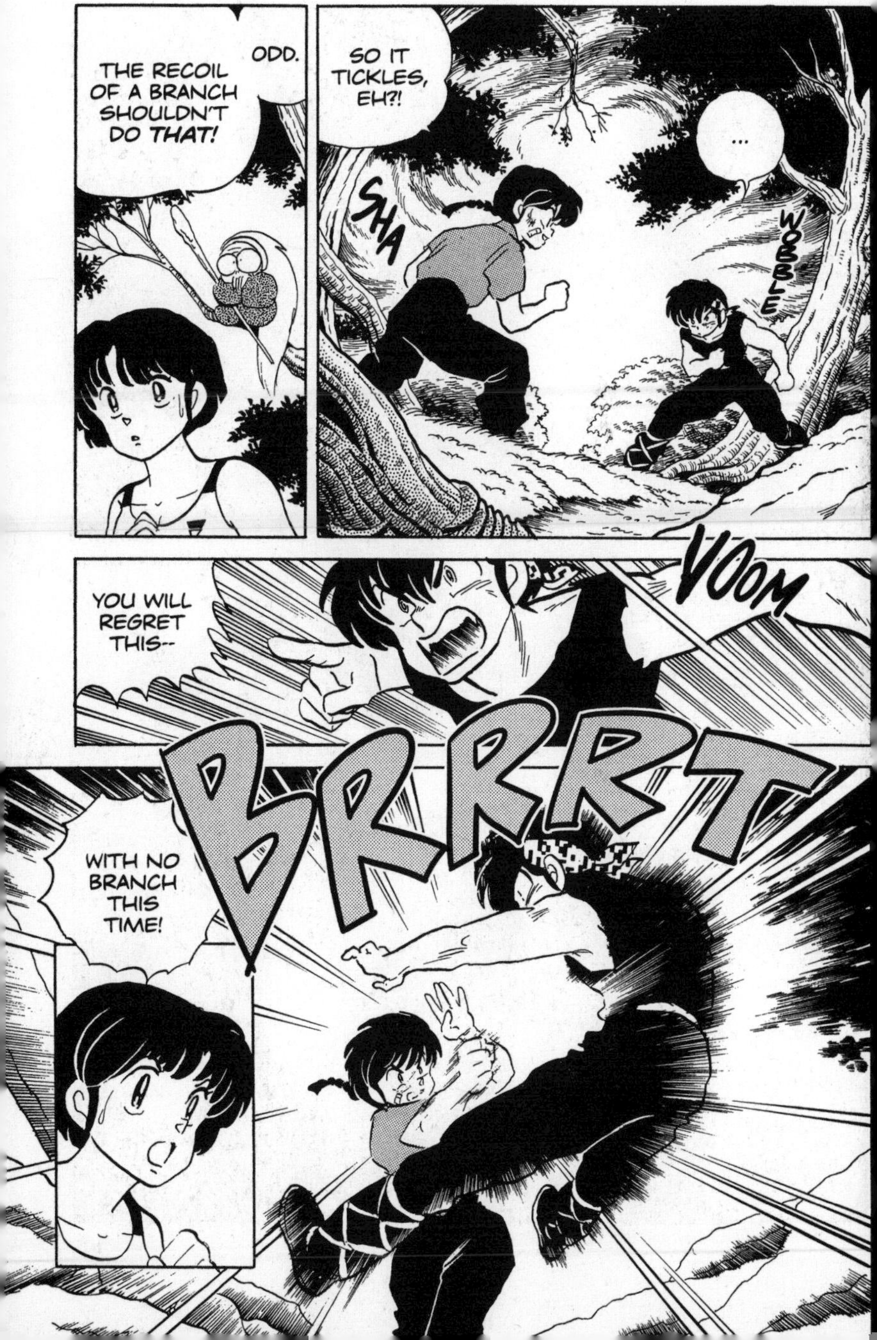
SO IT TICKLES, EH?!
...
SHA
WOBBLE
ODD.
THE RECOIL OF A BRANCH SHOULDN'T DO *THAT!*
VOOM
YOU WILL REGRET THIS--
BRRRT
WITH NO BRANCH THIS TIME!

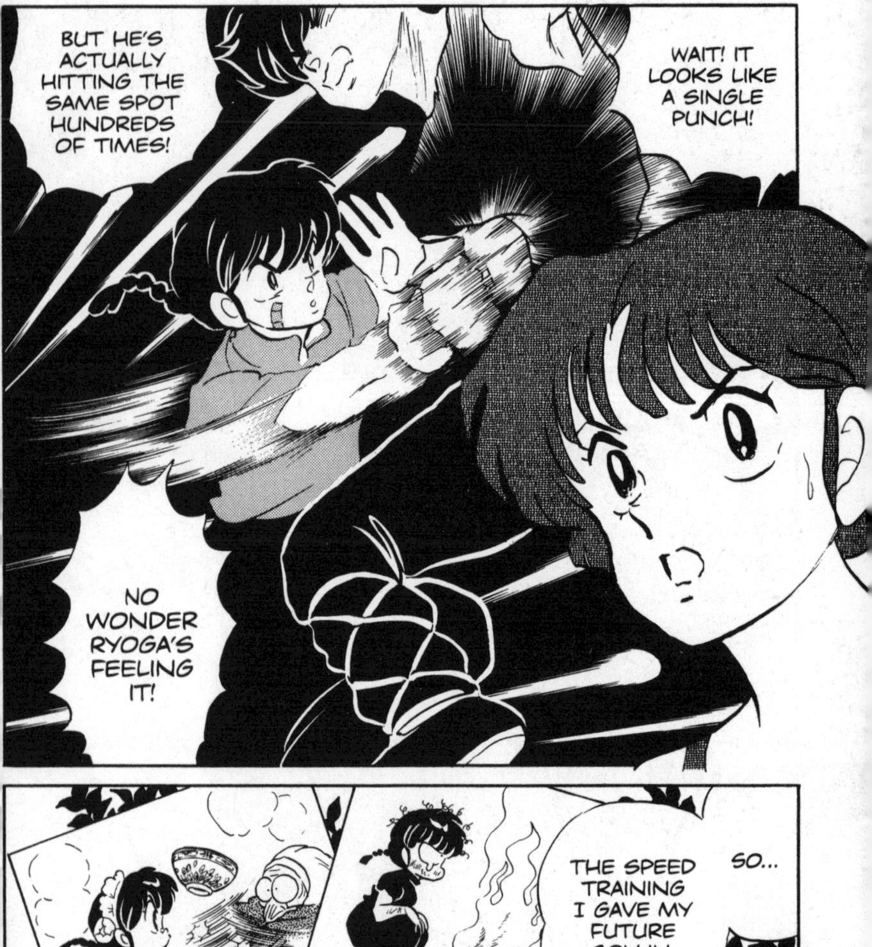
WAIT! IT LOOKS LIKE A SINGLE PUNCH!
BUT HE'S ACTUALLY HITTING THE SAME SPOT HUNDREDS OF TIMES!
NO WONDER RYOGA'S FEELING IT!
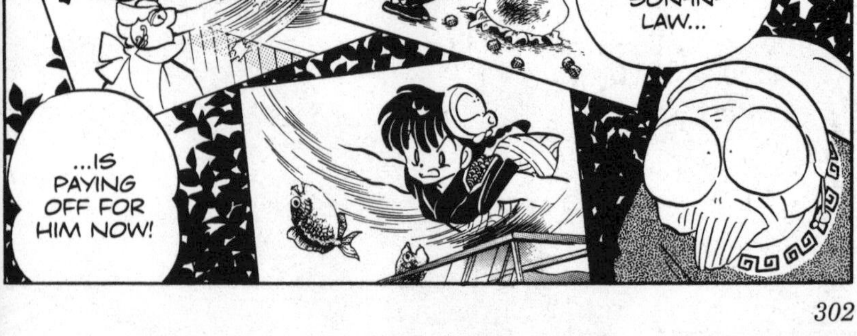
SO...
THE SPEED TRAINING I GAVE MY FUTURE SON-IN-LAW...
...IS PAYING OFF FOR HIM NOW!

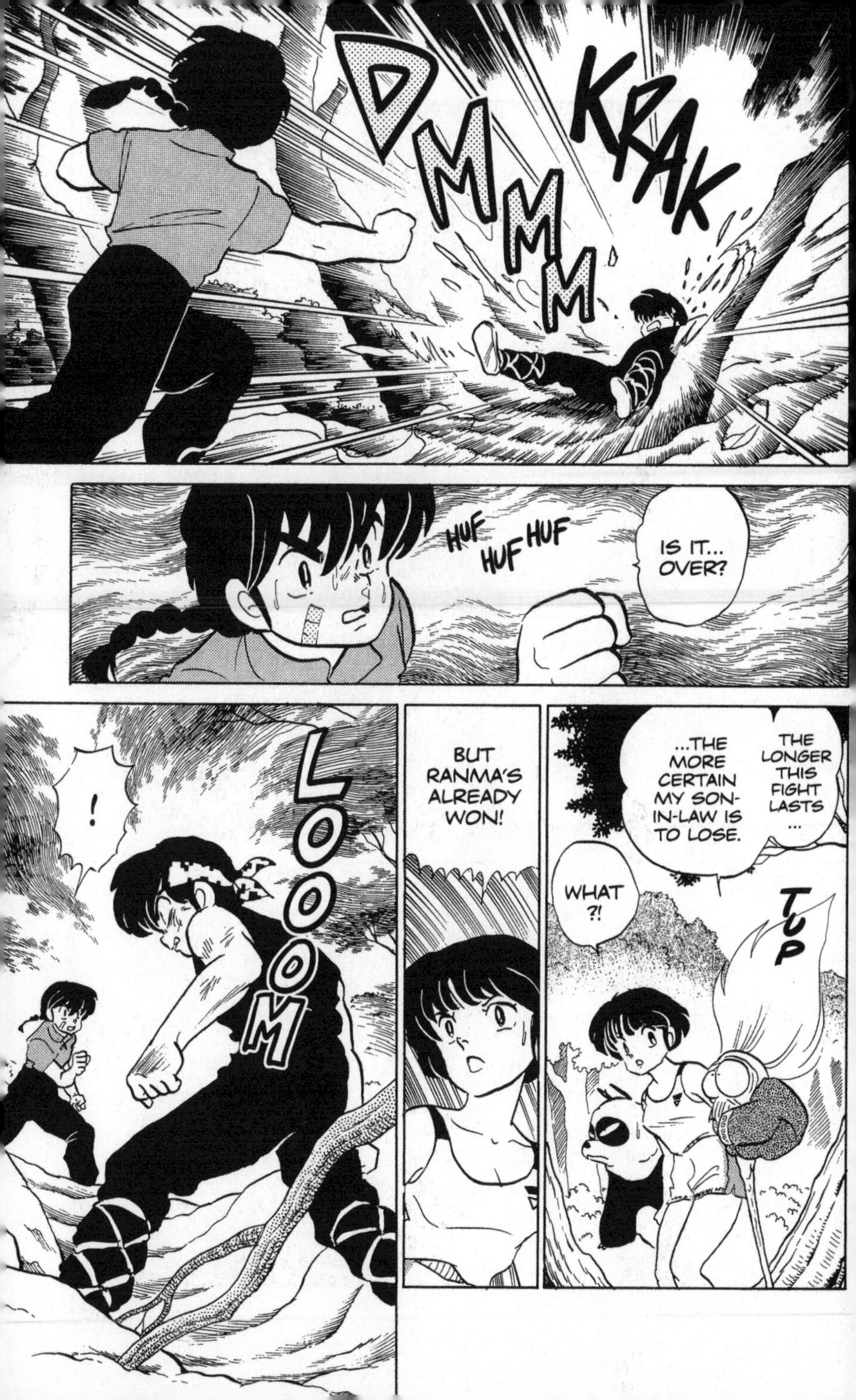
KRAK
DMMMM
IS IT... OVER?
HUF HUF HUF
THE LONGER THIS FIGHT LASTS...
...THE MORE CERTAIN MY SON-IN-LAW IS TO LOSE.
TUP
WHAT?!
BUT RANMA'S ALREADY WON!
!
LOOOOM

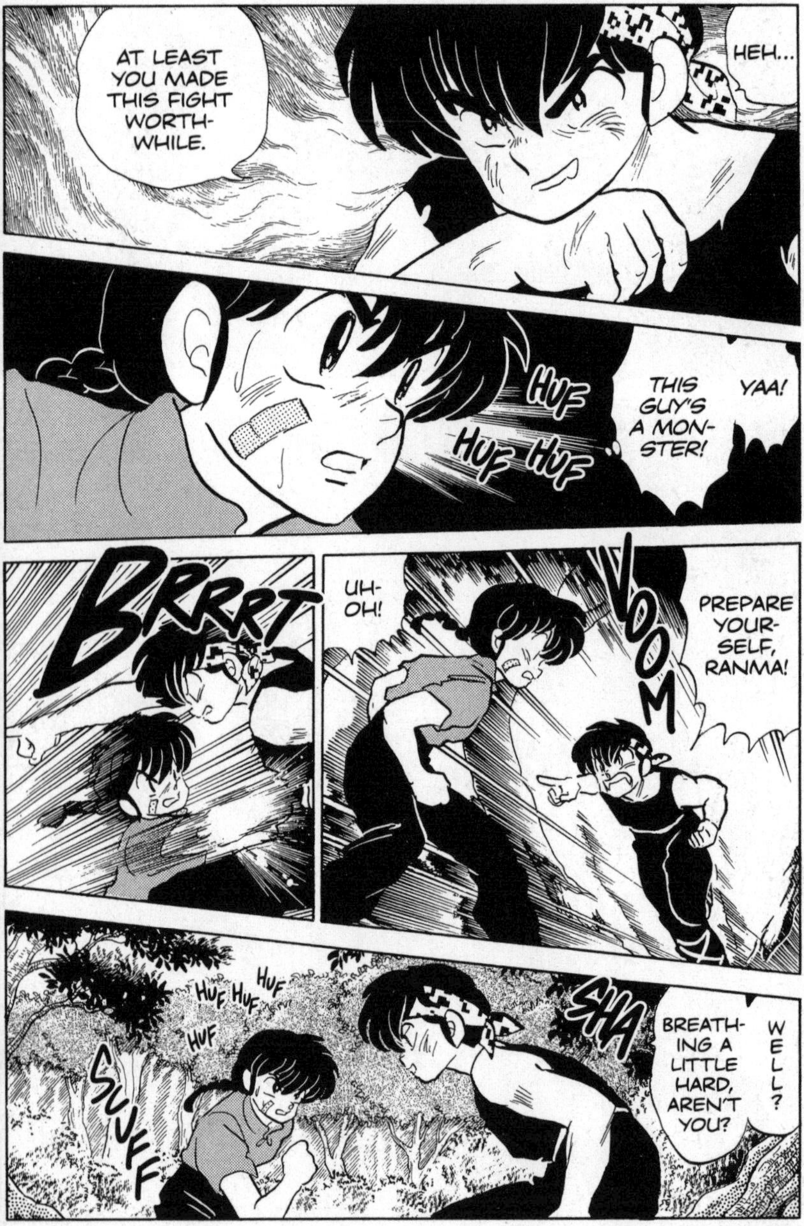
HEH...
AT LEAST YOU MADE THIS FIGHT WORTH-WHILE.
YAA!
THIS GUY'S A MON-STER!
HUF HUF HUF
PREPARE YOUR-SELF, RANMA!
VOOM
UH-OH!
BRRRT
WELL?
BREATH-ING A LITTLE HARD, AREN'T YOU?
SHA
HUF HUF HUF HUF
SNUFF

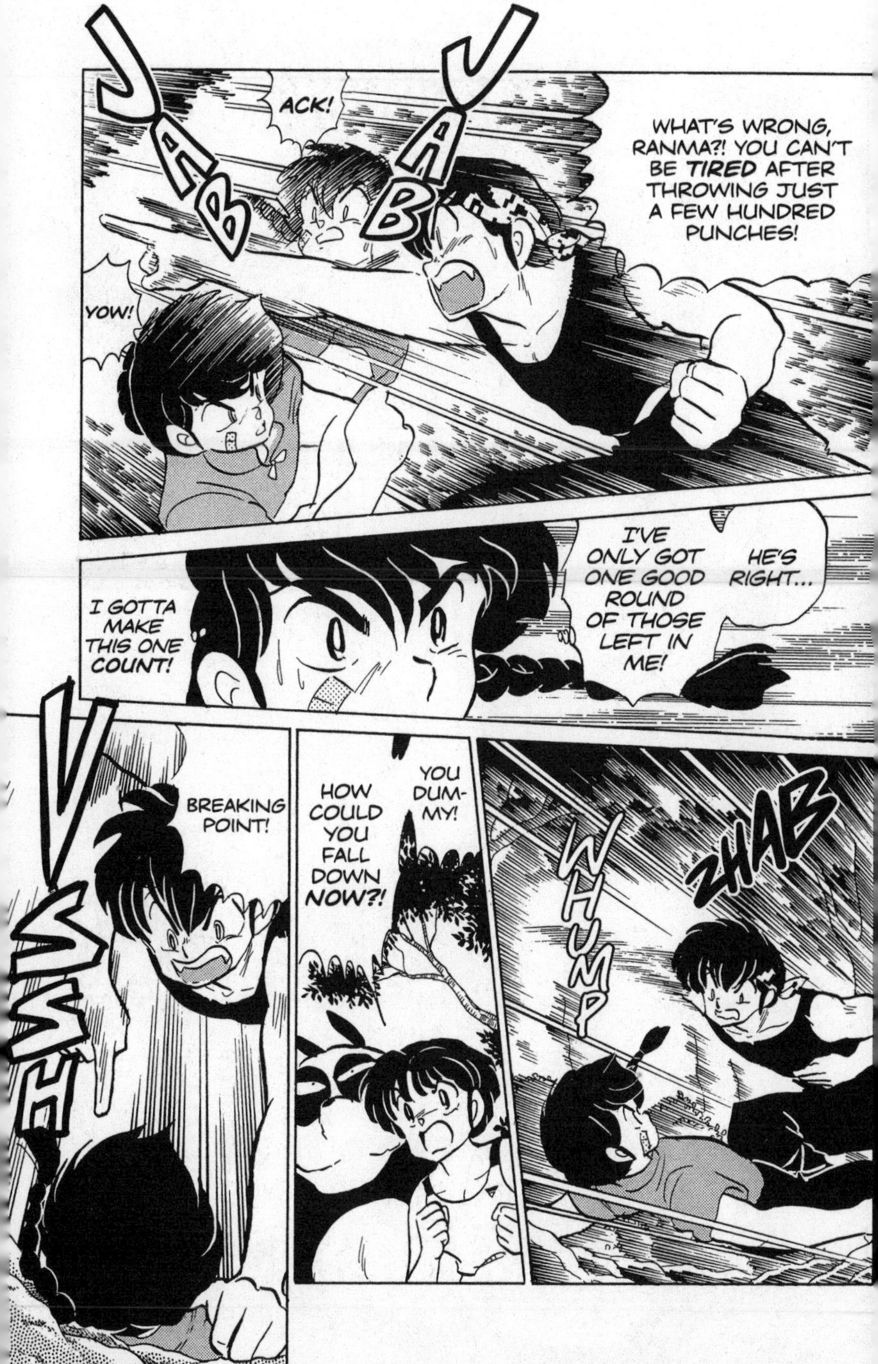
WHAT'S WRONG, RANMA?! YOU CAN'T BE TIRED AFTER THROWING JUST A FEW HUNDRED PUNCHES!
JAB
ACK!
JAB
YOW!
HE'S RIGHT...
I'VE ONLY GOT ONE GOOD ROUND OF THOSE LEFT IN ME!
I GOTTA MAKE THIS ONE COUNT!
ZHAB
WHUMP
YOU DUMMY!
HOW COULD YOU FALL DOWN NOW?!
BREAKING POINT!

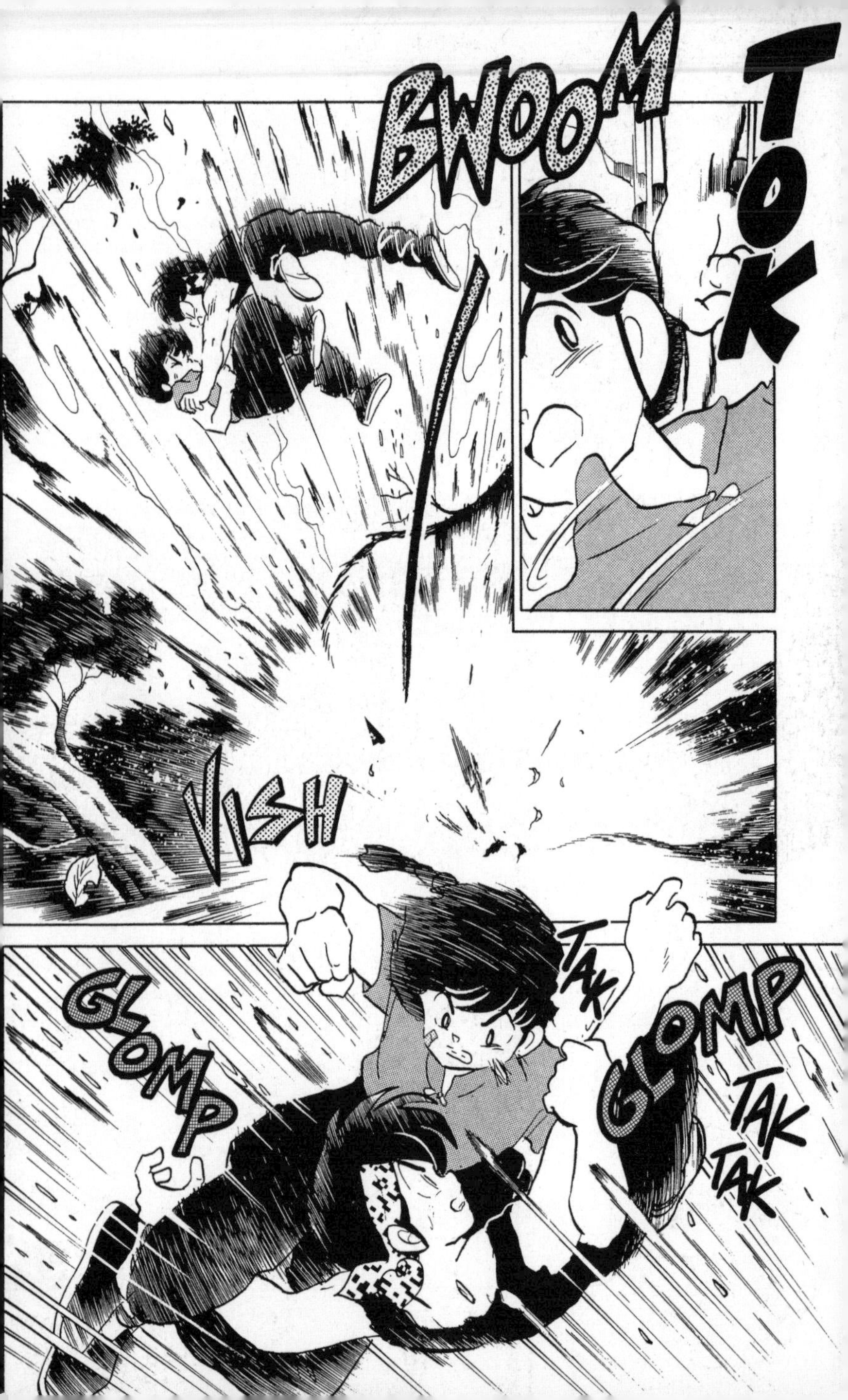
TOK
BWOOM
VISH
TAK
GLOMP
TAK
TAK
GLOMP

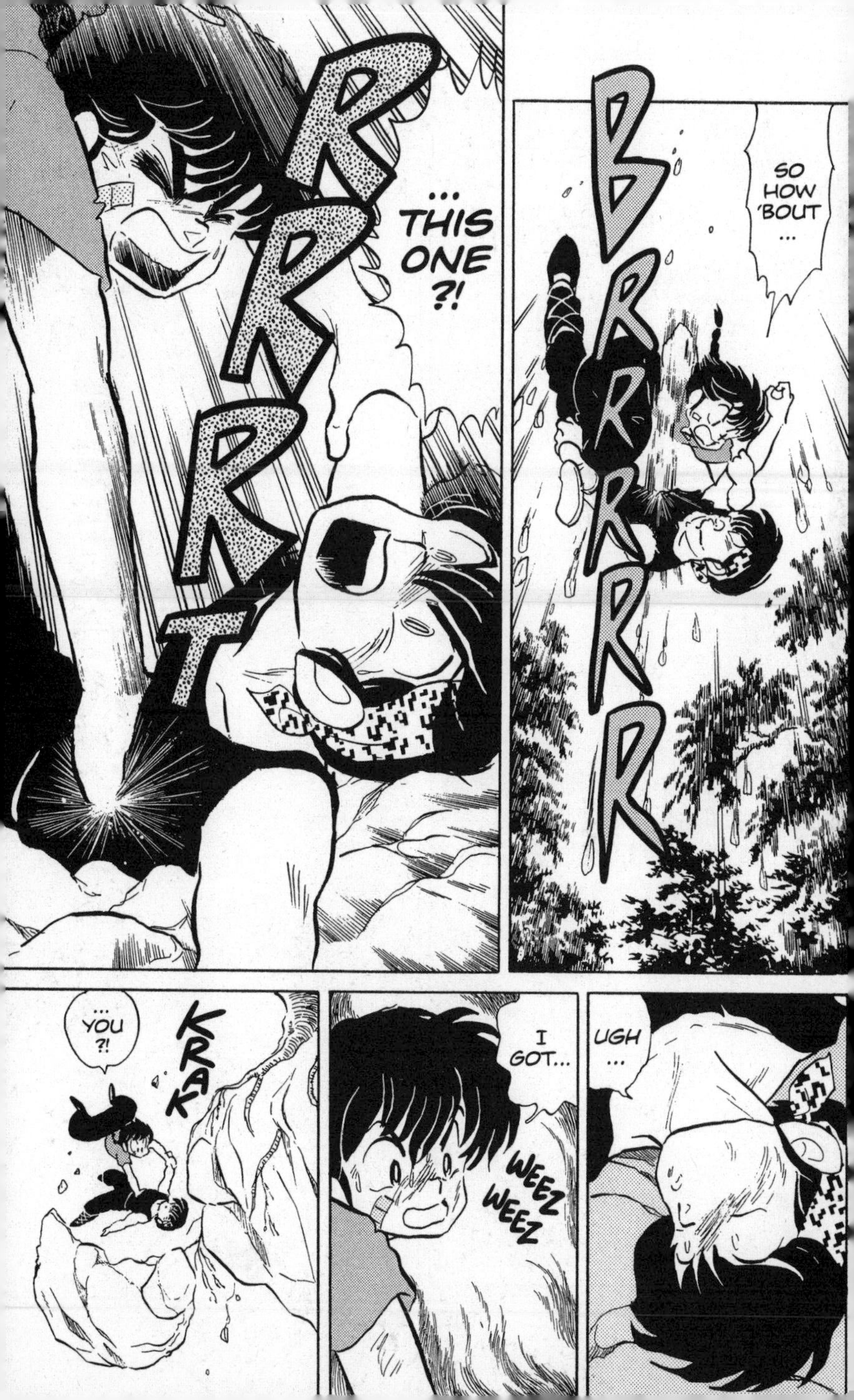
SO HOW 'BOUT ...
BRRRRRR
RRRRRT
... THIS ONE ?!
UGH ...
I GOT...
WEEZ WEEZ
... YOU ?!
KRAK

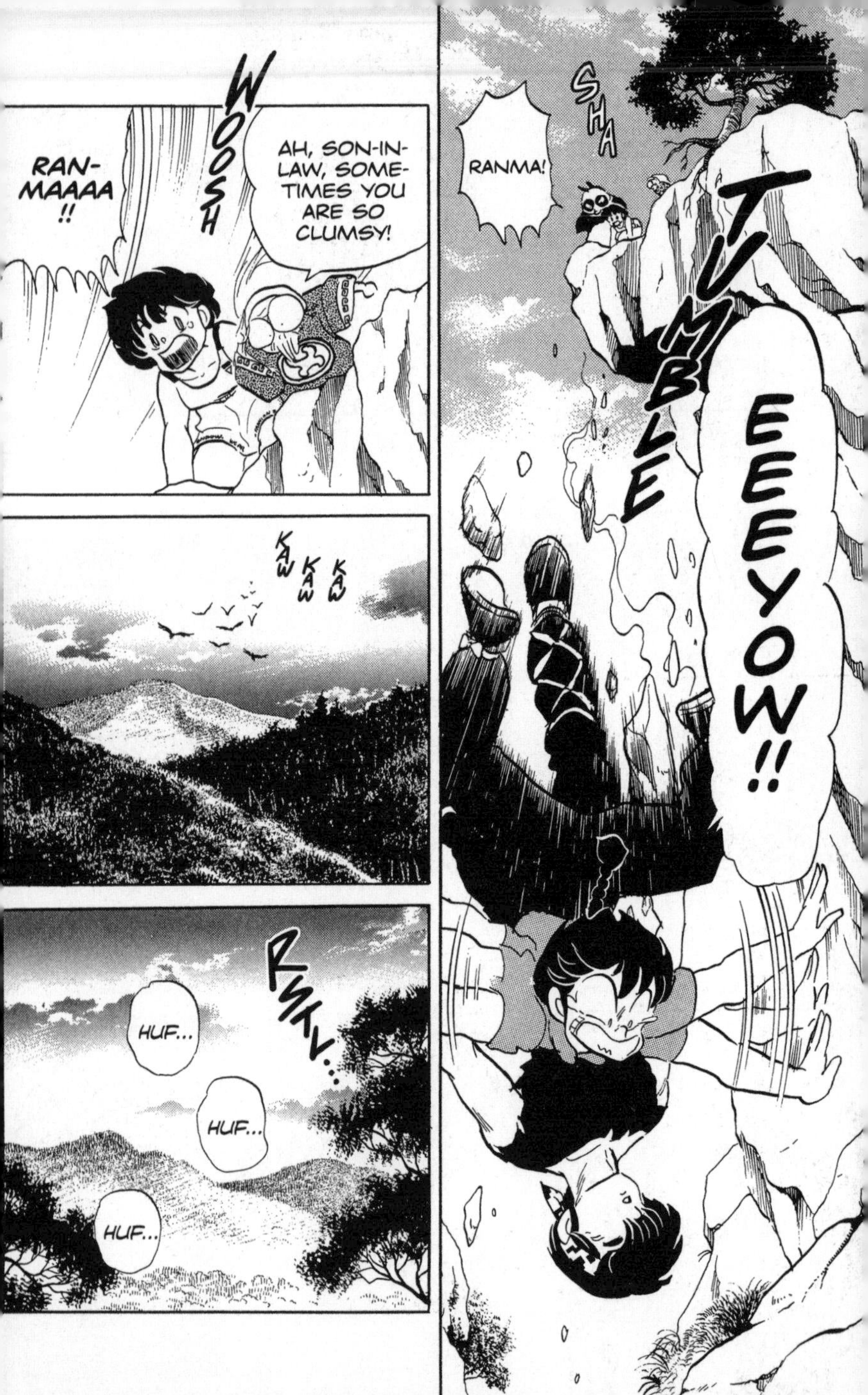
SHA
RANMA!
TUMBLE
EEEEYOW!!
AH, SON-IN-LAW, SOMETIMES YOU ARE SO CLUMSY!
WOOOSH
RAN-MAAAA!!
KAW KAW KAW
RSKV...
HUF...
HUF...
HUF...

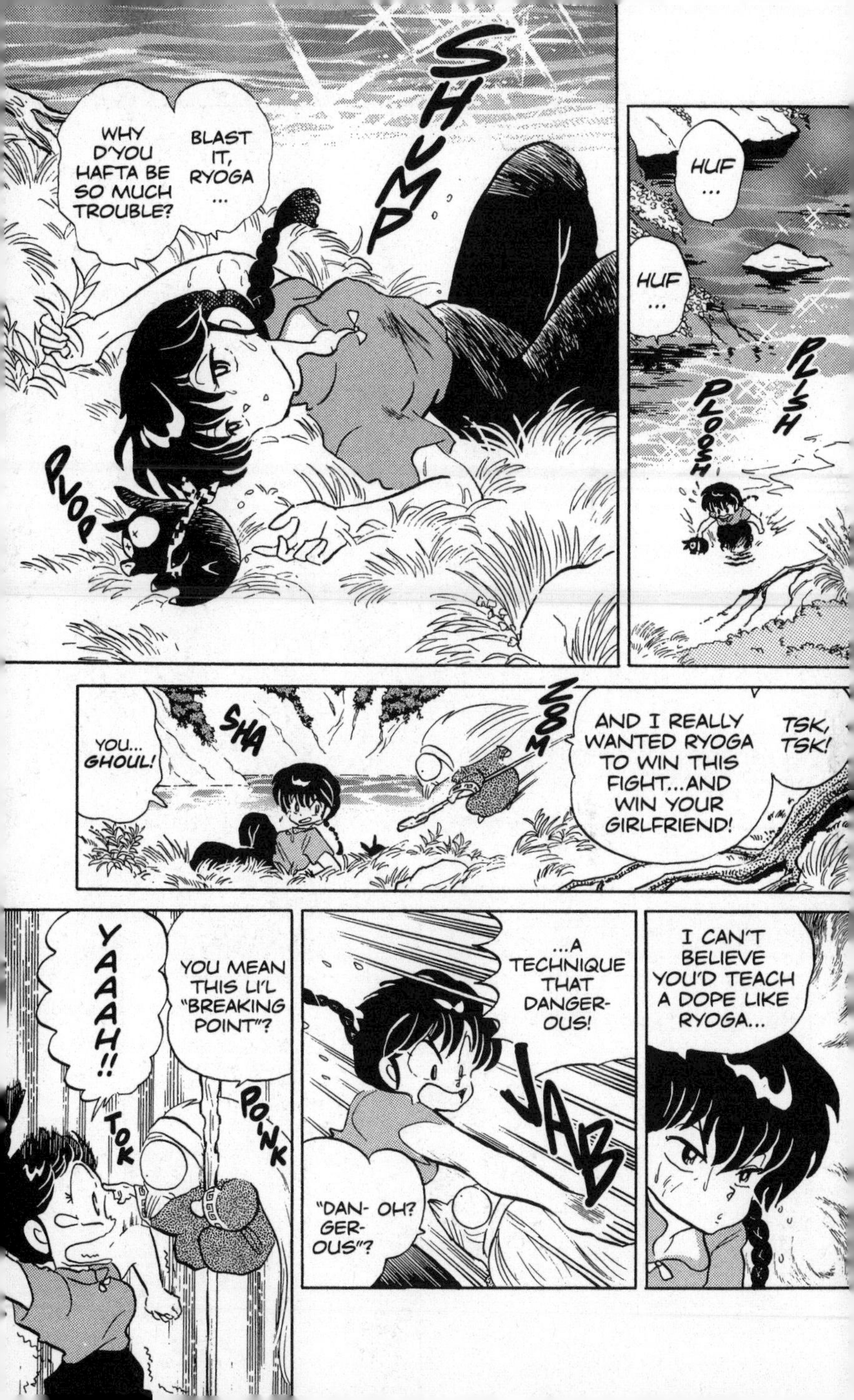
HUF ...
HUF ...
PLISH
PLOOSH
SHUMP
BLAST IT, RYOGA ...
WHY D'YOU HAFTA BE SO MUCH TROUBLE?
PVOP
TSK, TSK!
AND I REALLY WANTED RYOGA TO WIN THIS FIGHT...AND WIN YOUR GIRLFRIEND!
ZOOM
SHA
YOU... GHOUL!
I CAN'T BELIEVE YOU'D TEACH A DOPE LIKE RYOGA...
...A TECHNIQUE THAT DANGER-OUS!
JAB
OH?
"DAN-GER-OUS"?
YOU MEAN THIS LI'L "BREAKING POINT"?
YAAAH!!
POINK
TOK

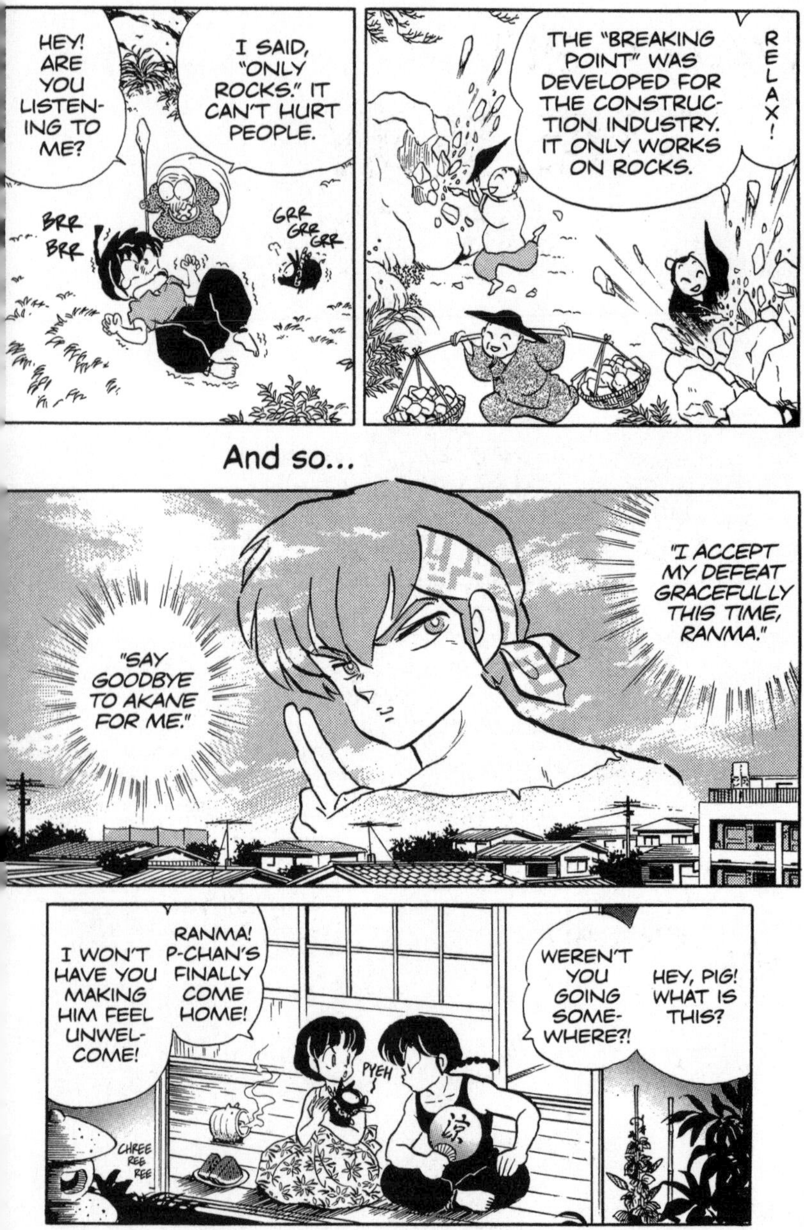
RELAX!
THE "BREAKING POINT" WAS DEVELOPED FOR THE CONSTRUCTION INDUSTRY. IT ONLY WORKS ON ROCKS.
I SAID, "ONLY ROCKS." IT CAN'T HURT PEOPLE.
HEY! ARE YOU LISTENING TO ME?
GRR GRR GRR
BRR BRR
And so...
"I ACCEPT MY DEFEAT GRACEFULLY THIS TIME, RANMA."
"SAY GOODBYE TO AKANE FOR ME."
HEY, PIG! WHAT IS THIS?
WEREN'T YOU GOING SOMEWHERE?!
RANMA! P-CHAN'S FINALLY COME HOME!
I WON'T HAVE YOU MAKING HIM FEEL UNWELCOME!
PYEH
CHREE REE REE

PART 20

THE WAY OF TEA

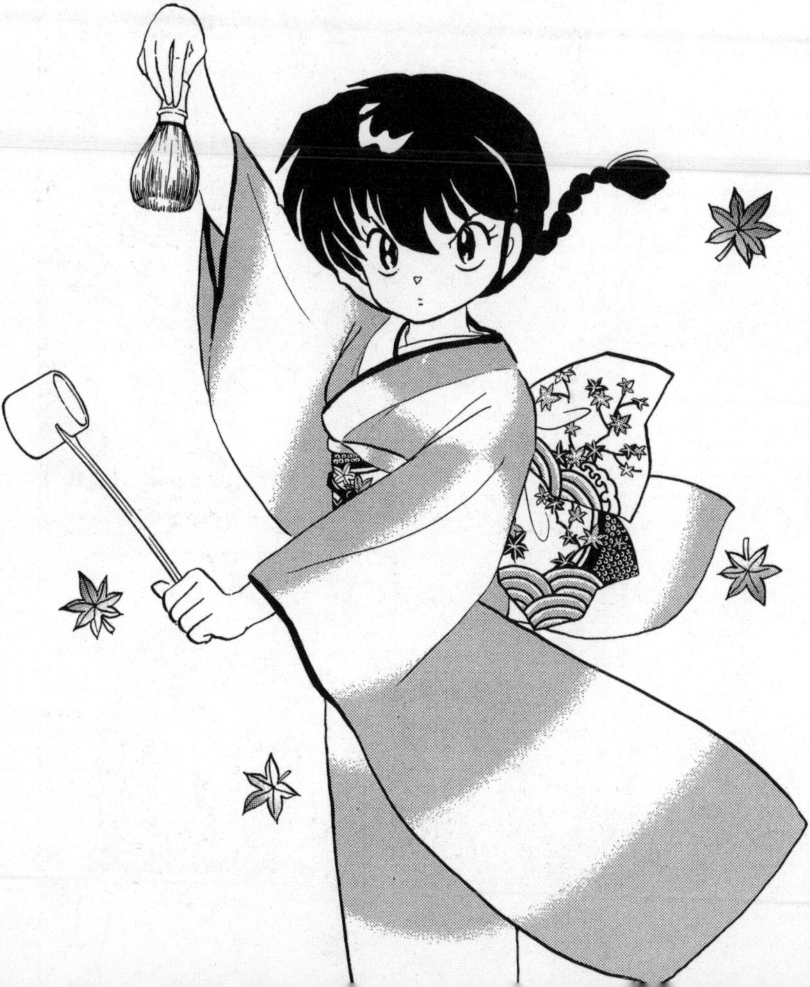

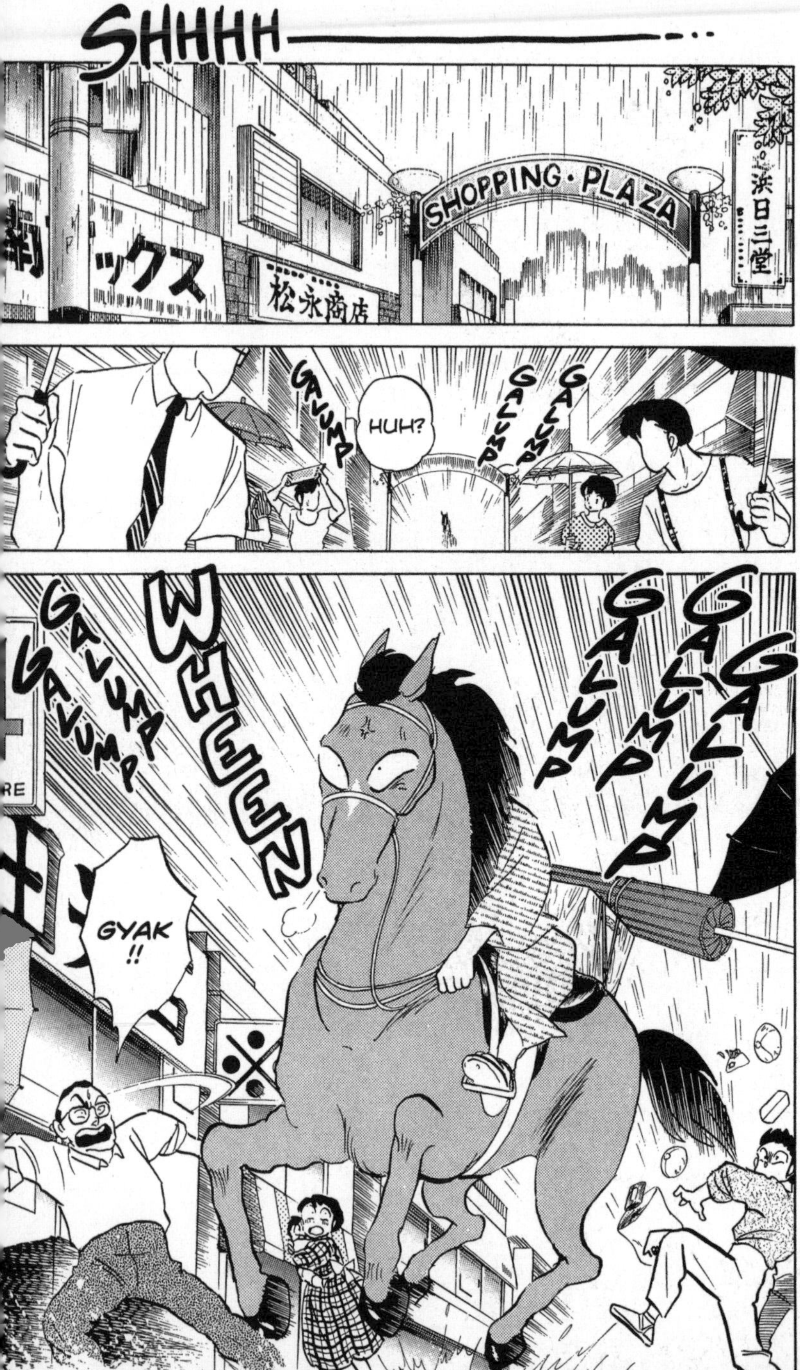
SHHHH
SHOPPING · PLAZA
松永商店
ックス
浜日三堂
GALUMP
HUH?
GALUMP
GALUMP
GALUMP GALUMP
GALUMP GALUMP
WHEEEN
GALUMP
GALUMP
GALUMP
GYAK !!

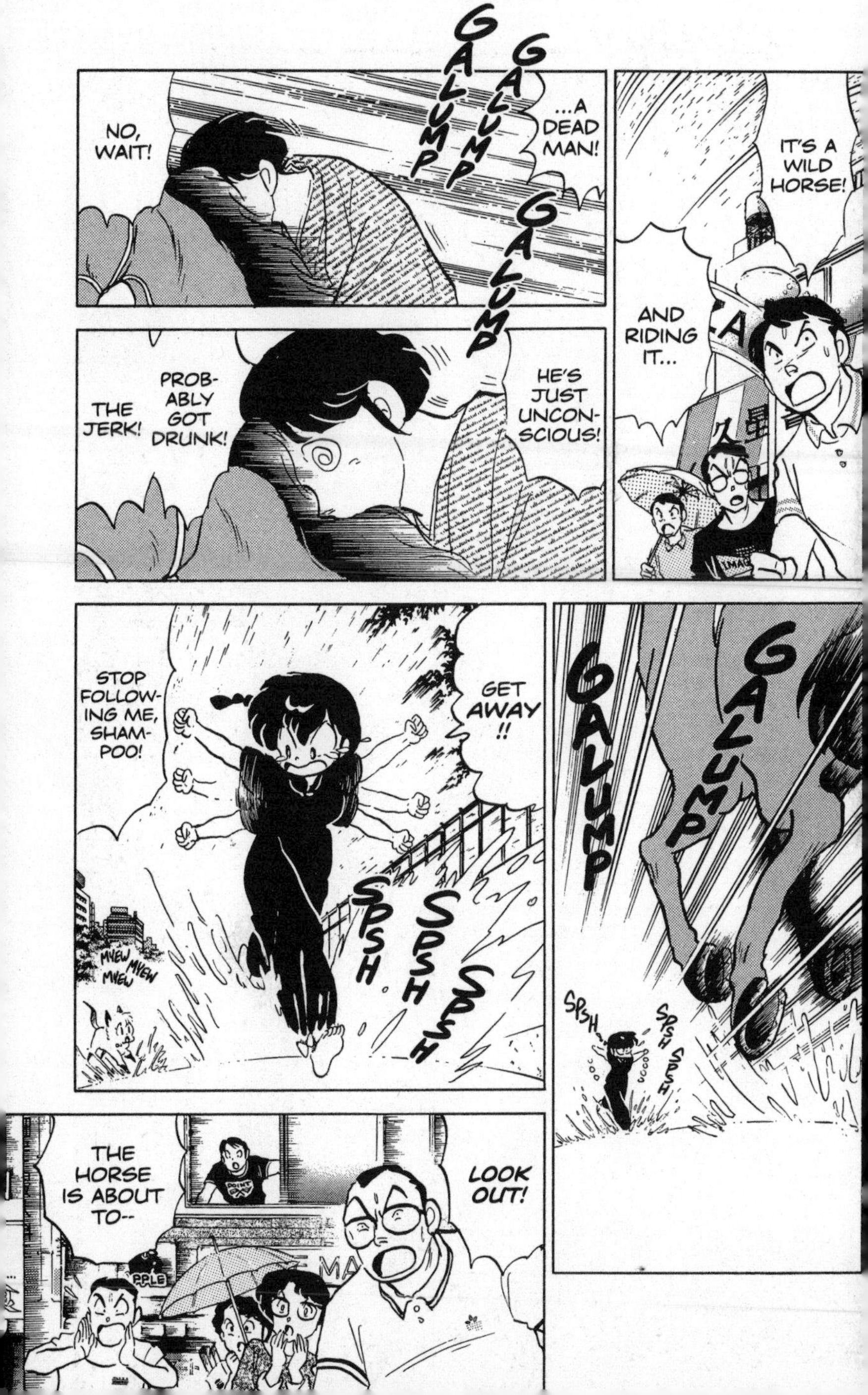
IT'S A WILD HORSE!
AND RIDING IT...
GALUMP
GALUMP
...A DEAD MAN!
NO, WAIT!
GALUMP
HE'S JUST UNCON- SCIOUS!
PROB- ABLY GOT DRUNK!
THE JERK!
GALUMP
GALUMP
SPSH
SPSH
SPSH
GET AWAY !!
STOP FOLLOW- ING ME, SHAM- POO!
SPSH
SPSH
SPSH
MVEW MVEW MVEW
LOOK OUT!
THE HORSE IS ABOUT TO--

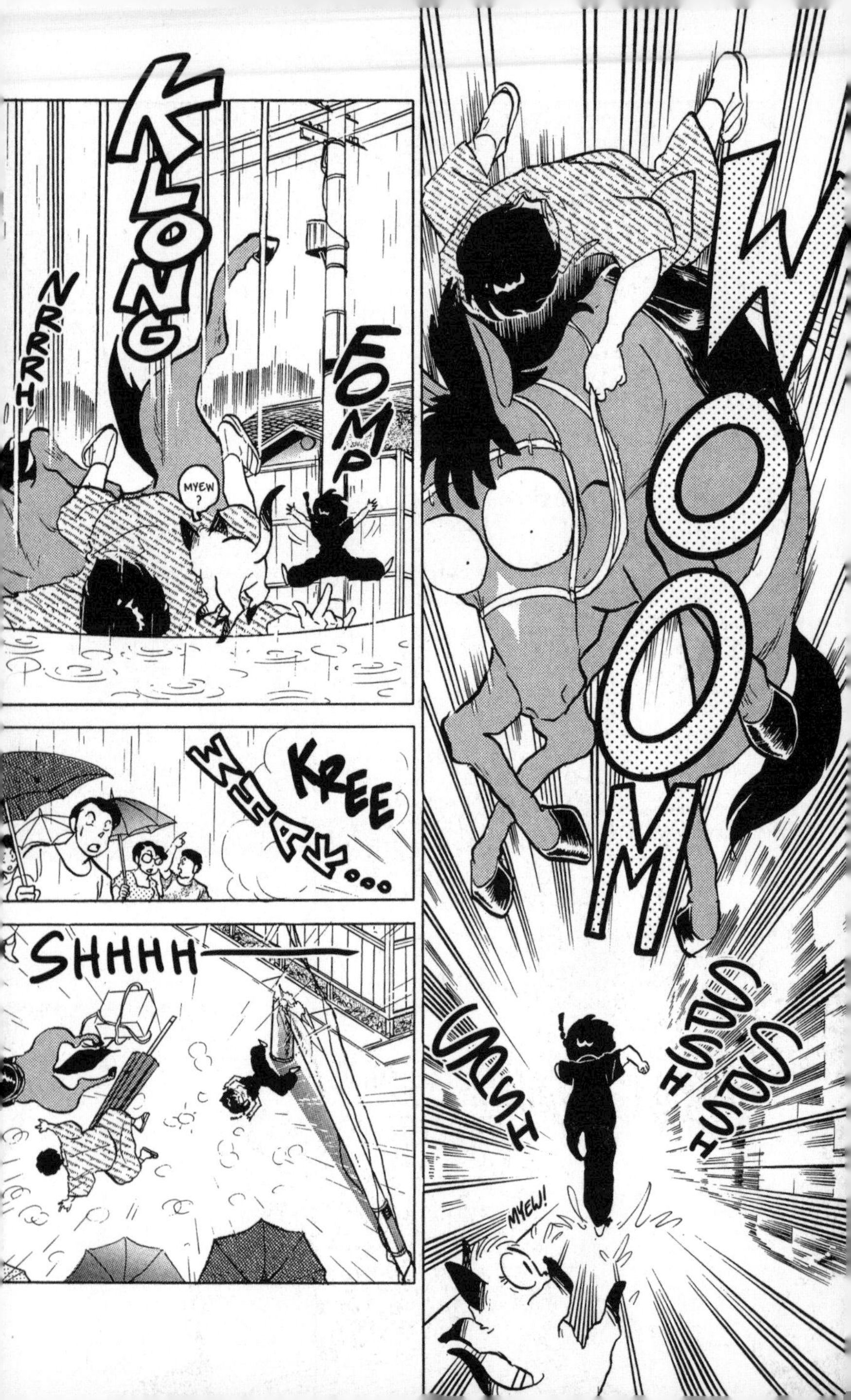
WOOOM
MYEW!
KLONG
NRRRH
FOMP
MYEW ?
KREE
SHHHH

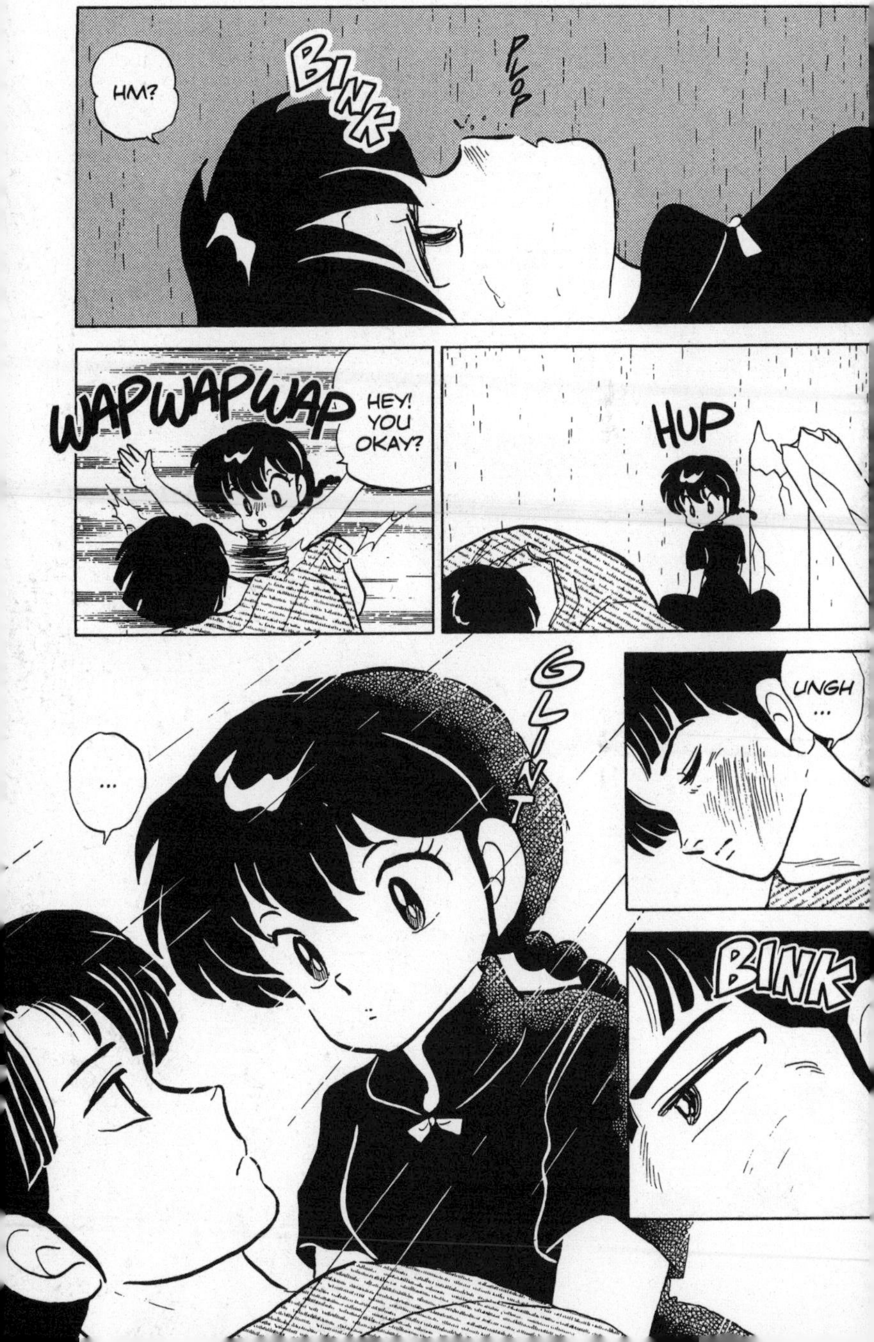
PLOP
BINK
HM?
HUP
WAPWAPWAP
HEY! YOU OKAY?
UNGH ...
BINK
GLINT
...

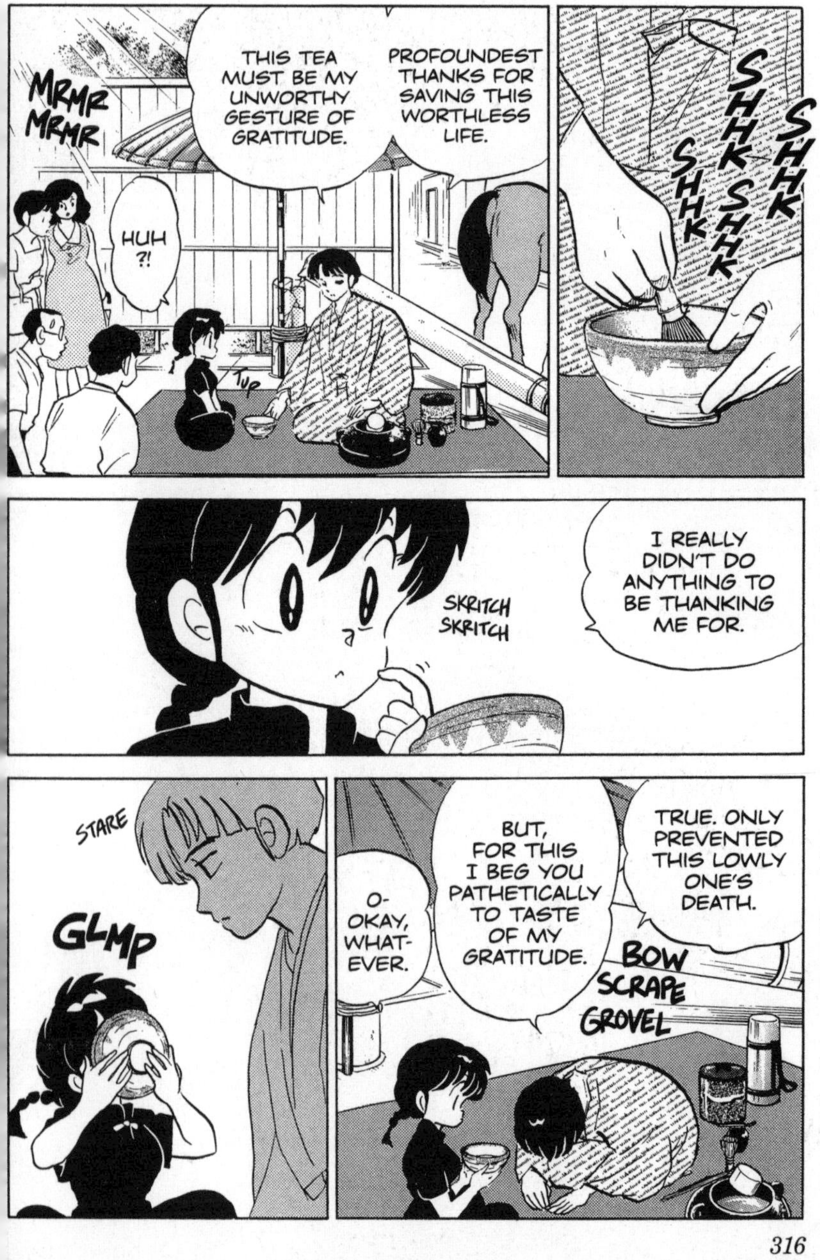
SHHK SHHK SHHK SHHK SHHK
PROFOUNDEST THANKS FOR SAVING THIS WORTHLESS LIFE.
THIS TEA MUST BE MY UNWORTHY GESTURE OF GRATITUDE.
MRMR MRMR
HUH ?!
TUP
I REALLY DIDN'T DO ANYTHING TO BE THANKING ME FOR.
SKRITCH SKRITCH
TRUE. ONLY PREVENTED THIS LOWLY ONE'S DEATH.
BUT, FOR THIS I BEG YOU PATHETICALLY TO TASTE OF MY GRATITUDE.
O-OKAY, WHATEVER.
BOW SCRAPE GROVEL
STARE
GLMP

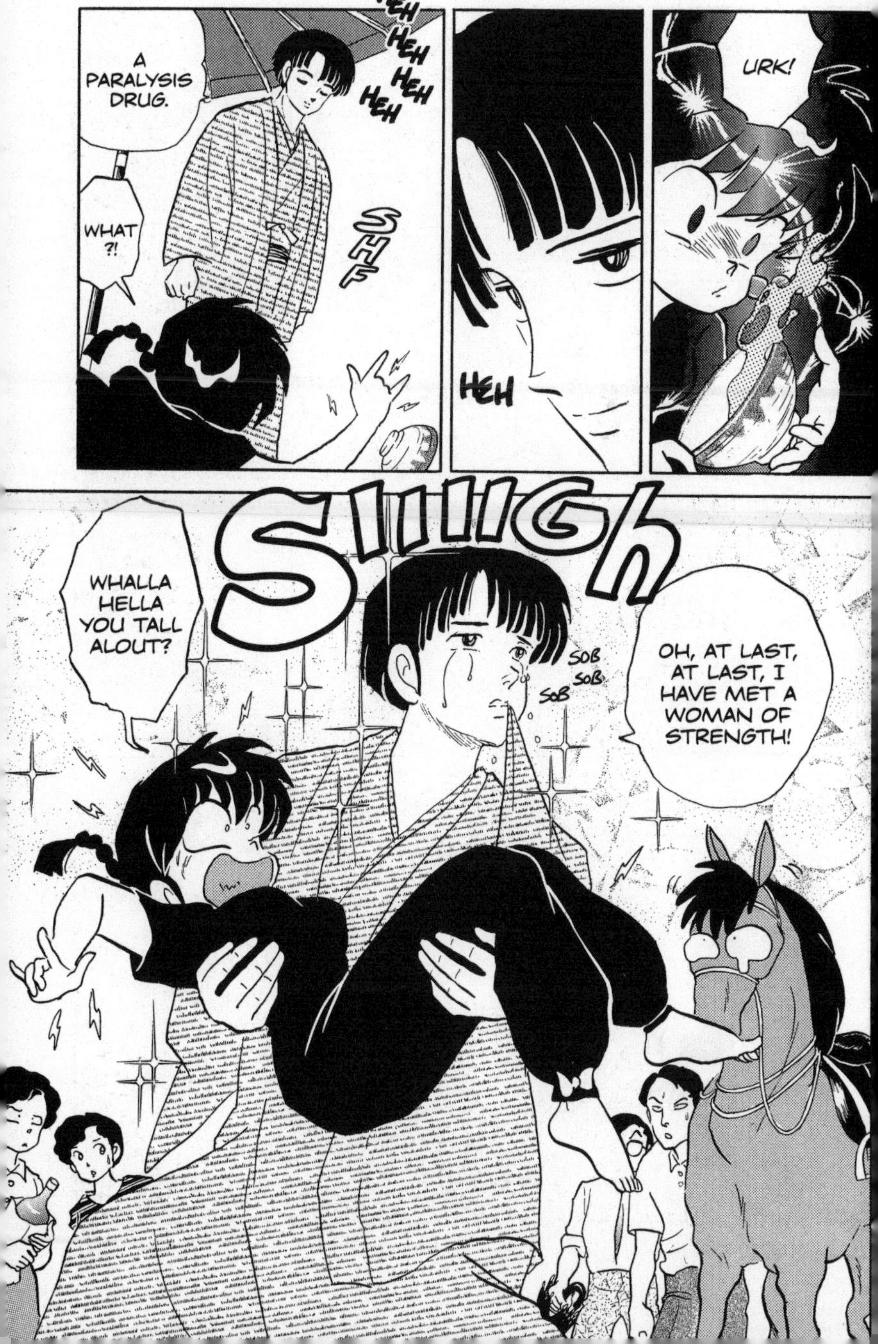
URK!
HEH
HEH HEH HEH HEH
A PARALYSIS DRUG.
WHAT ?!
SHF
SIIIGH
OH, AT LAST, AT LAST, I HAVE MET A WOMAN OF STRENGTH!
SOB SOB SOB
WHALLA HELLA YOU TALL ALOUT?

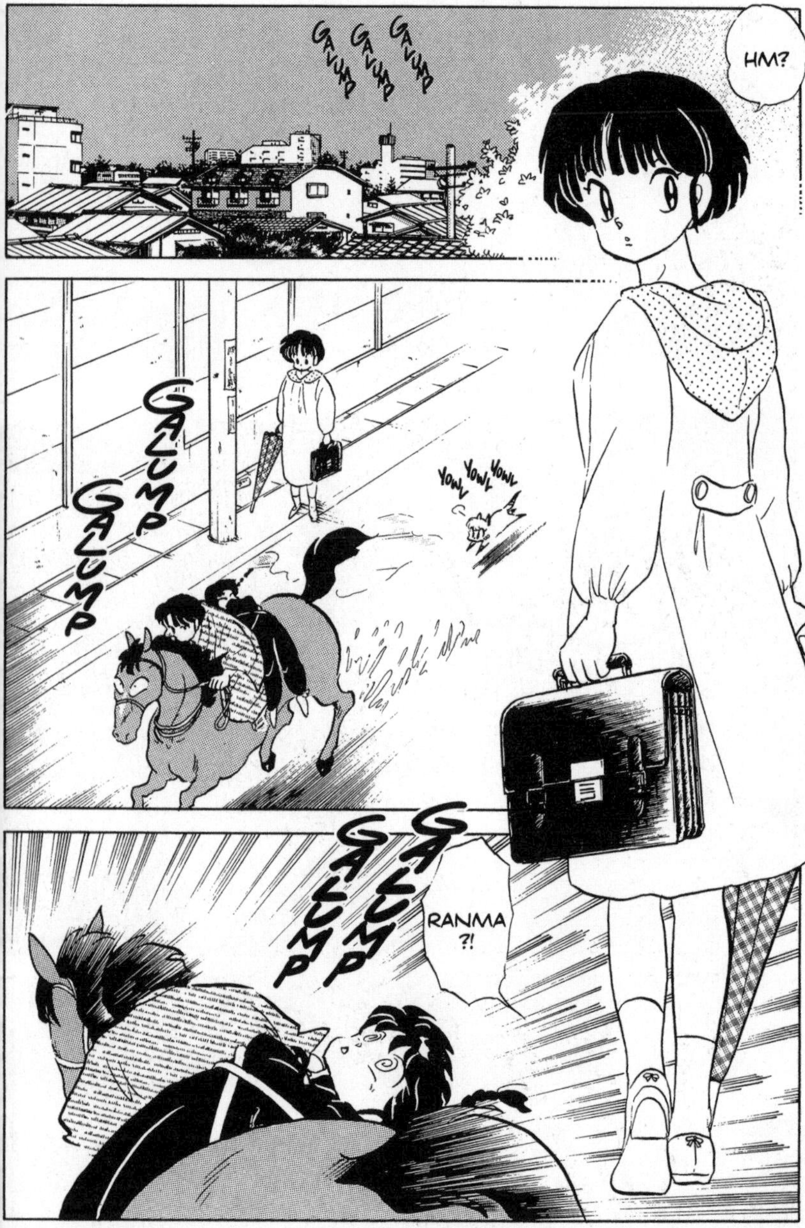
HM?
GALUMP GALUMP GALUMP
GALUMP
GALUMP
YOWL YOWL YOWL
GALUMP
GALUMP
RANMA ?!

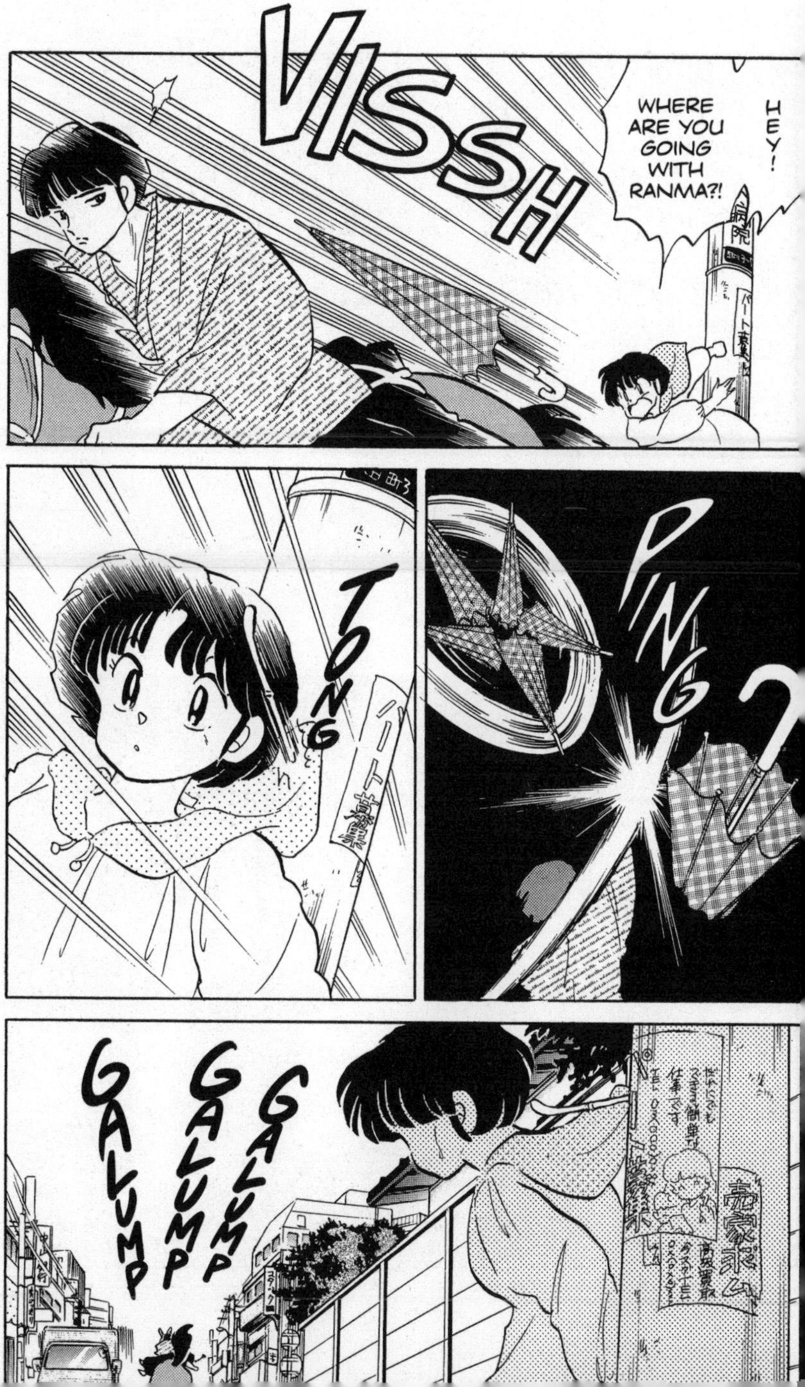
HEY!
WHERE ARE YOU GOING WITH RANMA?!
VISSH
PING
TONG
GALUMP
GALUMP
GALUMP

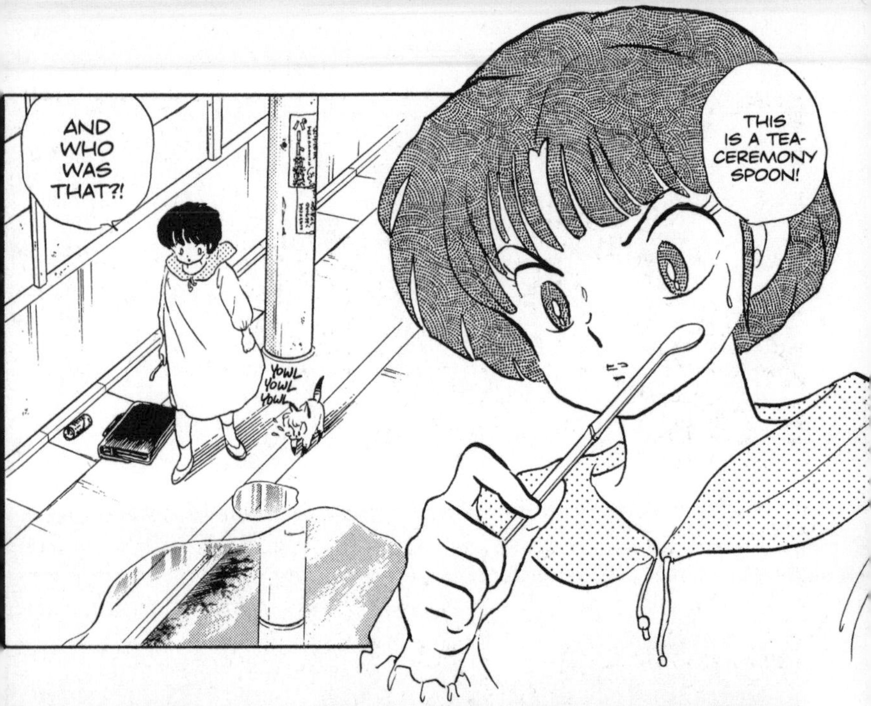
THIS IS A TEA-CEREMONY SPOON!
AND WHO WAS THAT?!
YOWL YOWL YOWL

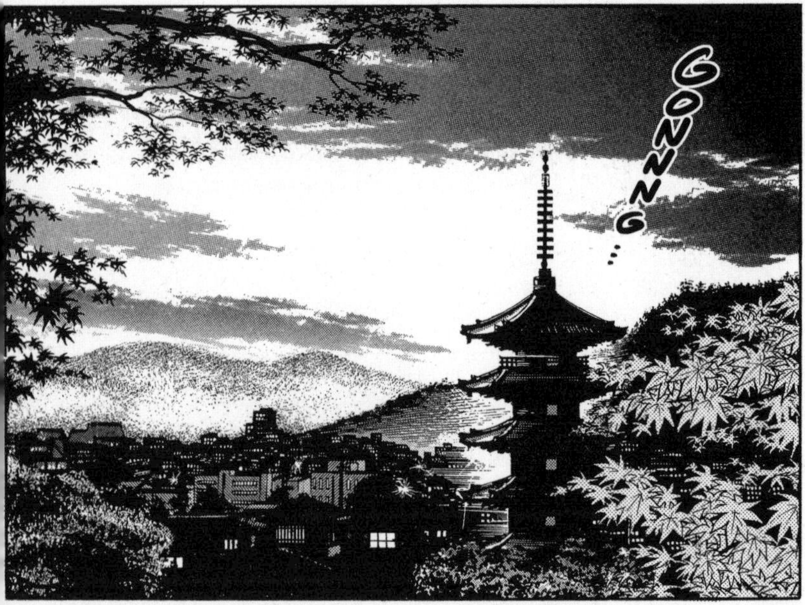
GONNNG...

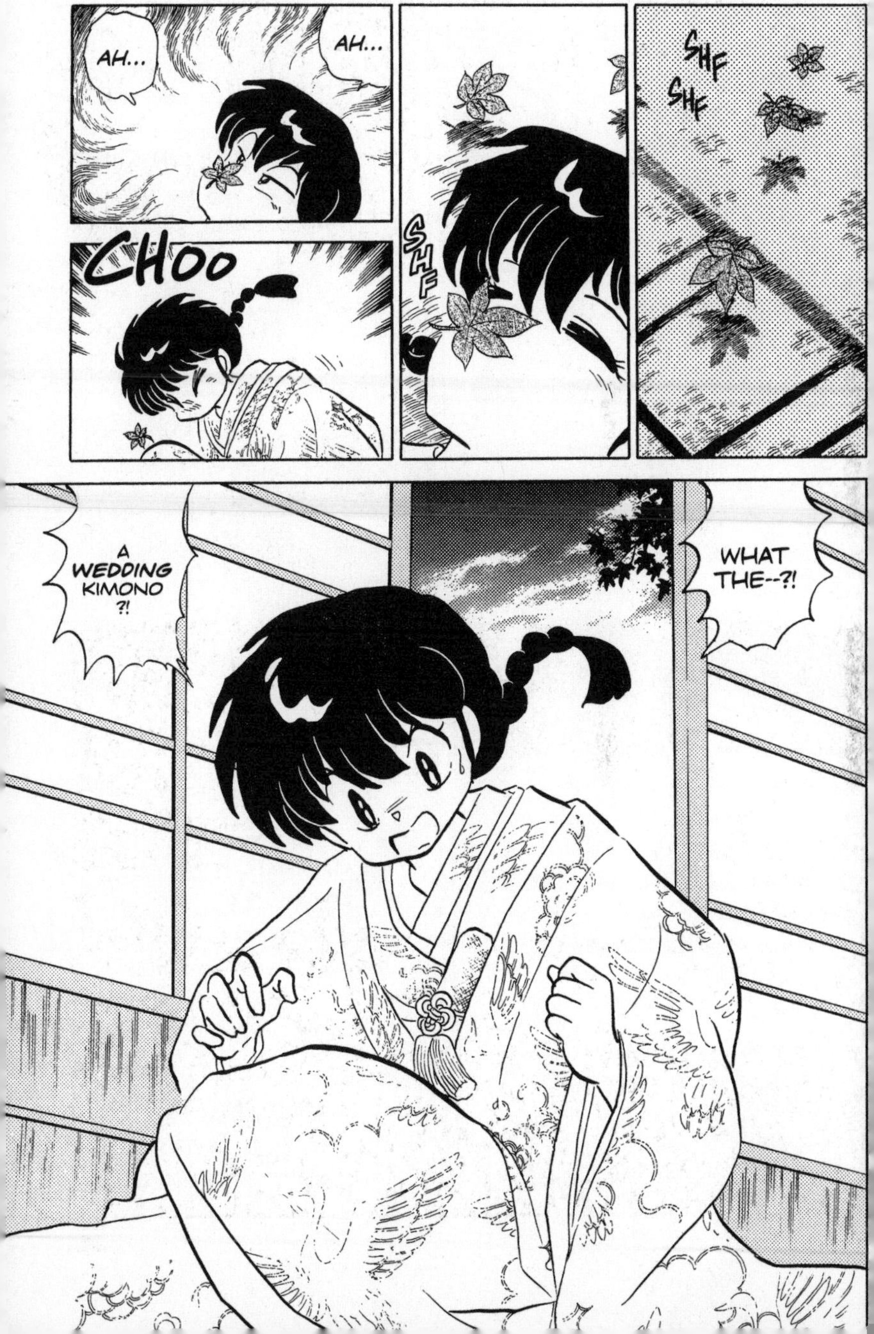
SHF
SHF
SHF
AH...
AH...
CHOO
WHAT THE--?!
A WEDDING KIMONO ?!

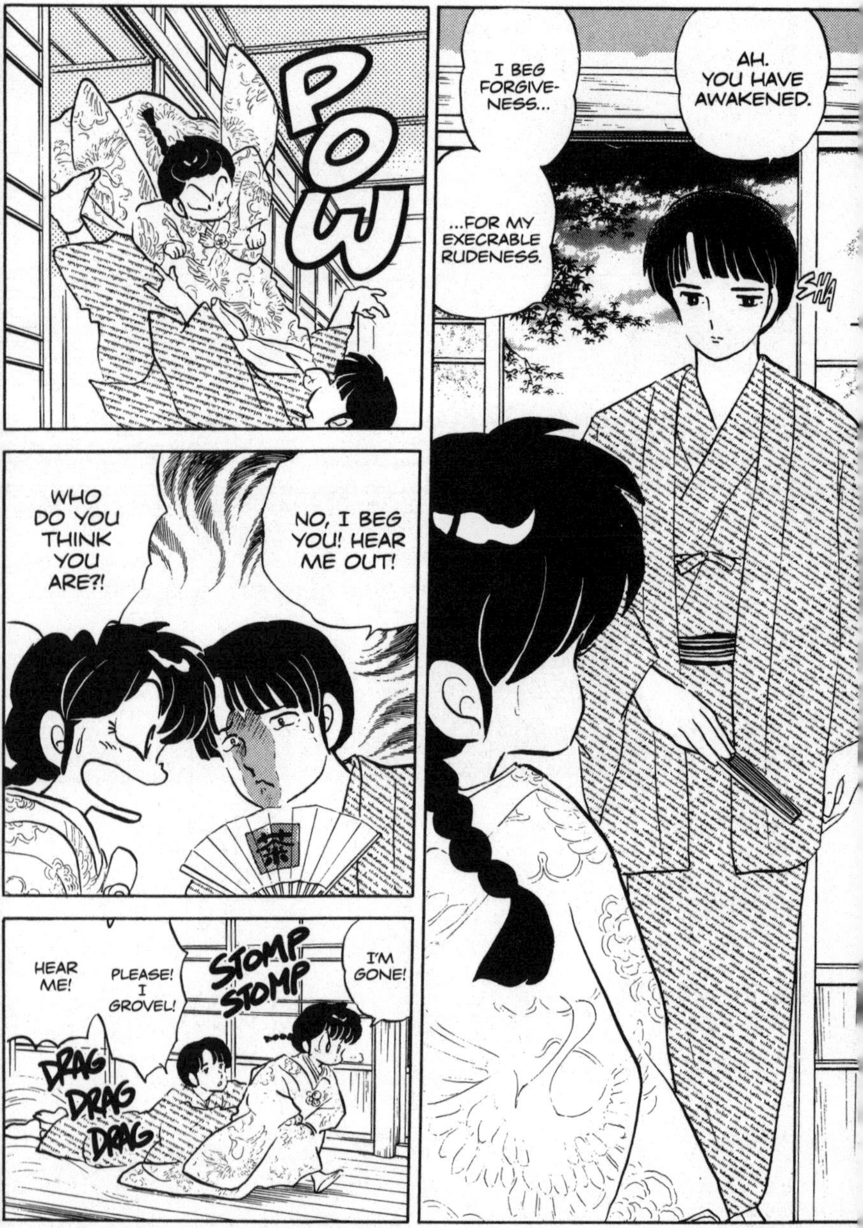
AH. YOU HAVE AWAKENED.
I BEG FORGIVE-NESS...
...FOR MY EXECRABLE RUDENESS.
SHA
POW
NO, I BEG YOU! HEAR ME OUT!
WHO DO YOU THINK YOU ARE?!
I'M GONE!
STOMP STOMP
PLEASE! I GROVEL!
HEAR ME!
DRAG DRAG DRAG

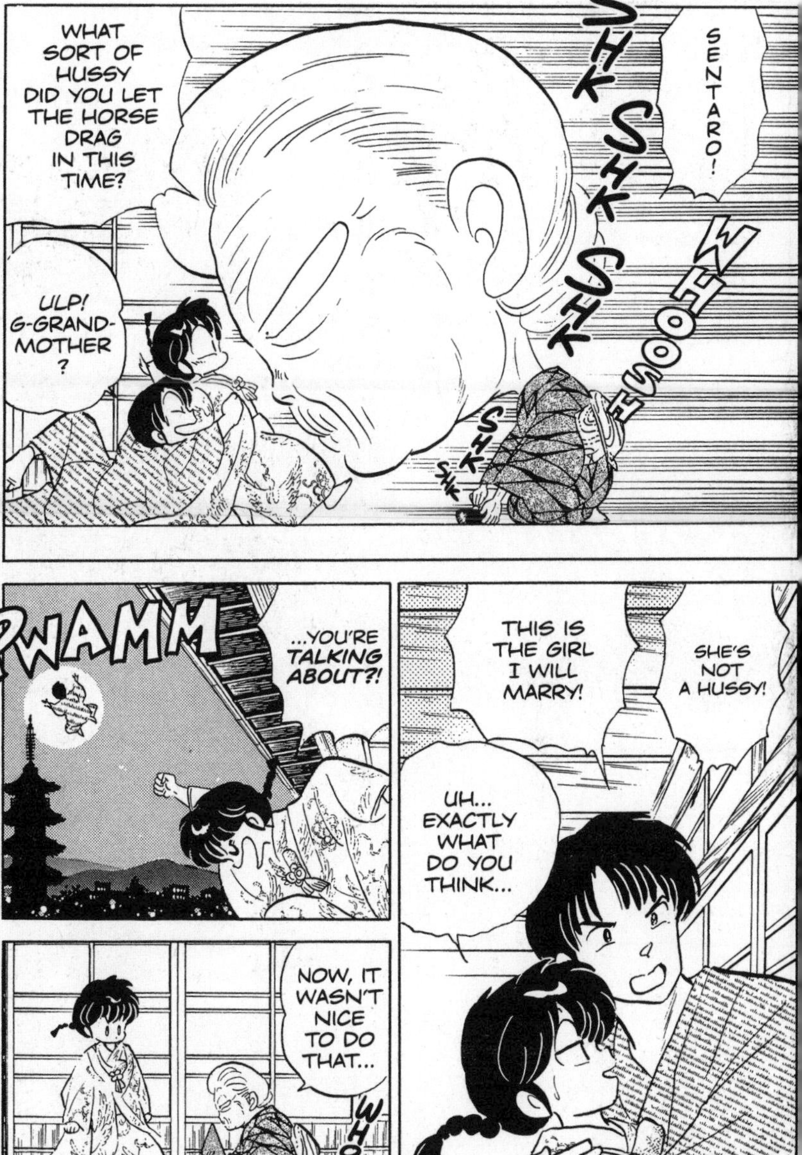
SENTARO!
SHK SHK SHK
WHOOSH
SHK SHK SHK
WHAT SORT OF HUSSY DID YOU LET THE HORSE DRAG IN THIS TIME?
ULP! G-GRANDMOTHER?
SHE'S NOT A HUSSY!
THIS IS THE GIRL I WILL MARRY!
UH... EXACTLY WHAT DO YOU THINK...
...YOU'RE TALKING ABOUT?!
PWAMM
NOW, IT WASN'T NICE TO DO THAT...
WHOOSH

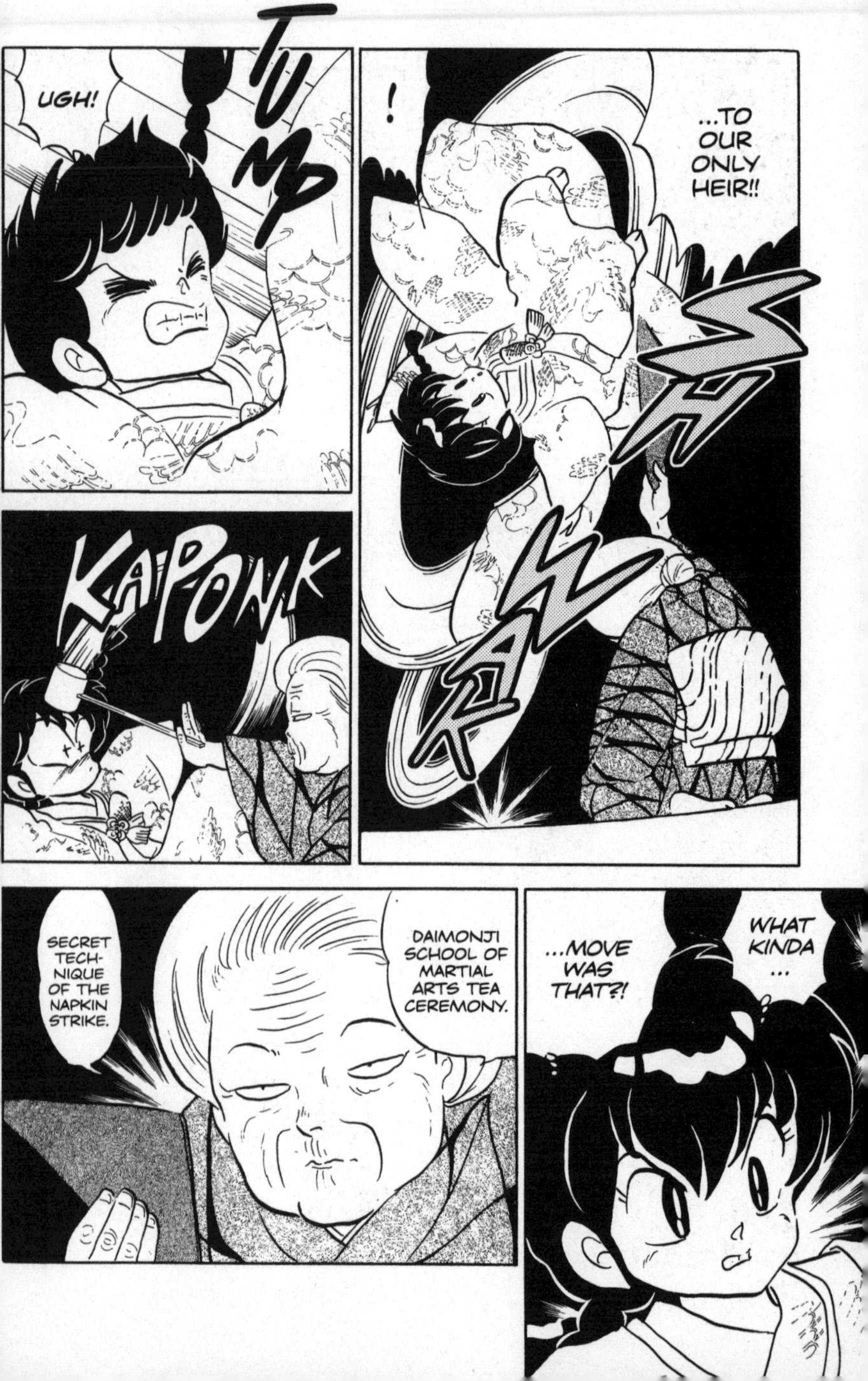
!
...TO OUR ONLY HEIR!!
UGH!
KAPONK
WHAT KINDA ...
...MOVE WAS THAT?!
DAIMONJI SCHOOL OF MARTIAL ARTS TEA CEREMONY.
SECRET TECH-NIQUE OF THE NAPKIN STRIKE.

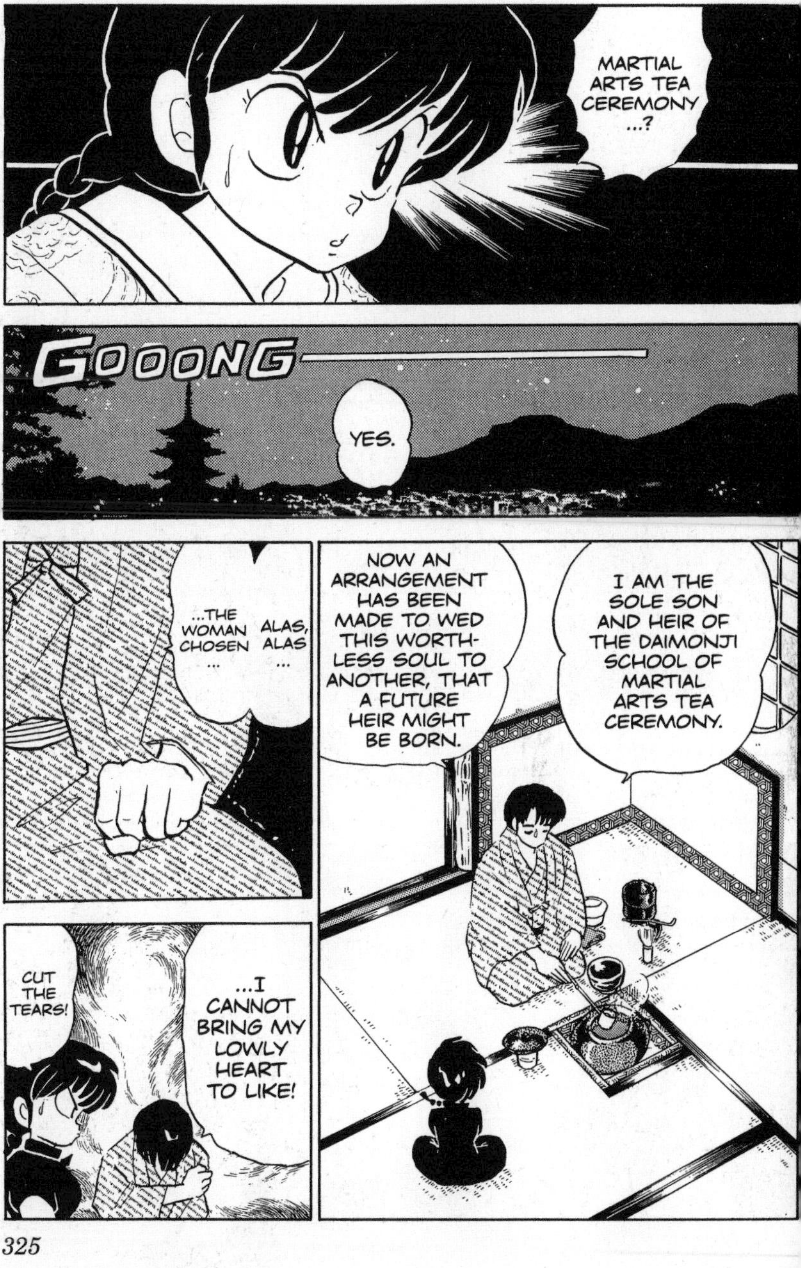
MARTIAL ARTS TEA CEREMONY ...?
GOOONG
YES.
I AM THE SOLE SON AND HEIR OF THE DAIMONJI SCHOOL OF MARTIAL ARTS TEA CEREMONY.
NOW AN ARRANGEMENT HAS BEEN MADE TO WED THIS WORTHLESS SOUL TO ANOTHER, THAT A FUTURE HEIR MIGHT BE BORN.
ALAS, ALAS ...
...THE WOMAN CHOSEN ...
...I CANNOT BRING MY LOWLY HEART TO LIKE!
CUT THE TEARS!

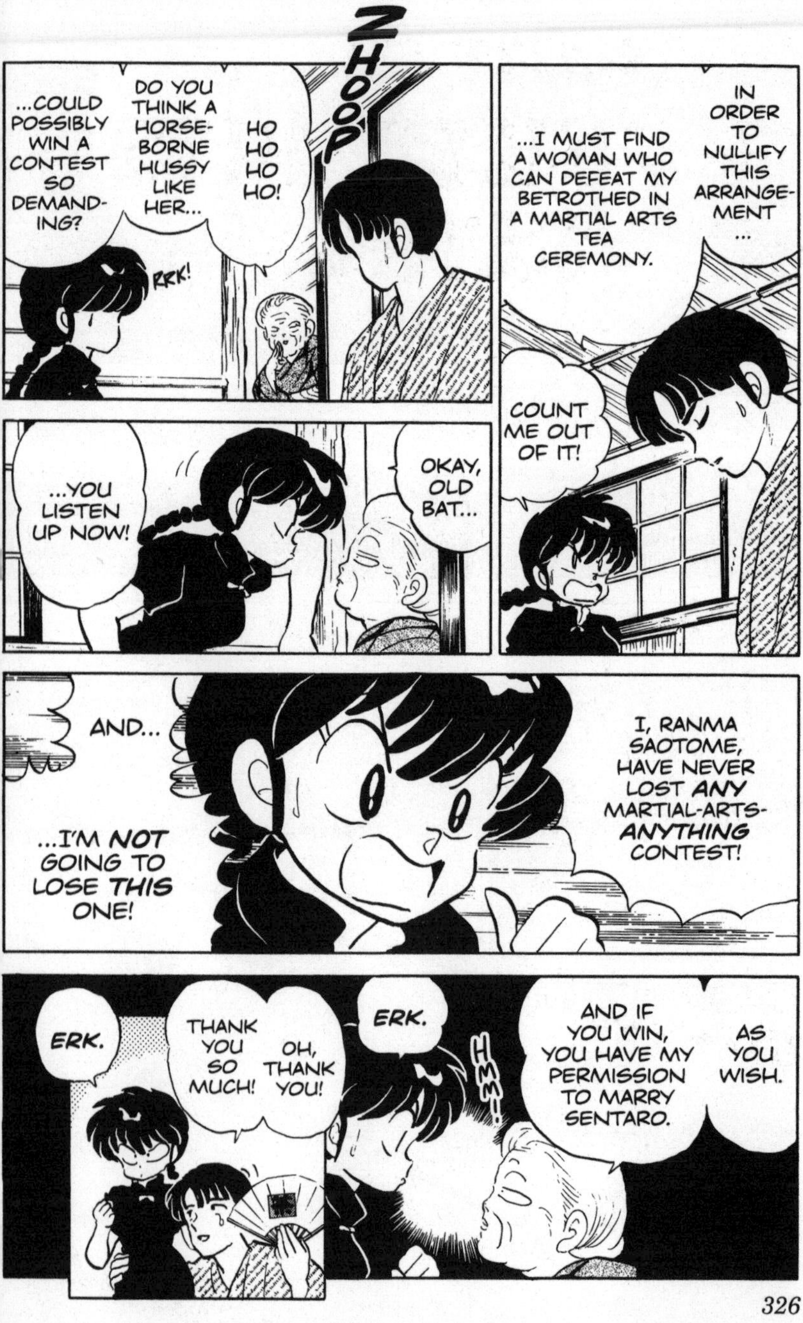
IN ORDER TO NULLIFY THIS ARRANGEMENT...
...I MUST FIND A WOMAN WHO CAN DEFEAT MY BETROTHED IN A MARTIAL ARTS TEA CEREMONY.
COUNT ME OUT OF IT!
ZHOOOP
HO HO HO HO!
DO YOU THINK A HORSE-BORNE HUSSY LIKE HER...
...COULD POSSIBLY WIN A CONTEST SO DEMANDING?
RRK!
OKAY, OLD BAT...
...YOU LISTEN UP NOW!
I, RANMA SAOTOME, HAVE NEVER LOST **ANY** MARTIAL-ARTS-***ANYTHING*** CONTEST!
AND...
...I'M **NOT** GOING TO LOSE **THIS** ONE!
AS YOU WISH.
AND IF YOU WIN, YOU HAVE MY PERMISSION TO MARRY SENTARO.
HMM!
ERK.
OH, THANK YOU!
THANK YOU SO MUCH!
ERK.

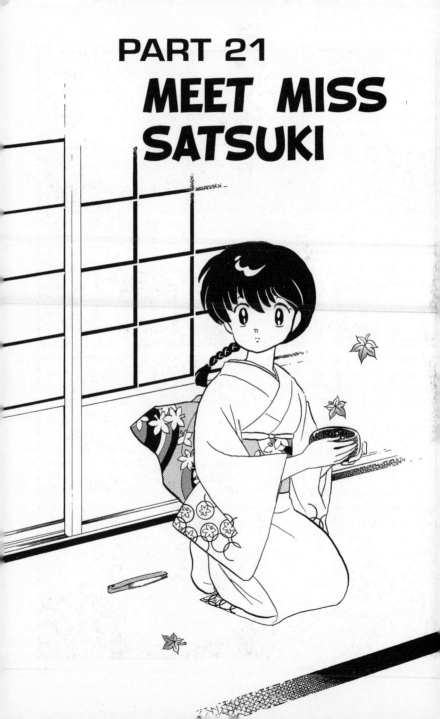

PART 21

MEET MISS SATSUKI

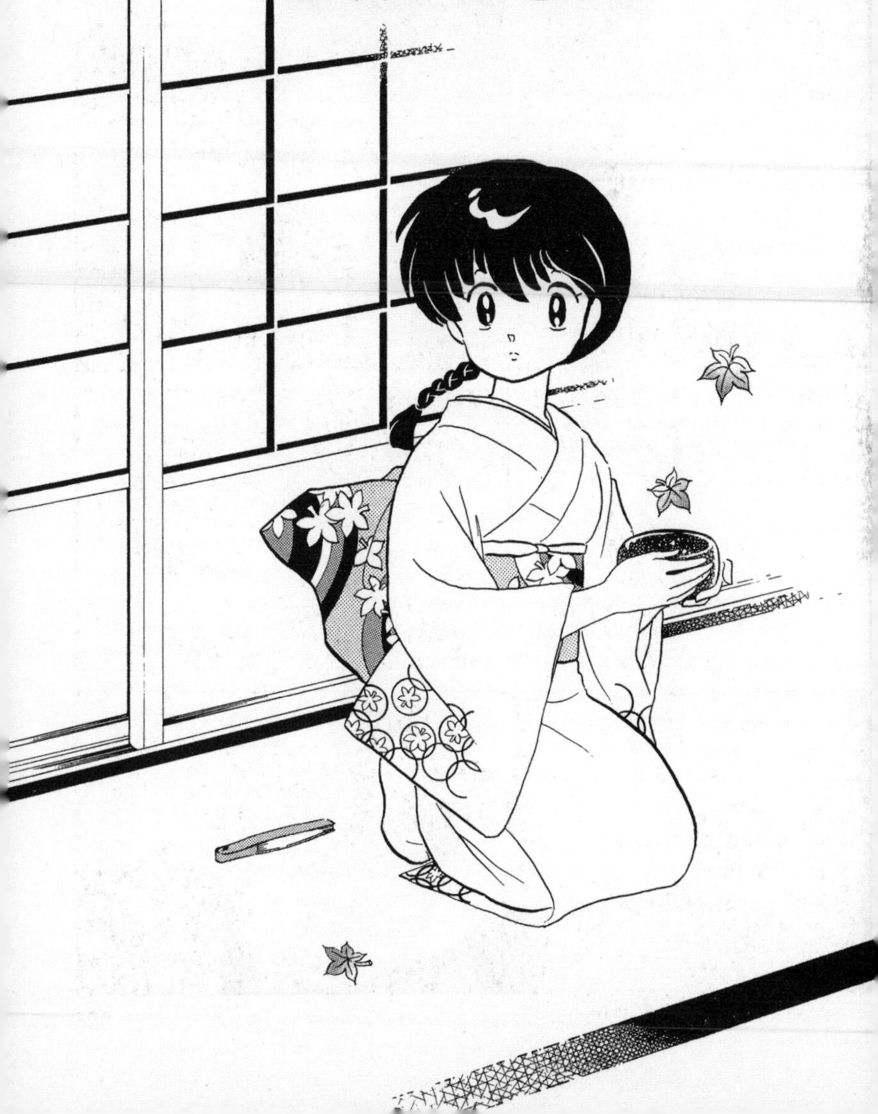

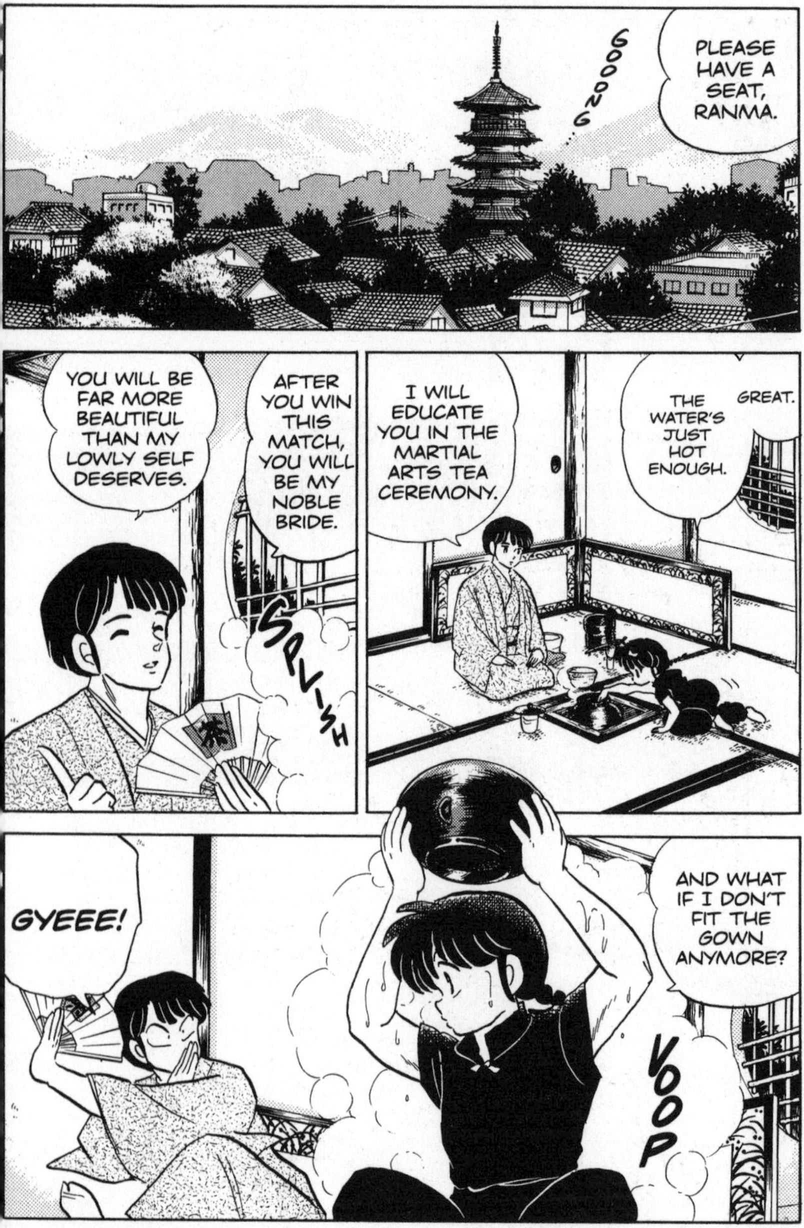
PLEASE HAVE A SEAT, RANMA.
GOOOONG...
GREAT.
THE WATER'S JUST HOT ENOUGH.
I WILL EDUCATE YOU IN THE MARTIAL ARTS TEA CEREMONY.
AFTER YOU WIN THIS MATCH, YOU WILL BE MY NOBLE BRIDE.
YOU WILL BE FAR MORE BEAUTIFUL THAN MY LOWLY SELF DESERVES.
SPLISH
AND WHAT IF I DON'T FIT THE GOWN ANYMORE?
VOOP
GYEEE!

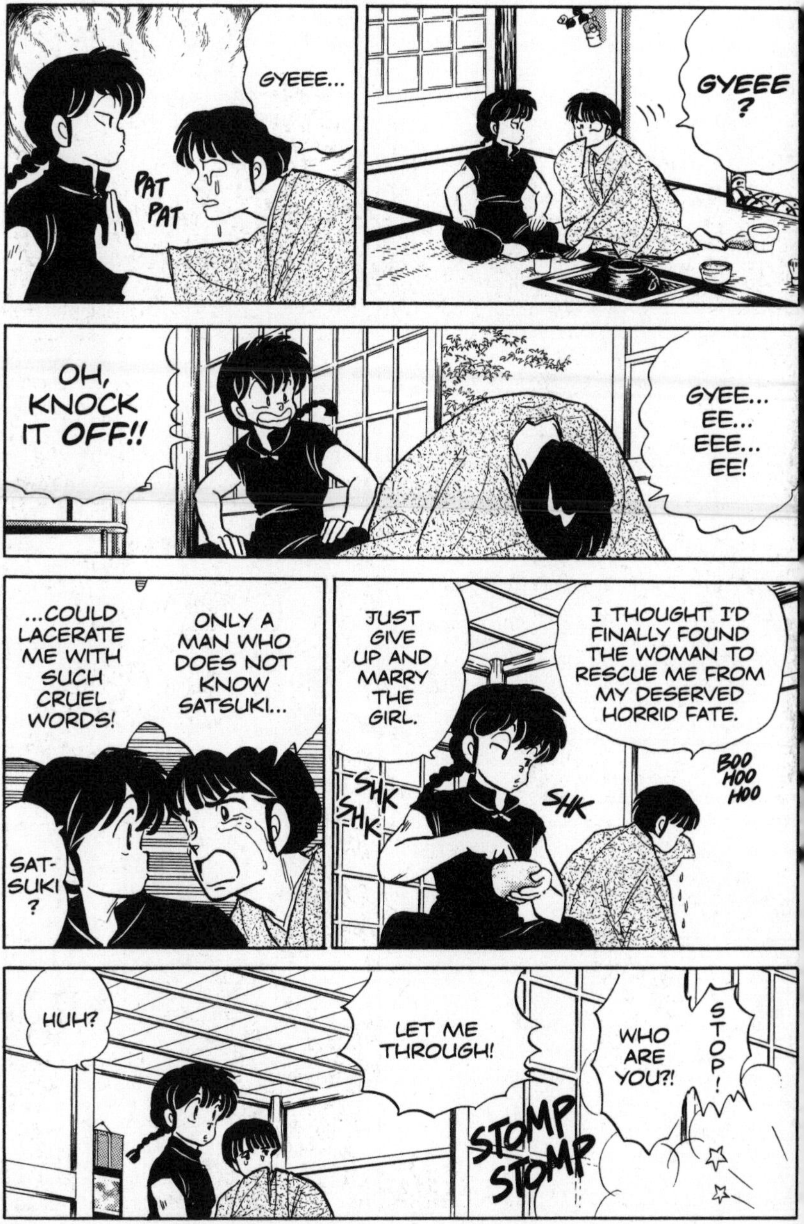
GYEEE ?
GYEEE...
PAT PAT
GYEEE... EE... EEE... EE!
OH, KNOCK IT OFF!!
I THOUGHT I'D FINALLY FOUND THE WOMAN TO RESCUE ME FROM MY DESERVED HORRID FATE.
BOO HOO HOO
SHK
JUST GIVE UP AND MARRY THE GIRL.
SHK SHK
ONLY A MAN WHO DOES NOT KNOW SATSUKI...
...COULD LACERATE ME WITH SUCH CRUEL WORDS!
SAT-SUKI ?
STOP!
WHO ARE YOU?!
LET ME THROUGH!
STOMP STOMP
HUH?

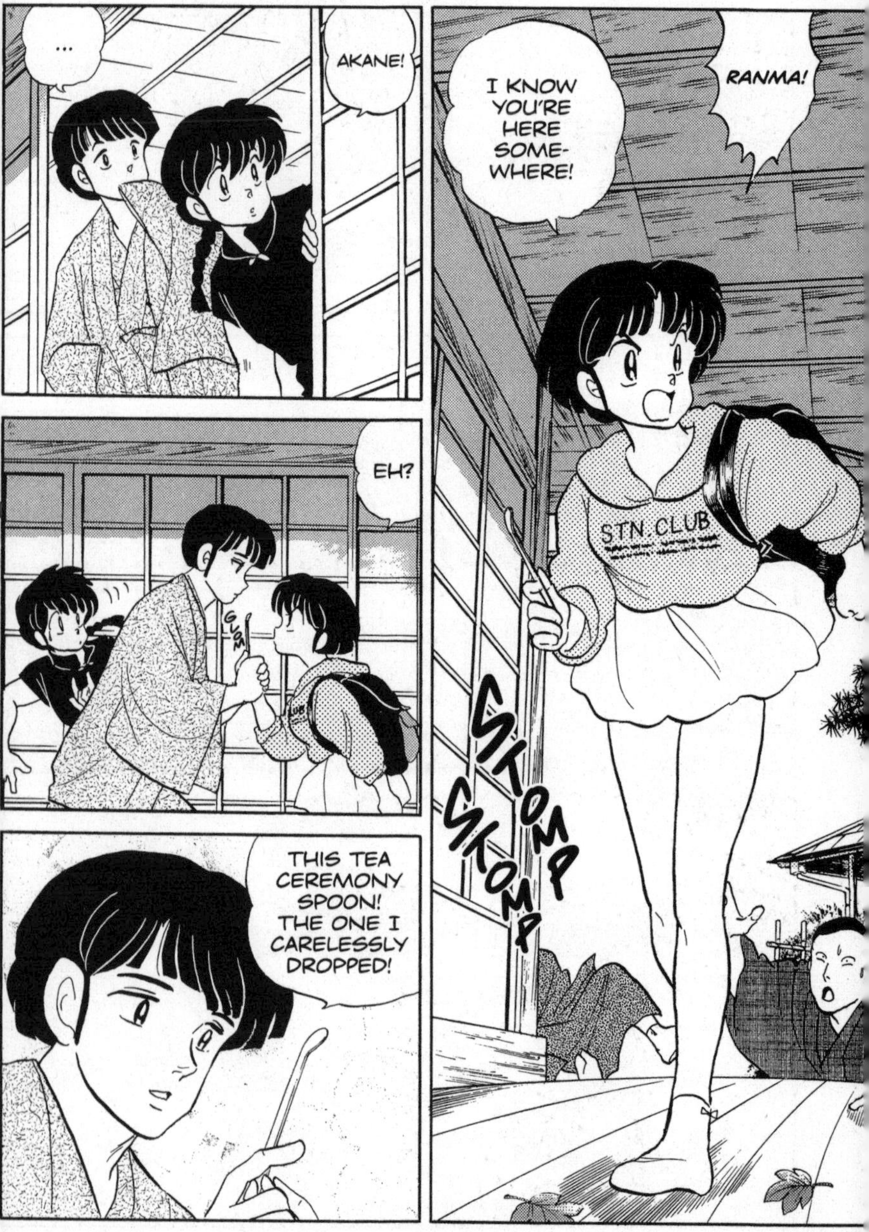
RANMA!
I KNOW YOU'RE HERE SOME-WHERE!
SKOMP
SKOMP
AKANE!
...
EH?
GLOM
THIS TEA CEREMONY SPOON! THE ONE I CARELESSLY DROPPED!

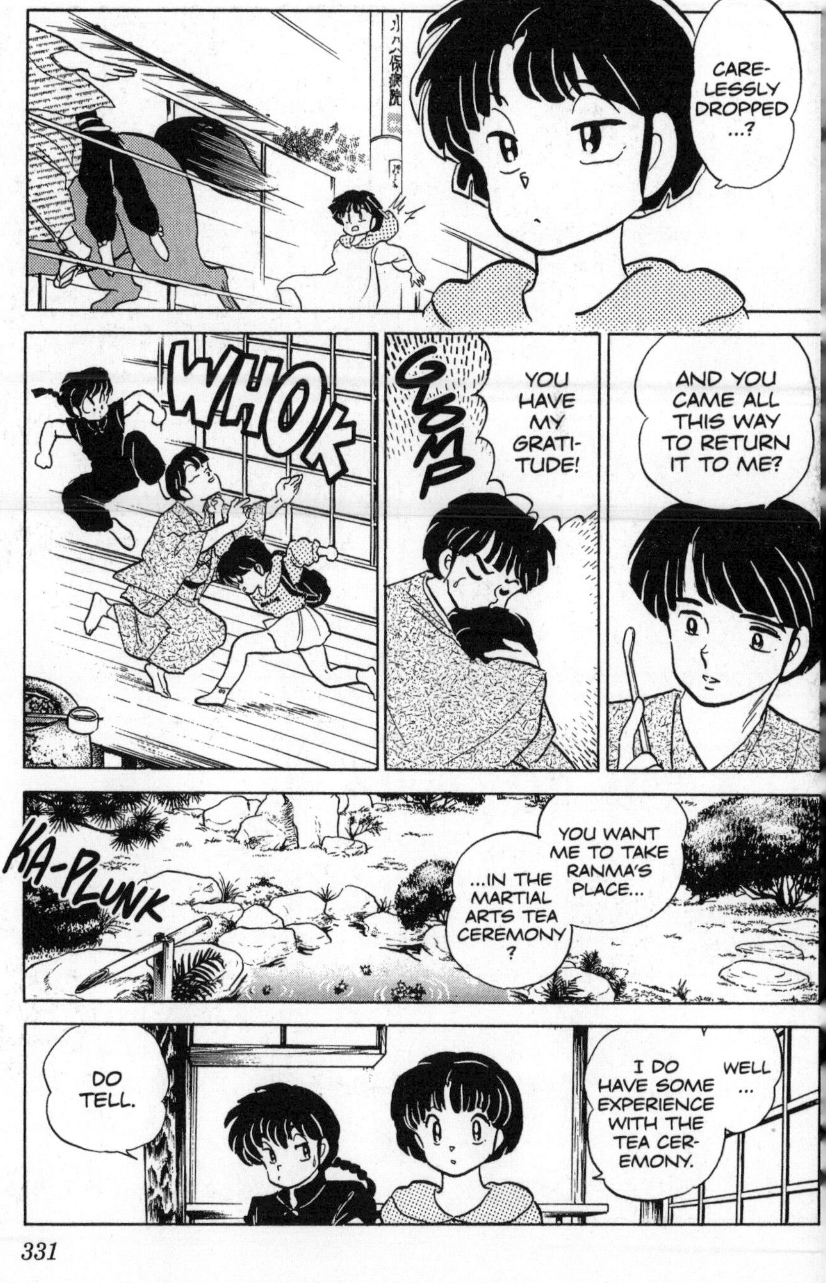
CARE-LESSLY DROPPED ...?
AND YOU CAME ALL THIS WAY TO RETURN IT TO ME?
YOU HAVE MY GRATI-TUDE!
GLOMP
WHOK
YOU WANT ME TO TAKE RANMA'S PLACE...
...IN THE MARTIAL ARTS TEA CEREMONY ?
KA-PLUNK
WELL ...
I DO HAVE SOME EXPERIENCE WITH THE TEA CER-EMONY.
DO TELL.

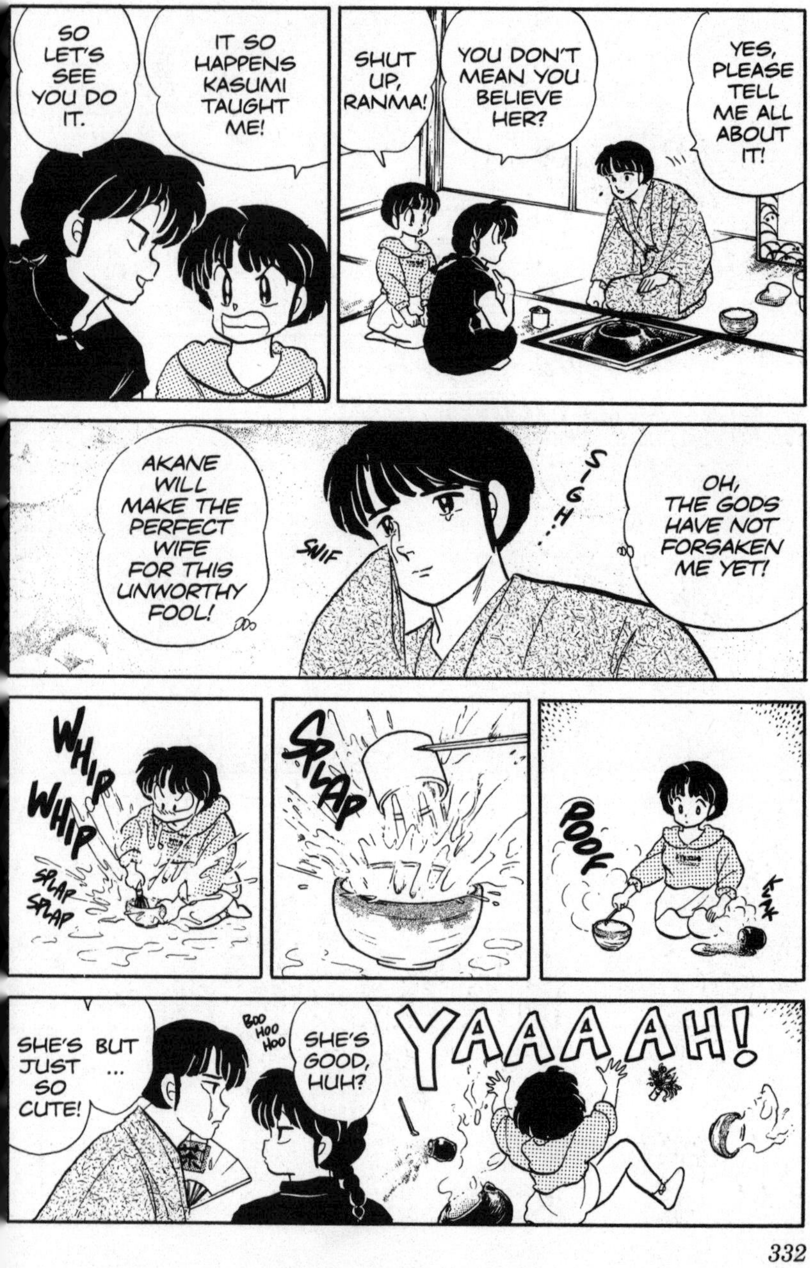
YES, PLEASE TELL ME ALL ABOUT IT!
YOU DON'T MEAN YOU BELIEVE HER?
SHUT UP, RANMA!
IT SO HAPPENS KASUMI TAUGHT ME!
SO LET'S SEE YOU DO IT.
OH, THE GODS HAVE NOT FORSAKEN ME YET!
SIGH...
SNIF
AKANE WILL MAKE THE PERFECT WIFE FOR THIS UNWORTHY FOOL!
POOK
KLINK
SPLAP
WHIP
WHIP
SPLAP
SPLAP
YAAAAH!
SHE'S GOOD, HUH?
BOO HOO HOO
BUT ...
SHE'S JUST SO CUTE!

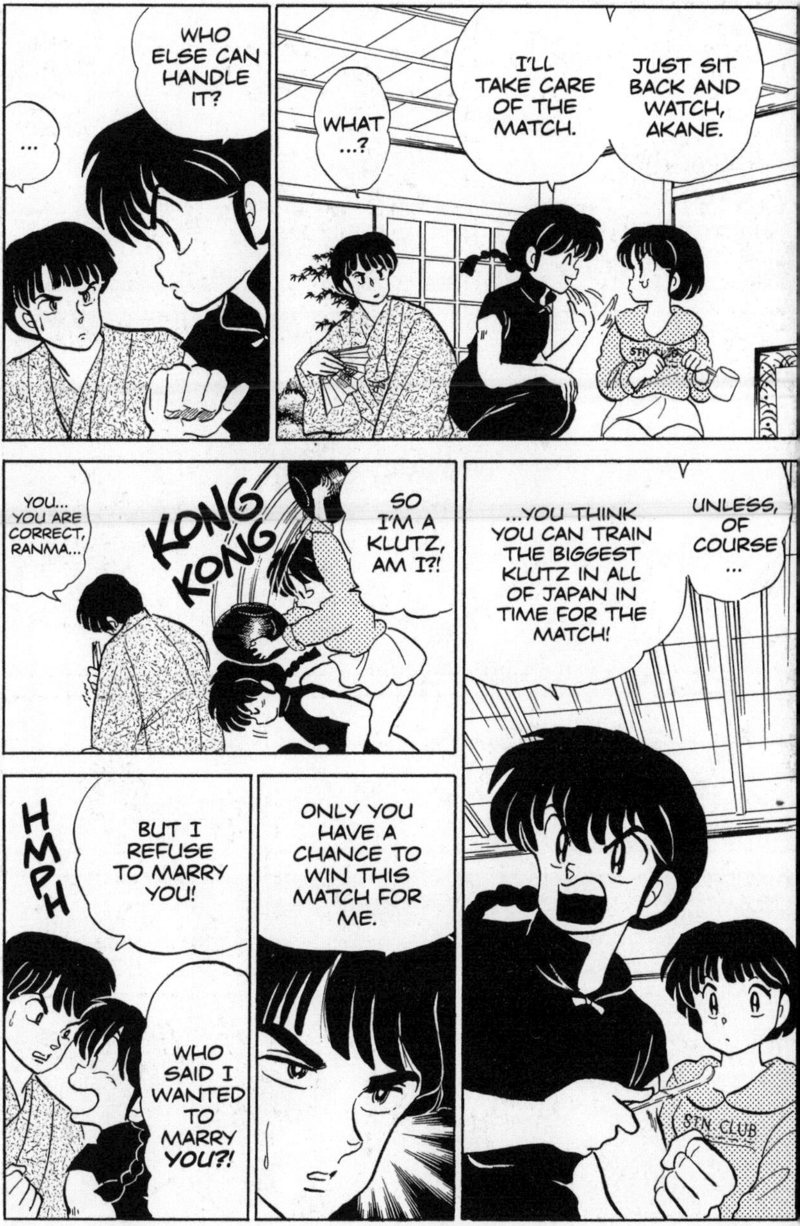
JUST SIT BACK AND WATCH, AKANE.
I'LL TAKE CARE OF THE MATCH.
WHAT ...?
WHO ELSE CAN HANDLE IT?
...
UNLESS, OF COURSE ...
...YOU THINK YOU CAN TRAIN THE BIGGEST KLUTZ IN ALL OF JAPAN IN TIME FOR THE MATCH!
SO I'M A KLUTZ, AM I?!
KONG KONG
YOU... YOU ARE CORRECT, RANMA...
ONLY YOU HAVE A CHANCE TO WIN THIS MATCH FOR ME.
BUT I REFUSE TO MARRY YOU!
HMPH
WHO SAID I WANTED TO MARRY YOU?!

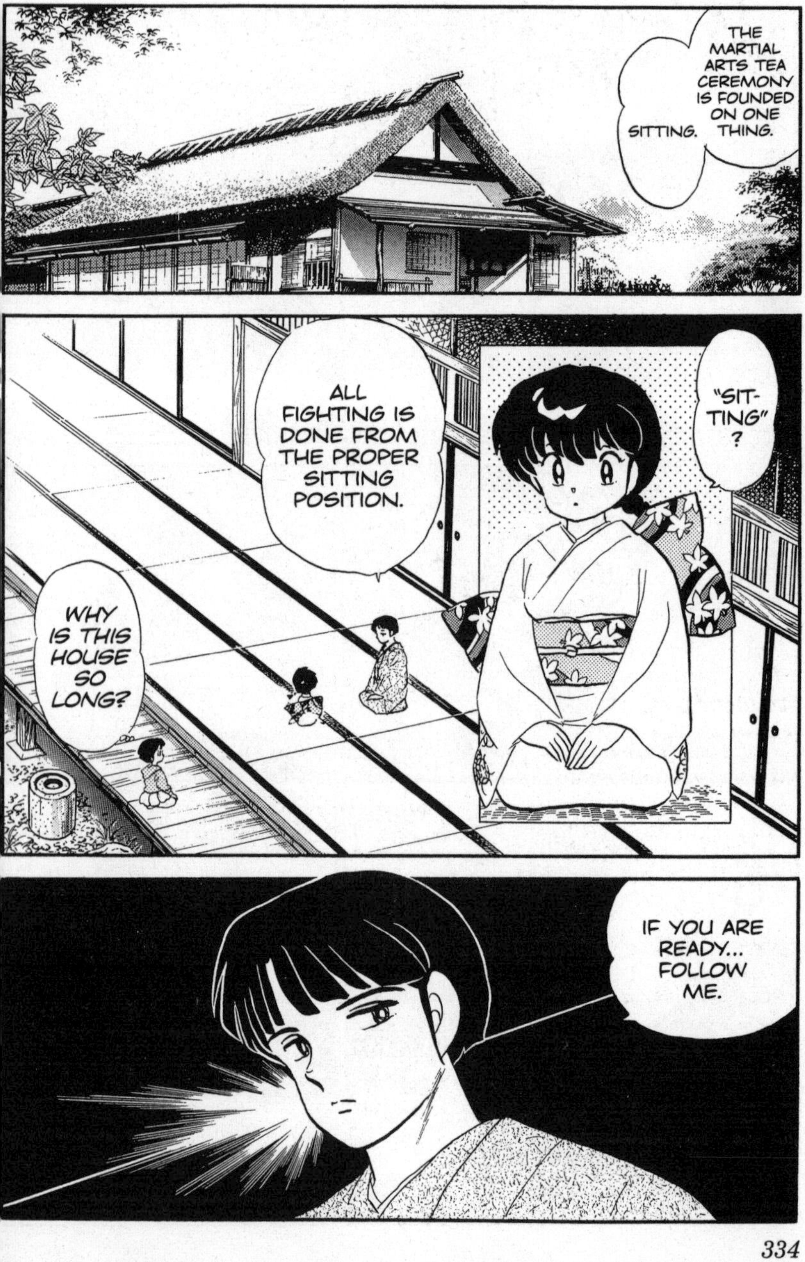
THE MARTIAL ARTS TEA CEREMONY IS FOUNDED ON ONE THING.
SITTING.
"SIT-TING"?
ALL FIGHTING IS DONE FROM THE PROPER SITTING POSITION.
WHY IS THIS HOUSE SO LONG?
IF YOU ARE READY... FOLLOW ME.

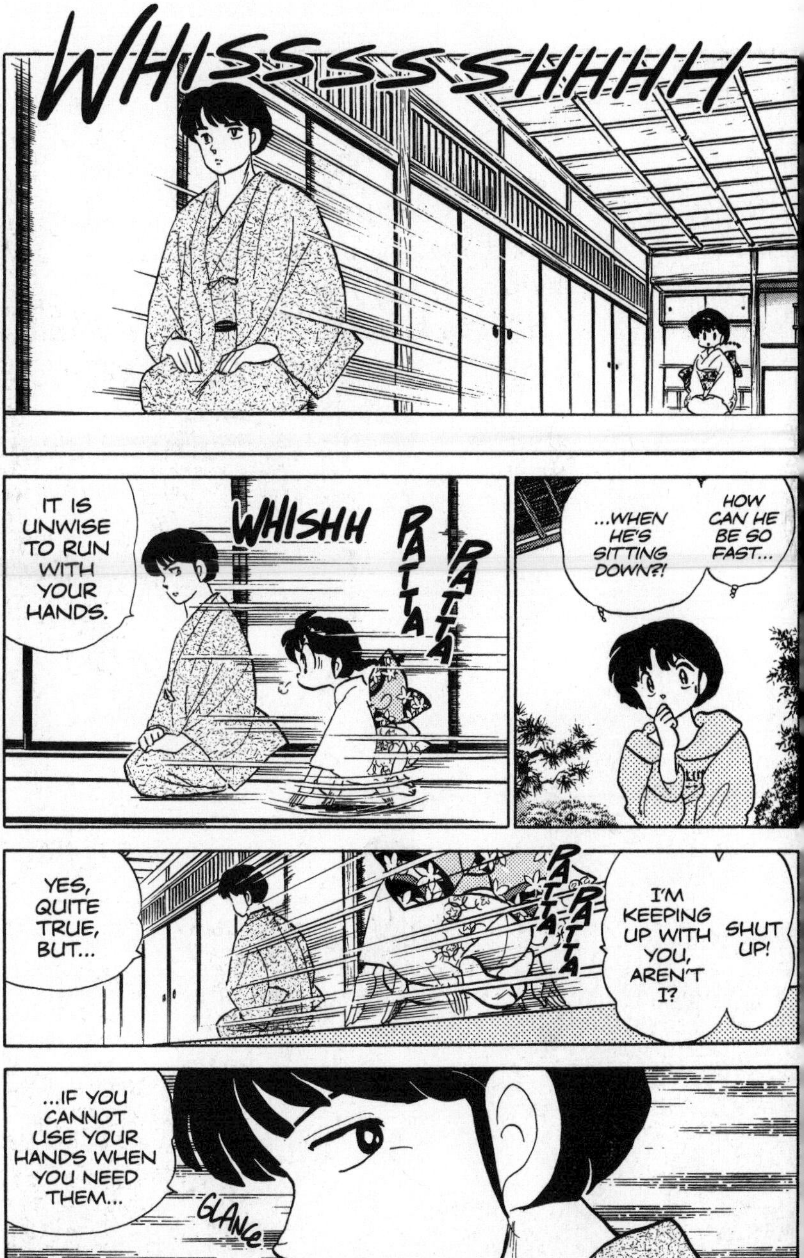
WHISSSSSHHHH
HOW CAN HE BE SO FAST...
...WHEN HE'S SITTING DOWN?!
WHISHH
PATTA PATTA
IT IS UNWISE TO RUN WITH YOUR HANDS.
SHUT UP!
I'M KEEPING UP WITH YOU, AREN'T I?
PATTA PATTA
YES, QUITE TRUE, BUT...
...IF YOU CANNOT USE YOUR HANDS WHEN YOU NEED THEM...
GLANCE

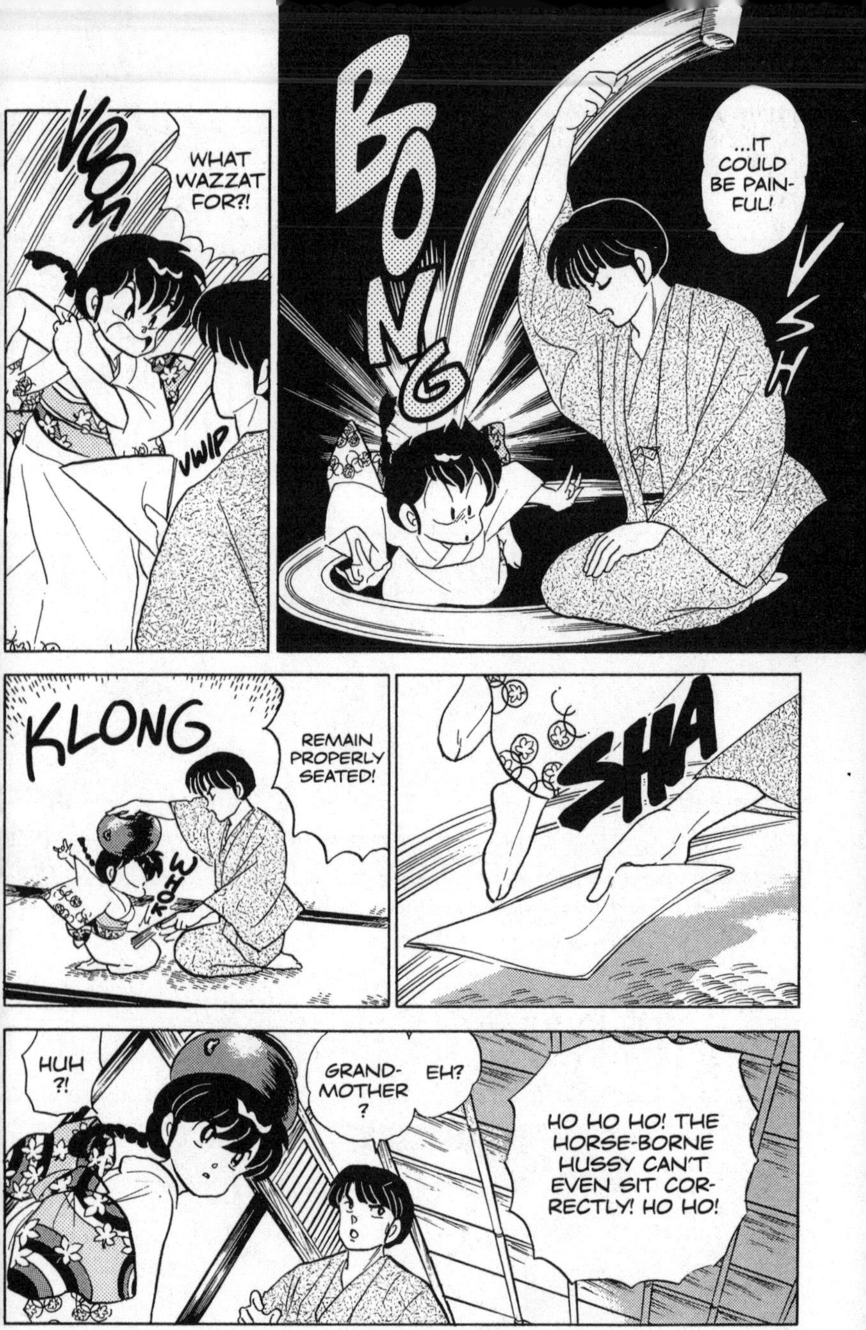
...IT COULD BE PAIN-FUL!
BOMG
VSH
WHAT WAZZAT FOR?!
VOOM
VWIP
SHA
KLONG
REMAIN PROPERLY SEATED!
WHOK
HO HO HO! THE HORSE-BORNE HUSSY CAN'T EVEN SIT COR-RECTLY! HO HO!
EH?
GRAND-MOTHER?
HUH?!

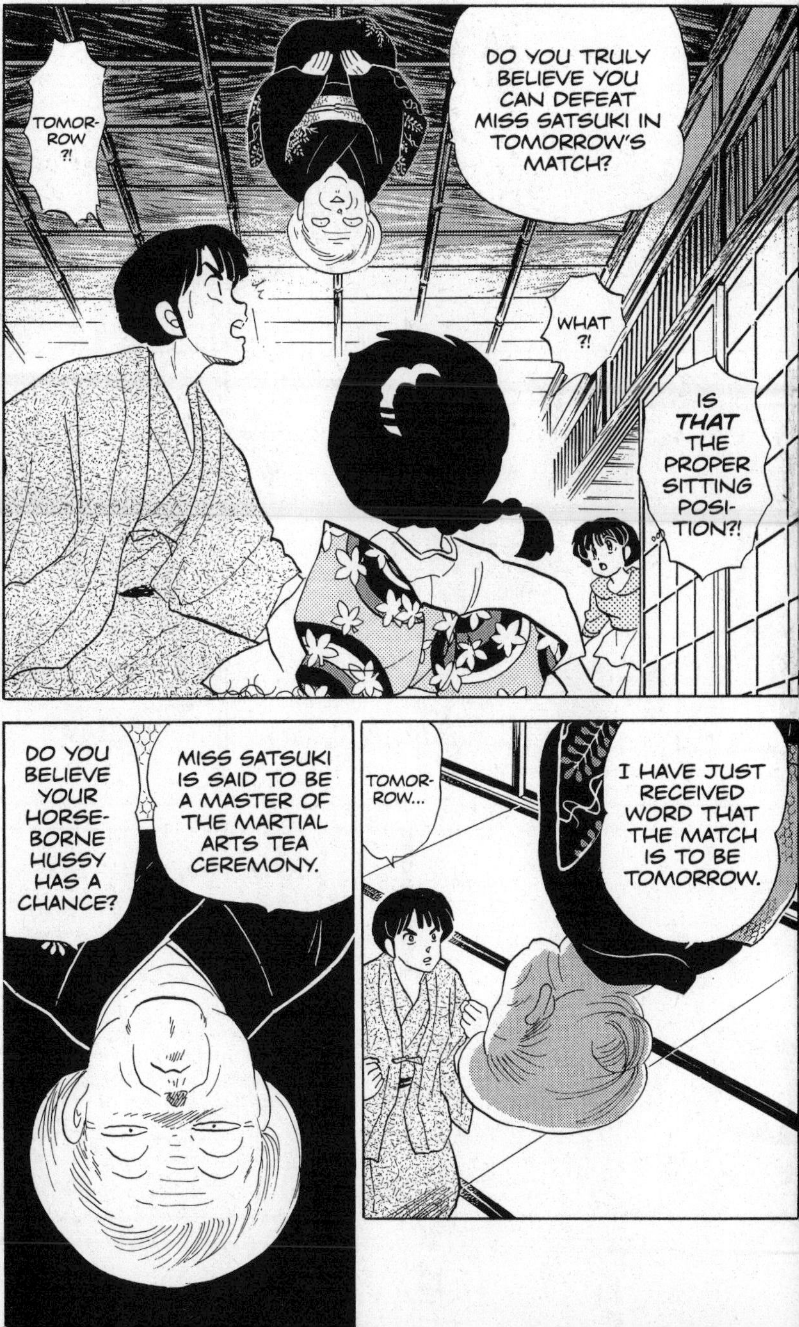
DO YOU TRULY BELIEVE YOU CAN DEFEAT MISS SATSUKI IN TOMORROW'S MATCH?
TOMOR-ROW ?!
WHAT ?!
IS *THAT* THE PROPER SITTING POSI-TION?!
I HAVE JUST RECEIVED WORD THAT THE MATCH IS TO BE TOMORROW.
TOMOR-ROW...
MISS SATSUKI IS SAID TO BE A MASTER OF THE MARTIAL ARTS TEA CEREMONY.
DO YOU BELIEVE YOUR HORSE-BORNE HUSSY HAS A CHANCE?

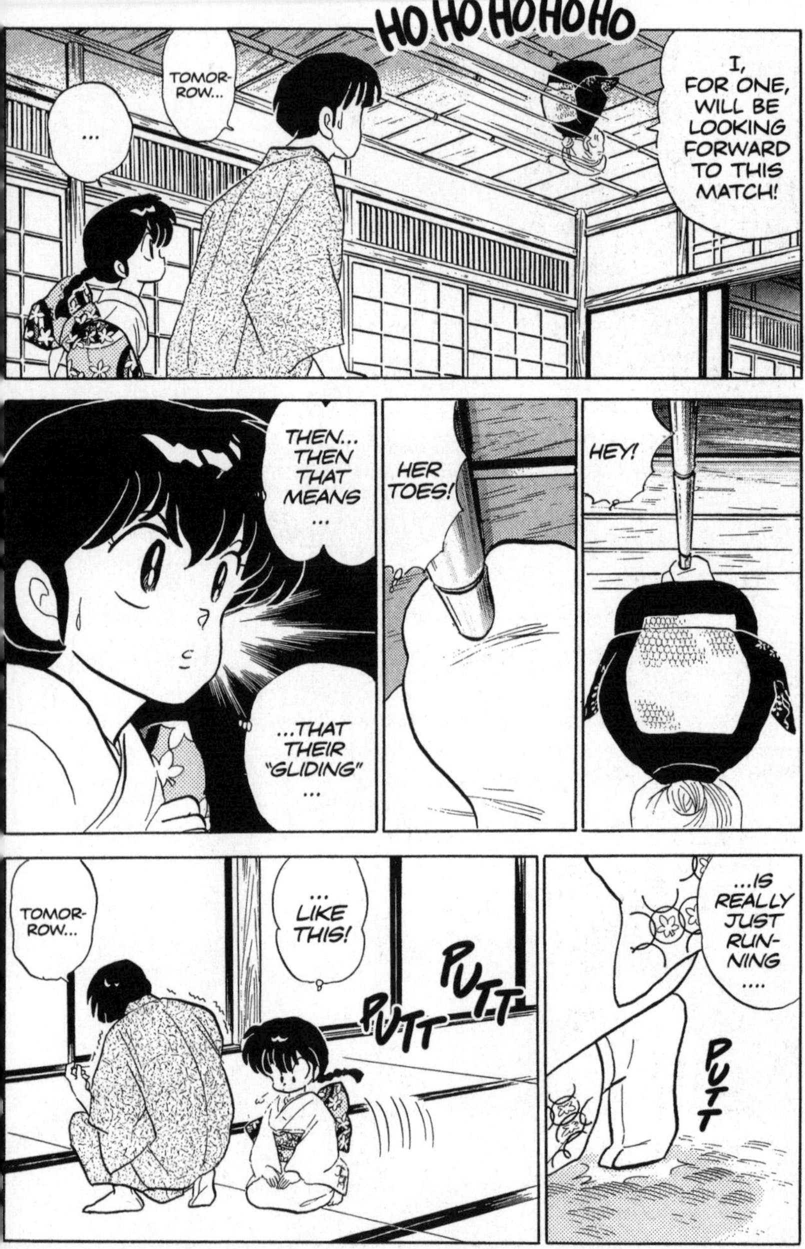
HO HO HO HO HO HO
I, FOR ONE, WILL BE LOOKING FORWARD TO THIS MATCH!
TOMOR-ROW...
...
HEY!
HER TOES!
THEN... THEN THAT MEANS...
...THAT THEIR "GLIDING"...
...IS REALLY JUST RUN-NING....
PUTT PUTT
... LIKE THIS!
TOMOR-ROW...
PUTT PUTT
PUTT PUTT

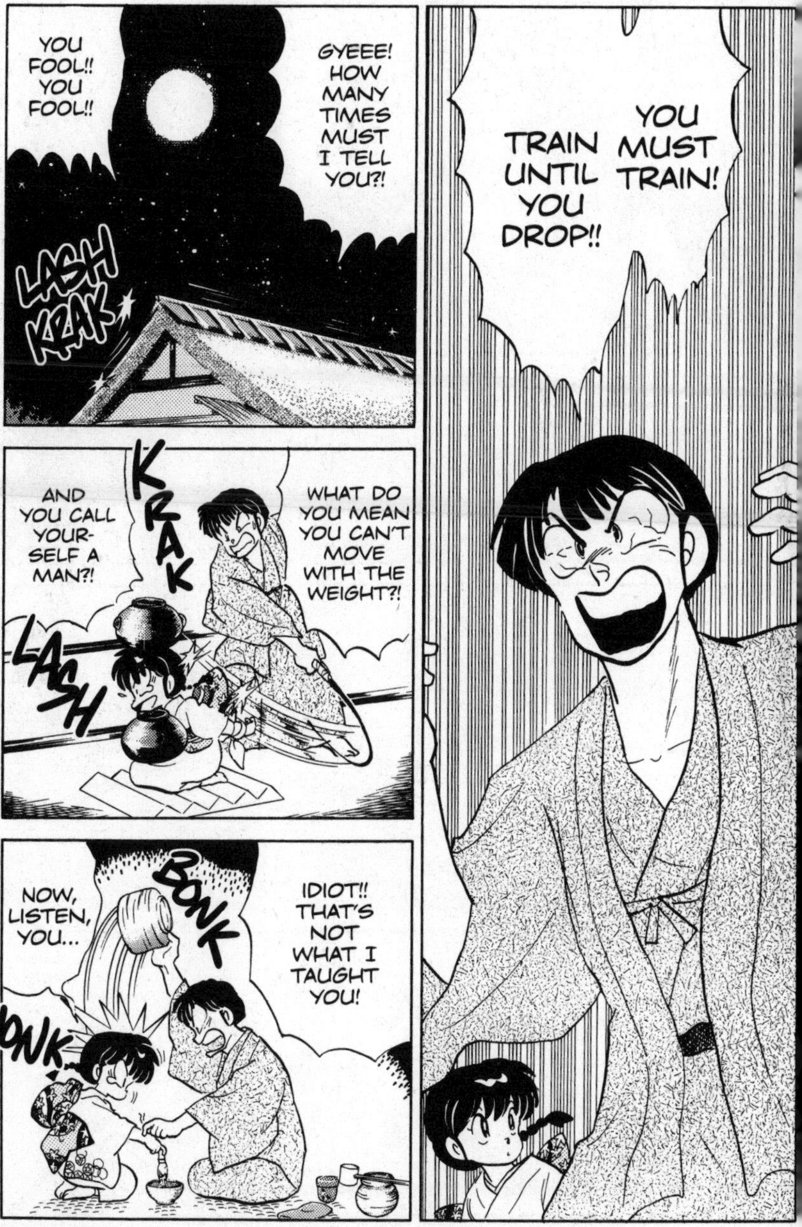
YOU MUST TRAIN!
TRAIN UNTIL YOU DROP!!
GYEEE! HOW MANY TIMES MUST I TELL YOU?!
YOU FOOL!! YOU FOOL!!
LASH KRAK
WHAT DO YOU MEAN YOU CAN'T MOVE WITH THE WEIGHT?!
KRAK
AND YOU CALL YOUR-SELF A MAN?!
LASH
IDIOT!! THAT'S NOT WHAT I TAUGHT YOU!
BONK
NOW, LISTEN, YOU...
WONK

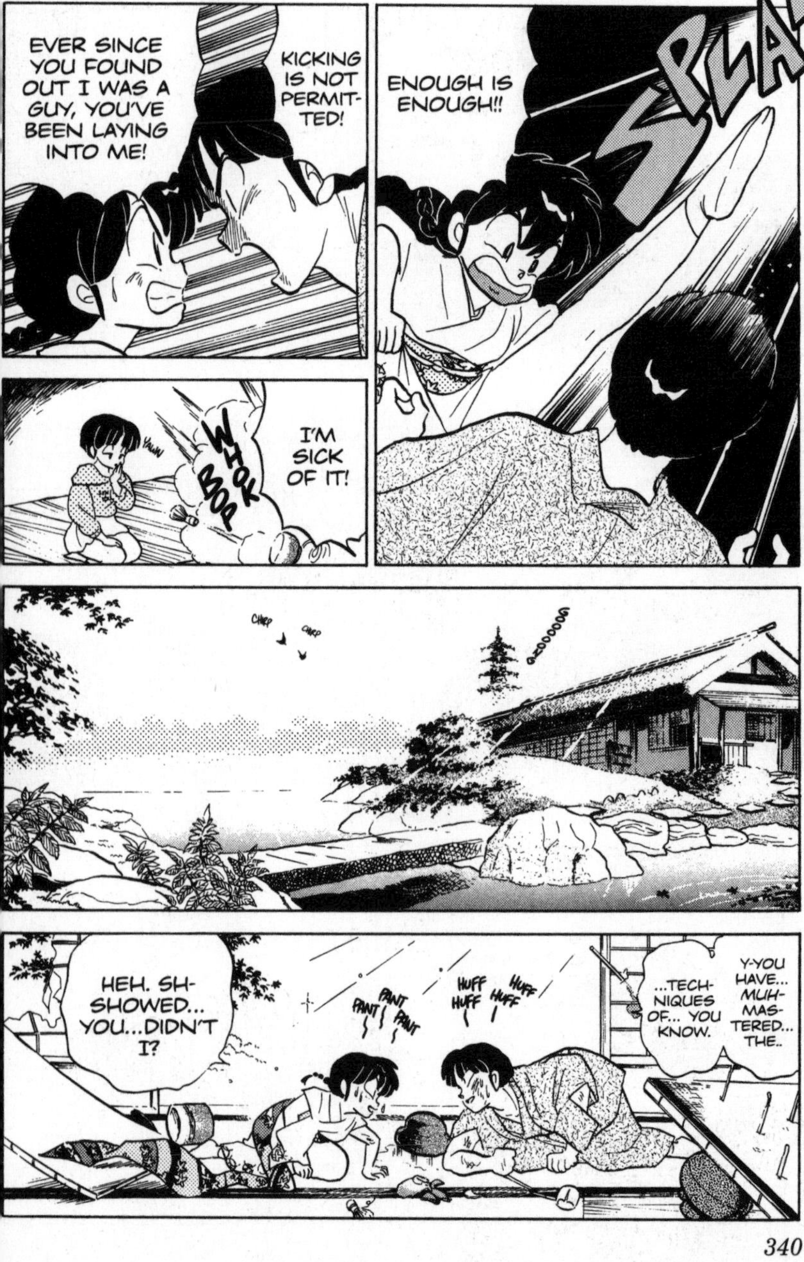
SPLAT
ENOUGH IS ENOUGH!!
KICKING IS NOT PERMIT-TED!
EVER SINCE YOU FOUND OUT I WAS A GUY, YOU'VE BEEN LAYING INTO ME!
I'M SICK OF IT!
WHOK
BOOP
YAWN
CHIRP
CHIRP
Y-YOU HAVE... MUH-MAS-TERED... THE..
...TECH-NIQUES OF... YOU KNOW.
HUFF HUFF
HUFF HUFF
PANT PANT
PANT PANT
HEH. SH-SHOWED... YOU...DIDN'T I?

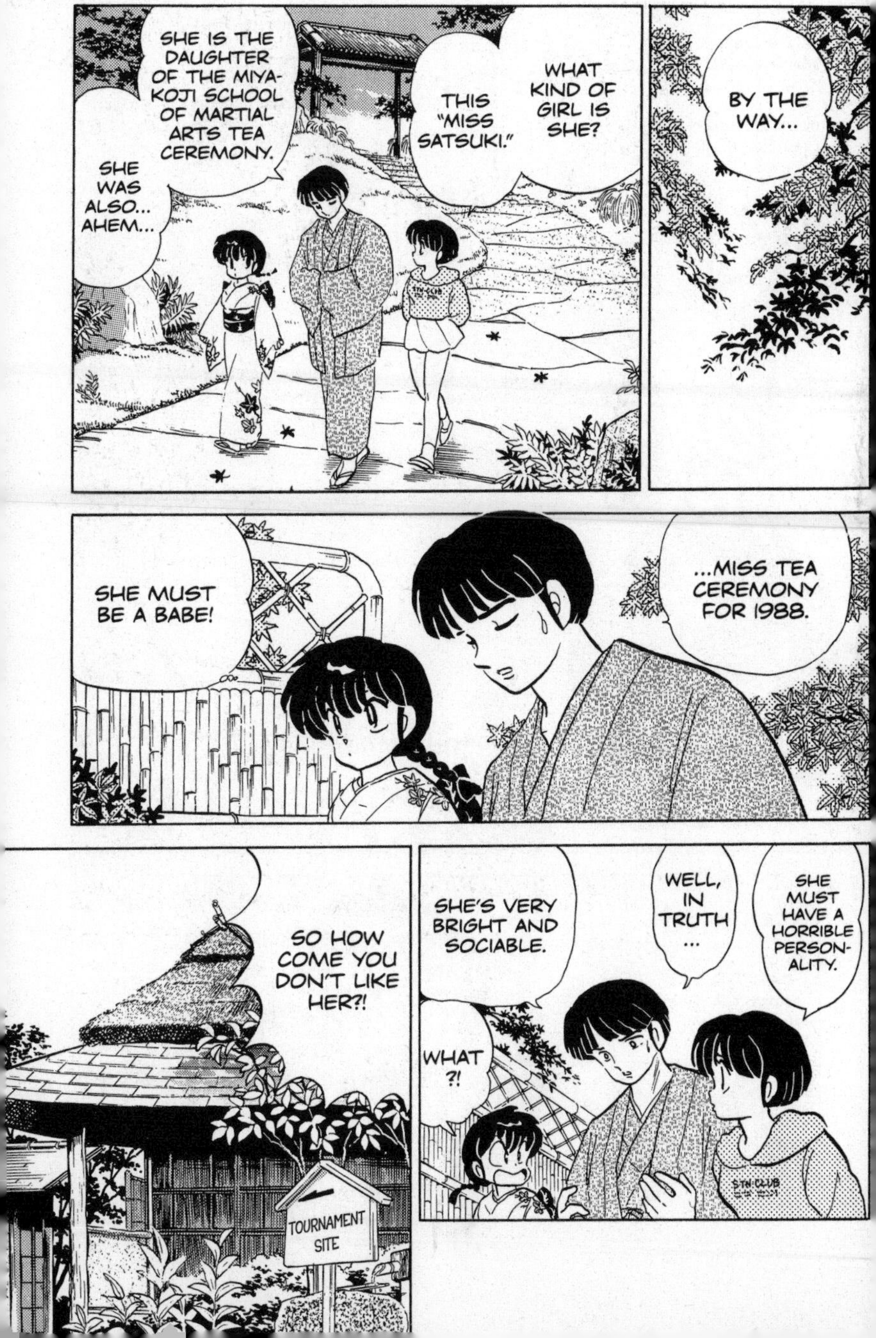
BY THE WAY...
WHAT KIND OF GIRL IS SHE?
THIS "MISS SATSUKI."
SHE IS THE DAUGHTER OF THE MIYA-KOJI SCHOOL OF MARTIAL ARTS TEA CEREMONY.
SHE WAS ALSO... AHEM...
...MISS TEA CEREMONY FOR 1988.
SHE MUST BE A BABE!
SHE MUST HAVE A HORRIBLE PERSON-ALITY.
WELL, IN TRUTH ...
SHE'S VERY BRIGHT AND SOCIABLE.
WHAT ?!
SO HOW COME YOU DON'T LIKE HER?!
TOURNAMENT SITE

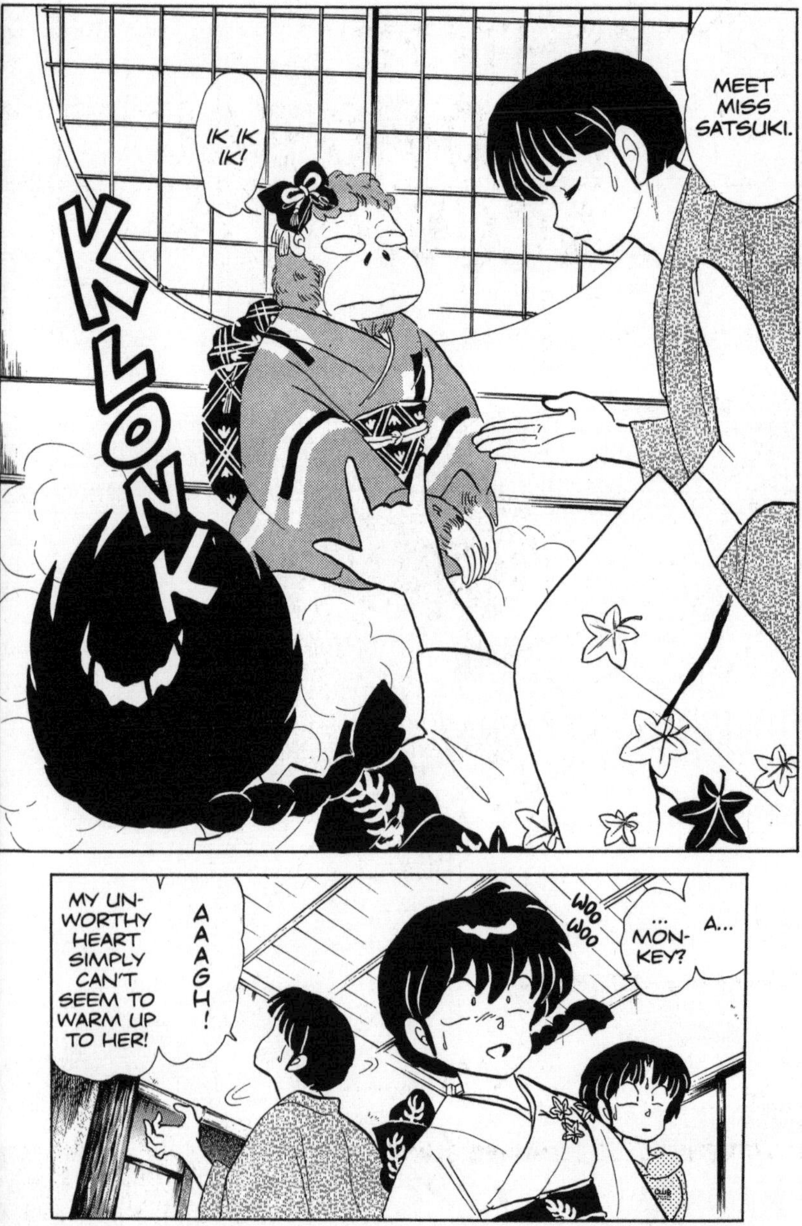
MEET MISS SATSUKI.
IK IK IK!
KLONK
A...
...MON-KEY?
WOO WOO
AAAAGH!
MY UN-WORTHY HEART SIMPLY CAN'T SEEM TO WARM UP TO HER!

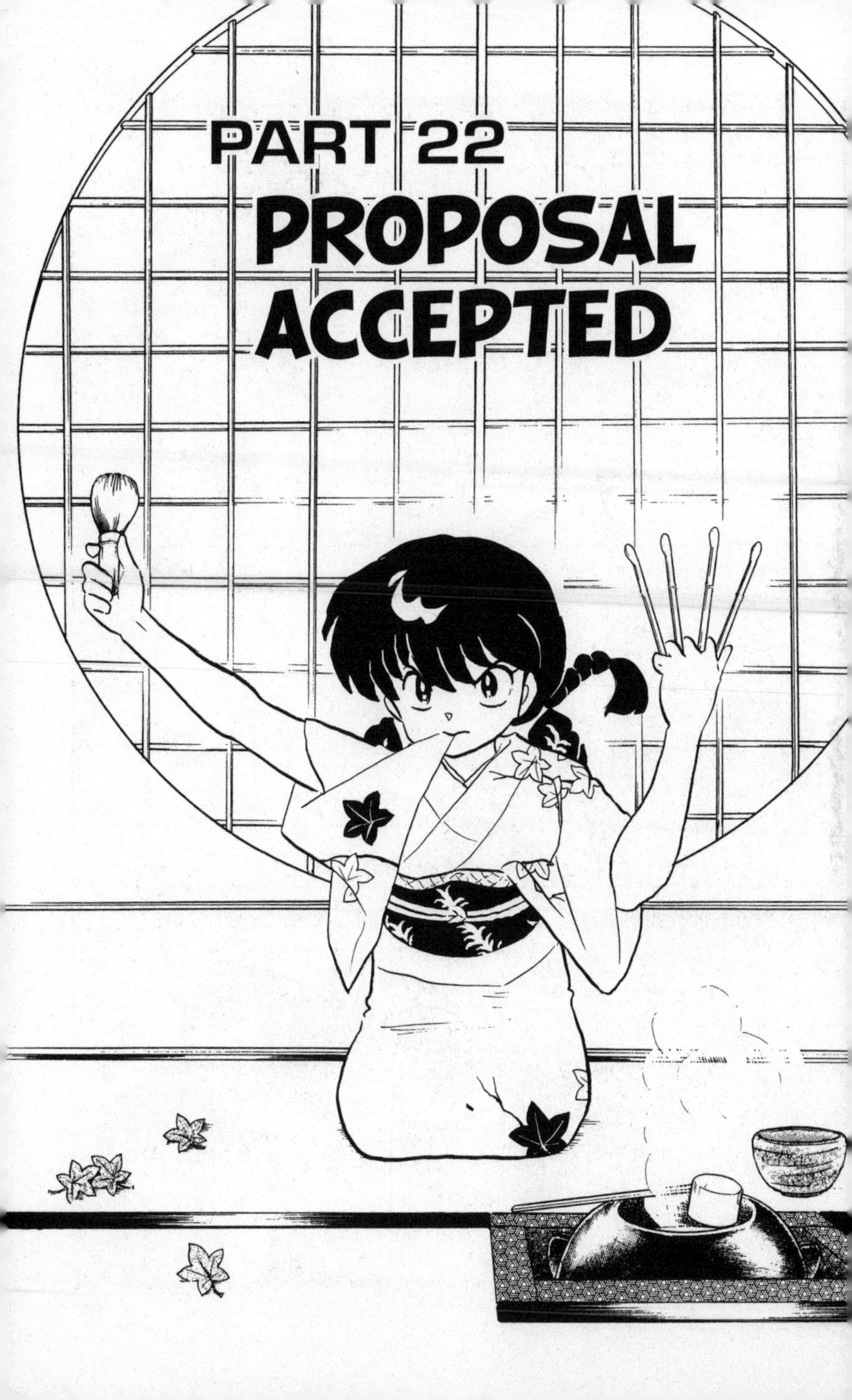
PART 22
PROPOSAL ACCEPTED

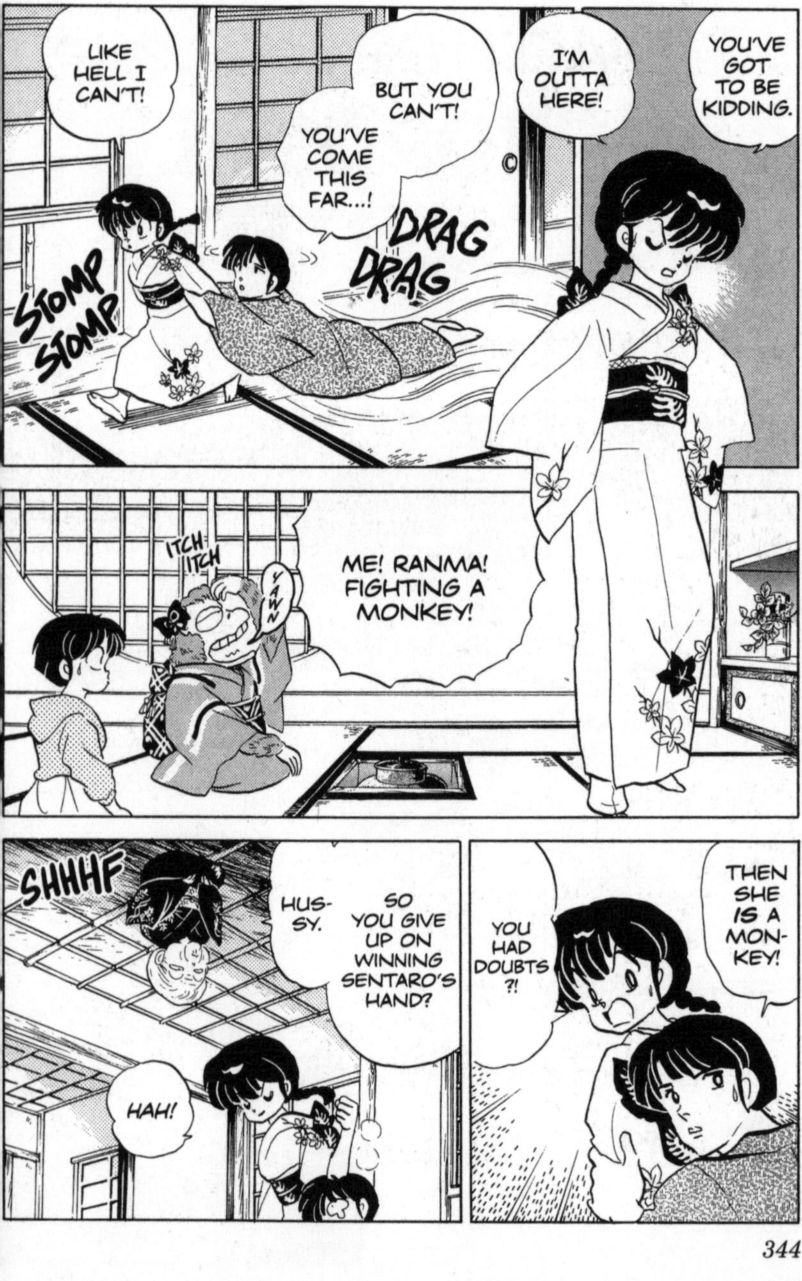
YOU'VE GOT TO BE KIDDING.
I'M OUTTA HERE!
BUT YOU CAN'T!
YOU'VE COME THIS FAR...!
DRAG DRAG
LIKE HELL I CAN'T!
STOMP STOMP
ME! RANMA! FIGHTING A MONKEY!
YAWN
ITCH ITCH
THEN SHE *IS* A MON-KEY!
YOU HAD DOUBTS ?!
SO YOU GIVE UP ON WINNING SENTARO'S HAND?
HUS-SY.
SHHHF
HAH!

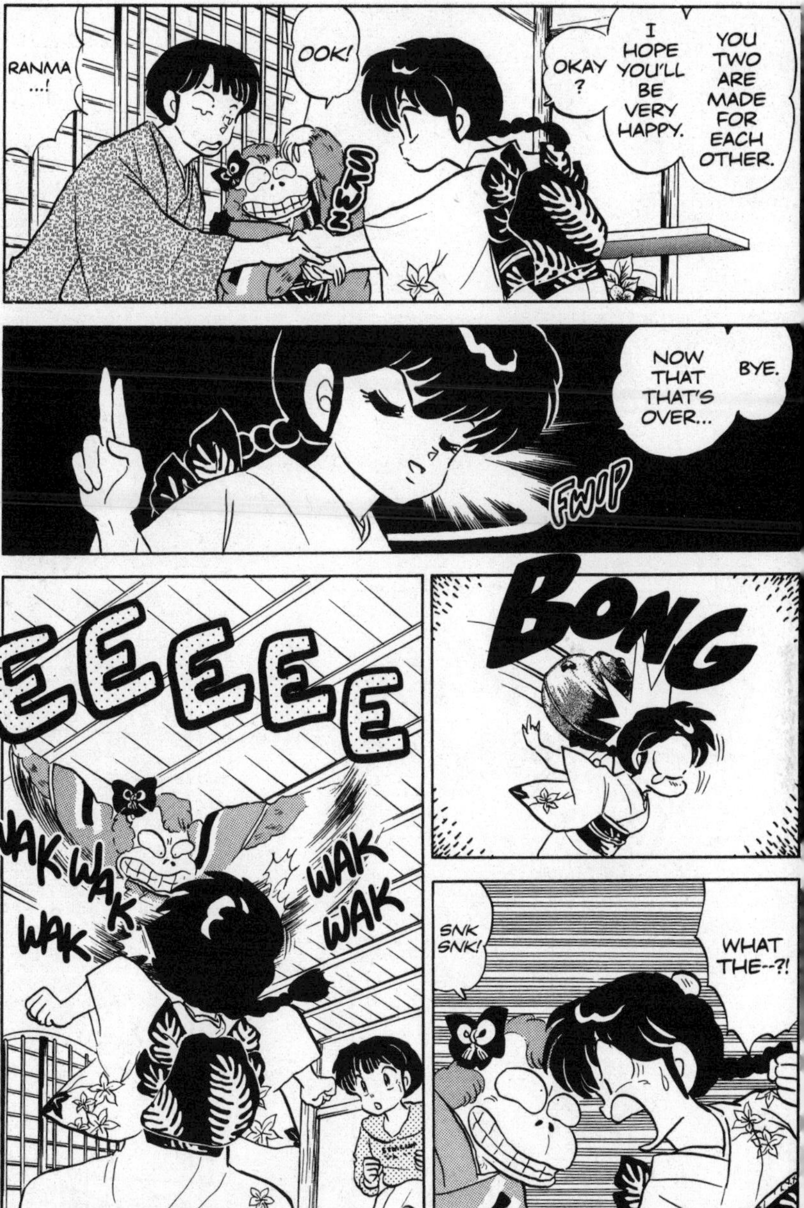
YOU TWO ARE MADE FOR EACH OTHER.
I HOPE YOU'LL BE VERY HAPPY.
OKAY ?
OOK!
RANMA ...!
NOW THAT THAT'S OVER... BYE.
FWIP
BONG
WHAT THE--?!
SNK SNK!
EEEEE
WAK WAK
WAK WAK
WAK WAK

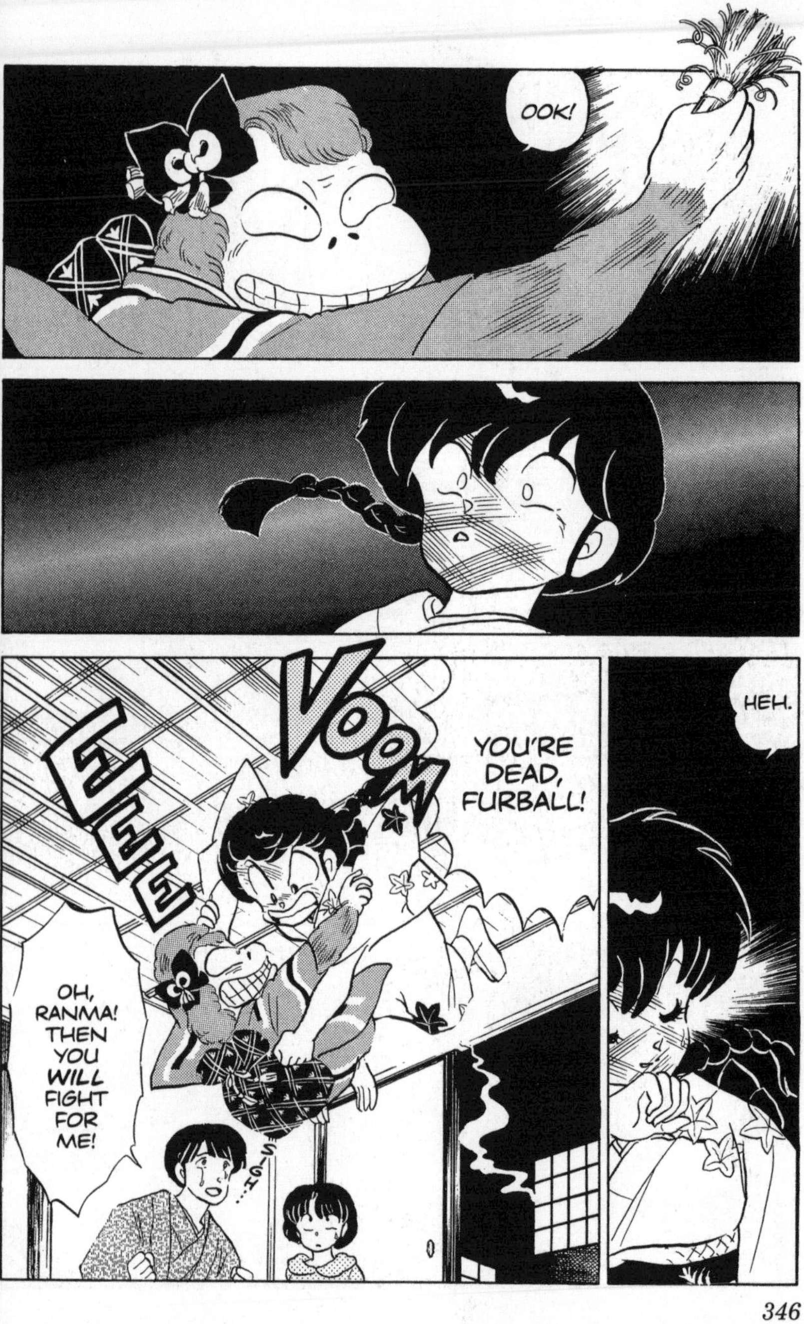
OOK!
HEH.
VOOM
YOU'RE DEAD, FURBALL!
OH, RANMA! THEN YOU WILL FIGHT FOR ME!
SIGH...

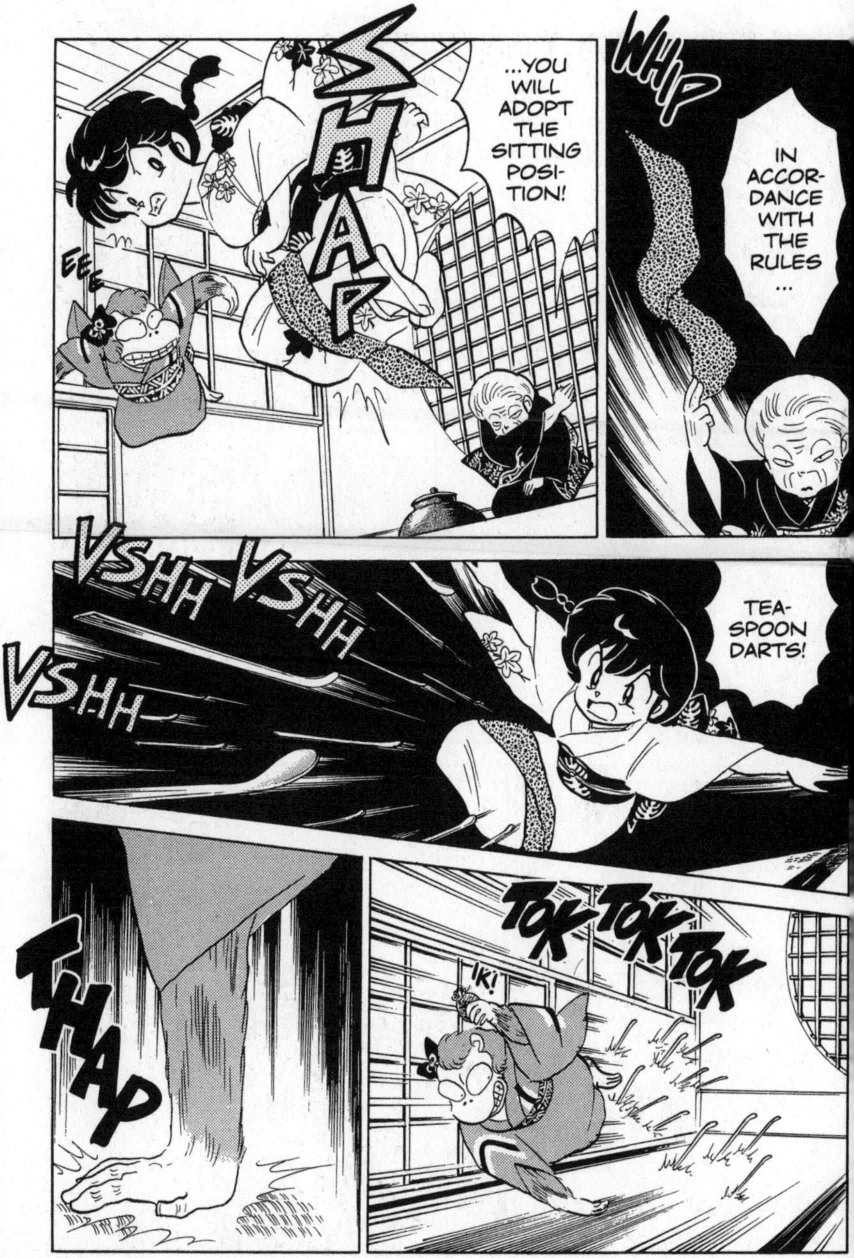
WHIP
IN ACCORDANCE WITH THE RULES ...
SHAP
...YOU WILL ADOPT THE SITTING POSITION!
EEE
TEA-SPOON DARTS!
VSHH
VSHH
VSHH
TOK TOK TOK
IK!
THAP

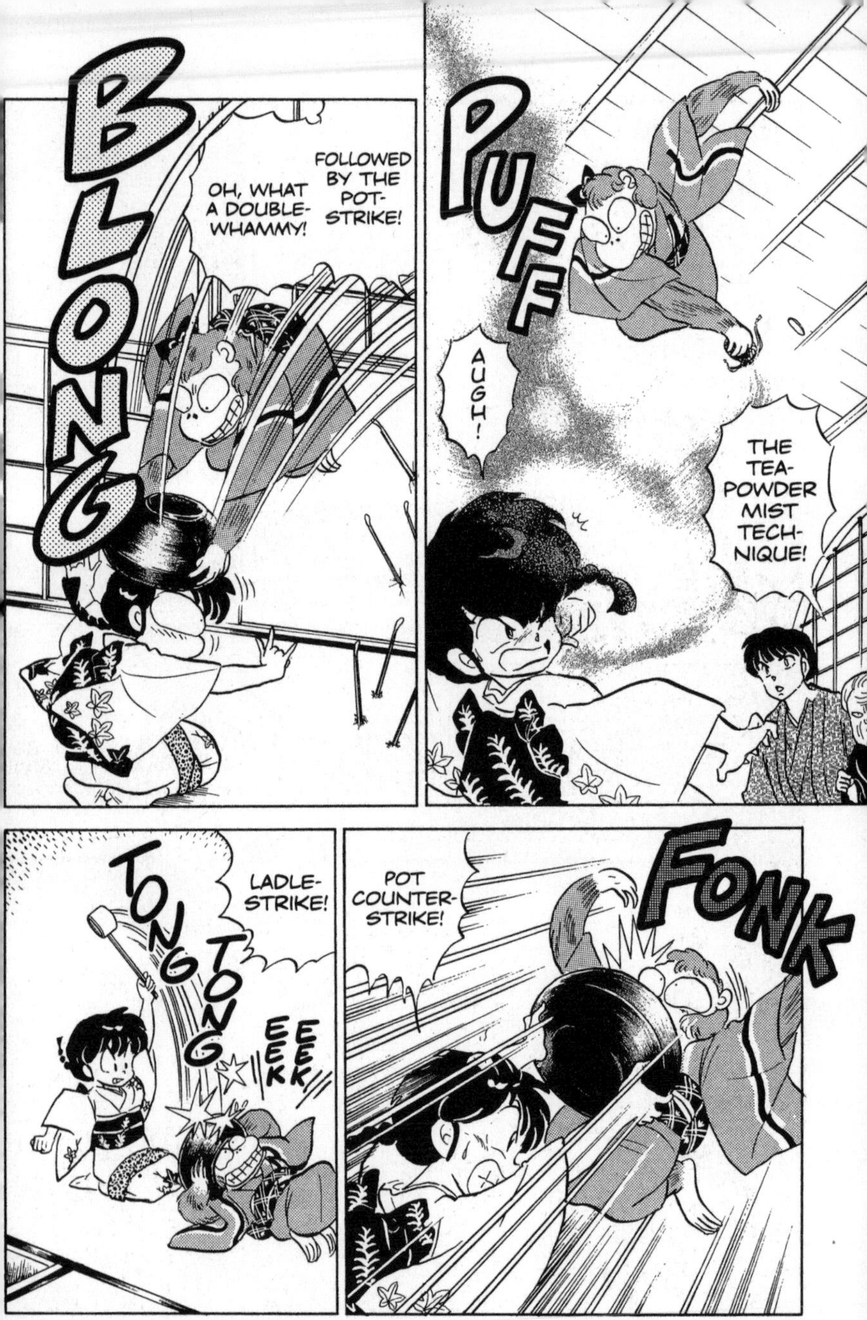
PUFF
AUGH!
THE TEA-POWDER MIST TECHNIQUE!
BLONG
FOLLOWED BY THE POT-STRIKE!
OH, WHAT A DOUBLE-WHAMMY!
FONK
POT COUNTER-STRIKE!
LADLE-STRIKE!
TONG
TONG
EEEK
EEEK

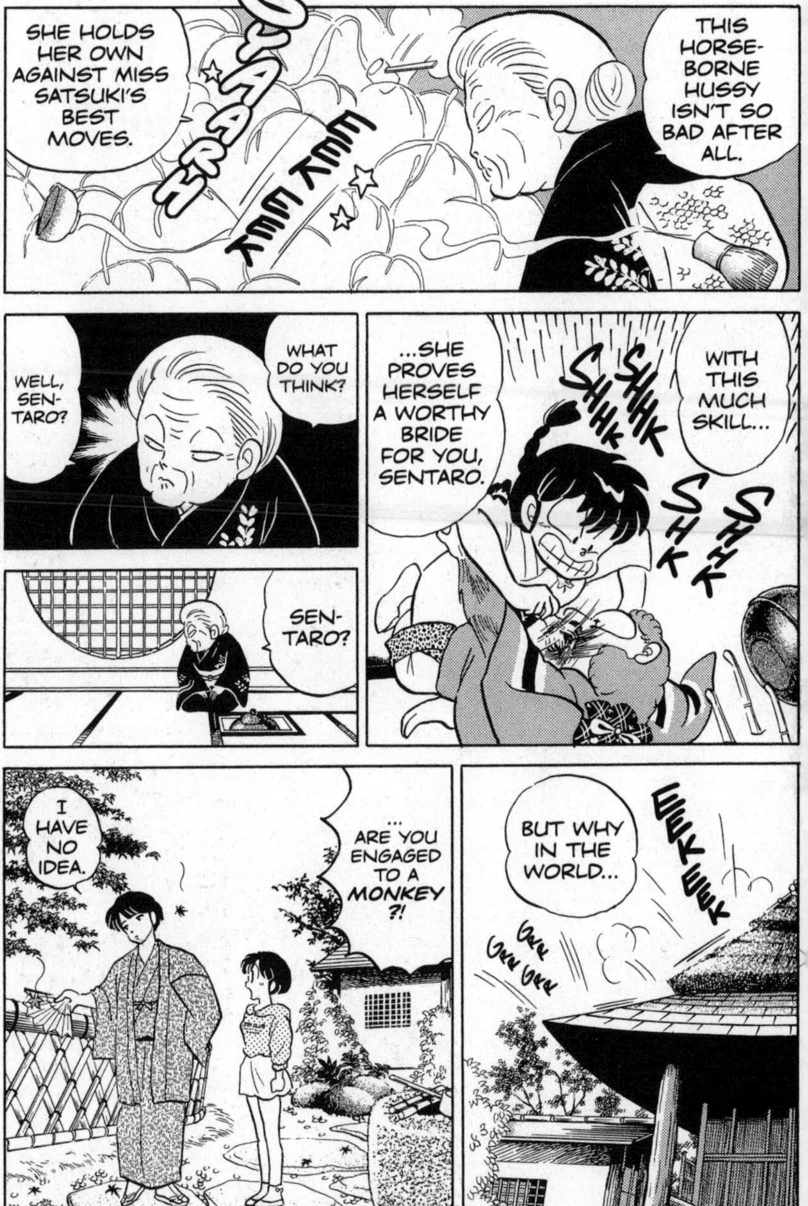
THIS HORSE-BORNE HUSSY ISN'T SO BAD AFTER ALL.
GYAARH
EEEK EEEK
SHE HOLDS HER OWN AGAINST MISS SATSUKI'S BEST MOVES.
WITH THIS MUCH SKILL...
SHHK SHHK
...SHE PROVES HERSELF A WORTHY BRIDE FOR YOU, SENTARO.
SHK SHHK
WHAT DO YOU THINK?
WELL, SENTARO?
SEN-TARO?
EEEK EEEK
BUT WHY IN THE WORLD...
GKK GKK GKK
... ARE YOU ENGAGED TO A **MONKEY** ?!
I HAVE NO IDEA.

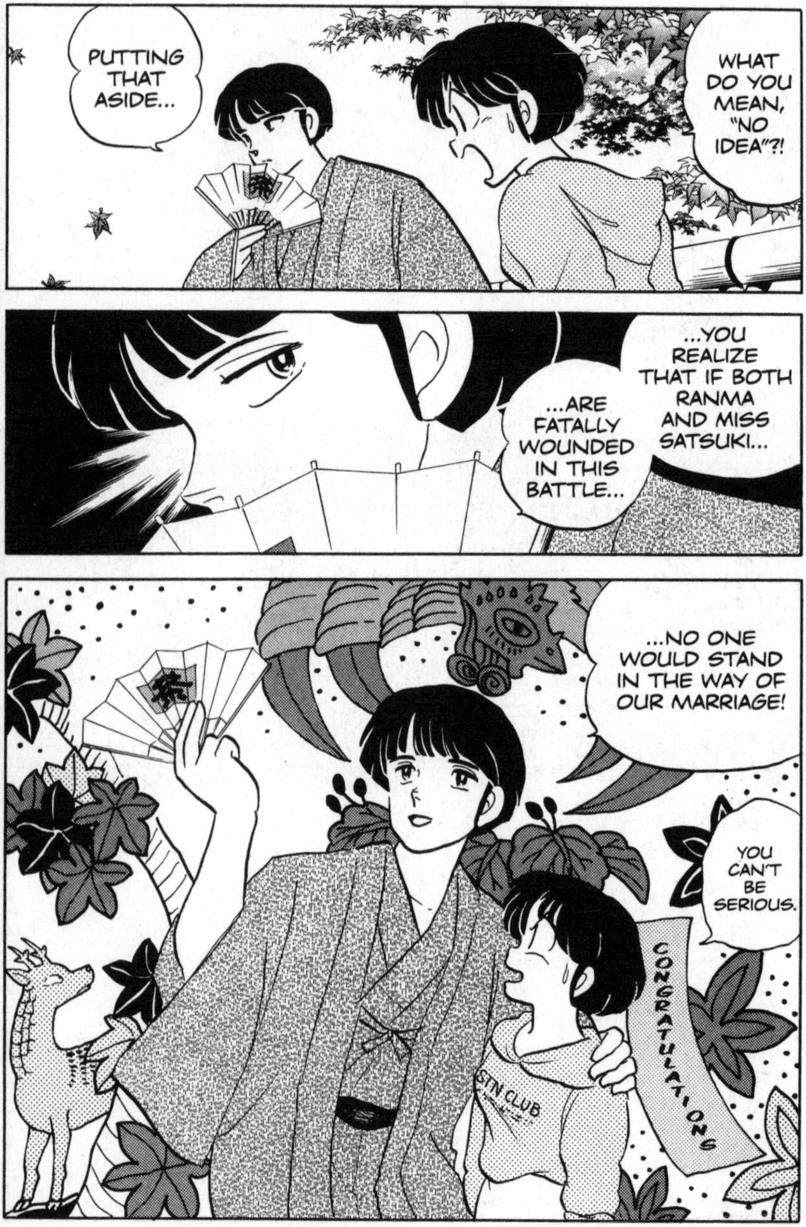
WHAT DO YOU MEAN, "NO IDEA"?!
PUTTING THAT ASIDE...
...YOU REALIZE THAT IF BOTH RANMA AND MISS SATSUKI...
...ARE FATALLY WOUNDED IN THIS BATTLE...
...NO ONE WOULD STAND IN THE WAY OF OUR MARRIAGE!
YOU CAN'T BE SERIOUS.
CONGRATULATIONS

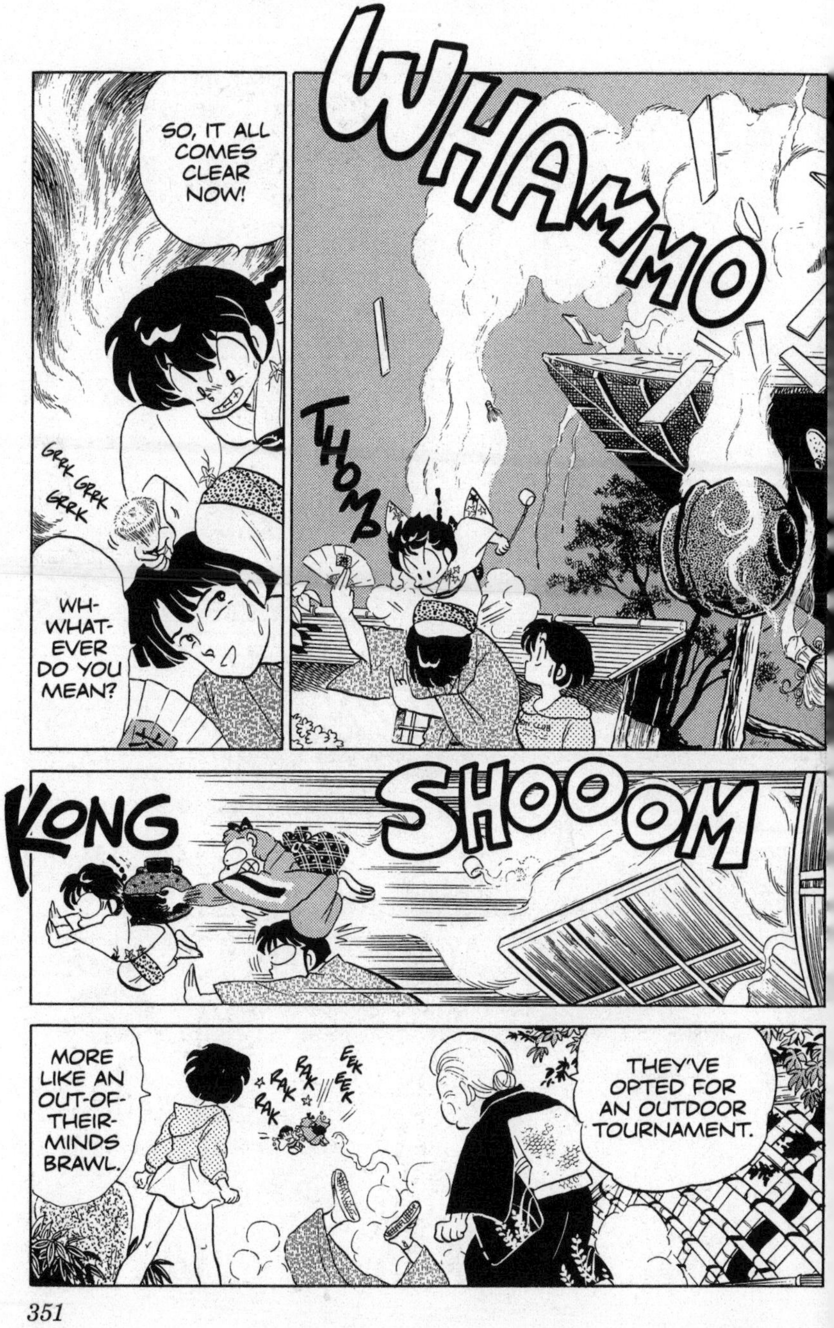
WHAMMO
THOMP
SO, IT ALL COMES CLEAR NOW!
GRRK GRRK GRRK
WH-WHATEVER DO YOU MEAN?
SHOOOM
KONG
THEY'VE OPTED FOR AN OUTDOOR TOURNAMENT.
EEK EEK
RAK RAK RAK
MORE LIKE AN OUT-OF-THEIR-MINDS BRAWL.

SWISH

Eeee

GET BACK HERE, FLEA-PICKER!

VISH

HYAH!

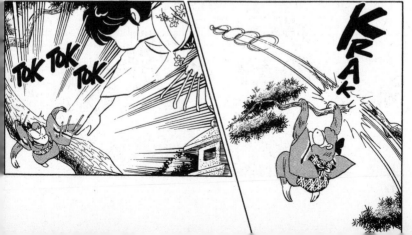

TOK TOK TOK

KRAK

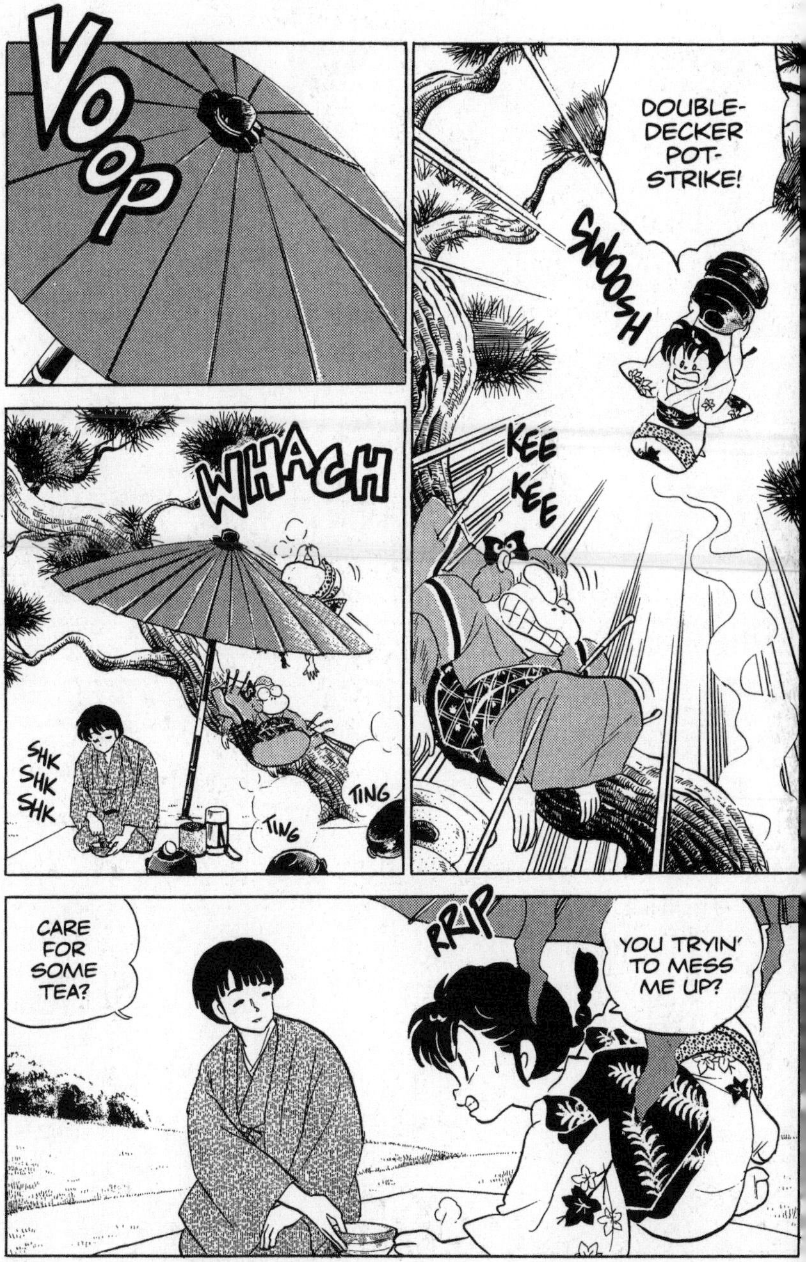
DOUBLE-DECKER POT-STRIKE!
SWOOSH
KEE KEE
VOOP
WHACH
SHK SHK SHK
TING
TING
RRIP
YOU TRYIN' TO MESS ME UP?
CARE FOR SOME TEA?

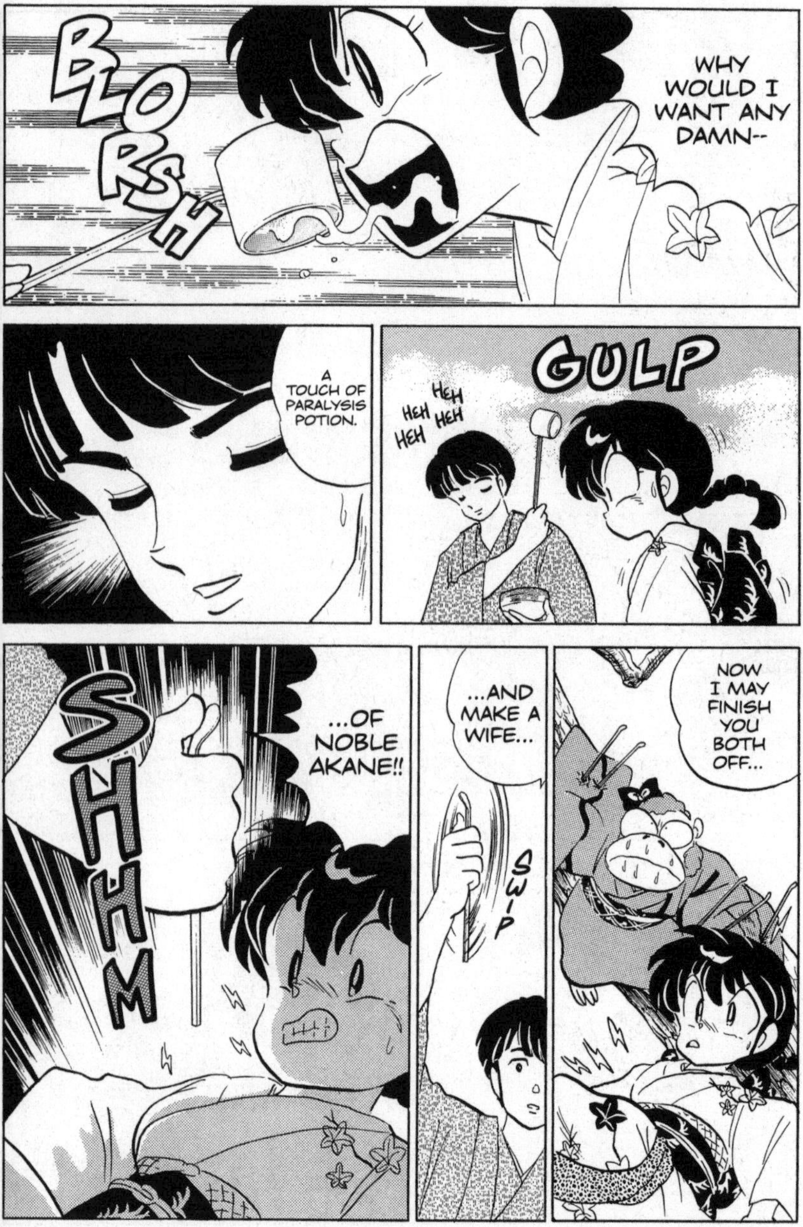
WHY WOULD I WANT ANY DAMN--
BLORSH
GULP
HEH HEH HEH HEH
A TOUCH OF PARALYSIS POTION.
NOW I MAY FINISH YOU BOTH OFF...
...AND MAKE A WIFE...
SWIP
...OF NOBLE AKANE!!
SHHHM

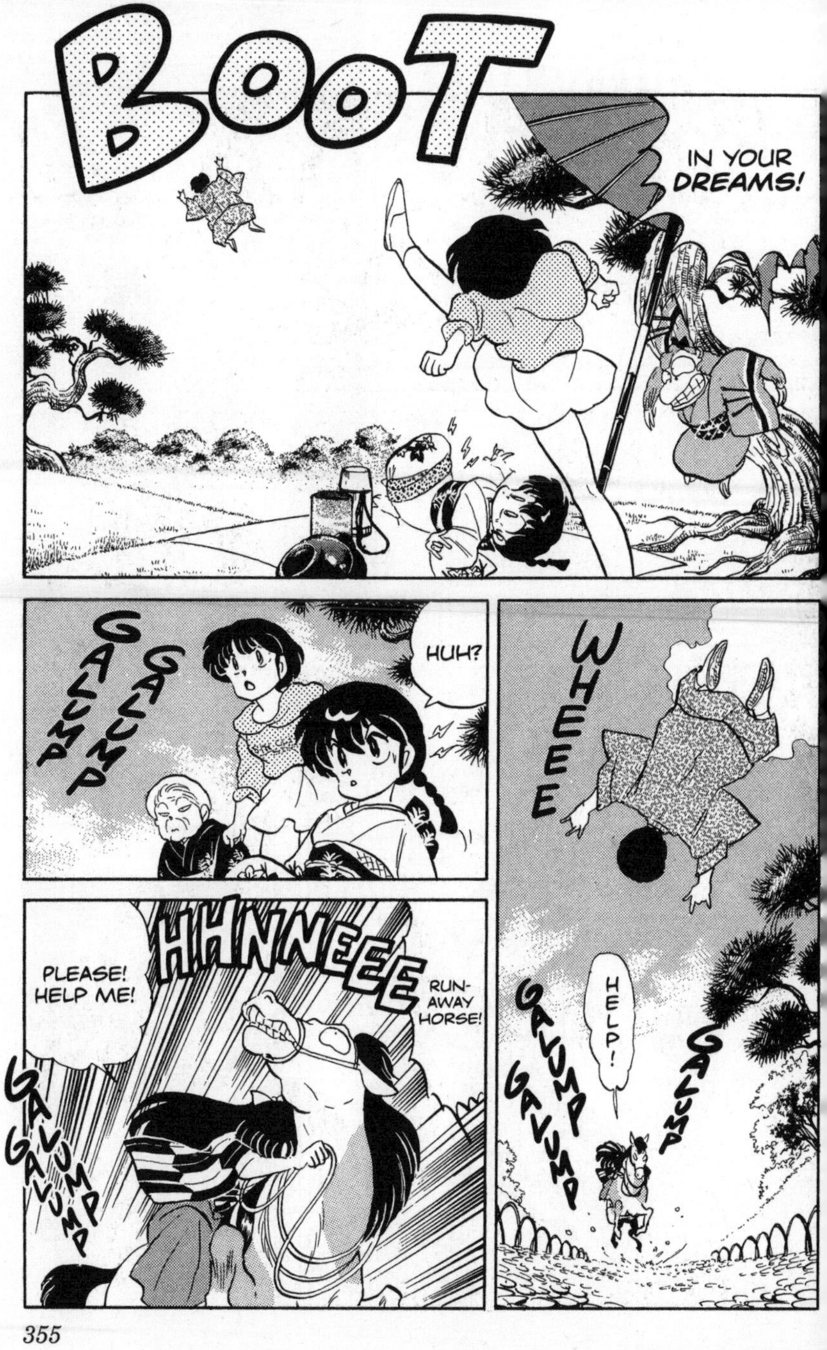
BOOT
IN YOUR DREAMS!
WHEEEE
GALUMP
HELP!
GALUMP
GAVUMP
HUH?
GALUMP
GALUMP
HHNNEEE
RUN-AWAY HORSE!
PLEASE! HELP ME!
GAVUMP
GAVUMP

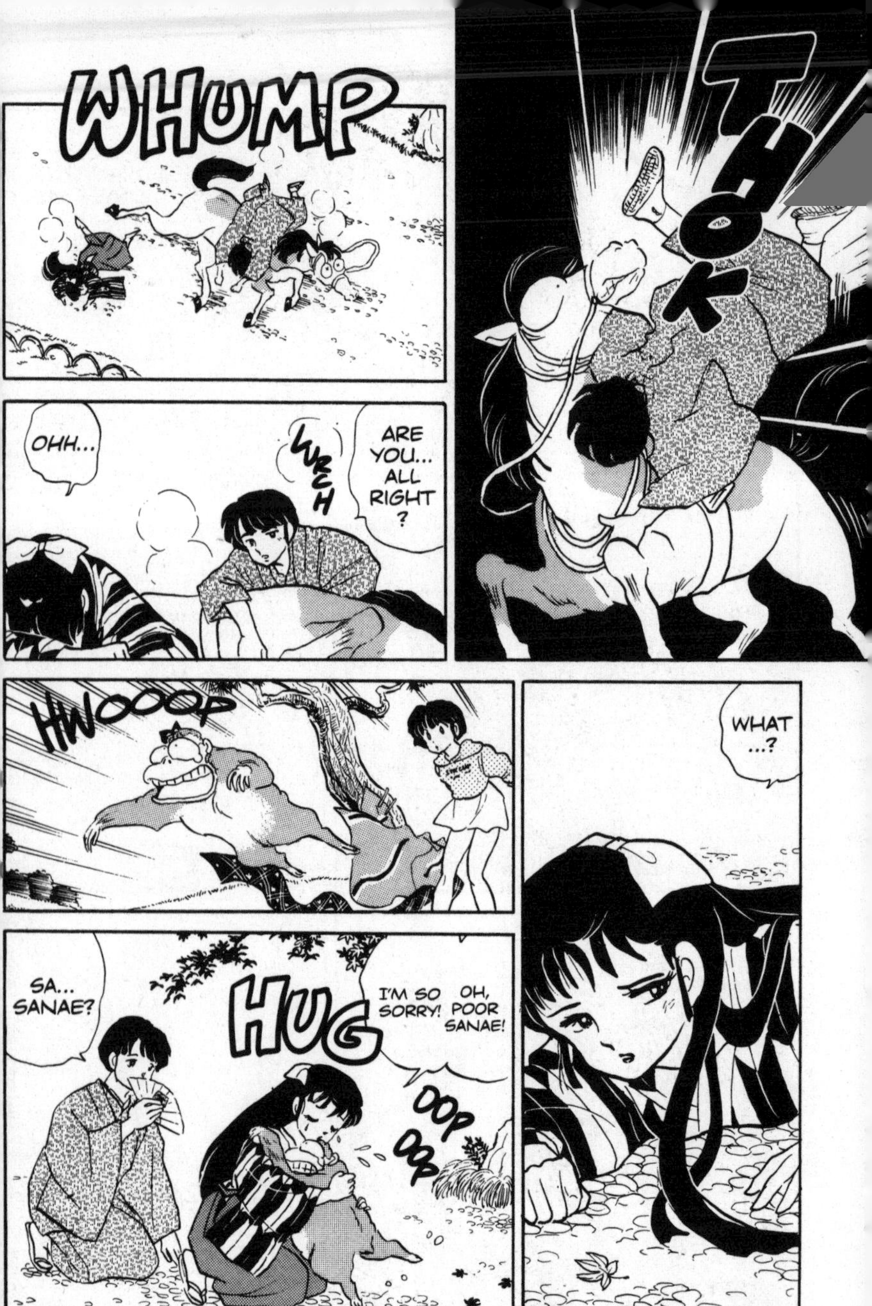
THOK
WHUMP
ARE YOU... ALL RIGHT?
LURCH
OHH...
WHAT ...?
HWOOOP
OH, POOR SANAE!
I'M SO SORRY!
HUG
DOOP DOOP
SA... SANAE?

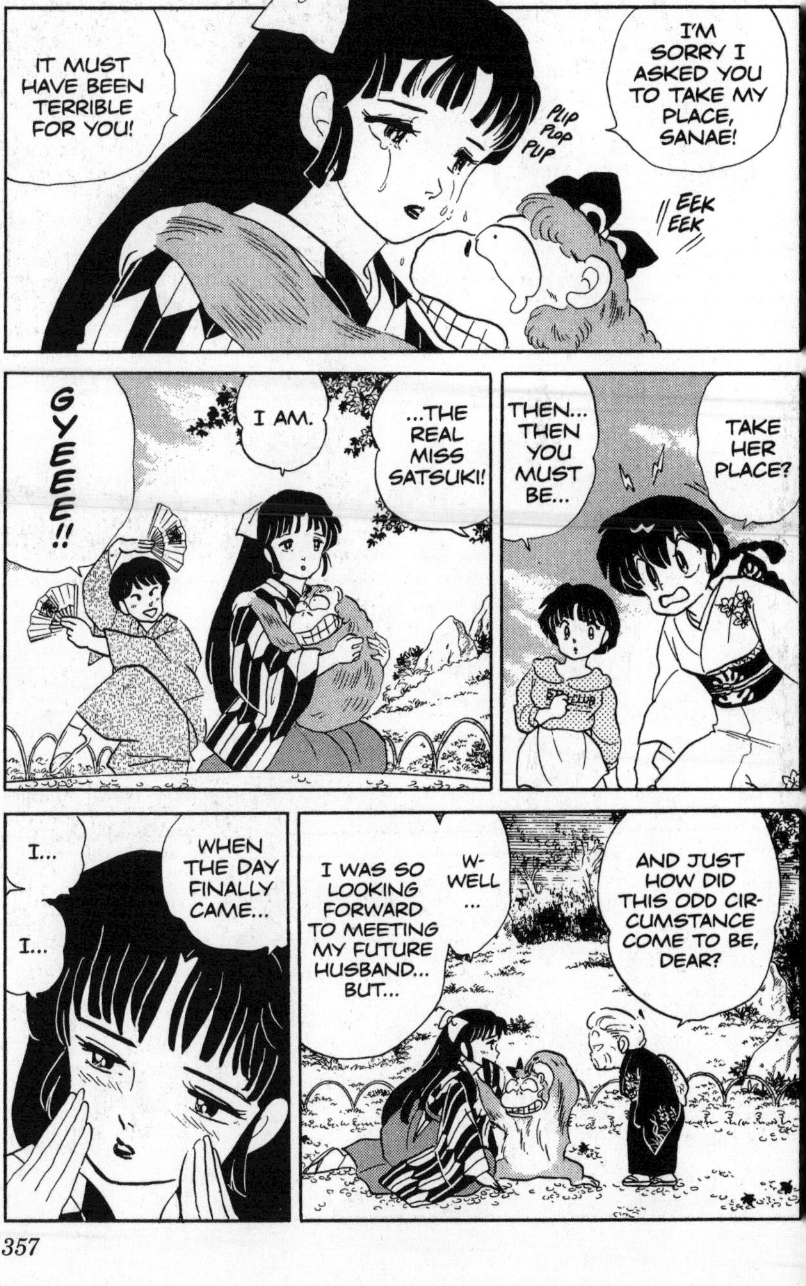
I'M SORRY I ASKED YOU TO TAKE MY PLACE, SANAE!
PLIP PLOP PLIP
IT MUST HAVE BEEN TERRIBLE FOR YOU!
EEK EEK
TAKE HER PLACE?
THEN... THEN YOU MUST BE...
...THE REAL MISS SATSUKI!
I AM.
GYEEEE!!
AND JUST HOW DID THIS ODD CIR-CUMSTANCE COME TO BE, DEAR?
W-WELL...
I WAS SO LOOKING FORWARD TO MEETING MY FUTURE HUSBAND... BUT...
WHEN THE DAY FINALLY CAME...
I...
I...

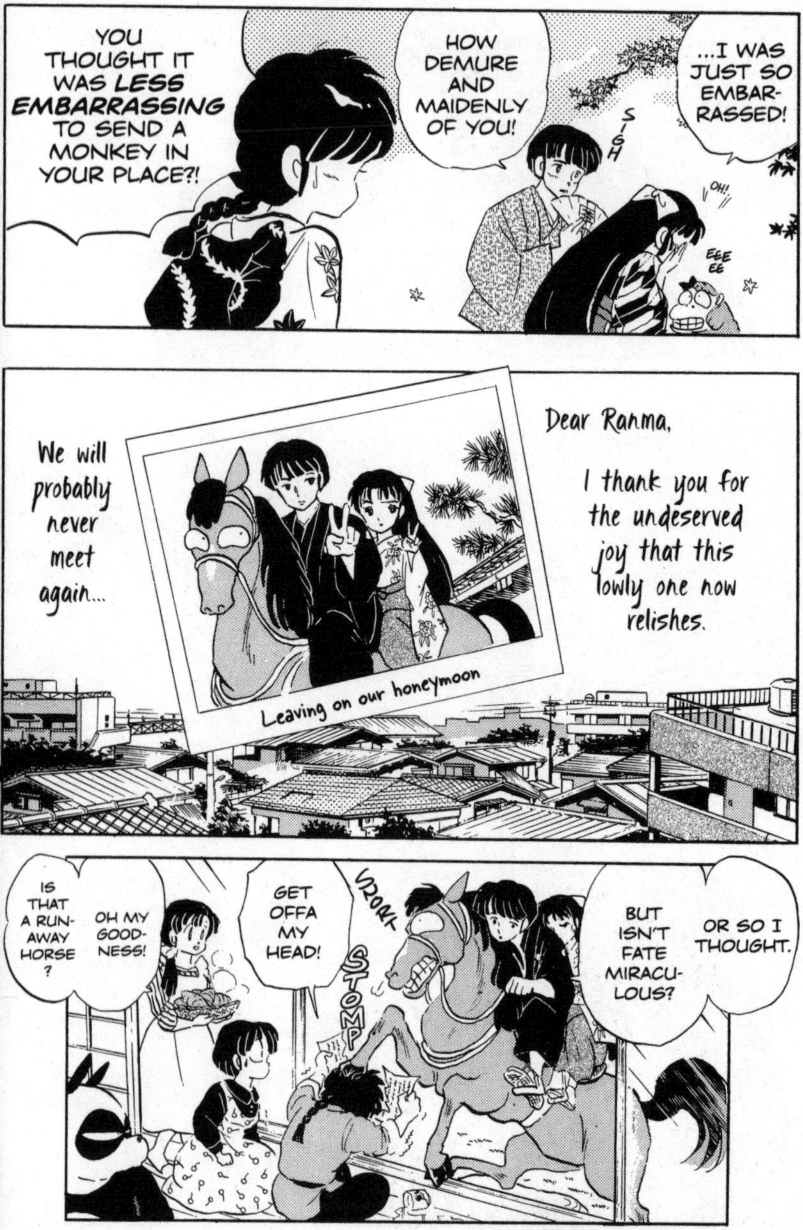
...I WAS JUST SO EMBARRASSED!
SIGH
OH!
EEE EE
HOW DEMURE AND MAIDENLY OF YOU!
YOU THOUGHT IT WAS LESS EMBARRASSING TO SEND A MONKEY IN YOUR PLACE?!
Dear Ranma,
I thank you for the undeserved joy that this lowly one now relishes.
Leaving on our honeymoon
We will probably never meet again...
OR SO I THOUGHT.
BUT ISN'T FATE MIRACULOUS?
VROOM
GET OFFA MY HEAD!
STOMP
OH MY GOODNESS!
IS THAT A RUNAWAY HORSE?

To Be Continued

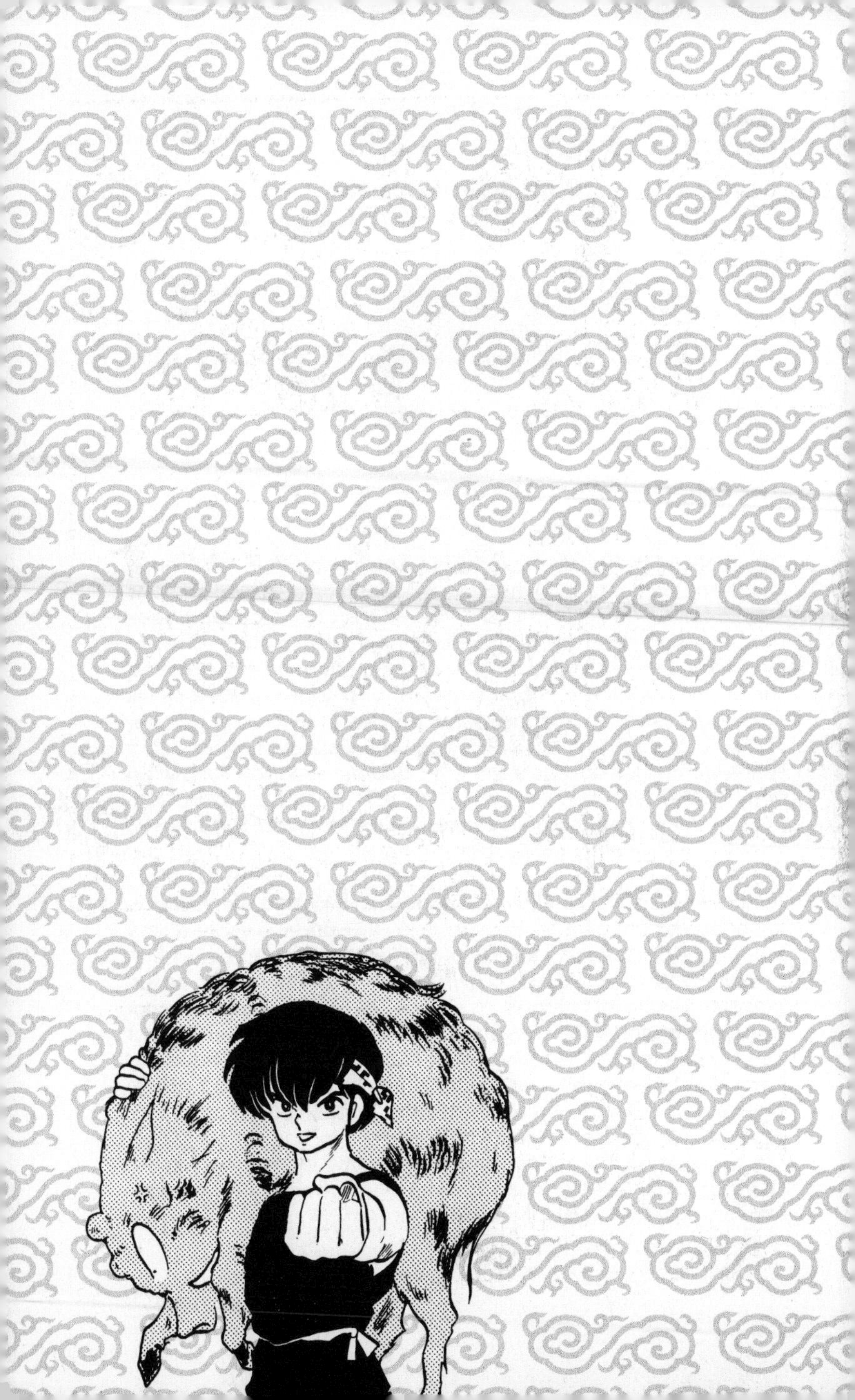

Rumiko Takahashi

The spotlight on Rumiko Takahashi's career began in 1978 when she won an honorable mention in Shogakukan's annual New Comic Artist Contest for *Those Selfish Aliens*. Later that same year, her boy-meets-alien comedy series, *Urusei Yatsura*, was serialized in *Weekly Shonen Sunday*. This phenomenally successful manga series was adapted into anime format and spawned a TV series and half a dozen theatrical-release movies, all incredibly popular in their own right. Takahashi followed up the success of her debut series with one blockbuster hit after another—*Maison Ikkoku* ran from 1980 to 1987, *Ranma ½* from 1987 to 1996, and *Inuyasha* from 1996 to 2008. Other notable works include *Mermaid Saga*, *Rumic Theater*, and *One-Pound Gospel*.

Takahashi won the prestigious Shogakukan Manga Award twice in her career, once for *Urusei Yatsura* in 1981 and the second time for *Inuyasha* in 2002. A majority of the Takahashi canon has been adapted into other media such as anime, live-action TV series, and film. Takahashi's manga, as well as the other formats her work has been adapted into, have continued to delight generations of fans around the world. Distinguished by her wonderfully endearing characters, Takahashi's work adeptly incorporates a wide variety of elements such as comedy, romance, fantasy, and martial arts. While her series are difficult to pin down into one simple genre, the signature style she has created has come to be known as the "Rumic World." Rumiko Takahashi is an artist who truly represents the very best from the world of manga.

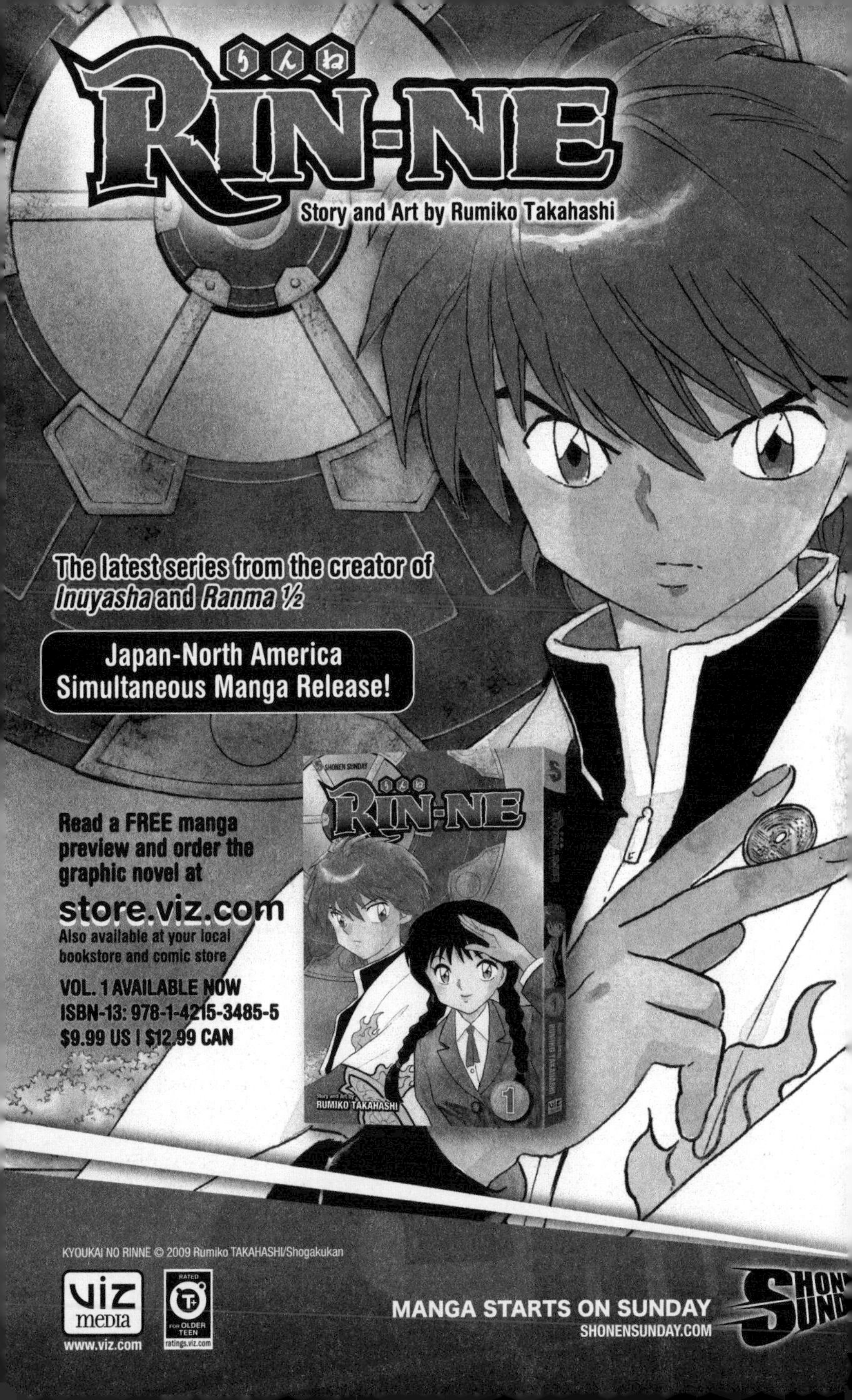
りんね
RIN-NE
Story and Art by Rumiko Takahashi
The latest series from the creator of Inuyasha and Ranma ½
Japan-North America Simultaneous Manga Release!
SHONEN SUNDAY
RIN-NE
Story and Art by RUMIKO TAKAHASHI
1
Read a FREE manga preview and order the graphic novel at
store.viz.com
Also available at your local bookstore and comic store
VOL. 1 AVAILABLE NOW
ISBN-13: 978-1-4215-3485-5
$9.99 US | $12.99 CAN
KYOUKAI NO RINNE © 2009 Rumiko TAKAHASHI/Shogakukan
viz media
www.viz.com
RATED T+ FOR OLDER TEEN
ratings.viz.com
MANGA STARTS ON SUNDAY
SHONENSUNDAY.COM

Ranma½ Returns!
REMASTERED AND BETTER THAN EVER!

One day, teenaged martial artist Ranma Saotome went on a training mission with his father and ended up taking a dive into some cursed springs at a legendary training ground in China. Now, every time he's splashed with cold water, he changes into a girl. His father, Genma, changes into a panda! What's a half-guy, half-girl to do?

Find out what fueled the worldwide manga boom in beloved creator Rumiko Takahashi's (*Inuyasha, Urusei Yatsura, RIN-NE*) smash-hit of martial arts mayhem!

Story and Art by Rumiko Takahashi

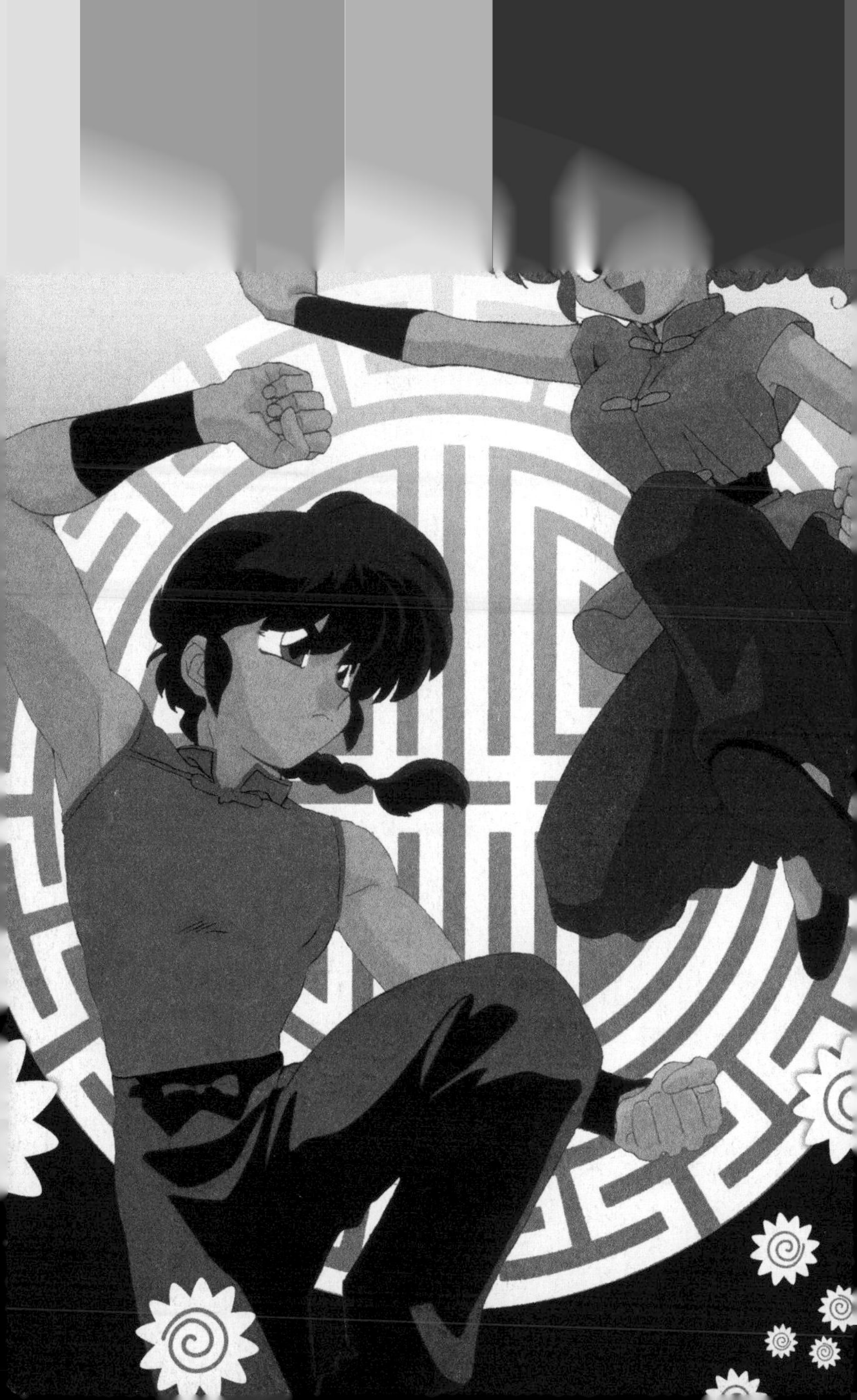

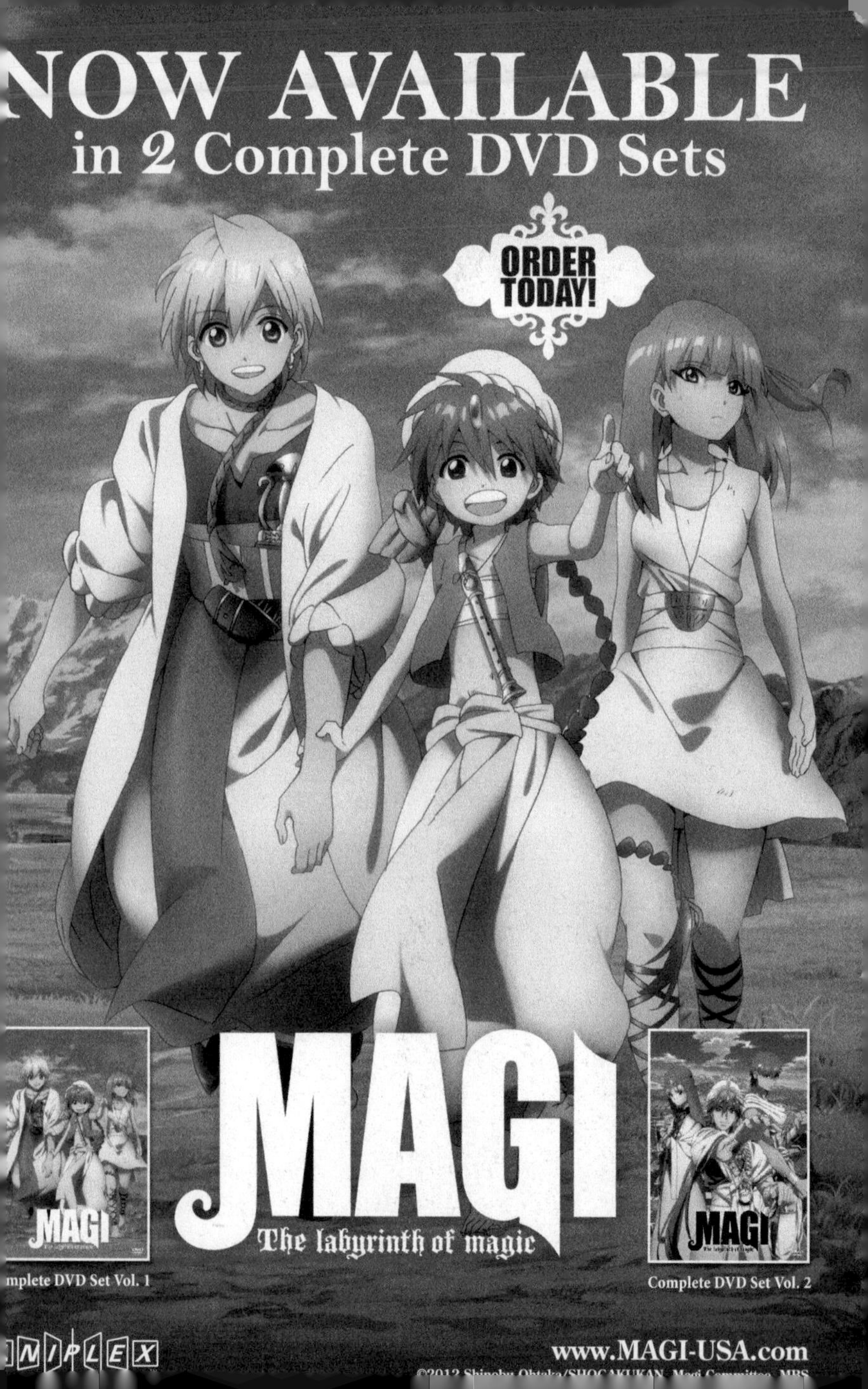
NOW AVAILABLE
in 2 Complete DVD Sets
ORDER TODAY!
MAGI
The labyrinth of magic
mplete DVD Set Vol. 1
Complete DVD Set Vol. 2
www.MAGI-USA.com
©2012 Shinobu Ohtaka/SHOGAKUKAN, Magi Committee, MBS

Hey! You're Reading in the Wrong Direction!

This is the end of this graphic novel!

To properly enjoy this VIZ graphic novel, please turn it around and begin reading from right to left. Unlike English, Japanese is read right to left, so Japanese comics are read in reverse order from the way English comics are typically read.

This book has been printed in the original Japanese format in order to preserve the orientation of the original artwork. Have fun with it!

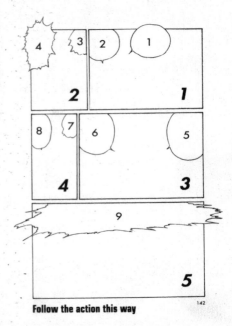

Follow the action this way

142